SIDE-SADDLE
on the
GOLDEN CALF

Social Structure and
Popular Culture in Amer

SIDE-SADDLE
on the
GOLDEN CALF

Social Structure and Popular Culture in America

Edited by GEORGE H. LEWIS
College of the Pacific

GOODYEAR PUBLISHING COMPANY, INC.
Pacific Palisades, California

TO CHERYL

CONTENTS

Concepts and Issues 1

PERSPECTIVE: WHAT IS POPULAR CULTURE?   2

Popular Culture: Notes Toward a Definition
                                            Ray B. Browne   5

Notes on Popular Culture
                                            Russel B. Nye   13

Thesis 21

POST-KOREA: THE ECONOMIC RISE OF THE WORKING CLASS   22

The Higher Meaning of Marlboro Cigarettes
                                            Bruce A. Lohof   25

Clean Fun at Riverhead
                                            Tom Wolfe   37

Prole Sport: the Case of Roller Derby
                                            George H. Lewis   42

The God-Hucksters of Radio
                                            William C. Martin 49

Singing Along with the Silent Majority
                                        John D. McCarthy,
                    Richard A. Peterson and William L. Yancey 56

Love and Sex in the Romance Magazines
                                            David Sonenschein 66

SUMNER'S FORGOTTEN AMERICAN TODAY   75

Playboy Magazine: Sophisticated Smut or Social Revolution?
                            Walter M. Gerson and Sander H. Lund 80

Patrons of Adult Bookstores and Movies
            President's Commission On Obscenity and Pornography   89

The Portrayal of War and the Fighting Man in Novels of the
Vietnam War
Clinton R. Sanders 100

The Creator-Audience Relationship in the Mass Media: An
Analysis of Movie-Making
Herbert J. Gans 109

A Conversation with Arthur Penn
Jacoba Atlas 120

The Social Meaning of Television Censorship
Eckard V. Toy, Jr. 127

Bureaucracy at the Bridge Table
Hugh Gardner 138

The Spyder (Sting-Ray, Screamer) Bike: An American Original
Arthur Asa Berger 154

Hamburgers, 18¢
Daniel and Susan Halas 157

The Social Stratification of Frozen TV Dinners
M. F. K. Fisher 167

HIGH SOCIETY: POPULAR CULTURE? 173

Pop Society and the *Nouveau Riche*
George H. Lewis 173

Antithesis 183

BLACK CULTURE 184

Courting the Black Billionaire
Media-Scope 186

The Impressions
Michael Alexander 191

Pop Art and the Black Revolution
Charles D. Peavy 201

The Black Art of Propaganda: The Cultural Arm of the Black
Revolution
Charles D. Peavy 208

On Cultural Nationalism
Linda Harrison 215

Revolutionary Art/Black Liberation
Emory 217

Black Poems, Poseurs, and Power

Nikki Giovanni 219

YOUTH CULTURE 224

Comics and Culture

Arthur Asa Berger 227

Rapping About Cartoonists, Particularly Robert Crumb

Harvey Pekar 236

Tattoo Renaissance

Amie Hill 245

Revolt for Fun and Profit

Nora Sayre 252

ROCK CULTURE 262

Rock Culture and the Development of Social Consciousness

Joe Ferrandino 263

The Times They Are A-Changin': The Music Of Protest

Robert A. Rosenstone 290

The Pop Artist and His Product: Mixed-Up Confusion

George H. Lewis 305

Rock for Sale

Michael Lydon 313

Altamont: Pearl Harbor to the Woodstock Nation

Sol Stern 321

STREET THEATER AS POPULAR CULTURE 341

The Making of the Yippie Culture

Garry Wills 343

Revolution or Tomatoes?

Barbara Falconer 358

The Hog Farm

Hugh Romney 367

Synthesis? 383

FURTHER READINGS 385

PREFACE

The central issue addressed in this collection of essays—the relationship between the social structure of a society and its popular culture—was perhaps hinted at most dramatically by John Lennon when he asserted that the Beatles, in their prime, were more popular than Jesus. What he meant, of course, was that the artifacts of popular culture created by the Beatles have had more impact in shaping the social structure of the present day world than have contemporary disseminations of the teachings of Christ. Since Lennon's statement, Jesus has been elevated within the world of popular culture to a status equal to that of the rock star by the appearance and great popularity of the rock musical, *Jesus Christ, Superstar.*[1]

In the late 1960's, Lennon and his wife, Yoko Ono, carried the concept implicit in Lennon's earlier statement some steps further in their attempts to commercially "sell" peace to the world via the mass media.[2] In their quest they reversed the adduced linkage of the two concepts, culture and social structure, that seem most widely held by American social scientists—that changes in culture always lag behind changes in social structure. For example, scholarly advice in the field of race relations has, until most recently, taken the form of attacking discrimination itself, rather than attempting to influence prejudicial beliefs.[3] American foreign policy toward preindustrial society has also taken as "given" this sequential linkage. Unfortunately, those anthropologists who question this design are not often listened to, either in sociological circles or in governmental ones.

Plato remarked in *The Republic* that musical "forms and rhythms are never changed without producing changes in the most political

---

1. Interestingly, John Lennon was originally invited to play the part of Jesus Christ in this musical. He declined.

2. As an example, they had a large billboard erected in Times Square, reading THE WAR IS OVER IF YOU WANT IT TO BE. They have sponsored peace messages in nearly all the media, as well as conducting their famous "bed-in' " press conferences for peace.

3. Richard A. Peterson, "The Manufacture of Culture: The Case of Popular Music," paper presented at the 65th Annual Meeting of the American Sociological Association, Washington, D.C., August 31–December 3, 1970.

forms and ways." Adolf Hitler recognized the power of the arts and mass media and utilized them well in terms of effecting political changes. Today, the concept of the cultural revolution is gaining in strength. Young radicals of the New Left, recognizing that culture is the way capitalism most immediately effects most of us (popular culture being the most everyday, immediate and consequently overlooked effector), are beginning to concentrate on developing the new cultural forms, confident that political and structural change will follow. In their song of revolution, the Beatles caution one not to look to the "institution" (social structure), but to "free your mind instead."

In the face of all this, why has there been so little interest on the part of American social scientists and policy makers in postulating culture (and more explicitly, *popular* culture) as an important and independent variable of social stability and change? In terms of political policy, one could hypothesize that it seems easier to attempt change of a social structure (i.e., the overthrow of a government) than it does to induce changes in "the hearts and minds of men" via manipulation of their culture. And yet evidence to the contrary seems to exist right before the eyes of the policy makers. The vast American market for artifacts of popular culture has had far reaching effects upon the social structure of Japan. Too, the introduction of American youth serving in Vietnam to marijuana and heroin has combined with the spread of these drugs from the "underground" youth and ethnic cultures to produce what I would hypothesize as the beginnings of some significant changes in the American social structure. The utilization of ping pong by the Red Chinese as a door opener in U.S.-Chinese relations in the Spring of 1971 is but another example of the importance of culture in relation to social structure.

Wylie Sypher has stated: "As a society changes, techniques change, along with the media of the arts and the modes of recording experience. So a style becomes an index to the structure of the contemporary consciousness and to the prevailing attitude toward experience in the contemporary world."[4] It would seem, therefore, that studies of the artifacts of a society's popular culture would be important in that these artifacts should roughly reflect (as well as predict) both the directions and rates of structural change occurring in that society.

In the academic world there has been little history of attention paid to culture by either researchers or theorists. Marxists and neo-Marxists have, until recently, downgraded culture as epiphenomenal superstructure (although it has interested them in so far as it reflects

---

4. Quoted in Marc Rosenberg, "The Underground Is . . . ," paper presented at the first Annual Meeting of the Popular Culture Association, East Lansing, Michigan, April 1971.

a society's political economy).[5] On the other hand, functionalists such as Talcott Parsons have conceptualized culture at such a high level of changelessness that it has been, in actual practice of research, taken as a "given" and ignored.[6] Debate between proponents of these two popular views (as well as the grave problems involved in operationalizing the concept) has led, in most cases, to the ignoring of culture as a variable in sociological research designs.

When contemporary culture has been academically examined, it has been primarily within the context of assertions of negative effects mass culture exerts upon society and/or "high" culture. The bulk of these assertions emanate from humanities departments and, according to Leo Lowenthal and Marjorie Fiske, seem directly traceable to elitist critiques and ideology of the eighteenth century.[7]

In the few instances of concern with popular culture by social scientists, the general opinion seems to be that popular culture lowers the level of taste in society, while rendering persons susceptible to techniques of mass persuasion. This, in turn, endangers the future of democratic social systems.[8] Aside from its ideological overtones, this argument is highly suspect because of the dearth of hard research addressed to the problem.

> Popular art confirms the experience of the majority, in contrast to elite art, which tends to explore the new. For this reason, popular art has been an unusually sensitive and accurate reflector of the attitudes and concerns of the society for which it is produced. Because it is of lesser quality, aesthetically, than elite art, historians and critics have tended to neglect it as a means of access to an era's—and a society's—values and ideas. The popular artist corroborates (occasionally with great skill and in-

---

5. Paul M. Sweezy, *The Present As History: Essays and Reviews On Capitalism and Socialism* (New York: Monthly Review Press, 1962). See Herbert Marcuse for an example of the new interest being taken in culture and capitalism, especially his *One Dimensional Man* (Boston: Beacon Press, 1964).

6. Talcott Parsons, *The Structure of Social Action* (New York: The Free Press, 1937).

7. Leo Lowenthal, "Historical Perspectives of Popular Culture," *American Journal of Sociology* 55 (1950): 323–32; Leo Lowenthal and Marjorie Fiske, "The Debate Over Art and Popular Culture in Eighteenth Century England," in *Common Frontiers of the Social Sciences* (edited by Mirra Komarovsky), (Glencoe, Ill.: The Free Press, 1957), pp. 33–96.

8. Ernest van den Haag and Ralph Ross, *The Fabric of Society* (New York: Harcourt, Brace and Company, 1957); Irving Howe, "Notes on Mass Culture," *Politics* 5 (Spring 1948): 120–23; Paul F. Lassarsfeld and Robert K. Merton, "Mass Communications, Popular Taste and Organized Social Action," in *Mass Culture* (edited by Bernard Rosenberg and David Manning White), (New York: The Free Press, 1957), pp. 457–73. It is interesting to note that the majority of these concerns about the dangers of popular culture were voiced in the repressive McCarthy era of the 1950's.

tensity) values and attitudes already familiar to his audience; his aim is less to provide a new experience than to validate an older one.[9]

The past decade has seen remarkable changes in American society, in terms of levels of technology, consumer power, and leisure time. All these variables have contributed their share to changes in the social structure of the society—all attain a focal point in the forms and formats of present day popular culture. As Alvin Toffler has noted, a man in a leisure-filled world has to structure his personality around differing clusters of values than the man in a work-centered society. "The decline of work creates a vacuum in which other values, once the property of a special elite, sprout."[10] It seems, therefore, that research designs employing popular culture as a variable would be not only worthwhile, but imperative undertakings for any social scientist interested in contemporary America. The sad fact is that little research of this sort has been reported upon within the academic boundaries of the social sciences. Those concerned have had to range far and wide among the media in their search for relevant material.

This collection is an attempt to bring together, from varied sources, essays of interest and relevance concerning social structure and popular culture. Because of the great variation in source areas, these pieces vary greatly in form; however, their content is in all cases addressed to differing facets of the theoretical problem—what is the relationship between social structure and popular culture?

The underlying assumption of this book is that study of the artifacts of American popular culture can shed light upon our society (most especially, its structural aspects). By presenting pieces from varied and cross-disciplinary sources, one is bound to step on some academic toes even while elevating the egos of others. This is as it should be. The perspectives, methodologies and modes of presentation of popular cultural artifacts range from quite qualitative literary discursions to the more quantitative studies of the social sciences. The purpose of this book, however, is to enable the reader to get a feeling of the scope and depth of some of the more problematic aspects of contemporary American society via study of artifacts of that society's culture—*whatever* the methodology or perspective employed.

In an area as new as that of the study of popular culture, there is yet no broad body of material from which to draw—methods and topics are only now becoming articulated. In examining the pieces in this volume, the reader should continually remind himself of this fact

---

9. Russel Nye, *The Unembarrassed Muse: The Popular Arts in America* (New York: The Dial Press, 1970).
10. Alvin Toffler, *The Culture Consumers* (New York: St. Martin's Press, 1964), p. 229.

—asking questions as to the relevance of the material and the reliability and validity of the studies reported. What future directions are suggested? What studies could be undertaken to "shore up" the findings reported on here? How could it be better done?

The essays in this collection are linked with a running commentary by the editor. In all cases, this commentary is designed to point out further directions for study as well as to provide a consistent context from which to view these stylistically varied pieces. The method of presentation is designed to raise questions and issues in the reader's mind which will aid him in attacking the individual essays and the commentary itself—not merely submitting to the material passively.

Finally, it is obvious that what is popular today may not necessarily be so tomorrow. Some of the artifacts reported upon in this book may hold vastly different positions within the cultural structure of the society by the time of the book's publication. (What was the fate of the movie industry with the advent of television? What happened to the Beatles?) The reader should be aware of this and utilize selections as examples of how to study (or how not to study) similar cultural artifacts. He or she might also speculate upon the *whys* involved in the shifting positions of artifacts within the American scene.

Marshall McLuhan once said; "we don't know who discovered water, but we are pretty sure it wasn't fish." It is the editor's hope that this collection will aid in stimulating more debate and research than the book itself contains. That is its justification. You are its judge.

George H. Lewis
Stockton, California
July 21, 1971

ACKNOWLEDGMENTS

The author wishes to thank the following for permission to reprint their material:

Ray B. Browne, "Popular Culture: Notes Toward A Definition," from *Popular Culture and Curricula*, by Ray B. Browne and Ronald Ambrosetti, copyright © 1970 by Bowling Green Popular Press. Reprinted by permission of Bowling Green Popular Press and the author.

Russel B. Nye, "Notes On Popular Culture," *Journal of Popular Culture*, Spring 1971, copyright © 1971 by Ray B. Browne. Reprinted by permission.

Bruce Lohof, "The Higher Meaning of Marlboro Cigarettes," *Journal of Popular Culture*, Winter 1969, copyright © 1969 by Ray B. Browne. Reprinted by permission.

Tom Wolfe, "Clean Run At Riverhead," reprinted with the permission of Farrar, Strauss and Giroux, Inc., from *The Kandy* Kolored Tangerine* Flake Streamline Baby*, copyright © 1963, 1964, 1965 by Thomas K. Wolfe, Jr., copyright © 1963, 1964, 1965 by *New York Herald Tribune*, Inc.

George H. Lewis, "*Prole Sport*: The Case of Roller Derby," prepared especially for this volume.

William C. Martin, "The God-Hucksters of Radio," *The Atlantic Monthly*, copyright © 1970 by *The Atlantic Monthly Company*, Boston, Massachusetts. Edited version. Reprinted with permission of the author and the publisher.

John D. McCarthy, Richard A. Peterson and William L. Yancy, "Singing Along With the Silent Majority," prepared especially for this volume. Printed by permission of the authors.

David Sonenschein, "Love and Sex In the Romance Magazines," *Journal of Popular Culture*, Fall 1970, copyright © 1970 by Ray B. Browne. Reprinted by permission.

Walter M. Gerson and Sander H. Lund, "*Playboy* Magazine: Sophisticated Smut or Social Revolution," *Journal of Popular Culture*, Winter 1967, copyright © 1967 by Ray B. Browne. Reprinted by permission.

The Report of the Commission on Obscenity and Pornography, "Patrons of Adult Bookstores and Movies," Washington, D.C., United States Government Printing Office, 1970. Edited version.

Clinton R. Sanders, "The Portrayal of War and the Fighting Man in Novels Of the Vietnam War," *Journal of Popular Culture*, Winter 1969, copyright © by Ray B. Browne. Reprinted by permission.

Herbert J. Gans, "The Creator-Audience Relationship In the Mass Media: An Analysis of Movie-Making." Reprinted with permission of The Macmillan

Company from *Mass Culture* by Bernard Rosenberg and David Manning White, copyright © 1957 by The Free Press, a Corporation.

Jacoba Atlas, "A Conversation With Arthur Penn," *Rolling Stone*, March 7, 1970, copyright © 1970 by Straight Arrow Publishers, Inc. Reprinted by permission of the publisher.

Eckard V. Toy, Jr., "The Social Meaning of Television Censorship," in *Challenges In American Culture*, edited by Ray B. Browne, Larry N. Landrum and William R. Bottorff, copyright © 1970 by the Bowling Green University Popular Press. Edited version. Reprinted by permission of the publisher.

Hugh Gardner, "Bureaucracy At the Bridge Table," prepared especially for this volume. Printed by permission of the author.

Arthur Asa Berger, "The Spyder (Sting-Ray, Screamer) Bike: An American Original," prepared especially for this volume. Printed by permission of the author.

Daniel and Susan Halas, "Hamburgers 18c," *Esquire*, July 1968, first published in *Esquire* magazine, copyright © 1968 by *Esquire*, Inc. Edited version.

M. F. K. Fisher, "The Social Stratification of TV Dinners," edited and retitled version of "What Is the Difference Between This Photograph and a Real TV Dinner?" *Esquire*, August 1970, first published in *Esquire* magazine, copyright © 1970 by *Esquire*, Inc. Reprinted by permission of Russell and Volkening, Inc.

George H. Lewis, "Pop Society and the Nouveau Riche," prepared especially for this volume.

Media-Scope, "Courting the Black Billionaire," *Media-Scope*, August 1969. Edited version. Reprinted by permission of *Media-Scope*.

Michael Alexander, "The Impressions," from *Rolling Stone*, December 27, 1969, copyright © 1969 by Straight Arrow Publishers, Inc. All rights reserved. Edited version. Reprinted by permission of the publisher.

Charles Peavy, "Pop Art and the Black Revolution," *Journal of Popular Culture*, Fall, 1969, copyright © 1969 by Ray B. Browne. Reprinted by permission.

Charles Peavy, "The Black Art of Propaganda: The Cultural Arm of the Black Power Movement," *Rocky Mountain Social Science Journal*, April 1970, copyright © 1970. Reprinted by permission of the author and the publisher.

Linda Harrison, "On Cultural Nationalism," *The Black Panther*, February 2, 1969.

Emory, "Revolutionary Art/Black Liberation," *The Black Panther*, May 18, 1968.

Nikki Giovanni, "Black Poems, Poseurs, and Power," *Negro Digest*, June 1969, copyright © 1969 by Nikki Giovanni. Reprinted by permission of *Black World* and the author.

Arthur Asa Berger, "Comics and Culture," prepared especially for this volume. Printed by permission of the author.

Harvey Pekar, "Rapping About Cartoonists, Particularly Robert Crumb,"*Journal of Popular Culture*, Spring 1970, copyright © 1970 by Ray B. Browne. Reprinted by permission.

Amie Hill, "Tattoo Renaissance," *Rolling Stone*, October 1, 1970, copyright © 1970 by Straight Arrow Publishers, Inc. Reprinted by permission of the publisher.

Nora Sayre, "Revolt For Fun and Profit," *Esquire*, August 1970, first published in *Esquire* magazine, copyright © 1970 by Esquire, Inc., copyright © 1970 by

Nora Sayre. Edited version. Reprinted by permission of John Cushman Associates, Inc.

Joe Ferrandiro, "Rock Culture and the Development of Social Consciousness," *Radical America*, November 1969, copyright © 1969 by Paul Buhle. Reprinted by permission of Paul Buhle and *Radical America*.

Robert Rosenstone, "The Times They Are A-Changin': The Music of Protest," a revised and updated version of an article that first appeared in *The Annals of the American Academy of Political and Social Science*, March 1969. Reprinted by permission of the author and publisher.

George H. Lewis, "The Pop Artist and His Product: Mixed Up Confusion," a revised and updated version of an article that first appeared in the *Journal of Popular Culture*, Fall 1970, copyright © 1970 by Ray B. Browne. Reprinted by permission.

Michael Lydon, "Rock For Sale," *Ramparts*, (December, 1969), copyright © 1969 by Michael Lydon. Reprinted by permission of Michael Lydon c/o International Famous Agency.

Sol Stern, "Altamont: Pearl Harbor to the Woodstock Nation," *Scanlan's*, March 1970, copyright © 1970 by Sol Stern. Reprinted by permission of the author and publisher.

Garry Wills, "The Making of the Yippie Culture," *Esquire*, November 1969. Reprinted by permission of *Esquire* magazine, copyright © 1969 by *Esquire, Inc.*

Barbara Falconer, "Revolution Or Tomatoes?" an expanded version of a piece first published in *California Living Magazine*, October 11, 1970. Reprinted by permission of the author.

Hugh Romney, "The Hog Farm," *The Realist*, November-December 1969. Edited version. Reprinted by permission of Paul Krassner.

SIDE-SADDLE
on the
GOLDEN CALF

Social Structure and
Popular Culture in America

Their idols are silver and gold,
The work of men's hands....
They that make them shall be like unto them;
Yea, everyone that trusteth in them ...
                    113TH PSALM

Things are in the saddle
And ride mankind ...
                    RALPH WALDO EMERSON

CONCEPTS AND ISSUES

PERSPECTIVE: WHAT IS POPULAR CULTURE?

The study of culture within the context of "mass society" has, since its inception in American scholarly circles of the late 1930's and early 1940's, been most often lodged within an evaluative context. More specifically, American intellectuals have divided themselves into two opposing camps with respect to what sociologist Leo Lowenthal has aptly pointed out as a basic dilemma concerning modern man's existence: "on the one hand, a positive attitude toward all instrumentalities for the socialization of the individual; on the other hand, a deep concern about the inner fate of the individual under the leveling powers of institutional and other organizational forms of leisure activity."[1]

> On the one side stand those . . . who find it possible to approve the major trends and patterns visible in the country today. If they are disconcerted by some of the excrescences of bad taste and unwise self-indulgence they see around them, they are nevertheless more than heartened by such things as the number of symphony orchestras, and the sales of books and classical records . . . .
> On the other side are arrayed those . . . who find themselves disconcerted, especially if they have had any Marxist background, by the fact that no people has ever been so free from material want, at the same time that, in the judgment of this group, the wealth is being spent in ways which are aesthetically and morally revolting. The responsibility for this phenomenon is attributed to some aspect of the mass-ness of the society and some dimension of the popular-ness of the culture.[2]

The dialogue that this ideological division created filled the scholarly journals of the 1940's, 1950's and early 1960's with debate, much of it heavily value laden.[3] The problem, as critic Leslie Fiedler so bril-

---

1. Leo Lowenthal, "Historical Perspectives of Popular Culture," *American Journal of Sociology* 55 (1950): 324.
2. Melvin Tumin, "Popular Culture and the Open Society," in *Mass Culture: The Popular Arts In America,* ed. Bernard Rosenberg and David Manning White (New York: The Free Press, 1957), p. 548.
3. Examples include the articles appearing in the Spring 1960 issue of *Daedalus,* as well as those in sections one, two and eight of *Mass Culture: The Popular Arts In America.* See also Norman Jacobs, *Culture for the Millions?* (New York: D. von Nostrand Company, 1961).

liantly pointed out, has a great deal to do with the fact of class distinctions in a supposedly democratic society. Distinctions among cultural artifacts are made in terms of their "worth." The more worthy the artifact, the "higher" the class level of those who consume it. In this manner, cultural artifacts serve the function of underscoring class levels, becoming "tags," or indicators, of one's stratum within the American class system. In Fiedler's words, the artifacts "suggest the intolerable notion of a hierarchy of taste, a hierarchy of values, the possibility of cultural classes in a democratic state."[4]

And so the debate raged on. Would the proliferation of "mass" or "popular" culture inexorably reduce the taste of the nation to its lowest common denominator, helping to create masses of the conforming and uninvolved, watched over and manipulated by the elite producers of these cultural artifacts (who themselves consumed the artifacts of "high" culture)? Or, would this proliferation of artifacts mean that individuals could actively choose their own unique configuration of cultural items, thus building individual identities rather than passively accepting the traditional and class-based configurations that had been thrust upon them in the past?

Sociologist Edward Shils, in 1959 at the Tamiment Institute seminar on mass culture, articulated this latter view—mass society has enhanced individuality because of the increasing number of choices or decisions that are not traditionally made for one, but are actively made by the individual.[5] This line of thought has since been pushed further by Alvin Toffler in a 1971 series of lectures and in his book, *Future Shock.*[6] Toffler's point is that the *early* stages of industrialization, with their attendant and primitive technologies produce standardization of products and hence severely limit the areas in which an individual can actively make decisions and choices. However, Toffler argues, this is only a first stage. In an advanced industrial society, such as present-day America, technology actually increases diversification of products and allows the individual the opportunity to make a greater number of decisions and choices—to the point of "decisional overload" on the part of many. Thus Toffler would argue that concerns about the leveling powers of societal institutions are no longer relevant to American society. What *is* relevant, according to Toffler, is a concern with the effects of forcing people to make *too many* individual decisions and choices in too short a time.

Those who equate mass culture with conformity would probably counter by asking about what *sorts* of options one has available. Does

4. Leslie A. Fiedler, "The Middle Against Both Ends," *Encounter* 5, (1955): 23.
5. Edward Shils, "Mass Society And Its Culture," in *Culture For the Millions?* ed. Norman Jacobs, p. 31.
6. Alvin Toffler, *Future Shock* (New York: Random House, Inc., 1970).

the option of choosing one of twenty brands of aspirin constitute a significant choice that reflects upon and reinforces the individuality of the chooser? As one cigarette company puts it, their cigarettes are for those individualists who break from the crowd. Yet, if this line were not effective in establishing a crowd of "individualists," would the company have continued to use the slogan as long as it did? Are the choices available those of *genus* or merely of *differentia?* And how are they perceived by the body of choosers?

By the early 1970's, the debates of the 1950's and early 1960's had seemed to lose much of their immediacy—mass society has *not* made automatons of us all. Other questions have become much more relevant, especially in the social sciences. What are the connections between life styles, interaction patterns, values, and the consumption, creation, and diffusion of cultural artifacts? And how do these produced artifacts relate to or reflect the changing social structure of American society? These are the questions to which contemporary social scientists are beginning to address themselves. These are the questions this book is all about.

> In my opinion, emphasis on cultural objects misses the point. A sociologist (and to analyze mass culture is a sociological enterprise) must focus on the function of such objects in people's lives: he must study how they are used; who produces what for whom; why, and with what effects. To be sure, value judgments cannot be avoided, but the qualities of the product become relevant only when related to its social functions.[7]

To study popular culture, one must first define it—not a simple task. In the following piece, Ray B. Browne, an academic deeply involved in American studies, surveys the various ways in which culture has been classified. Browne finally arrives at his own (broad) definition of popular culture. As he puts it, at this early stage (early in the sense that serious and systematic study of American popular culture began only in the middle-to-late 1960's), definitional *inclusiveness* is better than definitional *exclusiveness.* Do you agree?

---

7. Ernest Van Den Haag, "A Dissent from the Consensual Society," in *Culture For the Millions?* ed. Norman Jacobs, p. 53.

POPULAR CULTURE:
NOTES TOWARD A DEFINITION

Ray B. Browne

"Popular Culture" is an indistinct term whose edges blur into imprecision. Scarcely any two commentators who try to define it agree in all aspects of what popular culture really is. Most critics, in fact, do not attempt to define it; instead, after distinguishing between it and the mass media, and between it and "high" culture, most assume that everybody knows that whatever is widely disseminated and experienced is "popular culture."

Some observers divide the total culture of a people into "minority" and "majority" categories. Other observers classify culture into High-Cult, Mid-Cult and Low-Cult, or High-Brow, Mid-Brow and Low-Brow, leaving out, apparently, the level that would perhaps be called Folk-Cult or Folk-Brow, though Folk culture is now taking on, even among the severest critics of popular culture a high class and achievement unique unto itself. Most of the discriminating observers agree, in fact, that there are perhaps actually four areas of culture: Elite, Popular, Mass and Folk, with the understanding that none is a discrete unity standing apart and unaffected by the others.

One reason for the lack of a precise definition is that the serious study of "popular culture" has been neglected in American colleges and universities. Elitist critics of our culture—notably such persons as Dwight Macdonald and Edmund Wilson—have always insisted that whatever was widespread was artistically and esthetically deficient, therefore unworthy of study. They have taught that "culture" to be worthwhile must necessarily be limited to the elite, aristocratic, and the minority. They felt that mass or popular culture—especially as it appeared in the mass media—would vitiate real culture. This attitude persists today among some of the younger critics. William Gass, for example, the esthetician and critic, takes the extreme position that "the products of popular culture, by and large, have no more esthetic quality than a brick in the street. . . . Any esthetic intentions is entirely absent, and because it is desired to manipulate consciousness directly, achieve one's effect there, no mind is paid to the intrinsic nature of its objects: they lack finish, complexity, stasis, individuality, coherence, depth, and endurance."

Such an attitude as Gass' is perhaps an extreme statement of the elitist critic's point of view. Luckily the force of numerous critics' arguments is weakening such attitudes. Popular Culture has a dimension, a thrust and —most important—a reality that has nothing to do with its esthetic accomplishment, though that has more merit than is often given to it.

This point of view is demonstrated by the talented young stylist Tom Wolfe, who, perhaps writing more viscerally than intellectually, thumbs his nose at the prejudice and snobbery that has always held at arms length all claims of validity if not esthetic accomplishment of the "culture" of the masses.

Susan Sontag, a brilliant young critic and esthetician, is more effective in bludgeoning the old point of view. Far from alarmed at the apparent new esthetic, she sees that it is merely a change in attitude, not a death's blow to culture and art:

> What we are getting is not the demise of art, but a transformation of the function of art. Art, which arose in human society as magical-religious operation, and passed over into a technique for depicting and commenting on secular reality, has in our own time arrogated to itself a new function—neither religious, nor serving a secularized religious function, nor merely secular or profane. . . . Art today is a new kind of instrument, an instrument for modifying consciousness and organizing new modes of sensibility.

To Sontag the unprecedented complexity of the world has made inevitable and very necessary this change in the function of art. This is virtually the same attitude held by Marshall McLuhan:

> A technological extension of our bodies designed to alleviate physical stress can bring on psychic stress that may be much worse. . . . Art is exact information of how to rearrange one's psyche to anticipate the next blow from our own extended psyches . . . in experimental art, men are given the exact specifications of coming violence to their own psyche from their own counterirritants or technology. For those parts of ourselves that we thrust out in the form of new inventions are attempts to counter or neutralize collective pressures and irritations. But the counterirritant usually proves a greater plague than the initial irritant like a drug habit. And it is here that the artist can show us how to "ride with the punch," instead of "taking it on the chin."

An equally important aspect of popular culture as index and corrector is its role as comic voice. Popular humor provides a healthy element in a nation's life. It pricks the pompous, devaluates the inflated, and snipes at the overly solemn. For example, such organs of popular culture as the magazines spoofed Henry James' pomposity during his lifetime, spoofed his "high" seriousness and in general tended to humanize him.

A more reasonable attitude than Gass' and one that is becoming increasingly acceptable is that held by the philosopher Abraham Kaplan: That popular culture has considerable accomplishment and even more real possibilities and it is developing but has not realized its full potential. All areas draw from one another. The Mass area being largely imitative, draws from the others without altering much. Elite art draws heavily from both folk and, perhaps to a slightly lesser degree, popular arts. Popular art draws from Elite and Mass, and Folk, but does not take any without subjecting it to a greater or lesser amount of creative change. That popular culture has "no more esthetic quality than a brick in the street" or at least no more esthetic potential is a contention refuted by America's greatest writers—

Hawthorne, Melville, Whitman, Twain, to name only four—as well as the greatest writers of all times and countries—Homer, Shakespeare, Dickens, Dostoevski, Tolstoi, for example.

Melville provides an excellent case in point. *Moby Dick* is the greatest creative book written in America and one of the half dozen greatest written anywhere. Its greatness derives from the sum total of its many parts. It is a blend of nearly all elements of all cultures of mid-nineteenth-century America. Melville took all the culture around him—trivial and profound— Transcendentalism and the plumbing of the depths of the human experience, but also demonism, popular theater, the shanghai gesture, jokes about pills and gas on the stomach, etc., and boiled them in the tryworks of his fiery genius into the highest art.

Many definitions of popular culture turn on methods of dissemination. Those elements which are too sophisticated for the mass media are generally called Elite culture, those distributed through these media that are something less than "mass" that is such things as the smaller magazines and newspapers, the less widely distributed books, museums and less sophisticated galleries, so-called clothes line art exhibits, and the like— are called in the narrow sense of the term "popular," those elements that are distributed through the mass media are "mass" culture, and those which are or were at one time disseminated by oral and nonoral methods— on levels "lower" than the mass media—are called "folk."

All definitions of such a complex matter, though containing a certain amount of validity and usefulness, are bound to be to a certain extent inadequate or incorrect. Perhaps a workable definition can best be arrived at by looking at one of the culture's most salient and quintessential aspects—its artistic creations—because the artist perhaps more than any one else draws from the totality of experience and best reflects it.

Shakespeare and his works are an excellent example. When he was producing his plays at the Globe Theater, Shakespeare was surely a "popular" author and his works were elements of "popular" culture, though they were at the same time also High or Elite culture, for they were very much part of the lives of both the groundlings and the nobles. Later, in America, especially during the nineteenth century, all of his works were well known, his name was commonplace, and he was at the same time still High art, Popular (even mass) art and Folk art. In the twentieth century, however, his works are more distinguishable as parts of various levels. *Hamlet* is still a play of both High and Popular art. The most sophisticated and scholarly people still praise it. But *Hamlet* is also widely distributed on TV, radio and through the movies. It is a commonplace on all levels of society and is therefore a part of "popular culture" in the broadest sense of the term. Other plays by Shakespeare, however, have not become a part of "popular" culture. *Titus Andronicus,* for example, for any of several reasons, is not widely known by the general public. It remains, thus, Elite culture.

Wideness of distribution and popularity in this sense are one major aspect of popular culture. But there are others. Many writers would be automatically a part of popular culture if their works sold only a few copies—Frank G. Slaughter and Frank Yerby, for example. Louis Auchincloss also, though his works are of a different kind than Slaughter's and Yerby's, because his subject is Wall Street and high finance, and these are subjects of popular culture.

Aside from distribution another major difference between high and popular culture, and among popular culture, mass culture and folk culture, is the motivation of the persons contributing, the makers and shapers of culture. On the Elite or sophisticated level, the creators value individualism, individual expression, the exploration and discovery of new art forms, of new ways of stating, the exploration and discovery of new depths in life's experiences.

On the other levels of culture there is usually less emphasis placed upon, and less accomplishment reached in, this plumbing of reality. Generally speaking, both popular and mass artists are less interested in the experimental and searching than in the restatement of the old and accepted. But there are actually vast differences in the esthetic achievements attained in the works from these two levels, and different aspirations and goals, even within these somewhat limited objectives. As Hall and Whannel have pointed out:

> In mass art the formula is everything—an escape from, rather than a means to, originality. The popular artist may use the conventions to select, emphasize and stress (or alter the emphasis and stress) so as to delight the audience with a kind of creative surprise. Mass art uses the stereotypes and formulae to simplify the experience, to mobilize stock feelings and to 'get them going.'

The popular artist is superior to the mass artist because for him "stylization is necessary, and the conventions provide an agreed basis from which true creative invention springs." It is a serious error therefore to agree with Dwight MacDonald (in *Against the American Grain*) that all popular art "includes the spectator's reactions in the work itself instead of forcing him to make his own responses." Consider, for example, the reactions of two carriers of non-Elite culture, the first of popular culture, the banjo player Johnny St. Cyr. He always felt that the creative impulses of the average person and his responses in a creative situation were immense:

> You see, the average man is very musical. Playing music for him is just relaxing. He gets as much kick out of playing as other folks get out of dancing. The more enthusiastic his audience is, why the more spirit the working man's got to play. And with your natural feelings that way you never make the same thing twice. Every time you play a tune new ideas come to mind and you slip that one in.

Compare that true artist's philosophy with that of Liberace, to whom the "whole trick is to keep the tune well out in front," to play "the melodies" and skip the "spiritual struggles." He always knows "just how many notes (his) audience will stand for," and if he has time left over he fills in "with a lot of runs up and down the keyboard."

Here in condensed form is the difference between popular and mass art and popular and mass artists. Both aim for different goals. St. Cyr is a truly creative artist in both intent and accomplishment. His credentials are not invalidated merely by the fact that he works in essentially a popular idiom. Given the limitations of his medium—if indeed these limitations are real—he can still be just as great a creator as—perhaps greater than—Rubenstein. It is incorrect to pit jazz against classical music, the popular against the elite. They are not in competition. Each has its own purposes, techniques and accomplishments. They complement each other rather than compete.

Another fine example can be found among the youth of today and their rebellion against what they consider the establishment. They are obviously not a part of the static mass, to whom escape is everything. Instead they are vigorously active, and in their action create dynamic and fine works of art, as examination of their songs, their art, their movies, and so on, dramatically demonstrates.

It is also unfair to give blanket condemnation to mass art, though obviously the accomplishments of mass art are less than those of "higher" forms. Liberace does not aspire to much, and perhaps reaches less. His purposes and techniques are inferior, but not all his, or the many other workers in the level, are completely without value.

All levels of culture, it must never be forgotten, are distorted by the lenses of snobbery and prejudice which the observers wear. There are no hard and fast lines separating one level from another.

Popular culture also includes folk culture. The relationship between folk culture and popular and elite cultures is still debatable. In many ways folk culture borrows from and imitates both.

Historically folk art has come more from the hall than from the novel, has depended more upon the truly creative—though unsophisticated—spirit than the mediocre imitator. "Sir Patrick Spens," one of the greatest songs (poems) ever written, was originally the product of a single creative genius. Today's best folklore-to-be, that is the most esthetically satisfying folklore which is working into tradition today, is that of such people as Woody Guthrie, Larry Gorman and such individual artists.

To a large number of observers, however, folklore is felt to be the same as popular culture. To another large number folklore derives directly from popular culture, with only a slight time lag. To them, today's popular culture is tomorrow's folklore. Both notions are gross and out of line.

Esthetically folk culture has two levels. There is superb folk art and deficient mediocre folk art. Esthetically folk art is more nearly akin to Elite art, despite the lack of sophistication that much folk art has, than to popular. Elite art has much that is inferior, as even the most prejudiced critic must admit. In motivation of artist, also, folk art is close to Elite, for like the Elite artist the truly accomplished folk artist values individualism and personal expression, he explores new forms and seeks new depths in expression and feeling. But there are at the same time workers in folklore who are mere imitators, just trying to get along—exactly like their counterparts in mass culture.

Thus all elements in our culture (or cultures) are closely related and are not mutually exclusive one from another. They constitute one long continuum. Perhaps the best metaphorical figure for all is that of a flattened ellipsis, or a lens. In the center, largest in bulk and easiest seen through is Popular Culture, which includes Mass Culture.

On either end of the lens are High and Folk Cultures, both looking fundamentally alike in many respects and both having a great deal in common, for both have keen direct vision and extensive peripheral insight and acumen. All four derive in many ways and to many degrees from one another, and the lines of demarcation between any two are indistinct and mobile.

Despite the obvious difficulty of arriving at a hard and fast definition of popular culture, it will probably be to our advantage—and a comfort to many who need one—to arrive at some viable though tentative understanding of how popular culture can be defined.

Two scholars who do attempt a definition, following George Santayana's broad distinctions between work and play, believe that "Popular Culture is really what people do when they are not working." This definition is both excessively general and overly exclusive, for it includes much that is "high" culture and leaves out many aspects which obviously belong to popular culture.

One serious scholar defines a total culture as "the body of intellectual and imaginative work which each generation receives" as its tradition. Basing our conclusion on this one, a viable definition for Popular Culture is all those elements of life which are not narrowly intellectual or creatively elitist and which are generally though not necessarily disseminated through the mass media. Popular Culture consists of the spoken and printed word, sounds, pictures, objects and artifacts. "Popular Culture" thus embraces all levels of our society and culture other than the Elite—the "popular," "mass" and "folk." It includes most of the bewildering aspects of life which hammer us daily.

Such a definition, though perhaps umbrella-like in its comprehensiveness, provides the latitude needed at this point, it seems, for the serious scholar to study the world around him. Later, definitions may need to pare edges and change lighting and emphasis. But for the moment, inclusiveness is perhaps better than exclusiveness.

REFERENCES

Gass, William H. "Even if by all the Oxen in the World." In Ray B. Browne, et al. *Frontiers of American Culture*. Purdue University, 1968.

Hall, Stuart and Paddy Whannel. *The Popular Arts.* New York: Pantheon Books, Inc., 1964.

McLuhan, Marshall. *Understanding Media.* New York: McGraw-Hill Book Company, 1964. *War and Peace in Global Village.* New York: McGraw-Hill Book Company, 1968.

Shapiro, Nat and Nat Hentoff. *Hear Me Talkin' to Ya.* New York: Dover Books, Inc., 1966.

Sontag, Susan. *Against Interpretation.* New York: Farrar, Strauss, & Giroux, 1966.

Williams, Raymond. *Culture and Society, 1780–1950.* London: Chatto & Winders, 1960. *The Long Revolution.* New York: Columbia University Press, 1961.

Browne's suggestion of metaphorically visualizing popular culture as a flattened ellipsis, or lens, is intriguing. If one were to keep this in mind, while also musing on the role the *motivation* of the creator plays in shaping his product, one might indeed begin to come to grips with the concept of popular culture.

Browne's spatial depiction of the concepts involved helps clarify still another point. As he has noted, most observers have defined elite and folk culture along the "good-or-bad," "high-or-low" continuum—Browne himself falls into this trap with relation to folk culture near the close of his essay. Outside of the obvious value judgment inherent in this mode of classification, there is also a more subtle trap; that of the stability and staticity implied in the ranking.[8] The concept of *popular culture*, however, implies kinetics and transitivity—and most especially when thought of in terms of Browne's ellipsis. One is more apt to conceive in terms of what is "in or out" than in the more absolute and static terms of "good or bad." This sort of thinking leads one in the direction of a modular frame of reference, where only the framework (social structure) remains relatively constant while the units (artifacts) themselves are constantly shifting from position to position allowing an impression of novelty within the skeleton of the whole. It is on the concept of *novelty* that the process of the diffusion of the artifacts of popular culture depends—it is the novelty of artifacts that holds interest in them and it is this novelty that stimulates the diffusion processes of the social system.[9]

While many of the traditional debaters of the 1950's lamented the death of folk art and culture at the hands of the mass culture creators, and Browne includes folk culture as only one concept huddling

---

8. I am indebted to Mary Shy for this observation.

9. These are the processes labeled by Erving Goffman as the circulation of symbols within the system. Erving Goffman, "Symbols of Class Status," *British Journel of Sociology* II (1951: 294–304.

under his "umbrella-like" definition of popular culture, cultural critic and essayist Tom Wolfe has taken a slightly different tack. Wolfe contends that post–World War II leisure patterns of Americans have reflected the rising level of affluence of the entire society to the extent that "subcultures" now do *not* have to merely accept a mass culture handed down to them, as the traditionalists have suggested. Rather, these subcultures are creating and consuming their *own* cultural artifacts. This rise of "new" folk cultures, Wolfe suggests, has great relevance for the society as a whole—the introduction of new artifacts into a youth or ethnic subculture lodged in a society with the sophisticated transportation and communication network of present-day America, can only result in the swift diffusion of these artifacts throughout the larger system (even to those higher reaches of the social system that Wolfe labels "pop" society).[10]

> Practically nobody has bothered to see what these changes are all about. People have been looking at the new money since the war in economic terms only. Nobody will even take a look at our incredible new national pastimes, things like stock car racing, drag racing, demolition derbies, sports that attract five to ten million more spectators than football, baseball and basketball each year. Part of it is a built-in class bias. The educated classes in this country, as in every country, the people who grow up to control visual and printed communication media, are all plugged into what is, when one gets down to it, an ancient, aristocratic aesthetic. Stock car racing, custom cars—and, for that matter, the jerk, the monkey, rock music—still seem beneath serious consideration, still the preserve of ratty people with ratty hair and dermatitis and corroded thoracic boxes and so forth. Yet all these rancid people are creating new styles all the time and changing the life of the whole country in ways that nobody even seems to bother to record, much less analyze.[11]

This process of diffusion creates consequences not only for the larger society, but quite importantly for the members of the subcultures from which the artifacts originated. These consequences, I suggest, manifest themselves many times in the form of tensions, reactions, and the further alienation of those large subcultures (the youth, the black community, and others) within the society that are seeking to create and retain some sort of cultural identity. The tensions and strains involved are critical—and warrant much more and

10. For further insights into this point, see Georg Simmel's cogent discussion of the social significance of secrecy, adornment, and secrecy as adornment within the context of subcultural systems. Georg Simmel, *The Sociology of Georg Simmel,* translated by Kurt Wolf (Glencoe, Ill.: The Free Press), 1950, pp. 334–44.
11. Tom Wolfe, *The Kandy & Kolored Tangerine & Flake Streamline Baby,* (New York: Farrar, Straus, and Giroux, 1965), p. XV.

serious attention from social scientists than they have been receiving.[12]
As Charles Winick has pointed out:

> One reason for the great, recent success of pop culture is the
> speed with which rituals and artifacts have been taken out of
> the possession of the outsiders and priced at what the market
> will bear. The outsider culture serves an unanticipated function
> in providing our luxury and leisure markets with new games and
> toys. Once they get into the mainstream, the outsider tastemak-
> ers move on to find new ways of affirming their alienation from
> the respectable world.[13]

As Browne and Wolfe have pointed out, the tendency has been to dismiss these artifacts of popular culture as irrelevant because of their
"esthetic deficiencies." This should not be the case.

Russel Nye, first president of the Popular Culture Association,
points out in the following piece further reasons why the study of popular culture in contemporary America is so important. He goes on to
suggest that if we are serious about this study, we have to develop serious methodologies. As he states, "Popular culture can be considered
as a point at which the investigative techniques of the social sciences
and the humanities may converge. . . . There is, then, no single, approved methodology for the study of popular culture, but several."
Throughout this book, the reader should keep himself aware of this
point. He or she should critically examine the varied methods employed by the contributors in their studies of social structure and popular culture, noting their relative effectiveness, yet at the same time
always questioning how these pioneering efforts can be improved.

---

12. Ned Polsky is among the few who have noted these tensions. He labels this
type of diffusion as the stealing of signals from a subculture. This, in turn, generates attempts to create new symbols (the concept of novelty) to replace those
that have been appropriated. Ned Polsky *Hustlers, Beats and Others* (Chicago:
Aldine, 1967), pp. 144–82.
13. Charles Winick, *The New People* (New York: Pegasus, 1968), p. 16.

NOTES ON POPULAR CULTURE

Russel B. Nye

First, let us define terms. I use the word *popular* to mean that which is
widely diffused, generally accepted, approved by the majority. *Culture,* an
especially protean word, I use in the sense of Edward Tylor's definition as
"that complex whole which includes knowledge, belief, art, custom, and
other capabilities acquired by man as a member of society," a definition
which, of course, needs to be focused more precisely, depending on the
use of popular materials within particular academic desciplines. This is not

the occasion to trace the history of popular culture, or of attitudes toward it; this has already been done with distinction by others.[1] I am more concerned at the moment with considering briefly recent trends in the study of popular culture, as observed by cultural historians, literary critics, historians of ideas, and philosophers of aesthetics. Within the last decade there has been, if I read the signs right, the beginnings of a significant shift in our attitudes toward relationships among cultural levels and cultural values. Artists and audiences seem to be crossing borders they shouldn't; critics are asking whether the lines that presumably separate "highbrow" from "lowbrow" or "elite" from "popular" (those classic terms never quite clearly established but traditionally and uncritically accepted) ought to be so sharply defined, or perhaps ought to be there at all. People who know Beethoven and Bartok listen to the Beatles; *Time* and *Newsweek* and Leonard Bernstein have approved California and Liverpool rock; even the *New York Review of Books, mirabile dictu,* has published an admiring article on popular music. *Peanuts* is written about by theologians and philosophers; there are articles on Marvel Comics and horror movies; John Lennon and Leonard Cohen are studied the way graduate students used to study Eliot and Pound. *Playboy* has a centerfold in the ancient and honorable *Police Gazette* tradition, and also publishes essays by Leslie Fiedler and Harvey Cox. There is a rock-opera and a folk-mass; painters use soup cans and highway signs and hamburgers. Clearly, things are not what they used to be.

There are a number of reasons for this wave of interest in, and the recent reevaluation of, the aims, audiences, conventions, and artifacts of popular culture. I should like to identify five which seem to me immediately operative, although there are probably others equally important. First, the attention given by social scientists to mass communications and media study has revealed serious limitations in the older concept of society as composed of a naive, maneuverable mass on the one hand, and a self-controlled, cultural elite on the other. The real relationships between the mass media and their various publics is proving to be much more complicated than the simplistic picture drawn by the critics of the thirties and forties. Social psychologists find that audiences resist manipulation in ways not earlier suspected; that mass communications do more than merely transmit information; that if the media do distort reality, people have compensatory built-in resistances, of which critics have never taken full account. Furthermore, it also seems clear that attempts to convince mass audiences that they ought to reject popular culture are ingenuous and ineffective, and that the critics of popular culture too may have their own biases and limitations. I do not think we can afford to overlook the importance of those explorations of popular culture now being made by the more alert social sciences.

---

[1]See, for example, Leo Loewenthal's essay, "An Historic Preface to the Popular Culture Debate," in *Culture for the Millions,* ed. Norman Jacobs (Princeton, N.J.: Princeton University Press, 1961), 28–42.

Second, the study of popular culture has been demonstrably affected by the example of cultural anthropology and its belief that all parts of a culture are worth study. Cultural relativism, the idea that no part of a culture has—for purposes of understanding it—innate superiority over another, has provided those who wish to study popular culture with a useful, viable methodology, as well as welcome scholarly and moral support. If it is permissible to study the songs of a Bantu tribe, or the marriage customs of a Polynesian subgroup, it seems equally permissible to study the songs of teeny-boppers in California or popular stories from *True Confessions,* and for the same reasons.

Third, the insights of Marshall McLuhan—scattered, confusing, but often brilliant—have attracted the attention of a number of younger critics who are putting together a new aesthetic which includes, rather than excludes, a wider range of cultural levels than before. McLuhan has made at least two suggestions which, in their reverberations, have deeply influenced the study of popular culture. His assertion that the medium is as important as, or more important than, the message, changed the focus of cultural criticism by shifting attention from content to medium, from *what* was said to *how* it was transmitted. "Concern with effect, rather than meaning," he wrote in *Understanding Media,* "is the basic change of our electric time;" or again, "When a medium becomes a depth experience, the old categories of classical and popular, or of highbrow and lowbrow, no longer obtain;" and again, "Anything that is approached in depth acquires as much interest as the greatest matters."

Deriving from McLuhan, critics such as Susan Sontag, for example, have opted for a "new sensibility," challenging all the old boundaries between scientific and artistic, high and low, mass and elite. In addition, another seminal idea has been McLuhan's concept of modern communications as a "mosaic;" that is, he suggests that information flows in upon the individual in a random "mosaic" pattern which is unified by the individual, who experiences and orders it. If life, as McLuhan says, has "discontinuous variety and incongruity," then art may reflect and interpret it by building similar mosaic, experimental structures in imitation of life. The Beatles' *Abbey Road* album, for example, a collection of separate songs in various styles and settings, gains full effectiveness only when the listener perceives the relationship among them all or simply experiences them all as a totality. To use the current popular phrase, "putting it all together" is a simplified version of McLuhan's idea of "mosaic" disconnection and reconnection. A novel like Leonard Cohen's *Beautiful Losers* asks the reader to do just that —to put together a discontinuous series of events and characters, separated by time and space, juxtaposed in a pattern that is no longer accidental as the reader imposes his own design on the experience.

Fourth, I think we are seeing the results of having lived for two generations with mass culture. We are not afraid of it any more, and we know how to find meaning and value in it. The dire predictions of the thirties and forties about the social disintegration and cultural decay that would inevitably follow movies, radio, comic strips, television, and jazz have simply not come true. The Canadian National Film Board calculates (and the figures no doubt hold true for the United States) that today's average 18-year-old has seen 500 feature films and 15,000 hours of television, plus heaven knows how many commercials, advertisements, comics, or hours of disc-jockey music he has heard on his transistor. Yet he seems to be able to handle it with considerable sophistication and to respond to it in a number of interesting, subtle, and imaginative ways. We have lived for three-quarters of a century with mass culture, and we are culturally no worse off than before; in fact, there is reason to believe we may be better off.

Fifth, and this is important, popular culture and technology have made a unique merger, with interesting, powerful, and utterly new results. The customized car, to cite an example, is an authentic midcentury expression of the meanings of the automobile age; there are those who find similar technological and aesthetic validity in a Brabham taking the Thunder Valley esses at Elkhart Lake, or in the intricate kinetics of a freeway cloverleaf. The artist has become technician—sculptors are metallurgists, printmakers chemists, movie directors and editors highly skilled workmen in the use of cameras, lenses, lights, cutters, and other tools of the trade. Popular artists have taken eager advantage of technology, both its materials and techniques. Acrylic paints, welding torches, television cameras, and multitrack tape recorders (Apple Records uses as many as sixteen tracks) are as much cultural tools as commercial ones, and vice versa. Painters use real telephones and bathtubs, composers artificial noises, musicians instruments like the Fender bass and the Moog synthesizer. Popular music in particular has made imaginative use of electronic technology. The sound engineer's part in making music is as creative as the musician's, using reverberation, overdubbing and distortion techniques to create sounds and performances that never existed; the amplifier alone has virtually transformed the character of much popular music. By using three amplifiers on a violin, for example, the engineer can select and combine sound frequencies and levels to produce quite new and striking sounds; to cite another example, the "wa-wa" pedal, developed recently for amplified guitar, for the first time gives a stringed instrument voice-like qualities. Certainly none of this bears resemblance to what were considered culturally acceptable techniques and subjects in the arts a short generation ago. This mutual absorption of culture and technology on the popular level is an outstanding characteristic of our contemporary world.

As a result of these and other factors, real doubts have been raised about the customary division of culture into brow levels, and about ways of judging and investigating materials drawn from popular culture. I am not at all sure that the presumed dichotomy among "cultures" is real or natural. Do the culturally elite never search for entertainment, and the so-called "masses" never seek insight? Is culture *only* a matter of class, income, and education? If you stopped *Gunsmoke* next week, would there be larger audiences for *Oh Calcutta?* As for the argument that popular culture does not impart "genuine" values, how do you measure genuine-ness? Who can say that the TV watcher gets less "genuine" value—at *his* level of experience—than the professor reading James? I have never quite understood why, if a Ph.D. settles down with a Scotch and soda to read Ross MacDonald (who was recently favored with front-page *Times* and *Newsweek* reviews) it's sophistication, whereas a tool-and-die maker from Oldsmobile who watches *Mannix* on TV with a can of beer is automatically a slob. Whose values are the more genuine? These are some of the questions raised by the current explorations of the nature and uses of popular culture, and ones that should not only be raised but answered.

There are many more. What about standards of "good" and "bad," applied to the popular arts? Should we judge a popular novel as we would Faulkner? Is Aristotle applicable to paperbacks, Northrop Frye to television? Most of our critical standards are drawn from studies of eighteenth- and nineteenth-century fiction and poetry—what have they to do with twentieth-century media? As a result, what a good many critics are saying about popular culture is little more than that the aesthetic forms and aims that flourished in the nineteenth century do not satisfy the twentieth, a conclusion hardly profound. Furthermore, what do we mean by *popular,* in the critical sense? Is definition in terms of consumption, or economics, or sales, valid? Is a "good" book that millions of people read "popular" or not? What are we going to do with Charles Dickens? Or Charles Chaplin? Or *Hair?* I have no answers nor is it necessary here to make precise ones. The point is, that by continuing to ask questions the range of interest in the study of popular culture may be broadened, deepened, better understood, focused with greater precision.

The study of popular culture is still in the process of finding its methodology, primarily because it is a joint scholarly venture, involving several disciplines, borrowing and gaining something from each. I do not account this a weakness. It means, in effect, that in finding out what we want to know about the culture of a society at a given place and time, we can choose the most effective tools, whether they be sociological, psychological, historical, aesthetic, or philosophical. Popular culture can be considered as a point at which the investigative techniques of the social sciences and the humanities may converge. Where such interests draw together—in examinations of social behavior, cultural patterns, communications media, social and cultural values—the study of popular culture provides a common ground where different disciplines may combine. There is, then, no single, approved methodology for the study of popular culture, but several. Since many forms of popular culture depend for effectiveness on their collective appeal (and some, like contemporary popular music are even collectively produced), any approach to the study of them almost necessarily must be eclectic. We should be able to choose the method of investigation which allows us to find out what we want to know. What works best is the best methodology.

Borrowing from a Wallace Stevens' poem, I should like to suggest six ways of looking at popular culture, depending on what one wishes to find out and how one wants to define it. One way turns on the study of the means by which culture is transmitted. It assumes that popular culture includes those cultural elements which are not so complex and sophisticated that they cannot be effectively disseminated among a *majority* audience. This provides a useful distinction between popular and elite cultures—i.e., a painting versus a print—by focusing attention on the distributive process. A second way of approaching popular culture may be based on an examination of the differences in the production of popular cultural artifacts, distinguishing between the unique and the mass-produced—in other words, focusing on the creative *act,* and on whether or not it can be sustained or is reproducible. John Cawelti has refined this approach by defining at least a broad portion of popular culture as that which is "characterized by artistic formulas which arise in response to certain cultural needs for entertainment and escape." That is, if there exists a majority cultural need, the popular artist evolves a formula for meeting it—the Western movie, the Sinatra song style, the McKuen poem, the *True Romance.*

Third, it may also be useful to examine the product of popular culture on the basis of its function—that is, to ask, What is it used for? Comics, B movies, "listening music," the detective story—is the point relaxation or cerebration? In recognizing the difference in function between Conan Doyle and Tolstoy—both masters at their craft—it is also recognized that one does not judge either by the other's standards. What this functional approach does, and very usefully, is to acknowledge gradations of aim among serious work seriously received, unserious work unseriously received, and all stages between. Basically, this view of cultural grades derives from Santayana's famous distinction between *work* and *play* as basic human activities, between what must be done and what is done by choice. While this approach is perhaps overly generalized, it is especially useful as a tool for studying popular culture before the appearance of the mass media—one cannot, I think, study premedia and postmedia popular culture in the same ways.

A fourth approach is that suggested by Marshall Fishwick's characterization of popular culture as "that part of culture abstracted from the *total* body of intellectual and imaginative work which each generation receives," which is not narrowly elitist or aimed at special audiences, and which is generally (but not necessarily) disseminted via the mass media. Popular culture thus includes everything not elite, "everything spoken, printed, pictured, sounded, viewed and intended for other than the identifiable few." Professor Fishwick's concept is particularly useful for its inclusiveness, and for its adaptability to sociological, historical, psychological, philosophical or critical investigation. Abraham Kaplan has suggested a fifth, somewhat related approach, pointing out that the distinguishing mark of popular culture is the *kind* of taste it reflects and satisfies, rather than how widely it is disseminated. Popular culture thus becomes not dependent for definition on numbers and profits, or for uniqueness or lack of it, but rather is defined on the basis of its own nature and aims. Sixth, Ray Browne has suggested that differences among various levels of culture are to be considered matters of degree rather than of substance or audience. Culture, he has written, is not to be arranged vertically from "low" to "high," but in a kind of horizontal continuum, resembling a flattened lens or ellipsis, with Elite at one end, Folk at the other, and between, largest and most visible, Popular culture. Lines of demarcation are mobile, investigatory methods variable and pragmatically chosen, the purpose to treat culture in all its phases, to exclude none and include all. Although I cannot match Stevens' thirteen, these are six ways of approaching the study of popular culture, all valid for varying purposes, all useful and investigating what is, it seems to me, the most provocatively versatile field of academic study of our contemporary day.

The value of this pioneering conference, and of others which I hope will follow, lies in asking questions, testing boundaries, stretching conjectures. What the study of popular culture requires more than anything else at this point is this loosening of divisions and broadening of perspectives. The classic definition of culture as "the best that has been done or thought," or as "the upper 10 percent of a society's best accomplishments," has been valuable—and will always be—as a means of preserving and transmitting the cultural heritage. But on the other hand, to rule out the rest of the broad spectrum of human culural acivity as an area for exploration is a far too restrictive act. Certainly, the culture of the majority of society ought to be subjected to this kind of searching, intensive investigation by historians, literary critics, and humanists in general, if we are to know our modern, pluralistic, multileveled society.

The general perspective concerning popular culture followed in this book is somewhat akin to a combination of Nye's fifth and sixth perspectives. Building upon Ray Browne's definition of popular culture, the following diagram is an attempt to integrate Browne's ellipsis concept with the idea of social structure, both in terms of *stratification* (pop society, middle classes, working and lower classes) and *differentiation* (youth culture, racial and ethnic culture).

Mass Culture will be conceptually defined as all elements of life which are generally, but not necessarily, disseminated by the mass media and which fall within the boundaries of the ellipsis as diagramed above. *Popular culture(s)*, on the other hand, would include all aspects of mass culture *as well as* the elements of both youth and the larger racial and ethnic subcultures.

The remainder of the book is broken up into two major sections,

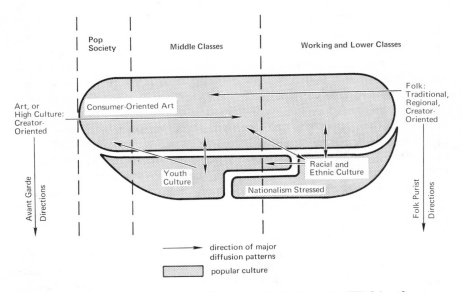

following from the diagram—*Thesis* and *Antithesis*. Within the section entitled *Thesis*, we shall examine the artifacts of popular culture as they relate to differing strata within the larger social system. Although the focus in *Thesis* is on existent American social classes, the section does not include a separate subsection devoted to the lower class. This is because the culture of the lower (non-working) class is mainly folk and ethnic, and thus not *popular* in the larger societal sense (Aspects of black ghetto culture are covered in another section of the book). As such, it is included in discussions of the working class. Similarly, upper class "high" culture, being creator-oriented art, is noted only in passing, as it also does not conform to a definition of *popular* culture. When the culture of the upper classes can be considered as consumer-oriented popular culture, it is presented and discussed.

Antithesis attempts to define, by means of their artifacts, major subcultural groupings that are presently exerting influence, both cultural and structural, upon the larger society. Obviously, there are many American subcultural groups whose cultural artifacts have not been included in *Antithesis*. The decision to include subcultural artifacts was made in terms of the importance, degree of diffusion and *popularity* of these subcultural artifacts within American society.

THESIS

POST-KOREA: THE ECONOMIC RISE OF THE WORKING CLASS

Although, as sociologist Herbert Gans has pointed out, the American working class has traditionally been America's dominant taste culture,[1] this public's values have found little expression in the artifacts of American popular culture. The reasons behind this lack of tangible expression of a dominant taste culture would probably include not only the fact that members of the working class have traditionally spent the largest proportion of their hours on the job, but also that this awareness of the centrality of the job to one's life excludes concern with more peripheral leisure-time pursuits.

> Alienation from work in a culture which gives work a central place in the life of the people means alienation from life. . . . It means unrelatedness to the inner sources of creative living, inability to feel free in the sense of freedom to express oneself.[2]

Hence, there have traditionally been few members of this class who have produced expressive and class based cultural artifacts. Ex-Beatle John Lennon expressed this well in his song "Working Class Hero."[3] He noted that those of the working class are so full of fear (confusion, anxiety and alienation) that they cannot function—they cannot express themselves, nor perform adequately even on the job.[4] Norman Mailer once remarked that the natural role of the twentieth-century man is anxiety. This may be underscored for the American working class.

On the other hand, the working class has traditionally had little money to spend on anything but the necessities of life. Hence, historically there have been few efforts to produce consumer goods that

---

1. Herbert J. Gans, "Popular Culture In America," in *Social Problems: A Modern Approach,* ed. Howard S. Becker (New York: John Wiley & Sons, 1966), p. 590.
2. Fred H. Blum, *Toward A Democratic Work Process* (New York: Harper & Row, 1953), p. 168.
3. John Lennon, "Working Class Hero," copyright © 1970, Mclen (Music) Ltd.
4. Melvin Kohn has found that, in general, the lower a person's class position in contemporary American society, the more generalized anxiety he evidences. Melvin Kohn, *Class and Conformity* (Homewood, Ill.: Dorsey Press, 1969), pp. 82-84.

would appeal to these persons. The market for such goods was non-existent. Since the end of World War II, however, this situation has been rapidly changing. With more income, the working class man has been able to escape the alienation and fear of his job centered life as he retreats further into the fantasies and material pursuits of leisure-time living.[5]

The rapid adoption of television by members of this class in the 1950's was only one (more expensive) means of escape. During the 1950's set ownership in the United States rose at a rate of 5 million a year—an adoption rate totally unprecedented in world history. Further, television ownership did not begin at the top of the economic scale and filter downward. From the beginning, television was known as "the poor man's luxury" because, as critic Max Lerner said, "it is his psychological necessity."[6]

In a later verse of "The Working Class Hero,"[7] John Lennon goes on to note that the working class has been kept, as he puts it, doped with religion, sex and TV. I would concur, while adding one further avenue of expression—sports. As Tom Wolfe has pointed out, the increasingly larger incomes and amounts of leisure time available (especially in post–Korea America) have helped create a taste culture that is now both sizable (in terms of leisure time consumption patterns) *and* articulate (in terms of the production of these class based artifacts). In the 1950's, working class consumption was more of packaged artifacts, produced outside the working class and beamed at members of this class. And, although this type of artifact is still very much in existence today, there are more and more instances of members of the working class themselves producing artifacts—today there *are* more working class heroes. The working class man is no longer as much of a passive player in terms of his job and his leisure-time activities as he was in the 1950's.[8] Today he is becoming much more of an active participant in the production and consumption of the artifacts of his own popular culture.

Herbert Gans has analyzed artifacts of working class culture with an eye to the types of values these artifacts reflect.[9] In the first place, members of this public reject strongly anything that smacks of the culture of the upper classes. Ideas by themselves are of little concern.

---

5. Arthur Shostak estimates that in 1969, the American working class male had 1,200 hours a year more leisure time than he did in 1880. Much of this shift has occurred since the close of World War II. Arthur B. Shostak, *Blue Collar Life* (New York: Random House, 1969), p. 187.

6. John Brooks, *The Great Leap, The Past Twenty Years In America* (New York: Harper & Row, 1966), pp. 161–64.

7. John Lennon, "Working Class Hero."

8. Joseph Kahl, *American Class Structure* (New York: Holt, Rinehart and Winston, 1953), p. 210.

9. Gans, "Popular Culture in America" pp. 590–2.

Substance, rather than the form in which the substance is expressed, is emphasized.

As Gans notes, much of the content of working class culture consists of modern and dramatic forms of the morality play (such as professional wrestling). Traditional values win out over temptation and impulsive behavior—external authority triumphs over individual self-expression.[10] There are no shades of grey—the world is peopled with heroes and villians.

Just as elements of the world tend to be classed as either all good or all evil, so there exists sharp segregation by sex in the working class.[11] One is all male or all female—those that are less are not to be tolerated. The male and female role are sharply differentiated[12] and there is, in the working class, relatively little social contact between men and women, except for sexual reasons.[13] Gans points out that this segregation is reflected in the artifacts of popular culture.[14] The action and adventure film, featuring male actors such as Clint Eastwood (Hang 'Em High, The Good, Bad, And the Ugly, A Fistfull of Dollars) are oriented toward the value structure of the working class male. Conversely, the romance and confession magazines reflect the values and value conflicts inherent in the working class female role. Males choose pin-up art that is more overtly erotic than that found in Playboy magazine. Females choose religious art and vividly printed land and sea scapes.[15]

In our first study, essayist Bruce Lohof points out the way in which the Marlboro Man reflects the values the working class assigns to its male public—the accepted role and behavior pattern of the individual facing a hostile environment. Lohof explicates this "merchandising of a metaphor"—utilizing his role as a member of the social system to trace historically the evolution of this cultural symbol and its evocation of a "cluster" of American values. Lohof's work is an example of the classical qualitative and impressionistic technique of the essayist. Of what worth do you feel it to be in the objective study of cultural artifacts?

---

10. This American lower and working class reliance on external authority as correct (and conformity to it), rather than reliance upon individual conscience, was an important finding of Melvin Kohn's. Melvin Kohn, *Class and Conformity*.
11. John Scanzoni, "Occupation and Family Differentiation," *The Sociological Quarterly* (Spring 1967), 2, pp. 187–88.
12. Elizabeth Bott, *Family and Social Network* (London: Tavistock Publications, 1957), pp. 53–55.
13. Herbert J. Gans, *The Levittowners* (New York: Pantheon Books, 1967), p. 183.
14. Gans, "Popular Culture in America," p. 591.
15. Ibid., p. 593.

THE HIGHER MEANING OF MARLBORO
CIGARETTES

Bruce A. Lohof

In 1960, S. I. Hayakawa—then a respected semanticist not yet foundered on the shoals of academic administration—delivered a lecture in which he related a personal and homely anecdote surrounding the birth of the Hayakawa's first child. "I was kind of thrilled and excited," he admitted:

> and so I wrote a poem about it. After it was written my wife pointed out to me:
> "It's a very nice poem, but you can't sell it."
> "Why not?" I asked.
> "Well, Pet Milk and Gerber's Food have taken over those emotions for commercial purposes."

Another reading of the poem told Hayakawa that it was straight copy for a baby lotion advertisement. "All the baby food suppliers, the diaper services, and so on," he discovered, were "exploiting the hell out of mother love for purposes of sale of products."[1]

This technique of exploitation—which Hayakawa calls the "poeticizing of consumer goods"—is, of course, not peculiar to the mother-love industries. Elemental in much effective advertising is the transubstantiation of soup or beer or laxatives into symbols of some higher and more holy good. Thus Brylcreem ceases to be merely a hairdressing and becomes a symbol of teenage sexuality. Volkswagens are turtlesque, nose-thumbing packets of the status which accrues to those who cannot afford, but delight in snubbing, the symbols of automotive hauteur—Cadillac, Lincoln, and Imperial. Pepsi Cola, once a humdrum soft drink, becomes symbolic of a whole generation of youthful and vigorous funseekers. The Pepsi Generation is:

> ... comin' at ya', goin' strong;
> Put yourself behind a Pepsi,
> If you're livin', you belong.

Teenage sexuality is worthy of our envy and Brylcreem, therefore, is worth buying. Those who cannot afford the status of a limousine can, nevertheless, take comfort in that certain eccentric nonchalance which cloaks the owner of every "bug." And Pepsi Cola is surely the found potation of those who have searched after the Fountain of Youth. But there is a breed of advertising that transcends the consumer's itch for sex, status, and eternal youth. The more perceptive of Madison Avenue's moguls sell

---

[1] S. I. Hayakawa, "The Impact of Mass Media on Contemporary American Culture," a lecture delivered at Sacramento State College, Sacramento, California, 1960. Portions of the lecture, though not the anecdote, appear as "Poetry and Advertising" in *Language in Thought and Action,* 2nd ed. (New York: 1964), pp 262–77.

products by identifying them with what Leo Marx has called a "cultural symbol," i.e., "an image that conveys a special meaning (thought and feeling) to . . . [the] large number of people who share the culture" with the advertiser and his product.[2] This transcendent form of advertising confronts the consumer with an image that will evoke a cluster of ideas and emotions which he holds in common with other Americans. It is not simply soap or soft drinks that are being sold. It is not even sex or security. It is, rather, the *merchandising of a metaphor* which will speak to and be understood by the collective imagination of the culture.

Doubtless the finest exemplar of the merchandised metaphor is the Marlboro Man who for the past half decade and more has served as the emblem of Marlboro Cigarettes. Rugged, vigorous, and robust, he strides across the television screen or through the pages of a magazine. He crouches before a daybreak fire to turn the crinkling bacon or pour coffee from a blackened pot. He rides his horse knee-deep in snow, his sheepskin coat warding off the howling winter winds. He gazes serenely over the sturdy neck of his stabled pony. In every case he is "lighting up," and suggesting that you follow his lead. He is the archetypical cowboy, to be sure. But he is much more.

There was a time when he was not even that. For 30 years the "man" in the Marlboro commercial had as often as not been a lady—and always in plush, upholstered surroundings. Marlboro Cigarettes in the days before the Marlboro Man had been "America's luxury cigarette," a genteel smoke available with either an ivory tip or a red "beauty tip." The affluent, textured salons in which Marlboros were smoked connoted a deep-pile luxury and velvet sophistication that bordered on the effeminate. Indeed, Marlboros were widely regarded as a lady's smoke 40 years before Virginia Slims Cigarettes congratulated the American woman on having come:

> . . . a long way, baby,
> To get where you've got to today;
> You've got your own cigaret, now, baby;
> You've come a long, long way.

Then the 1950's brought the first cancer scare and, subsequently, a bromide in the form of cigaret filters. A spate of filtered brands entered the market. Among them was the Philip Morris Company's early bid. "New from Philip Morris," the slogan said. Marlboros, an old brand in new clothing, now had a "filter, flavor, [and] fliptop box." Moreover, lest the effeminacy of old be augmented by the sissiness that surrounded the earliest filtered cigarettes, Marlboro was given a new, masculine image—the tattooed man.

By chance, the first tattooed man was a cowboy. No Marlboro Man, he was simply the result of an advertiser's desire to identify his product with "regular guys." As an agency executive later admitted, "We asked our-

---

[2]Leo Marx, *The Machine in the Garden* (New York: 1964), p. 4.

selves what was the most generally accepted symbol of masculinity in America, and this led quite naturally to a cowboy." No apparent effort was made to magnify this initial cowboy into the cultural symbol which would later emerge. Indeed, the tattooed man soon forsook the range in pursuit of other manly vocations. "Obviously," advertisers erroneously reasoned, "we couldn't keep on showing cowboys forever, although they could be repeated from time to time." In his place came a succession of he-men— explorers, sailors, athletes, and an occasional tuxedoed but no less rugged gentleman. In each case the common denominators were an elemental masculinity and, of course, the tattoo—emblem of those who look "successful and sophisticated but rugged . . . as though [they] might have had interesting experiences."[3]

But the tattooed man, like the imagination of the culture that smoked his cigarettes, kept returning to the open spaces of his birth. His Madison Avenue parents had meant for him to don cowboy regalia on occasion, but the costume became his natural clothing. In the early '60's the cowboy was promoted to supremacy over other tattooed men. By 1963 the tattoo had disappeared and the Marlboro Man had emerged as the exclusive inhabitant of Marlboro commercials. A cultural symbol had evolved; a metaphor was ready for merchandising.

The Marlboro image, though woven into whole cloth, consists of two elements, each illuminated in the neon of sloganeering. One, naturally, is the Marlboro Man himself. The other is expressed in the ubiquitous phrase: "Come to Marlboro Country."

Marlboro Country, in a sense, is Montana—the Montana which more than 25 years ago astounded that eastern, erudite Jew Leslie Fielder. "The inhumanly virginal landscape: the atrocious magnificence of the mountains, the illimitable brute fact of the prairies"—this is Marlboro Country. It is, as the license plates say, the "Big Sky Country." Had it not been for Rousseau's romantic myth of noble savagery, Fielder would have been psychologically impotent in the face of its virginal enormity. He would have had no way of comprehending it. There would have been nothing for him "to do with it . . . no way of assimilating the land to [his] imagination."[4]

But the Rousseauan legacy, held in trust by Natty Bumppo, Daniel Boone, and more recently Ben Cartwright, has made Marlboro Country not only mentally manageable but psychologically fascinating. Thus, what might have boggled the national imagination by its sheer immensity in fact evokes within the cultural consciousness a nostalgic and reverent image

---

[3]Leo Burnett, "The Marlboro Story: How One of America's Most Popular Filter Cigarettes Got that Way," *New Yorker* 34 (November 15, 1958): 41–43. See also "Marlboro Won Success by Big Newspaper Ads," *Editor and Publisher* 91 (December 6, 1968): 26; and "PR Man Fones, Adman Burnet Bare 'Secrets' of Modest Marlboro He-man," *Advertising Age* 29 (November 17, 1958): 3, 99.
[4]Leslie A. Fiedler, "Montana, or the End of Jean-Jacques Rousseau," reprinted in *An End to Innocence* (Boston: 1955), p. 131.

of its own mythical heritage. Marlboro Country is an environmental memoir, reminding Americans of where they have been and inviting them to vicariously return.

At first glance Marlboro Country is reminiscent of the pastoral ideal of a Vergilian poem. Folded, spindled, and mutilated, modern man views such vernal expanses with the envy of Vergil's exiled shepherd:

> Tityrus, while you lie there at ease under the awning of a spreading beech and practise country songs on a light shepherd's pipe, I have to bid good-bye to the home fields and the ploughlands that I love. Exile for me, Tityrus—and you lie sprawling in the shade, teaching the woods to echo back the charms of Amaryllis.[5]

The rustic garden, of course, is a potent symbol in the American mind. Leo Marx has shown the intrusion of "technology" into the "pastoral ideal" or *The Machine in the Garden*—to be a "metaphoric design which recurs everywhere in our literature" from James Fenimore Cooper and Washington Irving to Ernest Hemingway and Robert Frost.[6] Indeed, so envious are harried twentieth-century Americans of the pastoral ideal that it spills out of their serious art and across their commercial advertising. Once the consumer realizes that "You can take Salem out of the country, but you can't take the 'Country' out of Salem" he and some modern Amaryllis are only a pack of cigarettes away from a gambol through a field of waving grass toward a shadowy glade. Here Rip Van Winkle escaped from the village to a cozy repose in the midst of benign nature. Here menthol-puffing couples meander barefoot across an oaken bridge with never a thought of splinters. Here picnics are antless, summers are sweatless, and autumns are endless (which is to say winterless). Here one can find pleasant refuge from the responsibilities and encumbrances of civilization.

But the trill of shepherds' pipes and the wooded serenity of a Hollywood back lot are, upon closer inspection, strangers in Marlboro Country. They belong instead to the pastoral verdure of Salem Country, that Arcadian middle landscape that edges upon civilization. On the nether edge of Arcadia, however, is the wilderness—violent, primitive, occasionally malevolent. This is the incredible landscape of Fiedler's Montana. This is the monstrous, illimitable home of the noble savage. This is Marlboro Country.

The cursory distinctions between the garden and the wilderness are esthetic: the bucolic greenery of "take a puff, it's springtime," versus the rough-hewn realism of a Frederick Remington painting; the capricious gaiety of flutes versus the strident, robust brass of "The Magnificent Seven," the motion picture whose virile theme accompanies all Marlboro commer-

---

[5]Vergil *Eclogues,* trans. E. V. Rieu, quoted in Marx, p. 20.
[6]Ibid, p. 16.

cials.[7] Beneath the surface, though, lie more important differences. The pastoral ideal connotes a benign nature where conflict, danger, and tension are nonexistent. The primitive ideal, on the other hand, speaks of a wilderness which jeopardizes and makes demands upon its residents. Accordingly, the Vergilian shepherd lies in repose, unharrassed by either the complicated tensions of the town or the forbidding dangers of the marsh.[8] Meanwhile, his wilderness counterpart stands erect and vigilant. He is a man in conflict with his environment. He is of necessity a man of action and purpose. He is a Marlboro Man.

The Marlboro Man epitomizes the awesome, primitive environment in which he lives. His clothing, his habits, and even his face reflect the competitive spirit which the wilderness exacts from its inhabitants. His garb is not the fringed and bespangled costume of dimestore Texans and back-lot cowboys. Nor is it the casual drape of the classic shepherd. He wears instead a rough-spun shirt, sheepskin vest or coat, dungarees, and chaps —nothing for show, nothing for comfort, everything for facing down the elements.

His habits, like his clothing, are dictated by practical considerations. He is, as the jingle says:

Up before the sun,
Travel[ing] all day long.

Each commercial presents another vignette. He rescues a stranded herd from the snowbound uplands; he mends fence; he rounds up stray calves; he thwarts an incipient stampede. Even his leisure moments—gathering water for the morning coffee or competing in a local rodeo—are reflections of his real purpose. His habits are work-oriented, his work a way of life.

But the essence of the Marlboro Man finds its truest expression in his face. His visage does not reflect the placid serenity of the shepherd. Nor does it mirror either the cosmetic polish of civilization's winners or the sullen weariness worn by its victims. Like his clothing and his habits, the face of the Marlboro Man comes with the territory—sculptured, cragged, lined not by age but by the elements. He gazes out upon Marlboro Country through what Fiedler called the " 'Montana Face' . . . a face developed not for sociability or feeling, but for facing into the weather."[9] A rude sagaciousness of eye, a leathery tautness of skin, a wind-cured ruddiness of com-

---

[7]It is worth noting that advertisers have recognized that Remington's paintings "would be perfect for a series of outdoor Marlboro posters," and have erected his art work—blown to 300 times its original size—along California's highways. See "Giant Size Remington Reproductions become Marlboro Outdoor Boards," *Advertising Age* 40 (January 20, 1969): p. 32.

[8]Marx delineates the borders of Arcadia. "One separates it from Rome, the other from the encroaching marshland." Within these borders the pastoral shepherd is "free of the repressions entailed by a complex civilization," but still "not prey to the violent uncertainties of nature." *The Machine*, p. 22.

[9]Fiedler, "Montana, . . ." p. 134–35.

plexion—altogether a rugged handsomeness—signal his sturdy lifestyle.

The higher meaning of this Marlboro Man and the wilderness he faces down cannot be written in terms of tobacco. Not cigarettes but metaphors —or in this case a metaphor—are being merchandised. The Marlboro image is a cultural symbol which speaks to the collective imagination of the American people. It speaks of the virgin frontier, and of the brutal efficacy and constant vigilance which the frontier exacts from its residents. It speaks, as did Frederick Jackson Turner three-quarters of a century ago, of that:

> coarseness and strength combined with acuteness and inquisitiveness; that practical, inventive turn of mind, quick to find expedients; that masterful grasp of material things, lacking in the artistic but powerful to effect great ends; that restless, nervous energy; that dominant individualism, working for good and for evil, and withal that buoyancy and exuberance which comes with freedom. . . .[10]

In fine, the image speaks of *innocence* and *individual efficacy:* innocence in spite of the Marlboro Man's rude sagacity, efficacy because the territory demands it as the price of survival. It was the innocence of the Marlboro Man which prompted Fiedler to write that, in Montana, "there was something heartening in dealing with people who had never seen, for instance, a Negro or a Jew or a Servant, and were immune to all their bitter meanings.[11] In Marlboro Country one finds a breed of humanity untarnished by—indeed, ignorant of—the acrid fumes of modern civilization. The naivete of the Marlboro Man is as fresh as the unpolluted air that sustains him and as pure as the mountain stream which quenches his thirst. Unsullied is he by the guilt and terror that mingle in the civilized eye whenever it sees a race riot or a ghetto or a mushroom cloud. He stands beyond the city's fouled social relations, compromised political affairs, and clogged streets. He represents a reprieve from the malaise that hangs darkly over all who have been accessories to the crimes of civilization.

The Marlboro image, however, is not evocative of simple escape. To be sure, the Marlboro Man stands apart from civilization. But he stands apart also from Arcadia, from the simple, purposeless, unencumbered dawdling of Salem Country. Like civilization—and unlike the Vergilian garden—Marlboro Country makes demands upon its inhabitants. But responsibilities there are simple. The tasks require vigilance, rigor, and diligence, but there is resolution and accomplishment in the reward. Possessed of those virtues memorialized by Turner—"that practical, inventive turn of the mind . . . that masterful grasp of material things"—the Marlboro Man is "powerful to effect great ends."

---

[10]Frederick Jackson Turner, "The Significance of the Frontier in American History," reprinted in *The Frontier in American History* (New York: 1920), p. 37.

[11]Fiedler is quick to notice the darker side of noble savagery, pointing out that these same people "had never seen an art museum or a ballet or even a movie in any language but their own." "Montana, . . ." p. 135.

The Marlboro image represents escape, not from the responsibilities of civilization, but from its frustrations. Modern man wallows through encumbrances so tangled and sinuous, so entwined in the machinery of bureaucracies and institutions, that his usual reward is impotent desperation. He is ultimately responsible for nothing, unfulfilled in everything. Meanwhile, he jealously watches the Marlboro Man facing down challenging but intelligible tasks. He sees this denizen of the wilderness living as Thoreau would have: "deliberately . . . front[ing] only the essential facts of life.[12]

Innocence and individual efficacy are the touchstones of the metaphor employed on behalf of Marlboro Cigarettes. Despoiled by technology, Marlboro Country and the virtues which flourished therein are no more. But technology has a way of reconstituting for commercial purposes that which it has taken away. So it is with the Marlboro Man, his habits and appearance, his virtues, and his territory. A way of life which became a folk myth in the minds of people is conjured back into "reality" and sent into the marketplace.

A decade ago the editor of a trade journal questioned the "intrusion" of cowboys "into . . . advertising—as authorities on cigarets, bourbon and automobiles." Noting the cowboy's alleged penchant "for personal ornamentation, preening, drinking and brawling," his tendency toward "regarding females largely in the herd," and the aroma "of horses, dung and sweaty saddle leather" that follows wherever he goes, the editor thought it paradoxical that "civilized advertising men can parade him before us as someone whose habits are worthy of copying.[13] The resolution to this paradox, of course, is that the Marlboro Man is not simply a cowboy. He is a symbol of irretrievable innocence, and of that illimitable wilderness wherein, as Emerson said, one might have been "plain old Adam, the simple genuine self against the whole world."[14]

---

[12]Henry David Thoreau, *Walden* (New York: 1961), p. 105.
[13]"Saddlesoap, Please," *Advertising Age* 31 (March 28, 1960): 90.
[14]*The Journals and Miscellaneous Notebooks of Ralph Waldo Emerson,* ed. William H. Gilman et al. (Cambridge: 1960—), IV, p. 141.

Melvin Kohn and other social scientists who have studied in a more quantitative manner (utilizing attitude questionnaires and such) the social psychological aspects of American social classes, have pointed out that the contemporary American working class male is more apt to feel his environment threatening than is his middle class counterpart (who views his environment as essentially benign).[16] Lohof's qualitative comparison and contrast of the Marlboro and Salem commercials seems especially significant in this light.

---

16. Kohn, *Class and Conformity,* p. 87.

Unlike the frustrated urban working class male who can never succeed in terms of the American ideology of individual success, the Marlboro Man *can* master his environment. But to do so, he has to retreat to a time when "everything was simpler," when the danger inherent in the frontier dictated lightning-like assessments of good and evil and lightning-like actions. Through the Marlboro Man, the urban working class male can, for a time, vicariously participate in the fantasies of nonanxiety that a successful taming of the environment implies. The hero, thus, has the mandate to perform practically any kind and amount of violence, since he is the "good guy"—success in one's struggle with one's environment is what counts. The *means* of achieving this success are emphasized much less.

The wide acceptance of the "Westerner" as folk hero of the working class can be thought of in these terms. Adult Westerns (such as those starring Clint Eastwood) have been seen as "representing a revolt against complex rationalism and reason"[17]—any kind of violent means can be used by the Western hero in his never-ending quest for positive goals.[18]

This goal valuation is found reflected also in television programming. In a 1963 study of both juvenile and adult television programs, there was found in each a definite tendency to project content in which socially approved goals were most frequently achieved by means not socially approved—the most often utilized means involving physical violence.[19] Urban sociologist Arthur Shostak points out that members of the working class are able to minimize their contact with middle class values by *selectively* watching television.[20] Soap operas, Westerns and mystery shows, and sports "promote a *weltanschauung*, or philosophy of life, warmly held by many workers."[21] These shows are the type that most often portray the successful resort to violence to achieve goals. Shostak emphasizes the popularity of traditional Westerns that portray the hero as a moral man who defeats the immorality of the threatening outside world.[22]

---

17. Walter M. Gerson, "Violence As An American Value Theme," in *Violence and the Mass Media,* ed. Otto N. Larson, (New York: Harper & Row, 1968), p. 157.

18. Peter Homans, "Puritanism Revisited: An Analysis of the Contemporary Screen-Image Western," *Studies In Public Communication* 3 (Summer 1961): 73–84.

19. Otto N. Larson, Louis N. Gray and J. Gerald Fortes, "Goals and Goal-Achievement Methods In Television Content: Models For Anomie?" *Sociological Inquiry* (Spring 1963), 180–96.

20. Working class publics do not watch shows that imply that effective social control can be exercised by poised, adept, civilized, clever men—the types of men the working class do not believe themselves to be. Arthur Shostak, *Blue Collar Life,* p. 190.

21. Ibid., p. 189.

22. Ibid.

Similar reasoning could probably explain the fantastic popularity of traveling rodeo cowboys in Western American communities of today. Not only are these cowboys looked up to as role models by the working class males of the community, but they are most regularly seduced by enchanted females.[23] In a sense, bronco busting could as well be thought of as a sexual "morality play"—dramatizing the conflict and eventual sexual conquest by the male of the female as it could the dramatization of the physical conquest of an hostile environment.

The cowboy reflects another salient interest of the American working class—mobility. As Joseph Kahl suggests, the working class man soon learns that advancement in the ranks is not a reality for him."[24] As an example Sociologist Ely Chinoy reported that in an automobile manufacturing plant he studied and worked in, only ten or twelve workers a year out of a force of 6000 were promoted to supervisory levels.[25]

And so the working class man is mobile—always ready (but reluctant) to pick up and leave town if a more secure job (usually defined in terms of salary and fringe benefits) is in evidence.[26] Since his interaction patterns are mainly within his kinship structure (rather than stemming from job or neighborhood contacts),[27] the working class man normally has few ties that a move would break.[28]

This concern with mobility is not new in America. Again, it stems from the days of the frontier—the time of the plainsman, explorer, and the cowboy. There is another type of working class hero whose stature rests heavily on a valuation of mobility—the truck drivin' man. According to Fred Schroeder, the hero among the truckers is the distance driver who pushes a diesel rig on long drives—"six days on the road" with long drive goals of Boston, Memphis and Los Angeles.[29]

The sexual potency of the trucker, as reflected in the many popular country and western "trucker songs" serves only to underscore

---

23. Traveling country and western male singers enjoy similar receptions. The girls involved are normally known as "snuff queens."
24. Joseph Kahl, *American Class Structure,* p. 207.
25. Ely Chinoy, *Automobile Workers and the American Dream* (New York: Doubleday, 1953), p. 44.
26. The working classes are, in general, quite *ambivalent* concerning mobility. Since a dominant value is that of a secure job, they would rather not be mobile, however they do value mobility as they realize secure jobs for them are more ideals than reality.
27. Floyd Dotson, "Patterns of Voluntary Associations Among Urban Working Class Families," *American Sociological Review* 16 (1961): 687–92.
28. This is assuming, of course, that he has made his first traumatic move away from the vicinity of the immediate family.
29. Fred E. H. Schroeder, "A Bellyful of Coffee," *Journal of Popular Culture* (Spring 1967), pp. 679–86.

traditional values of mobility and independence. Yet the songs also reflect the working class value conflict between sowing wild oats and putting down roots.[30] Dave Dudley, the most important writer and performer of trucker songs, reflects this conflict in his song "Truck-Driving Man." Dudley sums up the song as being about a "guy that's got a lot of chicks everywhere, got one at home, but that don't make him married."[31] Yet in his "Sugarland, U.S.A.," Dudley sings of the trucker who this time is going to settle down and stay with his "sugar" in Sugarland, U.S.A.[32]

The idea of man and machine pitted against a hostile environment is perhaps expressed best in Dudley's song, "Six Days On the Road," which describes a trucker coming home from a six-day run, eyes bugged from the amphetamines he has taken, his log book two days behind, and a weighing station ahead. This type of alliance in the face of danger has been chronicled in song throughout the history of American popular culture, from the tradition of the cowboy and his horse *(The Chisholm Trail)* to the engineer and his throttle *(Casey Jones)* and now to the trucker and his rig *(Six Days On the Road)*.[33]

Tom Wolfe has noted another American example of the man-machine alliance—he labels Junior Johnson of stock car racing fame the last American hero. According to Wolfe, the sport of stock car racing was one direct consequence of the Appalachian whiskey distilling business. Those "good old boys" who learned to drive by running whiskey became the legendary winners in the early Southern stock car racing circuit.

> It wasn't just the plain excitement of it (whiskey running). It was something deeper, the symbolism. It brought into a modern focus the whole business, one and a half centuries old, of the country people's rebellion against the Federals, against the seaboard establishment, their independence, their defiance of the outside world. And it was like a mythology for that and for something else that was happening, the whole wild thing of the car as the symbol of liberation in the postwar South.[34]

As stock car racing became more popular, the larger automotive

---

30. Ibid., p. 685.
31. Dudley is quoted in John Grissim, *Country Music: White Man's Blues* (New York: Paperback Library, 1970), p. 246.
32. This song seems to reflect the "ancient rural bias" of the working class—looking to the simpler rural setting for clues to the "good life" and the meaning of existence. See Arnold W. Green, *Recreation, Leisure and Politics,* (New York: McGraw-Hill Book Company, 1964), pp. 192–93.
33. In this context it is interesting to note that the English working class slang usage of the term "rig" to signify the male sexual organ is becoming widely diffused and accepted in the American working class and youth cultures.
34. Tom Wolfe, "The Last American Hero," *The Kandy-Kolored Tangerine-Flake Streamline Baby* (New York: Farrar, Straus & Giroux, 1965, p. 139.

companies began paying attention. They found that there were significant shifts in Southern automobile sales patterns—depending on the model and type of automobile that was currently winning on the stock circuit. Today the larger Detroit-based companies finance the drivers of their specially designed and tuned cars, forcing the independent driver out of contention for top racing honors. The only thing the independent can hope for is to be flashy enough to catch the eye of a corporation scout. Stock car racing is now big business.[35] Yet the image remains—the hero—man and machine united in rebellion against a hostile environment.

Although the spectator can cling to this romantic image, many in the car world cannot. Not only has Detroit taken over the stock car circuit, but the corporations have also adopted the most popular innovations of the 1950's and early 1960's car customizers for assembly-line production. This diffusion of subcultural artifacts into mainstream American mass culture has helped propel a new artifact from the underground into the arena of working class popular culture—the motorcycle.

The years following World War II saw a tremendous demand for motorcycles on the part of urban youth (especially in California). Because of the scarcity of the machines, many youths took to stealing them and radically altering their appearance ("chopping" them) to escape detection.[36] For twenty-some years these "outlaw bikers" retained their image. The Hell's Angels rode chopped Harley-Davidson 74's almost exclusively. Frank Reynolds, while a member of the Angels, wrote down his feelings about his bike—his words sum up the values involved in this man-machine rapport better than most:

> It is hard to describe my motorcycle, yet it is within me— I have deep feelings for it. I always called it my old lady after I lost my wife. . . . My bike has replaced a woman in the sense of love for something near . . . she speaks with the throb of heartbeat as she stands still. I'll walk upon her in the light of any hour and gaze in love and wonder before I kick her over. I take my little blanket of many colors off of the tank that drapes down over the vertical engine. The wiring on her is very important as I raise up to give the healing thrust that brings her to life and roar off into any land together, forever . . . . This is hard to de-

35. Just how big can be seen by the fact that the 1971 Martini and Rossi American Driver-of-the-Year award went to Bob Petty, a stock car racer. By winning, Petty beat two past Indianapolis 500 winners as well as a Grand Prix winner. Stock car racing is now a *legitimate* American sport, having diffused from the Southern subculture to spread via the attention given it by the large Detroit automotive corporations. (At this writing, Petty is driving for Plymouth.)

36. Tom Wolfe, "Sissy Bars Will Be Lower This Year," *Esquire,* February 1971, p. 62.

scribe, if I could only do it in words fully it would be wonderful for my ears to hear.[37]

Today the outlaw image has abated and the cycle is an important artifact of working class popular culture.[38] Not only are many of the former car customizers now involved with cycles, but cycle racing tracks have sprung up all over America. But perhaps most important is the degree to which the cycle has reflected the working class American value of man and machine facing together an hostile environment. Cross-country cycle riding has always been popular—from the expeditions of the outlaw biker gangs to the more current weekend expeditions of members of local road riding clubs. Cross-country cycle riding, racing and jumping have always been major activities of the bikers—the competition involved seems to emphasize the man-environment conflict to a greater degree than the man-versus-man competition that has emerged as the more important emphasis in the working class car culture.

Sociologist Lee Rainwater has noted the importance of the automobile in the working class as a symbol of liberation, not only from the larger social environment (as Tom Wolfe suggests) but also from the ties of familial obligation.[39] For many working class American males, the highway is their hometown, the place where they feel most free and secure. "Many of them were conceived in automobiles and many of them will die in them."[40]

In American urban centers there exists at present another type of working class car sport whose participants seem to reflect many of the same values as did the whiskey runners/stock car racers. This sport is known as street racing. In the larger urban areas (New York City and Los Angeles being the two major areas), hundreds of spectators will gather to watch racers dragging on a city street (blocked off by the participants themselves). The racing will continue until word is received that the police are on their way.[41] In some instances, if the race is important enough and has attracted enough spectators, the police will ignore its illegality and allow it to be run. In other cases, they will simply send on their way any racers or spectators that are

---

37. Frank Reynolds, *Freewheelin' Frank* (New York: Grove Press, 1967), pp. 90–91.
38. As the motor scooter gains in popularity and the motorcycle is romanticized as it is presented to middle class audiences in films such as *Easy Rider,* the cycle, as the stock car before it, will no longer serve as an artifact of a subcultural group, but be diffused as an artifact and symbol of the general mass culture of America.
39. Lee Rainwater et al., *Workingman's Wife* (New York: Oceana, 1952), p. 192.
40. Michael E. Malone and Myron Roberts, *from pop to culture* (New York: Holt, Rinehart & Winston, 1971), p. 5.
41. Just as did the whiskey runners, street racers have radio-equipped cars monitoring police calls.

still in the area when the police arrive. In any case, the street racing is completely in the open and so highly organized it goes on "like clockwork" every Saturday night in various sectors of the larger American cities.[42]

Although not entirely a phenomenon of minority groups, street racing in Los Angeles originated in Watts and is primarily carried on by Blacks and Mexican-Americans. In New York a great deal of the street racing goes on in Harlem—although races have been known to be run on Long Island as well. Traveling in competition at speeds well over 100 miles per hour down the city blocks of the urban ghetto—that is the contemporary urban "thing" of the car as a symbol of revolt and liberation, just as it is a not well-publicized, but important facet of the popular culture of the American urban working class.

In the following piece, Tom Wolfe, utilizing his unique style as essayist-critic/interviewer-observer (Wolfe will sometimes spend months living with those he is to write about—immersing himself in and attempting to absorb their specific perspectives and attitudes toward the artifacts of popular culture they are producing and consuming) points up the role of the automobile in satisfying the aggressive tendencies of contemporary urban man. The generalized anxiety and frustration found in the working class, the tendency of its members to see things as either all good or all bad, and their emphasis on physical prowess and violence as means of combatting their hostile environment are combined in automotive terms to emerge as the phenomenon known as the "demolition derby."

Wolfe also points up here the importance of the "taste leader" in the diffusion process. For a sport such as the demolition derby to spread from its inception point in a small societal subgroup, it must be visibly endorsed and enjoyed by taste leaders. Wolfe gives as an example the arena fighting of Roman socialites and its effect on the diffusion of this type of sport in the Roman Empire. Do you feel the same sort of thing could be hypothesized with respect to demolition derby? How about stock car racing? Or motorcycling?

---

42. Joe Scalzo, "Street Racing—That's What," *Car Life,* April 1970, pp. 62–66.

CLEAN FUN AT RIVERHEAD

Tom Wolfe

The inspiration for the demolition derby came to Lawrence Mendelsohn one night in 1958 when he was nothing but a spare-ribbed 28-year-old stock car driver halfway through his 10th lap around the Islip, L.I., Speedway and taking a curve too wide. A lubberly young man with a Chicago boxcar haircut came up on the inside in the 1949 Ford and caromed him 12 rows up into the grandstand, but Lawrence Mendelsohn and his entire car did not hit one spectator.

"That was what got me," he said. "I remember I was hanging upside down from my seat belt like a side of Jersey bacon and wondering why no one was sitting where I hit. 'Lousy promotion,' I said to myself.

"Not only that, but everybody who *was* in the stands forgot about the race and came running over to look at me giftwrapped upside down in a fresh pile of junk."

At that moment occurred the transformation of Lawrence Mendelsohn, racing driver, into Lawrence Mendelsohn, promoter, and, a few transactions later, owner of the Islip Speedway, where he kept seeing more of this same underside of stock car racing that everyone in the industry avoids putting into words. Namely, that for every purist who comes to see the fine points of the race, such as who is going to win, there are probably five waiting for the wrecks to which stock car racing is so gloriously prone.

The pack will be going into a curve when suddenly two cars, three cars, four cars tangle, spinning and splattering all over each other and the retaining walls, upside down, right side up, inside out and in pieces, with the seams bursting open and discs, rods, wires and gasoline spewing out and yards of sheet metal shearing off like Reynolds Wrap and crumpling into the most baroque shapes, after which an ashblue smoke starts seeping up from the ruins and a thrill begins to spread over the stands like Newburg sauce.

So why put up with the monotony between crashes?

Such, in brief, is the early history of what is culturally the most important sport ever originated in the United States, a sport that ranks with the gladiatorial games of Rome as a piece of national symbolism. Lawrence Mendelsohn had a vision of an automobile sport that would be all crashes. Not two cars, not three cars, not four cars, but 100 cars would be out in an arena doing nothing but smashing each other into shrapnel. The car that outrammed and outdodged all the rest, the last car that could still move amid the smoking heap, would take the prize money.

So at 8:15 at night at the Riverhead Raceway, just west of Riverhead, L.I., on Route 25, amid the quaint tranquility of the duck and turkey farm flatlands of eastern Long Island, Lawrence Mendelsohn stood up on the back of a flat truck in his red neon warmup jacket and lectured his 100 drivers on the rules and niceties of the new game, the "demolition derby." And so at 8:30 the first 25 cars moved out onto the raceway's quarter-mile stock car track. There was not enough room for 100 cars to mangle each other. Lawrence Mendelsohn's dream would require four heats. Now the 25 cars were placed at intervals all about the circumference of the track, making flatulent revving noises, all headed not around the track but toward a point in the center of the infield.

Then the entire crowd, about 4,000, started chanting a countdown,

"Ten, nine, eight, seven, six, five, four, three, two," but it was impossible to hear the rest, because right after "two" half the crowd went into a strange whinnying wail. The starter's flag went up, and 25 cars took off, roaring into second gear with no mufflers, all headed toward that same point in the center of the infield, converging nose on nose.

The effect was exactly what one expects that many simultaneous crashes to produce: the unmistakable tympany of automobiles colliding and cheap-gauge sheet metal buckling; front ends folding todgether at the same cockeyed angles police photographs of night-time wreck scenes capture so well on grainy paper; smoke pouring from under the hoods and hanging over the infield like a howitzer cloud; a few of the surviving cars lurching eccentrically on bent axles. At last, after four heats, there were only two cars moving through the junk, a 1953 Chrysler and a 1958 Cadillac. In the Chrysler a small fascia of muscles named Spider Ligon, who smoked a cigar while he drove, had the Cadillac cornered up against a guard rail in front of the main grandstand. He dispatched it by swinging around and backing full throttle through the left side of its grille and radiator.

By now the crowd was quite beside itself. Spectators broke through a gate in the retaining screen. Some rushed to Spider Ligon's car, hoisted him to their shoulders and marched off the field, howling. Others clambered over the stricken cars of the defeated, enjoying the details of their ruin, and howling. The good, full cry of triumph and annihilation rose from Riverhead Raceway, and the demolition derby was over.

That was the 154th demolition derby in two years. Since Lawrence Mendelsohn staged the first one at Islip Speedway in 1961, they have been held throughout the United States at the rate of one every five days, resulting in the destruction of about 15,000 cars. The figures alone indicate a gluttonous appetite for the sport. Sports writers, of course, have managed to ignore demolition derbies even more successfully than they have ignored stock car racing and drag racing. All in all, the new automobile sports have shown that the sports pages, which on the surface appear to hum with life and earthiness, are at bottom pillars of gentility. This drag racing and demolition derbies and things, well, there are too many kids in it with sideburns, tight Levis and winklepicker boots.

Yet the demolition derbies keep growing on word-of-mouth publicity. The "nationals" were held last month at Langhorne, Pa., with 50 cars in the finals, and demolition derby fans everywhere know that Don McTavish, of Dover, Mass., is the new world's champion. About 1,250,000 spectators have come to the 154 contests held so far. More than 75 percent of the derbies have drawn full houses.

The nature of their appeal is clear enough. Since the onset of the Christian era, i.e., since about 500 A.D., no game has come along to fill the gap left by the abolition of the purest of all sports, gladiatorial combat. As late as 300 A.D. these bloody duals, usually between men but sometimes between women and dwarfs, were enormously popular not only in Rome but throughout the Roman Empire. Since then no game, not even boxing, has successfully acted out the underlying motifs of most sport, that is, aggression and destruction.

Boxing, of course, is an aggressive sport, but one contestant has actually destroyed the other in a relatively small percentage of matches. Other games are progressively more sublimated forms of sport. Often, as in the case of football, they are encrusted with oddments of passive theology and metaphysics to the effect that the real purpose of the game is to foster character, teamwork, stamina, physical fitness and the ability to "give-and-take."

But not even those wonderful clergymen who pray in behalf of Congress, expressway ribbon-cuttings, urban renewal projects and testimonial dinners for ethnic aldermen would pray for a demolition derby. The demolition derby is, pure and simple, a form of gladiatorial combat for our times.

As hand-to-hand combat has gradually disappeared from our civilization, even in wartime, and competition has become more and more sophisticated and abstract, Americans have turned to the automobile to satisfy their love of direct aggression. The mild-mannered man who turns into a bear behind the wheel of a car—i.e., who finds in the power of the automobile a vehicle for the release of his inhibitions—is part of American folklore. Among teen-agers the automobile has become the symbol, and in part the physical means, of triumph over family and community restrictions. Seventy-five percent of all car thefts in the United States are by teen-agers out for "joy rides."

The symbolic meaning of the automobile tones down but by no means vanishes in adulthood. Police traffic investigators have long been convinced that far more accidents are purposeful crashes by belligerent drivers than they could ever prove. One of the heroes of the era was the Middle Eastern diplomat who rammed a magazine writer's car from behind in the Kalorama embassy district of Washington two years ago. When the American bellowed out the window at him, he backed up and smashed his car again. When the fellow leaped out of his car to pick a fight, he backed up and smashed his car a third time, then drove off. He was recalled home for having "gone native."

The unabashed, undisguised, quite purposeful sense of destruction of the demolition derby is its unique contribution. The aggression, the battering, the ruination are there to be enjoyed. The crowd at a demolition derby seldom gasps and often laughs. It enjoys the same full-throated participation as Romans at the Colosseum. After each trial or heat at a demolition derby, two drivers go into the finals. One is the driver whose car was still going at the end. The other is the driver the crowd selects from among the 24 vanquished on the basis of his courage, showmanship or simply the awesomeness of his crashes. The numbers of the cars are read over loudspeakers, and the crowd chooses one with its cheers. By the same token, the crowd may force a driver out of competition if he appears cowardly or merely cunning. This is the sort of driver who drifts around the edge of the battle avoiding crashes with the hope that other cars will eliminate one another. The umpire waves a yellow flag at him and he must crash into someone within 30 seconds or run the risk of being booed off the field in dishonor and disgrace.

The frank relish of the crowd is nothing, however, compared to the kick the contestants get out of the game. It costs a man an average of $50 to retrieve a car from a junk yard and get it running for a derby. He will only get his money back—$50—for winning a heat. The chance of being smashed up in the madhouse first 30 seconds of a round are so great, even the best of drivers faces long odds in his shot at the $500 first prize. None of that matters to them.

Tommy Fox, who is 19, said he entered the demolition derby because, "You know, it's fun. I like it. You know what I mean?" What was fun about it? Tommy Fox had a way of speaking that was much like the early Marlon Brando. Much of what he had to say came from the trapezii, which he rolled quite a bit, and the forehead, which he cocked, and the eyebrows, which he could bring together expressively from time to time. "Well," he said, "you know, like when you hit 'em, and all that. It's fun."

Tommy Fox had a lot fun in the first heat. Nobody was bashing around quite like he was in his old green Hudson. He did not win, chiefly because he took too many chances, but the crowd voted him into the finals as the best showman.

"I got my brother," said Tommy. "I came in from the side and he didn't even see me."

His brother is Don Fox, 32, who owns the junk yard where they both got their cars. Don likes to hit them, too, only he likes it almost too much. Don drives with such abandon, smashing into the first car he can get a shot at and leaving himself wide open, he does not stand much chance of finishing the first three minutes.

For years now sociologists have been calling upon one another to undertake a serious study of America's "car culture." No small part of it is the way the automobile has, for one very large segment of the population, become the focus of the same sort of quasi-religious dedication as art is currently for another large segment of a higher social order. Tommy Fox is unemployed, Don Fox runs a junk yard, Spider Ligon is a maintenance man for Brookhaven Naval Laboratory, but to categorize them as such is getting no closer to the truth than to have categorized William Faulkner in 1926 as a clerk at Lord & Taylor, although he was.

Tommy Fox, Don Fox and Spider Ligon are acolytes of the car culture, an often esoteric world of arts and sciences that came into its own after World War II and now has believers of two generations. Charlie Turbush, 35, and his son, Buddy, 17, were two more contestants, and by no stretch of the imagination can they be characterized as bizarre figures or cultists of the death wish. As for the dangers of driving in a demolition derby, they are quite real by all physical laws. The drivers are protected only by crash helmets, seat belts and the fact that all glass, interior handles, knobs and fixtures have been removed. Yet Lawrence Mendelsohn claims that there have been no serious injuries in 154 demonlition derbies and now gets his insurance at a rate below that of stock car racing.

The sport's future may depend in part on word getting around about its relative safety. Already it is beginning to draw contestants here and there from social levels that could give the demolition derby the cachet of respectability. In eastern derbies so far two doctors and three young men of more than passable connections in eastern society have entered under whimsical *noms de combat* and emerged neither scarred nor victorious. Bull fighting had to win the same social combat.

All of which brings to mind that fine afternoon when some high-born Roman women were out in Nero's box at the Colosseum watching this sexy Thracian carve an ugly little Samnite up into prime cuts, and one said, darling, she had an inspiration, and Nero, needless to say, was all for it. Thus began the new vogue of Roman socialites fighting as gladiators themselves, for kicks. By the second century A.D. even the Emperor Commodus was out there with a tiger's head as a helmet hacking away at some poor dazed fall guy. He did a lot for the sport. Arenas sprang up all over the empire like shopping center bowling alleys.

The future of the demolition derby, then, stretches out over the face of America. The sport draws no lines of gender, and post-debs may reach Lawrence Mendelsohn at his office in Deer Park.

In the next piece, I am concerned with the diffusion of an artifact—this time, the violent and physical sport of roller derby. I chose to examine the sport as a case study—attempting to uncover the reasons for its large scale diffusion and popularity in the working class *with minimal coverage by taste leaders in the mass media.* Making some assumptions about the working class (and people in general), I present four underlying factors in the popularity of roller derby as a *prole* sport.

PROLE SPORT: THE CASE OF ROLLER DERBY

George H. Lewis

As Journalist Tom Wolfe has pointed out, *prole* sports (such as cycle racing and demolition derbies) attract more American spectators per year than even professional football. Yet one seldom hears these sports mentioned in the media. If they are covered at all, it is usually as a one-shot "feature of interest " on *Wide World of Sports.* What is it in the nature of the *prole* sports (or the media) that has created this curious situation?

The answer, I feel, lies in the unique historical pattern of American sports. Traditionally sports have been the product and domain of societal upper classes—those with the leisure time and money to afford them. The assimilation pattern, then, took the form of a downward flow—a sport created and first enjoyed by the fashionable and genteel became a diversion of the middle class and finally a society-wide "popular" sport.[1]

In America the post–World War II economic boom, coupled with increased leisure time, has given the lower and lower-middle classes the time and money to afford sports. This unique historical occurance has helped to create sports vastly different in style and structure from those created in the traditional upper-class manner. *Prole* sports seem to have evolved from existing and necessary artifacts of the world of work; i.e., automobiles, cycles, muscles (wrestling), etc.; they place more emphasis on speed and power (in relation to agility and finesse) than do the *bourgeois* sports. Variations in *prole* sports seem to be mainly in the expense of the necessary equipment and artifacts involved (demolition derby requiring more expensive equipment than roller derby).

Considering the location of American *prole* sports in the social structure and that until recently the media have taken general aim at the middle classes as their primary target group, perhaps this lack of *prole* sports exposure makes more sense. The media have mainly concerned themselves with the watered-down *bourgeois* sports that are now hailed as the most "popular" in America. (American football, as an example—having been "watered down" from its original bourgeois European form.) Yet the *prole* sports continue to draw their audiences. For example, in 1967, although the San Francisco Giants (baseball) had the highest attendance records of any sport in the Bay Area, the San Francisco Bay Bombers (roller derby) had the second highest figures, outrunning football, basketball, soccer and hockey.[2]

With little or no media exposure as a sport (but some nonprime-time television exposure as an amusement—much like wrestling), how is it that roller derby not only draws such large crowds but continues to grow substantially each season? The sport has sold out virtually every major hall in the country. League games are seen (usually by videotape) on some 75 independent television stations. Top skaters can pick up close to $40,000 for a nine-month season. Roller derby is one of the most widely diffused of the *prole* sports—and it is so because of its unique combination of the four vital aspects of "grand spectacle": (1) speed and power, (2) artifact deriva-

---

[1] In America, the history of football is an excellent example of the diffusion process.
[2] Joan Grissim, Jr., "Nobody Loves Us But the Fans," *Rolling Stone,* March 15, 1969, p. 18.

tion from *prole* culture, (3) player identification, and (4) spectator role as participant.

SPEED AND POWER

Roller derby rules are very simple. A team is composed of two platoons of five (one platoon men, the other women) who skate around a circular track during eight alternating two-minute periods. Each platoon consists of two jammers, two blockers, and one pivot man.

A period begins with two opposing platoons of the same sex skating together around the track. When the referee signals that both platoons are "in a pack," the jammers are given 60 seconds to break away forward from the pack and lap the field. The pivot man aids in this maneuver by blocking opposing jammers (he can do this only after the first jammer has left the pack), and more important, "springing" platoon jammers ahead of the pack. This latter is accomplished by the pivot man's joining one hand with the jammer and, by pivoting on the move, utilizing the stretch of the joined arms as a lever force to hurl the jammer forward. Once jammers are ahead of the pack, each attempts to knock those of the opposing platoon out of the action (which usually means blocking them off their feet or into the track railing). A jammer who laps the field receives one point for every member of the opposing platoon he or she passes during a jam. Blockers for both platooons stay to the rear of the pack to prevent opposing jammers from scoring.

There are penalties and exceptions, however; the rules seem to exist only to be broken. For instance, if a blocker suffers a fall, it is common practice for him or her to skate across the infield to catch the pack. Personal feuds abound and many times are allowed to interrupt scoring play—referees are constantly breaking up one fight after another. In a recent game a player grabbed a folding metal chair from the infield and began beating an already-felled member of the opposition with it.

Clearly the emphasis is on speed and power—agility and finesse take a back seat in the minds of roller derby fans—and "grace under pressure" would be hooted out of the arena. As in wrestling, of course, much of the power and violence is "hoked up." A skater can hit 35 m.p.h. on a banked track and few go a full season without a hip or back injury. If the lid were really taken off—if all things were as they seem—players would be routinely killed, or at least severely maimed. But, to the spectators, the authenticity doesn't matter. It is grand spectacle. It is what they want. As John Grissim, Jr. has remarked concerning the inauthenticity of much of the violence, "One could talk to a lot of ex-skaters who now own bars and bowling alleys and probably make a case but it would be wasted effort. One good judo chop and a hip block at full tilt carries more weight with the fans than any six . . . testimonials."[3]

---

[3]Ibid., p. 20.

ARTIFACT DERIVATION

As with all *prole* sports, the artifacts of roller derby are derived from lower class culture. A popular *prole* function has always been Saturday night at the roller rink—a place where youths could meet for the exhibition of individual prowess, as well as a convenient spot for the exchange of information, alcohol and drugs, and a spot for the convenient pickup (for either sex).

Skating around and around the circular track, "disinterested" eyes continually sweeping the sidelines, couples holding hands, youths executing figure-eights, skating backwards, being chased by rink officials for skating with notched wheel edges (which results in awesome noise and damage to the rink track), stopping in at the refreshment counter every 20th lap, nudging a rival over the rail, this was the 1940 to 1950 urban *prole* parallel to the middle class teen phenomenon of "cruising the main drag." In fact it served not only the same function of "cruisin' " but also many of those of the "teen hops"—all in one grand spectacle.

Roller derby is the logical sporting extension and abstraction of these "Saturday nights,"[4] just as stock car racing is the logical sporting extension and abstraction of Appalachian whiskey running.[5] Each utilizes existing artifacts of *prole* culture to create spectacle, while at the same time reinforcing audience fantasies. As active (or formerly active) users of the involved artifacts, spectators can not only understand player skills, but vicariously enact their own power fantasies.

PLAYER IDENTIFICATION

In all sports the star syndrome appears. Certain players are "crowd pleasers"—those upon whom spectators project their individual dreams and desires.[6] A unique aspect of roller derby is the fact that a team is made up of equal numbers of males and females (but note also they are strictly segregated by sex in terms of playing periods). Furthermore, *prole* cultural male-female values emerge and are symbolically acted out on the roller derby track (the male platoon as protector of the female platoon, as an example). This frequently approaches the ridiculous—an attack on female members of one team by female members of the other stimulates retaliatory attacks by the males of the offended team *on the males* of the offending team.

Media research has revealed that a significant number of females are

---

[4]In terms of its appeal to a mass *prole* audience. Its roots as a sport go back to the roller skating marathons of the 1930's. Roller Derby was founded in Chicago in 1934 by Lee Seltzer.

[5]Tom Wolfe, in "The Last American Hero," presents this extension. Tom Wolfe, *The Kandy-Kolored Tangerine-Flake Streamline Baby* (New York: Farrar, Straus & Giroux, 1965), pp. 105–44.

[6]Two of roller derby's most well-known figures of this sort are 15-year veteran Joan Weston of the San Francisco Bay Bombers, and 20-year veteran Ann Cavello of the Mid-West Pioneers.

spectators at sports events,[7] however; roller derby is one of the very few sports to recognize this and actually to incorporate female players in its structure. That roller derby is a *prole* sport makes this even more amazing.[8] In any event, roller derby allows its female audience the possibility of psychic identification that most sports preclude.

Reflecting another trend, an increasing number of black players have joined the ranks. The transition has been accomplished without any real opposition, yet the small percentage of black faces in the roller derby audience betrays a slight uneasiness with the changing character of the line-up. Roller derby is still, in essence, a *white prole* sport.

SPECTATOR AS PARTICIPANT

As Max Lerner has remarked, too much has perhaps been made of the passivity of spectator sports.[9] With relation to American *prole* sports, his point should be underscored. *Prole* spectators react to their alter-egos in the arena in a very physical and emotional way. Just as they will wildly cheer their heroes, the spectators will turn viciously on fallen idols. "They often attack them on the street, hiss at them in supermarkets, and write them obscene letters. In their more devilish moods they have been known to shoot at the skaters during the games with BB guns and throw objects of art ranging from beer cans to heavy chunks of metal."[10]

This type of violent physical activity not only involves the spectator in relation to the player, but also the spectator in relation to other spectators. "You can't call the crowd of 10,000 an audience. It is an organized mob—near hysterical men and women writhing in great paroxysms of emotion, by turns ecstatic, argumentative, despairing and vindictive. But never silent. If the action on the rink is sport, the behavior is spectacle. The two spheres are at times competitive, leaving the spectators to choose between Aristotelian catharsis and just plain raising hell."[11]

In sum, roller derby as a *prole* sport serves functions similar to the "circuses" of Roman culture. The sport allows spectators to take part in a crucial ritual that binds them to one another and to their *prole* culture. Physically tribal, at $3.00 per seat, roller derby guarantees their money's worth.

---

[7]Frank Reyson, "The Cluttered World of Sports and Media," *Media-Scope,* December 1969.

[8]*Prole* values have traditionally included an element of the female as breadwinner, so her active role in roller derby may not be so startling as a middle-class observer might think. Today this role may well appeal to the same middle-class females as some of the more extreme and physical women's liberation groupings do.

[9]Max Lerner, *America As Civilization* (New York: Simon & Schuster, 1957), p. 818.

[10]Bernard McCormick, "Porky Pig's Children: There's Something About the Roller Game That Brings Out Blood Lust in the Fans," *Philadelphia Magazine,* June 1968, p. 15.

[11]Grissim, "Nobody Loves Us . . ." p. 18.

Can you think of competing reasons that would lead to similar conclusions concerning roller derby? If so, how could one "test" these competing ideas within the arena of American society?

The violence of demolition and roller derbies can be seen in many other American sports, among them wrestling. Reul Denney claims that the wrestling public chooses to view the sport as drama, rather than as contest. "It is willing to give up the sense of pure competition between equalized or handicapped contestants in order to pay attention to a drama of alternative scenes of dominance and submission.[43] This dramatization of the forces of good and evil in the world as a spectacle performance of fictional violence serves again to reinforce working class conceptions of reality.[44]

The *prole*, or working class, sports are in the process of diffusing upward in the American social structure—stock car racing is fast becoming a legitimate middle class sport (just as sports car racing is diffusing downward from its origins in the upper classes). Motorcycle sports too, are becoming recognized as legitimate forms of activity by the middle class.

But just as these sports are diffusing upward, many other sports have diffused downward in the system. This process has been greatly aided by television, which has made many sporting events available for consumption by the working class.[45] Although its origins were in the upper class, baseball has been traditionally thought of as the great American pastime—the game of the working class American. Today it has been eclipsed in popularity by professional football.

Baseball, according to Marshall McLuhan, is a holdover from the early stages of industrial society.[46] It is elegant, but in a simple and mechanical way. Each player has his own individual territory to defend—there is little team action *or* body contact in the sport. Football, on the other hand, is more complex, violent, and team oriented. Team territory is defended, and time, rather than the mechanical virtuosity of the pitcher-batter duel, is of prime importance.[47]

The effects of the media itself upon the popularity of a sport are

---

43. Reul Denney, *The Astonished Muse* (Chicago: University of Chicago Press, 1957), p. 133.

44. Arthur Shostak has pointed out that a major working class belief is that "everyone has his price" and that "the world is a racket." He asserts that many of the working class lean on the seamier aspects of commercial sports such as wrestling (and boxing) for support of this world view. Shostak, *Blue Collar Life,* p. 202.

45. As *Car and Driver* magazine has ruefully remarked many times, the popularity of "stick-and-ball games" among the lower classes is perpetuated by the "whores of the stick-and-ball press." Leon Mandel, "Can A Machine Kill A Man?" *Car and Driver,* September 1968, p. 8.

46. Marshal McLuhan, *Understanding Media* (New York: McGraw-Hill, 1966), pp. 211–12.

47. Ibid.

important also to keep in mind. Baseball was a type of sport well suited to presentation by radio. The announcer could easily describe all the relevant action as the game proceeded. Football, however, is much more difficult to cover in the verbal medium. Then, too, in terms of live attendance, it does not matter much where one sits at a baseball game. One can observe the slow and mechanical "one-thing-at-a-time" type action from nearly every seat in the stadium. Yet in order to experience the many simultaneous and relevant aspects of a football game, one should sit as close as possible to the 50-yard line. Television has changed all this—baseball becomes boring on TV, while football is eminently suited for the medium. Similarly, sports such as basketball and ice hockey may become more popular as the television camera crews learn *how* to telecast the games.

The rising popularity of cable television may well have an impact on the world of sports. As it stands today, a television station can broadcast only one program at a time. This means that advertising prices are very high and sponsors are reluctant to take chances on financing the presentation of sports with potentially limited appeal.[48] A cable station, however, can broadcast many programs at once (the coaxial cable of cable television can carry 20 or more programs simultaneously). Thus a station can run more specialty shows, beamed at smaller target audiences. This could, in the future, spell doom for the exorbitantly priced commercially beamed sports (such as professional football), as it ushers in an age in which American subcultures (whether regional, ethnic, age, or class based) could all enjoy watching the sport that appeals to them most—for a modest subscription price on cable television.

Frank Reyson, editor of *Media-Scope* (a magazine oriented toward executives of commercial firms) has pointed out that although some research has been done in terms of the demographic characteristics (age, sex, ethnicity, class, and so on) of differing sports audiences, most of it locked away in the vaults of corporations such as *Coca-Cola* or *Gillette*. Also, there has not been as much research done in this area as many assume.

> Sports audience research is still in "the dark ages," according to Bob Stolfi, vp for sports sales at the CBS-TV network. "The best we do is quantitative," he explains. "The agencies do some research, but not as much as you might think. For example, nobody ever tested the relative effectiveness of a commercial on the NFL telecasts versus one on a hockey game."[49]

48. Many sponsors are even becoming hesitant to pay the enormous prices involved in professional football sponsorship today.
49. Frank Reyson, "The Cluttered World of Sports and Media," *Media-Scope,* November 1969.

Can you think of ways in which to set up studies that would test the effectiveness of commercials? What variables would be involved? How would you handle them? Perhaps a first step would be to ask yourself how you could determine the demographic characteristics of a local (and live) sports audience.

Until more research is done by (and released to) social scientists concerning the demographic characteristics of sports audiences, speculations such as the one above on the effects of cable television will have to remain speculations. Does this imply anything about the roller derby article?

As we turn from sports and television to the medium of radio, sociologist William C. Martin explores the role of the evangelist as religious spokesman and articulator of the values of the American working class. Combining participant observation and content analysis (analysis of scripts, documents, and so on) with the techniques of informal interviewing, Martin has gathered what most sociologists would term "soft" data on these disseminators of religious artifacts of popular culture.

THE GOD-HUCKSTERS OF RADIO

William C. Martin

You have heard them, if only for a few seconds at a time. Perhaps you were driving cross-country late at night, fiddling with the radio dial in search of a signal to replace the one that finally grew too weak as you drew away from Syracuse, or Decatur, or Amarillo. You listened for a moment until you recognized what it was, then you dialed on, hoping to find *Monitor* or *Music Till Dawn.* Perhaps you wondered if, somewhere, people really listen to these programs. The answer is, they do, by the tens and hundreds of thousands. And they not only listen; they believe and respond. Each day, on local stations that cater to religious broadcasting and on the dozen or so "super-power" stations that can be picked up hundreds of miles away during the cool nighttime hours, an odd-lot assortment of radio evangelists proclaims its version of the gospel to the Great Church of the Airwaves. . . .

The format of programs in this genre rarely makes severe intellectual demands on either pastor or flock. C. W. Burpo (Dr. Burpo accents the last syllable; local announcers invariably stress the first) and Garner Ted Armstrong usually give evidence of having thoughts about the broadcast ahead of time, though their presentations are largely extemporaneous. Some of the others seem simply to turn on the microphone and shout. Occasionally there is a hint of a sermon. J. Charles Jessup of Gulfport, Mississippi, may cite Heroditas' directing her daughter to ask for the head of John the Baptist as illustrating how parents set a bad example for their children. David

Terrell may, in support of a point on the doctrine of election, note that God chose Mary for his own good reasons, and not because she was the only virgin in Palestine—"There was plenty of virgins in the land. Plenty of 'em. Mucho virgins was in the land.". . . Often, however, a program consists of nothing more than a canned introduction, a taped segment from an actual "healing and blessing" service (usually featuring testimonials to the wondrous powers of the evangelist), and a closing pitch for money.

The machinery for broadcasting these programs is a model of efficiency. A look at station XERF in Ciudad Acuña, Coahuila, Mexico, just across the border from Del Rio, Texas, illustrates the point. Freed from FCC regulations that restrict the power of American stations to 50,000 watts, XERF generates 250,000 watts, making it the most powerful station in the world. On a cold night, when high frequency radio waves travel farthest, it can be heard from Argentina to Canada. Staff needs are minimal; less than a dozen employees handle all duties, from the front office to equipment maintenance. The entire fourteen hours of programming, from 6 P.M. to 8 A.M., are taped. Each week the evangelists send their tapes to the station, with a check for the air time they will use.

All announcing is done by Paul Kallinger, "Your Good Neighbor along the way." A pleasant, gregarious man, Kallinger has been with XERF since 1949. In the fifties, he performed his duties live. At present he operates a restaurant in Del Rio and tapes leads and commercials in a small studio in his home; he has not been to the station in years. A lone technician switches back and forth between the preachers and Kallinger from dusk till dawn. . . .

Who listens to these evangelists, and why? No single answer will suffice. Some, doubtless, listen to learn. Garner Ted Armstrong discusses current problems and events—narcotics, crime, conflict, space exploration, pollution—and asserts that biblical prophecy holds the key to understanding both present and future. C. W. Burpo offers a conservative mixture of religion, morals, and politics. Burpo is foursquare in favor of God, Nixon, and constitutional government, and adamantly opposed to sex education, which encourages the study of materials "revealing the basest part of human nature."

Others listen because the preachers promise immediate solutions to real, tangible problems. Although evidence is difficult to obtain, one gets the definite impression, from the crowds that attend the personal appearances of the evangelist, from the content and style of oral and written testimonials, from studies of storefront churches with similar appeals, and from station executives' analyses of their listening population, that the audience is heavily weighted with the poor, the uneducated, and others who for a variety of reasons stand on the margins of society. These are the people most susceptible to illness and infirmity, to crippling debts, and to what the evangelists refer to simply as "troubles." At the same time, they are the people least equipped to deal with these problems effectively. Some men in such circumstances turn to violence or radical political solutions. Others grind and are ground away, in the dim hope of a better future. Still others, like desperate men in many cultures, succumb to the appeal of magical solutions. For this group, what the preachers promise is, if hardly the Christian gospel, at least good news.

The "healers and blessers," who dominate the radio evangelism scene, address themselves to the whole range of human problems: physical, emotional, social, financial, and spiritual. . . .

The continually fascinating aspect of the healing and blessing ministries is that they do produce results. Some of the reported healings are undoubtedly fraudulent. One station canceled a healer's program after obtaining an affidavit from individuals who admitted posing as cripples and being "healed" by the touch of the pastor's hand. Police officers have occasionally reported seeing familiar vagrants in the healing lines of traveling evangelists, apparently turning newly discovered disorders into wine. But these blatant frauds are probably rare, and a faith healer need not depend on them to sustain his reputation. He can rely much more safely on psychological, sociological, and psychotherapeutic mechanisms at work among his audience.

The testimonials that fill the broadcasts and publications of the healers point to two regularities in a large percentage—not all—of the reported cures. First, the believer had suffered from his condition for some time and had been unable to gain relief from medical or other sources. Long illness or disability can weaken emotional and mental resistance to sources of help that one would not consider in other circumstances. Second, most of the cures occur at actual healing services, when the deep desire to be made whole is transformed into eager expectation by a frenzied whirl of noise, anxiety, and promise, and the pervasive power of the gathered group of true believers.

In recent years, the miracle-workers have turned their attention to financial as well as physical needs. They promise better jobs, success in business, or, in lieu of these, simple windfalls. A. A. Allen urges listeners to send for his book *Riches and Wealth, the Gift of God.* Reverend Ike fills his publications and brodcasts with stories of financial blessings obtained through his efforts—"This Lady Blessed with New Cadillac," "How God Blessed and Prospered Mrs. Rena Blige" (he revealed to her a secret formula for making hair grow), "Sister Rag Muffin Now Wears Mink to Church," and "Blessed with New Buick in 45 Minutes." Forty-five minutes is not, apparently, unusually fast for Reverend Ike. He regularly assures his listeners, "The moment you get your offering [and] your prayer requests into the mail, start looking up to God for your blessing because it will be on the way."

These men of God realize, of course, that good health and a jackpot prize on the Big Slot Machine in the Sky are not all there is to life. They promise as well to rid the listener of bad habits, quiet his doubts and fears, soothe his broken heart, repair his crumbling marriage, reconcile his fuss-ing kinfolk, and deliver him from witches and demons. No problem is too trivial, too difficult, or past redemption. Brother Al will help women "that wants a ugly mouth cleaned out of their husband." A. A. Allen claims to have rescued men from the electric chair. Glenn Thompson promises "that girl out there 'in trouble' who's trying to keep it from Dad and Mother" that if she will "believe and doubt not, God will perform a miracle."

The radio evangelists do not cast their bread upon the waters, however, without expecting something in return. Though rates vary widely, a fifteen-minute daily program on a local radio station costs, on the average, about $200 per week. On a superpower station like XERF the rate may run as high as $600. The evangelists pay this fee themselves, but they depend upon their radio audience to provide the funds. For this reason, some take advantage of God's Precious Air Time to hawk a bit of sacred merchandise. Much of it is rather ordinary—large-print Bibles, calendars, greeting cards, Bible-verse yo-yos, and ball-point pens with an inspiritional message right there on the side. Other items are more unusual. Bill Beeny, who tends to see the darker side of current events, offers $25-contributors a Riot Pack containing a stove, five fuel cans, a rescue gun, a radio, and the marvelous Defender, a weapon that drives an attacker away and covers him with dye, making him an easy target for police. Ten dollars will buy a blue-steel, pearl-handled, tear-gas pistol, plus the informative and inspirational Truth-Pac #4. Or, for the same price, Evangelist Beeny will send his own album of eighteen songs about heaven, together with the Paralyzer, "made by the famous Mace Company." Presumably, it is safer to turn the other cheek if one has first paralyzed one's enemy.

The most common items offered for sale, however, are the evangelist's own books and records. Brother Al's current book is *The Second Touch:* "It's wrote in plain, down-to-earth language, and has big print that will heal any weak eyes that reads it." For a $5 offering C. W. Burpo will send his wonderful recording of "My America," plus a bonus bumper sticker advertising his program, The Bible Institute of the Air—"Be a moving billboard for God and Country." Don and Earl, "two young Christian singers from Fort Worth, Texas," offer for only $3 "plus a extra quarter to pay the postage back out to your house," albums of heart-touching songs and stories that include such old favorites as "Just One Rose Will Do,". . . "Lord, Build Me a Cabin in Heaven," "Streamline to Glory," "Remember Mother's God," "A Soldier's Last Letter,". . . "Just a Closer Walk with Thee" (featuring the gospel whistling of Don), and that great resurrection hymn, "There Ain't No Grave Gonna Keep My Body Down."

In keeping with St. Paul's dictum that "those who proclaim the gospel should get their living by the gospel," the radio ministers do not always offer merchandise in return for contributions. In fact, the books and records and magazines probably function primarily as links that facilitate the more direct appeals for money almost sure to follow.

Brother Al, sounding like a pathetic Andy Devine, asks the faithful to send "God's Perfect Offering—$7.00. Not $6.00, not $8.00, but $7.00." An offering even more blessed is $77, God's two perfect numbers, although any multiple of seven is meritorious. "God told me to ask for this. You know I don't talk like this. It's got to be God. God told me he had a lot of bills to pay. Obey God— just put the cash inside the envelope.". . . Seven's perfection stems from its prominence in the Bible: the seven deadly sins, the seven churches of Asia, and so forth. . . .

Brother Glenn Thompson, who also names God as his co-solicitor, claims that most of the world's ills, from crabgrass and garden bugs to Communism and the Bomb, can be traced to man's robbing God. "You've got God's money in your wallet. You old stingy Christian. No wonder we've got all these problems. You want to know how you can pay God what you owe? God is speaking through me. God said, 'Inasmuch as you do it unto one of these, you do it unto me.' God said, 'Give all you have for the gospel's sake.' My address is Brother Glenn, Paragould, Arkansas."

In sharp contrast, Garner Ted Armstrong makes it quite clear that all publications offered on his program are absolutely free. There is no gimmick. Those who request literature never receive any hint of an appeal for funds unless they specifically ask how they might contribute to the support of the program. Garner Ted's father, Herbert W. Armstrong, began the broadcast in 1937, as a vehicle for spreading a message that features a literalistic interpretation of biblical prophecy. The program has spawned a college with campuses in California, Texas, and London, and a church of more than 300,000 members. Characteristically, the minister of the local churches, which meet in rented halls and do not advertise, even in the telephone book, will not call on prospective members without a direct invitation. This scrupulous approach has proved quite successful. *The World Tomorrow,* a half-hour program, is heard daily on more than 400 stations throughout the world, and a television version is carried by 60 stations.

Several evangelists use their radio programs primarily to promote their personal appearance tours throughout the country, and may save the really high-powered huckstering for these occasions. A. A. Allen is both typical and the best example. An Allen Miracle Restoration Revival Service lasts from three to five hours and leaves even the inhibited participant observer quite spent. . . .

Despite the blatantly instrumental character of much radio religion, it would be a mistake to suppose that its only appeal lies in the promise of health and wealth, though these are powerful incentives. The fact is that if the world seems out of control, what could be more reassuring than to discover the road map of human destiny? This is part of the appeal of Garner Ted Armstrong, who declares to listeners, in a tone that does not encourage doubt, that a blueprint of the future of America, Germany, the British Commonwealth, and the Middle East, foolproof solutions for the problems of child-rearing, pollution, and crime in the streets, plus a definitive answer to the question, "Why Are You Here?" can all be theirs for the cost of a six-cent stamp. . . .

To become a disciple of one of these prophet preachers is, by the evangelists' own admission, to obtain a guide without peer to lead one over life's uneven path. Though few of them possess standard professional credentials, they take pains to assure their scattered flocks that they have divine recognition and approval. . . . According to David Terrell, Jesus came into his room on April 17, about eight-thirty at night and told him there was too much junk going around. "Bring the people unto me." . . . Other evangelists simply promise, as does Brother Al, "I can get through to God for you." In support of such claims, they point to the testimony of satisfied disciples and to their own personal success; the flamboyance in dress affected by some of the men obviously capitalizes on their followers' need for a hero who has himself achieved the success denied them.

In the fiercely competitive struggle for the listeners' attention and money, most of the evangelists have developed a novel twist or gimmick to distinguish them from their fellow clerics. C. W. Burpo does not simply pray; he goes into the "throne room" to talk to God. The door to the throne room can be heard opening and shutting. David Epley's trademark is the use of the gift of "discernment." He not only heals those who come to him, but "discerns" those in his audience who need a special gift of healing, in the manner of a pious Dunninger. A. A. Allen emphasizes witchcraft on most of his current broadcasts, blaming everything from asthma to poverty on hexes and demons. In other years he has talked of holy oil that flowed from the hands of those who were being healed, or crosses of blood that appeared on their foreheads. David Terrell frequently calls upon his gift of "tongues." Terrell breaks into ecstatic speech either at the peak of an emotional passage or at points where he appears to need what is otherwise known as "filler.". . . Terrell defends his "speaking in the Spirit" over the radio on the grounds that he is an apostle—"not a grown-up apostle like Peter or Paul; just a little boy apostle that's started out working for Jesus."

Once one has made contact with a radio evangelist, preferably by a letter containing a "love offering," one is usually bombarded with letters and publications telling of what God has recently wrought through his servant, asking for special contributions to meet a variety of emergencies, and urging followers to send for items personally blessed by the evangelist and virtually guaranteed to bring the desired results. One runs across holy oil, prosperity billfolds, and sacred willow twigs, but the perennial favorite of those with talismaniacal urges is the prayer cloth.

Prayer cloths come in several colors and sizes, and are available in muslin, sackcloth, terrycloth, and, for a limited time only, revival-tent cloth. As an optional extra, they can be annoited with water, oil, or ashes. . . . One woman told Reverend Ike that she had cut her cloth in two and placed a piece under the separate beds of a quarreling couple. She declared the experiment an unqualified success, to the delight of Reverend Ike—"You did that? You rascal, you! Let's all give God a great big hand!"

These scraps of paper and cloth serve to bind preacher and people together until the glorious day when a faithful listener can attend a live service at the civic auditorium or the coliseum, or under the big tent at the fairgrounds. It is here, in the company of like-minded believers, that a person loses and perhaps finds himself as he joins the shouting, clapping, dancing, hugging, weeping, rejoicing throng. At such a service, a large Negro lady pointed into the air and jiggled pleasantly. Beside her, a sad, pale little woman, in a huge skirt hitched up with a man's belt, hopped tentatively on one foot and looked for a moment as if she might have found something she had been missing. On cue from the song leader, all turned to embrace or shake hands with a neighbor and to assure each other that "Jesus is *all right!*" Old men jumped about like mechanical toys. Two teenage boys "ran for Jesus." And in the aisles a trim, gray-haired woman in spike heels and a black nylon dress, danced sensuously all over the auditorium. She must have logged a mile and a half, maybe a mile and three quarters, before the night was over. I couldn't help wondering if her husband knew where she was. But I was sure she liked where she was better than where she had been.

If a radio evangelist can stimulate this kind of response, whether he is a charlatan (as some undoubtedly are) or sincerely believes he is a vessel of God (as some undoubtedly do) is secondary. If he can convince his listeners that he can deliver what he promises, the blend of genuine need, desperate belief, reinforcing group—and who knows what else?—can move in mysterious ways its wonders to perform. And, for a long time, that will likely be enough to keep those cards and letters coming in.

Were you to study this phenomenon of the radio evangelist, what similarities and differences would you employ in your research methods? Why?

Martin's findings reflect much that we have already seen in other studies of artifacts of working class popular culture: the desire for practicability in a complex and changing world and the search for reinforcement of simplistic notions of good and evil, right and wrong.

Sociologists McCarthy, Peterson and Yancey, employing the more quantitative techniques of the sociological survey in Nashville, Tennessee, point out that country and western marks the musical core of lower and working class popular culture, especially in the South. Again, the value of the self-reliant man overcoming a hostile environment is pointed out as a central concern of this type of music, as well as the strong and romantic rural bias of the working class. Further, McCarthy, Peterson and Yancey point out an important (and often overlooked) distinction with respect to working class values as found in country and western music—the difference between social and economic conservatism.

In studying the audience of this music, McCarthy, Peterson and Yancey have presented differences between country and western listeners and other working class respondents of Nashville. They have also mentioned that there is a strong correlation between preference for country and western music and race (poor whites comprising the largest audience). Are the differences they point to between country and western fans and others due primarily to the racial factor involved? They do not tell us. What are your guesses? And what relevance would an answer to this question have in terms of the study of social structure and popular culture?

SINGING ALONG WITH THE SILENT MAJORITY

John D. McCarthy, Richard A. Peterson,
William L. Yancey

While the Kennedy Administration patronized the fine arts, and the Johnson Administration was more likely to support well-known popular entertainers, the Nixon Administration, like none of its predecessors, has embraced "country-western music."

The president not only invited Johnny Cash and Merle Haggard, widely known country-western recording artists, to the White House for performances, but he followed by proclaiming October, 1970, as "Country Music Month." Thus the first president in history to claim roots in middle class suburbia has identified himself with the nasal twang sound of the songs of poor southern whites—a sound scoffingly referred to as "hillbilly music." It remained for Burl Ives, however, to explicitly link country-western music with true Americanism. He proclaimed from the stage, at the recent 44th birthday celebration of the Grand Ol' Opry, "Country music is *the* music of this great land of ours."

President Nixon's embrace of country-western music raises a number of significant questions about this music and its devotees. What are the important themes in this music? Who are its devotees? Do these devotees exhibit a coherent ideological position which would put them solidly in the Nixon camp? Answers to these questions will be derived from several larger studies in which the authors are presently engaged.

The country songs which have received the most notoriety in recent months express patriotism, regionalism, self reliance, and displeasure with indolent youth—presumably views held by members of that fabled constituency, the Silent Majority. The wide popularity of two recent Merle Haggard recordings—"Okie from Muskogee," which castigates hippie life styles while extolling the small town virtues of football, liquor and sex, and "The Fightin

Side of Me," an affirmation of two-fisted patriotism—has led many casual observers to class the entire range of country-western music as ideologically conservative.

President Nixon has apparently drawn such a conclusion, as his invitation to Johnny Cash to perform at the White House included a request for Cash to sing, "Welfare Cadillac," a song explicity denigrating welfare recipients by rehearsing all of the old saws about welfare chiselers. The fact that Cash balked at singing this song in the face of presidential pressure and did not perform it at the White House illustrates very dramatically the point we will argue below: country-western performers, their music, and their audience cannot be neatly fitted into the conventional left-right ideological categories.

For example, most songs written by Merle Haggard deal with the problems of little men in their struggles in a complex society. His "My Momma's Hungry Eyes" is such a song. He has also written, but has not been allowed to record, "Irma Jackson," a song compassionately chronicling the suppression of an interracial love affair. What is more, during the popularity of Haggard's "conservative" recordings, two other recordings — Johnny Cash's "What is Truth?" a plea for tolerance for the younger generation, and his brother, Tommy Cash's "Six White Horses," an expression of grief over the killing of Jesus, John F. Kennedy, Robert Kennedy, and Martin Luther King—were also high on the country-western hit tune charts.

Conservative political themes in country-western music are not a recent phenomenon, however. Indeed, there has long been an "underground" market for right-wing and racist records in the deep South. These records have been sold in dime stores but are not normally played on the air. Most of these records are made by unknown artists, but Marty Robbins, who campaigned for George Wallace in 1968, has recorded songs under the alias "Johnny Freedom." One of these, "Ain't I Right" is a song depicting college youths who come south to foment trouble in the cause of communism, and another, "My Native Land," asserts that our national leaders have betrayed the people and wish to see the nation on its knees. But while such themes have always been present and have received wide publicity recently, they have made up a very small part of the mass-market-oriented country music.

Country and western music, while simple in melody and rhythm, has always featured complex and varied lyrics. Since the beginning of commercial country-western music in the 1920's, the dominant lyrical themes have most often stressed individual troubles. A number of different themes are treated, but as with other forms of popular music, most country-western songs deal with love. The matter-of-fact treatment of the love problems of mature men and women are most often portrayed as a war between the sexes, as, for example, "I Cried All the Way to the Bank," and "Thank God and Greyhound You Are Gone."

Unlike the temperance songs of an earlier generation, liquor is now most often viewed in the context of an omnipresent view of love, economic, and family troubles and is normally seen as dissolving personal responsibility if not felt guilt. And while over-the-road truckers have replaced cowpunchers and railroad men as folk heroes, work songs continue to celebrate the victory of the strong, self-reliant, long-suffering working man over all obstacles of nature, the limitations of his body, and technology. A typical song depicts an overworked driver on pep pills highballing an overheated rig through an ice storm, in defiance of company orders, in order to get home to his wife.

A number of songs extol rural ways, as, for example, "Louisiana Man" and "That Little Brown Shack Out Back," which fondly recalls country plumbing. This genre is increasingly explicit in its criticism of urban ways, as in "I Wouldn't Live in New York City if You Gave Me the Whole Dang Town." Even many of the satirical novelty songs are set in the context of "trouble" as, for example, Johnny Cash's recent "A Boy Named Sue."

Unlike the labor union organizing songs of the 1930's, the many troubles which are chronicled in country-western music are rarely set in larger political perspective. More often fate, luck, the power of love, and liquor are the explanations for trouble. What is more, solutions to such problems are most likely to be stated in individual terms—self-reliance is the key here, a self-reliance which presumes a sort of frontier-like communalism. Thus, while political themes are rarely stated in overt terms, the values most often expressed in country music do have political connotations. We will return to examine these after dealing with the question, "Who comprises the audience for country and western music?"

During the summer of 1969 we interviewed 700 adult heads of households in Nashville, Tennessee concerning, among other things, their music preferences. These data taken in the context of the wide variety of other information gathered from these respondents afford us the opportunity to learn something more about the country music devotee. Our sample is not representative of the Nashville population because we purposefully oversampled lower and working class families. This sampling design, as we will show, is particularly appropriate for the analysis of country-western music fans, beyond the obvious utility of using respondents from Nashville, the home of country-western music.

WHO PREFERS COUNTRY MUSIC?

Though the president and Burl Ives may believe that country-western music is the music of the nation, our data suggests that, in Nashville at least, the music has its strongest appeal to the southern white working and lower class. To no one's surprise, only about 5 percent of our black respondents preferred country music, while approximately 45 percent of our white respondents preferred it. We found a very strong relationship between social class and preference for this music among whites, where 75 percent of the respondents with less than a ninth grade education preferred country-western music. With increasing education and income, preference for this music declines, so that among persons who have graduated from college we find that only 16 percent prefer country-western music. We expect that the rate of preference among this group for country-western music is probably far lower outside of Nashville for obvious reasons. Though there are few Nashvillians who were reared in the North, those with less than a high school education are quite a bit less likely to prefer country-western music (30 percent). Their southern counterparts are more likely to prefer it—where about 65 percent prefer country-western music. Also, persons who were reared on farms and in small towns are more likely to prefer this music than are those who are reared in large cities.

There is independent evidence of the regional preference for country-western music in that the majority of radio stations which operate on an exclusive country-western format are located in the South. Of the ten states with the largest number of exclusively country-western radio stations, according to the Country Music Association, eight are in the South (Texas, Florida, North Carolina, Georgia, Tennessee, Alabama, Louisiana and Virginia), while the other two (California and Oregon) are in the West.

BLUE COLLAR BLUES

Assistant Secretary of Labor Jerome M. Rostow said in a speech to the American Compensation Association (October 29, 1970):

> American workers expect that a steady, full-time, conscientious performance will pay off in an acceptable quality of life for them and their families.
>
> Unfortunately, numbers are getting increasingly frustrated by a system they think is not giving them a satisfactory return for their labors.
>
> Instead, millions of full-time workers—I mean get-there-on-time type workers—find themselves in an almost intolerable three-way bind: (1) the legitimate, basic needs of their families have grown beyond the capability of their take-home pay, even though that check has increased; (2) they are unhappy with their jobs, but they see no way of breaking out; (3) their total life-patterns are less than satisfactory.

Our evidence suggests that this characterization fits the lower and working class respondents we interviewed in Nashville. It is significant that while those respondents drawn from this class fit the image painted by Rostow (the bulk of the country-western fans come from this class), the country-western fans are only a slightly exaggerated version of this image. In addition to being members of the working and lower classes—in itself meaning that their level of income is either below the poverty line or at best marginal —they do not see, at least in the near future, much hope of improvement in their economic circumstances. Fifty-eight percent of our working and lower class respondents indicated that their jobs would not improve during the next five years. Country-western fans were even less optimistic about their future job prospects than were other blue collarites. Fifty-eight percent of the working and lower class respondents believed that their incomes would not change or would worsen in the next five years. Middle-class respondents were far more optimistic about the future with respect to jobs and income.

Yet in the face of economic deprivation, with little hope or expectation for a change in the near future, working and lower class respondents indicated a very strong belief in the "American Dream." This is especially true with respect to the role of hard work and self-reliance in occupational and economic success. Even though most of these respondents came from families who were also working class, only 25 percent expressed agreement with the statement, "Because of my family origin, I won't be able to get ahead much." Eighty-seven percent agreed with the statement, "You can succeed in this country with ability and effort." Lower and working class country-western supporters were no different from their counterparts who preferred other music styles, with respect to these beliefs.

But when we look at beliefs about the importance of work and work values, we find that the country-western supporters place somewhat more emphasis upon determination and ambition than their counterparts. So while 77 percent of the working and lower class respondents who prefer other music styles agreed that "the most important qualities of a real man are determination and ambition," 83 percent of the country-western fans agreed. Further, country-western fans were somewhat more likely than their counterparts to agree that "the best way to judge a man is by success in his work." The fact that only 43 percent of our middle class white respondents agreed with this statement suggests that a stereotype of the working and lower class as lacking ambition and placing little emphasis upon work is faulty.

Previous research on the working and lower class has suggested that rather than blame themselves for failure to succeed, the dream of success is supplanted by a focus on small goals in the workplace, an intense concern with security, and a continual accumulation of material possessions. This group is said to value a steady job over insecurity which offers the possibility of increased economic payoff, and to rationalize such choice. Yet, in a society which strongly emphasizes economic achievement, we see that members of the working and lower classes continue to value highly hard work and economic success in spite of their own lack of achievement. We might expect this situation to produce personal psychological problems for these Americans, and indeed our evidence suggests that our working and lower class respondents (both country-western fans and those who prefer other styles of music) exhibit low levels of self-esteem, high levels of psychosomatic symptoms of stress, and high levels of anomie, compared with middle class respondents. It seems clear that their situation produces troubles of many sorts.

Previous observation of the working and lower classes in the United

States has suggested that beyond the strong emphasis upon work as an adaptation to the conflict between lack of success and belief in the American dream, there is also an adaptation revolving around the dream of a small town and rural life. Apparently a large number of working and lower class urban whites dream of some day resigning from their jobs and moving to the country to earn a living on a small farm. Though both those who prefer country-western music and those who prefer other styles among the lower and working class respondents in our sample are highly likely to agree to such statements as "life in small towns is better, even though there may not be as many good jobs as there are here in the city," the country-western fans are substantially more likely to agree with this statement.

The Americans who prefer country-western music, then, are clearly confronted with economic problems and problems of justifying their own personal failure in the light of their strong beliefs in the American system. The music, as we have seen, emphasizes many of the problems which these Americans have in common, probably providing some solace in demonstrating that indeed others also have similar troubles. Further, some of the themes in this music hold out the possibility of solutions to the common problems—though the solutions remain stated in individual terms.

SINGING ALONG WITH THE SILENT MAJORITY

At first glance, there are obvious connections between ideological conservatism and the situation of country-western music fans. They are predominantly southern and white, and are commonly thought to be one of the more conservative groups in America—especially in the matter of civil rights. As working and lower class whites, they have been left behind by the civil rights and poverty movements of the 1960's. William Brink and Louis Harris demonstrate that approximately 70 percent of a national sample of poor whites disapproved of the "War on Poverty" in 1968, and the most important reason for such disapproval was a belief that the program was designed for blacks. Perhaps reflecting in part their experience with these attempts at relatively radical social change, more than 60 percent of our working and lower class respondents agreed with the statement, "if you start trying to change things very much, you usually make them worse." The country-western fans among this group were stubstantially more likely to agree with this statement (where about 71 percent of the respondents agreed). We know that this group was more likely than any other in the South to prefer the candidacy of George Wallace in 1968, we might be led to believe that politically this group prefers a status quo, anti-black political platform.

On the other hand, we have seen that this group is confronted with a wide range of personal troubles. Do their prejudices get the better of their realization of their own disadvantaged economic position? The answer must be negative, based upon our survey evidence. When asked whether the federal government should provide health insurance, somewhat over 60 percent of the working and lower class respondents agreed, making them far more likely to agree than middle class respondents. When asked whether the government should have more power to deal with the problems of the poor, the majority of these respondents agreed, and country-western fans were quite a bit more likely to agree, where approximately 74 percent agreed with this statement. So we see that the country-western fans surveyed, even though white southerners, fit the characterization of economic liberalism and civil libertarian conservatism which has been applied to this class nationally.

Unlike the black American, lower and working class whites have no clear and obvious barrier or corresponding ideology which can be used to explain their failure to achieve success in the American system. The recent emphasis on politicized themes in country-western music, as seen especially in such songs as "Welfare Cadillac," "The Fightin' Side of Me," "Okie from Muskogee," and "Bus Them Children," are symptomatic of the emergence of an explanation of troubles for those who have been apparently left behind by the systemic changes which have taken place over the last decade. Yet in this case, the blame for failure is not placed upon the system—this would not fit in with the strong belief in the American dream—but rather on the agents of social change. The songs identify these agents: The Department of Health, Education and Welfare is the force behind school integration and busing; the poverty program and the welfare system are blamed for the presence of Cadillacs among the very poor, hippies and peace-niks are identified as causing crime in the streets, disruption, and the lack of support of our fighting men in Viet Nam; and weak national leadership is blamed for having allowed the country to drift. All of this is summed up by the anguished song, "Where have all Our Heroes Gone?"

Yet the strong belief in the viability and sanctity of the American way of life does not solve the troubles experienced by this group of Americans, and we have some indication that they also favor change which would serve to confront some of their economic problems—changes that would be characterized as liberal in common parlance. This is so, even though they are suspicious of change as an abstract notion. This evidence, then, suggests some validity to the statement made by Albert Gore, unsuccessful incumbent candidate for the United States Senate from Tennessee, during his recent campaign, "Scratch a Wallacite and you will find a populist." In Davidson County (Nashville) Senator Gore ran 20,000 votes ahead of Nixon's candidate, William Brock, in spite of the fact that Wallace had taken Davidson County in 1968 and Brock had stressed themes very similar to the themes we find in "political" country-western music. Gore did find many populists through his stress upon the gut economic issues which our evidence suggests should appeal to working and lower class whites in general and country-western music fans among them, in particular.

Our evidence suggests that in spite of the recent popularity of presumably "conservative" songs in country-western music which reflect the strong beliefs in patriotism, individualism, and self-reliance among country-western fans, there is a large reservoir of liberal economic sentiment among these Americans. A politician who is conservative on both economic and social issues and who mistakes the strong feelings of primitive patriotism and support for the frontier virtues among the fans of country-western music as support for a conservative economic program may be making a serious error. The economic troubles of the affluent remain different from the economic troubles of the poor and the marginal poor. President Nixon may discover that this segment of the Silent Majority, when it finds its tongue, will speak with a forked one.

An important aspect of this study is that it is an attempt to identify quantitatively the consumers of a popular cultural artifact and to study, not only the demographic characteristics of that audience, but its attitudes and values as well. Interestingly, the findings are very close in many respects to those more qualitatively arrived at by essayists and critics such as Lohof and Wolfe. What methodological implications does this have for the study of popular culture.

Although McCarthy, Peterson and Yancey confine their study to the Southern lower and working classes, country music is also the preference of the Southern white migrant to the Northern or Western city. According to a sociological study done by Lewis Killian, urban social life for these migrants centers around the "hillbilly" tavern, where country music, both live and recorded, is played.[50] Essayist John Grissim has chronicled the rounds of the traveling country and western singer—the circuits do include urban areas as well as rural regions.[51] Hence one might suppose the lower and working class popularity of this type of music to be in evidence in many of the urban areas of America, as well as in its rural Southland.

In the early portions of this section it was pointed out that the most important aspects of the popular culture of the working class seemed to revolve around sex, religion, sports and television. The traditional importance in the American working class of the comic strip and the comic book appears in recent years to have declined dramat-

---

50. Lewis M. Killian, "The Adjustment of Southern White Migrants to Northern Urban Norms," *Social Forces* 32 (October 1953): p. 681.
51. John Grissim, *Country Music*.

ically[52]—most probably due to the increasing importance of television in the lives of this class. There are, however, some few types of printed material that are consumed by working and lower class publics. The popularity of the more vivid sex magazines with the working class male has been mentioned previously. Other working class reading material generally divides itself into two major categories—the tabloids (police magazines and exposé sheets) and the home repair and handicraft magazines.

In a study of the content of American magazines, Herbert Otto found the working class–oriented police and detective magazines to lead the field with respect to the descriptions of incidents of rape and to be just barely nosed out of first place by working and lower middle class men's magazines (such as *Male, Rogue* and *Stag*) in terms of their treatment of the topics of sex and torture.[53] With respect to the crime coverage of the tabloids (such as *The National Enquirer*), the race of the accused (if black) will be stressed along with the power of the defendant (if a politician or Mafia type) and the inadequacy of watered-down penalties and the Supreme Court. While good "plain folk" police may win occasional praise, greater attention is paid to scandals that expose the bribing of law enforcement officials by criminal organizations or the actual participation in criminal activities by the police. The star attraction, however, for the tabloids is the sensational trial that mixes sex, mayhem and violence.[54]

The importance of the sports sections of the modern tabloid cannot be overestimated. These articles furnish information for discussion and argument, both on the job and in the neighborhood bar.[55] Incidently, this working class preoccupation with sports is also buttressed by a preoccupation with betting. As editor and social critic Peter Schrag has pointed out, baseball is not the national pastime; racing is.[56] Betting gives the working class male a chance to "beat the system"; a chance in a small way, to control his world. Sociologist Irving Zola has remarked, "gambling seems to operate to deny the vagaries of life and to give the working class male a chance to regulate life."[57] Do you agree?

---

52. See Leo Bogart, "Adult Talk About Newspaper Comics," *American Journal of Sociology* 61 (1955): 26–30 and David Manning White, *The Funnies: An American Idiom* (New York: The Free Press, 1963).

53. Herbert A. Otto, "Sex and Violence on the American Newsstand," *Journalism Quarterly,* Winter 1963, pp. 19–26.

54 Arthur Shostak, *Blue Collar Life.*

55. Ibid., pp. 194–95.

56. Peter Schrag, "The Forgotten American," *Harpers,* August 1969.

57. Irving Kenneth Zola, "Observations on Gambling in a Lower Class Setting," in *Blue Collar World,* ed. Arthur Shostak and William Gomberg (Englewood Cliffs, N.J.: Prentice-Hall, 1964), p. 360.

Home repair and hobby magazines are a further staple of the male working class, reflecting many of the values of this class in the style and content of their articles. *Popular Mechanics*, in an advertisement, labeled its readers as not being "beatniks, potheads, or playboys." In contrast, readers would "rather look at a picture of auto racing champion Dan Gurney in a G.T. than go shopping for a dress with their wives. They'd rather buy a boat than take a cruise. They'd rather build a summer house than spend a month at Greenbrier. They'd rather paint the house than the town. They'd rather have a new outboard than wall-to-wall carpeting."[58] In short, they *would rather be* working class.

It has been pointed out that the working class exercises strict segregation between the roles of male and female. The great majority of the material in this section has articulated the dominant male values of the working class—and although the female participates in many of these aspects of popular culture (especially with respect to the religious and musical artifacts), her exposure is primarily to the ideal male role model.[59] There is little in these artifacts that relates to her place in the social structure as anything but an object for the satisfaction of the sexual appetite of the male.

There are, however, some artifacts of working class popular culture produced primarily for the consumption of the female. One of these is the daytime television "soap opera,"[60] but the more important and explicit artifact is the romance or confession magazine which deals primarily with the working class female's conflict between being sexually responsive to be popular with men and remaining virginal until marriage.[61]

In the following piece, social scientist David Sonenschein, analyzes the content of documents (romance magazines) to uncover the hidden functions of socialization these magazines perform upon their read-

---

58. Ad appearing in the *New York Times,* August 18, 1966. Quoted by Arthur Shostak, *Blue Collar World.*

59. This in turn leads her to *expect* "ideal type" behavior from the males surrounding her—leading to disappointment on her part and to a further intensification of feelings of insecurity, anxiety and frustration on the part of the working class male.

60. The polar values of the lower class are reflected in viewer responses to daytime soap opera machinations. These responses are "cast in vivid blacks and whites; they want good rewarded with permanent joy, they want evil punished with hideous extinction, and they don't have the slightest use for a fictional world that works in any other way." Edith Efron, "You Are Finks," *TV Guide,* April 17-23, 1971, p. 18.

61. Incidentally, Herbert A. Otto found the romance magazines to rank *second* (in terms of all types of magazines studied) with respect to the number of descriptions of rapes they presented. Herbert A. Otto, "Sex and Violence on the American Newsstand."

ers. Notice that he analyzes advertisements as well as articles—what can you tell about a population from the advertisements beamed at it? What would William Martin have said about that?

Unfortunately Sonenschein has not attempted to determine the characteristics of the readers of these magazines in a very systematic fashion, relying upon some old commercial surveys and his own "initial observations." What implications might this have for his total study? Can you thing of methodologies that might aid in solving this problem?

While reading note the size and composition of Sonenschein's sample of magazines. How much faith would you place in it as being representative of all such magazines published in the United States? As much as Sonenschein does? Why?

LOVE AND SEX IN THE ROMANCE MAGAZINES[1]

David Sonenschein

It is fairly common to say that the mass media and popular culture contain suggestions as to many of our culture's values. There may be some disagreement as to the exact boundaries of these systems, but a general consensus among social scientists on this seems to exist. The anthropologist in particular is prone to examine textual material for value and symbolic content, for it is within this realm that he sees the very essence of culture. This area is our concern here.

Two major interests have motivated the present analysis: one in cultural conceptions of "pornography" and the other in forces of cultural socialization. A great deal of the mass media has been identified with, even defined as, "pornography," "obscenity," or "objectionable" material. Hardcore erotica (the sole, specific depiction of sexual action) has been referred to as "the mass media of sex," but now we find sex permeates much of the media around us; items readily available on the market that deal directly (girlie magazines) or indirectly (advertising) in erotica have been called "soft-core" pornography. Thus, the traditional and perennial question of obscenity—what are its effects?—is asked of a far wider range of

[1]A revised version of a paper presented to a special session on "The Issue of Obscenity and Pornography in the Contemporary Media" for the American Association for Public Opinion Research (May, 1969). In operationalizing this, I am grateful to the following people who commented critically on earlier drafts: Eva Hunt, Nancy O. Lurie, Nancy L. Gonzalez, H. C. Dillingham, Brenda E. F. Beck, Alice Marriott, Carole Rachlin, Edward Sagarin, W. Cody Wilson, James L. Mathis, M.D., J. W. Mohr, Gunther Schmidt, and Roger Abrahams. Co-workers Mark J. M. Ross, Richard Bauman, and Morgan Maclachlan join in colleagueship in the newer project.

material than before; in fact, many are asking that question of what they see to be no less than their total environment ("it's all around us").

In addition, however, to the mere mention of acts, an extremely crucial aspect of erotica is the way in which sex is described with attendant values. It is this total configuration that becomes the major variable in socialization. Through this process of "social scripting,"[2] acts, contexts, and consequences are spelled out as behavioral alternatives in various interpersonal settings. It is this that determines for the observer or reader whether the sex is arousing or not, moral or immoral, and consequently, pornographic or not.

Beyond the immediate action in the stories, we find that sexual behaviors and attitudes are inseparably linked to broader cultural symbol systems, and it is within these that we begin to find and understand what it is that may be "wrong" with certain kinds of activities. We know that sexuality, previously thought of as a monolithic "drive" that motivates and determines a number of behaviors and dispositions, is in fact much more diffuse in human personalities and social systems.[3] We may gain a sense of this linkage in the ways sex is connected to nonsexual values and activities in the lives and thoughts of people in the magazine stories.

With regard to socialization interests, it is known that many of the readers of confession magazines are adults, usually younger married lower-middle or lower class housewives, living in the Midwestern United States.[4] On the other hand, there are indications from initial observations by this author that many readers of the magazines are of a different sort: younger girls of preteen years, usually from ages 9 to 12, are also attracted to the magazines. This population needs further definition in terms of its motivations and characteristics, but the need for socialization considerations for an age group younger than previously thought is established.

Eight different romance or confession magazines with a total of 73 fictional stories form the basis of the analysis. They were purchased from a downtown Austin newsstand and represent *all* of the magazines available on the stand at that time (one month's availability). While they are a "universe" of material at that point in time and space, they are a "sample" of a larger universe of published magazines. In 1966, there were 32 different confession magazines available; total readership was about 13½

[2]William Simon and John Gagnon, "Pornography—Raging Menace or Paper Tiger?" *Trans-action* 4 (1967): 41–48.
[3]William Simon and John Gagnon, "On Psychosexual Development," in *Handbook of Socialization Theory and Research,* ed. D. Goslin (Chicago: Rand McNally, 1969), 733–52; John Gagnon and William Simon, "Sex Education and Human Development," in *Sexual Function and Dysfunction,* ed. P. Fink and V. Hammett (Philadelphia: Davis, 1969), 113–26.
[4]Fawcett Publications, Inc., *Reader Characteristics* (New York: 1953); Look Magazine, *The Audiences of Nine Magazines: A National Study* (New York: Politz Research, 1955).

million.[5] The magazines used here were published by five different publishers though there seems to be little difference among them with regard to editorial policies. Each magazine averaged about nine stories per issue.

An initial survey of their content was made by coding for aspects of format, characteristics of the narrator and main partner, sexual events and situations, and other factors that figure in the plots of the stories.

For those who have seen the magazines, it is clear that the most salient characteristic of them is sex. Throughout all of the format features, the themes of sex and the physical nature of people are heavily played upon. The immediate and initial appeal, however, is to the femininity of the potential buyer, an image with which she may most readily identify. For example, six of the eight magazines carry cover pictures of young females of a very wholesome sort; even those depicted in a "seductive" kind of pose (i.e., facial expressions, body postures, clothing arrangements and types suggesting eroticism) may still retain a look of innocence.

Surrounding the picture are the titles of the magazine itself and of the stories for that month, but, upon inspection, one is struck by the apparent incongruities of the two sets of images. The names of some of the magazines in the sample were such ones as *Real Confessions, Secrets, Intimate Story, Daring Romances,* and so on. The titles imply what is to be the nature of the stories. They promise to be stories of an intensely personal sort, the kind that one would confide only to one's closest friend. There is a strong element of wickedness and even sinfulness about the relationships to be described inside. Such large-type statements as

> One Night A Week We Were Wicked—We Were
> Single Girls on the Prowl For Men!
> I Lost My Virginity—And Reputation—In The
> Boys' Locker Room!
> He Left Sex Out Of Our Dates—If He Loved Me,
> Why Didn't He Show It?!

all serve to heighten the anticipation for sex in a way that finds some correspondence with many popular judgments of what is seen to be "obscene": *illicit* sex. Such activities as abortion, premarital sex, incest, and adultery are explicitly mentioned on the covers of the magazines.

In the table of contents, the stories are listed with a short statement of what is to be the basic theme, a kind of "abstract" of the story. Again, these statements serve to set up the reader for access to an illicit affair of the narrator. Some examples are:

---

[5]*Standard Periodical Directory,* 2nd. ed. (New York: 1967). A larger number of magazines for the new study has been obtained. However, due in part to the formalized nature of the stories, the present sample sufficed in yielding significant themes in proper proportions. General agreement was also found in the present study with two earlier surveys. See George Gerbner, "The Social Role of the Confession Magazine," *Social Problems* 5 (1958): 29–40; and Wilbur Schramm, "Content Analysis of the World of Confession Magazines," in *Popular Conceptions of Mental Health,* ed. J. C. Nunnall (New York: Holt, Rinehart & Winston, 1961), 297–307.

"When I Say It Baby, You Do It—Anything And Everything!"
His Vile Commands Ring In My Ears, And There Is Nothing I Can Do
To Escape His Ugly Desires!

"My Stepfather Taught Me Sex!" It's My Wedding Night—I'm In
My Bridal Bed. But The Arms That Hold Me, The Lips That Seek Mine,
Belong To My Mother's Husband!

There begins to appear a message that the narrator seems to have little control over the situations she finds herself in. All in all, however, 77 percent of the story titles directly implied some sort of *sexual* activity as the *main* theme for the story.

For each story, there is an accompanying photograph supposedly depicting some main event in the story. These were coded in a broad way for the kind and style of posing in the picture. Photos of couples predominate, with 22 percent involving kissing (some with partial undress), and 15 percent depict the couple in a situation that can be described as "erotic," that is, there is a salient sexual intent between the two individuals. In most of these latter cases, the couple is touching or is in some kind of physical contact. Consequently, 37 percent of the format pictures involve a sexual or at least physical relationship. Thirty-three percent of the pictures represent some kind of fight, argument, or anguish, usually between a couple or in a family setting. This latter theme becomes significant as we shall see in the content of the stories.

Advertising was also coded for simple content and kind of appeal. Ads selling material of a mail-order dime store variety comprise a large category, 37 percent of all ads. However, the general category of "improvement" was the largest and most significant. In this there were two varieties. One was labeled "appearance improvement," and included such things as bust development, weight losing ads, fashions, and beauty aids; this comprised 36 percent of all the ads. Other kinds of ads based on a direct appeal to the improvement of one's self and position, such as loans, medicine, and religion, comprised 27 percent. In total, "improvement" advertising amounted to 63 percent.

The values of oneself as a physical being, more so as an appealing and in some ways a marketable physical being, are thus played upon heavily from the beginning. But we also start to get a sense of some of the risks that simply being a woman may entail. The relationships that await one, and the path through them that one must necessarily take, begins to seem more and more difficult. To what extent merely living life and being a woman means enduring punitive experiences are themes further elaborated upon in the texts of the stories.

Story types were classified into four general categories according to a classification set up by the editors of *True Story* magazine (one from 1958—not included in the sample) as a guide to potential authors. The resultant distribution on this basis was as follows:

Marriage story types	36%
Love story types	30%
Family story types	20%
Teenage story types	14%

It may be noted that the stories that deal with home life, marriage and family stories, total over half of the sample: 56 percent. The contextualization of the activities in the stories (recall the titles) are not as exotic, or erotic, as originally anticipated; they turn out to be settings that involve the basic values and symbols of our culture: the Home, Family, and love.

Overwhelmingly, the narrator is female (90 percent), young in age (teenage, 36 percent, or in her twenties, 22 percent), fairly religious (34 percent of the narrators mentioned a Christian affiliation or a "general belief in God"), and usually a housewife, 41 percent (other occupations are secretarial/clerical/sales: 22 percent, or student, usually high school, at 16 percent). Race was, with one exception, unspecified but implied white. Fifty-one percent were married, 38 percent were single with no previous marriage. Married women usually had a small family of one or two children. The settings of the stories were usually in small towns, but if set in a large city, the narrator was mentioned as having come from a small town or rural area. The depiction of the narrator then is that she is just "average." Even her physical appearance is not especially gorgeous, but she is explicitly described many times as being "pretty." She is at the same time like all other girls, yet like all other girls want to be.

The life of the narrator is also "average," with problems that arise in any family which are not of a totally disabling sort. Money problems, for example, occur in 25 percent of the stories, housing problems in 21 percent, health difficulties in 16 percent, and occupational troubles in 14 percent. The complications in the lives of the narrators, however, derive not from aspects of a larger world or "society" (indeed, there is little that can be called social consciousness in the stories), but rather problems come from the people in life, especially those close to the narrator, and from within the narrator herself. Life is a series of personal involvements, the management of which constitutes "life" or "living," and the existence of which "makes life worthwhile." Satisfaction comes from having a loving mate and having a supportive environment of "people you can get along with."

To return to the characters of the stories, the main partner of the narrator usually had fewer specified qualities. The main "other" was usually a male (69 percent), older in age, either the narrator's spouse (34 percent) or a previously unmarried single male (25 percent). His religion and race are unspecified but he appeals less to religion or the name of God, and no question ever arises over miscegenation. His occupation is given in general terms but usually set in skilled jobs or middle class office work.

Given the anticipation for sex as set up by the format, the actual incidence of activities was not as frequent as expected. Coitus is the most frequently occurring singular activity (63 percent of all stories) but more diffuse in its setting, "scripting," and consequences. Kissing occurs in second place (60 percent) but with more partners than coitus. Heavy petting is mentioned least of all in its specifics but occurs in 18 percent of the stories. Other kinds of sexual activity are rare. Incest is mentioned in only a few of the stories, homosexuality hinted at only once, and oral-genital activity never considered. Extramarital sex occurs in less than 5 percent of the married cases. It is of note that the partners with whom the narrator has sex are either the spouse (27 percent for coitus) or a single male (i.e., only one: 25 percent). In most of the cases, therefore, sex takes place within the boundaries of an emotional relationship with one male. Despite the lure of the titles, promiscuity in the sense of frequent and indiscriminate sexual behavior does not occur as a behavioral mode. In those few cases where it does happen, the punishments for indiscriminate sex are swift and severe; they are dealt out in an almost destructive fashion so as to indicate that those kinds of consequences were what was to be expected anyway.

The disruptive troubles that beset the stories are those that have personalistic references; that is, as we indicated before, "people" are the causes of trouble and the kinds we see in the stories are of a particularly damaging sort. Relationships are volatile, hostile, and even dangerous; in contrast to male-oriented erotica, it is trauma, rather than sex, which is "just around the corner." In those relationships where sex occurs, the results for the people involved were destructive. In relations where sex occurred, 54 percent of the relationships worsened because of the event. Much of this, of course, happened in cases of premarital sex, but even in many instances of marital sex the message was that when sex is attempted to be used as a solution for a problem, or the basis for forming a relationship, it became evident very quickly that it was not the answer. According to the stories then, guilt, anxiety, and personal difficulties for the narrator as well as damages to others are the costs of misusing or even just having sex.

Other themes of disruption occur significantly and regularly. Some are as follows:

Fight or argument in stories	70%
Mention of violence of any kind	53%
Loss of partner	36%
Guilt felt by narrator for coitus	34%
Loss of virginity by narrator	33%

Each of these, of course, may be elaborated upon separately, but we may mention here only how they cumulatively contribute to the feeling of uneasiness underlying each story. In nearly all the stories, the narrator goes through some sort of crisis; the crux of each, and the attraction for the readers, seemingly, is the *consequences* of events and their resolutions.. This is in itself a separate topic for investigation, but story endings give up a clue. Forty-eight percent end on a note of the narrator having mixed feelings of guilt and hope, punishment and salvation. This derives from the narrator having gone through a basic and fundamental crisis that seems to involve one's psychological self, particularly as felt through the emotions of love and sex. Nineteen percent of the stories end on a completely sad tone, where punishment has come about with the tacit admittance by the narrator that she deserved what she got in the end. Even though others are in the environment who will, perhaps by their very nature, take advantage of the narrator, the burden of villainy is assumed by her. She has misused or misapplied her self and her sex in a way that brings not only punishment but retribution.

We noted that the crucial and emotionally involving aspect of the stories is not so much the sex itself but the "social scripting" of sex, the perception of the partner and the narrator as "responsible" (as opposed to "responsive") beings, and the consequences of interpersonal commitment. The emphasis in the stories is that the purpose of life is the establishment of a series of dependable and stable sets of interpersonal relations, ideally to be founded upon that most stable and enduring of all forces, Love. To this, sex is only secondary; sex can be generated by love but love may be degenerated by sex. When we spoke of the "misuse" of sex, we were referring to the settings in the stories where relationships were attempted to be founded and sustained by sex. It couldn't be done.

We spoke of sex as being "diffuse" in both personality and sociocultural systems. We wish to place particular emphasis upon the latter and suggest that in addition to sex being connected to such things as roles, preferences, and activities, sex is at least distributed through, and at most generated by, a broader system of values which contains views of the world and the social order.[6] It is this latter set of orientations that determines the place and propriety of sex. From the scriptings in the romance magazines, a very explicit sense of what that value and symbolic order is can be obtained.

The basic theme of each story is the stabilization of one's personal life. This may occur in a variety of settings (as with our story types on marriage, etc.) and with a variety of results (getting married, getting divorced, getting pregnant, etc.), but the essence of life is the search for continuity through dependable relationships. It is very obvious in the stories that the most desired manifestations of this essential quality for life are marriage, a family, and love. These are the stable blocks on which daily life, and hence our culture and society, is built. These institutions are the resources for the relationships that allow for the expression of our "real nature." The crises in our stories all seem solvable by recourse only to love; love is the

[6]David Sonenschein, "Pornography: A false Issue," *Psychiatric Opinion* 6 (1969): 10–17; *ibid.,* "Pornography and Erotica in America," in *Sex and the Contemporary American Scene,* ed. E. Sagarin (New York: Dell, 1970).

overriding context of sex and any use of sex beyond this is taboo and destructive.

Here are the links between the values of legitimate versus illegitimate behavior. The condemnation of sexual activities and relationships is discussed not so much in terms of themselves but in terms of their consequences. Thus, activities and attitudes that threaten or violate the symbols and values of love, marriage, and the family are acts which endanger their very existence. The stability of these institutions is threatened by the volatile nature of sex itself and the enduring values of the institutions are threatened by sexual and emotional exploitation, "taking" rather than "giving." Sex cannot occur without love; by itself it is immoral, illicit, and even "obscene." Outside the institutions of the family and marriage, it is even worse: it is "unnatural."

What we are led to is the conclusion that the condemnation and negative sanctioning of sex occurs when the continuity and stability of basic cultural institutions is perceived to be threatened or denied as valid and necessary. "Obscenity" and "pornography" in this sense are those acts and attitudes which violate fundamental and symbolic realms in our culture. We know historically the perception of this has varied with time and place, but we may explain the great variety of judgments that have occurred in the past on this basis.

The issues of obscenity and pornography are basically symbolic issues; they are connected to what is perceived to be the essential tradition of our society in its cultural values and social structures. Violations of these are what call forth the cries of the impending End of Civilization As We Know It. Judgments of obscenity and pornography can be applied to a wider variety of things and behaviors, many of them non-sexual in nature. It is believed that widespread and continued indulgence in "obscene" and illicit acts creates a "moral collapse" and social destruction. The family is the fundamental sociocultural unit and the institution of marriage through love is necessary for its origin and continuance. "When these go, what else is there?" ask the magazines.

Contrary to our initial expectations, then, the romance magazines really appear to be paragons of virtue, arguing with a traditional, cultural morality for the necessity of love and the family and the minimizing of sex if one is to survive personally or socially. The effects and consequences of acting outside these values are spelled out in a fashion that explicitly details the risk. For the reader, the result is not a pretty picture.

Contained in the romance magazines and their explicit treatments of sex is the argument for the continuity of the American mode of life. Obviously, one of the main ways of establishing cultural continuity is to define the borders of deviance and state the consequences for going over. This is done by imbuing specific areas of interpersonal relations with the aura of heavy negative sanctioning. If a young female reader acquires the language of sex in the punitive terms that are portrayed in the magazines, we may wonder what the cost is of maintaining cultural continuity. The alternatives are limited for us in the media and the penalties are severe for the wrong choices. Yet the social order continues to be questioned and challenged. The problem is one that is demanding attention by its very protestations.

SUMNER'S FORGOTTEN AMERICAN TODAY

At the turn of this century, William Graham Sumner referred to that class of Americans caught between the rich and the poor—the broad, strong middle class—as America's "forgotten men."[1] This broad class, today estimated as 40 to 50 percent of the American population, is comprised of many subclasses and taste cultures. Nevertheless, the middle class as a whole shares certain values, beliefs, and life styles which distinguish its members from those above and below.[2] In terms of popular culture, the middle class is the largest consumer class in America today.[3]

According to Herbert Gans, this middle class public is, in *one* respect, similar to the working class. Its members are not interested in the "culture" of the upper class (although Gans does admit that some of the female members do express an interest in becoming "cultured").[4] The middle class, for the most part, rejects the intellectual and cosmopolitan sophistication of the upper class—yet it does accept some simplified forms of upper class culture, such as film versions of certain plays and novels.

Although the middle class does not place so strong an emphasis on substance (as opposed to form) as the working class does, the tendency to do so can most definitely be seen in many of the artifacts of middle class culture. Dramatically presented materials express and reinforce the values of the middle class.[5] Although some questioning of these values occurs, doubts *must* be resolved at the conclusion of the drama.

Gans also notes the rise of a "progressive" element in the middle class culture—an element that is more interested in Van Gogh than in

---

1. William Graham Sumner, *The Forgotten American and Other Essays,* ed. Albert G. Keller, (New Haven: Yale University Press, 1918).
2. Jack L. Roach, Llewellyn Gross, and Orville Gursslin, *Social Stratification In the United States* (Englewood Cliffs, N.J.: Prentice-Hall, 1969), p. 167.
3. Herbert J. Gans, "Popular Culture In America," in *Social Problems: A Modern Approach,* ed. Howard S. Becker, (New York: John Wiley & Sons, 1966), p. 589.
4. Ibid.
5. The popular film *Love Story* can be cited as a good example.

Grandma Moses, in *Playboy* than in *Life*. As America passed through the 1960's, this progressive element of middle class culture grew in strength and influence. Today its importance can be attested to not only by the traditional-progressive tension reflected in many artifacts of middle class popular culture,[6] but also in the increasing interest of the middle class in some selective forms of the "culture" of the upper classes. Alvin Toffler identified this trend in 1964 when he pointed out that one out of six to one out of four Americans is involved with what he called the "culture industry."

> It is clear . . . that the culture consumer is a new breed. . . . He is not part of the old, settled aristocracy, certain of its place in the world and confirmed in its interests, its judgments and its tastes . . . nor is he part of the shrinking world of the blue-collar worker or the farmer. Yet neither is he the sadly limited, provincial middle-class man of the past. He is, for one thing, too educated. He is also too traveled. . . . [His wife is] no longer homebound. She has an automobile available to her and time for activities outside the house. . . . She has some ties with the outside world. Her husband is no longer Mr. Babbitt. And she is not Mrs. Babbitt.[7]

The artifacts of middle class popular culture are somewhat different than those of the working class. Although certain sports (such as tennis, skiing, or golf) are emphasized,[8] for the most part the sporting world is less important to the members of the middle class than it is to the working class.[9] Games (such as bridge, *Monopoly*, or poker), however, loom large in the lives of the middle class, reflecting the middle class' belief in self-control and ability leading to success in a competitive situation.

Having, on the whole, pursued education further than members of the working class, the middle class public tends to read a good deal more. Hence books, newspapers and magazines are more important for them as carriers of popular culture.

Films have come to be of more importance (especially for the upper middle class—perhaps because they can better afford the costs of attendance[10] (admission fees plus sitter fees for children). However,

---

6. Many television advertisements utilizing sex draw effectively on this tension.

7. Alvin Toffler, *The Culture Consumers* (New York: St. Martin's Press, 1964), p. 51.

8. Perhaps because these are typically thought of as upper class sports, those members of the middle class with aspirations of upward mobility are more apt to play tennis, ski or golf.

9. This is not to say sports are unimportant to the middle class. Only that they are *less* important than to lower class publics.

films as an artifact of popular culture are, in no American social class, so important as they were prior to the advent of television. The middle class, like the lower and working classes, places a great deal of importance upon television—however, their viewing habits differ. The lower and working classes tend to pay more attention to the action films, the sports events, and the afternoon soap operas, while the middle class audience is more inclined to watch the "prime time" fare and the talk shows. This emphasis on prime time fare is no accident. The middle class consumer has much more to spend than his working class counterpart—and both advertisers and the television industry are aware of this. Hence prime time television is consciously "tailored" for the largest segment of the middle class audience possible. Because of its purchasing power, the middle class public can claim a great proportion of American advertising as an aspect of its popular culture.[11]

Purchasing power also means greater leisure-oriented mobility. The middle class family is more apt to take automobile trips and weekend excursions than the working class family. As sociologist Arnold Greene has pointed out, not only do the working and lower classes do very little camping, they also are not much interested in tourism (except as it is involved in the visiting of relatives in other states). Outside of the economics involved, Greene points out further reasons for the reluctance of working and lower class persons to participate in camping and tourist activities.

> One must relate to strangers, adroitly take and step out of roles, and competently meet unexpected developments of high stress character. Fears of "being taken" or "suckered" combine here also with provincial ignorance of where one might go, smugness in concluding little elsewhere is really worth visiting, and preference for the hometown version of things.[12]

The relative emphasis on the highway as a means to leisure activities has led to the emergence of the freeway culture of drive-in food dispensaries as an aspect of middle class culture (as are other artifacts of prepackaged or frozen foods—reflecting the middle class future-oriented belief that "time is money").

---

10. Although, in an age of television, theatre owners have attempted to lure the lower and working class to "family nights" at the drive-in theatre—where three to four grade D features will be shown for a very modest admission fee (usually a standard price per carload). Most drive-ins pipe in country and western music during intermissions. In this context it is interesting to note that many drive-in theatres double as "drive-in churches," featuring fundamentalist services on Sunday mornings.

11. Gans points out the usually unsuccessful efforts the media exert to convince manufacturers to advertise to their lower and working class audiences. Gans, "Popular Culture in America," p. 592.

12. Arnold W. Greene, *Recreation, Leisure and Politics* (New York: McGraw-Hill, 1964), p. 198.

Sex is an important aspect of middle class popular culture, just as it is with the working class. Although the hard drivin' physical working class image of the male has been traditionally rejected by the middle class public (with its emphasis on respectability and self-restraint), this repression and the use of sexual allusion and innuendo is breaking down within middle class culture. *Media-Scope* magazine has explored, from the point of view of the advertiser, the foment that seems to be going on in middle class publics with respect to the *presentation* of sex in everyday life:

> Throughout communications the barriers are down. It is hard to find a monthly magazine without sex in a coverline. This is not counting those that specialize in the subject. Classics of the field are being challenged, too, by newcomers, including *Penthouse* and a new dual-audience offshoot of a computer-dating service. This is *Checkmate*, a magazine for sophisticated singles. Last month in New York the Society of Publication Designers scheduled a meeting to answer the question, "Do magazines use sex or abuse sex?"
>
> The subject is not being neglected by the business press, either. *Art Direction* not long ago questioned excesses in an editorial titled, "Taste 1969: The Age of the Whore?" The Canadian weekly, *Marketing*, ran a special report in August on nudity in advertising.
>
> Editorial sex is also having its day on the air. ABC-TV launched its series, "Love, American Style," with a farce about teenagers, parents, and "the pill." Dr. Hip Pocrates has emerged from the underground press to FM radio with medical insights on sex. The subject is discussed routinely on TV panel shows, and specials abound. Metromedia Program Sales is syndicating "Anything Goes," on sex and the arts. Capital Cities Broadcasting Corp. is doing the same with "Sex and the Search for Adventure" with F. W. Winkler, M.D.
>
> Checking out audience attitudes on news media, *Time* had Louis Harris include some sex questions. "By nearly three to one, readers deny that papers are 'too full of sex,'" *Time* reported, and "nearly one in three finds TV news too full of sex. . . ."
>
> Men seem to be missing from the landscape. Short of Marlboro men, there is little for women to admire but other women. Dr. Charney (co-founder of *Psychology Today*) quotes his wife as feeling that TV commercials may be missing a bet when they make no attempt to appeal to female interest in the male body. It may be, the psychologist speculates, that focusing on men would turn off the male audience. "Men don't like to look at other men because then you get the sort of Silva Thin homosexual undercurrents, which is another element of sex in advertising."
>
> To the editor of *Cosmopolitan*, (Helen Gurley Brown), the absence of men from the scene has to do with emancipation for

both sexes. "Traditionally, I think, we still would rather look at women than men because so far, women have been prettier. They have rad a lot of hair and their faces have been beautifully made up, and they have these nice bosoms. So far, we haven't been able to show male genitalia, which are very showy also. We haven't gotten that far yet, and also men have had to have crewcuts and they all looked just alike.

"I think the time will come, as we gradually get more emancipated, when you will be seeing more beefcake." Right now, men are abandoning crewcuts and "old puritanical tweed" suits, Mrs. Brown notes. "The next step is that nude males will be as interesting to look at as nude females, but part of that, I think, has to do with woman's emancipation. We are on the pill now. We are much freer sexually than we have ever been, thank goodness, and as a woman gets free to enjoy herself sexually, she is going to start being turned on by a man's body. She never was before."[13]

In working class popular culture, the emphasis in terms of sex and action seems to be focused more on the male than it is in the middle class (Marlboro man, truck driver, auto racer). What sort of explanation would you offer for this observation? Do you suppose it has anything to do with dissimilar expectations of role behavior across classes (with respect to sex differences), or does it have to do with the market audience and whatever "turns the consumer on?" Who is most exposed to the media, by class? And who *does* make what types of economic decisions in the family?[14]

Sociologists Gerson and Lund, in the following selection, take a look at *Playboy* magazine. Using a similar type of content analysis as did Sonenschein, they argue that although *Playboy* does emphasize the female body in its pages, the primary function of the magazine is the socialization of the young urban middle class male. Thus the image of the ideal man, as presented in *Playboy* is vastly more important than the Playmate of the Month.

It is instructive to keep in mind the contrasting rural working class image of the Marlboro man while exploring Gerson and Lund's presentation of the urban middle class image of the Playboy. Are these images of "ideal" and respected types? Or are they actual role models utilized for socialization purposes by their audiences? Within this context, Gerson and Lund's discussion of the "safety-valve" function of the image is provocative. Can questions of this sort be resolved without study of the *consumers* of the artifacts?

---

13. "The Bad, the Bare and the Beautiful," *Media-Scope,* November 1969. Quoted by permission.
14. See Mirra Komarovsky, "Class Differences In Family Decision-making on Expenditures," in *Household Decision-Making.* ed. by N. Foote, (New York: New York University Press, 1961).

PLAYBOY MAGAZINE: SOPHISTICATED SMUT OR SOCIAL REVOLUTION?

Walter M. Gerson
and
Sander H. Lund

Since publication of the Kinsey reports, much commotion has been raised about the so-called "American Sexual Revolution." Many social scientists and laymen alike claim that recent American social history has witnessed a marked, revolutionary, general relaxation of the restrictive cultural norms governing human sexual behavior. This general loosening of American sexual norms, it is claimed, is manifested in both the findings of scientific research and in the operation of the contemporary popular cultural milieu. It is often asserted that the "decline" in American sexual morality is reflected in both sociological and social psychological research and in such areas of American popular culture as fashion (the bikini and miniskirt), mass entertainment (topless dancers and "sexy" movies), and the mass media ("raw," uncensored books and nudie magazines).

Those who contend that the "sexual revolution" is but a popular myth, however, have pointed out many weaknesses in this argument. They have noted, for example, that the conclusions drawn by Kinsey may have been biased, since his sample came from volunteers who may have overrepresented that portion of American society which is sexually active. Critics of a "sexual revolution" have also pointed out that the term has never been adequately defined. There is no absolute and necessary relationship between verbal statements and actual behavior.

However one reacts to the notion of a "Sexual Revolution," one point is clear, obvious, and indisputable: there has been a massive increase, at least at the verbal level, in popular concern with sex and sex-related topics.

This increase is clearly manifest in the continuing rise to eminence of sophisticated men's magazines—magazines which, to a greater or lesser extent, are oriented toward sex and the glorification of scantily clad beautiful young women. The magazine perhaps most representative of this field is *Playboy,* owned and edited by Hugh Hefner. Before the advent of *Playboy,* sexuality and sophistication occupied opposite ends of a continuum. Sexual magazines for men had been aimed at the lower classes and were consequently rather crude. Sophisticated men's magazines apparently deemed it impolite and improper to allude to sex overtly. Into the gap thus generated moved Hugh Hefner and *Playboy* in the early 1950's. *Playboy* allowed the more urbane men of the middle and upper classes—who tended to be repelled by the raw and often adolescent level of other men's magazines—to indulge their desire for sexual material at a more sophisticated level. In a real sense, the magazine was a response to a new demand in the popular cultural milieu. Overt interest in sex was no longer defined by higher-status men as a sign of immorality and degeneracy.

Moreover, *Playboy* accelerated this acceptance of sex as healthy by dispensing with crude, suggestive pictures and stories of rape and murder, and substituting urbane and literate essays, intellectual articles, and "artistically sensual" drawings and photographs. Burgeoning *overt* masculine interest in sexuality precipitated by an increasingly permissive moral climate (at the verbal level) was satisfied then by *Playboy*. The magazine was a first venture, so risky, in fact, that the first issue was not dated, with the expectation that there might not be another. Today, however, supported by accelerating popular interest in sexuality, it is one of the nation's most popular magazines.

Playboy serves one significant function today—socialization, as a largely informal content analysis of randomly sampled issues published during the period December 1965 through June 1967 will demonstrate. In this analysis it has been necessary to rely, perhaps inordinately, on some form of "sociological imagination" rather than purely quantitative methodology. The conclusions, therefore, are tentative and exploratory and are hypotheses for further study.

When one speaks of a magazine's functions, one must answer the question: "Functional for whom?" Obviously the way a magazine is used varies from reader to reader, and one publication can serve different purposes for different people. *Playboy's* main function is the socialization process. Not all of *Playboy's* readers use the magazine for these purposes. But analysis of *Playboy,* even a very informal analysis, reveals certain regularities and consistencies in style and content which when compared to the magazine's impressive success, appear functional in at least a minimal sense.

Playboy seems to supply its readers a goal to achieve, a model of behavior to emulate, and an identitly to assume. In essence, the reader is taught how to become a "Playboy." Throughout the magazine—in advertisements, editorials, pictorial essays, cartoons, articles, and works of fiction—the Playboy model, or what we shall call the "Playboy stereotype" is pounded into the reader. This stereotype generally consists of a sophisticated, cosmopolitan, urbane, diverse, affluent, intellectual, promiscuous (if that is the word), mature bachelor. This goal is, perhaps, what most American men have long desired as a perfect style of life. *Playboy* was not only the first magazine to delineate the stereotype in a systematic and explicit form, but also the first systematically to suggest means for achieving the ideal.

The single most salient concrete representation of the "Playboy stereotype" is the *Playboy* rabbit, self-acknowledged symbol of the magazine. The rabbit is almost inevitably shown in the company of one or more beautiful and adoring young women. He is always dressed impeccably (and expensively) in the latest styles, which range from formal dinner-wear to Bermuda shorts and cashmere sweaters, and is frequently depicted engaging in such diverse and sophisticated activities as skin diving, mountain climbing, yachting, or driving a foreign sports car. One of the rabbit's most striking and revealing characteristics, however, is his sophisticated blase attitude. Although he appears to lead the life of an ideal Playboy (which includes being in intimate surroundings with spectacularly beautiful and alluringly unclad young women), his expression never changes. His eyes are always half-closed in a bored fashion and his mouth is constantly turned up at the corners in an almost smug smile of self-satisfaction. Every aspect of his style of life reflects sophistication. He is, in every sense of the word, a man (or rabbit) of the world.

It is reasonable to hypothesize that a good many of *Playboy's* readers are men who for one reason or another (typically youth and inexperience) do not meet the levels established by the *Playboy* criteria. Hypothesizing further that these men accept the stereotype standards, then the second aspect of the *Playboy* socialization process begins to operate. *Playboy* at this stage begins to serve as a means of educating its readers in how to achieve the stereotype. It teaches them how to look, think, and act like Playboys. This instruction takes two forms: (1) formal or overt and (2) informal or covert.

Readers of *Playboy* are instructed on the formal level through such conventional channels as informative articles, advice columns, and certain kinds of advertisements. The instruction is often quite straightforward and direct, seemingly consciously aimed at teaching its readers some aspects of playboy living. From June 1966 through June 1967, there appeared in *Playboy* 82 factual-informative articles (features defined as "articles" in the magazine's table of contents). A rough classification of the articles by topic appears in Table I. Each article was classified according to the primary

TABLE I

CLASSIFICATION OF FACTUAL-INFORMATIVE ARTICLES IN *PLAYBOY* MAGAZINE FROM JUNE, 1966, TO JUNE 1967.

Topic	No. of Articles	% of Total
Fashion	13	15.9
Grooming	3	3.7
Interior Decorating	2	2.4
Cars	2	2.4
Music (Jazz)	2	2.4
Food	5	6.1
Drink	3	3.7
Parties ("how to . . .")	6	7.3
Travel ("where to go; what to do")	3	3.7
Sports	4	4.8
Entertainment	13	15.9
Modern Society—Human Problems	10	12.2
Popular Culture	7	8.5
Business—Money	5	6.1
Women—Sexual Freedom	3	3.7
Cameras	1	1.2
TOTALS	82	100.0

subject topic the article dealt with; hence, each article is tabulated only once in the table. Note that the vast majority of the articles are in some manner instructive. They show the reader what to wear and how to wear it, what cars to drive, what food and drink to consume, how to throw parties, and where to travel. For the young, the socially ignorant, the uninitiated, *Playboy* functions as an operating manual. It teaches them how to achieve the "Playboy Stereotype." For the more blase and cosmopolitan, *Playboy* functions to reinforce or validate what they already know about being a playboy.

A high standard of quality typifies the "Playboy Stereotype." The food and drink, for example, are exceptional and of gourmet quality (old Cognac and exotic foods); the cars are inevitably sports models; and the clothes are expensive and in the latest fashion. In other words, the stereotype is consistent with the image of an upper class playboy.

Another source of formal instruction can be found in the "Playboy Advisor," an institutionalized feature in the magazine. Confused and troubled readers can find therein information to solace their troubles and advice to solve their problems. The questions raised (and apparently answered) range from normal problems ("Should I have sexual intercourse with girls other than my fiancee?") to fashion and etiquette ("When is it proper to wear a white dinner jacket?") to gourmet matters ("What is the difference between imported and domestic wine?").

Other avenues of formal instruction are exemplified by features such as "The Playboy Forum," where readers debate and discuss salient issues such as sexual morality and exchange ideas and pieces of important information, and various other regular editorial features such as "Playboy After Hours," and "The *Playboy* International Datebook." *Playboy* also regularly reviews books, records, movies, Broadway plays, nightclubs, and other such attractions. All of these features, in some manner or other, demonstrate to the reader how a "Playboy" should behave—what books he should read, records he should listen to, movies and plays he should attend, where he should travel, what food and drink he should consume, where he should be entertained, and so on. . . .

Examples of informal avenues of instruction are such features as cartoons, fictional stories, and certain aspects of advertisements. It may be that the key difference between the formal and informal avenues of instruction, besides their degree of manifestness, is that the formal avenue teaches the reader *what* to do, and the informal teaches him *how* to do it. In other words, on the formal level *Playboy* teaches its readers the symbols, artifacts, and rituals which proclaim a playboy's status, and on the informal level it teaches him the subtle action, the attitudes, the beliefs, and the style of living which goes with them. The two categories are not mutually exclusive. Both are found pervasively throughout the magazine. Some aspects of formal instruction are found in works of fiction, and some aspects of informal instruction are found in informative articles. In terms of emphasis, however, the formal means of instruction is generally most salient in the direct and straightforward informative article, while the informal means of instruction is most salient in the more subtle and indirect works of fiction.

The style of living which *Playboy* seemingly attempts to teach could probably be best described as "cool but active sophistication." The other traits implicit in the "Playboy Stereotype" (i.e., sexuality and intellectuality) are oriented to this basic value theme. Since there are so many traits associated with the stereotype, however, and since they are interrelated, it is unfortunately difficult to extract the value's essence in a clear and unconfounded manner. Fortunately, at least an indication of its existence can often be seen in the content of many of the magazine's cartoons, advertisements, and works of fiction. A typical cartoon, for example, shows a husband suavely serving his wife and her lover cocktails in bed. The wife's reaction is: "Henry, I think you're taking this like a cad." The husband, true to the highest *Playboy* tradition, has "kept his cool," and effectively demonstrated his unruffled sophistication.

The subtle influence of the "Playboy Stereotype" is also reflected in many of the magazine's advertisements. As with the *Playboy's* symbol, the rabbit, the men depicted inevitably appear to behave in a suave, cool, and sophisticated fashion. They are always impeccably dressed in the latest fashion. Their female companions are usually lovely, adoring, and pliant. They are always in diverse but sophisticated surroundings (from sky diving to skin diving, from formal dinners to intimate bedrooms). Their most significant characteristics are their sublime "coolness," their self-assurance, their command of the situation. They do not represent the "man next door" who drives a Ford station wagon and has two children. They are self-assured, inimitably cool, and elite. As with the rabbit, they represent to some readers both a goal and a means of achieving that goal.

In addition to cartoons and advertisements, a third vehicle for indirect socialization in *Playboy* is, of course, the works of fiction. The process of learning is essentially the same as with other indirect avenues: instruction through identification and imitation on the part of the reader. With works of fiction, however, it is slightly more complex and diverse. The stereotype is generally the same. But works of fiction allow the Playboy's intellectuality and personality to be brought forth and rounded out. The stereotyped Playboy becomes multidimensional. He can quote Ibsen, Sartre, and Mailer. He is at home at formal dinner parties and "hippie" beer bashes, and as a consequence he seduces with equal facility sophisticated debutantes and female bohemians. Sarcasm and a "cool" sense of social awareness are his weapons. His morality and intellectuality are cool; he is the true individualist making his way towards some sort of secular nirvana.

The essential process involved in indirect socialization is, first, identification with the "Playboy Stereotype" and, second, imitation of the stereotype's behavior as presented in the advertisements, cartoons, and works of fiction. Therefore, as one assimilates the essential features of the "Playboy" image through identification and imitation, one tends to develop a "Playboy" self-conception and becomes, in essence if not in fact, a playboy.

A third facet of *Playboy's* socialization process is the dual function of motivation-reinforcement. That is, having given its readers a goal and providing them with a method of achieving that goal, *Playboy* provides them with some motivation for starting the process and reinforces them for continuing it. We shall consider these two functions as one, for the stimuli which initiate the reader into the socialization process are the same stimuli which keep him going.

The obvious initial desire which probably motivates many of *Playboy's* readers to embark upon the socialization process is sexual interest. Much of the intent in adopting the "Playboy Stereotype," aside from increases in status, prestige, and the like, appears to be to increase one's sexual activity. Overall, nonmarital sexual intercourse is still probably largely disapproved of in American society. Social punishment, in the form of legal sanctions and/or adverse public opinion, and psychological punishment, in the form of anxiety and guilt, are often the result for those who violate the traditional norms. *Playboy* functions to motivate the adoption of its stereotype and reinforces its continued assimilation by attempting to create among its readers the belief that not only is nonmarital sexual intercourse all right, but that it is good, healthy and desirable. Once the readers have largely accepted this contention, *Playboy* further facilitates the adoption of its stereotype by fostering the impression that belief in the morality of nonmarital sexual intercourse is a widely held opinion by people of high status.

The first stage in this motivation-reinforcement process, creation of the belief that nonmarital sexual activity is both healthy and normal, is manifest in the "Playboy Philosophy," a regular feature of the magazine. The essence of the morality found therein is that *it is indeed morality.* Sex is taken out of the gutter, cleaned off, and put back in its rightful place in "polite society." The unhappiness caused by Victorian repression is depicted, and at the same time it is demonstrated that a more liberal moral atmosphere is conducive to a happier, more well-adjusted society.

The "Playboy" morality is a logical, well thought out, possibly valid rationalization for the existence of the "Playboy Stereotype." The psychological punishment of guilt is alleviated by the demonstration that nonmarital sexual activity is in most cases moral, and that it is the traditional morality which is wrong. Thus it functions to motivate and reinforce the acceptance of the "Playboy Stereotype" by freeing the reader from the grasp of the traditional moral code.

The second stage of the motivation-reinforcement process (creation of the belief that the "Playboy" morality is widely accepted by high status people) can be found in such features as "Dear Playboy" (Letters to the Editor) and the "Playboy Forum." In the first place, it can be seen that an unusually high number of high-status individuals (psychologists, psychiatrists, heads of citizens' committees, ministers, and professors of sociology) write to the magazine heartily praising the "Playboy Morality." Such feedback may tend to create in the reader the impression that the "Playboy Stereotype Morality" is largely accepted by the elite, people whom they know they can trust. In the second place, although *Playboy,* in the interest of impartiality, does print the letters of some of those who disagree concerning its morality, the vast majority of letters published do in fact support it. Moreover, as an aside, it seems that somehow letters supporting *Playboy* are always literate and logical, while critical letters often tend to be irrational and fanatical (depicting Victorian reasoning at its worst). Be that as it may, however, the main point is that the large number of pro-*Playboy* letters create a feeling of "we-ness," a sort of abbreviated ethnocentrism. The person who adopts the *Playboy* morality and through it, the "Playboy Stereotype," is supported by the impression that he is a member of a large, high-status group. This is functional for him in two ways: First, the high status of his supporters tends to legitimize and strengthen his belief in the "Playboy" morality, which decreases the effects of guilt. Second, the large number of his supporters enhances his impression that belief in the morality of nonmarital sexual intercourse is increasing in American society which, in turn, tends to convince him that the social and legal sanctions elicited by violations of the traditional norms will be less painful. In any case, the supporter of the "Playboy" morality is freed to a certain extent to pursue the "Playboy Stereotype."

Another source of reinforcement-motivation is *Playboy's* treatment of women. Since, as we have noted, the "Playboy" morality is presented as morality, women cannot be shown being manipulated and exploited in this magazine, as they are in the lower class media. They must enjoy sex; it must be good for them. The contention that sex should be and is moral and healthy for women is a cornerstone of the "Playboy" morality. Rape and manipulative seduction are totally absent in *Playboy.* Those women who are seduced are usually experienced and of age, but even if they are not, the seduction is "for their own good," they enjoy it, and afterwards are grateful it was performed. The essence of this attitude is reflected in a statement of one foldout "Playmate": "I am my own woman . . . I lead my life according to my own standards, . . [which is] the pursuit of intellectual pleasure."

A fourth facet of the *Playboy* socialization process, what we refer to as the safety valve function, is also a form of reinforcement. Although the readers may be motivated to accept the "Playboy Stereotype," many are simply not able to live up to all its standards. Some men are not affluent enough, or intellectual enough, or "cool" enough (they might have some rather permanent personality characteristic which is not consistent with the "Playboy Stereotype"). Furthermore, there may be those who do not wish overtly to become playboys. They may be insufficiently socialized, or they may implicitly realize that the stereotype is beyond their reach. At any rate, for those who accept at least minimally the "Playboy Stereotype," but refuse to pursue it overtly, *Playboy* provides them with potential vicarious satisfactions. It provides an imaginary world in which they can be playboys without having to be intellectual, sophisticated, and affluent. They can do exciting things, go to exotic places, and seduce voluptuous young women, all in their imaginations, without having to risk the ego-shattering experience of failure and rejection.

The center page foldout, a monthly feature which depicts various beautiful young women in gaping stages of nudity, is a key factor in the safety valve function. The young Aphrodites function to a certain extent as the reader's vicarious lovers. The pictures easily convince the viewer that the girl could be his sexually and he could be in the picture. Thus, for example, the young women always stare directly into the camera and their expressions are intimate and willing. An example is the November 1966 foldout which reveals a young girl lying completely nude on the floor, gazing expectantly into the camera which looms directly above her. The impression is of a man looking down at his lover who reclines at his feet. This impression is enhanced by the *two* glasses of wine in the picture. One for the girl, the other apparently for the viewer, her lover. Another example, in the December 1965 issue, shows a nude young woman, lying in a mussed-up double bed. There are two pillows, the one on which she rests and one beside her which is indented as though it had been slept on. The reader can easily feel that he has just arisen from bed, and is now looking back at the woman with whom he has spent the night.

Between the December 1964 and the June 1967 issues, *Playboy* published 30 centerfold "Playmate" pictorials. Of 26 of these photographs (February, March, April and July 1965 being unavailable), 50 percent (13) depicted a girl either in or near a bed or wearing a negligee. Another 30 percent (8) showed a girl in the process of undressing, and 7 percent (2) revealed a young woman emerging from a shower or bath. The latent and overt sexuality of many of the poses demonstrates graphically that the playmate may easily function as more than mere sensual art.

The safety valve function is also somewhat of a reinforcer for those who perhaps intend to adopt the "Playboy Stereotype" morality in their overt behavior. The centerfold and other pictorial features foster the impression that many respectable and lovely young girls are willing to engage in nonmarital sexual activities. The reader is motivated, firstly, by the graphic depiction of the sensual pleasures that await him if he adopts the stereotype morality. Secondly, he is reinforced by the apparent willingness of the girls. He discovers he will not be forced to try to manipulate or exploit them, and he therefore knows he will be able to avoid the potential guilt of success and potential anxiety of failure. Thirdly, he is reinforced because the girls are respectable. They are assumedly on his level socially, so he will not have to experience the discomfort of a sordid and "raw" affair.

Thus, we have *Playboy* magazine, a contemporary American phenomenon. To most observers, reasons for the magazine's instant and continuing success are probably self-evident. However, all too often, books, movies, and magazines are examined only in terms of their entertainment value while their latent functions remain relatively unnoticed. Social phenomena like *Playboy* are significantly part of the popular culture of contemporary American society. Serious students of American culture and social life cannot afford to continue to ignore them as unworthy of scholarly investigation.

What are the similarities and differences in Gerson and Lund's technique as compared with Sonenschein's study of the romance magazine? Can you think of ways to improve the content analysis involved (such as attempting to specify more explicitly the criteria utilized for classification)? What assumptions do Gerson and Lund make concerning *Playboy* readers? Do they have any evidence to back up these assumptions?

Throughout the last few pieces, it has been repeatedly pointed out that little research has been done on the composition of specific consumer audiences—much of the data in this area comes from educated guesses and informal observation from which general conclusions are drawn. McCarthy, Peterson and Yancey presented one means (survey analysis) of obtaining this type of information. But suppose the public involved was reluctant to be identified with the artifact? (This could be, by the way, one reason why Sonenschein and Gerson and Lund did not attempt to survey the publics involved in their studies.) How would one then approach this problem?

This methodological issue was faced by the members of the President's Commission on Obscenity and Pornography. The solution of their researchers? Observation of members of the audience, especially the visual clues to their position within the American social structure. From here, supporting interviews were obtained from a few of these persons. By checking the representiveness of those who responded to the interviews as to the demographic characteristics (age, sex, ethnicity, marital status, and so on) of the total number observed, inferences were made in terms of the representativeness of the interview data obtained.

It has long been a strong American middle class belief that patrons of pornographic bookstores and movie theatres are, in the majority, single, lower class, deviant, and deranged. The studies reported on in the following selection help to explode this myth, showing that the typical customer is married, middle class, white, and quite respectable in both dress and manner. What does this suggest about educated guesswork as a basis for identifying the consumers of a cultural artifact, their motivations and beliefs? Can you think of other means by which data of this sort could be obtained?

PATRONS OF ADULT BOOKSTORES AND MOVIES

The Report of the Commission on Obscenity and Pornography

The "consumer of pornography" has been a vague and shadowy concept in American folk myth, not well defined but nevertheless obviously an undesirable type. Yet, in spite of the debate regarding the legal control of obscenity that has been growing the past 15 years, not one empirical study had been reported on the characteristics of people who bought erotic materials when the Commission came on the scene. The Commission has funded a few pilot studies of the patron of adult bookstores and movie theaters, and these together begin to sketch in a more definite image of the "consumer of pornography."

ADULT BOOKSTORE PATRONS

Massey (1970) observed 2,477 people who entered two bookstores carrying sex-oriented materials in Denver, Colorado. The observations were made over a six-day period in August 1969. One of the stores carried exclusively sex-oriented materials, while the other was a segregated section of a larger bookstore-newsstand. The sex-oriented sections were clearly marked "for adults only." Trained observers attempted to classify each patron in terms of sex, age, ethnic group membership, type of dress and the presence or not of a wedding band.

The patrons were almost exclusively male. Almost three-quarters (74 percent) were estimated to be in the age range of 26-55, while 22 percent were 21-25, and 4 percent were over 55; less than 1 percent were possibly under 21. Eighty-nine percent of the patrons were white, 4 percent black, and 5 percent Spanish-American. Over half the sample were casually dressed, 26 percent wore suits and 13 percent were blue-collar workers; the remainder were soldiers, students, tourists, hippies and clergymen. One-third of the patrons whose left hands were observable had on wedding bands. Jewelers estimate that roughly half of married males wear wedding bands, so well over half of these patrons were probably married.

Massey also inserted postcards in the purchases of 500 customers asking for demographic information. Only 52 of these postcards were returned, but the results were very similar to the observations. The purchaser who returned the postcard was male, age 26–35, had some education beyond high school, was married, a resident of the city, had an annual income of $10,000–$15,000, and had a professional or white-collar occupation. . . .

Massey attempted to interview some of the patrons, but soon gave up. The customers were quite skittish and generally silent while in the store; they appeared poised for flight. If someone spoke to them, they tended to respond in monosyllable and move away. Customers did not interact with each other and interacted with the cashier-clerks as little as possible. . . .

Booksellers' descriptions of their customer populations were quite consistent with the objective observations. Most of the stores claim a steady clientele who buy materials regularly, as well as transients who rarely come in more than once, but no estimates of the proportions of these two types could be made.

Nawy (1970) observed 950 customers in 11 adult bookstores in San Francisco. Only 3 percent of these were females and they were mostly accompanied by a male escort. About 8 out of 10 of the customers were over 25 years old and less than 1 percent were possibly under 18. The ethnic composition of the customers approximated the ethnic composition of San Francisco as given in the United States Census; predominantly white with a small proportion of blacks and orientals. Middle-class customers, as indicated by dress style, predominated. It is estimated, based on the number of wedding bands observed, that most customers were married. Nine out of ten shopped alone. Approximately one customer in every five made a purchase.

Winick (1970a) reports observations of 1800 patrons of bookstores, 300 in each of six cities; Mid-town Manhattan, Los Angeles, Chicago, Detroit, Atlanta, and Kansas City. Ninety-nine percent of the patrons were male. Approximately 80 percent were white, 15 percent black, and smaller percentages were Spanish-American and oriental. The variations across cities in ethnic composition of customers seemed to reflect the differing ethnic composition of the cities. . . . The age distribution was roughly the same across the cities. Twenty-six percent of the patrons wore business clothes, 41 percent casual, and 33 percent work clothes; few military uniforms were observed. There were considerable variations from city to city regarding costume: Atlanta, New York, and Kansas City had lower proportions of business attire and higher proportions of work clothes; Chicago and Los Angeles had higher proportions of business attire. The observers estimated the social class of the patrons as 44 percent lower class, 47 percent middle class, and 8 percent upper middle class. The downtown Manhattan figures inflated the lower class proportions considerably. Almost all (96 percent) shopped alone.

The profile of the patron of adult bookstores that emerges from these observations in different parts of the United States is: white, middle aged, middle class, married, male, dressed in business suit or neat casual attire, shopping alone. . . .

ADULT MOVIE THEATER PATRONS

Winick (1970a) observed 5,000 customers of adult movie theaters in nine different communities that provided a considerable spread of size, geographic, cultural, ethnic, and socioeconomic characteristics. The observations in eight of these locations were relatively consistent, but one was quite different from the others. We will describe the results of the observations on the eight and then discuss the ninth location.

Seventeen percent of the attendees were estimated to be in the age category 19–27, 32 percent in the 28–40 category, 41 percent in the 41–60 age group, and 10 percent were estimated to be over 60 years old. These figures did not vary significantly from city to city. Eighty percent were white, 14 percent black, 5 percent Spanish-American, and 2 percent oriental. These figures did vary from city to city, but the variation appears to reflect the ethnic makeup of the community. Ninety-eight percent of the patrons were male; more females were observed in suburban locations than in downtown locations. All the females were with a male escort or in a mixed-gender group. Ninety percent of the men attended alone. Attending alone was even more characteristic for the downtown theaters; roughly 15 percent of the patrons of neighborhood theaters attended in groups of two or more males. Twenty-nine percent of the patrons were estimated to be lower class, 55 percent middle class, and 16 percent upper middle class. These proportions differed widely from situation to situation reflecting the character of the area in which the theater was located. For example, 62 percent of the patrons of New York neighborhood theaters were lower class, 69 percent of those in Kansas City were middle class, and 48 percent of patrons of New York suburban adult theaters were upper middle class. Forty-one percent wore suits and ties, 50 percent wore neat casual clothes, and 10 percent wore work clothes. This also varied by community. Downtown and suburban theaters had more suits and ties and neighborhood theaters had more work clothes; Los Angeles had more casually dressed patrons. Approximately 15 percent of the customers scrutinized the outside display and a similar proportion exhibited a conflicted demeanor in entering the theater. Very few juveniles were observed looking at the displays outside the theater.

The one theater whose patrons did not fit this general description was a theater in a relatively small city that contained several colleges. The patrons of this theater were more likely to be younger, white, and casually dressed; there was also more attendance of male-female couples.

Winick (1970b) also conducted interviews with 100 patrons of an adult movie theater which provided validation for the classifications based on external observation. He classified each of the patrons in terms of age, ethnicity, and social class on the basis of external observations before the interview and then again after the interview on the basis of the interview data. The two sets of classifications correspond very closely, the main difference was reclassification of a few cases from upper middle class to middle class. These data confirm the possibility of making such judgments accurately from external observation and heightened our confidence in the descriptions provided by such observations.

Nawy (1970) observed a total of 2,791 customers at three adult theaters in San Francisco. Ninety-seven percent of these customers were male. Blacks are underrepresented and Chinese overrepresented in comparison to their population in the city. Thirty-nine percent wore suit and tie, 49 percent wore neat casual clothes, 6 percent were dressed in sloppy casual clothes, 4 percent were in "hip" costumes, and 2 percent in blue collar work clothes. Thirty-one percent wore a wedding band, 58 percent did not, and 11 percent could not be observed; this provides an estimate that about 60 percent are married based on the assumption that half of married men wear wedding bands. Eighty-five percent of the customers entered the theater alone, 6 percent were with the opposite sex, and 8 percent were in a group of the same sex. Twenty-three percent of the patrons appeared to be regular customers.

Nawy (1970) also collected questionnaire data from 251 of these adult movie theater patrons. The demographic data of this questionnaire sample is very similar to the description of the total sample of patrons based on external observation. . . . Thus, the external observations are validated and amplified by the self reports.

Patrons of adult movie theaters may be characterized on the basis of these observations to be predominantly white, middle class, middle aged, married, males, who attend alone. This contrasts very much with the characteristics of patrons of general movie theaters who tend to be young heterosexual couples (Yankelovich, 1968).

Nawy (1970) reports that his observations revealed that over half of the adult movie theater business is conducted during the 9:00 a.m. to 5:00 p.m. working day. This may be less true for neighborhood and suburban theaters than for downtown theaters. This business pattern contrasts sharply with that of the general motion picture theaters which often do not open until 6:00 p.m. . . .

ARCADE PATRONS

Two pilot studies of adult film arcade patrons have been made (Massey, 1970; Nawy, 1970). Both of these indicate that females are not allowed in these arcades.

Massey (1970) observed 236 persons entering an adult film arcade in a single day's complete coverage. He concludes that, "the general type and characteristics of consumers observed in the bookstores continued to be seen in the arcade."

Nawy (1970) observed a total of 367 patrons in all six of the known adult film arcades in San Francisco. The characteristics of these customers were similar to those of the patrons of the bookstores and the movie houses: white, middle aged, middle class, married males. Chinese were less often found in the arcades than in the movies. During business week lunch hours and around 5:00 p.m., three out of four patrons of the arcade were dressed in suit and tie.

INTERVIEW AND QUESTIONNAIRE STUDIES OF
CONSUMERS OF EROTIC MATERIALS

Several investigators (Goldstein, et al., 1970; Massey, 1970; Nawy, 1970; Winick, 1970b) have attempted to study patrons of adult bookstores and adult movie theaters. All have reported a great deal of difficulty in securing the cooperation of members of these potential subject populations, Customers in adult bookstores appear more reluctant to participate in a study than patrons of adult movie houses. The response rates in the successful studies were all less than 50 percent. This low response rate may introduce an undetermined bias into the results because those who agree to filling out the questionnaire or to the interview may be different in some other way from those who do not agree to participate. The distribution of demographic data on the people who participated in the more intensive studies is very similar to that found for the larger samples of observed customers, however; this would suggest that the other data may be fairly representative, too. . . .

Nawy (1970) administered questionnaires to two samples of patrons of adult movie theaters, using two different methods. In one case, questionnaires were left at an accessible place in the theater to be filled out and returned; of 800 questionnaires, 190 or 24 percent were returned. In another case every third person leaving the theater was approached and requested to complete the questionnaire; 44 percent of those approached complied with the request, and this resulted in 61 completed questionnaires. The distribution of demographic variables was very similar and the two samples were combined for analysis. The distribution on demographic variables for this combined sample was not statistically significantly different from the total sample of over 3,000 patrons observed.

Nawy (1970) found that the patrons of adult movies generally lead active and varied sex lives. Ninety-three percent have a regular partner; most have intercourse twice a week or more often; and most report having had intercourse with more than one person during the past year. Most of these viewers of adult movies say that their sex partners are aware of their interest in sex films. Fifty-four percent report that sex is more enjoyable since they have been viewing sex films and less than 1 percent report that attendance at such films has had a negative effect on their sexual relations. Seventy-nine percent report that the films have motivated them to introduce new variety into their sex lives. This variety was within fairly circumscribed limits, however, for these people were overwhelmingly heterosexual; only one of the respondents indicated an interest in experimenting with sadomasochism, and none indicated a desire to engage in bestiality or pedophilia.

Thirty-six percent of these patrons report attending adult movies once a week or oftener. They do not feel guilty about such attendance. Their reported reasons for attending these movies are: for entertainment only, 45 percent; to get new ideas, 36 percent; viewing is satisfying in itself, 35 percent; to pass time, 24 percent. Seventy-one percent of the movie patrons have purchased material at adult bookstores. Forty percent of these people report having spent more than $100 in the past year on erotic materials.

These customers of adult movie theaters manifest a good deal of upward socioeconomic mobility. Consistent with this upward mobility is that they report larger percentages delaying first intercourse experience until after high school years than does a national sample of men generally (Kinsey, 1948) or a national sample of college students (Berger, et al., 1970).

Goldstein and his colleagues (1970) interviewed 52 volunteer customers of adult bookstores and adult movie theaters using standardized clinical interviews of approximately two and one-half hours length that inquired intensively into history of experience with erotic materials, attitudes toward sex, and sexual history. The responses from this sample are compared with responses from 53 control subjects to the same interview. The two groups are fairly similar in terms of a variety of demographic variations except that the consumers of erotic materials are better educated and have higher level current occupations.

The buyers of erotic material tend to report more parental permissiveness when they were growing up regarding nudity around the home and exposure to erotic materials than do the controls, but there were no differences in the amount of either erotica around the house or conversation about sex. The two groups report essentially the same source of sex information, but the buyers of erotica tend to have been less likely to have had a sex education course in school.

The buyers are more likely to have had their first sexual intercourse after age 18 than are the controls, and they report less experience with erotica during adolescence.

As adults, the buyers of erotica report frequencies of intercourse fairly similar to that of the controls and a similar degree of enjoyment of intercourse. They are more permissive toward a variety of sexual practices, feeling that every individual should be free to decide for himself what to do in the sexual realm. In practice they also are more likely to have extramarital sexual experience and more often to achieve orgasm through nonintercourse means. The buyers of erotica differ from the controls most in the amount of experience that they have had with pictorial and textual erotic materials; they do not differ, however, in exposure to live erotic shows.

Most patrons of adult bookstores and movies houses appear to have had less sexually related experiences in adolescence than the average male, but to be more sexually oriented as an adult. The high degree of sexual orientation in adulthood encompasses, in addition to pictorial and textual erotica, a variety of partners and a variety of activities within a consensual framework. Activities most frowned upon by our society, such as sadomasochism, pedophilia, bestiality and nonconsensual sex, are also outside the scope of their interest.

REFERENCES

Berger, A., Gagnon, J., and Simon W. Pornography: High school and college years. *Technical reports of the Commission on Obscenity and*

Pornography, Vol 9. Washington, D. C.: U. S. Government Printing Office, 1970.

Finkelstein, M. M. Traffic in sex-oriented materials, Part I: Adult bookstores in Boston, Massachusetts. *Technical reports of the Commission on Obscenity and Pornography,* Vol. 4. Washington, D. C.: U. S. Government Printing Office, 1970. (a)

Finkelstein, M. M. Traffic in sex-oriented materials, Part II: Criminality and organized crime. *Technical reports of the Commission on Obscenity and Pornography,* Vol. 2. Washington, D. C.: U. S. Government Printing Office, 1970. (b)

Goldstein, M. J., and Kant, H. Exposure to pornography and sexual behavior in deviant and normal groups. *Technical reports of the Commission on Obscenity and Pornography,* Vol. 7. Washington, D. C.: U.S. Government Printing Office, 1970.

Kutschinsky, B. Pornography in Denmark: Studies on producers, sellers, and users. *Technical reports of the Commission on Obscenity and Pornography,* Vol. 4. Washington, D. C.: U. S. Government Printing Office, 1970.

Massey, M. E. A market analysis of sex-oriented materials in Denver, Colorado, August, 1969—A pilot study. *Technical reports of the Commission on Obscenity and Pornography,* Vol. 4. Washington, D. C.: U. S. Government Printing Office, 1970.

Nawy, H. The San Francisco erotic marketplace. *Technical reports of the Commission on Obscenity and Pornography,* Vol. 4. Washington, D. C.: U. S. Government Printing Office, 1970.

Winick, C. A study of consumers of explicitly sexual materials: Some functions served by adult movies. *Technical reports of the Commission on Obscenity and Pornography,* Vol. 4. Washington, D. C.: U. S. Government Printing Office, 1970. (a)

Winick, C. Some observations of patrons of adult theaters and bookstores. *Technical reports of the Commission on Obscenity and Pornography,* Vol. 4. Washington, D. C.: U. S. Government Printing Office, 1970.

Yankelovich, Inc. Public survey of movie-goers—1967. In *A year in review.* New York: Motion Picture Association of America, 1968, pp. 11–12.

Turning once again to the artifacts involved, critic Benjamin De Mott has remarked that one way of separating mere occurrences from significant developments in popular culture is to look for a success in a declining medium.[15] *Playboy* is an excellent example of this—the era of the American mass magazine seems to be quite definitely approaching its end. Although some few mass magazines are still in existence, they are nearly all in financial trouble. What seems to be taking their place are the *specialty* magazines, aimed at certain narrowly defined taste subcultures.[16]

15. Benjamin De Mott, "The Anatomy of Playboy," *Commentary* 35 (January 1963): p. 112.
16. Examples include *Street Chopper, Ski, Rolling Stone, Avant Garde* and *Black World.*

The increasing importance of the paperback book may also have something to do with the decline in popularity of the mass magazine.[17] Most of these magazines were built around short fiction stories, novels (continued from month to month) and nonfiction "lives-of-great-men" features. Some of the most interesting research in the field of social structure and popular culture has been content analysis of the mass magazine. Studies have pointed out the shifting themes of the stories and articles, both in terms of the types of characters portrayed and the locale of the stories.[18]

The heroes of the very early American magazines (1787–1820) were patriots, gentlemen, and scholars—reflecting the dominant values of the upper class readers of these costly magazines. However, as industrialization ushered in the era of the mass magazine, the type of hero portrayed in its pages changed. During the years 1894–1903, the hero was more likely to be the powerful individualist who succeeded in *laissez faire* capitalism.[19] Between the two world wars, however, the hero went through further changes. Two types of hero emerged: one the little man with traditional virtues in an agrarian setting (in the fiction articles), the other the "organization man" in his urban setting (in nonfiction).[20] One could hypothesize that the two models reflected the difference between the traditional values of the ideal middle class American hero (as reflected in fiction) and the reportage of the successful behavioral role model of the male in the real middle class world (as reflected in the nonfiction). As Orrin Klapp pointed out in 1962, "Modern man is caught in a dilemma between two ideals, standing on his own feet (according to the Protestant ethic) and complying with groups."[21]

Today, as Theodore Greene has hinted, if the mass magazines had survived one would suspect they would reflect a middle class hero who is more socially conscious and concerned with the structure of

---

17. Richard Lingeman found, on a 1967 visit to "Middletown (Muncie, Indiana) that the city's three bookstores relied mainly upon paperback sales. Lingeman concluded that the real function of paperbacks in Middletown may be to replace the magazines that people were reading in the 1920's and 1930's when Robert and Helen Lynd did their famous studies of that city. Richard R. Lingeman, "Middletown Now," *New York Times Book Review,* February 26, 1967.
18. For an excellent time series study of this sort, see Theodore P. Greene, *America's Heroes: The Changing Models of Success in American Magazines* (New York: Oxford University Press, 1970).
19. Ibid.
20. Patricke Johns-Heine and Hans H. Gerth, "Values In Mass Periodical Fiction, 1921–1940," *The Public Opinion Quarterly* 13 (1949): pp. 105–13; and Theodore P. Greene, *America's Heroes.*
21. Orrin E. Klapp, *Heroes, Villains and Fools* (Englewood Cliffs, N.J.: Prentice-Hall, 1962), p. 45.

urban bureaucratic America.[22] This is a reasonable picture of the hero as pictured in the few mass magazines that *are* still in existence, such as *Readers Digest, Ladies Home Journal,* and *Cosmopolitan.* (One could easily check this hypothesis with a study of his own.) If one accepts the contention that paperback books have, to a great extent, *functionally* replaced the mass magazine, then one should look also to them for reflections of middle class heroes. The increasing importance of science fiction in paperback form, and science fiction's increasing concern for just this theme, seems to lend support to the argument.[23] Also supportive is the current and vast quantity of paperback nonfiction sold that addresses itself to the lives of socially conscious leaders.[24]

Another important aspect of the study of the mass magazine has been the discovery of a great deal of discrimination against minorities in the stereotyping of fictional characters in the stories. White Anglo-Saxon Protestant Americans seem to play the leading roles in most of the stories; they command the most in the way of material goods and occupy the superordinate roles in most human relationships.[25] Criticism of stereotyping has also been launched at television and has been partially responsible in the last few years for programming that is perhaps a *bit* more equitable.[26]

Stereotyping and discriminatory portrayals are prevalent in the

---

22. Greene, *America's Heroes.*
23. See the works of Robert Heinlein, Arthur C. Clarke, J. G. Ballard and Brian Aldiss. Also note the theme of social rather than technological evolution as expressed in Stanley Kubrick and Arthur C. Clark's film, *2001: A Space Odyssey.* As John Baxter has pointed out, a major concern of the science fiction film is with the loss of individuality from technology run out of control. See John Baxter, *Science Fiction In the Cinema* (New York: Paperback Library, 1970).
24. Examples include Martin Luther King, Jr., John and Robert Kennedy, Jerry Rubin and Che Guevara.
25. Bernard Berelson and Patricia Salter, "Majority and Minority Americans: An Analysis of Magazine Fiction," *The Public Opinion Quarterly* 10 (1946): pp. 168–97.
26. This charge is also reflected in the many critiques of television by racial minorities, especially of the working and lower classes. The contention is that the situations and values depicted have no relevance at all—they are perceived by these persons as pure fantasy and not as any reflection either of their own lives of those of anyone they know or aspire to be. Similar problems have been pointed out in the area of primary and secondary school educational materials. Michael B. Kane has studied the stereotyping of minorities in school textbooks. Michael B. Kane, *Minorities In Textbooks* (Chicago: Quadrangle Books, 1971). The same sorts of charges Kane levels have been launched against primary school educational materials that use white middle class situations and people as role models. These role models are not recognized by the lower class child as relevant, and hence the content of the school lesson passes him by. Reaction to this charge has included the highly successful television program *Sesame Street,* which utilizes the media of television to project situations more relevant as examples for lower class children.

world of paperback books as well. A case in point is the best selling
novel, Arthur Hailey's *Airport*.[27] This novel describes the events at
"Lincoln International Airport" (Chicago) during a stormy evening.
A bomb has exploded on the Trans-American Airlines Chicago-to-
Rome flight (the *Golden Argosy*) and the emergency landing of this
flight is delayed because an Aero-Mexican jet is stuck on the runway.

All the heroes and heroines of *Airport*—those who perform their
jobs efficiently and well—are identifiable by name as White Anglo-
Saxons. Captain Vernon Demerest of Trans-America's *Golden Argosy*
is described as a "tall, broadshouldered, striking figure who towers
above others around him and conveys an impression of authority; pos-
esses strong aristocratic features.[28] The Trans-American stew-
ardesses, although indulging in illicit sexual behavior with Demerest
and other pilots were, "neither whores nor easy lays. They were, however, alive, responsive, and sexually endowed girls who valued quality,
and took it when it was so obviously and conveniently close to hand."[29]
One is left with the impression that these super Anglo-Saxons are superior not only intellectually, but biologically as well.

In contrast are the blunderers and villains of the book who are
almost all ethnic group members. The jet that is causing the trouble at
Lincoln Airport (by having become mired in the mud) is a Mexican
jet. Furthermore, the Mexican crew is lazing inside the warm pilot's
lounge while the American ground personnel are out in the freezing
weather attempting to remove this hazard from the runway. The
Mexicans are further complicating the American operations by their
hostility and uncooperativeness.

Another example of discrimination is the portrait of Perry Yount,
a black air traffic controller who is found derelict in his duty, is fired
and later has a mental breakdown. The other controller involved in
the incident that caused Yount to be fired, however, (Keith Bakers-
field) is not fired and finally proves himself by guiding the crippled
Golden Argosy safely onto the runway.

The "mad bomber" who cripples the *Golden Argosy* in flight is a
Mexican, Cuban, or Puerto Rican called D. O. Guerrero (whose ini-
tials just happen to be DOG).[30] He is described as "a gaunt, spindly
man, slightly stooped-shouldered [as compared to Captain Demerest's
broad shoulders] with a shallow face and protruding narrow jaw . . .

---

27. This novel has also been made into a successful film, nominated for the 1971
Academy Award. I am indebted to a review of the book by John J. Lennon for
a good deal of the information that follows. John J. Lennon, "The Case of Airport," *Journal of Popular Culture*, Fall 1969, pp. 355–60.
28. Ibid.
29. Ibid.
30. Ibid.

he needed a shave and a clean shirt, and was perspiring."[31] Harry
Standish, one of the Anglo-Saxon Customs officials, knew just by
observing this man that something was wrong.

The minor characters in the novel reveal similar biases and stereotypes. Floyd Zanetta is a loudmouth and inconsiderate troublemaker.
Mrs. Ackerman is a psychotic. Bonnie Vorobioff is portrayed as a dumb
peasant and Mrs. Harriet DuBerry Mussman is a loud-mouth, social-
climbing Jew. Marcus Rathbone disagrees with and dislikes everything,
including the White-Anglo-Saxon plan to disarm Guerrero.[32] Terry
O'Hale is an ignorant, Italian-hating, stupid, "rough, tough Bostonian
with a reputation for meanness in the ring, as well as out of it."[33] Joe
Patroni is a master craftsman in the bedroom—a "cocky-stocky
Italian-American."

The ultimate stereotyping in Airport is, of course, the changing
of Chicago's O'Hare International Field to Lincoln International Airport. O'Hare becomes, in Airport, relegated to the status of O'Hagen
Inn.

One should consider how much reinforcement of "traditional"
middle class biases and prejudices a book such as Airport can command
—especially with the circulation it received as a best seller.[34]

In the following piece, Clinton Sanders notes the stereotyping of
the Vietnam War in American novels, which he claims can be generally classed as evidencing either patterns of affirmation or patterns of
despair that reflect the divided (and ambivalent) mood of the American middle class concerning the Asian adventure.

Although Sanders' sample of novels is small, he notes that his
conclusions seem to fit well with empirical work that has been reported in sociology concerning war and the attitudes and actions of
its participants. With his methodology, Sanders focuses the issue of
social structure and popular culture that has been implied throughout
this section of the book (most especially with respect to the content
analysis of magazines and novels). That issue is: How much reality
can one expose by analyzing the more subjectively created artifacts?
(such as works of literature). Do you agree with Robert Gliner and
R. A. Raines (a sociologist and English professor respectively) when
they make the following statement?

> ". . . literature can provide a needed approach to academic
> discussion of American society, especially since growing numbers

---

31. Ibid.
32. Rathbone's objections foil the plan and precipitate the explosion on the
Golden Argosy.
33. Lennon, "The Case of *Airport.*"
34. Not only did *Airport* top the best-seller list for over 55 weeks; it was also
circulated in condensed form by the *Readers Digest* book club and has made
the rounds as a popular film.

of social scientists are questioning the possibility of an "objective" social science. Literary artists often convey very involving descriptions of society. They are sometimes able to show the direction a given society is taking, and to describe inconsistencies within it—they are often prophets of the future. The literary artist does not avoid value judgments, for in portraying the lives of members of society, he is able to show that life *is* value judgments. The literary artist is not a passive reporter, an "objective" observer; he swims through the mud with the characters he creates. Many literary artists have taken it upon themselves to portray the anguish of American society and to assume responsibility for commenting upon the social issues of which they are a part . . . you cannot be neutral, nor can you remain indifferent.[35]

How would one's stand on the above statement relate to one's reactions to the study of social structure via artifacts of popular culture?

35. Robert Gliner and R. A. Raines, *Munching On Existence* (New York: The Free Press, 1971), pp. ix–x.

THE PORTRAYAL OF WAR AND THE FIGHTING MAN
IN NOVELS OF THE VIETNAM WAR

Clinton R. Sanders

In his discussion of the novels which rose phoenix-like out of the ashes of World Wars I and II, literary critic Malcolm Cowley states:

> War novelists are not sociologists or historians, and neither are they average soldiers. The special training and talent of novelists lead them to express rather special moods. They are usually critical in temper and often they are self-critical to the point of being burdened by feelings of guilt. They are sensitive—about themselves in the beginning; but if they have imagination (and they need it) they learn to be sensitive for others, including the conquered peoples among whom American soldiers were forced to live.[1]

War novels are shaped by their subject as are the individuals who take part in the boredom, death, camaraderie and degradation of war. While—as Cowley states—war novelists are not sociologists, it is likely that the sociologist can learn much from the analysis of reality based "fictional data" dealing with this highly social phenomenon, war, and the values, attitudes and relationships of those who participate in it.

The novelistic portrayals of the war in Vietnam are unusual when compared with previous war fiction, in that they are being written and presented to the reader while the war is in progress. The works which developed out

[1]Malcolm Cowley, *The Literary Situation* (New York: Viking Press, 1947), p. 25.

of World Wars I and II were largely written after the conclusion of each war. The appearance of war novels while the war is still in progress (stalemate, regress?) may be accounted for by the highly emotional debate about the war which is taking place at home. The controversial nature of the war in Vietnam not only creates a lively market for the novels but also—because the novelists generally take implicit or explicit sides on the morality, tactics and goals of the war—it makes it useful for purposes of analysis to divide the novels into two rough pro and con categories. I have decided, as Eisinger does in his discussion of war fiction[2] to describe the prowar works as evidencing "patterns of affirmation," and the antiwar novels as showing "patterns of despair." The former are either overt or covert apologetics for the war in which the style is commonly romanticised naturalism and there is usually little questioning of the basic moral aspects of the war and business of killing by the main characters. As Eisinger states:

> The rhetorical novel is one that is unblushingly patriotic in intention, written to persuade us that the war was a noble effort. These novels justify the brutality of the war by arguing that fighting against the nation's enemies somehow completes a man; the only effective rebuttal to brutality is brutality.[3]

Novels displaying patterns of despair are generally antiromantic and often rather surrealistic in style. The war is questioned, the killing and destruction of property are questioned, and the callousing effects of the war upon the characters is often a major theme. For the disillusioned writer "the army robs all men of life; they are dead because the army deprives them of will. They must be blank and inhuman, they must be nobody, they think nothing and stand for nothing, if they are to adapt to the army.[4]

This discussion is based on a reading of a rather limited number of novels (9) written between 1965 and 1968. Although this sample is small it is representative of what seems to be the stylistic, ideological, and literary quality continuum, and I am confident that the following analysis would not be significantly altered if it were based upon a larger selection.

"THIS AIN'T NO DEMOCRACY. THIS IS THE ARMY."[5]

In general, the portrayal of the U.S. Army in Vietnam is rather bleak. Even in the novels of affirmation the Army, as an organization, is often seen as a hindrance to the winning of battles. Any respect for the organization is quickly erased by the routinized stupidity and inefficiency of the Army in action. As John Sack states in his blackly humorous novel, *M,*

---

[2]Chester E. Eisinger, *Fiction of the Forties* (Chicago: University of Chicago Press, 1963).
[3]Ibid., p. 45.
[4]Ibid., p. 31.
[5]Daniel Ford, *Incident at Muc Wa* (New York: Pyramid Books, 1967), p. 71.

"the army is a device built by geniuses to be driven by—idiots is too strong a word, men of average intelligence is fairer."[6]

The Army is pictured as a total institution with absolute control over the lives of its participants. On the one hand this absolutism is resented by the characters, and on the other it is looked upon as being an acceptable part of the "job" of soldiering. Beaupre, the disillusioned antihero in David Halberstam's novel, *One Very Hot Day,* says:

> "That's the name of the game, taking crap, being nice, being patient. That's why we're here, and that's what we're paid for, and it's my job and it's your job . . ."[7]

A major fault in the organization is often that of failing communication—communication down the chain of command from combat to supply, from air to ground, and between soldiers.
For example, Sack writes:

> In actual fact, the cavalry's big lieutenant colonel had given his captains the order; insure that positive identification be made—a sniper in the house, destroy it; otherwise spare it. But through the iteration of imperatives and the abolition of qualifiers and a wise apprehension that the colonel couldn't be serious, his order had been almost unrecognizable when it got through channels to Demirgian's Sergeant Gore. Gore had heard the order as, 'Kill everything. Destroy everything. Kill the cows, the pigs, the chickens—everything![8]

The bureaucratic structure of the Army is portrayed not only as an impediment to the short-range goals of the organization, but is also seen as destructive to the characters of the individuals involved. The individual must sacrifice his personal values to those of the group and must "struggle constantly against the impersonality of his military organization and the meaninglessness of his activity."

In descriptions of professional soldiers and officers presented in the novels, the distinction which Janowitz makes between the heroic and technocratic leader is especially apparent.[9] The heroic leader—the personification of military glory and tradition—is described in Gene D. Moore's novel of affirmation, *The Killing at Ngo Tho.*

> He was completely loyal to those of his command who had earned his faith, thought that God had created no finer thing on earth or in heaven than a good soldier, and was utterly fearless. In battle, in the face of civilian criticism of the military, in any endeavor, once he had committed himself he went all the way, and like his friend Patton, he had often seemed completely out of step with times of peace.[10]

---

[6]John Sack, *M* (New York: Signet Books, 1966), p. 54.
[7]David Halberstam, *One Very Hot Day* (Boston: Houghton-Mifflin, 1968), p. 65.
[8]Sack, *M,* p. 159.
[9]Morris Janowitz, *The Professional Soldier* (New York: The Free Press, 1960).
[10]Gene D. Moore, *The Killing at Ngo Tho* (New York: Pyramid Books, 1967), p. 23.

Daniel Ford describes the technocratic military leader who is "concerned with the scientific and rational conduct of war" in *Incident at Muc Wa.*

> The lieutenant was young. . . . Soon the army would be commanded by men like Lieutenant Schultz, who knew all about computers, and who regarded World War II as something for the history books.[11]

Both the novels of affirmation and the novels of despair are critical of the military manager. The former because he makes the job of the main character (always an heroic leader) more difficult due to bureaucratic regulations, and the latter because of the depersonalizing effects of the regulations upon the individual.

The antibureaucratic theme of the novels of affirmation may also be seen in the antipolitics and antiPentagon positions of the heroic major characters. In Robin Moore's *The Green Berets* the antipolitician stance is particularly apparent. Many of the actions which the unconventional forces define as necessary to the "winning of the war" run counter to political and international agreements.

> "By God Damn! Those Vietnamese generals—stupid! Dangerous stupid. Two hundred fifty my best men that sneak-eyed yellow-skin bastard corps commander takes out of here yesterday—and our big American generals? Politics they play while this camp gets zapped."[12]

In a recent article dealing with the combat soldier in Vietnam, Charles Moskos comments on the pragmatic nature of primary relations in combat.[13] Moskos' view that the soldier's social relationships in situations where death or injury are ever-present possibilities are determined by his definitions of his life chances is supported by the data culled from the fictional literature. Like the infantryman's weapon, his buddy is another means of staying alive. The grizzled first sergeant tells M Company:

> "Now this battalion is good—know why? Why, because we help our buddies. . . . I want you troops to say, 'If there's anywhere in the world I want to get wounded, it's in this battalion! Because my buddies'll bring me in, they're not going to leave me.' "[14]

In the Vietnam war novels as in the novels of World War II there is an unbridgeable social gulf between the enlisted men and the officers. Cowley and Eisinger both attribute this separation to the fact that officers have more privileges than do the enlisted men rather than due to the enlisted men's defining their officers as incompetent.[15] However, the latter

---

[11]*Ford, Incident at Muc Wa,* p. 103.
[12]Robin Moore, *The Green Berets* (New York: Avon Books, 1965), p. 33.
[13]Charles Moskos, "Why Men Fight," TRANS-*action* 7 (November, 1969): 13–23.
[14]Sack, *M,* p. 99.
[15]Cowley, *The Literary Situation,* pp. 31–32; Eisinger, *Fiction of the Forties,* p. 24.

explanation is common in the novels of this most recent war. The officers
are separated from their subordinates by their own incompetence and the
resulting distrust which this creates.

"The Army wouldn't be so bad if it weren't for the officers," Stephen
said. . . .

"Heck, Steve, somebody's got to give the orders."

"If you put all the possible orders in a hat, mixed 'em up, and pulled
one out whenever you wanted to make a decision, you could run this army
better than General Hardnetz."

"Yes, but!" Lieutenant Hamilton's pink corn-fed face bloomed with
inspiration. "Officers are for Wartime, Steve. Don't you see? When we get
out there in a real fight, somebody has to give the orders. Otherwise—
bang! Chaos!"

"I'd trust chaos before I'd trust General Hardnetz," Stephen said.[16]

"IT'S THE ONLY WAR WE'VE GOT"

More than anything else, the novels dealing with the war in Vietnam
are set apart from those dealing with the world wars by the portrayal of
the character of the war itself. The novels of despair are particularly concerned with this frustrating, senseless, strange war in which no final victory seems possible.

> Now he was becoming frightened again, aware of his age
> and the senselessness of the war—not the killing but the endless
> walking each day and the returning to My Tho with nothing done, noth-
> ing seen, nothing accomplished, nothing changed, just hiking each
> day with death. . . .[17]

Generally, the novels of affirmation can escape the despair which the
foreign character of the war calls forth by concerning themselves with the
description of limited battles which in the end resolve themselves in limited victories. Yet, even the "blood and guts" war novel must occasionally
touch upon the broader picture. In the following passage from Moore's
The Killing at Ngo Tho the Vietnamese commander is explaining the war
to his heroic American counterpart.

> "Your experience has only been with short wars, wars settled
> in a short span of years and where there has been recognizable defeat
> of one force and victory for the other. This plus the fact that your
> country has existed as a culture for only a few hundred years gives
> you a short-sighted view of problems as they exist here in Viet Nam
> and an impatience to solve all these problems in a single masterful
> stroke."[18]

In the novels of affirmation, therefore, the goal becomes death to as

---

[16]Ford, Incident, p. 22.
[17]Halberstam, One Very Hot Day, p. 126.
[18]Gene Moore, The Killing, p. 127.

many Viet Cong as possible. The more existential novels contain less mass slaughter but often indicate that, not only does the war situation itself brutalize its participants, but also this unconventional war with its vague goals and questionable morality is particularly destructive to those who are assigned to fight it. Sack describes the action taken to neutralize the feelings of ineffectualness generated by the unfamiliar character of the war.

> Once as their APCs passed some yellow Vietnamese houses where a sniper or two mightn't inconceivably lurk, the prudent caval-rymen paused and burned the pathetic little hamlet down, an act that any American whose heart goes out to the homeless will censure with a vehemence that is proportional to his range from the houses in question. Demirgian joined in with gusto, throwing his hand grenades into the thatch. Far from seeing this as senseless, Demirgian's inevi-table GI point of view was—finally! Finally he could do something with a clear bearing on America's war effort, clear in a physical sense if hazy around the edges in the sense of grand strategy.[19]

Moskos' finding that to the American GI all Vietnamese are potential enemies is strongly supported by the fictional data. The war is often pre-sented as a war against all Asians. The experienced sergeant advises the novice in William Wilson's novel of despair, *The LBJ Brigade:*

> "Ya ain't gonna have no trouble knowin' who ta shoot. If he ain't white shoot 'em. This is a race-war kid. A hundred-year-old hag can kill ya just as dead as a hot charlie. So can a ten-year-old kid. If he ain't white, screw the questions, shoot."[20]

While it is difficult for the characters to tell the enemy from the allies, a great respect for the Viet Cong is evident, particularly in the novels of affirmation which place considerable value upon the soldierly virtues.

While the enemy is often portrayed with hate-tinged respect, the South Vietnamese (ARVN) soldiers are generally represented as totally incom-petent.

> Sace smiles. He has smiled the whole time. He smiles because he has American soldiers under his command instead of Vietnamese soldiers. He calls the Arvin dirty names. I have heard him say, 'The fartin' fools. All they do is cough un fart, fart un cough. If they'd all get in tune they could make a million bucks. They couldn't ambush a rock.'[21]

This derogatory portrayal of the South Vietnamese soldier is particu-larly apparent in the novels of despair. The novels of affirmation generally represent the soldiers as being incompetent because of the inferior and

---

[19]Sack, *M,* p. 146.
[20]William Wilson, *The LBJ Brigade* (New York: Pyramid Books, 1966), p. 69.
[21]Ibid., p. 55.

corrupt leadership of the Vietnamese officers. When an American officer takes command the Arvin fight as well as American soldiers.

The most basic ingredient of war novels is death. The novels which do not glorify the war present death as an ever-present and always terrifying possibility. These works are soaked in blood and the lives of the characters are completely shaped by the presence of death. The novels of affirmation tend to be less concerned with the fear of dying while "not measuring up" in combat is presented as a much more frightening possibility. Death is often seen as simply a matter of chance. One increases his chances if he is careful, but in the long run there is no escape if "a bullet has your name on it." At the height of battle the principal character in *Incident At Muc Wa* thinks:

> "It's all a matter of statistics now. So many men, so many cubic meters of air, so many bullets flying across . . There's not a damned thing I can do to better my chances."[22]

THE "UNIFORMED CIVILIAN" AND THE
PROFESSIONAL SOLDIER

In the vast majority of previous war fiction the American soldier was portrayed as a "uniformed civilian"—a man to whom the war was simply an interruption which did not have a lasting effect upon his values or morals. In the Vietnam novels one finds an increasing emphasis upon the professional soldier. This can probably be accounted for by the fact that much of the literature available at this point deals with the early stages of the war in which professional soldiers acted largely in an "advisory" capacity. The novels of affirmation have a tendency to deal with the professional soldier more than do the novels of despair which emphasize the effects of war upon the novice warrior to whom war is a horrible interlude rather than a permanent way of life. The professional soldier in the "blood and guts" war saga is presented as a "fighting machine" who unquestionably obeys orders (". . . I am a soldier and I have written orders which cannot be misunderstood, and soldiers obey orders whether they like them or not.[23]) and who, at the same time, has the capacity for making instant decisions and insuring that the decisions are translated into action. When he is portrayed in the novels of despair, the professional soldier is usually a completely controlled machine who had adapted perfectly to a life of danger and authority. He has also learned how to cope with the varied demands of authority. A recruit describes the experienced sergeant in *The LBJ Brigade:*

> "We sit at attention, but Sace has a trick, to the captain he appears to be at attention, to us he seems to be slouching, he is an expert soldier, he can satisfy everybody at the same time."[24]

---

[22]Ford, *Incident,* p. 186.
[23]Moore, *The Green Berets,* p. 216.
[24]Wilson, *LBJ Brigade,* p. 21.

As can be expected, the theme of masculinity is central to many of the novels. Hard drinking and sex are highly valued and there are often passages which indicate the antiintellectualism of the masculine ethic. These passages usually take the form of a confrontation between a college-educated soldier and a professional in which the former is questioning the morality and politics of the war.

The hedonism and violence of the fictional portrayal of the soldier are often tempered with a goodness and gentleness, particularly toward the Vietnamese children. The warriors are practical, manly, yet gentle men who are simply doing their jobs. This is particularly apparent in novels of affirmation such as Robin Moore's *The Green Berets*. And so, while stupidity and callousness and carousal are presented, the American soldier is rarely portrayed as being inherently evil or corrupt. What seems to the civilian to be morally questionable is pictured as the obeying of orders or as the groping response to the unfamiliar character of the war.

Moskos's study of the combat soldier and Cowley's analysis of war novels both point to the lack of any clear-cut ideological justification for the war on the part of the American soldier.[25] There is, however, a definite "underlying commitment to the basic American ideals of family, materialism, Americanism and anti-Communism."

In the novels of affirmation, America must win because it never loses. The soldier fights for his home and so that his children will not have to fight the Communists in the States. The Americanism which the soldier possesses is material as well as familial. As Moskos observes:

> By far and away, the overriding feature in the soldier's perception of the American way of life is the creature comforts that life can offer.[26]

The members of M Company in John Sack's novel quickly find what they are fighting for soon after their arrival in Vietnam.

> Twenty-four hours at this foreign address and M's new immigrants had learned that the American way of life packages easily— that if given enough corrugated steel containers the quartermaster corps can deliver it to the antipodes, the touch of the entrepreneurial hand, the ring . . g of the magic register, and there in the horrible jungle are Lady Pepperel Percale sheets.[27]

The majority of the overtly ideological statements made by the characters in the novels are usually in the form of anti-Communism ("First, I am a professional soldier and I take orders and do what I am told. Second, I don't want my children fighting the Communists at home."[28]) in which the

---

[25]Moskos, "Why Men Fight," pp. 19–21; Cowley, The Literary Situation, p. 26.
[26]Charles Moskos, "The American Soldier in Combat," (unpublished manuscript, Northwestern University, 1967), p. 25.
[27]Sack, *M*, p. 110.
[28]Robin Moore, *Green Berets*, p. 152.

"domino theory" plays a large part. Sack parodies this position in his novel of despair.

> One week later when M was being whisked to the ends of the earth to fight against the communist way, it couldn't have quoted two consecutive words of Johnson's why it was going there—and M didn't need to. M firmly believed—or rather it firmly believed that it firmly believed—in the principle of perpendicular geography, the article of American faith that all this world's sovereign countries stand on their ends and if one topples over the rest will follow, that if Vietnam is allowed to fall to its enemies the cursed tide of communism shall flow across the Pacific as inexorably as the Japan current.[29]

Apart from ideology, the primary reason for fighting presented in the novels is simple survival. The characters are put into situations in which death is so immediate that ideology is unimportant. As the experienced sergeant tells the soldiers in Wilson's *LBJ Brigade:*

> "Screw what ya been told in the States. You ain't fightin' the Communists, you ain't fightin' Charlie. You ain't fightin' for liberty or America or the cunt next door. You're fightin' to stay alive."[30]

Rather than being bound by various "buddy relations" as described by Janowitz, Little, Stouffer and others,[31] the GI in the novels dealing with the war in Vietnam is portrayed essentially as an atom floating free of social bonds other than the formal ties of army organization.

This asocial depiction of the soldier in Vietnam is particularly apparent in the more existential novels of despair, whereas the atomism of the characters in the novels of affirmation is derived from their "rugged individualism" and self sufficiency.

Rather than the character in the novel attempting to "realistically improve the chances of his own survival" through the encouragement of social relationships, often the opposite is true—the soldier defines the chances of his own survival by being bettered by his avoidance of social ties. In the novels of despair, social relationships are meaningless in the individual's very personal confrontation with death and the brutality of war. In the novels of affirmation, social relationships limit the prized individualism of the heroic character and may be dangerous because of the nature of a war in which "When you've seen as much war as me, you'd know you can't trust nobody" is a major tenet.

We see, therefore, in the novels coming from our latest and most controversial war the portrayal of the soldier as an individual possessing a

---

[29]Sack, *M,* p. 131.
[30]Wilson, *LBJ Brigade,* p. 68.
[31]Roger Little, "Buddy Relations and Combat Performance" in Morris Janowitz, ed., *The New Military* (New York: Russell Sage, 1964), pp. 195–223; Samuel A Stouffer, *The American Soldier: Combat and Its Aftermath* (Princeton, N.J.: Princeton University Press, 1949); Morris Janowitz and Roger Little, *Sociology and the Military Establishment* (New York: Russel Sage, 1965).

vague (latent) ideology of Americanism, materialism and anti-Communism, confronting death and brutality in a frustrating, unconventional war in which all supposed allies are potential enemies and learning to cope with the absolutism, rigid stratification and anti-individualism of the military.

In general, because of the massive disagreement as to the wisdom, utility, and morality of this present war, the novels are much easier to divide into two categories than are those of previous wars. The writer is forced to take sides, either depicting the heroic soldier and playing upon the public's desire for vicarious excitement, therefore explicitly or implicitly justifying the violence in Vietnam, or condemning the war through a portrayal of its absurdity and its brutalizing effect upon its willing or unwilling participants.

Herbert Gans takes some further steps with Clinton Sanders' idea that there are two major publics in the American middle class mass audience (with respect to the Vietnam War). Addressing himself to the film industry, Gans envisions numerous publics in the mass audience, each with its own taste or opinion leaders. The creator of a film, then, has to define *his* target audience.

As a film progresses from concept to script to image, there may be many persons involved, each with his own "audience image." Thus the creative process becomes actually a series of negotiations—and the final product is determined to a large degree by those negotiators with the most power. The power of the negotiator is, however, dependent upon the audience and its values—for if the product is *not* accepted, the negotiator's ideas will be perceived as of less worth the next time around.

Gans illustrates his ideas with respect to *The Red Badge of Courage*. Although the movie is of the late 1940's, it does point out the roles of power, feedback and decision-making with respect to the film industry of that time.

THE CREATOR-AUDIENCE RELATIONSHIP IN THE MASS MEDIA: AN ANALYSIS OF MOVIE MAKING

Herbert J. Gans

One of the elements in the process by which movies (as well as other mass-media products) are created is the feedback that takes place between the audiences of that product and its creators. The creators referred to here are the movie-makers, i.e., the producers, directors, writers, actors and others whose decisions and actions create the movie. These creators get some feedback from the box office and from audience research. However, this paper argues that there is another, prior feedback which operates within the movie-making process itself.

The general feedback hypothesis suggests that there is active, although indirect interaction between the audience and the creators, and that both affect the makeup of the final product. This is in contrast to earlier models of the relationship, in which one or the other of the participants were pictured as passive. Thus some critics have suggested that Hollywood products are so similar that the audience has no real choice, but must passively accept what is offered. Others have argued the opposite, that the movie-makers are virtually passive, and give the people "what they want." Neither statement is accurate, but each has some truth. The audience is obviously limited by what is offered, but what is offered to it depends a good deal on what it has accepted previously. The movie-makers try to create pictures good enough to attract the audience, but at the same time they try to make sure that people will be satisfied with the movie they have chosen, by guessing and anticipating what will please them. Here, they use audience research to find out what people want, and make inferences from the choices people have previously expressed at the box office.

However, such inferences are complicated by two factors—the wants of the individual movie-goers and the nature of the total audience. Whether the movie-goers have specific and manifest wants is a moot question. Most likely they do not, and are satisfied to select from what movies are available, but *then* they expect to be entertained by the choices they have made. Being entertained means, on the one hand, that people want to satisfy various latent needs or predispositions, and on the other hand, that they want to be surprised with something new or different. Because people have these predispositions, their choices follow some analyzable pattern. But while there may be enough of a pattern to encourage the movie-makers to inferences about future choices, there is never enough to provide reliable predictions.

The process of prediction is further complicated by the composition of the audience. The movie audience can be described in many ways. From the box office it may look like a mass. To the sociologist,[1] it appears as an aggregate of youthful clique members who have followed the advice of their opinion leaders.[2] The creator sees the audience in its reaction to his product. For him, it is important to recognize that the members of an audience who have made the same choice at the box office may have done so with different predispositions. The audience for each movie can be classified into a large number of publics, each public being an aggregate of peo-

---

[1]For an exhaustive critique of the concept of mass, and an analysis of the audience in terms of sociological data, see Eliot Freidson, "Communications Research and the Concept of the Mass," *American Sociological Review* 18 (June 1953): 313–17.
[2]See Elihu Katz and Paul Lazarsfeld, *Personal Influence* (Glencoe, Ill.; The Free Press, 1956).

ple who have made a choice with the same predisposition, or set of related predispositions. Every ticket-buyer will respond to several themes in a single movie, and thus "belongs" to a number of publics.[3] Moreover, since he will look for different gratifications in a musical than in a western, he will "belong" to a different set of publics for every type of movie. The total potential movie audience is thus composed of innumerable publics, and every movie attracts a distinctive combination of them.[4]

There are so many publics that market research can never do more than skim the surface in providing information about the present audience, or inferences about future ones. Yet the movie-makers continue to make successful pictures. One reason for this is the existence of a further feedback mechanism which exists within the creative process itself, and literally permits the audience to follow the creators into the studio. Let us see how this takes place, and how it seems to shape the final product.

Every creator is engaged to some extent in a process of communication between himself and an audience, that is, he is creating *something* for *somebody.* This somebody may be the creator himself, other people, or even a nonexistent stereotype, but it becomes an *image* of an audience which the creator develops as part of every creative process. For analytical purposes this *audience image* can be isolated from the creative process as a whole.

This image, though projected by the creator, functions as an external observer-judge against which he unconsciously tests his product even while he is creating it.[5] As a result, the creation of any product may be described as a series of steps in which the creator selects one solution out of several possible ones, partly on the basis of the supposed judgment of this audience image. Obviously, the literary and other requirements of the product to be communicated are also involved in the selection between alternatives, but in the mass media product, these are often less important than the expectations of the audience image.[6]

---

[3]For example, from the audience for a Western movie, one might be able to isolate a public that has come to see a conflict between good and evil, another that has come primarily to see a heroic individualist, and a third that wants to commute for a few hours to the wide open spaces. Undoubtedly there are many other such publics. In addition, each theme is probably interpreted somewhat differently by different people, so that publics are further stratified by age, sex, socio-economic characteristics, education and taste level.

[4]In addition, there is that sizeable but probably decreasing band of people who go to the movies regardless of what is playing, or who come with limited expectations. They provide a "cushion" for predictions, and soften the effects of wrong guesses by the movie-makers.

[5]The relation between creating and judging aspects of the creator might be compared to the "I"—"me" relationship of George Herbert Mead. See Anselm Strauss, ed., *The Social Psychology of George Herbert Mead* (Chicago: University of Chicago Press, 1956), esp. pp. 242ff.

[6]The similarities and differences between mass-media creator and artist here remain to be explored.

The audience image is not a unified concept, but a set of numerous impressions, many of which are latent and contradictory. These impressions deal primarily with how people live, and how they look at, and respond to the roles, personalities, relationships, institutions and objects that movies portray. These impressions develop and accumulate in the mind of the creator in his contacts with potential audiences. The experienced movie-maker must have some image of the audience response to all of the innumerable situations and characters that he is apt to work into different movies. As he begins to work on a specific picture, what probably happens is that he pulls together a group of more or less consistent impressions which will evolve into his audience image for *that* movie. This image is broad enough to permit him to communicate with many of the publics who will come to see the picture, although only rarely can he reach all publics. Also, his image changes somewhat from movie to movie, but it can do so only within limits which are imposed on his sensitivity and skill by the familiarity he has with the social, cultural and psychological experiences of the total audience.

It must be emphasized that the creator not only anticipates his audience, but tries to create or attract one for his product. In order to do this, the movie-maker concentrates on the product itself, and tries to make a "good" movie. He may succeed if his work on the product (and his audience image) are sensitive to the predispositions of any part of the total movie audience. The "great" movie-maker may be able to create a loyal audience precisely because he knows or feels something, perhaps within himself, that is shared by a large number of publics, but has not been sensed by other creators who are perhaps equally bold or adept in other aspects of movie-making.

Every creator has a somewhat different life history and consequently a distinctive image of the audience. Sometimes, he shares enough of the characteristic of an actual audience so that by creating for himself, that is, for his self-image, he is also communicating to a larger audience. This perhaps describes the folk artist in preurban societies, whose audiences were relatively homogeneous. The mass media creator, however, works for a large number of publics. Many of these publics have tastes and predispositions that vary from his own, and in many cases, these are evaluated socially as inferior, or "lower" than his. As a result, the creator may feel somewhat intolerant of his audience.[7] Much of our popular culture is produced by creators whose personal tastes are "higher" than those of their

---

[7]He may even consider that he is prostituting himself. This is so partly because the artist, whose norms he still follows, traditionally created for himself, or for a like-minded audience. Many observers have called attention to the desire of mass-media creators to gain the approval and respect of critics, intellectuals and others who follow the norms of "high culture." The fact that the mass-media creators are wedded to the demands of their audiences while retaining the norms of the artist might explain the intensity of their desire for approval, as well as their dilemma.

audiences. Although this relationship breeds problems of role, morale, and product quality, it may also provide the creator with enough emotional distance between himself and the audience to permit him to create for an audience of so many different publics.

In summary, the audience image thus functions to bring the moviemaker in contact with one of his major reference groups. Other reference groups affect the creator's total image, e.g., colleagues, superiors, critics, and respected creators in other fields. Their demands may sometimes conflict with those of the imagined ticket-buyers, and will remind the creator of his role conflicts, although they may also broaden and diversify his own audience image. In addition, pressure groups are able, through their clamor, to win a place in the creator's audience image, and may also limit his communications with other publics, or force it into devious channels. Empirical research would undoubtedly permit refinement of the audience-image concept, especially of its latent aspects.[8]

The audience participates in the making of a movie through the audience image held by the individual creator. Since a movie needs a large audience to be commercially successful, it must be made as attractive to as many publics as possible, within the literary elasticity of the screen play. Consequently, its creation involves several different audience images.[9]

The making of the picture itself can be viewed as a decision-making process. As each creator applies his audience image in the decisions that have to be made, he is "representing" some of the publics who will eventually see the movie. The completed picture is a combination of the decisions made by its creators, and also a compromise or perhaps more correctly, a "negotiated synthesis" of their individual audience images. However, this synthesis takes place within a power structure, and the final decisions are often made by studio executives who point the compromise in a direction that seems to assure the largest box office. Thus, the final product has some of the characteristics of a political party platform, seeking to please as many as possible. The making of a movie can be studied much like any other political decision-making process (such as a party caucus, or a labor-management conference), and it is possible to observe how each creator makes decisions in terms of his position in the power structure, his audience image and his other reference groups, all of which have implications for the makeup of the actual audience.

---

[8]These might be studied in four ways. First, through the creator's cultural background, his education, work and leisure history, his various reference groups, and the audiences and cultures he knows. Second, through his aspirations, the kinds of things he would like to create, the audiences he would want to create for, and the career goals he has generally. Third, through his personal tastes and preferences, both as a creator and as a member of audiences. And finally, through his role in the making of the product, and the decisions he makes in those situations that have implications for the eventual audience.

[9]The exception might be the "great" producer or director, whose audience image is so multifaceted that he is able, by himself, to command a large number of publics.

The portion of each creator's audience image that is most important in the making of the movie depends partially on the role he plays in the production process. The studio executives work intimately with financing, and their images are likely to seek out the largest number of people. They are perhaps especially conscious of the audience as a mass with a lowest common denominator of interest. The director and writer are probably able to give fullest rein to their audience images, and have served as models for much of the foregoing discussion of the mass media creator. The producer occupies the ambivalent position of the foreman, and his audience images must take into account the studio as profit-making institution, and his own image as creator.[10] The actors may not develop audience images, for their work is frequently dependent on the director, or, if they are stars, they have a ready-made audience in their fans.[11]

Descriptions of the movie-making process suggest the multiplicity of potential audience images involved.[12] The process may begin with a product created for another audience entirely, such as readers or theater-goers. The studio's readers may see it as suitable for movie audiences. If the executive producer agrees, he may assign it to a producer, director and writer. Presumably his choice of specific persons is related to his feeling that they will agree with his audience image for the eventual movie. Quite often several writers are employed before a satisfactory screenplay is achieved. Perhaps they function to assure the movie's appeal to more publics by adding their own images. When stars are chosen, the picture may be rewritten further to strengthen their parts, in order to attract the audiences that they bring with them.[13] The cameramen and technicians may also play roles beyond their technical ones.[14]

When the shooting itself is completed, the cutter will edit in his or her image. After the sneak previews, when the movie has been tested against a sample ritually presumed to represent all future publics, the picture may be reworked to add appeal for publics left unconvinced by the preview.

---

[10]Rosten's study of a sample of 144 producers indicated that 52 had held jobs as movie writers and 21 as directors. See Leo Rosten, *Hollywood* (New York: Harcourt, Brace, 1941), p. 270.

[11]Many actors undoubtedly have audience images, and those who do are probably considered to be the better actors.

[12]See for example Dore Schary (as told to Charles Palmer), *Case History of a Movie* (New York: Random House, 1950), and Rosten, Ch. 11.

[13]Leo Handel advises producers "to increase the potential audience for a film by combining, in one picture, players appealing to different audience sectors." See Leo Handel, *Hollywood Looks At Its Audience* (Urbana: University of Illinois Press, 1950), p. 150.

[14]David Riesman suggests the role of the camera crew as a "near audience" (personal communication). Since these people are involved in the instrumental, rather than the substantive aspects of movie-making, and in their own leisure choices are more like the rest of the audience than others involved in the production, they may provide the creators with the earliest preview of the validity of their audience images.

Even before completion of the picture the advertising department has begun to build expectations among what it considers to be the potential audience and its opinion leaders. Their various ads are calculated to reach as large a number of specific publics as possible. This process may continue even after the picture is released, for if a movie proves to be weak at the box office, the studio suddenly rewrites its ads in the hope of seeking other publics that will make the picture profitable.[15]

Many of these hypotheses can be illustrated from a study Lillian Ross made some years ago of the production of the movie, *The Red Badge of Courage*.[16] Her account first appeared in the *New Yorker,* and combined reporting with many personal (and satirical) interpretations. However, on the assumption that the main facts can be abstracted from her report with some reliability, the data can be reanalyzed to show how the creators of the picture sought to affect it in terms of their audience images, and how the picture changed when different images were applied during its making. The description will be quite brief, and will therefore rely, for summary, on the highbrow, middlebrow, lowbrow terminology. These terms will be used as oversimplified but objective categories of audience preferences, without any value connotations attached to them.[17]

The Red Badge of Courage had three main creators: John Huston, the writer-director, Gottfried Reinhardt, the producer, and Dore Schary, the studio production head.

John Huston is a successful and many-faceted director. In this picture he was trying to bring a famous novel, and the novelist's conception, to the screen with maximum fidelity to both media.[18] His aims suggest that he was making the movie primarily for his colleagues, critics, and himself—and with a highbrow audience image. However, while working on this picture, he was already planning his next one, *The African Queen,* for a much larger audience.

Schary, the studio head, wanted to have "a wonderful picture and a commercial success,"[19] and his audience image was somewhat larger than Huston's and more middlebrow. At the time, Schary was involved in a

---

[15]For example, according to a story in *Variety,* " 'The Harder They Fall' is being given a campaign overhaul as the result of a reportedly spotty box office . . . ads focussing on prizefighting seem to have discouraged femme ticket-buyers. As a consequence, a switch will be made to emphasis on the racket angles. While 'Fall' does deal with boxing, a criminal element associated with that sport forms the basis of the story." *Variety,* April 18, 1956, p. 4.

[16]Lillian Ross, *Picture* (New York: Harcourt, Brace, 1952).

[17]The best recent description of these terms is by Russell Lynes, although he mixes analysis and evaluation freely. See his *Tastemakers* (New York: Harper's, 1954), Chap. 13.

[18]". . . Like Stephen Crane, he wanted to show something of the emotions of men in war, and the ironically thin line between cowardice and heroism." Ross, *Picture,* p. 8.

[19]Ibid., p. 21.

struggle over control of production in the studio with Louis B. Mayer. Mayer was bitterly opposed to making *The Red Badge of Courage* because he felt that its lack of plot and romance would mean box-office failure, at least in terms of the audience for whom he had been creating. For many decades, he had been identified in the studio with gay musicals and sentimental family trade pictures, such as the *Andy Hardy* series.

Reinhardt, the producer, came from a well-known German theatrical family. He was caught between Huston's image of the highbrow publics, which he seemed to share, and Schary's desire for an audience large enough to make the movie profitable.

Huston shot the picture much as he wanted it. However, Reinhardt felt that the first version lacked both the kind of story and the element of surprise that he felt necessary for *his* image of the audience, and just before the first sneak preview, he persuaded Huston to make the necessary changes.

However, this review and a second one made it clear that the two movie-makers were not communicating to a considerable portion of the publics represented at the preview. Then the transformation of the picture began. Schary wanted it made into more of a battle picture, with an eye on the publics who liked a war story. Reinhardt, trying to hold on to Huston's audience, and his own, persuaded him not to touch the picture itself. Instead, he added a narrated introduction that urged people to enjoy the movie because it was based on a literary classic. This appeal to cultural duty was perhaps intended for what Russell Lynes would call an upper middlebrow audience.

However, the third sneak preview showed that the actual audience was not persuaded. Huston had meanwhile left for Africa and Schary now took over production. He proceeded to simplify the movie by taking out several of Huston's favorite scenes, in which the director had tried to portray the novelist's conceptions of men's emotions in war. He also changed the order of events to allow the plot to move more directly and toward a single and final climax.

Reinhardt described the process in a letter to Huston:

> . . . Dore had secretly higher hopes for the picture box office wise than I . . . [he] . . . wanted to conquer the resistance of the audience which he clearly, and we both, felt. . . . I seriously questioned our ability to win the hearts of those who objected to the picture basically; those who hated it. On the other hand, we might easily, in trying to win them, lose those who were already our friends, those who loved the very things the others hated.[20]

He also described the new version of the movie:

> . . . The picture had lost some of its complexities and colors. It was now a straighter, simpler picture. The consensus was, you can

---

[20]Ibid., p. 222.

follow it now, you can understand it. . . . It is probably a very fine picture. Everybody tells me it is. But I would have to lie if I said it was the picture I had hoped for. . . .[21]

After these changes were made, a fourth preview was held, and this time 70 percent of the people present were willing to recommend the movie to their friends.[22] It was finally released and was well received by the critics, but the box-office results were disappointing.

Afterwards, Nicholas Schenck, then the president of the studio, explained to Miss Ross that he had questioned the commercial potential of the movie from the start, but had given his approval to the film in order to support Schary in his struggle with Mayer. Schary he seemed to consider a young, promising executive whose audience images were likely to mean profits for the studio in the future. Mayer, on the other hand, appeared to represent a set of lowbrow publics who were either decreasing in number or were finding satisfactory entertainment on television.

For the purpose of our analysis, it must be noted that *The Red Badge of Courage* was in many respects an atypical movie, and the differences in audience images among the participating creators were unusually extreme. Nevertheless, it is likely that the processes described here take place in the making of every movie, though in different ways. In a more representative picture, other kinds and combinations of audience images are likely to be involved. Differences of opinion between creators might focus on such topics as the characteristics and social roles of hero and heroine, the actors to interpret them, the portrayal of complex social relationships and issues, the depiction of emotional and moral conflicts in the story, and the solution of these in the ending. However, what a sociological study of movie-making ought to investigate is precisely what audience images are represented, and what major issues have to be resolved in the more representative kinds of Hollywood movies.

The ideas illustrated here by the movies could, of course, be tested in other mass media as well—for example, by a study of the staging of a TV spectacular, or of the editing of any magazine emphasizing features rather than news. One could even investigate the writing of a popular novel, although many of the audience-image struggles take place within the mind of a single person.

The preceding analysis can be placed in a broader context by suggesting that it has dealt with the role of the audience (through the audience image) in the *creation* of the mass-media product. One implication of this role is that the audience also affects the *content* of the product. This can be observed most clearly when the content of a product changes as it is communicated to new audiences. For example, it is possible to observe the changes made in a novel when it is brought to the screen, and to relate

---

[21]Ibid.

[22]These were presumably opinion leaders, scouting for the publics they represented.

these to the creators' desire to appeal to different publics.[23] Similar altera-
tions in content take place in a stage play as it prepares on hinterland try-
outs for the larger set of publics it will meet on Broadway, or when scientific data are popularized in the Sunday supplements. An important problem
for study is the extent to which audience characteristics affect the content
that is being communicated, and the amount and kind of deviation from the
creator's original intent that takes place.

An understanding of the role of the audience in affecting content can
also contribute to the clarification of mass-media criticism. The critic addresses himself to the content of a product, but in this process he makes
assumptions and judgments about the audience. For example, the critic
who condemns the changes made in a novel by the producer of the screen
version is assuming that the book which appealed to a smaller reading audience ought to be made into a movie for the same kind of audience. What
is offered as criticism of the content is really in part—though only in part
—a value statement about the proper audience to be sought. Further analysis of this example would show the extent to which the standards used to
judge the mass media today are based on single audience assumptions
more applicable to a past European leisure class than to contemporary
America.[24] Research on the relationship between content and audience
might contribute to the reformulation of the critic's role, and the development of standards appropriate to the heterogeneous set of publics served
by the mass media.

It can be shown that the role of the audience extends beyond the creation and the content of the mass-media product, but affects the structure
and the culture of the mass media industries themselves. For example, note
the indirect part the audience has in the oft-mentioned insecurity of the
mass-media creators, and the apparently irrational decision-making patterns that have sometimes been observed. Every mass-media creator, whatever his skill, is to some degree dependent on the validity of his audience
image for his status and standing in the industry. However, publics are so
numerous and so fickle in their infinite combinations that it is impossible to
tell in advance whether a once-successful image is still accurate. Every
new product is thus a gamble, and each time the problem of what the audience is like, and which publics are to be sought, must be determined and
negotiated again. In this process, the creator who was successful the last
time has the most status, and his ideas are influential until he guesses incor-

---

[23]This is in addition to the changes required by the technical difficulties in the
media. See Lester Asheim, "From Book to Film," in *Reader in Public Opinion and
Communication,* ed. by B. Berelson and M. Janowitz (Glencoe, Ill.: The Free Press,
1953), pp. 299–308.
[24]Paul Lazarsfeld and Robert K. Merton, "Communication, Taste, and Public Action,"
in *Communication of Ideas,* ed. Lyman Bryson (New York: Harper's, 1948), p. 111.

rectly.[25] Often the decision-making process can become a struggle between creators with various audience images, none of which can be tested
before the release of the product. Consequently decisions may be made on
the basis of irrelevant, but enforceable criteria. In the movies, only the top
creators, the big stars, and a few formulas and stereotypes seem to be able
to escape this insecurity, and to achieve a somewhat more permanent and
more stable level of acceptance. The stars do it by typing themselves, and
by establishing quasi-personal relationships with fans. At the same time, the
turnover of creators probably also reflects the role of the audience and the
turnover of publics within it.

No attempt has been made to list all the roles played by the audience
in the relationship with the mass media. In summary, it can only be suggested that the explanation of various media phenomena by looking for
possible audience roles might be a promising one for future research. Such
research might also provide insights useful for the evaluation and perhaps
even the creation of mass-media fare.

---

[25]When a group of movie-makers is successful in creating an audience for a new
product, the product is soon copied by others pursuing what they imagine to be an
empirically verifiable set of publics. In Hollywood, this initiates the phenomenon
known as the cycle.

Do you feel Gans' model is as applicable today as it was when he
formulated it? What changes, if any, would you suggest? Do you
feel it to be applicable today to media other than the film industry?

In the following interview, Arthur Penn, the American film director, touches on many of the points Herbert Gans has made. Penn
has his own subject-audience image and cannot conceive of himself
operating outside the American context, as this would entail the creation of alternative images on his part. He suggests the existence of
many American middle class values and the part myth (as reflected
in film) plays in reinforcing these values. Penn does not feel that film
creates values—like the mass magazine, it is an expression of society,
not a mover of it.

Penn feels that the director is the true creator of a film—but that
the studios have yet to realize this. He notes, however, that he (as
director) is in constant contact with the entire creative process—
even to supervising the editing of the film. As Gans would probably
point out, a less powerful director (or one less committed to his own
individualistic expression) would be much less influential in the shaping of the final form and content of his film—given the power structure of the industry within which he would have to operate.

In addressing himself to this power structure, Penn notes the limitations that *are* imposed by its members with respect to the shape and tone of the final product. He sees the American trend to be one of a breakaway from the studio and its attendant power structure to allow more freedom of expression, pointing to the film *Easy Rider* as an early and awkward step in this direction.

A CONVERSATION WITH ARTHUR PENN

Jacoba Atlas

There seems to be, within this country, a kind of instant identification with the outlaw, outcast. You've dealt with that fascination in most of your films. Do you feel that involvement with outside the mainstream of accepted behavior is fundamental to the American character?

Well, I think it's inherent within the American character to change the law by moving outside it. Laws have a habit of becoming antiquated just like everything else. There's an aging process to laws and it seems to me that at a certain time somebody who changes the law can be called an outlaw, and at another time he can be called a revolutionary, and at another time he can be called a fearless statesman. So, in consequence, we have to say what is the law and what is its context, and I think that is more appropriate.

For instance, whose law is the proper law when people are marching on the streets of Washington? It's clearly not the Justice Department as far as I'm concerned. It's got to be somebody else's. I'm not necessarily in defense of people like Bonnie and Clyde—but I am speaking in the defense of others who, at a certain time, moved outside the law and became revolutionary and placed his life in jeopardy to change and create another state of being. I have great admiration for people like that.

In Mickey One *you created what seems to be the ultimate paranoic movie. When the hero says, for instance, "What am I guilty of? I'm guilty of not being innocent"—that's an incredible line—*

That's right—

Do you feel, in fact, that whole concept seems so totally American . . .?

Definitely. I don't think it's so much an inherent guilt, but I think it is an American phenomenon which says if you are not part of the kind of system which is guilt-induced, then you find yourself guilty before the fact. You're guilty of not being innocent.

You can't maintain innocence, I believe, in a society which is mainly mafia oriented, or if it's not mafia oriented, it's big business oriented, which is almost the same thing; they're very close to being interchangeable. Also, in wartime, you have the military structure and that makes you ask yourself in what capacity are you innocent and in what capacity are you guilty. And that's the kind of dilemma. It wasn't just paranoia, as it was to say there's a certain justification in paranoia. You're not just freaking. There *is* some-body coming after you, you just have to know who it is. But there is some-one coming. . . .

You stayed in America making films when a lot of other directors—your peers in creativity and age—left and went to Europe. Lester, Losey, Kubrick. Was there a conscious decision on your part to stay in this country.

There was a very conscious decision to stay here and do what I know I can do, which is the American Scene. I don't know if I could do it in another country. I may try one like that, but I think eventually, no matter what, I would come back. I know this country, I know its behavior, I know what people will do. And I don't know that I would know that about France or Italy no matter how familiar I became with that country. Then, too, I think you sort of have an obligation to remain. For some of the people you mentioned, it was different. Losey left because he couldn't work, he was blacklisted. That wasn't true with Lester, he went there and started work-ing in television and developed an English personality, he completely re-lates to that country. My youth, my childhood is related to this. For better or worse. I have to stick to it.

Did you find any kind of optimism in the people in Alice's Restaurant? *I don't mean Arlo Guthrie, specifically, but the people in the commune.*

Yeah, I did find it. But optimism is a relative word. What I did see, and it gives me pleasure, is a generation of people doing something about their own destiny. You know, there was a whole generation who grew up in the McCarthy era that just took things as it came, and what came was the whole middle class. What I see with this group, and groups like it across the country, is that they are fighting for a different kind of identity. How suc-cessful they'll be in their fight, I don't know. I don't think human beings have ever been terribly successful in their fight for identification. But the fact that they're fighting for one, and the fact that they're repudiating a lot of values that they find—empty values, forced values—and searching for values of their own, it seems to be really admirable and also the kind of salvation of their souls. So I think . . . if I think it can be saved, and I'm not entirely sure I do think it can be saved, if I did think so, then I would feel that this was cause for optimism about that generation.

What about Ray and Alice? In the film they seem to be supplementing their own lack of a basis for their relationship with other people and other problems.

It's not very uncommon that you find people like Alice and Ray who, in their own generation, were renegades, but who because they were just loners in it, didn't find a definite way of life. What happened is now the kids have caught up to where Ray and Alice's impulses were. Now, whether Ray and Alice's impulses are still there or not, I don't know. . . . I would question . . . I don't know if they still are, I don't think they are, I think the aging process has passed them by. In that sense there's almost something sad and tragic about them—I mean the fictional Ray and Alice—not the real ones. The fictional Ray and Alice were the aspirations of another generation that hoped to do what this generation is doing so naturally.

How did you feel about the criticism that was lashed out at the film?

I take criticism seriously, but I can't do anything about it and I don't know . . . criticism comes and some of it's good and some of it's bad. But you can't do anything about it because the nature of criticism is that it's after the fact. It's easy to be a second guesser. Sure I would change a lot of everything I've ever done if I had the opportunity to go back over the films and re-make them. But I don't have the opportunity, the only people who have that opportunity are the critics. I hope they make good movies.

Were you ever uncomfortable with the scene with Arlo's father?

Uncomfortable in terms of narrative or in terms of portraying Woody?

In terms of portraying Woody.

Well, only because this was the one case where we were having an actor impersonate somebody who was a real person, and we hadn't done that in the picture. At least not in terms of Arlo's past. We had in terms of Alice and Ray. But Woody *was* such and *is* such a significant character in American legend that it seemed a shame to have to impersonate him, but there was no other choice. The scene was to me absolutely vital so that we could understand the relationship between Arlo and Woody. I don't think we could have left it out of the picture and had the picture be as meaningful as it was, at least as meaningful as it was to me, without that scene.

Were you conscious of how episodic the film was?

Episodic in terms that there wasn't a tight narrative; the picture seemed to be going off into many different areas at once. Yes, I would; but I would suggest that maybe there is another way of putting that, maybe there's another way of understanding narrative these days which is to say that it doesn't go in a straight line. It just doesn't go, "this happened and then this happened and then this happened," as if each thing were the consequence of what had immediately gone before. The fact that Arlo has a dying father, in a certain sense leaving him both a heritage of brilliance and a heritage of an illness, seems to me to be an on-going story at the same time Arlo is fighting for a life style and a way of dealing with his kind of crisis that is more immediate to him. You can't say that one should be there and the other one shouldn't or one should come there and the other should follow. I think they should both just run parallel. I think new stories should be ungangly.

You seem to try with each movie to find a new pacing. With Left Handed Gun *you had an almost Greek tragedy pacing, with* Bonnie and Clyde *you went quickly from one emotion to the other. . . .*

Yeah, I think there's a certain style. I think each material has it's own style. One seeks that out. This *Little Big Man* has it, an ever so faintly comic sense under everything that happens. Even when the door on the stage coach started to bang on the gambler's head I thought that was very good, although I never planned it.

Do you agree with the theory of the director as the "author" of a film?

Yeah, I think that's pretty much it, sure. I work with DeeDee Allen on the editing (she also edited *Bonnie and Clyde, Rachel, Rachel* and *America, America)* and we communicate constantly during all the phases of editing, although she does the actual physical work. It's just a question of screening the film again and again, a hundred times to get where you want to put the emphasis and all that. The same is true with the writing and pretty much the whole movie. It's gotten to be a director's thing. It always was, but the studios kept wanting to deny the fact.

There seems to be a lack of directors in their Forties who are willing to deal with what it means to be that age. Everyone is concentrating on youth, with the exception of John Cassavetes (later Richard Brooks with The Happy Ending). *What happens when you get older?*

Well, I think that's one of the things that's going to change. I don't think we recognize that there is a 35-to-40-year-old bracket in America. We've been so youth oriented that nobody seems to recognize that at 35–40 you're entering into a distinctly different phase of your life, and I don't think anyone has been very successful in bringing that sort of thing to the fore-front either psychologically or dramatically. But I think that that time has come to an end because a certain number of film-makers are 40 now, and although I hate to number myself among them, somehow I got there. And I think that what interests us in our lives is perforce what will interest us on the screen. So, eventually, that sort of subject matter will come under scrutiny.

How much would you say American mythology shapes our lives? Do you feel films have made much of an influence on shaping what we think of ourselves?

I don't think it comes very much from our films really. I think our myths started 'way back. For instance, the myth of Billy the Kid was a created myth. A man came out of the West and started writing stories and sending them back East about the adventures of Billy the Kid. *The Adventures of Bonnie and Clyde* was the result of a comic book issued by the FBI actually about the exploits of Dillinger and Bonnie and Clyde and other bank robbers. It was a creation of mythology in order to have a solution to it. The solution in both cases happened to be violent ones. I think that we have a mythology that exceeds films, although I think film will begin to be a part of it. I don't even know that you could call it mythology. I think it's just tales, yarns. You know, it's a young country, and we only really have a spoken history in that sense. I think the yarns are now coming down to us and, of course, they're very full, loaded material.

Do you think there's a danger that the tale—as in the case of Billy the Kid—will take over from reality until both are blended out of control?

Yes, I thing that's a grave danger. Not so much the tale as I think the values implicit in the tale. If you think that things are good and true and beautiful and help little old ladies across the street, then by definition you're going to be a successful industrialist; I mean that's the kind of Tom Swift tale that's come down. But I think what we've discovered is that if you're nice to old ladies you're very apt to get sent off to a war. And that's not so good.

I understand that you've had observers from the American Film Institute[1] on your films. How do you feel about the AFI?

Well, I think it's pretty good. I don't thing it's the answer because I don't think that sort of quasi-State-run-altruistic-let's-help-the-young-people sort of thing is any kind of answer. But it's better than nothing. That's all. It's better than nothing. I'm on the board, but I'm actually pretty ambivalent about it. But as I said, I know it's better than nothing.

How are you dealing with the Indians in this new film?

It's not accurate in terms of actual fact, but I think it's going to come out a little closer to the spirit of the Indians than anything else. I mean nothing that we're showing do we have any reason to believe actually happened quite as we're showing it. But I suspect that there was a good deal of this kind of treatment of the Indians around. And, consequently, there was a reciprocal kind of treatment of whites, but as someone recently said, the white man brought them smallpox, tuberculosis, and bad treaties. And we rendered them a kind of interior prisoner.

But we're not treating the Indians in those terms. As I say, this is oddly comic and maybe that's not the appropriate way to deal with something as important and as meaningful as this, but on the other hand maybe it is the way. Maybe one way to make entry into this kind of established superstition is to go by a more opaque way than saying this is a direct representation of what went on. That's not our intention.

What's been the reaction of the Indians working on the film?

They said that for the first time we're telling it a little like it was. There's no question but that the whole script is very supportive of the Indians. We report Custer as an absolute fool. More than that, as a megalomaniac with Presidential aspirations. There's a body of historical material supportive that he thought that because the Democratic convention was going to take place four days after the Battle of Little Big Horn, one of his hopes was that if he won a significant victory he would go to the convention as a really important candidate. He would be a candidate by acclamation.

Shades of Chicago. . . .[2]

Shades of Chicago, indeed! So we have that very much as a part of

---

[1]The American Film Institute is a non-profit organization to promote film studies, preserve rare prints, make grants to film makers, etc. It was funded originally by the Ford Foundation and the National Council of the Arts.
[2]Referring to the 1968 Democratic convention in Chicago—(editor).

our film. Not to say so much that this is contemporary, but more to say that what is contemporary is also antique and history does repeat itself.

How much do you feel film can be viewed as a cause for social action? As a revolutionary force?

As a source of engendering action on the part of the people, well, one would hope that would be true, but I won't really think it is. I think that what you do is contribute to a climate and when the climate is right for action, maybe a lot of things will eventually end in action. I don't think any one thing causes it any more than I believe that old canard that people have seen too much sex and violence and that's why we have sex and violence in our lives. I also can't believe that if we have too much activism in the movies we will have activism in society. I think we have activism in society because society is damn well ready for it. Change is going to have to happen, if change doesn't happen at the right rate I don't think it's so much the fault of activism as it is the fault of the people who are holding onto the Establishment. If they're not going to give, then they're going to be made to give.

Do you feel that your films offer any kind of releases from the natural frustrations that must arise out of what you've just said?

Well, I hope. I don't know if it releases, but what I think it does, it brings recognition of your own agony, frustrations, and emotional dilemma and so forth. You go to Ingmar Bergman films and it's another country and another time and yet I know these experiences, I know them viscerally, I know them right at the center of my gut. And you say with the shock of recognition, yes, I know that to be the truth and that, to me, is what art is all about. And if you have even a little bit of that in your films you're doing well.

Do you feel that any American films have reached that level; that universal feeling of recognition? Easy Rider *just doesn't hold up to the films of Bergman or Robert Bresson. ...*

Not yet they don't, not yet, but we're getting there. You know we had the problem of kind of liberating our films from the industry. They don't. They start out in a comparatively free state. We start a film and it has to go through American unions, through American organized labor and then do that and try to come out and say something that might be antithetical to everyone of their positions. It's a very difficult thing to do. But what's happening is that a lot of film-makers are strong enough in their commitment to go off and make films that say what they want to say without that. And it's going to be free of the studios and I think the studios are going to be happy to be free of them.

What first attracts you to a film? Like Little Big Man?

The identity crisis from one culture to another. Can we really indulge in the idea that there are red men and black men and yellow men and keep up these distinctions? I don't think we can, and that's posing an identity crisis for this nation.

After having read Penn's interview, attempt now to utilize it as data—a case-study, in effect. How substantially does Penn support Gans? Where do they differ? What difficulties does the introduction of the power and decision-making process (which both men discuss) in the creation of the artifacts of popular culture introduce to the study of such artifacts?

Because of television's commitment to the largest possible audience and its reliance on commercial concerns as monetary sponsors, there are a great many persons involved in making the decisions in this medium. Generally speaking, the idea is to produce a show that will *not* offend (1) any segments of the anticipated mass audience, (2) sponsors or probable sponsors, (3) regulatory agencies, (4) the federal government, (5) regional and local network affiliates. It is, therefore, a long and tortuous route from the conception of a television program to its eventual airing. As Gene Roddenberry, the producer of *Star Trek* said:

> The television writer-producer faces an almost impossible task when he attempts to create and produce a quality TV series. Assuming he conceived a program of such meaning and importance that it could ultimately change the face of America, he probably could not get it on the air or keep it there.[36]

Roddenberry's *Star Trek* had many problems of just this sort. The network at first rejected the character of the alien, Mr. Spock. They felt that his pointed ears made him look too much like the devil and that this would alienate "the big religious group in this country."[37] When Roddenberry refused to drop Spock, the network's sales department prepared brochures on the show in which they airbrushed out Mr. Spock's pointed ears and gave him rounded eyebrows.[38] Even then, the network executives were concerned about the integrated crew of the depicted space ship *Enterprise.*

> By putting a Negro in the crew they might lose the Southern states, by putting a Mexican in the crew they might lose Texas, Arizona, and parts of California, and so forth. The overseas sales representatives were also greatly concerned about the matter. A Chinese crew member could lose sales for the show in Indonesia, etc. . . . Gene began to realize that if he listened to all these people, the *Enterprise* would end up with an all-white, Protestant, Causasian crew.[39]

---

36. Stephen G. Whitfield and Gene Roddenberry, *The Making of Star Trek* (New York: Ballantine Books, 1968), p. 21.
37. Ibid., p. 125.
38. Ibid., pp. 126–27.
39. Ibid., p. 127. This, of course, was the fate of *Airport's Golden Argosy.*

Fortunately this did not happen—but it does go to show that the type of jockeying and decision-making that is done in this industry is similar to (if perhaps even more complex than) that Herbert Gans depicted in the film industry.

Even the television talk shows are subject to this sort of control. Guests are carefully screened—not only who shall appear, but even what subjects shall be discussed. Prospective guests are "interviewed" by network "talent coordinators" and certain subjects (noncontroversial, nonboring) are selected. The talk show host has this information when he comes on the air—he asks only the selected questions. In most cases, he gets back only the anticipated answers.[40] And, according to most of the talk show programmers, the answers are not the important thing anyway.

> The kind of information we're disseminating is not so much words and ideas as how people look, how they act, what their face is like. . . .[41]
>
> I really don't care what's being said as long as it's being said well. . . .[42]

What then *could* one conclude from a content analysis of television shows concerning the values and social structure of their audiences? Librarian Eckard Toy, utilizing "inside" material gleaned from scripts and production schedules of television shows, explores in more depth the many ways in which an artifact is shaped by the television decision-makers in its translation from script to screen.

---

40. Chris Welles, "The Sociology of Dumb," *Esquire* (May 1971).
41. Ibid., p. 177.
42. Ibid.

THE SOCIAL MEANING OF TELEVISION CENSORSHIP

Eckard V. Toy, Jr.

Mark Twain once observed that Americans had three precious things: freedom of speech, freedom of conscience, and the prudence never to practice either.[1] Commercial television appears to confirm this observation. It is commonly acknowledged that government agencies, networks, sponsors, and local stations all regulate the content of television, but the daily routine of

---

[1] Paraphrased in Morris L. Ernst and Alexander Lindey, *The Censor Marches On: Recent Milestones in the Administration of the Obscenity Law in the United States* (New York: 1940), 269–70. See Ralph E. McCoy *Freedom of the Press: An Annotated Bibliography* (Carbondale, Ill., 1968). for an extensive survey of literature about censorship. McCoy includes many titles that deal with television.

this editorial hierarchy is usually not visible. The University of Wyoming has several hundred scripts and production schedules of *General Hospital, Gidget, The Flying Nun,* and *Peyton Place* in its archival collections. These source materials lack the significance of the controversies stirred by the firing of the Smothers Brothers, the silencing of opponents of the ABM, or the resignation of the head writer on *Laugh-In,* but they are probably more representative of day-to-day censorship practices.

These television programs, which were all products of the American Broadcasting Company, appeared between late 1963 and early 1968 and paralleled in time the presidency of Lyndon Baines Johnson. But these series projected an image of society that betrayed class biases and institutional conservatism and seemed far removed from the Great Society. Debates about good taste have sometimes obscured the essentially conservative social content of programs whose entertainment role was also a means of social education—establishment theatre as opposed to guerrilla theatre.[2]
. . .

Nearly everyone is familiar with racy dialogue and humorous incidents that editors have overlooked. *Laugh-In* strikes so quickly that much of the content is lost. This is unlike the satirical stumbles of the Smothers Brothers. And on the *Tonight Show* there was the artful scene when Ed Ames clobbered an outline figure of a cowboy right in the crotch with a trusty tomahawk. Although this episode was on videotape, it had a spontaneity that made it acceptable (in much the way that instant replays take on more meaning than the original). An example of planned deviation, with subliminal overtones, was in an episode of *Get Smart,* when the camera focused over the Chief's shoulder to reveal five telephones to foreign countries hanging from the wall. Those phones to Berlin, Paris, London, and Tel Aviv were hanging vertically, while the center phone to China was conspicuously cross-ways. Or there was the time when Johnny Carson told about giving the peace sign to a striking cab driver and getting only half of it returned.

Too often, perhaps, we think of censors protecting us from naughty things like those, but Mason Williams has described it better in his poem that explains the censor as cutting holes in the mind. There was the incident when the sponsor's representative objected to a scene where Petula Clark touched Harry Belafonte on the arm. And there was Bill Cosby's routine about religion on the *Tonight Show* when word after word was silenced. This merely made the context seem worse. What or who determines good taste? . . . Two years ago, a Milwaukee, Wisconsin, television

---

[2]See, for example: Bob Tweedell, "CBS' Jencks, TV Writer Barrett Raise Questions on Taste," Roundup Section, Sunday Denver *Post,* November 2, 1969, pp. 21, 27; Charles Winick, *Taste and the Censor in Television* (New York: 1959) [An Occasional Paper for the Fund for the Republic on the Role of the mass Media in The Free Society]; Harold C. Gardiner, S.J., *Catholic Viewpoint on Censorship* (Garden City, New York: 1958); and Edith Efron, "You Can Take Your Choice," *TV Guide,* (November 1, 1969), pp. 12–16.

station owned by the liberal Milwaukee *Journal,* refused to show a cleansed version of *Never on Sunday.* The same evening, a much less politically liberal station in Madison, Wisconsin, showed the movie. Why? Audience rating, organized opposition, or station censoship? Where was the controversy when the movies *Georgy Girl, Fail Safe,* and *Tom Jones* were shown in the fall of 1969? Again, on news programs, signs in student demonstrations have sometimes been shown with their four-letter words emblazoned for all the world to see. Yet it is virtually impossible to present the words audibly, as an ETV production about the Chicago demonstrations recently proved. . . .

Time magazine has defined "Pastore's Complaint" as "A phobia against violence and sex on television, exacerbated by recent disturbances in American society and by the Noxzema 'take-it-all-off' commercial."[3] Unlike *Portnoy's Complaint,* the Pastore ailment hinges on the belief that there has been too little motherly (translate government) concern for the welfare of the child. But is Senator John O. Pastore's carrot-and-stick procedure with the television industry and with the Federal Communications Commission sufficient to reconcile the problems facing the viewer? These arguments about violence and sex on television have been with us for nearly two decades.[4] On the one hand, some persons who reject the nude theatre, the sexual revolution, and sex education in the schools demand a reduction in sexuality on television. And there are many other persons, who do not fear sex, demanding that more be done to regulate violence on TV. In 1954, Walter Lippmann wrote: "believing as I do in freedom of speech and thought, I see no objections in principle to censorship of the mass entertainment of the young . . . the risks to our liberty are . . . less than the risks of unmanageable violence."[5] Now the National Commission on the Causes and Prevention of Violence has criticized the television industry: "Television entertainment based on violence may be effective merchandising, but it is an appalling way to serve a civilization—an appalling way to fulfill the requirements of the law that broadcasting serve the 'public interest, con-

---

[3]"Premieres: The 'New' Season," *Time* 94 (September 26, 1969): 80.

[4]Bob Tweedell, "Networks, NAB Claim Violence Data Is Old; Progress Cited," Roundup Secion, Sunday *Denver Post,* October 19, 1969, pp. 25, 31; "What Is TV Doing to Them," series in *TV Guide,* October to November, 1969; Robert D. Kasmire, Vice President, National Broadcasting Company, Inc., October 17, 1968, before the National Commission on the Causes and Prevention of Violence"; Richard W. Jencks, President of CBS/Broadcast Group of the Columbia Broadcasting System, Inc., "The Problem of Violence in Television Entertainment," a talk before the Radio and Television Society of Hollywood, June 17, 1969; Statement by Frank Stanton, President, Columbia Broadcasting System, Inc., before the Subcommittee on Communications, Senate Commerce Committee, March 12, 1969; and "Remarks" of U.S. Senator John O. Pastore at the National Association of Broadcasters Luncheon, March 24, 1969.

[5]Walter Lippmann, "The Young Criminals," *New York Herald Tribune,* September 7, 1954.

venience and necessity'."[6] This concern about violence and sex brings into focus question about what extent television should reflect society as it is, as it ought to be, or as it is thought to be.

During the administration of President John F. Kennedy, this nation was on a narcissistic binge, and criticism—preferably self-criticism—was acceptable. In some ways, there was an easing of the internal control mechanism in the TV industry, and it appeared as if there might be improvement. Educational television failed to challenge commercial TV, but there was hope. It is common in our pluralistic society to have tension between the ideal and the real, between conformity and pluralism. It seemed for a while that the Kennedy style might reconcile rather than polarize. In McLuhanese, President Kennedy's cool image was made to order for a cool medium in a potentially hot time. But he also failed. The pseudoenvironment of Camelot was as false as Dwight D. Eisenhower's small town or the electronic pseudoenvironment of television. Today, President Nixon serves as our link between the artistically bland and the socially blind. Too often the television images created by and about white middle-class America have neglected this conflict of values. To what extent does the image of this homogenized middle-class society carry over into the ghetto? To what extent should the ghetto subculture be packaged for middle-class consumption? Which is the more misleading, *Julia* or the *Tonight Show?*. . . .

E. B. White wrote in *Harper's* magazine in 1938: "I believe TV is going to be the test of the modern world, and that in this new opportunity to see beyond the range of our vision we shall discover either a new and unbearable disturbance of the general peace or a saving radiance in the sky. We shall stand or fall by TV—of that I am quite sure."[7] As a mass medium, television tends to be conservative in its political and social content, partly because of the fear of offending any large portion of the audience and also because it is a business and its goals often clash with the role of the intellectual as a critic of society. In 1936, William S. Paley complained about radio: "Too often the machine runs away with itself . . . instead of keeping pace with the social needs it was created to serve."[8] Television faces a similar dilemma. . . .

Television is a Gulliver-like product of the technological revolution and social and economic centralization. Unlike radio, television began full-size as a child of the networks. Its growth coincided with the maturing of the associational impulse in American life that contributed to the development of organized ethnic groups, church associations, and patriotic societies.

---

[6]Robert Gruenberg, "U.S. Commission Deplores TV Violence," *Denver Post,* September 24, 1969, p. 6. Also see "How Much Violence Is There on Television?" *TV Guide,* July 12, 1969, pp. 26–30.

[7]Quoted in Gary A. Steiner, *The People Look at Television: A Study of Audience Attitudes* (New York: 1963), p. 3.

[8]Quoted in Fred W. Friendly, *Due to Circumstances Beyond Our Control . . .* (New York: 1967), p. xi.

These organized external influences combined with governmental, network, and commercial bureaucracies to give television a supervision that radio had lacked when independent stations and untried performers created auditory chaos. The solution lay in organization and centralization. The network system imposed new rules. Ad-lib talk was virtually banished, professionalism developed and controls were imposed as most programs were written and rehearsed. Prior censorship or prior restraint became common. Room for error was eliminated and opportunities for experimentation were reduced. As corporate controls were reinforced, public demands for censorship diminished. . . .

The Federal Communications Commission licenses individual television stations, but it does not license the networks. The National Association of Broadcasters, which represents only about two-thirds of the television stations in the country, adopted a television code in 1952. Each network has between 30 and 50 editors and assistants who attempt to enforce that code. In addition, they are also guided by network regulations, sponsors' restrictions, and the characteristics of the audience. . . .

. . . The former head of NBC's broadcast standards department, Ernest Lee Jahncke, Jr., summed up the network viewpoint in an article in 1969.

> We believe that TV is and should be a mirror of society, but that it should only reflect society up to a certain point. TV will always be the most conservative of the performing arts—not only because of the kids in the audience, but also because people over 30 have sensibilities and moral standards that must be recognized. You could say we try to stay just a step or two behind the times.[9]

Frank and Doris Hursley, the creators of *General Hospital* and a new series, *Bright Promise,* soon to be produced by Bing Crosby Productions, state that they have never had trouble with censorship. Possibly, as they admit, this is because they are familiar with "network objections to controversial subjects, violence and such topics as suicide, [and] overt sexual material." Yet the Hursleys have written about "artificial insemination, birth control, drug abuse, and the common types of social injustice,"[10] and their experience seems to confirm the observations that daytime serials often are regulated less than evening programs.

General Hospital evolved from an outline called "Pulse of Life" written in October 1962. When the Hursleys first proposed the series, they cited an analysis of daytime audiences indicating that the most effective plots concerned love triangles of married people in their thirties. In addition, the authors planned "young love, occasional melodrama and other identifiable problems, emotionally treated."[11] In this first phase of creativity, a kind of

---

[9]Quoted in Bob Tweedell, "Interesting Aspects to Smothers Poll," *Denver Post,* June 2, 1969, p. 24.
[10]Frank and Doris Hursley to author, June 26, 1969.
[11]"Notes on a Medical Daytime Serial," October, 1962, Frank and Doris Hursley Collection (University of Wyoming Archives, Laramie, Wyoming).

reverse censorship took place. Editors suggested: all of the characters were too nice, so make one "bitchy," make another character "quite unsympathetic" because "We're not going to make villains of doctors, so a single civilian is a god send." . . .

The Hursleys have demonstrated that writers who know their audience and their editors can work virtually unchallenged. *General Hospital* is essentially *Peyton Place* in a hospital. With well-established precedents and rather confining plots, the series maintains the facade of middle-class respectability and professional competence amidst considerable sexuality and emotional distress. . . .

When we shift from the daytime serials and game shows to evening entertainment, we note a distinct difference in the variety and composition of programs. *Peyton Place* succeeded in establishing itself in the evening hours, but similar efforts have generally failed. The variety hour or the situation comedy has been more common in prime time, and *Gidget* and the *Flying Nun,* both produced by Screen Gems for ABC, fit this latter category. *Gidget* was based upon Frederick Kohner's short novel of the same name, which had already been successfully exploited by Hollywood in three movies, *Gidget, Gidget Goes Hawaiian,* and *Gidget Goes to Rome.* In a kind of critical obituary notice, James and Renee Munoz analyzed the viewer response for *TV Review.*[12] The Munoz' gave the program a high rating based upon the transformation of the father into a positive character from the negative role in the movies. The television series focused on the relationship between Gidget and her father, and the generation gap idea was implicit in the production. The ratings tended to confirm that the network got the audience for which it aimed. *Variety* described *Gidget* as a "middle-class fanatsy,[13] and the network editors, an advertising agency, and Frederick Kohner, the original author, sought to keep it that way. . . .

. . . Attempting to avoid the beach bum image, the producer reminded the casting director: "It is vital that those episodes of Gidget involving school sequences be peopled by clean-cut, attractive-looking youngsters."[14] Throughout the series this was the theme.

One female editor ordered deletion of a beach scene showing "voluptuous" girls and she also objected to a "close-up of Gidget on her knees on the bed facing her father where her night clothes reveal her well-rounded bosom."[15] It was not clear whether the editor feared incest or believed that a 16-year-old girl should not be so equipped. Three other censors took turns editing the scripts and rushes, but the result was similar. Whether male or

---

[12]James Munoz and Renee Munoz, "Gidget: A Viewer Analysis," *TV Review* in William Sackheim Collection (University of Wyoming Archives, Laramie, Wyoming).
[13]Quoted in Munoz, "Gidget: A Viewer Analysis," p. 67.
[14]William Sackheim to Bob Ellsworth, June 9, 1965, Sackheim Collection.
[15]Editorial report, April 20, 1965, Sackheim Collection.

female, they generally reacted against vigorous dancing, tight sweaters, and skimpy bathing suits. . . .

These examples of editorial actions are common to most programs, although perhaps more stringent with those intended for juveniles. But there are other censorship activities that extend beyond the NAB Code and simple editorial questions. At one point an editor reminded the director to "be sure this allergy bit in these scenes will be acceptable to your sponsor."[16] The script described a character as allergic to soup, and the sponsor was Campbell's Soups. Another example was a reference to aspirin, and the editor noted: "the 'aspirin' mention is contrary to your sponsor's interests. Please check with your ABC Co-ordinator for possible conflict."[17] . . .

Each episode was also reviewed by Frederick Kohner, the original author. In one segment, entitled "All the Best Diseases Are Taken," the script called for Gidget to engage in social protest and demonstration. Kohner condemned this script as "a very disturbing entry and one that could do harm to the series." He explained:

> Gidget is made the speaker of a fringe movement . . . De facto Gidget is here the exponent of a minority group. References to "demonstration," "Berkeley," "bomb," "hammer and sickle!" [this was 1965] have too serious connotations today to be treated lightly. . . . Obviously this is not the stuff Gidget pictures are made of. I for one couldn't find anything to laugh about here. The father being warned and almost threatened by University functionaries seems to be as unreal as his subsequent wishy-washingness. [sic]
> The first eight segments were so delightful and so engaging that I feel new writers coming into the series should make it a point to read and *study* these excellent scripts in order to adapt themselves to the happy and healthy climate in which our girl thrives.[18]

The ABC editor had nothing to add. Perhaps, though, there was one redeeming feature of this series. Several times the Casting Department had been reminded; "In accordance with studio policy to employ minority groups, please consider casting such persons for the following roles:"[19] Sergeant Kulpepper, Officer Joe Hanley, a waiter, Miss O. Stoddard, a janitor, and another officer. Toward the end of the series a memo requested up-grading minorities to minor character roles. . . .

Peyton Place was based on the well-known novel by Grace Metalious about life in a small New England town. Some ABC executives worried about adapting this novel to television, but the ABC Director of Broadcast

---

[16]Editorial report, December 10, 1965, Sackheim Collection.
[17]Ediorial report, February 3, 1966, Sackheim Collection.
[18]Frederick Kohner to Sackheim, July 31, 1965, Sackheim Collection.
[19]Memo, Legal Department to Sackheim, May 11, 17; August 19, 1965; February 9, 1966, Sackheim Collection.

Standards reported that after a few letters opposing the effort, mail was generally favorable and many viewers identified closely with the characters.[20] . . . *Peyton Place* had a freedom of characterization not permitted many other evening programs, and the editors faced a dilemma in attempting to reconcile the conflict between soap opera subjects and prime time viewing. Although not considered a family program, *Peyton Place* attracted a composite audience and the editors were especially concerned with physical actions, teenage mannerisms, word substitutions, and violence. There was a constant effort to portray teenagers as only slightly more worldly than those shown on *Gidget.* Yet, the general story lines were seldom challenged. Superficial changes in characterization were more common. Despite the relative freedom of subject matter, the editorial guidance seemed aimed at eliminating innuendo rather than directness. Explicit relationships were less vulnerable than implied ones. In a scene where a sexually frustrated father attempted to stroke his daughter's hair, the editor ordered: "Please substitute something with less incestuous overtones."[21]

Although the number of incidents depicting physical violence was not great, an automobile accident scene was softened, a bloody fight was made less bloody, and an editor requested that an episode about an autopsy not be shown on Thanksgiving Day. The director was also reminded not to let a gun "fire into the camera—i.e., living rooms of America."[22]

The evidence of editorial involvement was constant, but the level of concern varied. Fully one-third of the changes involved word substitutions, primarily in the area of sexual relationships. While word substitutions were quite common, other violations of the NAB Code were not as apparent. In fact, there were more recommended changes because of real or potential conflicts with sponsors than with the Code. Tobacco companies were among the most important sponsors of *Peyton Place,* and this caused numerous problems. When *Peyton Place* was scheduled to have two cigarette sponsors in the fall of 1967, the director was told to eliminate as much smoking as possible because of their competitive situation.[23] Cigarettes were not to be used or abused in certain ways: "do not grind cigarettes out on the floor in deference to . . . sponsors:" They were not to be "stubbed out in cold cream jars . . . in deference to cig sponsor;" ashtrays were to be clean; use of pipes and cigars was to be cleared with sponsors; chain-smoking was to be modified; and cigarettes were not to be ground out under foot, thrown to the ground, or dangled from mouths. And one scene was changed after the warning that "smoking and narcotics often arouse

---

[20]Grace M. Johnsen to author, September 24, 1969.
[21]Editorial report, June 4, 1964, Paul Monash Collection (University of Wyoming Archives, Laramie, Wyoming).
[22]Editorial report, October 31, 1966, Monash Collection.
[23]Editorial report, May 15, 1967, Walter Doniger Collection (University of Wyoming Archives, Laramie, Wyoming).

cigarette sponsors."[24] Even potential sponsors were not neglected, and one editor cautioned: "a possible coffee or food sponsor won't like the line about Allison not liking coffee."[25] . . .

. . . In *Peyton Place* doctors and lawyers were prominent among the characters and their professional images were protected: "eliminate the idea that country doctors are inferior;" "caution [not] to destroy the public's confidence in women doctors;" patients and nurses were not to abuse or challenge the doctor's roles as father figure and humanitarian; and doctors were not to cause undue pain to their patients. "Insistent" was substituted for "bullying" in reference to a lawyer, and there was to be no implication that the police were "heavyhanded" or brutal. Even the success ratio of the police was to be improved: "all this talk about the inadequate police work doesn't build up respect for law and order."[26]

Religion was to be defended, the marriage ceremony was to be revered, and affairs and adultery were to be condemned:

> Sharon can be in love with a married man—but this cannot be an affair—and since crime cannot be rewarded—somewhere ahead *she* must learn the sorry lesson of fooling around with a married man. Betty must also rebel—so our viewers will learn the error of this way of life. Caution—caution.[27]

A reference to one character intending to do humanitarian work in Peru was questioned because the statement implied Peruvian inferiority. The editor asked that the speech be modified "so we won't seem to downgrade our South American friends."[28] One of the most extreme examples concerned a scene that was deleted from an episode in 1966: "we must be certain Webber's dislike is against Rod's nonchalant attitude toward money rather than any slur on the credit card practice [sic]."[29] . . .

Obviously, the problems considered in this paper are not as serious as some of the more recent manifestations of censorship. Irving Wallace, whose movie the *Chapman Report,* was virtually unrecognizable after editing for television, was active on a committee opposing the ABM. On the committee's behalf, Arthur Goldberg asked the networks to sell them air time. NBC and CBS refused because they claimed this position had received adequate news coverage and because they were reluctant to get involved with the equal-time provisions. ABC did not respond at all, and several independent stations turned the committee down.

In October, 1969, it was reported that Paul W. Keyes, the producer and head writer of *Laugh-In* had resigned. After vigorously defending the pro-

---

[24]Editorial reports, October 7, 12, 1964; January 6, 1966, Monash Collection.
[25]Editorial report, June 30, 1965, Monash Collection.
[26]Editorial report, Monash Collection.
[27]Editorial report, Monash Collection.
[28]Editorial report, Monash Collection.
[29]Editorial report, Monash Collection.

136 SIDE SADDLE ON THE GOLDEN CALF

gram last summer, he has now been quoted as saying that *Laugh-In* is "slanted, vulgar and dirty."[30] He implied that the trend had accelerated during the past few months. If this is true, why should *Laugh-In* be protected and the Smothers Brothers fired? Is content less important than ratings? Is it merely the approach? An examination of censored scripts of the Smothers Brothers confirms that the controversy was not simply a question of good taste. Richard W. Jencks, an executive of CBS, countered arguments against the network: "If [critics] mean that we should not reject

> entertainment material because it has topical comment of a controversial nature, then we agree wholeheartedly. If, on the other hand, they mean that we should allow any performer who by his talent has earned exposure to a microphone or camera to voice his own personal political views at any opportunity he chooses, then we disagree.
> Someone has to be the judge of the difference between entertainment and propaganda.[31]

The Smothers Brothers engaged in political and social satire, and they lost ground in the ratings. Either situation was sufficient to cause trouble for them. Perhaps we might borrow a few words from the David Steinberg sermonette about Jonah that was cut from one program and suggest that the Smothers Brothers in their *New Testament* way literally grabbed the establishment by the *Old Testament.*

---

[30]*Playboy* Interview: Rowan and Martin.
[31]Bob Tweedell, ". . . Smothers Poll.

The censorship of television materials brings up an important point. If one expects these artifacts to reveal values of the social structure of the creator and consumer, one must take the censors into consideration as an intervening variable. With respect to many topics (sex being one), the values reflected on television may be those the censor believes to be acceptable by the TV public; these values, however, may well *not* be the ones this public actually practices. This difference between "public" and "private" values is an important one to take into account when studying popular culture. One must, as Herbert Gans implied, be aware of the total context within which the artifact was created.

The *purpose* for which the artifact was created is also important. In a tongue-in-cheek content analysis of television, Allan Sherman came to the conclusion (by watching only weekly series programs) that money and bathrooms do not exist in America.[43] By watching only commercials, he concluded that "America is money-mad and bathroom

---

43. Allan Sherman, "The Martian Report," *TV Guide,* April 17, 1971, pp. 37–40.

happy."[44] The only constant finding he could come up with in watching varied television fare was that the Average American does not watch TV![45] One must, in studying the artifacts of popular culture, be aware of their limitations as data, as well as their strengths.

In turning to the question of what constitutes play in the American middle class, Sociologist Hugh Gardner contends that sports (both spectator and participant) are not the only form, nor necessarily the most popular. Irving Crespi has examined the popularity of card playing in American life and has noted that it is one of the few leisure-time activities that can compete successfully with the American mass media.[46] Crespi has gone on to point out that card playing allows groups in mass society to play at highly competitive situations that parallel the situations of their lives.[47] As Marshal McLuhan has remarked, *games* as popular art are social reactions to the action of any culture.

> As extensions of the popular response to the workaday stress, games become faithful models of a culture. They incorporate both the action and reaction of whole populations in a single image.[48]

A 1963 review of studies of adult game preferences in the United States revealed that games of chance (such as poker) are associated with high routine responsibility training, punishment for the display of initiative, and a belief in the benevolence of the gods; they are preferred by members of the lower status groups. On the other hand, games of strategy (such as chess and bridge) are associated with severe upbringing as children (primary socialization), psychological discipline, and complex culture; they are preferred by members of the higher status groups.[49] Utilizing historical analysis and a witty and perceptive eye, Hugh Gardner analyzes the game of bridge with respect to its position and function in the American social structure.

---

44. Ibid., p. 38.
45. Ibid., p. 40.
46. Irving Crespi, "The Social Significance of Card Playing as a Leisure Time Activity," *American Sociological Review* 21 (1956): 717–21.
47. Irving Crespi, "Card Playing as Mass Culture," in *Mass Culture*, ed. Bernard Rosenberg and David Manning White (New York: The Free Press, 1957), pp. 418–21.
48. Marshall McLuhan, *Understanding Media* (New York: McGraw-Hill, 1964), p. 208.
49. Brian Sutton-Smith, John M. Roberts and Robert M. Kozelka, "Game Involvement In Adults," *The Journal of Social Psychology* 60 (1963), pp. 15–30.

BUREAUCRACY AT THE BRIDGE TABLE[1]

Hugh Gardner

Once upon a time, baseball was the American national pastime. Now, everyone knows that football has assumed the throne, and that baseball, despite its best efforts to modernize, is becoming as out of date as courtesy and home-cooked meals. Marshall McLuhan, with his splendid off-the cuff omniscience, explains this transition in terms of technology's impact on our culture; in this electronic age, you know, the complex simultaneity of football is more appropriate to the times than the machine-age linearity of baseball.[2] Others seem to feel that the gridiron supplanted the diamond because our society has become more mentalistic and effeminate. By this interpretation, the flabby desk-ridden Americans of today have a greater need for vicarious aggression than did Americans of more robust eras; needless to say, the street-riot mayhem of football fills this order better than the gentlemanly tedium of baseball. I am sure that there is great truth in either of these explanations, but I am equally sure that they both tend to ignore how the majority of our nation really passes its time.

Regrettably, both theories automatically assume that our national pastime must have something to do with physical sports. No doubt this makes some sense, for we are a sporty nation. But where are the ladies? For various reasons, mostly male reasons, they generally have plenty of idle time to pass. And regrettable though it may be to male theorists who have to take account of them and male pragmatists who have to live with them, ladies are, I suspect, a part of the nation. But they don't give a donut about football, despite the fact that TV networks and impatient males have expended enormous energies trying to get them to. Yet if the millions of women who regularly play social bridge could be counted, a female national pastime would emerge of such proportions as to drive TV executives mad with frustrated greed . . . for as yet there is no known way to mechanize cards, coffee, and neighborhood gossip. These days, if one omits the ladies from his considerations, he runs a risk far greater than the scrutiny of academic truth; he may not escape with his hide.

Bridge is not just a woman's game; in fact, bridge's aggressive flavor marks it as more of a man's. The most recent survey of bridge's popularity, conducted by the U.S. Playing Card Association, estimated that there are upwards of 35 million American adults who play bridge, of whom about 75 percent are women.[3] Thirty-five million are a lot of decks of cards, and a lot

---

[1]The author would like to record his thanks to professors Warren Hagstrom and Schalom Schwartz for their criticisms of an earlier version of this manuscript, and to Jayne Branting for typing help and general yeomanry.

[2]Marshall McLuhan, *Understanding Media: The Extensions of Man* (New York: McGraw-Hill, 1964), pp. 234–45. Also see Mackey, note 7 below, p. 125.

[3]Cited by Jack Olsen, *The Mad World of Bridge* (New York: Holt, Rinehart and Winston, 1960), p. 237.

of people, probably no fewer than pay any attention to football telecasts. More than 10,000 books have been written about bridge,[4] which may be more than have been written about football (football's vast popularity was some 20 years later in arriving).[5] *Books in Print* currently lists 129 nonfiction football books to 117 about bridge. Every newspaper carries a regular bridge column or two, ETV teaches it on television, and there are thousands of bridge clubs all over America. Yet it is the most difficult of all card games, and it takes time and effort to become even modestly good at it.

All of this, ideally, would be by way of introducing the proposition that bridge itself is a choice candidate for whatever honors are deserved by being America's national pastime. But that would be a fatuous proposition in a country where tastes are more often created than spontaneous, where traditional and folk culture have been all but obliterated, where an endless variety of ostensible play activities have become hard work and big business, and where most of the leisure-seeking citizens have become royally passive subjects of The Tube. In these times of merchandized professional play, it is no longer as much a question of what the people want; it is more accurately a question of how much they can stand.[6] The point of studying national pastimes is that they may tell us something significant about culture and people. But when play is administered from above, we're not in a very good position to comment on the meaning that play has to the everyday lives below. We can only trot out numbers—numbers that represent good sales technique rather than the way our play and our lives are knitted together. If we are to find connections, we are forced to look at the quality of play instead of its quantity. To understand what our pastimes tell us about our character, we have to look at the character of the play itself.

Contract bridge, as we know it today, was invented in 1927 by the millionaire card buff Harold S. Vanderbilt while on an ocean cruise.[7] There already existed a game called bridge, a faintly modified version of a still older game called whist, but apparently, to Harry, the thrill was gone. He wanted to make it more exciting, more like reality. His main contribution to the limping game of bridge was to introduce the idea of *contract*. In the old game, players got points for as many hands, or tricks, as they could take. Vanderbilt's innovation was that players should bid against each other, as in a marketplace. Whoever claimed he could take the most tricks then entered into a "contract" to either win that many or suffer penalties. It was all very much like the capitalism Vanderbilt knew: one bids for a piece of work, or auctions a service, and the winner of the bid signs a contract to deliver.

---

[4]Ibid.

[5]Gregory P. Stone, "American Sports: Play and Dis-Play," in *Mass Leisure,* ed. Eric Larrabee and Rolf Meyersohn (New York: The Free Press, 1958), pp. 253–64.

[6]See John Kenneth Galbraith's discussion of "the revised sequence" in *The New Industrial State* (New York: Houghton Mifflin, 1967), pp. 211–19.

[7]Rex Mackey, *The Walk of the Oysters: An Unholy History of Contract Bridge* (Englewood Cliffs, N.J.: Prentice-Hall, 1965), pp. 1–8.

He then delivers or goes to court and pays damages. Along with introducing the "contract," Vanderbilt revised the scoring system so that shirkers and greedy optimists were made to pay "penalties" when they bit off more than they could chew. At the same time, those who did better than their contract called for were awarded "bonuses." If they did so well as to bid and deliver a contract to make all or all but one of the 13 tricks, they received a fabulous reward called a "slam bonus." With these scoring changes it became possible to amass much larger scores than it had been before, and people who like their winnings big were very pleased. The scoring also included points for having a string of high cards in one suit, which are called "honors." No bridge expert has ever been able to explain to me why such dumb luck in the draw of the hand should be rewarded, especially in a game which tries to emphasize skill and intelligence. Perhaps Vanderbilt felt there was some inherent aristocratic virtue in being blessed with a pedigreed suit of high face cards, like having a nice respectable family or a nice art collection. At any rate, Vanderbilt's capitalistic innovations caught on like the booming stock market. Almost overnight the entire upper class was playing bridge, but—unlike the stock market bubble—bridge never burst.

Thus Harry Vanderbilt brought the game up to date with modern capitalism, giving it the structure and atmosphere of the dizzy, harsh world of big business. A few years later, Ely Culbertson came along and gave it sex appeal. Culbertson, who has been variously described by bridge historians as a genius, an egomaniac, a con-man, and a dirty old man, came onto the the bridge scene in 1929 with a magazine called *Bridge World*.[8] Ely's intentions in founding the magazine were to become the game's premier authority and to become rich. He was successful in both areas. Culbertson had a colorful personality and a brilliant mind. He knew how to play the publicity angles, he was a good card player, and best of all, he had a System. Americans seem to love Systems, especially in difficult games where money or something else of value might be involved. But Culbertson's was more than just a system; he made himself a household word all over America by making it a *sexy* system and by cultivating an audacious, rakish, and outrageously conceited public image of himself. Like all sharpies he loved to brag. This is how he once explained his conquest of the bridge world to the Sales Executive Club of New York:

> I have formed the greatest advertising and publicity organization in the world. I have sold bridge by appealing to the instincts of sex and fear and by false presentation of my own character and that of my wife. I am not the cocky, smart-aleck, conceited, and ready-to-fight person I have tried to make the world believe. My wife is not the shy, diffident, cool, calculating woman I have tried to make the public

[8]Compare Olsen, *The Mad World of Bridge* and Mackey, ibid., though you will find the same thing in either.

believe. It is all a stunt calculated to make the name Culbertson syn-onymous with contract bridge.

First we had to build a system. That took six years. Then we had to sell the system. We appealed to women, to their natural inferiority complex. Bridge was an opportunity for them to gain intellectual parity with their husbands. We worked on their fear instincts. We made it almost tantamount to shame not to play contract.

I have sold bridge through sex—the game brought men and women together. I used the words "forcing bid" and "approach bid" because there is a connotation of sex to them.[9]

Culbertson also introduced bridge expressions like "squeeze," "vul-nerability," and "going to bed with my king." Until Culbertson, bridge term-inology was mainly the language of power and profit: violent words like "slam" and "killing defense," business words like "contract," "transporta-tion," and "bonus." What Ely Culbertson did was give the masculine, smoke-filled world of Harry Vanderbilt the lure of the boudoir, and in so doing he brought millions of women into a male's game (and with them, millions of new males as well).

Culbertson's expressions are still used in bridge play today. In the wake of his sexual revolution one now hears such modern derivations as "strength but not length," "covering my honor," and "having enough for a raise." Even standard bridge jargon seemed to take on double meanings after Culbertson made the game racy . . . terms like "rubber," and "trick," and phrases like "a stiff Ace," "let's see what you've got," and even "laying down the dummy." Through the aroma of sex and the calculated mystique of himself and his marriage, Culbertson may have doubled the popularity of the game he once called "the world's second-most-popular indoor sport."[10] His own humble confessions show us that his success was obvi-ously an example of first-class salesmanship. These confessions are also as clear a statement as has ever been made of the principle of modern ad-vertising. If Harry Vanderbilt was the game's first Capitalist, Ely Culbertson was its first Ad Exec and PR Man.

The rise (blush) of bridge may indeed have been the first great exam-ple of modern merchandising. Thanks to Culbertson, bridge swept the na-tion more rapidly than a play form ever had—more rapidly, perhaps, than a play form has since. Culbertson's techniques were quite precocious in the 1930's. It was not until quite a bit later that playing on the fears of being socially unacceptable and tickling sexbuds became institutionalized ap-proaches in advertising. What Culbertson accomplished is made all the more remarkable by the fact that he did it without television, the ultimate medium for the sex-sell. Of all the fads that swept the 30's and kept minds off the depression, very possibly bridge was the most remarkable and un-questionably the most enduring.

---

[9]Quoted in Olsen, *The Mad World of Bridge,* pp. 153–54.
[10]Mackey, *The Walk of the Oysters,* p. 33.

One reason bridge endured was, no doubt, that it was fun to play. But when a phenomenon of that magnitude catches on and steadily grows for 40 years, without any assist from television or sophisticated postwar promotional campaigns, it must be touching some profound nerve endings. Perhaps a look at the kind of people who play bridge will give us some clues as to what those nerve endings are.

As mentioned before, bridge, is a derivative of an earlier game called whist. Whist was a game of the upper classes, and, in its early days, bridge was too. After Culbertson popularized it, bridge was reduced in chic to the middle class, and it remains an overwhelmingly middle class game today (though it is widely played among the upper classes as well). As a popular card game, bridge is rivaled only by poker; as an intellectual's game, it is often compared to chess. But the difference among these three games, and among the social classes whose members play them, are well worth noting.

The main difference among the games of poker, chess, and bridge is the kind of aptitude required to play them well, and hence to enjoy them. Poker, on one hand, is a game of emotion, aggression, and luck. Conceptually simple, it is nevertheless difficult to play well without the "guts" to bet good cards and take chances, the ability to interpret "hunches" correctly and "figure the odds," and the ability to keep a "poker face" while reading the feelings of other players. It is a visceral, cunning, and chancy game. As everybody knows, it is played most widely among the working classes, where aptitude for poker and aptitude for living come to much the same thing.

Bridge, on the other hand, is a game requiring coolness, restraint, and intellectual skill. Men who are experts at both poker and bridge, like Charles Goren, generally estimate that successful poker involves about 90 percent chance and 10 percent skill, while good bridge varies between 60 to 85 percent skill.[11] In addition to greater levels of intellectuality, bridge also requires greater emotional reserve. There are not just "rules" to bridge; there are "laws," and they are published in a small, hardcover book rather than a small softcover pamphlet, as if to give them more authority.[12]

These laws do more than just defiine the mechanics of play; they also cover, in great detail, the proper way to behave at the bridge table. "Plays should be made without emphasis, gesture, or mannerism," for instance, "and so far as possible at a uniform rate." Of course, in the home, where most bridge is played, these rules are not followed all that closely; but then again, the bridge that's played there is severely looked down upon by devotees and experts. When the game is serious, some rather shocking interpersonal punishment can befall an offender. In duplicate tournaments, where the best players are found, an infraction may result in an invitation to leave and not return; it will always result in painful official penalties. In any

---

11Charles Goren, *Contract Bridge Complete* (New York: Doubleday, 1951).
12*The Laws of Contract Bridge* (New York: Crown, 1963).

case, emotion is thought to cloud a player's mind and stand in the way of playing well. It is not surprising, then, that this is so heavily a middle class game—an aptitude for calculation, uniformity, and restraint serves one well in the office too.

Chess also requires unemotional thinking and perhaps even more logical skill. The difference between it and bridge is that chess is *purely* logical. Bridge, however, is sociological and psychological as well as logical. Chess is so unsocial that it can be played across great distances by *computers.* Bridge, by contrast, is a four-person social-psychological encounter. The essence of bidding is to read your partner's mind and reach perfect agreement, while the essence of playing is to read your opponents' minds and fake them out. In fact reading everybody's mind all the time is the nature of the game. In other words, it helps in bridge to be an experienced adult and a good intuitive psychologist. Chess requires no such maturity at all; it merely requires an analytical mind (to be really good, an *obsessive* analytical mind). This point is demonstrated by the fact that child prodigies are forever popping up in chess, able to handle the greatest masters even though unable to handle alcohol. But there are no pubescent geniuses in bridge. A kid with little social experience is simply not very capable of penetrating other minds and understanding complex social-psychological events. Neither is a computer, and bridge will never be as successfully programmed as chess. As Ely Culbertson once said. "I play men, not cards."[13]

It is doubtful if there are any distinct differences in the social class of chess players and bridge players. Both would no doubt be lumped into either the middle or the upper-middle class. But there do seem to be occupational differences. I remember clearly from my compulsive game-playing days in college that bridge players always seemed to be students of the humanities, business, or society, while chess players always seemed to be majors in hard science or philosophy. It makes sense to suspect the same sort of thing is true in the world of adults. Though I am unable to find any hard figures on the matter, it is my observation that chess players tend to be skilled professionals who work with purely analytical problems like computer programming or theoretical science. There aren't many jobs like that, even in this age. Perhaps that's one reason why there aren't that many chess players either. Bridge, on the other hand, is much more diffuse in its occupational appeal. Wherever intellectual calculations are required that must be more than just analytic and mechanical, calculations that must take personalities and social settings into account as well, there bridge will thrive.

As we know, bridge players are estimated to be 75 percent women and 25 percent men. The bridge-playing public divides itself into three rather

---

[13]Mackey, *The Walk of the Oysters.*

distinct categories: casual players, tournament players, and experts. The
sex factor enters into each of these categories differently—there are
unique things to learn at each level.

Women outnumber men among casual players because they are
more inclined to use bridge as a medium (male cynics would say excuse)
for informal socializing. Bridge sophisticates regard these casual afternoon games as little more than coffee-klatsches—the lowest form of
bridge life. In any case they don't tell us much except that housewives
have a lot of lonely time on their hands, though for women that is a fact
of desperate significance. A phenomenon of far greater interest for our
purposes here is what has sometimes been called "conjugal bridge," or
bridge played by married couples. Bridge is a partnership game, and
cooperation between partners is essential to winning. Among casual
players conjugal bridge is very common, but frightfully often it turns
out to be not so very casual after all. The thing that distinguishes conjugal bridge, it seems, is that latent husband-wife hostilities tend to be
vented openly during play.[14] The difficulties of cooperating in a bridge
partnership so often display the difficulties of a marital partnership that
the game might be considered a microcosm of the reality. More than
once what begins as a pleasant evening over at the Bennetts has ended
up in mayhem (and even murder). Why?

The reason may lie in the fact that bridge is a great equalizer, the
latter-day Colt .45 of the married middle class. It is basically a man's
game, emphasizing supposedly masculine aptitudes: restraint, logic, and
so on. As a play form, it duplicates a male world—the world of pressure,
achievement, and strategic ploys down at the office. But as a social experience, it puts all the players on an equal footing . . . "sheltered"
housewives along with hard-nosed breadwinners who "know what the
real world is like." It thus gives a woman an opportunity to participate in
her husband's sense of reality, and it forces the husband to relate to his
wife as if she were a business partner. It is no wonder, then, that tensions often rise to the breaking point. What is supposed to be a partnership of cooperation easily becomes a competitive dogfight, with the wife
trying to show her husband that she is competent in his world and the
husband trying to show her back that he's better at it than she is. In
other words, it mixes up the distribution of power in the marriage and
confuses the clarity of the sex roles. Women are supposed to be illogical
and emotional, and when they try to be logical and clever like their husbands think of themselves, the husbands get itchy . . . and angry. A
bridge game gives a woman a chance to tell her husband something
she may have secretly suspected for a long time . . . that he's stupid. A
husband might feel in turn that his silly dingaling wife just has no right

---

[14]See Olsen, *The Mad World of Bridge* or talk to any married bridge player.

to say something like that or try to assert that she's better than he is at this game. Explosion. *C'est l'amour.*

Sex figures somewhat differently in the second level of bridge expertise, the players who go to duplicate tournaments. Here, one tournament organizer of my acquaintance estimates, there are about twice as many women players as men. In part they are similar to the women who play coffee bridge in the afternoons, they obviously take the game a lot more seriously. Anyone who has ever attended a duplicate tournament knows that these are not little social affairs; they have all the solemnity of a summit conference or a battlefield. Duplicate tournaments are officially organized by The American Contract Bridge League (which has about 165,000 members, 53 percent of whom are women). It takes a fee to play in them, as well as steel nerves. The main purpose of participating is to win what are known as "Master Points," and the ultimate aim is to accumulate enough of them to work your way up through the various ranks and become a "Life Master"—a status as significant to bridge players as Supreme Court Justice is to the rest of us. The world of serious bridge is a highly competitive world, as internally stratified as large corporations or 18th-century England. The pressures are intense, the atmosphere electric, and the stakes—intangible though they may be—are high. In every way duplicate tournaments "duplicate" the business world outside (though that is not the meaning of the term). It follows, then, that women who seek out this sort of experience are a different breed. A good guess would be that they seek an outlet for a great deal of personal ambition—ambition thwarted by the male-dominated world around them, business and otherwise. The chances are also good that they are the wives of successful professionals and executives, seeking an accomplishment that will put them on a more equal footing with their husbands.

Despite all this, women almost never make it to the top. The third level of bridge players, the expert, consists almost entirely of men. In the last 20 years only a handful of women have risen to take their places among the best. Only two women have played in the last 16 world championships. This has usually been explained in bridge circles as yet another demonstration that women are just too irrational, too flippant, etc., etc., to become really good at something like bridge. This explanation, quite obviously, need not be taken seriously.

Marvin Reznikoff and Tannah Hirsch, two psychologists writing in *Psychology Today,* have proposed instead that "what separates the men from the girls" is aggressiveness.[15] Noting that bridge is basically aggressive, even as it is restrained, the psychologists cited studies showing that little boys are more aggressive than little girls and pointed out that the two best-known women experts play very aggressive bridge. But very

---

[15]Marvin Reznikoff and Tannah Hirsch, "Bridge Over Troubled Water," *Psychology Today,* May 1970.

possibly that is a lot of baloney as well. Everybody knows that there are plenty of aggressive women running around, and their supposed passivity does not prevent them from greatly outnumbering men in those rigid and ruthless duplicate tournaments. The best explanation probably lies in the diffculty, from a woman's point of view, of living the kind of life one must in order to become a recognized expert. It requires a great deal of travel to attend enough tournaments to acquire a lot of master points, and it is a rather lonely life of hotels and strangers. Women's lot in the world makes this life singularly unrealistic. For one thing, there are children. For another, there are husbands, who sometimes begin to get itchy when their wives get *too* good at something or are inclined to be away from home a lot or "drag them around." Women who are truly good at bridge ultimately find themselves in the same sex-role bind as their conjugal or coffee-klatching sisters in the suburbs: There is an upper limit, for most of them, to the extent they can compete in a male world and get away with it.

Social class and sex thus have a great deal to tell us about bridge and the people who play it. Race and religion have something to tell us too. The importance of both shows up most clearly within the highest stratum of bridge. It is common knowledge among bridge buffs that a great many of the best players, probably even the majority, are Jews. From Charles Goren to Ira Corn, Jewish names have dominated the game throughout its modern history. While Jews are vastly overrepresented among the best, names like Polanski and O'Brian are scarcely seen at all. Recalling that bridge skill requires high ambition, it's not so hard to understand why this is the case. What psychologists call "achievement motivation" is stronger among Jewish families than it is among Protestant families, and it is *least* strong, in our society, in Catholic families. Jews are largely barred from the WASP-dominated corporations, but in the more liberal professions they have found safe passage and participate in these professions out of all proportion to their numbers. There is more than fancy to the stereotype of every Jewish mother wanting her son to be a doctor or a lawyer and pushing him hard to make it. They do want, and they do push. Catholics, on the other hand (for reasons that are a little too complex to go into here) occupy fewer places in the corporate and professional establishment than their numbers in our population would imply. In other words, bridge is a Protestant game which Jews flock to and Catholics do not strongly care much about. In this sense, as in so many others, bridge is a microcosm of our society.

The case of blacks in bridge is something else again. The Jews have been excluded from the corporations but not from the professions. The blacks have been excluded from everything—until, perhaps, recently. The American Contract Bridge League (American as it most certainly is) banned blacks throughout most of its history. The blacks thus formed their own league, The American Bridge Association, which still exists today.

But the ACBL was officially integrated in 1967 after years of being unofficially integrated in most parts of the country, so the black league is mainly a thing of the past.

Still, there are reminders. Only a few years ago a national tournament was scheduled to be held in Jackson, Mississippi, only to be moved at the last minute for reasons mysteriously having to do with the amount of playing space available. The question of blacks and bridge is not easily answerable when the deck, until recently, has been so stacked against them. Even so, there are two things worthy of note in this matter. One is that black tournament players are very much of the black upper class, which is to say they correspond to the American middle or upper-middle class at best, thus confirming the middle class character of the game. Another is my observation that blacks were inordinately attracted to the game at the university where I went to graduate school; they were among the best players, too. Like the Jews, where they are accepted, they are high achievers.

Bridge is a complex social phenomenon in which things like social class, sex, religion and race all play major roles. Is there any way to reduce this complexity and find a single, simple motivation that all bridge players share in common? While bridge has not received much attention from psychologists, it has been put on the couch a few times.

One explanation of why people play bridge was advanced by Professor C. G. Shaw of New York University.[16] Shaw believed that bridge attracts a particularly weak and lethargic kind of person who normally leads a dull, unrewarding life. Without the energy to do much else, he plays bridge to bring some excitement into his life. "The habitual bridge player lacks adequate emotional power," Shaw said, "and must play to stimulate his nerves." It may be true that some people play because they're bored, but what is "adequate emotional power"? So "adequate" that one never plays games? If anything, bridge seems more an outlet for *excess* emotion than mere titillation for the lifeless.

Another explanation of bridge-playing has been offered by the famous psychoanalyst Alfred Adler:

> Bridge players are usually suffering from an inferiority complex and find in the game an easy way to satisfy their striving for superiority. Most people play cards to waste time. Time, if a man is not courageous, is his greatest enemy. Bridge is a great invention. A little of it is relaxation but a lot becomes a mental habit, an attempt to satisfy a striving for superiority. It offers an opportunity to conquer others.[17]

There is certainly some truth to this. Phrases like "killing defense" and "bridge for blood" are not only common in bridge play, but they also hap-

---

[16]Quoted in Olsen, *The Mad World of Bridge,* pp. 65–66.
[17]Ibid.

pen to be the titles of two popular books on bridge strategy.[18] Bridge can be a very aggressive game of not-so-polite conquest. Anyone who plays the game is familiar with the sadistic gloating that often accompanies winning and the gruesome persecution of partners that often accompanies losing. And as one bridge writer put it, "What is the inveterate card-slammer doing when he slaps down that ace but symbolically whacking his opponent in the mouth?"[19] Surely this sort of thing is satisfying to many who play the game, but it's not a very good explanation, nevertheless. Those familiar with the history of psychology will recall that Adler invented what he called "the power principle." He explained *everything* in terms of conquest and a striving for superiority. Explaining everything with one principle is usually tantamount to explaining nothing, and Adler, in consequence, did not have much of an impact on the development of professional psychology. A general striving for superiority need take no particular form, and hence fails as an explanation of why some particular form is widely sought out in preference to others.

Yet another psychological explanation is that bridge is an escape from reality, a release-valve for inner tension. As Dr. Harold Hays argued in *Bridge World:*

> . . . contract bridge is the greatest outlet for excess nervous energy that one has at hand. There are thousands of people who are 'bottled up,' who are full of nervous explosive material which is in constant turmoil. Many such individuals can let off steam by reading an exciting detective story; others must get rid of this energy in some other way, and contract is the solution.[20]

This position was put somewhat less favorably a while back by the *Christian Century,* which described a famous bridge match as "a Tom Thumb Congress of the American mind—a mind which prefers to dawdle over mythical difficulties and fence with hard situations which never exist, while men are asking for bread."[21] The *Christian Century* is as uncharitable as Professor Shaw in denying human beings their inevitable diversions, while Dr. Hays gives us no good reason why bridge is any more an ideal solution to the problem of nervous energy than it is for Adler's impulse to conquer.

All in all, the psychologists haven't done very well. They seldom do when trying to explain complicated social phenomenon, particularly one of the magnitude of bridge. Social phenomena always add up to more than the sum of the individuals involved in them, and to explain them satisfactorily one must usually go beyond biography and ego and look

---

[18]Ray Young, *Bridge For Blood* (Chicago: Follett, 1966); Hugh Walter Kelsey, *Killing Defense at Bridge* (New York: Hart, 1967).
[19]Olsen, *The Mad World of Bridge,* p. 66.
[20]Quoted by Olsen, pp. 68–69.
[21]Ibid.

at the social context which gives them birth. Individualistic psychology may help us to understand some players' motivations, but it is of little use in understanding the bridge phenomenon itself. The history and character of the game, the medium of its popularization, the aptitudes required to play it, and the way it is socially organized—these things tell us a great deal more. They all identify bridge as a game appealing to middle-class bureaucrats and professionals—and their wives.

Contract bridge today is played almost exactly the way it was upon its invention in 1927 by Harry Vanderbilt. Before Vanderbilt, it was a game of limited appeal to the upper classes.[22] It was a game of some skill among other games of skill, but it possessed no especially popular features.

Vanderbilt wanted to make the game of bridge more exciting, more like reality, and he made it both with his capitalistic innovations. Vanderbilt knew intuitively what social scientists know today about what makes something "exciting": something is exciting for a person if it touches on something intensely real to him in the form of play, ritual, or art.[23] In other words, "excitement" duplicates "reality," but puts it in a bottle and limits its fatefulness. An exciting game brings reality and fantasy together in play in a way that makes it different from either of its components. The play form is not so fantastic that it can't be taken seriously, yet not so realistic that it is as threatening as the world outside. A good, involving game, in other words, makes fantasy manifest and reality subject to control; it puts the player more or less in command of a little bottle full of reality for the time being.

Harry Vanderbilt's world was the complex, legalistic, bureaucratic reality of big business—a world full of contracts, deals, lawsuits, government, and calculated risk—a world where large amounts of money and large numbers of people had to be manipulated and administered. His innovations in the game of bridge were designed to give it more a flavor of that reality, and hence to make it more exciting. Harry Vanderbilt and his fellow corporate capitalists ruled America in those days, and the game of bridge, as he developed it, gave anyone who would play it a symbolic opportunity to play in the rulers' world. Bridge was not, and is not, a trivial game. It did not pass like the other fads of the 30's because the game Harry Vanderbilt invented is still an accurate and meaningful analog of the realities dominating America. Though bridge has since passed from the upper class to the middle class, so too has America passed from domination by wealthy entrepreneurial families to domination by im-

---

[22]Mackey, *Walk of the Oysters* and Olsen, *Mad World of Bridge*.
[23]See McLuhan, *Understanding Media* or Johan Huizinga, *Homo Ludens: A Study of the Play Element in Culture* (Boston: Beacon Press, 1955), for ethnological and phenomenological points of view. Several empirically oriented studies of "excitement" have been done by Dr. Elaine Walster and various students of hers at the University of Wisconsin.

personal organization men and corporate technocrats.[24] Bridge has also become a great deal more sophisticated in technique than it once was, but then so too has the science of business administration. Bridge has remained appropriate and grown in popularity in good part because the fundamental principles of both bridge and corporate reality are similar.

Nevertheless, it took the precocious merchandizing genius of Ely Culbertson to bring bridge to the middle class *masses.* And masses they were, or were quickly becoming. In the 19th century, America was still, for the most part, a two-class society: the upper class in the parlors and board rooms and the working class in the factories and farmland. The middle was made up of a comparatively small class of merchants and petty clerks. Only in the 20th century has our modern middle class, engineering and administering the steady growth of industrialization and huge corporations, become significant in numbers and in the economy. By the 1930's and the 1940's the middle class, as we now know it, was well on its way to becoming the dominant, or at least the largest, class in America. Industry was on the way to great changes too, with the rise of advertising and the consequent development of need-creation and controlled markets.

Ely Culbertson recognized these changes, and capitalized on them while they were still in their infancy. The new middle class was still threatened by sex, but it was better educated and not so puritanical about it as the rural and working class consumers (then declining in marketplace importance). They could enjoy a little sexuality in their daily lives as long as it was just politely titillating and not overtly vulgar. The conditions were right to attach a little sex to commodities.[25] If sex had been either completely repressed or frank but "dirty" in the new middle class, (as it largely was in the declining working-rural classes), there would have been no opportunity to sell things by making them a little risque; such an approach would either offend or it would have to sell the real thing—whores or pornography. The new class was liberated just enough, and yet still repressed enough, to make it work. Ely Culbertson did make it work, stimulating the game's appeal by attaching to it the tasteful perfume of double-entendre, and making himself a great deal of money in the doing. Culbertson may have been the first of the sex-as-commodity merchants who rose to prey on the new class and who dominate consumer marketing today.[26]

The other dimension to Culbertson's technique was to exploit the insecurities of the new middle class—insecurities which have always accompanied upward social mobility. He played on the new class' fear

---

[24]See Galbraith, *New Industrial State*, pp. 211–19.
[25]Herbert Marcuse, *Eros and Civilization: A Philosophical Inquiry into Freud* (Boston: Beacon, 1955).
[26]Vance Packard, *The Hidden Persuaders* (New York: David Makay, 1957); or Marcuse, ibid.

for social acceptance, and *created* the fear that if they did not play bridge they might not get that acceptance from their middle-class friends and neighbors. As Culbertson said himself, "we made it almost tantamount to shame not to play contract." But the brunt of Culbertson's strategy, as he also admits, was the appeal to women. Polite sexual innuendo was one way, but not the most important way. Most of Culbertson's success in captivating middle class women with bridge came from his accurate comprehension of the sense of insignificance they felt when compared to their husbands. In the earlier days of industrialization, women were rather the equals of men; if their work was hard and sweaty, their husbands' was probably even more so. With a move up to the middle class, however, things changed. Labor-saving devices reduced the wife's importance as a housekeeper; child care was largely taken out of her hands by more strict school attendance laws and earlier ages for school enrollment; still more of her functions were taken away by affordable processed foods, affordable hospitals and retirement homes, and the development of other service institutions both affordable and unavoidable. And all the while her husband worked in the faraway offices of some big important company doing big important business. At the same time, a middle-class woman's new respectability and affluence made it both unnecessary and somewhat embarrassing for her to share work and exchange favors with other women in the neighborhood—a sharing that had once been a major part of her social life. Yet she was not offered much of a social life in exchange; she had little knowledge of the world her husband worked in, and with his business friends she was made to feel more like an appendage than a partner.

The women of the new middle class were lonely, and they felt inferior. But as Culbertson said, "bridge was an opportunity for them to gain intellectual parity with their husbands," to show that women could be smart and clever too, to show that wives could work with their heads as well as their bodies. Bridge also provided a medium—or again, an excuse—to get together with other women and escape the lonely misery of the mechanized, empty houses they lived and waited in. For their husbands, on the other hand, bridge was an opportunity to fantasize in play the prowess they wished they exercised on their jobs, to celebrate all the careful calculations of middle class office life by reducing them to somewhat more understandable terms, and to expel their frustrations by pretending that they were really capable of controlling all this (especially if they got really good at "systems").

Middle class worklife is complex and requiring of calculation because, first, it is not self-sufficient work, and second, it is so largely "teamwork." It was once much easier for a man to say "screw the system" and go off and farm than it is today; there were once more jobs where "promotion" and "not making waves" were not things to be worried about; and there were once more jobs where one didn't have to work in close dependent interrelation with a lot of other people. Today, a middle class employee must be rather good at amateur public relations to succeed.

This is subtle stuff, and it requires good logic and good psychology to "succeed" in the modern world. As one writer put it while comparing corporate success with the complex game:

> "Well-established rules dictate play—and logic prevails. Gambits may improve the player's position on the board. The laws of probability often govern decisions on whether to make one move or another. Success accrues particularly to the player who can think more than one move in advance. The ultimate champion is one who, with a sweep of his eye, visualizes the entire board before him and plans every move that might help him reach victory, taking into account at the same time the likely moves of his opponents."[27]

As it happens, the author of these words was referring to chess. But as we have established, chess is logical and nothing else. Bridge is logical and social-psychological besides, and hence much more realistic in terms of the office downtown.

Man does not live in a vacuum, nor does he play in one. He lives within social reality systems, and it is from these systems that he gets his sense of what the world is like. In turn, it is from this sense of what the world is like that he chooses his play forms. Certain games are more attractive than others because games differ in the images of reality they represent to the player. A person in search of the liberating euphoria of play will choose a game or games that most nearly represent in their internal structure the way he sees the external structure of the world around him. Thus a *macho*-obsessed Spaniard chooses bullfights and an American bureaucrat chooses bridge. As Johan Huizinga showed in *Homo Ludens*[28] (and Emile Durkheim showed before him in *The Elementary Forms of Religious Life*[29]), all social rituals have this quality of mystically reproducing the order of the universe as seen by a particular culture. Primitive ceremony involves the acting out of nature as imprinted in tribal consciousness, with the effect that this acting out maintains and verifies the tribal sense of cosmic order and refreshes the participants; it assures that all is right with their world. Modern social rituals are basically no different, and bridge is no exception.

A middle-class man may use bridge to create a more agreeable form of his own office world, while his wife uses it to enter that world as an equal or to have an independent social life apart from it. It is a game of middle class existential survival. Perhaps that is why it is so often played in deadly, ruthless earnest. It is a psychological battle of wits to survive with dignity in the disoriented and unstable world of the corporate

---

[27]Hal Higdon, "Executive Chess," *Playboy*, March 1971, p. 193.
[28]Huizinga, *Homo Ludens*.
[29]Emile Durkheim, *The Elementary Forms of Religious Life* (New York: Humanities Press, 1964).

middle class. Bridge makes it seem possible to gain control over that world at least for awhile, at least in play, and it makes it all seem challenging, exciting, and most of all *real* and *manipulable.* The pause that *really* refreshes—for those immersed in the realities of bridge, it is a temple of Life.

Can you think of further methodological approaches to the study of a culture's games that might be fruitful? Could similar analyses be applied to more physical games, such as football, golf, or tennis? In this context what significance (if any) should one place upon politicians' borrowing the terminology of the sports world to describe national and international events? Is the *type* of game utilized as analogy significant in any way to the study of social structure? (As an example, football—like chess—is a game set up with the idea of *team* defense of common territory.)

Although the games played later in life perhaps perform more of a supportive than socializing function, just the opposite can be posited when examining the world of play of the American child. The recent furor over the inclusion or noninclusion of sexual organs on dolls quite dramatically reflects middle America's sexual ambivalence, while the toy manufacturers' large scale production of weapons as toys dramatizes the importance Americans place on violence as a means of attaining one's goals. Children learn early that it is un-American to be a "chicken."

The artifacts of play thus reveal a good deal about the values of those who construct them—and about the anticipated roles to which the child is, by means of his play, being socialized.[50] Examination of the toy boxes of America would, I feel sure, reflect many important aspects of our culture—one among those aspects being great differences in children's toys with respect to the social class of the parent.

Using a "loose" methodology of observation, sociologist Arthur Asa Berger examines the role of the bicycle in the socialization patterns of youthful middle America.

---

50. It is within this context that the violence of much of middle America's child-oriented television fare has been criticized.

THE SPYDER (STING-RAY, SCREAMER)
BIKE: AN AMERICAN ORIGINAL

Arthur Asa Berger

If you want to know what is "going on" in a society, sometimes it pays to look at things that are so obvious and so ordinary that they have the status of being invisible, so to speak. I am talking about the everyday and common matters that we tend to dismiss without concern, while we search for "important" things; but our everyday assumptions and commonplaces *are* important. As the distinguished Dutch cultural historian Johan Huizinga wrote in *The Waning of the Middle Ages;* "We may even say that the true character of the spirit of an age is better revealed in its mode of regarding and expressing trivial and commonplace things than in the high manifestations of philosophy and science."

The same can be said of the spirit of a country, and an examination of commonplaces often reveals values and social processes that are of some significance. For example, look at the relatively recent phenomenon—the Spyder or Sting-Ray or Screamer bike.

What are we to make of these bikes, these flamboyant, ill-proportioned grotesques which are beginning to dominate the American bicycle scene? The bicycle is a ubiquitous, and until recently, relatively uniform type of transportation. Most bikes are thin-wheeled, with light frames—similar to what we used to call "English style" in reference to a popular English brand, the Raleigh. In America, however, we developed the balloon tire bicycle in the thirties, an innovation from the English style.[1] This led, ultimately, to Spyder bikes, or "Sting Rays," as one manufacturer calls them. These bicycles are important because they are unique—this type of bike is *an American original*—and because the bikes reflect, in graphic form, many of the forces at work in America society.

The bicycles are studies in self-deception. They are bikes which think they are motorcycles. Thus we find they have "high rise" handlebars, and various other items found on many motorcycles. Thanks to the rear tires (which come in various styles, depending upon what is to be done with the bicycle), it is possible to do one-wheel stands—a popular motorcycle trick.

These bicycles are relatively expensive, and can run up to $100 dollars if one wishes to indulge in all the flashy extras and deluxe features.You can get five-speed stick shifts,[2] souped-up banana seats called "glitter sit-

---

[1]Although the ballon tire bicycle was not developed until the thirties, the pneumatic tire was invented in 1890 and was perhaps the most important factor in precipitating the turn-of-the-century American bicycling craze (even as the bicycles involved were derivations from an English model and could not be thought of as American originals). See Sidney H. Aronson. "The Sociology of the Bicycle," *Social Forces* 30 (1952): 305–12.

ters," bright "glitter grips" for highrise handlebars, and chrome plated fenders, to mention a few of the "options." In addition, the manufacturers are beginning to introduce *model changes* every year, just as in the automobile industry. For example, Schwinn has introduced a new model called the "Ram's Horn," which is a lightweight, highrise five-speed Sting Ray with handlebars that curve around like a Ram's horn.

The development of the Sting-Ray and its brethren only carries to a somewhat mad conclusion what was evident in the old balloon tire bike— itself a vehicle fashioned by American character and culture. The balloon bikes, called "trucks" in the trade, represented American ruggedness and masculinity. That they were stupidly inefficient did not matter. The thick tires and cumbersome frame forced the American child to pump strenuously and use a tremendous amount of energy, since weight and friction were considerable. But it was "worth it" to have a rugged bike for future "rugged individualists," instead of those effeminate European thin bikes, with their narrow tires and gears.[3] The balloon tire bike represents a simplistic Americanization of the bicycle, however, the genius of America was yet to manifest itself—one had to wait for the likes of the Spyder Bike, the *ne plus ultra* of Americanism.

As I see it, the Spyder Bike reveals a great deal about contemporary American society. For one thing, it symbolizes the lost youth of the American child. Despite all the talk in America about how glorious childhood is, the various pressures in America all "conspire" to eliminate more and more of childhood, and make young people want to be "old" as soon as they can. We put young boys into long pants at a very early age, and once in long pants they learn, subtly, to act as grown ups. Young children imitate grownups by transmogrifying their bicycles into grotesques such as Sting-Ray bikes, whose proportions are, quite simply, monstrous.

In addition, there is the matter of "education for consumption," with the introduction of "style" into bikes, the young person learns to "go through the motions" as his father does when buying a car. There are options to consider, there is "status" to be gained, "life style" to be revealed. A few years of spyder bikes and you are ready for the next step: buying automobiles, then anything and everything else.

The spyder bike, then is a grotesque. In its garishness and vulgarity it stands for the chrome-plated, plastic-coated ugliness that is so widespread

---

[2]Sears advertises "five-on-the-floor" stick gear shifts, which suggests the four-on-the-floor gearshifts of sportscars. Also you can get "chopper forks" (for the "Easy Rider Look") and billboard tires, an automotive wheel (instead of handlebars), etc., etc. This styling is now available on tricycles and scooters, so that even infants can be indoctrinated.

[3]Given the proliferation of traditional American values in the present-day working class, it is interesting to note how many of the children of this class still ride balloon bikes *(editor)*.

in American culture—what many call our "plastic" society. But it also symbolizes a perversion of values, a somewhat monstrous application of merchandising and salesmanship that, I believe, has gotten out of control and
has led to grave distortions in American society.

Young boys and girls ride around on bikes whose names suggest potency and death, bikes which suggest to them that they are grown-ups and
which initiate them into the fine art of consumption. They learn to consider
options of just the sort that will be useful when they start purchasing automobiles and are led to equate status and perhaps "happiness" with the
gadgets they load on to their bikes. There is, perhaps, a logical progression: bicycle, motorcycle and automobile, each of which involves all sorts
of style decisions, since the items involved are not just utilitarian but are
invested with great symbolic signiflcance.

Curiously enough (and this is hopeful) there also seems to be some
kind of a counter-revolution. There has been a remarkable surge in the
popularity of bicycling on thin wheel ten-geared bikes. These bikes, austere
and basic (though often quite mechanically elaborate and expensive) represent a complete repudiation of all that the spyder-bike stands for. The rise
of sport bicycling may have been stimulated by the development of concern
over our ecology and by the whole "youth rebellion," (which has repudiated
so much of American culture), but whatever the case, it is an extremely
interesting and hopeful development. In this "war" of bicycle styles we see
the outward manifestation and expression of deep conflicts that are going
on in the American psyche and in American society, and which deal with
our values, goals, and aspirations on the cultural as well as the individual
level.

What we have is the Madison Avenue "merchandising mentality," exploitative and lacking social consciousness on one side (the Sting Ray),
and on the other, the whole counter-culture, "self-realization," nature syndrome, which is so critical of our institutions (the ten-speed touring bike).
What happens in the bike world will be a valuable indicator of where our
culture is moving as well as *how* (on Screamers or touring bikes) it is getting there.

Is Berger correct? Can you think of alternative interpretations
that fit the data as well?

The majority of middle class Americans do not get where they are
going by means of bicycles. "Time is money" and the illusion of the
added speed and worth of individual modes of transportation, the shift
to suburbia, plus the fantastic post-World War II proliferation of the
American highway system have combined to instill in the middle
American a strong dependence upon the automobile. This dependence
in turn, has led to the rapid rise of what some call "freeway culture":
neon-sculpted industries built along the freeways of the nation, cater-

ing to the twin middle class values of time as money and substance over form. Journalists Daniel and Susan Halas examine in detail one of the more popular aspects of freeway culture, the franchise-food operation.

HAMBURGERS 18¢

Daniel and Susan Halas

Some people are born common, some attain commonness and some have commonness thrust upon them. We were doubly damned: drafted, and stationed in Indianapolis to protect Indiana. If we were not common in the beginning, we are common now. Membership in the ranks of the Army and residence in Indiana guarantees participation in the "prole life"—a mode of existence which most of America lives and the rest never hears about—the life of the common man. . . . While it would be laudable to be a poet of the common man, true commonness is the denial of poetry—the poetry of the common man (humble and strong) is only a fiction.

To be common is not even to be poor. The poor we read about live in ghettos; when they get pregnant they are put on welfare, and their children are bitten by rats. To be common is to be beneath notice—like a particularly well-known stretch of road—completely familiar and generally ignored.

We are surrounded by people who lead common lives, work at common jobs, earn common salaries, have common ambitions, even common dreams. The manufacturers who promise a free Cannon dish towel inside every box of detergent really have their number; the Shell Americana Game was made for them. Common problems are only truly depicted in the common man's media: told in *True Confessions,* aired on *Search For Tomorrow,* forgiven in church, and enumerated in Country-Western songs which begin, "I quit my job in the car wash. . . ."

In Indiana, where the prevailing idea of a good time has not progressed far beyond going into town and standing in front of J. C. Penney's, hands in pockets, rocking back and forth on your heels, talking Chicago hog prices, our particular notion of a good time disintegrated rapidly and dissolved into looking for new magazines at the shopping center and driving up and down Pendleton Pike trying out all the roadside eating places.

Pendleton Pike, Indiana route 36/67, runs northeast out of Indianapolis. Route 36 starts in the center of town as a two-lane truck route—the curse of the semi—complete with three railroad crossings, right-angle turns and no passing. At Thirty-eighth Street, in a burst of neon lyricism, it spreads to four lanes and promises the open road. Here where the city greets the superhighway wilderness, where the Holiday Inn sign is king, here where the shopping center dominates either side of the road are the *déjà vu* used-car lots, cut-rate department stores, trailer camps, the endless succession of gas stations and drive-in restaurants. If we had the impression of having been here before, it is because this scenery duplicates itself nationwide. This is the marketplace the automobile has made possible. This is where the life of the common man is not only enjoyed with the aid of a car, but actually sustained from coast to coast.

Artists, city planners and others who fail to appreciate the common man generally deplore the blight of roadside architecture—especially that species of restaurant which sells the 15-cent (now 18-cent) hamburger. These sirens of the highway, these chromium, glass and neon conglomerations of popular taste, attack the sensory system of the driver and lure him off the road to satisfy what must be an hereditary American craving for grease. The wizardly excesses of the McDonald's or the Burger Chef signs have a dream merchant's mind behind them. Their animated explosions of light create the nighttime atmosphere of desire and further the conviction that the dollar which buys two hamburgers, two milk shakes and an order of French fries is the dollar well spent. That *is* what a dollar will buy, delivered with lightning speed by the beauteous hand of Linda or Flo, prepared by the back line, bagged, boxed, plastic-covered, sales-taxed; as closely as modern industrial processing can manage it will duplicate every other hamburger, milk shake and French fry in the history of the firm. This is the food of the common man. This is prole food.

We became interested in prole food the way we became interested in corn—it was all around us. On Pendleton Pike that which is not corn is trailer camp and that which is not trailer camp is someplace to eat. On or with access to Pendleton Pike await the following establishments: Mr. Fifteen, Frisch's Big Boy, Dunkin' Donut, Burger Chef, Dog 'N' Suds, A & W Root Beer, Sizzler's Steak House, Bonanza Sirloin Pit, Colonel Sanders' Kentucky Fried Chicken, Chicken Delight, Shakey's Pizza, Lum's (Hot Dogs Steamed in Beer), and White Castle, America's answer to Gothic architecture.

The prole-food business is the franchise business. Some prole-food outlets are chain-operated and company-managed, and some are one-of-a-kind small businesses, but the real money and the reason the road is lined with these establishments is the franchise.

Quality in the traditional sense is not the key to the popularity of franchised food, which is popular because it is standardized and partakes of all the guarantees that come with quality control. It may not be splendid, but it is always the same. At the price it is surprising any of it is edible. Our working hypothesis postulated that edibility is inversely proportional to the number of processes the food undergoes before being fried and to the length of time it remains in grease.

Franchise food is designed primarily with the young in mind—the teenager, the young adult and the young family. The hamburger, French fries and milk shake may be as American as apple pie, but have precisely the opposite implication—of a "triple treat" representing the ultimate abnegation of home, Mom, and Mom's home cooking. They represent freedom of choice, speed and mobility, friends, cars, excitement, fun, and just what America has to offer the common man.

The franchise-food operation indicates a limited menu. Give or take a few side dishes, only seven substantial items are served along the nation's highways: hamburger, hot dog, pizza, chicken, steak, and, to a lesser extent the fish sandwich and barbecued ribs. In an effort to create a standardized product each has developed something bearing a family resemblance to one of these familiar foods, but decidedly something new and all its own. Take pizza, for example: it may look like a pizza; it is round, it is covered with tomato sauce, cheese, mushrooms, sausage, pepperoni, and sometimes anchovies—but it is not just a pizza. It is a Shakey's Pizza (one of their twenty-one varieties). What is sold as a hamburger along the highways may differ in size, in the way it is cooked and in the kind of bun that contains it, but no matter the variety it is our native, dearest and best-loved national dish. You can get a patty as small as a silver dollar, frozen and then refurbished by frying, broiling or charcoal burning, enveloped in a toasted—or untoasted—sponge bun. But if you stop at a Burger Chef place, you can be sure that the patty, before being broiled, will be three and a half inches in diameter and that the hamburger placed before you in California is identical in every way to the one you've had in Indiana.

There are almost as many reasons for eating prole food as there are common men—but only rarely is the food the main attraction. True, the 18-cent hamburger is a quick meal. Eating is a habit and at certain times during the day people feel called upon to fill their mouths, even when driving along the road. At these times they want their food fast and they want it cheap, but unless they are under the age of twelve they are not eating prole food in preference to anything else. The $1.29 steak, on the other hand, is selling "the good life" and a restaurant atmosphere for a quarter of what a real restaurant would charge. If the steak happens to be a little tough and tasteless, it only proves you get what you pay for. A minimal expenditure purchases an evening out, a break in the routine, and a sense of refinement, even if the sign proclaims "Watch us cook." The most compelling reason that people, common or swell, eat out is to have fun. Tough proles go to the Big Boy where on Saturday night they cruise the lot, appraise the girls, harass the hired cop, and have fun. The more refined go to Shakey's where they eat pizza, drink beer, sing along with the ragtime banjo, and have fun. Though food may figure in the initial expectation, the goal is social—to see and be seen, to have a good time.

An industry has been built around food to which the need or desire for food is largely incidental. Selling prole food on the basis of need is like the pitch of a popcorn man we heard: "Who needs popcorn?" No one *needs* popcorn and no none *needs* prole food.

The 18-cent hamburger buys the common man a half hour to do something else as well as eat; the 99-cent box of chicken is a meal Mom didn't have to fix; the $2.80 giant pizza is the long-awaited good time. At these prices and these motives for eating it, prole food is here to stay. In addition to being wildly popular with the common man, the average developed franchise restaurant returns to its management 13 to 22 percent net profit. In America, where the profit motive is still strong, it can be expected prole food will flourish and multiply.

The franchise-business agreement is as old as the Romans. Then the right of franchise was sold to coiners of money. Its more recent profitable application has been to businesses associated with the automobile. Car dealers, car rentals, car accessories, gas stations, repair and servicing operations, motels, and drive-in restaurants are almost all exclusively franchised. Postwar production of the automobile transformed America almost overnight from a pedestrian economy to an automobile economy. As a result the mutual dependence between the automobile and the roadside industries has produced, if not the right to coin money, the opportunity to make a great deal of it.

In the prole-food business a franchise is the right granted by a manufacturer to an individual distributor to make and market its line and to use the company name. For this right the buyer usually pays a flat fee and a yearly percentage of his gross. The initial investment, including building and land leases, can run in excess of $50,000. In return the buyer is helped in site location, financing, training and advertising, and given additional services in product development and quality control. As a member of a system, he has increased purchasing power; the discounts he receives on paper goods alone make him look like a cutthroat operation to the individual entrepreneur.

And he gets the name. The name is the key. A successful name assures instant product recognition from coast to coast. It becomes part of the language, like Chevrolet, or Holiday Inn, or Big Boy. The right to use the name is the right to a place in America's communal memory. To the buyer of the franchise this the assurance that his drive-in restaurant could and should be an overnight success.

Not everyone wins at the franchise game. Indiana, which once led the nation in automotive production with such cars as the Marmon and the Duesenberg, failed to free itself of the notion that the automobile was a luxury, and so lost out to Detroit, which sold the idea that everyone can own a car. Today, the sight of a boarded-up would-be prole-food outlet that never caught on is not uncommon, but the success stories are phenomenal.

McDONALD'S

McDonald's invented the 15-cent hamburger, and at last count has sold over 3 billion of them. A chart of its growth rate looks like a geometric progression. In ten years its sales have mushroomed from zero to $219,000,000 gross in 1966. Just when the sign that proclaims this feat of business acumen will flip to 4 billion is a secret, and whether the man who eats McDonald's 4 billionth will get a free one or be sung to by angels is unknown.[1] McDonald's 15-cent idea illustrates the first and leading principle of the prole-food industry: the amount of money spent by the customer should be beneath his conscious consideration. Prices should be so low that anyone, whether from impulse or design, can eat out. The $1.29 steak and the $2 pizza are both logical outgrowths of an affluent society where anything under a $5 bill looks like small change.

COLONEL SANDERS' KENTUCKY FRIED CHICKEN
(it's finger-lickin' good)

He really is a Kentucky Colonel and he's cooking country-fried chicken seven days a week nationwide. Who could fail to be touched by the story of a man who at 65, when the new highway bypassed his lowly chicken emporium, put a frozen chicken under each arm and barnstormed the border states? He discovered and exploited, and in time franchised and sold, at a 2-million-dollar profit, his secret recipe (the seasoning is still *his* secret). Who would have guessed part of that secret recipe was in pressure-cooking the chicken before frying it?

Colonel Sanders is the exception that proves the rule. He *is* selling food. It would be hard to find even homemade fried chicken that tastes better. The Colonel is also selling the idea of carry-out food. His case underlines a second leading principle in the franchise-food business: franchise foods do not compete with one another. All contribute to the "food-away-from-home" idea, and all compete with the grocery store for America's food dollar.

Colonel Sanders' is hardly vying for the McDonald's market. Chicken does not compete with steak, nor steak with pizza. Even Burger Chef does not compete with McDonald's, despite their obvious similarities. Battle lines can be drawn. The supermarket appeals to Mom with the message: Home, Family, Safety and Security. The franchise restaurant appeals to the kids with: Fun and The Freedom of The Road. Colonel Sanders' is fortunate to have it both ways—you *go out* to buy it, and *bring it home* to eat it. Prepackaged food of such exotic delights as frozen tacos and egg rolls undoubtedly takes its toll. However, even though chicken is the cheapest commodity in the grocery store, millions of Americans are finding that they would rather take home a carry-out order of his "finger-lickin' good" variety than sweat over the traditional hot stove.

THE BURGER CHEF SYSTEM

Indiana's own answer to prole/franchise food, Burger Chef, provides the convenient case for detailed study. Its headquarters are located in downtown Indianapolis' industrial section, and here we learned why they call it The System.

---

[1] At the time this goes to press, the count is up to over 8 billion *(editor)*

Burger Chef Systems, Inc. and the man behind it, Frank Thomas, president, constitute a local success story. Thomas (whose father owned a frozen custard stand), using McDonald's 15-cent hamburger idea, built one outlet to show off a line of food processing equipment. The food met with instant success. Since then there's been no stopping him. In less than ten years Burger Chef has grown into an operation of 710 outlets in 40 states. The company has set itself the goal of a 1000 stores in 48 states by 1970. In 1967 General Foods bought Burger Chef for more than $15,000,000.

From the consumers' point of view, Burger Chef and McDonald's are virtually indistinguishable. Both feature a mind-expanding sign, and both specialize in courteous, instant service and the miniscule hamburger. (Burger Chef broils, McDonald's fries, but we can't tell the difference), and their French fries are tasty. On our last visit, the counter girl suggested we try an item recently added to the menu—the apple turnover. It cost a quarter and weighed half a pound—a real tooth breaker.

Thomas hopes that the addition of tables and booths will increase Burger Chef's appeal to families with children out for a night on the town, as well as to the tired driver who has had enough of his automobile while on the road. In this world of extremely fine distinctions, this single difference could prove crucial. While McDonald's expects the customer to eat in his car (making few provisions for sit-down eating), Burger Chef invites the customer to pause over a brief meal in a restaurant atmosphere—admittedly not a very classy restaurant, but a restaurant nevertheless. . . .

Thomas related the growth of the "food away from home" idea to the growth of the automobile. "After the war there were a limited number of automobiles," he said. "Then there were several years where they made 6/8/10 million cars. Cars more than doubled on the highway in the ten years after 1945. You had twice as many customers drive in. The market, in a sense, doubled. Families with kids wanted a place to eat away from home. The school-lunch program had come into being. Kids were used to eating away from home. When I was a kid, I *had* to come home to eat. *My* kids don't have to come home to eat, now." As an extension of the school-lunch program, and capitalizing on America's growing mobility, Burger Chef Systems, Inc. and Frank Thomas have become rich.

Why are there no Burger Chefs in New York City? It would be ridiculous to try to sell a product specifically designed to reach a mobile economy to New York pedestrians, answered Thomas.

With the automobile in mind, all Burger Chef locations have the same requirements—and the main requirement is a *road*. The traffic should be in excess of 10,000 cars per 24-hour period and speed should be controlled at no more than 40 miles per hour. As traffic passes the Burger Chef on Pendleton Pike, stoplights keep it to about 30, and the cars never stop coming. The population of the city should be no fewer than 15,000 with an industrial climate favorable for young families. An adjacent school or shopping area adds substantially to the value of the location. Our Burger Chef is next to a large shopping center and its proximity to Fort Benjamin Harrison's military and civilian population makes it an ideal location. Added to this is the fact that the U.S. Army Finance Center, after the Pentagon the second largest military building in America, is at Fort Harrison.

As for the food, Frank Thomas assured us they use the very best beef, constantly striving for a meat-to-fat ratio that results in the tastiest hamburger (lean beef does not make the best hamburgers, at least for the palate of the common man). The Burger Chef hamburger is three-sixteenths of an inch thick and it weighs 1.6 ounces, which comes out as ten to the pound. Thus the customer pays $1.80 a pound for Burger Chef hamburger *and* convenience. A gallon of Coke mix makes 56 drinks and 100 pounds of potatoes peel into 230 servings of French fries. Overall, food cost is held to 35 percent of the total cost. Labor for preparing and serving is not more than 20 percent, which may explain why "union" is a dirty word throughout the industry.

The 18-cent hamburger advertised on the flashing sign brings customers into the store, but management would be happier if they bought the Big Shef. At 45 cents, the double-decker Big Shef not only bites a bigger chunk out of a dollar, but also rings up a greater margin of profit. Give or take a little tartar sauce and an extra piece of bun, all that separates two Burger Chefs at 36 cents from a Big Shef is nine pennies of profit. If management had its way, every customer would order the profit leaders—a Big Shef, an orange drink and French fries. Frank Thomas said enough to convince us, however, that in the case of fluctuating costs, Burger Chef would probably go the route of 11 hamburgers to the pound, rather than sully the product or raise the present 18-cent price ceiling.

If Frank Thomas' office was the very model of the modern executive, Walter "Bud" Lough's looked as if it had been taken directly from the pages of Sinclair Lewis. Lough is vice-president in charge of training, research and development. On his desk sits a huge free-form ashtray initialed with a silver embossed "L." Two bronze plaques proclaim his ten years of loyal service to the Sani-Serv and Burger Chef System. On one wall hangs an imitation oil painting: Christ dressed in flowing robes is exchanging pleasantries with a businessman dressed in 1947 grey flannel. The office is further graced by a set of chromoliths, including the most popular picture in Indiana, *The Big Moment*—when Pa hands the reins to Sonny as the buckboard fords the stream. In addition there is a wall clock in the shape of a wristwatch, a toy Pepsi-Cola dispenser, Optimist Club literature, *Enthusiasm Makes the Difference* by Norman Vincent Peale, the collected works of Edgar Guest, a thick volume entitled *Psycho-cybernetics,* and a bust of Abraham Lincoln.

Bud Lough painted an optimistic picture. Product development? Yes. They were developing a product. They were developing a ham-and-cheese sandwich. Right now they were field-testing the identical sandwich in five different markets to determine which of five different prices would yield the biggest return. Marketing? Bud Lough didn't put much faith in it. There was a man from the dehydrated-onion industry (yes, there is a dehydrated-onion industry) testing customer response to dehydrated onions. But for all of Bud Lough, his nine-point graduated response scale failed to impress him. Lough could tell in advance that when a man buys an extra half hour, it doesn't matter if it comes with or without dehydrated onions.

Bud Lough knew he was not selling food—he was selling The System. As a spokesman for The System no one could preach and teach the central tenets of Burger Chefdom more effectively, creatively or sincerely than Bud Lough. Bud Lough teaches the prospective Burger Chef managers to care about Burger Chef. They care because they have a minimum of $25,000 of their own money tied up, or because they are being trained to manage the company-owned units at a salary larger than they have ever made before.

We watched them, earnest, sincere, and trying, trying, trying—a paunchy 50-year-old man, a young man in his middle twenties, and a big ex-football-player type—all trying to remember to put into practice the 25 points of effective counter selling.

If the manager fails to learn his lessons in the three-week training school, it is not because his schooling isn't thorough. Teaching machines and on-the-job training increase its effectiveness. A mock-up, complete in every detail, of a Burger Chef sales counter provides the reality factor for the student. A closed-circuit television system records his sales demonstrations, and moments later instant playback points up his deflciencies and encourages him to see himself as others see him. A classroom sales problem begins at point of contact and ends when the student/customer has the requested order in hand. The student strives for a 45 second optimum service time. During these 45 seconds has he practiced effectively each of the 25 points? Has he remembered to say courteously, "Can I help you, sir?" in his opening, remembered to suggest the orange drink, and if he is presented with a $5 bill for the sale, has he remembered to lay it by the side of the cash register to scotch all questions of whether it was a five or a one? He must know every trick, for it will be his responsibility to teach and supervise his own staff. His success in the business will largely depend upon how well he motivates his help and insists on their absolute fidelity to The System.

It is not every man who genuinely wants to learn to assemble and take apart a condiment dispenser, or who considers neatness and punctuality serious matters. The missing bow tie, the five minutes late were major offenses against The System—a system whose incantation is, "Thou shalt be neat," and "Thou shalt not be tardy." The System—a masterful creation of the time-and-motion man—is a studied and codified pursuit of the dollar. It is the dollar that lures, motivates and eventually beatifies the man in his own eyes. It is The System that brings in The Dollar.

Quality is where you find it. For Burger Chef it is in The System. Quality is the preplanned, preselected, prebuilt, presold, every-contingency-fore-seen System. The System is encompassed in the Burger Chef operator's manual, a thick orange book, which devotes itself in depth to the whims of the Idaho potato when deep fried, employee relations, getting the customer in and out fast, pushing items with the biggest net return, bookkeeping, maintenance of the equipment and its suppliers, and how to mop the floor.

The System is spelled out in The Book, drilled in classes, and practiced in stores.

The System is so simple and so complete that even a child, possessed of 25,000 dollars and the overwhelming desire to succeed could make it work. . . .

Owning a Burger Chef franchise is not like owning a corner grocery. Burger Chef does not attract the kind of people who want to work in the store during the day and sleep over it at night. A typical buyer hopes that one franchise will lead to another and a third and a fourth, *ad infinitum*. There are already many multiple owerships within The System. What worked once will work again, and the chain-within-a-chain idea is what the smart franchise buyer has in mind. Holding ten going franchises in Burger Chef could easily put the owner with only a limited management responsibility in the $100,000-a-year bracket. That's what it is all about. Franchising is one of the ways still open to the man who has no particular talent or education to become wealthy. Owning a successful franchise makes it possible for a man who never heard of the term to become nouveau riche.

The prole-food business in its franchise form is only ten years old. It is not hard to see the shape of its future on Pendleton Pike. A yet unnamed Italian place is being snapped into its prefabricated form. A Howard Johnson's is coming, and what used to be 40 acres of corn will be 40 acres of Motor Inn Restaurant with parking lot. Farther down, a site has been picked for the new franchise wunderkind—Indianapolis will get its first Arby's Roast Beef. Given this kind of proliferation, can market saturation be far off? Though these establishments do not yet compete with each other, eventually they must, for along with the supermarket, they are all after the same food dollar. That food dollar can be stretched to include just so many hamburgers, pizzas, steaks and fried chickens.

There are still miles and miles of waiting highway left, but it holds just so many choice locations. When these are taken, the customer will have to decide whose hamburger he *really* wants.

The prole-food industry, faced with a seemingly unlimited mass appetite, has not had to worry about competition. When the highway (like the West) is settled, instead of range wars over sheep and cattle, we will have road wars over steak and pizza sites.

With such eventual stiff competition in mind, The System is experimenting with wider menu variety and higher-priced items. These are radical departures for a business that has as its base the limited menu and the premise that the amount of money spent should appear insignificant—to the customers at least.

The System is experimenting so that when competition becomes a reality, profit margins narrow and, as with the automobile, the fine distinction is the telling one, Burger Chef shall not only survive but endure.

Every once in a while the highways of America will harbor a culinary find. Somewhere along the road from nowhere to nowhere we have stopped to eat something so delicious and at the same time so common that the instant desire is to tell the world: The plate of spaghetti in a little place in New York State just before the Thousand Island Bridge on the St. Lawrence River; the ice-cream-soda perfection of a place in Sydney, Nebraska; and the archetypal waffle in a café in Shelbyville, Kentucky. But these are rare and isolated incidents—common things done uncommonly well. Do not expect this from the nationwide prole-food outlets. . . .

No, in the nationwide franchise restaurant system is found the ultimate in prole food—where quality is defined in terms of standardization and consistency. There are no surprises (perhaps we are fortunate in this)—only the familiar, the known, the recognized, the dependable, from coast to coast, nationwide, from sea to shining sea.

You are what you eat. In what ways do you find the Halas' reportage on culinary standardization relevant to the study of social structure and popular culture? What important changes in American society of the 1960's and 1970's do you see reflected in the franchise-food operation?

Speaking about this culinary standardization, Arthur Berger notes how members of the American middle class have sacrificed their individuality for a few pennies and a little time. The desire for a McDonald hamburger is, in Berger's estimation, the next best thing to a death wish.

> A McDonald hamburger reminds you how very mortal you are, how you too will be thrown away some day in the moral equivalent of a paper bag.[51]

Are there other aspects of food (or drink) as popular culture that you feel would be useful to study? Why and how would you go about it?

The American middle class ethic reflected in the popularity of the franchise-food operations, is seen in still another culinary artifact. In the final piece in this section, critic M. F. K. Fisher explores the impacts frozen dinners have on social classes in America and how this impact differs by class level.

---

51. Arthur Asa Berger, *The Evangelical Hamburger* (New York: MSS Educational Publishing Company, 1970), p. 1.

THE SOCIAL STRATIFICATION OF
TV DINNERS

M. F. K. Fisher

Newcomers to our country find the flat rectangular packets, frozen stiff in every grocery store from the biggest supermarket to the smallest cross-roads "general," an amusing thing to play with, and gradually to depend on. They seem, and too often they prove to be, unreal, unbelievable . . . and then routine. On the outside is a brilliant fakey picture in full color of the gastronomical bliss within. The directions for attaining it are in basic language, with the required oven temperature often in blacker, larger type for those of us who can read numbers but not words.

The process of hopefully turning the flat block of ugly, lumpy grey ice back into an appetizing collection of nourishing tidbits for human consumption is kept as simple as possible. After the final chef of a long series of them sees how hot the oven should be and how long the meal will take to emerge at its peak of perfection, the foil top is left alone or loosened or partly removed, according to what will finally emerge (French fries and rolls are "exposed" while their accompaniments steam along under cover), and presumably one's taste buds ready themselves as the tray with its neat compartments turns into exactly what the pretty pic-ture promised: a "juicy tender all-sirloin chopped steak with gravy, fluffy whipped potatoes with extra pat of butter, peas-n-carrots just like Mom's." . . . Yummy Eatin, one nationally distributed brand calls it.

Another popular purveyor offers, of course in its own little depres-sion in the foil tray, what it calls an exclusive feature as well as "an extra 'home style' touch": a *muffin!* A full-page color ad in national maga-zines directed at Togetherness in the Home suggests that this bonus can turn any meal into a festive birthday treat by having a little candle stuck into it. Such whimsy contradicts the original and always preferred prac-tice of eating TV meals in the half-dark in almost any position, but pref-erably on the floor or on the southernmost tip of the spine if in a chair: the bright cartoon shows a cretin-like little boy actually sitting at a table, probably because it is a Special Occasion. He is grinning, perhaps with anticipation. Mom, rushing in from right, is grinning with self-satisfaction at how loving and generous she is, to stick the candle in the fluffy free muffin which in turn has soothed her last-minute qualms about forgetting Junior's birthday . . . and all this thanks to the benevolent thoughtful home-style chefs who watch over our national diet in their sanitized factories. . . .

Mexicans who come to our western states for work, usually migratory, find TV meals not only handy but glamorous. Living conditions are seldom more than rudimentary, but somehow a way to heat an oven to 450 de-grees for half an hour is generally procurable, and people who live in every seasonal-crop area along our border have told me that often one stove will run 24 hours a day, while families wait their turns. No pots and pans, no plates, no garbage: all are real problems to people who live in cramped cabins or tents and must follow the harvests in whatever beat-up car will hold the most children and cousins.

My grocer, by now one of the last small-town holdouts against supermarkets (which he knows tacitly that I go to for things he cannot possibly afford to stock), worries every summer when pickers move into our California valley for the prune and grape crops. Exhausted men will come into his store and buy 12 or 15 frozen meals every night after work, he says. He hates to take most of what they have earned that day in the blazing sun, stooping over the vines and stretching into the trees. But they tell him their children love the surprise of the exciting dishes, and will eat every crumb. He sometimes reminds them in his anxiety that he carries good dried beans and fresh chili powder and that they can feed a hell of a lot of kids for what one frozen meal will cost them. They laugh happily and say they can eat beans in Jalisco. This is vacation, they say. "We take it easy in your country," they say, and they keep right on laughing, so that my friend is not sure what the joke might really be.

They buy without regard to price, but by the pictures on the packages, and they pay from an occasional 39 cents or "today's special smash bargain 3 for $1.19" to a rarer 79 cents, as do perhaps a hundred million other visitors and residents of America. The choice is wide, and while most combinations of food are straight Yankee (Swiss steak in beef and tomato gravy, French fries, mixed vegetables in seasoned sauce, vanilla pudding with macaroon crumbs), there are available dinners called Italian (spaghetti and meatballs), Chinese (chicken chow mein), and even "Continental" (beef Burgundian).

One production our spendthrift stoop-laborers never seem to buy is called Mexican Style. There are several versions of this, depending on the distributor and perhaps the locality, but a typical one (59 cents on sale will include in its three compartments two cheese-stuffed enchiladas in a mild chili gravy, some pinto beans, and a portion of corn with bits of red and green pepper in it. The package will give some sensible hints on adding tomato soup, a salad of avocado and grapefruit, a custard of some kind for dessert.

Not too coincidentally, a costlier version of the same feast, grandly specifying three courses, has almost exactly that menu in its dimples, except for the salad, which would not survive too gracefully a half hour in a hot oven. (Neither does the pudding, unless one really likes one's custard bubbling. . . .) This "typical Mexican feast," still costing less than a dollar, has five places in its foil tray, filled with good bland tomato soup with bits of toasted tortillas floating limply in it, a bean enchilada and a beef tamale in chili-flavored gravy. "Spanish-type" rice, refried beans with grated cheese and, for a special surprise, an apple-custard pudding. Even gringos, whose palates are abashed by most seasoning south of the border, admit that such so-called Mexican frozen meals are almost taste-less, but that the quality of the food is somewhat above the usual level for some reason. They are popular . . . unless you come from Jalisco!

Pressed-foil trays are as standard as the ubiquitous "fresh peas in seasoned sauce" which in eight out of ten menus fill the top right-hand compartments, and an afficionado will know exactly where to put his fork or spoon if he stares at the television or the wall, and exactly what will go into his mouth, and how it will taste, depending upon which brand his girl patronizes (or oftener, which one the nearest supermarket stocks. . . .

There seem to be three main levels of dining on frozen meals. The first one is mass-produced and mass-distributed, all over the nation, mostly by reputable companies which are often local subsidiaries of huge firms like Campbell's and General Foods. (For this reason I use the word "reputable," in spite of some personal qualms, but with legal approval.) The locations of their production plants are strategically near main dis-tribution centers for vegetables and meats, and are as awesome in their combining of the mechanical and the computer ages as a secret missile site. Words like "countless" and "untold" and "myriad" are ridiculous in describing the daily output of these plants, for not only every completed foil tray, correctly labeled, but every milligram of food it holds has been computerized. Precision is of the essence in the enormous vats that do their controlled simmerings and blanchings in the sterilized air-conditioned laboratories, and then the tons of seasoned nutritives shoot down to their separators, and when they fall at a blinding speed into exactly their right compartments on each tray as it whizzes along the belts, they will all look like the labels that are finally stuck on their sealed covers. They will vary a little in content, according to local and ethnic appetites, but usually one can buy the same meal in Vermont as in California or Wisconsin, and its additives will follow exactly the electronic decision: this much MSG and that much riboflavin per serving . . . and precisely the same number of those round green things in the upper right-hand compartment.

The second level of frozen foodery is comparatively amorphous. Its practitioners or disciples or victims usually live (usually alone) in small apartments. "Our junior executives," one serious and youthful manager of the frozen-food department of a stylishly located store assured me, "are real gourmets. They ignore the complete dinners, and don't seem to care how much they spend on the fancy stuff in small packages . . . frozen can-apés, maybe stuffed Cornish hen with wild rice and the special sauce in a little bag inside, and then green beans in butter with fresh mushrooms. They go wild! This is when they entertain, you understand. At home, like. They always get a good bottle of wine, too. If it's for a girl they get some frozen pastry. They just don't care about the cost . . . and they love to cook, gourmet-style. They have little kitchenettes, mostly." (The young man sounded wistful. I asked him if he liked cooking too, and he said almost apologetically, "Well, you see, I'm of Italian descent. So what I like is to start a good sauce on my day off . . . my girl grows basil and parsley like crazy in her window box . . . and then I pick up some fresh capellini . . ." and we were off, while the frozen gourmet stuff lay stiffly in his counters).

A less extravagant side to this middle level of buying is maintained by people who are literally too housebound, too fragile or convalescent, too old to prepare decent meals for themselves, but who for one reason or another are still free from the hypnotic bonds of the enclaves built to receive them, the Rest Havens, the Golden Years Villages.

Much as I dislike TV dinners for my own self, at least now when I can still choose, I have often introduced them to gallant older friends, and have shown how to cope with the almost idiot-proof modes of preparing them. Even after half an hour in a hot oven, one of those pressed-foil trays is not actively dangerous in the wobbling grasp of an old man in his one-room flat, and there is usually pap-like food in the tidy compartments that will not need strenuous mastication, in either the mouth or the belly. . . .

Such maneuverings as the Junior Executive goes through, needing pots and casseroles and plates for his Lucullan and wily tidbits, are impossible for the very weak, the elderly. They often find real succor in the makeshift but attainable food provided by an average frozen meal, and I am glad for that.

The third level of patrons of the galloping ready-to-heat food industry is strictly high-cost luxury living, with no heed for the bills but with an often finicky palate. It is made up of people who are used to good restaurants in many countries, to good chefs in the classical European attempts at *la haute cuisine.* They know something about sauces, either innately or by forced sophistication as their incomes have burgeoned. They pay for, and usually get, the best there is to be had and, much as I begrudge admitting it, that can be very good.

They are furnished by small outfits, usually headed by a noted and retired chef. They learn the lists of packaged foods they can choose from, as well as their own and their guests' tastes, and they stock their yacht reefers twice a year or oftener, and send hundreds of pounds of fine precooked frozen courses to their mountain lodges. When they recognize their own brand in First Class on a jet to Paris or Teheran, lusciously bubbling from the stewardess' infrared oven, they smile possessively, for they know that they are indeed flying high. Sure, it would cost little more to hire a good chef of their own. But 50 carefully wrapped packages of breaded breast of chicken with prosciutto don't have tantrums. They don't quit in the middle of dinner. They sit there in the fridge, waiting silently, worth every ounce of gold they cost. . . .

There are small, quiet top-drawer freezing kitchens all over the country . . . near affluent centers, that is. I know one north of San Francisco that does nothing but make entrées for a single airline noted for its worldly meals. A famous chef-emeritus from one of the very great restaurants in

Paris supervises the immaculate kitchen. The packaging is done without any outward splash in colored advertising and so on, since the whole operation is discreetly under wraps . . . committed . . . pledged.

Another small factory south of Los Angeles takes care of a certain amount of summer Carriage Trade when there is anything to spare, but is tacitly devoted to provisioning the yachts which rest between cruises in Newport Beach or San Diego or Santa Barbara. Its list is fairly simple, and its quality apparently unwavering. Of course it is run by a former chef, and he keeps his tidy light kitchen humming quietly in the hand of a mixed batch of French, Italian, Swiss cooks, in a fascinating ballet of puff paste here, puree of abalones there, sauce for a wild-rice stuffing at the big range, cheese sticks being cut at a long corner table. . . . As in all small successful operations like this one, the setup is basically uncomplicated, with one man at the head, perhaps a couple of moneybags in the background, and a carefully chosen and dedicated crew to watch everything from the deep-freeze room to the temperature of a pot of sauce on the stove. (It will be poured into a big flat pan, on crushed ice, to cool on a kitchen table, and then moved directly to the flash-freeze room kept at 50° below zero. Once well frozen, it will go to the deep freezer kept at 10° to 20° below, depending upon it ingredients and purposes.) . . .

There is comparatively little demand, even in specialty shops, for this third and most elegant type of "TV" food. It needs careful attention, and proper serving utensils in the private kitchens it is prepared for. And it can be good, for it is fastidiously prepared from the best procurable ingredients, and by knowing cooks. It costs a lot. A single portion of Chicken Burgundy, for instance, costs about $2.50, and if one likes that type of food it would be hard to equal it in a fine restaurant. On the other hand, a box of 100 artfully fabricated canapés, correctly frozen according to their ingredients and flavors, can cost a moderate $11. Or there will be things like an excellent baked chicken-liver pâté for about $2 a pound, and a fancy sweet tart to serve eight people for $3. No fuss, no muss, again . . . and who could duplicate them for less?

The trouble with all such small, dewy-eyed, and idealistic ventures is that Expansion is almost bound to take over. I am sure that is why I was sick after eating the stuffed chicken from the little place where deep-freezing had started before the food was properly chilled. And once I could focus my bilious eyes I read the tiny print on the label, and was astonished as well as further nauseated to learn that the sauce contained pork, lard, MSG, and soy! There is no need for any one of these in a proper stuffing made of rice and mushrooms, and the label spelled doom to whatever dreams were left in the head chef's heart. His was neither a huge mass production, able to market a "gourmet delicacy" for 79 cents, nor was it a ruthlessly small operation selling packages for $2.50. His stamped price was $1.29 . . . and there are cheaper and easier ways to die. . . .

Frozen packaged food is an increasingly important part of our culture. Its rapid adoption will give much thought to future historians, if there are any left to think, by the end of this century. One slightly macabre comfort is that by then the additives so calmly if tinily noted on every package, including such current dreads as the cyclamates and others possibly as dangerous, will probably have killed any semblance of healthy clean hunger in us, and we will welcome the predicted diet of the future, all tasteless pills and capsules. What such a regime will do to our two other basic needs, for warmth and for love, has had less study devoted to it, and in that lapse may lie our salvation, even gastronomically.

HIGH SOCIETY: POPULAR CULTURE?

My following presentation of pop society points out how one can use secondary sources (many, admittedly, qualitative and impressionistic in nature) as data in the presentation of linkages between social structure and popular culture. Here I am concerned with the *diffusion* of artifacts from one part of the social structure to another, their utilization as "boundary-maintaining" symbols, and the different meanings placed upon these artifacts by different consumers within the class structure. Is meaning inherent and discoverable within the artifact itself? Or is its meaning (and consequently, importance) determined by the socio-cultural milieu? If the latter, does the artifact also help define its socio-culture milieu? If so, then where and how should one break into this circular system of "feedback" to study it?

POP SOCIETY AND THE *NOUVEAU RICHE*

George H. Lewis

In much of the critical literature concerning popular or "mass" culture the implicit assumption has been made that a strong correlation exists between the social class level of a person and the type of culture he consumes[1]—*superior, mediocre,* or *brutal* being examples of cultural labels applied to artifacts with respect to the class level of consumer.[2] This assumption does have some validity, especially when one is addressing oneself to the lower, working or middle classes. However, even within these levels, a great deal of slippage occurs—the diffusion and the ease of artifact reproduction in present-day America has resulted in a relatively free "circulation" of artifacts from one subculture (or class level) to another. When one speaks of associations of certain artifacts with certain class

---

[1]See, for example, the articles by Bernard Rosenberg, José Ortega y Gasset, Leo Lowenthal, Dwight MacDonald, Clement Greenberg, T. W. Adorno, Marshall McLuhan, Irving Howe, Ernest van den Haag, Leslie Feidler and Melvin Tumin, in *Mass Culture,* edited by Bernard Rosenberg and David Manning White, (New York: The Free Press, 1957). Also, Norman Jacobs (ed.), *Culture For the Millions* (Princeton, N.J.: Van Nostrand, 1961), as well as D. Duane Braun, *Toward A Theory of Popular Culture* (Ann Arbor, Mich.: Ann Arbor Publishers, 1969).

levels, one can do so only very generally. To become more specific than "middle," or "working" class, for example, would be to introduce false precision in the data.

This correspondence between the type of culture consumed and the social class of the consumer becomes even less valid when one turns to the upper class in American society. Herbert Gans draws a distinction between creator-oriented and consumer-oriented culture at this class level.[3] Creator-oriented culture, emphasizing *method* (as opposed to content), is exclusive and original and cannot be thought of as *popular* culture.[4] The cultural artifacts of creator-oriented "high" culture are not distributed by major media, nor are they intended to be.

> Its art takes the form of originals distributed through galleries; its books are published by subsidized presses or commercial publishers willing to take a loss for prestige reasons; its journals are the so-called "little magazines"; its theater is concentrated largely in New York's off-Broadway and occasional university repertory companies, although it may share a few Broadway plays with the upper-middle class.[5]

Consumer-oriented high culture, on the other hand, *can* be thought of as popular culture. The end of World War I in this country brought the beginnings of a breakdown of conventional "high society." Although the old property-based establishment still remained, holding its coming-out balls and relaxing in its private clubs, the newer "cafe society" sprang into being—a grouping composed of persons whose status rested not on property and ancestry, but on consumer-oriented sorts of things: show business, advertising, public relations, the arts, journalism. These, the *nouveau riche* of the 1920's, congregated in America's large urban areas and looked for styles to symbolize their newly won positions. As these styles became institutionalized components of the cafe society culture, a problem arose—how to maintain the boundary between the evolving life style and that of the aspiring upper-middle class. Since the artifacts of cafe society were for the most part consumer oriented, it became an increasingly difficult task to prevent the diffusion of these artifacts to the upwardly mobile. The continuing affluence of post–World War II America, with its concomitant creation of new and varied positions of professional and managerial responsibility served only to complicate the boundary-maintenance tasks.[6]

Since the middle and late 1950's, the successful adoption of many of the cultural artifacts of cafe society (such as European auto racing, skiing,

---

[2]Edward Shils, "Mass Society and Its Culture," *Daedalus,* Spring 1960.
[3]Herbert J. Gans, "Popular Culture In America," in *Social Problems: A Modern Approach,* ed. Howard S. Becker (New York: John Wiley & Sons, 1966), pp. 584–87.
[4]See this book, page 19 for a working definition of popular culture.
[5]Gans, "Popular Culture in America," p. 585.
[6]C. Wright Mills, *White Collar* (New York: Oxford University Press, 1956)

sailing, and art appreciation) by the upwardly mobile has led to a search on the part of cafe society for newer and differing artifacts of identity. As in London during the affluence of the Regency period of the early 1800's, the members of America's "high society" of the early 1960's began looking to the lower orders and subcultures of society for artifacts they could adopt as their own.

> The various modes of *nostalgie de la boue* were in large part the young aristocrats' means of setting themselves apart from the middle classes. Wealth was no longer a buffer between the classes; but the old aristocratic manner of *confidence* was. The middle classes had money but lacked the confidence to be anything but ever more ornately respectable. The aristocrat had the confidence to be as shocking and outrageous as a navvy and get away with it. The bourgeois was hipped on gentility—genteel language, genteel conduct, the *gravitas* of the good burgher. The aristocrat shone by his own brilliance without regard to popular opinion, by which he usually meant the middle classes.[7]

In 1964 Susan Sontag pointed to one aspect of the new style in her "Notes On Camp.[8] Camp values frivolity, rejects the Puritan work ethic, approves of the ostentatious and shocking, and provides one source of content which can be used to maintain the boundary against upper-middle culture.[9]

The advocacy of camp justifies borrowing artifacts from the lower and subcultural strata. The first subclassifications of camp were high, middle and low camp—this distinction permitting members of the high culture public to borrow without impairing their own status. In the mid 1960's, for example, the Beatles were not high camp. The Rolling Stones were.

> I mean, it's *exciting,* they're all from the lower classes, East End-sort-of-thing. . . . They're all young, it's a whole new thing. It's not the Beatles. Bailey says the Beatles are *passé,* because now everybody's mum pats the Beatles on the head. The Beatles are getting fat. The Beatles—well, John Lennon's still thin, but Paul McCartney is getting a big bottom. . . . The Stones are thin. I mean, that's why they're beautiful, they're so thin. Mick Jagger—wait'll you see Mick.[10]

Pop society, then, created by the affluence of post World War II America—whose artifacts are derived from the lower and subcultural strata —whose leisure styles are shaped around these deliberately chosen and *unrespectable* totems.

---

[7]Tom Wolfe, *The Pump House Gang* (New York: Farrar, Straus and Giroux, 1968), pp. 169–70.
[8]Susan Sontag, "Notes On Camp," *Partisan Review* 31 (Fall 1964): 515–31.
[9]Gans, "Popular Culture in America," pp. 586–7.
[10]Tom Wolfe, *The Kandy-Kolored Tangerine-Flake Streamline Baby* (New York: Farrar, Straus, and Giroux, 1966), p. 173.

POP ART

In the late 1880's and early 1900's, America's new millionaire industrialists began looking to the arts as a forum within which to legitimize their social status. Dealers such as Joseph Duveen made millions selling cultural immortality to men such as John D. Rockefeller, Sr., and J. Pierpont Morgan, in the form of European Art.[11] After World War I, this practice continued. As Tom Wolfe notes, the New York Museum of Modern Art was not founded by intellectual revolutionaries. It was founded in John D. Rockefeller, Jr.'s living room, with the Goodyears, Blisses, and Crowinshields in attendance.

> They founded the museum in order to import to New York the cultural cachet of the European upper classes, who were suddenly excited over the Impressionists and post-Impressionist masters such as Cézanne, Picasso, and Braque. In either case, Old Masters or New, the route was through art that had been certified in Europe.[12]

By the 1950's the social world of certified art, even modern art, was controlled by the upper class. The artifacts of identity were, quite simply, nearly all owned by a select social grouping. In an essay on the reopening of New York's Museum of Modern Art (after the addition of a wing to the building), Tom Wolfe divides the people attending into the very important (that is, those who either gave big money or could attract big publicity) and the little ones (the "five thousand people, haunch to paunch, who merely gave a hundred dollars or a couple of thousand or something of the sort to the building fund.")—the striving *nouveau riche,* there to be enlightened by the "true illuminati."

> The wife of the President of the United States delivers the re-inaugural address. The Cabinet is there, the diplomats are there, (the) Ambassador to the United Nations is there. The clergy is there; some noted Chicago preacher is reading the text of an address by Paul Tillich, the theologian, who prepared a sacred discourse for the occasion. The new realm of man's holy spirit . . . Art . . . (had) become the center of social rectitude, comparable to the Episcopal Church in Short Hills.[13]

Then, in the late 1950's and the early 1960's, *pop art* "happened." By 1962 pop art had become a focus of social excitement in New York. A world of new cultural artifacts was suddenly opened. Those in the upper class, threatened by the increasing pressure the upper-middle class was putting on the world of museum society, began adopting the artifacts of pop art as their own. Rauschenberg, Johns, and Warhol became the darlings of pop society—the creators of their adopted and "shocking" new art form. The reaction from the upper-middle class press was predictable.

---

[11]Aline Saarinen, *The Proud Possessors* (New York: Random House, 1958), pp. 58–62.
[12]Wolfe, *The Pump House Gang,* p. 144.

The truth is, the art galleries are being invaded by the pin-headed and contemptible style of gum-chewers, bobby soxers, and worse, delinquents.[14]

Pop society has indeed found a series of artifacts they could safely utilize as totems of identification—artifacts that would seemingly never be adopted by the striving and respectable upper-middle class. This is, however, becoming less and less the case. As pop art becomes more acceptable as an art form, the *nouveau riche* become more attracted to it, causing pop society of the early 1970's to abandon the now respectable artifacts (such as Andy Warhol's early [1962] soup can, Coca-Cola bottle, and Marilyn Monroe series) for the newer and emerging creations of the op, modular and kinetic schools.

> The future of art seems no longer to lie with the creation of enduring masterworks but with defining alternative cultural strategies, through series of communicative gestures in multi-media forms. As art and nonart become interchangeable, and the masterwork may only be a reel of punched or magnetized tape, the artist defines art less through any intrinsic value of art object than by furnishing new conceptualities of life style and orientation. Generally, as the new cultural continuum underlines the expandability of the material artifact, life is defined as art—as the only contrastingly permanent and continuously unique experience.[15]

FILM

The introduction of network television in 1948 signalled the decline of film as a medium of American popular culture. Although the film industry is today attempting to woo the lower classes by means of multi-feature drive-in theater shows with low admission prices, and the middle class by means of films tailored for prime time television, they are having little luck in either direction. In 1969 the film industry sold an average of 21 million tickets a week; however, as Richard Schickel points out, this means that "all the movies on view in such a period attract(ed) an audience no greater than that of the weekly episode of a television show that is close to the peril point in the ratings."[16]

Film is increasingly becoming the medium of both the highly mobile upper-middle class and pop society. "They (films) are the playthings of The New Class, those who are custodians (or, perhaps, prisoners) of the technostructure."[17] The *nouveau riche* lean most especially toward foreign films.

---

[13]Tom Wolfe, *The Kandy-Kolored Tangerine-Flake Streamline Baby*, p. 226.
[14]Max Kozloff, "Pop Culture, Metaphysical Disgust, and the New Vulgarians," *Art International*, February 1962, quoted in John Russel and Suzi Gablik. *Pop Art Redefined* (New York: Praeger, 1969), p. 10.
[15]John McHale, "The Plastic Parthenon," *Dotzero Magazine*, Spring 1967.
[16]Richard Schickel, "The Movies Are Now High Art," *New York Times Magazine*, January 5, 1969.
[17]Ibid.

Just as the millionaire industrialists would not buy a painting unless the artist were European, and the emerging American high society of the 1930's and 1940's would not accept art unless it were certified in Europe, so the striving upper-middle class public place value almost solely upon European-made films.

> If the notion that the film is the central art of our time has any validity, it lies simply in the fact that (the *nouveau riche)* is the most significant socio-economic group of our time. They are the great consumers, not only of culture but of all the other doodads of affluence— notably such items as foreign food, foreign cars, and foreign travel.[18]

Pop society, on the other hand, consumes more of the American product—older "camp" American films (such as Humphrey Bogart movies) and, most especially, the works of American "underground" film makers.[19] Andy Warhol, having abandoned his earlier canvas-based art for the kinetic art of the film, emerged in the middle 1960's as an important figure in the world of the underground film. By so shifting his medium, Warhol remained as a significant creator of pop societal artifacts, leaving his earlier (and now respectable) artifacts behind for consumption by the *nouveau riche.*

MUSIC

In 1961, Chubby Checker recorded a Hank Ballard tune entitled "The Twist." In a year of mediocre music, the song (and more important, its attendant dance step) caught on in the youth culture. Soon its popularity began to spread to the "over–21" crowd. Journalists wrote satirical articles on the Twist and *The Peppermint Lounge,* just off Times Square in New York City, hired a group (Joey Dee and the Starliters) to play Twist music all night long. Pop society then took over. In the 1950's, modern jazz was the thing—Miles Davis, the Modern Jazz Quartet, even Thelonious Monk. But not rock and roll. As modern jazz became a "respectable" artifact of the rising upper-middle class, pop society discovered rock and roll in the form of the Twist.

> This is where it started, the hysterical adulation of pop singers by the rich. . . . It became hip to know Joey Dee, hipper to know (Chubby) Checker. Huge status to be publicly snubbed by Phil Spector. A bit later it was paradise to be entirely ignored by the Beatles. And by 1966, Mick Jagger was the most wanted guest in the world, the final face, the ultimate. For one pout of his red lips, any millionairess hostess going would have promised away her life.[20]

---

[18]Ibid.

[19]Some foreign films *are* viewed by Pop Society—even as they are shared with the *nouveau riche.* In these cases, the idea is to extract a certain content from the film —a content that differs radically from that absorbed by the upper-middle class viewer.

[20]Nik Cohn, *Rock From the Beginning* (New York: Stein and Day, 1969), p. 76.

Artifacts from the arenas of music and film have since been melded by Jean-Luc Godard, who cast Mick Jagger and the Rolling Stones in the revolutionary film-collage, *One Plus One.* Donald Cammell has also utilized Jagger in his brilliant *Performance.* Andy Warhol, in the late 1960's, moved in similar directions, putting together a multi-media show entitled *The Exploding Plastic Inevitable,* which featured the hard rock sound of The Velvet Underground, as well as Warhol's explorations in the media of film and light projection. Since then, the worlds of Warhol and the rock superstar have been further melded with Warhol's 1971 album cover for the Rolling Stones' *Sticky Fingers.*

With the waning of rock superstars evidenced in the early 1970's, the attention of pop society is turning more and more to the black "soul" performers. It is now super hip to have black performers (musical *and* political) attending one's party and snubbing one's guests. Elaborate performances, mixing rock with more "traditional" forms, are also gaining in importance. This is akin to introducing the works of daring young painters to the walls of the status museums of America; for the hoi polloi, *Jesus Christ, Superstar;* for pop society, Bernstein's *The Mass* (or at least its premiere performances in the newly opened John F. Kennedy Cultural Center in Washington, D.C.).

LANGUAGE AND COSTUME

Just as its media appropriations, pop society draws many of its artifacts of language and costume from the lower and subcultural strata. Deliberately nongenteel and "shocking," both men and women of pop society have delighted in utilizing words such as *fuck* as routine expletives. There are further usages of what Tom Wolfe describes as "more elaborate but quite common expressions (referring) to quaint anatomical impossibilities."[21] Expressions from the black ghetto subculture are also important as acquired artifacts of pop society, as is the black form of the "put on."

Costumes have their origins many times in other subcultures. The more risqué and daring the style, the more heavily it is applauded. Topless evening wear, "high camp" clothing, "super funk" (or "bad ass") black stylings, flowers and feathers, "hip" and "Afro" hair styles, beads, denim, and pearls are all examples of subculture artifacts that were, during the late 1960's, assimilated, produced, packaged, and sported as artifacts of pop society.

DRUGS AND DRINK

Marijuana has had a similar status in pop society as did alcohol in the cafe society of Prohibition times. It is a minor vice that carries with it the flavor of illegality—the scent of the underworld. One should, as a host or hostess, have marijuana on hand. In any case, one should never object to

---

[21]Wolfe. *The Pump House Gang,* p. 171.

one's guests using it. In the early days of pot and pop society (1963–64), users made a big point of claiming they did not drink—alcohol was labeled as dangerous, sloppy and not 'in." However, this attitude changed. By 1968, marijuana was being smoked just like any cigarette (and not with the furtive ceremony that accompanied its introduction as an artifact). Alcohol had again become acceptable (even as it remained "low" status) and could be sipped while smoking marijuana. Hashish, however, was taking the place of marijuana as the high status artifact of pop society. As the use of marijuana spread in society, it became less and less unique to be discovered smoking it. Hashish, with its higher potency and price and more exotic history, became the new drug of pop society.

Moving on from hashish, pop society had, by 1970, delved into European high society of the last century to resurrect cocaine as an artifact of their status group.[22] Again, the romanticism was there (along with even more of an underworld flavor). And the price was even more dear than that of hashish—just as the "hit" was stronger.

As with other adopted artifacts, the idea seems to be to consume those things that define one as a member of a certain status grouping. Because of their high price, illegality, and unacceptability to traditional "high" society, artifacts such as cocaine flourish in pop society. The *nouveau riche* do not dare to risk their future status by adopting these sorts of artifacts. Rather, they *overconform* by heavily adopting the conventional artifacts of high society (or ones as near to them in outward appearance as possible), becoming "junior" art patrons and avid foreign film watchers. The members of high society are too busy defending their own traditional status artifacts from the *nouveau riche* to threaten seriously the autonomy of pop society's new and changing culture.

MEDIA SOCIETY: A NOTE

The utilization of the media for definition has led some to label pop society as "media society," although they are not exactly the same thing.

> . . . how did you qualify? You . . . had to be a face. And what was a face? Roughly, it was when you walked into any snob restaurant anywhere and everyone sensed you come in behind them and automatically turned around. You were young, flash, international. *Vogue* said you were Now. Exactly, you were the beautiful people.[23]

The most important factor that establishes membership in media society is frequent exposure in all the media—from *Vogue* magazine to the television talk shows.

One can be a member of the traditional high society with no public exposure at all—and even the members of cafe society were allowed time

---

22Sir Arthur Conan Doyle's Sherlock Holmes (against the best advice of Dr. Watson) was an avid cocaine user.
23Cohn, *Rock from the Beginning,* p. 76.

away from the public eye for private vacations and creative activities. However, the media society has to keep a fairly steady exposure or risk total image diffusion.

Becoming a member of media society is nearly as difficult as remaining a member when one has "arrived." Many members of pop society are also members of media society—making it because of their economic status and the name they have made for themselves within their pop social circle. Tom Wolfe chronicles one mid-1960's example in Baby Jane Holzer, who lives in a 12-room apartment on Park Avenue in New York City and is an heiress to a real estate fortune.

> Jane Holzer in *Vogue*, Jane Holzer in *Life*, Jane Holzer in Andy Warhol's underground movies, Jane Holzer in the world of High Camp, Jane Holzer at the rock and roll, Jane Holzer is—well, how can one put it into words? Jane Holzer is This Year's Girl, at least, the New Celebrity, none of your old idea of sex pots, prima donnas, romantic tragediennes, she is the girl who knows . . . The (Rolling) Stones . . .[24]

On the other hand, Mick Jagger of the Rolling Stones can be classed as a member of media society (even though he should probably be thought of more as an *artifact* of Pop Society, than a member of it).

In a word, media society encompasses the "faces"—those whose images are projected as fresh and vital, who successfully tread the media tightrope between oversaturation and underexposure. Although members of pop society are well represented in media society, the two are not the same. "All the world's a stage," but most men and women are sitting in the audience. Members of media society refuse to be seated.

---

[24]Wolfe, *The Kandy-Kolored Tangerine-Flake Streamline Baby*, p. 172.

This book has, thus far, presented many methodological alternatives in the study of popular cultural artifacts of the established American social structure *(Thesis)*, ranging from the insightful (although impressionistic) literary discourse of the critic to the more quantitative sampling and obtrusive observation of the social scientist. The pieces were deliberately arranged with respect to their degree of methodological quantification—from the qualitative studies of Lohof and Wolfe, through more quantitative efforts of McCarthy, Peterson and Yancey and the researchers of the President's Commission on Obscenity and Pornography, to the qualitative methodologies of the Halas' and my own reportage of various studies of pop society.

Throughout this section, emphasis has been placed on critical examination of the studies presented, both in terms of their methodologies and their utility as indicators of cultural-structural links in American society. To this end, not only were supportive (and sometimes nonsupportive) researches pointed out in the running commentary, but further, many methodologically oriented questions were asked of the reader as he or she progressed through the section.

As we consider now *Antithesis*, the perspective is shifted somewhat. Because the focus is upon large subcultures antithetical to the established social structure (and its critics and social scientists), a good deal of the reportage involved is qualitative—outsiders looking in, insiders looking out. The editor assumes the reader is, by virtue of his or her exposure to the materials in *Thesis*, able to carry over and pose in *Antithesis* the relevant methodological questions.

A final note: In *Thesis*, prime concern was placed upon uncovering *established* value patterns and structural configurations of American society. *Antithesis* is concerned with *alternatives*. Therefore, the issues raised with respect to the study of subcultural artifacts and lifestyles are more in the realm of *competing* value patterns and structural configurations. What new forms might work? Why and why not? And, if established, how does one retain autonomy as an alternative grouping, considering the swift patterns of cultural diffusion within the contemporary American social system? (one example of which was presented in the study of pop society).

ANTITHESIS

BLACK CULTURE

The publication in 1939 of E. Franklin Frazier's *The Negro Family In the United States*[1] emphasized the commonly held belief that the American Negro had no cultural past, that the institution of slavery had indeed destroyed all vestiges of culture that were carried to this country from West Africa on the slave ships. Abram Kardiner and Lionel Ovesey, in 1951, wrote that the Negro "had no culture . . . he was quite green in his semiacculturated state . . . (he had) no pride, no group solidarity, no tradition."[2] And in 1964 Charles Silberman, in his *Crisis In Black and White* noted that "the Negro has been completely stripped of his past and severed from any culture save that of the United States."[3] Yet, as sociologist Charles Kiel has pointed out, these writers have overlooked what he terms

> that special domain of Negro culture wherein black men have proved and preserved their humanity. This domain or sphere of interest may be broadly defined as entertainment from the white or public point of view and as ritual, drama, or dialectical catharsis from the Negro or theoretical standpoint. . . . These entertainers are the ablest representatives of a long cultural tradition— what might be called the soul tradition—and they are all identity experts, so to speak, specialists in changing the joke and slipping the yoke.[4]

From the Harlem Globetrotters to Muhammid Ali to James Brown, one can note the distinctive Negro style of the creator—the transformation of the event into the dramatic ritual of popular culture.

Thus, there seems ample evidence of the existence of black popular culture, even though there has been little recognition of its exis-

---

1. E. Franklin Frazier, *The Negro Family in the United States* (Chicago: University of Chicago Press, 1939).
2. Abram Kardiner and Lionel Ovesey, *The Mark of Oppression* (New York: World Publishing Co., 1951), p. 384.
3. Charles Silberman, *Crisis In Black and White* (New York: Random House, 1964), p. 109.
4. Charles Keil, *Urban Blues* (Chicago: University of Chicago Press, 1966), p. 15.

tence nor study of it.[5] Diffusion of black culture into white has long been an overlooked fact of the American scene. In 1958 Melville Herskovits asserted there were substantial survivals of African culture among black Americans, with many Africanisms spilling over into white American culture.[6] Charles Keil estimates that 90 percent of the words that appear in the Sunday supplement slang glossaries can be traced to black culture.[7] Eldridge Cleaver, Leroi Jones, and others have noted the importance the diffusion of black musical artifacts has had in shaping white popular music.[8]

Diffusion has operated in the opposite direction as well. With the spread of television in the lower classes and the post–World War II emergence of the black community as a consumer public, images of white popular culture surrounded the black American as never before. S. I. Hayakawa has hypothesized that television may have had more to do with the stirrings of unrest in the black communities of the late 1960's than many would think.

> You discover that there is a caste system that the television set has told you nothing about—and that as a member of the wrong caste, most of the privileges of being an American, except for paying taxes and serving in the armed forces, are in whole or in part denied to you. ... What would *you* do?[9]

As the consumer power of the black community began to be felt in American business and as the civil rights movement gained momentum, blacks began to gain some exposure in the media, yet they were employed as *actors* and not as *creators*, reflecting white concepts of black life. Writer John Oliver Killens has remarked that not one television show in America gives an honest picture of black life in this nation. As he says, "TV was more truthful when there was no black exposure.[10]

The post–World War II emergence of the black as consumer has been sustained and strengthened. As Charles Keil states, many blacks offer a near-parody of the American lust for material possessions.

---

5. One reason for the lack of visibility of black culture is probably the fact that cultural artifacts have traditionally been appropriated by white artists and entrepreneurs, altered slightly to fit the values of the white audience, and presented to them (with no recognition given as to the origins of the artifact). This has been especially true in the field of popular music.
6. Melville J. Herskovits, *The Myth of the Negro Past* (Boston: Beacon Press, 1958).
7. Charles Keil, *Urban Blues*, p. 17.
8. Eldridge Cleaver, *Soul On Ice* (New York: Dell Publishing Co., 1968) and LeRoi Jones, *Blues People* (New York: Morrow, Williams & Co., 1963).
9. S. I. Hayakawa, "Television and the American Negro," Etc., 20, no. 4: 405.
10. John Oliver Killens, "Rappin' With Myself," in *Amistad 2*, ed. John A. Williams and Charles F. Harris (New York: Vintage Books, 1971), p. 110. See also Marquita Jones, "Racism In Television," *Black World*, March 1971, pp 72-78. The 1972 comedy series *Sanford and Son* may be a sign that things are changing, however slowly.

The American status-symbol quest becomes an obsession in the Negro community, where conspicuous consumption—the acquisition of the biggest cars and the flashiest clothes—sometimes takes precedence over adequate food and shelter. Like his fellow Americans, the Negro is addicted to TV, loves baseball, and to a certain extent he even loathes and fears the Negro.[11]

In the following article, corporation-executive-oriented *Media-Scope* magazine reports on advertising agencies and their reactions to the black American consumer. Of what impact is the media in creating needs and desires on the part of blacks for these white-produced artifacts of "popular" culture? And what might this have to do with the desire of black Americans to create their own cultural artifacts?

---

11. Keil, *Urban Blues*, pp. 11–12.

COURTING THE BLACK BILLIONAIRE

Media-Scope

On the screen, the speaker is a renowned black actor named Ossie Davis. In the audience are mostly white advertisers and agency executives, eager to learn more about "The Black Billionaire."

As the theater darkens for this eight-minute promotional film sponsored by Zebra Associates, Inc., a fully integrated new agency run by black principals, Davis advises his attentive viewers: "You know something? We wouldn't mind buying your products if we felt that your product made us feel special too—not separate . . . not different, but a real part of that dream, that seemingly empty American dream. But that's what we want to be able to feel part of. Don't talk to us separately, but talk to us so that we see ourselves and know that you also see us as a real part of that dream."

If Davis had the opportunity to talk directly with his audiences, he might be surprised by the results. Advertising directors in many industries and media experts in both general and black-oriented agencies unmistakably reflect a growing awareness of the Negro consumer and his estimated $30 billion in annual purchasing power. A majority of companies that have developed special marketing and advertising programs directed at the black consumer are more than willing to discuss their ethnic efforts, though few lines of universal accord can be determined on any of the main issues: How do you define the Negro market? How do you reach it most effectively? What are its future directions?

SOUNDS OF SILENCE

The sensitive subject evidently stirs guilt feelings among many of those contacted, who either refuse to comment or, more often, suddenly announce plans for prolonged business trips or vacations. In fact, some of the artful dodgers should be as inventive with their advertising as they are with their escape and evasion tactics. A few are candid enough to admit what a lot prefer to conceal: "We'd just as soon stay out of this because we'd look bad in comparison to what the beer boys are doing"; or "We'd like to do some ethnic advertising, but our budget is too small"; or "Frankly, our efforts are a token thing, so please don't mention us.". . .

NOT A HOMOGENEOUS MARKET

To be sure, the sentiment is spreading that we are not all talking about a homogeneous Negro market, and many lament the scarcity of more specific demographic breakdowns. An emerging school of thought, based on scattered and frequently impressionistic evaluations, recognizes the Negro as a heterogeneous community, with the same kinds of demographic differences as whites. This view is supported by one of the more extensive and refined compilations of Negro data, assembled by Miss Terry Pellegrino, assistant to the executive vice-president and media director of Young & Rubicam, Inc. In this encyclopedic study, which is periodically updated, the Negro is further delineated by such characteristics as age, sex, education, average remaining lifetime, geographical location and concentration, literacy, employment, hours worked, income level, financial expectations, psychological factors, product usage, and media habits. "We collect and interpret everything that's available on the subject," she says, "and our conclusions differ account by account.". . .

PRODUCT GOVERNS DECISION

. . . "We start by looking at the Negro as buyers and consumers like anybody else," explains Louis Fischer, senior vice-president/media director at Dancer-Fitzgerald-Sample, Inc. "Our advice to the client is to examine the entire market in relation to the product he's selling. This might involve separate efforts against the Negro, Spanish, Jewish, rich, old, young, etc., or it might not. We're not separatists. The product governs the decision.". . .

THE ROLE OF BLACK AGENCIES

In recent years new agencies have been springing up to serve the needs of articulating and reaching the black market. Simultaneously the established general agencies have been broadening their attempts to meet the same requirements. . . .

One of the largest advertisers to try the black agency route is P. Lorillard Co., makers of Kent and Newport cigarettes. Bob Carey, the firm's advertising manager, reveals why: "For several years we felt the Negro market was different and separate copy and media were needed at times. We had a white agency developing our copy for use in Negro media, but we found we weren't getting anywhere. Adaptation of our general market advertising just didn't come off in the Negro market. So we decided to seek someone more attuned to the Negro market, someone who knows the right way to go.". . .

TOWARD AN IDEAL MEDIA MIX

No matter if the agency is general or black oriented, the biggest challenge is to decide on the most effective media mix for zeroing in on the overall Negro market or any of its segments. The relevant questions are formidable: Should you use Negro media exclusively or combine them with prime media? Can nonethnic-oriented media do the job just as effectively as specialized broadcast and print outlets? If Negro media are employed, which are best for a given product or service? Do ads and commercials intended for the black consumer have to include Negro symbols, or can they be product oriented?. . .

A CANDID LOOK AT BLACK MEDIA

Of course, depending on the advertiser's goals, each medium has pros and cons. In contrast to many spokesmen, who are wary of giving offense, Howard Sanders[1] is notably outspoken on this subject.

Radio is the fastest medium for selling, he says, and if it's the Negro teenager you're after, he might recommend general radio instead of black stations, now that the prime stations have integrated their on-the-air personalities as well as their program formats. He'd get an argument from Dick Severance, director of advertising and promotion for the F & M Schaefer Brewing Co., who discovers a high incidence of Negroes tuning into general stations for newscasts and flicking back to their own stations for soul sounds.

As for newspapers, Sanders believes they don't necessarily sell products, but they do a very creditable job of merchandising the idea of a company's social involvement. This explains why his first campaign to dramatize the equal opportunity program of the R. J. Reynolds Tobacco Co. is running exclusively in over 80 Negro papers. . . .

Negro magazines and supplements such as *Ebony* and *Tuesday* are "fine for glamorous color advertising to justify a company's involvement in the black community." Moreover, they are read by every member of the household. This view is substantiated by many advertisers, large and small, who hint or state, "If you're trying to reach only the Negro market, these are the books to do it."

Sanders also makes use of subway station billboards in Negro neighborhoods, a technique that excels when black faces are clearly identifiable in the ad.

As for TV, Sanders doesn't think it should aim ads exclusively at the Negro because the cost per thousand would be too great. However, he applauds the trend toward increased use of black models in commercials. . . .

---

[1]President of Howard Sanders, Ltd., a Manhattan-based black agency (editor).

NEGRO SYMBOLS?

Another controversy surrounds the wisdom of using only product-oriented ads, or messages addressed directly to the Negro, in general or special media. . . .

Several years ago, Rheingold Breweries, Inc. turned up a catchy campaign with special appeals to diversified ethnic groups including the Negro. Though earning laurels for creativity, the TV commercials failed in their main purpose: to boost beer sales. One of the reasons cited is that the campaign was not run in ethnic media. In any event, the brewery has switched to a product- and taste-oriented campaign, extolling the "Ten-Minute Head." Appearing in prime and Negro media, the campaign has thus far been a gratifying success.

Schaefer Brewing Co. undertook research on the use of Negro symbols in advertising, and the lessons are instructive. No appreciable difference was evident in Negro response to print ads with and without black models, so most of the firm's print advertising is product-oriented. Radio is a different story, however. In the past, Schaefer would advertise on Negro radio without using the vernacular. "We committed the error of using Robert Merrill and others equally unsuitable on Negro stations," Severance confesses, "and it stuck out like a sore thumb." Then the company experimented with Negro disc jockeys relating the commercials in their own style and it proved a big hit. Currently all radio commercials feature young vocal groups discovered by Schaefer's annual talent hunt. Three of the ten groups selected are black, and their renditions of Schaefer commercials are played on soul as well as general stations. Some elements of Negro culture, like soul music and humor, seem to work anywhere.

The firm's TV commercials are especially conscious of Negro symbols "but, recognition has been a real problem with this," Severance discloses. Witness the skit with Millie Mosconi demonstrating his skill on the pool table, while observers are enjoying their favorite brew. Some of them are black, but except for one brief closeup you'd never know it in the semi-darkness of the background. Then there's the oft-seen "catcher" commercial, which shows a baseball catcher conning a batter into striking out. What problems this caused for Schaefer's and its agency! First of all, they had to decide which principal figure should be black: the catcher, batter, or umpire. If you picture a black catcher outwitting a Puerto Rican batter, you risk offending another minority. But if the distracted batter happens to be white, a large group of white beer drinkers might feel slighted. And what about the umpire, that traditional pillar of baseball authority? White or black? The outcome: a black catcher and umpire, plus two batters, white and non-white. As every baseball fan knows, some days you're better off staying in the dugout. "Do you know we got letters accusing us of tokenism?" Severance moans. "The ump wears a mask and one of the batters is on screen only briefly, so I must admit it looks that way."

It all adds up to the dictum of many companies and agencies that attempt integrated advertising: Negro models must be used in the most natural manner. In doing so, you are not so much meeting an obligation as reflecting the realities of American life. . . . Pepsi spotted the natural hairdo trend among blacks almost three years ago and came up with a powerful ad to depict it. Insisting that "our reading of the black community saw this thing coming," the special markets staff brushed aside objections within the company, and established a successful pattern that others have followed.

At TWA, realism in advertising is seen as a reflection of realism within the airline. "In a group scene, we never try to force either the role of the Negro or their number," explains Catlin. "We show Negroes as pilots, hostesses and baggage handlers because TWA employs them in all these capacities. Moreover, we try to use our own workers in our ads." A case in point is the "Jones" commercial, now playing on TV. The star of this spot is a black skycap who hustles his passenger through the line. "We wouldn't think of using a white model to play Jones because we won't go out of our way for unnatural situations," Catlin emphasizes. . . .

CHALLENGES FOR THE FUTURE

The ideal of assimilation is a hope of all reasonable men, but not even the most optimistic humanists look for the Negro market to vanish overnight. How this affects advertisers is thoughtfully expressed in a basic statement by the National Association of Market Developers: In a marketplace that can and often does become an arena where black consumers act on an individual, personal level, many Negroes are inclined, or can be persuaded, to favor the products or services of those manufacturers who are contributing most to the economic and social well-being of the Negro community. One can expect the black consumer to patronize those companies which show the same appreciation for his dollar as they do for other consumers. . . .

More and more white Americans are getting the message that Negroes are on the move, and the definition of special markets can only alter in the direction of more sincere involvement by all industries in the process of social change. Today, it's still an enlightened minority of advertisers, but tomorrow it may be a large consensus, who realize that by being relevant to blacks, they are also being relevant to America.

The importance placed on the conspicuous consumption of white-produced material goods has posed a psychic dilemma for the black American. Should he pursue these symbols of white America or should he create and consume artifacts of his own black popular culture? For the black artist, this dilemma is pushed one step further. Should he create artifacts of black culture for dissemination to the white world and accept white status symbols in return, or should he create solely for the black community, producing artifacts that will help the black in discovering, shaping and accepting his identity?

Curtis Mayfield and the Impressions,[12] a black popular musical group, has faced just this dilemma in its performances to both black and white youthful audiences. Too, what are the "symbols of success" the black entertainer should display? Fast (white) cars and sharp (white) clothes or soul stuff? Michael Alexander, on tour with the Impressions, depicts their life-style, their rationalizations and reasons for it.

---

12. Mayfield has, since this piece was written, left the Impressions and attempted to make it on his own as a solo artist.

THE IMPRESSIONS

Michael Alexander

The white kid dressed in revolution hip stood in the audience at Fillmore West, listening to the Impressions run through their remarkable string of hits: "Gypsy Woman," "People Get Ready," "Keep on Pushing," "We're a Winner," "This is My Country." They swung into "I'm So Proud," a likable love ballad with none of the social overtones of their more recent songs. . . .

As he finished, lead singer Curtis Mayfield stepped to his mike and said softly, "America, with all your hangups we're proud of you too."

The white Political Conscience turned suddenly away. "Black Capitalists," he said, and left.

The show was over. Out front the rentafuzz were helping out the last of the $3.50-per-head audience who were too stoned to navigate through the spilled soft drinks, cigarette butts and candy wrappers littering the Fillmore's basketball court. Backstage a black with Afro hairdo has cornered Mayfield to protest the lyrics of the Impressions' current hit, "Choice of Colors." . . .

"We *don't* have a choice of colors," said Afro. "We don't. We don't have a choice at all."

Mayfield listened quietly, trying to reason. "You aren't listening to the words." He repeated them, a tiny touch of annoyance in his voice. The lyrics were clear to him. . . .

. . . In this case one had the feeling that Afro's real, although unexpressed complaint was that the song wasn't very militant, that [it] did not come on strong against the power structure.

"You listen to that song again," Curtis said. "If you still don't understand it, we can talk about it again tomorrow night."

NO TIME TO WRITE

At eleven o'clock the following morning Mayfield, still in a robe, opened the door of his sixteenth-floor "garden" room facing the swimming pool of the San Francisco Hilton. He'd finished his breakfast steak and fruit cocktail.

A huge press party at Basin Street West and the opening at Fillmore West were behind him. There would be two more nights headlining the Fillmore, then four at Basin Street. . . .

Fred Cash and Sam Gooden dropped in. Sam is the handsome Impression, tall and trim with the high cheekbones of his Indian grandmother. Fred had a cold and was complaining mildly about the wet weather. He is nearly as tall as Sam, but everything about him is thicker—his features, his body (lots of soul food and barbecue there), even somehow, his movements and speech. The Impressions were going shopping. . . .

They went through the lobby of the Hilton, past a woman earnestly discussing her glands, and out to Mason Street where Benny the driver was waiting with the Blue Cadillac sedan. The four of them were enveloped in soft leather and eight-track stereo tape from speakers poking out of everywhere. They spent the trip discussing the Playboy Club where they went for dinner after the Basin Street press party. Bunnies bringing them the finest food, the manager personally welcoming them, everybody bustling around making sure everything was just right, and all just for the three of them, these South Side Chicago cats. They couldn't get over it.

Finding the right clothes proved troublesome. Their initial excitement at seeing what they liked gave way to frustration at getting fitted. Sam, the only one of average build, was buying matching black and brown leather vests, and shirts with puffy sleeves while Curt was entwined in a shower curtain doubling as a dressing room, trying on pants with little success. He is a compact five foot seven and solidly built but complained, "I can't get into anything. It's my ass, sticks out and throws everything out of whack." He finally found a pair with a buckle in back that allowed him to cinch the waist, picked out a couple of shirts; plopped a Napoleon hat on Marv the Manager as a gag, and paid with a hundred dollar bill. . . .

Fred Cash was in his room. If you need to find Fred when he's on the road, chances are very good that you will find him in his room. Fred likes hotel rooms, he likes motel rooms even better. "There's none of that fuss with lobbies and stuff." He lounged on the bed, feet up and arms folded, the TV, stuck too low in a dresser across the room, tuned to *The Dating Game.*

"I could stay in the hotel room all the time. I could stay in here for seven days. I wouldn't get lonely. Long as I've got the TV, got a little radio here, I'm happy. We eat most of our meals in the hotel, unless we know a good soul food place. I can send out for everything." Saying it, he called room service to send up a pack of Marlboros.

'GOODBYE,' AND HE HUNG UP

"I was in school in Chicago, when I joined the group. This came along and it was a chance to make money, and I was in school to learn to make money, so I said, why not? I was seventeen or eighteen at the time, about in there. When I left school I had about five months left. But I'm planning on going back and get the paper."

The phone rang. Fred mumbled some uhuhs, then suddenly said, "Baby, I'm not going to give you any *money*, understand? I'm sorry, but *no*. Goodbye." and hung up.

"It was this girl who tried to see me yesterday. I don't know how she knew I was here. She says her mother works here. She wants money! Says she has to visit her grandmother or something. I told her—I'm not going to give you money.

"We don't get hustled like that very often. I can count the girls like that on one hand. We don't hang around with that kind of people." He shook his head and changed the subject. . . .

"We played the the-a-ters up until about three years ago. It was hard, hard." (Remembering, his accent is even flatter than usual, as if he were back in his Chattanooga boyhood before he was an Impression.) "We'd get up at eight or nine in the morning and do four or five shows, man, and work to two AM. and then get up the next morning at eight or nine again and do it for seven days. It wears you *out*. The worst place was the Royal The-a-ter in Baltimore. You play the Royal they don't like you, you come onstage and they throw bottles, eggs, *everything*. At the Royal, they request a song, you stop your singing and do the request, man, or *else*. They finally closed it when somebody got killed.

"We lost our band about a year ago. The three of us had driven into Atlanta about two hours ahead of the group. It was night and they were going pretty fast, I guess. They were in a station wagon we used to use, towing a trailer with all our gear in it, and they were coming down a big double highway to a bridge. The bridge had this curve in it and it went over this river." Fred moved his hands like two planes banking. "They must have been doing 90 or a 100 miles an hour and," one of the hands suddenly shot straight ahead, "they just never got across that bridge. They just went through that rail and they went 210 feet in the air clear across the river and hit the bank on the other side. A farmer found them about eight o'clock the next morning. We had to go to the morgue to identify the bodies, and I didn't think I could go in. Then I got there and somehow I did. Lord, they was messed up, the guitar player had his arm all twisted and . . .

"The Lord must have been telling us something. We all used to have sports cars. In '63 Curt had a Jag and Sam and me had Corvettes and that Jag wasn't fast enough, we used to run away from it. So Curt got a 427 Cobra, and then we got 427 Corvettes. We used to run 150 miles an hour every day. We used to drive a lot, especially during the summer. Drive, drive, drive. None of us liked to fly, and we'd drive to concerts all over the Midwest and the South. After that accident we sold the Corvettes right then. We were going from Atlanta to Indianapolis and around Greenville, I think, somebody wrecked Curt's Cobra. I drive a Cadillac now.

"After we lost the band, it's hard trying to get a new one going. We've been trying for a year. This one looks like it may make it. It *limits* us. All we can do is our big hits. Our old band could do anything we wanted."

It was time to get ready for the show. We sent out for some of Leonard's good Fillmore Street barbecue and Fred called room service for a coke. He showered and shaved, singing along with an Impressions record on a battery-powered phonograph and with a cigarette, burned off the loose threads on his new shirt. "I can't *stand* loose threads," he said.

WE SPEAK OUR MINDS

Everyone was still sleepy. It was midmorning, and the performance at the Fillmore the night before had been wearing. The Impressions had a radio interview to tape at a local R&B station. They sat in the back seat of the gold Cadillac Eldorado, Curt's car, gawking at the city and all the pretty girls blossoming on the first sunny day in two weeks. Benny casually steered the car towards the Bay Bridge.

At the station they were welcomed and led into KDIAs somewhat untidy studio. The show they were to pre-tape was one of those Sunday night interview affairs.

The interviewer kept fishing for weak spots, and the Impressions suffered it all with quiet dignity. "You try to present yourselves as ordinary people, but you're not ordinary."

"Well," Curt replied, "we're just simple people. Just down to earth." The interviewer kept looking for big ego. It wasn't there. All those songs of social comment they're singing now—"This is My Country," "Choice of Colors"—weren't the Impressions trying to set themselves up as spokesmen?"

Curt answered, "I like to call these songs of inspiration, songs of faith. We don't try to be spokesmen, although we speak our minds. We're entertainers. We're complimented that they look on us as spokesmen, but we just think we're singing what all the brothers feel."

"The black performer isn't a shuffler anymore," said Sam.

"They're getting hip to themselves," added Fred. "James Brown wouldn't sing about pride three years ago."

They went through the Impressions' history: Fred and Sam's Chattanooga origins; all of them singing in South Side Chicago gospel choirs (Curt belonged to The Travelling Soul Spiritualists Church), the gathering of five high school kids into a group, naming themselves the Impressions because, honest to God, they wanted a name to live up to. And where were they going from here?

"Being ambitious fellows," Curt laughed, "we want to share in more of the profits."

HOW YOU DOIN', BROTHER?

. . . Motown's big group, the Four Tops, came by Basin Street West to see the show. The Tops were playing the Crown Room at the Fairmont

Hotel, playing to a white audience and making a lot of money. They're old friends of the Impressions, and Curt introduced them from the stage. After the show they came by the dressing room and a quiet, tired 2 AM scene simply exploded. Everybody was shaking hands, grabbing thumbs, "How you *doin'*, brother?" Laughing, telling latest stories, talking about the gigs they were doing, slapping hands after each good remark, slapping one hand, slapping *two* hands, hands slapping everywhere, and everybody talking so goddam blackass *flat*. (Later, Curt would confess that after a road trip, being around Sam and Fred and their Chattannoga accents, he would get home and catch hell from his three little kids for talking funny.) The Tops' lead singer asked about the audience at the Fillmore and the Impressions were all talking at once. "You wouldn't be-*lieve* that smoke when you walk out there it's like to knock you *over*." "There's cops standing right next to it and I think *they's* high, *too*." The Impressions were down *home*. . . .

IT'S JUST COMMON SENSE

Curtis Mayfield moves with the times. The songs today are not the songs of a few years ago. They are tougher, not necessarily more militant. "I believe that with all the problems, our biggest problem is ouselves. 'Choice of Colors' isn't for Whitey, its for us. We have to get together. If we united behind our leaders we'd be much stronger. Even Martin Luther King who had the biggest following and it was too small.

"There's 20 million of us and that's not enough. But that doesn't mean you just lay down all the time either. You should be pushing, even scaring sometimes." He doesn't support the Black Panthers as a scare group because "they aren't a national organization; they don't have the muscle. . . .

There have been conflicts with the message songs. WLS in Chicago, a white pop station which controls 14 percent of the national market, was among many that refused to play "We're a Winner." There have been other cases of station censorship. You sense it frustrates him more than it hurts. Decisions like that keep the Impressions from the security of knowing they'll never fall back in the ghetto. But they do the songs.

"We thought of not doing them. 'Choice of Colors'; 'Mighty, Mighty (Spade and Whitey)—but sometimes they're just right. They sound right. You *have* to do them."

MAN, WE'RE BLACK . . .

. . .[Curtis] had been writing songs again, suddenly withdrawing into his room, taking his guitar out and trying a new line in his head. But it was coming in spurts and that annoyed him. He enjoys composing, but he also feels the pressure. One of the Impressions' strong points is that they do original material, and all of it comes from Curtis. . . .

"I want to write stories, too. But I can't get it down the way I want to. Once for a week I had dreams every night that were complete stories. They were like movies—I could see the things.

"Did you see *2001?* I like movies like that. They didn't explain every-thing and it lets you wonder what it was about.

"My education didn't give me any background, not even any back*bone,* as a black. It just didn't mean anything. My whole education for whatever I do know was brought to me right here on the road. I left school at 15. Actually, I was singing with the Impressions when I was 13. We got a break at 14 and I was singing at the Apollo The-a-ter at 15, my birthday was the first or second day we arrived at the place.

"At one time I thought of going back to school, probably to take busi-ness. . . . Well, I don't know . . . I still don't like doing the business end of this and I try to leave it for others."

It's tough enough just traveling and performing. The road wears a man down after 12 years. "I'm tired. I'm tired. But this life, and you know we're nowhere near the peak of it—entertainment is such a gas you be-come addicted to it. And despite of its hangups, if you're anywhere near successful it becomes a part of you. That's the way I am, I can't help it. There's nothing else I want to do. There's nothing else I could do any-way, but if I could do something else I wouldn't want to do it because this life, if you live it in such manners, can be beautiful for you.

"Being an entertainer, even though it's beautiful and it's nice in the public's eye and to have people gawking at you, it has its hangups. We don't have as much privacy as we would like. I resent it, but I find my re-sentment's in vain simply because I brought it to be. I wanted to be suc-cessful, I wanted the money, I like doing what I'm doing. I wanted to be just what I am. Now I've got to give up some of those other things. . . .

Was his family poor?

"Were we poor? Man, we're *black.* Of course we were poor!

"I imagine we've done what most guys would want to do. We're all married. We have families. I have three children. Which means responsi-bilities, securities, college for the children and a place to try and finally lay out for them. As well as our own selfish pleasures, y'know, sports cars and big time, but no more than anybody else. Now that I have money I spend it less than I used to, but we still blow it, still get hung up with little material things and what have you."

"Choice of Colors," the latest entry in the Impressions' search for a hit, was number seventeen on the Cashbox list and had a bullet before it. It was rising fast.

He is writing the songs of the coming black middle class. The songs of aspirations. A good home, a nice car, decent neighbors, money, educated kids, travel, security. You can't knock it until you've had the opportunity to reject it, which is what the White Political Conscience at the Fillmore didn't understand.

Curtis Mayfield is 26 years old.

For the lower class ghetto black, the dilemma of whether to pursue or create artifacts of white or black popular culture is not so intense—the culture of the ghetto is mainly shaped by those who live within it. Just as religion, radio, and entertainment are culturally important in the lives of the working and lower class white, so black versions of these artifacts are important in the black ghetto. Ulf Hannerz has remarked, with relation to these artifacts, that, "while (they) have no authority over the community as such, they engage in symbolic action aimed at the entire ghetto, and in this sense they come as close to overarching institutions as anything in the community.[13]

Religion, radio and entertainment in the ghetto are primarily concerned with music. In black popular culture, music seems to be not only the major ingredient of the "shared perspective," but also the primary vehicle for its communication. Ghetto preachers work with collections of motifs which they expect to be familiar to the members of their congregations—these many times take the forms of lyrics to the popular songs of black artists or the lyrics of the gospel hymns.

The more secular components of the ghetto cultural apparatus work in a similar way. The black radio stations have hit music—nearly all soul and rhythm and blues—on their programs more or less around the clock. As the black playright Imamu Amiri Baraka (LeRoi Jones) has pointed out:

> A lot of the music on the soul stations the people feel is necessary to themselves. They feel that they could not really conduct their lives correctly without it.[14]

The black disc jockies, leading personalities in the community, have developed their own "raps" concerning black ghetto life. They express their enjoyment of music in cries, shouts and comments interjected into it; addressing themselves to the subjects of women, soul food, hustling and other aspects of ghetto life.[15]

In turning to the world of black music and entertainment, one has to deal very early with the man LeRoi Jones has called America's number one poet—James Brown. James Brown is, as Mel Watkins has recognized, the embodiment of the black life style. His significance lies in his fidelity to that life style and his deft evocation of its nuances and subtleties."[16]

---

13. Ulf Hannerz, *Soulside* (New York: Columbia University Press, 1969), p. 150. Hustling and playing the numbers might well be added to Hannerz's religion, radio and entertainment as overarching institutions of the ghetto.
14. Quoted in Mike Coleman, "What Is Black Theatre?" *Black World,* April 1971, p. 33.
15. This same type of frantic patter was adopted by the early white rock and roll disc jockies; Murry the K being perhaps the best known example.
16. Mel Watkins, "The Lyrics of James Brown," in *Amistad 2,* ed. John A. Williams and Charles F. Harris (New York: Vintage Books, 1971), p. 22.

It can be pretty scary up where I am. I mean like every-body's watching. Know what I mean? The whole world. Black and white. I'm carrying the whole thing. Right now, in what I'm doin, I'm doin' more for the Negro cause than *any* of them *other* cats. I'm talkin' about *Soul*. Forgettin' that other stuff. That's silly. I'm talkin' about bein' *alive*, man. About *feelin'*. (James Brown)[17]

The majority of James Brown's audience could be described as the "grass roots" segment of the black community—those who react to and reject white America, both in terms of life style and point of view. Charles Keil has posited that the predominant modes of expression of black culture are auditory and tactile, not visual and literate as are those of white America.

The prominence of aural perception, oral expression, and kinetic codes or body movement in Negro life—its sound and feel—sharply demarcate the culture from the . . . white world outside the ghetto.[18]

In the world of James Brown, you have to feel, not think it.

The black alternative to the meaninglessness of the bureaucratic, abstract world of white America has taken the form of an intense concern for the personal, the immediate, the emotive. One's status is not assessed in terms of socially defined positions, rather it is *situation*-oriented and dependent upon the outcome of each personal confrontation and interaction.[19] This aspect of black status is best seen in the phenomenon known as "rapping"—a form of verbal behavior that is "gut-deep, salvation-oriented, ego-meshed, and ultimately directed toward the one-on-one confrontation of individuals—of either competition or sex or both."[20] This quality of rapping is what seems to engage James Brown's audience—his status in this area (as evidenced in his song lyrics) is unquestioned.[21]

The characteristic of transforming actions to drama—the theatrical aspect of black life—can be seen in James Brown's stage performances. His entrance is always accompanied with grand orchestral fanfare and marked with a great deal of posturing in his costly tailored suits. As his act progresses, the impeccable clothes become meaningless as he sweats, strains, and even gets down on the stage floor while evoking the last ounce of emotion from his songs.

---

17. Doon Arbus, "James Brown Is Out Of Sight," in *The Age of Rock,* ed. Jonathan Eisen (New York: Random House, 1969), p. 290.
18. Keil, *Urban Blues,* p. 17.
19. Watkins, "The Lyrics of James Brown," p. 31.
20. Ibid., p. 36.
21. Muhammid Ali, in his earlier days of boxing fame, was especially well known and respected in the black community for his "rap." One could also think of the performance of the Harlem Globetrotters as a vocal *and physical* rap.

> His shoulders heave and he flops to his knees, dragging the microphone with him. . . . The crowd is hysterical, shattering the stillness. . . . The five girls high up on their platform are jerking in mourning. Isolated screams from the audience (erupt) out of its momentary silence. . . . He is in an ecstasy of agony. Or tears. Or both. Screaming out his misery in that coarse voice which rakes relentlessly over the vowels. . . .[22]

As the show reaches its close, members of his band take the microphone from him, drop a luxurious robe about his shoulders and begin leading him from the stage. But James Brown refuses, tossing off the robe and resuming the song. This is repeated several times, each time with a more ornate robe and more dramatics until Brown stands by himself, unfastens his jeweled cuff links, flings them into the audience and with no help, strides to the stage wings. Brown's act is a put-on, a parody of posturing, a symbolic "act" in affirmation and acceptance of the absurdity of the American system. This, as Mel Watkins states, is the adhesive which binds James Brown "to blackness and to his audience."[23] As he has entitled one of his most popular songs, "Say It Loud—I'm Black and I'm Proud."

The value of the immediate in black ghetto life is reflected in that part of the life style known as "begging."[24] Mel Watkins points out how clearly this reveals the distance the black community is from the "abstract conceptual ideals" of white America. Begging is an act without consequence in terms of personal evaluation. If it works, it is accepted. This value is clearly reflected in many of James Brown's songs.[25]

Traditionally men and women in black America have considered themselves to be separate from and antagonistic to each other.[26] Men are stereotypically seen to be primarily interested in sexual satisfaction and independence—they are strong sexually[27] and are thought to take favors from anyone who will grant them.[28] Women, on the other hand, have been said to be primarily interested in emotional support and in maintaining their families.[29] The black woman has traditionally been seen by the black male as a symbol of his impotence. The connections the female has had with the white world and her usurpation of

---

22. Arbus, "James Brown is Out of Sight," p. 294.
23. Watkins, "The Lyrics of James Brown," p. 27.
24. Ibid., p. 35.
25. Examples being "Please, Please, Please," "If You Leave Me," and "You've Got the Power."
26. Roger D. Abraham, *Positively Black* (Englewood Cliffs, N. J.: Prentice-Hall, 1971).
27. Eldridge Cleaver has pointed out the black male's acceptance of sex as an outlet for his social emasculation by white America. Cleaver, *Soul on Ice.*
28. Keil, *Urban Blues,* p. 9.
29. Ibid.

many facets of the male role (with respect to the family structure) has resulted in her many times being typed by the male as self-righteous, money-grabbing, treacherous and domineering. This symbolism of resentment and scapegoating is breaking down in the black community as the stance of the black male toward the larger society becomes more militant. The songs of James Brown have chronicled this shift in attitude, from "Prisoner of Love," and "Money Won't Change You," to "It's A New Day," and "Say It Loud—I'm Black and I'm Proud."

As James Turner has remarked, most sociological studies of the black community have failed to come to grips with the *subjective* meaning of the emerging black consciousness—they have been content merely to describe the fledgling black organizational structures and their members.[30] Pop cultural analysis of the music of the black American and its reflection of his new group consciousness, the changing role relationships between males and females, the self-assertion of the black male and the black concern with cultural identity may be important steps in this neglected area.

Just as white culture has appropriated aspects of black culture (notably the blues song), so the new self-assertion of the black creator has led to his appropriation of certain aspects of white popular culture in an attempt to shape black artifacts of revolution. Black studies scholar Charles Peavy chronicles one such appropriation.

Is the following a description of a revolutionary artifact of black popular culture or only a fantasy based on a mirror image of the white man's superiority as described in the white media from which the symbols were borrowed? *Can* a revolutionary minority borrow cultural symbols from the dominant society from which it is rebelling?

---

30. James Turner, Editorial, *Black World,* January 1971, p. 8.

POP ART AND THE BLACK REVOLUTION:

Charles D. Peavy

Dr. J. Denis Jackson, a Negro physician and cultural psychiatrist[1] in Atlanta, Georgia, is the author of an extraordinary novel entitled *The Black Commandos*.[2] The book, written under the pseudonym Julian Moreau,[3] is undistinguished as literary art, for its is seriously marred by stylistic crudities and numerous errors in punctuation and spelling, doubtlessly the result of uncorrected printer's errors. To concentrate myopically on these technical imperfections, however, is to miss the significance of *The Black Commandos*, a book which is at once a revolutionary treatise,[4] an autobiographical fantasy, and a science fiction novel—all couched in the images and idiom of pop culture. There have been, of course, many efforts on the part of black revolutionary artists to utilize various media as agents or propaganda, for example, the dance, painting, theatre, and literature.[5] *The Black Commandos,* however, represents the first attempt to incorporate the standard devices of pop culture manifested in comic books, television, science fiction, and spy-thrillers as a vehicle for black consciousness.

For instance, the stereotypic pop culture hero is immediately perceivable in the protagonist of the book, Dr. Denis Jackson, a fantasied projection of the author. Jackson is described as extremely handsome, fabulously wealthy, immensely strong, and extraordinarily intelligent, possessing as he does "a half-dozen degrees—a B. A., M. A. LL. B, M. D., Ph. D, as well as a B. S. in Engineering." In addition, he has "mastered over two dozen languages" and holds patents on half a dozen discoveries and inventions" (note how his accomplishments are always measured by the dozen and half dozen). In short, the hero of the book represents a Negro Superman (in both the Nietzschean and the comic book senses of the word), and the extensive use of pop culture symbols and situations in the action of the novel indicates how fully the contemporary mass media

---

[1]Jackson refers to himself as a cultural psychiatrist (he is listed as both physician and cultural psychiatrist in the yellow pages of the Atlanta telephone directory). He is currently developing his own theories of psychology, which include the concept that Freud is irrelevant to the needs of the masses of people, particularly black people. Middle class, Austrian referents, feels Jackson, are not applicable to the millions of black Americans.

[2]Julian Moreau, *The Black Commandos* (Atlanta: The Cultural Institute Press, 1967).

[3]Paradoxically, Jackson uses a pseudonym in writing the novel, then gives his real name to the hero of the book. Jackson claims direct descent from African Moors who conquered Spain and Southern France (his maternal great grandfather, a "Frenchman of color," was named Julian Moreau).

[4]There are long digressions in the novel which examine the sociological and psychological implications of white racism in America.

[5]See, for example, my "The Black Art of Propaganda: The Cultural Arm of the Black Power Movement" in *The Rocky Mountain Social Science Journal* 7, no. 1 (April 1970). This article is reproduced in this volume, pp. 208–214.

has captured the author's imagination. The novel also illustrates the author's rebellion against a white racist society (the book, says Jackson, was written in anger). What *The Black Commandos* does, in effect, is to create a black Clark Kent-Bruce Wayne, a Negro Superman-Batman folk hero who battles the forces of evil (white racism and bigotry) oppressing his people.

The first two sections of the book describe the events that shaped the hero's personality when he was a child: the brutal slaying of his young playmate by a rural southern sheriff and the killing of his father by two white policemen. The child witnessed both of these murders, and as a result vowed to dedicate his life to avenge his friend, his father, and his race.

In the third section, entitled "Big Bad John," the child has matured into the mysterious multimillionaire, Dr. Denis Jackson. The doctor is searching for people with violent tempers and excessive brutality, for murderers, and for psychopaths to be used by him in the implementation of his plan—a plan "as horrible as it was necessary" (p. 22). Jackson is recruiting candidates for his secret organization, the NSPNPA (National Secret Police of the Negro People of America) later to be known as the "Black Commandos." His search for a "killer breed" is restricted to Negro males who have been desensitized by prolonged periods of racial injustices, enforced poverty, and ignorance. In this section he succeeds in "recruiting" Big John, a psychopathic killer who looks like the "reincarnation of John Henry" and who combines the size and strength of that folk hero with the ferocity and sadism of the title character in the popular ballad of a decade ago—"Big Bad John."

At this point in the text Jackson (the author-psychiatrist) digresses in a long commentary on the recruiting procedures of his persona and name sake, Dr. Denis Jackson. He examines the old cliché that contends that the white man kills strangers while the black man kills his friends and relatives, noting that there is some truth in this idea if one is speaking of "tendencies and not totalities." The Negro's world is small and circumscribed, and his cultural limitations prevent him from including a diversity of social or cultural types within his circle of acquaintances, which is made up almost exclusively of his friends and relatives. Often ignorant, the ghetto male is also an accumulation of hurts, sufferings, and frustrations. He is filled with resentment and often a diffuse, helpless hatred, but he is prevented by ignorance, history, negative tradition and a profound sense of racial inferiority from striking out against his true enemies—racial bigots. When the Negro's frustration becomes unbearable he often explodes in violence against his brother simply because the real enemy is not around.

> An argument over an owed quarter may erupt with one or the other consciously striving to verbally reduce his victim to a level lower than human excreta. Somewhere in the process, usually aided by alcohol, the poor unfortunate across the table becomes a sym-

bol. A symbol of all the hurt, the suffering he has undergone. Now! Now! He must smash it! Destroy it! when it is over and his malignant passion is spent he may find that he is one brother less. No man ever really kills his brother over a quarter! (p. 26)

It is the intention of the book's hero to channel this rage, and to direct it at its proper target—"to kill for a higher purpose." The recruits for Jackson's Black Commandos are taken to a secret island headquarters where they are "conditioned" to absolute loyalty in a special Indoctrination Unit containing electronic hypnotic devices. The commandos are kept in excellent physical condition by daily training in a large, hangar-like gymnasium, where they receive instruction in body building, Judo, and Karate. The psychological and physical conditioning received by the men on this island prepare them to be Black Commandos, a group formed to combat the Ku Klux Klan and "other bigots who would resort to violence and terror against the Negro people" (pp. 72–3).

The island headquarters complex also includes a Scientific Unit where the secret weapons of the Black Commandos are developed. These include huge flying saucers powered by "negative cosmic magnetism," thermonuclear devices detonated by a remotely controlled ruby laser apparatus, and a highly sophisticated nerve gas (the "Pink Mist") which may be used to render unconscious or kill the enemy with predictable results. The description of the island's futuristic laboratories (which come equipped with the inevitable mad-genius scientist) attests to the author's familiarity with the science fiction tradition. The subtle blend of science fiction with the basic revolutionary thesis that permeates the book should not, however, be overlooked. For instance, in a description of one of the flying saucers, Jackson writes:

> The Black Saucer—the amazing giant flying saucer, flew at the speed of light and made no sound above a slight stirring of breeze. Its power source and flying dynamics were both secretly discovered by Denis Jackson and they were a thousand years ahead of anything the present world was aware of! Jackson (not like another Negro Genius, George Washington Carver) did not feel disposed to give his technological advances to a white society which would be so ungrateful as to use his "gifts" to further subjugate his people. He chose to use his discoveries in his fight for Human Rights! (pp. 162–63)

The descriptions of the commandos' raids on the American mainland are even more characteristic of typical pop culture narrative than the use of "fantastic" science fiction elements, although here again the revolutionary thesis is at least subliminally omnipresent. For instance, the assassination of the governor of Alabama shows kinship with the humor of Al Capp (Governor Malice is an obvious parody of the real Governor Wallace) as well as the characters and situations of widely known comic book and television series. The elaborate planning that goes into the crashing of the gates at the State Capitol and the liquidation of the Capitol guards by a detachment of Black Commandos is reminiscent of the skilled teamwork displayed in CBS-TV's "Mission Impossible" (a Black Commando raiding party is divided into "triarms" or groups of three—"one creative thinker, one muscle man, and a coordinator." The coordinator leads the trio and gives the orders.) The actual assassination of Malice, however, is accomplished by Denis Jackson and Al Ghandi, the "dynamic duo" of the Black Commandos. The term "dynamic duo," from the tongue-in-cheek alliterative dialogue of the popular TV series "Batman," has become a familiar phrase to millions of television viewers. Jackson and Gandhi, the "fearless fighters" for the freedom of black people, are described as "the dynamic duo" twice in the novel (p. 86 and p. 186).

Jackson decides that the assassination of the governor must be done in the manner of the old Tong hatchet men, another group which has captured the imagination of generations of movie serial fans and comic book readers. As Jackson explains before the assassination, the "Tong murder" will be symbolic:

> . . . I think the lesson of the hatchet man is a good thing to learn and to apply at appropriate times in human history. The hatchet man . . . remained true to his high purpose so long as he felt needed and faded apparently into oblivion thereafter. I intend that the Commandos do likewise—to be resurrected if and when they are needed again. (p. 81)

There are, of course, other reasons for using this method of extermination, for it made the operation look like the work of "agents of a foreign government sent in to create chaos in America" (cf. Ian Fleming's James Bond mysteries and the TV series. "The Man from U.N.C.L.E.") "The hatchet in Governor Malice's skull caused most of the suspicions to fall on Red China. This is exactly what Jackson had planned and white America was reacting exactly as he knew it would" (p. 89).

The final execution at the State Capitol is described as occurring in the improbable, hyperbolic fashion common to comic book illustrators:

> The hatchet literally whistled past Jackson and the State Trooper to catch Governor Malice smack between the eyes and continued on its way through more than half the governor's skull. The body of Governor Malice was thrown backwards with tremendous force—knocking over a chair and crashing against a desk twelve feet away . . . before coming to rest on the floor in a grotesque spread eagle position of death! At the moment Al's hatchet had done its work, Jackson had shot the remaining guards between their eyes. (p. 86)

It might be added that it is not uncommon that the commandos' victims are shot "between the eyes"—this seems to be a characteristic of their marksmanship (and again, of comic book illustrators).

There are other characteristics of the commandos that have their sources and analogues in the comic book clichés and the mannered speech of radio and TV serials. For instance, it is the custom of Jackson, the leader of the commandos, to shout "O.K. Commandos, let's go!" before speeding away from the scene of their latest attack. This exclamation becomes so characteristic of Jackson that by page 166 of the novel the author notes "The leader of the Commandos uttered his now familiar cry." Older readers of this passage will recall the traditional cry of "Heigh ho, Silver! Away!" of the radio serial "The Lone Ranger." The same generation of readers will recall that Superman was "faster than a speeding bullet" when they read that Denis Jackson "streaked across an intersection like a bolt of zig zag lightning. Several police fired at the blurr [sic] but were totally frustrated in trying to get this incredible human form into focus!" or "Jackson came to a halt and tossed a grenade. . . . The explosion which followed occurred in three seconds, but Jackson was already more than a hundred yards away!" (p. 203). Again, images of Superman or Captain Marvel are conjured up in the description of Jackson's rescue of Oliver Williams:

> Jackson saw Oliver fall and streaked toward his fallen comrade like a meteor—as usual a dazzling display of speed and power—sweeping back a half dozen guardsmen with one mighty swing of his left arm, he scooped Oliver up with his powerful right arm and sprang over a heap of dead bodies so lightly it was easily apparent that Oliver's weight (190 lbs) did not slow him up in the least. (p. 212)

Sophisticated white readers might find the aspects of the novel described above quite amusing, but it should be remembered that at the time *The Black Commandos* was written the author was in dead earnest. I can personally attest to the impact the novel had upon militant black students on the campus of the University of Houston, who did not find the book at all "funny." If *The Black Commandos* is viewed against the proper psychological and sociological referents, an understanding of the students' attitudes should not be difficult.

As one might expect, there is a great amount of violence—even sadism in *The Black Commandos*. Again, this could be a trait shared with such "popular" books as Mickey Spillane's Mike Hammer series, or some of the more sadistic tortures devised by Ian Fleming in his James Bond books. It is reasonable to assume, however, that there is more behind the cruel execution of the white racist, Judge Green, than a stereotype:

> When the Judge regained consciousness, Al had inserted a large needle in his radial vein. The needle was attached to the bottom half of a twenty cc syringe. Attached to the back of the syringe was a piece of rubber tubing leading to a small air pump. The pump had its own motor, and it was pumping vigorously—flooding the Judge's system with air, creating a giant air embolus! (p. 177)

If violence and sadism— elements so common in the contemporary popular novel—abound in *The Black Commandos*, another element, sex, is notably absent. Though the protagonist often observes prostitutes plying their trade, and though he himself is very attractive to women, he never indulges in sex or romance, but remains the celibate messiah bent upon the salvation of his people with an almost monomaniacal singleness of purpose. Indeed, the god-like qualities of the hero are hinted at more than once in the novel. But the hero is an Old Testament God, a god of vengeance. For example, see the chapter entitled "An Eye for an Eye and Something More!" (pp. 95–105) and Jackson's pronouncement of doom on the Klansmen, "All members of the Klan are arbitrarily held to be guilty of the crimes of that group and therefore all are sentenced by me here and now to be executed for their common guilt." (p. 74) Jackson's Black Commandos are described at one point as black angels of death. They bring retributive justice to the undesirable elements in American society (the Ku Klux Klan, the Mafia, racist governors, redneck bigots), purging America in a series of little Armageddons (the Battle of Los Angeles, the Battle of Jackson and the Siege of Mississippi).

That the Black Commandos are agents of retributive justice is indicated in their emblem: ". . . a black fist enclosed by a steel gray triangle and struck across by a bolt of golden lightning. The fist represents power—violent and final; the lightning indicates striking fast and with the elusive power of a thunderbolt; and finally the steel gray triangle represents strong defense by the organization of itself and the Negro people." Underneath this emblem appears the motto of the Black Commandos, "Those Who Won't Do Right for Love of God, *Must* Do Right for Fear of Him!" (p. 83)

In an interview in Atlanta, Jackson told me that he had difficulty in getting *The Black Commandos* published because most whites considered the book destructive, indeed—considered him destructive. Jackson, however, contends that he is a liberal humanist but that in the area of human dignity he believes in revolutionary, rather than evolutionary, change. "I am not interested in destroying the white people," he said, "but in saving them. White people need to see that the sickness of racial prejudice which motivates them against the Negro is ultimately self-destructive and will only lead to disaster." Jackson feels that there are but three possibilities left to the whites: genocide, the removal of the motivation for the emergence of the Black Commandos, or an ultimate confrontation with such a force as the Black Commandos.

Jackson admits that *The Black Commandos* was written in anger, that it was in part intended as a kind of catharsis for him, and that his views have been somewhat modified since the book's publication. Nevertheless the book continues to exercise a powerful attraction for young black people who have managed to obtain a copy. This popularity can be explained in part by the book's extensive use of the materials of pop culture. In his "The Last Days of the American Empire (Including Some Instructions For Black People)"[6] black revolutionary LeRoi Jones inveighs against white American

---

[6]LeRoi Jones, *Home: Social Essays* (New York, 1966), pp. 189–209.

pop culture icons. Jones contends that many of these "heroes" are manifestations of the oppressive and racist elements in white society.

> Do you think that the television series "Burke's Law," where the
> hero is a white millionaire who is also chief of police, is *accidental?*
> This is the way these folks think, and what they legitimately aspire to.
> Ditto, in the case of James Bond, the suave, unbeatable fascist. All
> these things merely prepare the Americans psyche for his role in
> world domination. (p. 198)

The Black Commandos offers a cultural hero to whom black readers can
easily relate; indeed they may assimilate such a figure into their own dreams
and fantasies in a manner that would have been impossible with the white
Anglo-Saxon or Teutonic superheroes of American popular film and fiction.

The same sort of phenomenon that Peavy examines in *The Black
Commandos* is present in film as well. Critic Robert Christgau has
noted that the "unannounced" Jim Brown film festival that has been
going on in 42nd street movies houses in New York City for years has
recently been replaced with black produced films, such as Melvin Van
Peebles *Sweet Sweetback's Baadasssss Song.*

> Ever since black power began, whites accustomed to taking
> sustenance from black culture have been foundering. At first,
> most of us were outraged at being read out of a vital synthesis in
> which we had invested emotion and often time and effort. In what
> may be the decade's most original contribution to political con-
> sciousness we came to regret our own arrogance—that is, we
> came to understand that the oppressed have an unduplicatable
> vantage on their own oppression . . . Now we are in phase three, in
> which we relate to black culture only sporadically if at all . . . I
> suspect contemporary black culture often appears awkward to us
> because it is in the process of understanding itself. We relate to
> blues because its few pretensions are natural, but the pretensions
> of Funkadelic are not. No doubt, a lot of the art coming down
> from black people right now will some day be perceived by every-
> one as pure jive . . . (But remember), the oppressed have an un-
> duplicatable vantage on their own oppression . . . The obviousness
> of *Sweetback's* symbolism might be related to the ghetto process
> of signifying. The white police commissioner can be understood
> as an obverse Stepin Fetchit, a caricature of establishment power
> every bit as cruel and inaccurate—and telling—as the caricatures
> of black subservience which have such an endless history in
> American culture. When we think about the film's sexism we
> should remember that alienation from his own sexuality is the

substance of Sweetback's oppression as the movie begins; then, too, we might just compare it to *Goldfinger* . . .[31]

In the following article, Charles Peavy goes on to contend that the strongest dissemination of black cultural nationalism (as distinct from Super-Spade funkadelic) has been through the presentation of black drama in black communities; particularly in the semiliterate communities of the ghetto.

---

31. Robert Christgau, "Soul On Screen," *Fusion,* 65, October 29, 1971, p. 47.

THE BLACK ART OF PROPAGANDA: THE CULTURAL ARM OF THE BLACK POWER MOVEMENT

Charles D. Peavy

"We must make warriors out of our poets and writers. For if all our writers would speak as warriors our battle would be half won. Literature conditions the mind, and the battle for the mind is the first half of the struggle."[1] This statement by Black nationalist Maulana Ron Karenga epitomizes the sentiment shared by most of the artists in the Black Arts movement, which has become a vital part of the Black Power movement in America. The nationalists and the Black Power advocates differ from the assimilationist- or integrationist-oriented civil rights groups in their insistence upon separation. Black Power adherents are opposed to integration primarily because they feel that implicit in the concept of integration is the belief in white superiority. For example, the integrationist philosophy contends that in order for the Negro to have decent housing or proper education, he must move into a white neighborhood and send his children to a white school. In addition, the token integration which has already occurred has had the tendency to drain the skills, energies, and intelligence of the Black ghetto into the white community, further perpetuating the economic and cultural poverty of the Black neighborhoods. But most importantly, the Black Power advocates in general have the tendency to reject white society because they feel that it is sick, immoral, deceitful, and bigoted toward all non-whites. Because of this, they feel any true integration or assimilation into this society to be not only impossible, but also undesirable; impossible because of the racism, discrimination, and segregation in American society, and undesirable because of the identity problems and negative self-images that have been produced in the minds of Black men by even token integration. Black consciousness, then, is an important step toward the Negro's sense of identity

---

[1] From *The Quotable Karenga,* ed. Clyde Halisi and James Mtumc (Los Angeles: US Organization, 1967), p. 13.

and self-esteem, conditions which are necessary if Black Power is ever to be achieved.

The urgency to overcome the sense of inferiority instilled in most Negroes by more than three centuries of white supremacist thought explains SNCC's insistence upon Negro leadership in the Black community, for only Black men can convey the revolutionary idea that Black people are able to do things for themselves.[2] The same desire to combat the psychological damage inflicted by centuries of racism has caused much of the work produced by the Black Arts movement to be decidedly antiwhite in its bias. Indeed, some of it is hostile in the extreme, although this should be understandable after some realization of the sociological and psychological impetus behind it.

Despite the militancy and hostility of many of these works, however, they should not be classified as "protest" literature, for in general the members of the Black Arts movement shun this type of writing. Concerning this, militant poet Etheridge Knight has said that "any Black artist who directs his work toward a white audience is, in one sense, protesting. And implicit in an act of protest is the belief that a change will be forthcoming once the masters are aware of the protester's 'grievance' (the very word connotes begging, supplications to the gods). Only when that belief has faded and protestings end, will Black Art begin."[3] All of the work produced by the Black Arts movement, then, is directed exclusively toward the Black audience, addressing itself to the fears, frustrations, and aspirations of Black America. Using a language that is meaningful to their people, the Black artists attempt to "tell it like it is" about themes relevant to all Black men.

The chief spokesmen for the Black Arts movement are Ron Karenga, the founder and chairman of US, the Black Nationalist Cultural Organization; LeRoi Jones, founder of the Black Arts Repertory Theatre and School in Harlem and of Spirit House in Newark; and Ed Bullins, co-founder of the Black Arts/West in San Francisco and Minister of Culture of the Black Panther Party for Self-Defense. A brief review of some of their statements should suffice to characterize the motivation of the movement. Karenga, for instance, has consistently indicated the revolutionary duty of the Black artist:

> Black Art, like everything else in the Black community, must respond positively to the reality of revolution. It must become and remain a part of the revolutionary machinery that moves us to change quickly and creatively. We have always said, and continue to say, that the battle we are waging now is the battle for the minds of Black peo-

---

[2]See Stokeley Carmichael's "Power and Racism," *New York Review of Books,* September 22, 1966, and Nathan Wright, Jr.'s "The Crisis Which Bred Black Power," *The Black Power Revolt* (Boston: Porter Sargent, 1968), pp. 103–18.
[3]"Black Writers Views on Literary Lions and Values," *Negro Digest,* 17 no. 3 (January 1968): 87.

ple, and that if we lose that battle, we cannot win the violent one. . . . For all art must reflect and support the Black Revolution, and any art that does not discuss and contribute to the revolution is invalid. . . .[4]

LeRoi Jones is closely allied with Karenga in his conception of Black Art. Karenga has stated that "Black Art must expose the enemy, praise the people, and support the revolution."[5] In an even more militant vein, Jones writes:

> The Black artist's role in America is to aid in the destruction of America as he knows it. His role is to report and reflect so precisely the nature of the society and of himself in that society, that other men will be moved by the exactness of his rendering and, if they are Black men, grow strong through this moving, having seen their own strength, and weakness; and if they are white men, tremble, curse, and go mad, because they will be drenched with the filth of their evil.[6]

Jones, who has been called the poet laureate of the Black Revolution, founded the Black Arts Repertory Theatre in Harlem in order to produce the revolutionary theatre that he had described in his essays.[7] He is currently the director of Spirit House, a Black community theatre in Newark, New Jersey. Spirit House, often considered the spiritual center of the Black Arts movement in America, offers plays as well as films, poetry readings, lectures, and music to the community. The Spirit House Players and Movers also tour out of the state with their repertory of Black drama. Also, Jihad Productions, an affiliate of Spirit House, makes available through the mail pamphlets, books, records, and films dealing with the Black Revolution. A typical sampling of titles should give an indication of the revolutionary nature of the material available through Jihad Productions: "Arm Yourself or Harm Yourself," a one-act play by Le Roi Jones; "Black Revolutionary Songs" by Yusef Iman; a pamphlet entitled "The Black Woman's Role in the Revolution"; a 33⅓ LP record entitled "Black and Beautiful"; and a documentary film entitled "Black Spring."

Ed Bullins, who is presently Playwright-in-Residence at the New Lafayette Theatre in Harlem, has strong convictions about the relationship between the artist and politics. Bullins believes that Black Theatre must be established as an institution in all Black urban communities because "the theatre will reinforce Black consciousness by exposing the lies that white culture has foisted upon us. The growth of Black theatre signals the end of our domination by white cultural values, a domination which has kept us in psychological and spiritual bondage."[8]

The dissemination of the cultural nationalism expounded by Karenga, Jones, and Bullins is increased by the existence of many magazines and

---

[4]Ron Korenga and Black Cultural Nationalism, *Negro Digest* 17 No. 3 (January 1968): 5.
[5]Ibid., p. 6.
[6]"State/Meant" in *Home: Social Essays* (New York: William Morrow, 1966), p. 251.
[7]See particularly Jones' "The Revolutionary Theatre," *Home: Social Essays,* pp. 210–15.

journals devoted to Black culture and philosophy. Typical of the "general interest" in magazines, which contain articles, poetry, fiction, and reviews, are *Black Dialogue* and *Soulbook,* both West Coast publications, and the *Liberator,* published in New York. There are journals devoted exclusively to Black drama, such as *Black Theatre: A Periodical of the Black Theatre Movement,* edited by Ed Bullins under the auspices of the New Lafayette Theatre in Harlem, and *Black Arts Theatre Magazine,* edited by David Rambeau of the Concept East Theatre in Detroit, Michigan. There are also journals devoted to poetry and music, such as *The Journal of Black Poetry,* edited by Joe Goncalves in San Francisco, and *The Cricket: Black Music in Evolution,* edited by LeRoi Jones and others in Newark, New Jersey. *The Cricket* should not be confused with such journals as *Downbeat, Metronome,* or *Jazz Review,* for unlike these publications, *The Cricket* is truly revolutionary in content.[9]

Despite the myriad magazines and journals available on the subject, however, the greatest dissemination of Black cultural nationalism (and the concomitant spread of the Black Revolutionary philosophy) has been through the presentation of Black drama in the Negro communities. This is due primarily to the immediacy and the psychic impact that these plays have had upon Black audiences, particularly those in the ghettoes, who would be disinclined to read the formal presentation of Ron Karenga or the essays of LeRoi Jones.[10] The plays are usually short, one-act dramas, and the dialogue is highly colloquial and realistic. The plots are simple and contain situations familiar to the audience, which has no difficulty in relating to the protagonist or his problems. These plays may be inexpensively mounted in the many Black Theatres which have emerged in the urban areas throughout America or in the neighborhood community houses in the ghettoes.[11]

---

[8]*Ebony,* 22 no. 11 (September 1968): 101.

[9]In the second issue of *The Cricket,* James T. Stewart says: "We reject, more emphatically than our predecessors, most of the Western white musical criterias. Our music has always rejected the established musical norm of the West. . . . We are challenging, more than ever before, the entire musical construction of the Western World" (p. 13). The opening lines of a poem by Stewart, printed in the same issue of *The Cricket* (p. 16) further emphasizes the revolutionary aspects of the new Black music:

> Our music must bring down the white empire.
> We come down on them like marauders breathing
> black chrysalis of sounds smashing their cellos,
> climbing down the walls
> to perform execution on all
> tempered music teachers in
> iron-eyed do-ra-mes
> ramming terrible beauty to their minds
> knocking plugs from their ears.

[10]LeRoi Jones has noted that "it is easier to get people into a consciousness of Black power, what it is, by emotional example than through dialectical lecture." See his "The Need for a Cultural Base to Civil Rites & Bpower Mooments" [sic] in *The Black Power Revolt,* pp. 119–26.

[11]For a directory of Black theatre groups in America, see *The Drama Review* 12 no. 4 (Summer 1968): 172–75.

The Black theatres, which for the most part are located in the "inner city" or in areas within or very near the concentration of the Negro population, use Black personnel in their productions. There are several such theatres in Los Angeles, the most notable being the one established by the Mafundi Institute in the Watts area.[12] Similarly, San Francisco has a number of active Black theatres, among them the Black Arts/West group, a Black Art revolutionary group allied with the Black Arts movement, the Black Panther Party, and other Black Revolutionary groups. One of the many programs of Black Arts/West was the setting up of a Black Communications Project in collaboration with the Black Students Union of San Francisco State College, the group which acted as a catalyst for the recent disturbances at that institution. The Black Communications Project was made operational in the spring of 1967 by the Black Students Union of San Francisco State College. Black cultural programs were held in Black communities throughout the state of California; much literature, consisting of newsletters, broadsides, and leaflets was distributed; political rallies were held in areas of Black population; and "Black Spring," a documentary film on Black culture and revolution, was made with LeRoi Jones, Ed Bullins, and the Black Arts Alliance, an organization of Black theatre groups.

Of the three Black theatres in Detroit, the most significant is the Concept East Theatre, founded by Woodie King, Jr. in November 1959. It is a Black Revolutionary theatre concerned with involving the Black populace in urban areas in militating for rapid change. Like Jones' Spirit House in New Jersey, Detroit's Concept East is a repertory theatre whose actors also travel outside the state. At present there are also branches of Concept East in operation in New York, Chicago, Cleveland, and Berkeley. The New York troupe of Concept East recently produced *Slave Ship* by LeRoi Jones, and *The Message,* a drama which takes place in an America of the future, where all the Negroes are systematically transported to concentration camps and eliminated. There are several Black theaters in New York City, but the most significant of the permanent groups is The New Lafayette Theatre, where Ed Bullins is Resident Playwright. Bullins directs his plays toward Black audiences, and most of them, he says, "are about Black people who have been crushed by the system, turned into gross distortions of what they can and should be, because they were denied knowledge of themselves and a space to grow." Although Bullins avoids long sermons or protests to and about "whitey," the whites have a "psychological presence" in most of his plays. "I don't deal with white society and culture," he says, "because I des,ise what it has done and still attempts to do to us."[13]

Early in 1968 Bullins formed "The Black Troupe," which made its first

---

[12]"Mafundi" means artist in Swahili. The Mafundi Institute, which is funded through the Brooks Foundation, has an actor's workshop and a resident musical group. The Institute is also developing the cinematic arts within the Black community.
[13]*Ebony,* 23 no. 11 (September 1968): 100.

appearance at a Black Panther benefit held in May of that year to raise bail for Eldridge Cleaver and six other Black Panthers imprisoned in Oakland, California. At the same benefit the "Theatre Black," a group formed in Cleveland in 1966, appeared and performed ghetto songs and dances. Le-Roi Jones' group from Spirit House was also there, performing his blatantly antiwhite play, "Home On The Range."

In the Deep South, the Free Southern Theatre in New Orleans travels to nearby rural areas, bringing free theatre to the Black comunities. Despite the fact that the theatre as an art form is quite foreign to the cultural experience and heritage of the Black audiences in these areas, the Free Southern Theatre has been successful in presenting plays that are relevant to the community.[14]

From a strictly psychological or propagandistic point of view, the most powerful form the Black theatre has assumed is in the development of street theatre. This type of theatre is represented by short dramatic pieces or skits which are especially adapted for presentation in urban streets. These brief dramas subliminally project Black consciousness while presenting contemporary themes or satires on counter-revolutionary figures or conditions. Large masses of the Black populace, particularly those who would not normally go to the theatre, are reached by these plays. The production procedure in these plays is to attract a crowd by the use of drums, recording equipment, dancing girls, or barkers, or else to begin the play amidst an already assembled crowd. The plays are performed in the street itself or atop a platform or flat-bed truck. Thus the old soap box oratory and street haranguing is given dramatic dimension and psychological impact by adapting itself to a visually-oriented audience—that is, audiences who exhibit a functional illiteracy.

The special problem posed by the widespread illiteracy among Southern Blacks in rural areas has been considered by a group called Southern Media, an organization based in Jackson, Mississippi. Southern Media is a program administered by Black people working to provide communication links between Black community groups. At present, most rural Black communities are isolated from one another, and their main contact with the outside world is through the TV and radio sets owned by the few families that can afford them. There are very few telephones, and only the local white newspapers are available in the area. These conditions, coupled with the high rate of illiteracy in the region, have resulted in the failure of Mississippi's Black communities to build permanent, progressive, state-wide political, economic, and social institutions. Southern Media seeks to overcome the failure in communications through the medium of the movies. The problem

---

[14]There are excellent essays on the Free Southern Theatre in the April 1967 *Negro Digest,* pp. 40–44, 95–98, and in *The Drama Review* 12, no. 4 (Summer 1968): 70–77. For an extensive documentary of the group, including photographs, journals, letters, and essays, see *The Free Southern Theater By the Free Southern Theater,* ed. Thomas C. Dent, Richard Schechner, and Gilbert Moses (New York: Bobbs-Merrill, 1969).

of illiteracy is overcome through the visuals of the motion picture, and the self-image of the Negro, who has seen himself only through the eyes of the Southern white, is improved. The instructional potential of the movies are vast (the subjects of the films range from the organization of a boycott to the setting up of a vegetable cooperative), and the production of the films opens up a new avenue of self-expression, for Southern Media trains local Blacks who both photograph and take part in the films.

There has been, of course, some "Black consciousness" programming on the television networks, but because of the white control of that communications medium, these programs have been limited. National Educational Television continues to have its "Black Journal," a series devoted to news coverage from a Black point of view and items of general or cultural interest to Black viewers. New York's WABC-TV has a Black weekly supplement called "Like It Is," a program which features specials on Black history, such as Garvey's "Back to Africa" movement or the founding of the Black Panther Party, as well as interviews and panel discussions with Black leaders and artists. There have also been notable specials, such as CBS's "Of Black America" and NET's "Blacks, Blues, Black."

More time, however, needs to be given to Black topics in the programming of the entertainment and educational programs on the national networks, for it is imperative that white America heed the significant cultural and philosophical developments that have resulted concomitantly with the rising Black nationalism in this country. At a time when newscasts are filled with daily reports of rioting and unrest in the nation's cities and universities, white Americans can no longer afford to be unaware of the frustrations and rage of its Black citizens. Indeed, although the Black Arts movement is directed toward Afro-Americans, other Americans should learn from its message to develop their own "Black consciousness" and thus, possibly, avoid what now seems to be an inevitable and violent confrontation between the races.

Black activist Linda Harrison critiques the concept of cultural nationalism in a colonial order. She argues that, by looking to the past (and Africa) for the values of a nationalistic culture, American blacks are closing their eyes to their present reality. Would Miss Harrison, who claims cultural nationalism to be "a myth and a fantasy," be more inclined to view *The Black Commandos* as an artifact of revolutionary black culture? Why?

Charles Peavy noted that *all* Americans should be exposed to black cultural nationalism, as they learn from it. Linda Harrison, on the other hand, contends that a *revolutionary* culture, born through face-to-face confrontation "on equal grounds with one's enslaver," is the only valid culture of the oppressed.

Following Linda Harrison, Emory, the Black Panther artist and cartoonist, describes revolutionary art (and culture). Is Emory's work revolutionary art or propaganda? Can one differentiate between the two?

ON CULTURAL NATIONALISM

Linda Harrison

Cultural nationalism is recognized by many who think in a revolutionary manner as a distinct and natural stage through which one proceeds in order to become a revolutionary. Such is not always the case, and many people remain at the level of a cultural nationalist all of their lives. In the United States, cultural nationalism can be summed up in James Brown's words—"I'm Black and I'm Proud."

Cultural nationalism manifests itself in many ways but all of these manifestations are essentially grounded in one fact: a universal denial and ignoring of the present political, social, and economic realities and a concentration on the past as a frame of reference.

This phenomenon is not unique to this stage of the revolution in which we find ourselves; neither is it unique to the United States Black "citizens" struggle for freedom. Frantz Fanon in *The Wretched of the Earth* said of this phenomenon that "There is no taking of the offensive—and no redefining of relationships. There is simply a concentration on a hard core of culture which is becoming more and more shrivelled up—inert and empty."

Those who believe in the "I'm-Black-and-Proud" theory believe that there is dignity inherent in wearing naturals, that a buba makes a slave a man, and that a common language—Swahili—makes all of us brothers. These people usually want a culture rooted in African culture—a culture which ignores the colonization and brutalization that were part and parcel, for example, of the formation and emergence of the Swahili language. In other words, cultural nationalism ignores the political and concrete, and concentrates on a myth and fantasy.

A man who lives under slavery and any of its extensions rarely regains his dignity by rejecting the clothiers of his enslaver; He rarely regains his dignity except by a confrontation on equal grounds with his enslaver. All men can die, and this is the only thing that equalizes them. Under many systems those with money die less often. Any confrontation which gives men, no matter what their social or economic position, an equal chance to die under equal conditions is uplifting for those who consider themselves at the bottom and degrading and toppling for those who are at the top. To see himself on an equal plane with his enslaver is to realize that the ones who enslave and oppress do not have the divine right to do so. There is nothing to be proud of in colonization and slavery and only out of the initiative of the oppressed can come something meaningful and amending to his existence.

Quoting Fannon, "The desire to attach oneself to tradition or bring abandoned traditions to life again does not only mean going against the current of history but also opposing one's own people. . . . Cultural Nationalists in their finery support many of the evils which have put them in the position of servitude. In the absence of constructive platforms and actions, the support and profit from "Being Black" they become profit seekers selling earrings at 400 percent mark up and buba's from dime store yardage at Saks-5th-Avenue prices. Sort of a hustler trying to become respectable. Exploiting those with weaker minds and weaker pocketbooks.

And because cultural nationalism has no political doctrine as a rule, the limits of being black and proud are proximate. Where is there to go after a woman has got a natural—to the natural shop of course!!—and pay $5.50 for a hairdo, $2.00 for oil spray, $2.00 for comb out conditioner, $3.50 for a line and comb-out, and then to the dress shop for a traditional wrap priced at $25.00 to $50.00. On the way from this shopping and spending they are still observing the oppression and exploitation of their people—in different clothes.

Because cultural nationalism offers no challenge or offense against the prevailing order; the influx of "Black and Proud" actors, movie stars, social workers, teachers, probation officers and politicians is tremendous. Bourgeoise and upper class standing is no handicap to the "Black" and vice versa. The power structure, after the mandatory struggle, condones and even worships this newfound pride which it uses to sell every product under the sun. It worships and condones anything that is harmless and presents no challenge to the existing order. Even its top representatives welcome it and turn it into "Black Capitalism" and related phenomenon. Everyone is black and the bourgeoise continue to hate their less fortunate black brothers and sisters; and the oppressed continue to want. The "Black" social worker continues to work for the degrading welfare system, and the "Black" probation and parole officers continue to violate their probationers and parolees.

We have no nation without a fight against those who oppress us. We have no culture but a culture born out of our resistance to oppression. "No colonial system draws its justification from the fact that the territories (and people) it dominates are culturally nonexistent. You will never make colonialism blush for shame by spreading out little known cultural treasures under its eyes." The people of Africa had cultures. It is only racism and economic necessities and whims that enslaved these countries and people. Apes have cultures—they are put into zoos. Economics transcends cultures in the capitalistic context. That is to say that capitalism will always use as its basis for expansion a real or imagined economic necessity. It will of course justify with racist conclusions and explanations of the progress that they bring to the "Natives" and "Savages," and no culture in the world, except a revolutionary culture will stop or halt or destroy that advance. Colonialism, slavery, neocolonialism, and other extensions of capitalism thrive over a thousand and one cultures. . . .

How can a cultural nationalist claim to love and be proud of a country —and a continent that has suffered for hundreds of years in colonialism and slavery, and is still suffering in all the cleverly disguised and open forms of these institutions? How can he himself deny the political realities of his own life in America by dressing up in a maternity smock (brightly colored) to participate in the culture of a people torn by revolution and revolt? How can a cultural nationalist claim adherence to the cultures of Africa, when the culture of Africa is a revolutionary culture? Solidarity with the revolutionary people all over the world has brought about a common culture to people who know nothing of each other except that they suffer under similar systems of exploitation; degradation, and racism. That their people have undergone much the same changes and that in no case will the people regain their dignity and find their freedom except through a face-to-face and equal confrontation through revolutionary tactics and actions. "A revolutionary culture is the only valid culture for the oppressed!!"

REVOLUTIONARY ART/BLACK LIBERATION
Emory

Besides fighting the enemy, the Black Panther Party is doing propaganda among the masses of black people.

The form of propaganda I'm about to refer to is called art, such as painting, sketching, etc.

ART AS REVOLUTION
The Black Panther Party calls it revolutionary art—this kind of art enlightens the party to continue its vigorous attack against the enemy, as well as educate the masses of black people. We do this by showing them —through pictures—"The Correct Handling of the Revolution."

BRIDGES BLOWN UP
We, the Black Panther artists, draw deadly pictures of the enemy— pictures that show him at his death door or dead. His bridges are blown up in our pictures, his institutions destroyed—and in the end he is lifeless.

We try to create an atmosphere for the vast majority of black people —who aren't readers but activists. Through their observation of our work, they feel they have the right to destroy the enemy.

To give you an example of where revolutionary art began, we must focus on a particular people, our brothers, the Vietnamese. In the beginning stages of their struggle against U.S. Imperialism—so as to determine the destiny of their own community—they had no modern technical equipment, such as, tanks, automatic weapons or semi-automatic weapons.

In these days of struggle for Black Liberation, here in America, we have no modern technical equipment compared to that of our oppressor. Going back to Vietnam, as time progressed, the Vietnamese people have the same kind of technical equipment as the U.S. imperialists, which also is made by the same manufacturer. . . .

ONE BULLET, 40 PIGS

So, here is where we began to create our revolutionary art—we draw pictures of our brothers with stoner guns with one bullet going through 40 pigs taking out their intestines along the way—another brother comes along, rips off their technical equipment; brothers in tanks guarding the black house and the black community—also launching rockets on U.S. military bases—Minister of Justice H. Rap Brown burning America down; he knows she plans to never come around; Prime Minister of Colonized Afro-America Stokely Carmichael with handgrenade in hand pointed at the Statue of Liberty, preaching we must have undying love for our people; LeRoi Jones asking, "Who will survive America?" "Black people will survive America"—taking what they want—Minister of Defense Huey P. Newton defending the black community—two pigs down, two less to go.

STANDARD OIL MOLOTOVS

We draw pictures that show Standard Oil in milk bottles launched at Rockefeller with the wicks made of cloth from I. Magnin and J. Magnin— pictures of Chinese fireworks in gunpowder form aimed at the heart of the enemy—Bank of America. Pictures of pigs hanging by their tongues wrapped with barbed wire connected to your local power plant.

This is revolutionary art—pigs lying in alleyways of the colony dead with their eyes gouged out—autopsy showing cause of death: "They fail to see that majority rules." Pictures we draw show them choking to death from their inhuman ways—these are the kinds of pictures revolutionary artists draw.

The Viet Cong stabbing him in his brain, black people taking the hearts of the enemy and hanging the hearts on the wall (put one more notch on our knife); skin them alive and make rugs out of them.

We must draw pictures of Southern cracker Wallace with cancer of the mouth that he got from his dead witch's uterus.

Pictures that show black people kicking down prison gates—sniping bombers shooting down helicopters, police, mayors, governors, senators, assemblymen, congressmen, firemen, newsmen, businessmen—Americans.

"We shall conquer without a doubt."

Black poetess Nikki Giovanni, in her critique of the revolutionary pose, again points out the ambivalence that exists in the black community. As she suggests, the first order of a revolution is to "get it together"—fragmentation of the sort that exists in the black community today renders revolution (or even much concerted change within the system) hopeless. As John Killens has said,

With the battle ever raging in the World Series of Blackness to see who will emerge the declared winner of the World Champeenship of Our Black and Beautiful Selves, cutthroat competition, back-stabbing, brother versus brother, all in the loverly name of Black Unity, with the air conditioner in perpetual motion and the shit flying every which away, sometimes a man must take time out and take stock, lest he become unable to differentiate between the bullshit and the reality and begin to qualify for the degree of BSA (Bull Shit Artist) par excellence.[32]

Whether this fragmentation is a product of the black community itself ("We got to get ourselves together") or a product of the white social system within which blacks find themselves ("Divide and conquer"), it does exist. Miss Giovanni notes that until black leaders refuse to allow themselves to be co-opted, the situation will remain the same, no matter how much black culture is produced—popular or otherwise—and no matter how much of a display of sexual potency the male black revolutionary offers his black woman.

---

32. Killens, *"Rappin' with Myself,"* p. 97.

BLACK POEMS, POSEURS AND POWER

Nikki Giovanni

I like all the militant poems that tell how we gonna kick the honkie's backside and purge our new system of all honkie things like white women, TV, voting and all the ugly bad things that have been oppressing us so long. I mean, I wrote a poem asking, "Nigger, can you kill?," 'cause to want to live under president-elect no-Dick Nixon is certainly to become a killer. Yet, in listening to Smokey and The Miracles sing their Greatest Hits recently, I became aware again of the revolutionary quality of "You Can Depend On Me." And if you ask, "Who's Loving You," just because I say he's not a honkie you should still want to know if I'm well laid. There is a tendency to look at the Black experience too narrowly.

The Maulana has pointed out rather accurately that "The blues is counterrevolutionary," but Aretha is a voice of the new Black experience. It's rather obvious that, while "Think" was primarily directed toward white America, Ted White could have taken a hint from it. We must be aware of speaking on all levels. What we help to create we will not necessarily be able to control.

The rape of Newark in the past election was criminal. If revolutionaries are going to involve themselves in politics, they should be successful. And while I'm sure poems are being writtten to explain the "success" of the Newark campaign, and essays and future speeches are being ground out on brand new Scott tissues, in living color, blaming the Black community for not supporting The United Brothers, I would imagine the first problem The United Brothers encountered that they were unable to overcome is that they were not united.

LeRoi Jones, for whatever reason, had no business appearing on a show with Anthony Imperiale issuing joint statements about anything at all because he (LeRoi) did not have equal power in his half of the joint. Joint statements and meetings with the governor did not encourage the Black people of Newark to support The United Brothers. Because of the prestige of LeRoi, no Newark voice is being lifted to analyze what went wrong. In the all-Black central ward, of the people who turned out to vote, only 50 percent of them voted for councilmen, period. They did not vote against The United Brothers but they would not vote for them, either. In a year when Black people showed little to no interest in national politics the stage was set for massive involvement in Black Power. There was no opposition— the people were not involved in another camp. So what went wrong?

Militarism—for one thing. To enter the main headquarters of The United Brothers one had to sign in. This turned most people off. Then you were asked quite tersely, "What do you want?" And if you couldn't answer concisely and accurately, you were dismissed. The height of this attitude at headquarters was reached when a man carrying $600.00 to give to the campaign was requested to sign in, then engaged in conversation by one of the keepers of headquarters. The man turned from the conversation to speak with someone else and was told by a second headquarters-keeper, "The brother wasn't finished with you." When the man's response wasn't satisfactory, they pushed him up against the wall and the brothers "guarding" him were told. "Do anything necessary to keep him in line." The man with the money finally made his way upstairs and complained to Karenga and LeRoi and was told his treatment was "an honest mistake."

It was a disaster. If that kind of treatment was accorded a man with as much prestige as he had, we shudder to think what happened to those who just drifted in to see. They offered an apology to the offended brother, but that missed the point entirely. The people of Newark became more afraid of the Black candidates and their organization than they were of the present scandal ridden, Black-hating administration. And at this writing not a single Black candidate was elected (Leon Ewing has contested the election and asked for a recount). This is too bad—to put it mildly. The contradictions are too great.

Revolutionary politics has nothing to do with voting, anyway. But if we enter electoral politics we should follow the simple formula that every Black person is a potential vote and must be welcomed and treated as such; with or without dashiki, with or without natural.

The latent militarism of the artistic community is even more despicable—art and the military have always been traditionally opposed. We saw the epitome of the new alliance at the recent Black Power Conference at

Philadelphia. Every artist "worth his salt" had a military wing attached to him. The conference had guards; the artists had guards; the guards had guards even. One of the highlights of the conference, to me, was Karenga's guards complaining about Stanford's guards. This is foolish because it has already been proven beyond a reasonable doubt—with the murders of Martin Luther King Jr. and Robert Kennedy—that anybody the honkie wants to take off he not only can but will, whenever and however he wants to stage it. The artist-guard syndrome seems to center around the impression we can make with the various communities. The artist impresses the white community with his militancy and the guards impress the Black community with their power. It's a sick syndrome with, again, the Black community being the loser. There is no cause for wonder that the Black community is withdrawing from involvement with the Black artist.

Watching *Soul,* which appears on educational TV in New York, the same simplistic crap was taking place. *Soul* is funded by the Rockefeller Foundation and the Negro Ensemble Company is funded by the Ford Foundation. Yet the people on *Soul,* after giving Barbara Ann Teer credit for founding NEC, put it down as not being Black enough. And The Last Poets, which is probably a truer title than they know, performed "Die Nigga." It's just not the same concept as Kill. It would seem to me that the most important and valid aspect of cultural nationalism would be the support of other Black cultural ventures. Especially since one cultural function is funded by the same white folks who fund the group being put down.

Since Black people are going to look at TV they should look at *Julia.* Diahann Carrol is prettier, *i.e.,* more valid, than Doris Day any day of the year. And while the idea of cops is bad to me, period, and extra-legal Black cops are even worse, if Black people are going to watch cops shows on TV then *Mod Squad* beats the other white vigilante shows. And if *I Spy* is, indeed, as I've been told, the new Lone Ranger, then Bill Cosby, by becoming the new Tonto, should help make us aware that we are the Indians of this decade. The parallel institutions that we hear so much about must certainly have reached their apex with *I Spy. For Love of Ivy* is as fine a movie as we've had since *Nothing But A Man.* And it's certainly more valid to us than *Planet of the Apes, Space Oddessy 2001,* and those other white things we are forced to watch. It would sometimes appear some elements of the Black artistic community are against popular success unless it's theirs. Sidney Poitier has moved into the area where we have said we want actors to go—only we didn't mean and make money, I guess. Everybody knows *Guess Who's Coming To Dinner* is a bad movie, but it is neither the beginning nor the end of Poitier's career; and the righteous indignation we spout is really quite out of place. Black people will soon quit listening to us if we can't get in tune with them. I would imagine it's a question of wigs.

Everybody has done his wig poem and wig play. You know, where we put Black people down for not having taken care of business. But what

we so easily forget is our own wig. While we put down commercially successful artists we scramble to the East Side to work, we fight for spots on
TV, we move our plays downtown at the first chance we get—we do the
very things we say are not to be done. Just because our hair is natural
doesn't mean we don't have a wig. We are niggers-in-residence at white
universities and talk about voting as a means to take over a city, then put
James Brown down for supporting Hubert Humphrey. It's all a wig. We
obviously have no concept of power because, if we did, we'd recognize
that the power of Black people forced James Brown to go natural. Everybody can't come up through the Civil Rights Movement 'cause it just
doesn't exist any more. When Black boys and girls from Mississippi to Massachusetts write James Brown letters complaining about "This Is My
Country Too" (or was that a John A. Williams book?) then we ought to
rejoice that Brown changes his position. The people we purport to speak
for have spoken for themselves. We should be glad.

And it's not as though—if we just like to complain—there isn't an abundance of issues to complain about. What was John Coltrane doing with
music that made some people murder him? Why isn't Otis Redding's plane
brought up from the lake? What about the obvious tie-ups in the murders
of John and Robert Kennedy with Martin Luther King's death? What elements in this country conspired to murder both Richard Wright and Ben
Bella? What did Malcolm and Nkrumah say to each other that caused one
to die and the other to be overthrown? Why have so many Arabs and people of Arab descent been recently arrested for murder or conspiracy to
commit murder? And I'd like to know what the cultural nationalists think
about James Forman living with a white woman who has borne his children controlling and directing SNCC while Stokely, married to a Black
woman, was kicked out? These are cultural questions—relating to survival. But it sometimes seems that the only thing that culturalists care about
is assuring themselves and the various communities that they are the vanguard of the Black revolution. They have made Black women the new jews
while they remain the same old niggers. We have got to do better than this.

Our enemy is the *New York Times,* not the *Amsterdam News;* its *Look*
and *Life,* not *Ebony;* and we ought to keep our enemy in sight. If we're going to talk about parallel institutions then we have to recognize the parallel
institutions we have. It is just not possible to have a crisis of Negro intellectualism unless we recognize that Negro intellectualism exists. Young
writers ought to recognize that an old writer can't put down other old
writers to our benefit. A nonswimmer flailing around in a turbulent lake is
sometimes better left to drown than that swimmers, in trying to save him,
should go under also. This may, however, be a personal decision.

One of the main points I'd like the culturalists to remember is that the
jews had over 100 art festivals while in concentration camps. The Warsaw
ghetto itself became the cultural place to play until the Germans carted
them off. And while it pleases me to know that we are making cultural

strides, it also worries me that we are failing to make political connections. Poems are nice, but as Don L. Lee points out, "they don't shoot many bullets." "We must," as Malcolm X says, "read our own poems. As a group we appear to be vying with each other for the title Brother and Sister Black. That will not get us our freedom. Poor people have always known they are Black as Rap Brown pointed out, just as poor honkies have always known they are white. These are facts. We need to know where our community is going and to give voice to that.

The Onyx Conference recently showed just how far from the community we had strayed . . . we didn't even want people there who weren't artists. And while Onyx will probably come out with an issue now that they have properly impressed the proper people, we are in grave danger of slipping away from our roots. The new hustle, starting with Claude Brown, and brought to its finest point by Eldridge Cleaver and Bobby Seale, with their hustle of Huey Newton in Huey's biography (serialized by that great known Black militant magazine Ramparts[?]), seems to be: who can get the ear of the enemy for enough money and/or prestige to float on a pink damn cloud to the concentration camps. Everyone who is breathing easy now that Wallace wasn't elected ought to check again—that's gas you're smelling, artist—and it will take more than a Black poem or your Black seed in me to rid this country of it.

YOUTH CULTURE

Sociologist Edward Shils has noted the emergence of American youth as a consumer public in the 1950's.[1] As Michael Malone and Myron Roberts point out in *from pop to culture* the "teenager" is perhaps the most revolutionary American invention since the automobile.

> In the years just prior to World War II, there were no teen-agers, no teenage magazines, teenage music, or teenage culture. The word itself had not even been invented.[2]

There were, of course, young people—but they were usually thought of as either children, students, or workers. The teenager of the 1950's was none of these. He . . . "(like smog) can be viewed as a by-product of the technological economy, in a real sense the creation of machines."[3] As America's postwar affluence continued into the 1950's, it (along with the concomitant flowering of American technology) ushered in the beginnings of youth culture in the form of the teenager.

As has been mentioned earlier, the postwar infusion of money in American society allowed classes of people whose styles of life had been practically invisible (such as the working and lower classes) to build monuments to these styles. This infusion also helped create the affluent leisure class of the American teenager. The teenager of the 1950's was not concerned with jobs or studies—he was not preparing for The Good Life, he was living it.[4] Or so it seemed to adults.

In point of fact, although American teenagers were labeled as "a privileged caste,"[5] this caste was probably the only totally disfranchised minority group in the country. As sociologist and educator Edgar Friedenberg has pointed out, the state retained the right even of stripping the teenager of his minority status. He had no right to

---

1. Edward Skills, "Mass Society and Its Culture," *Daedalus,* Spring 1960.
2. Michael E. Malone and Myron Roberts, *from pop to culture* (New York: Holt, Rinehart and Winston, 1971), p. 178.
3. William Braden, *The Age of Aquarius* (Chicago: Quadrangle Books, 1970) p. 52.
4. Malone and Roberts, *from pop to culture.*
5. Ibid., p. 179.

demand the protection of *either* due process *or* the juvenile administration procedure.[6]

The teenager also had informal aspects of minority status imputed to him. He was seen as:

> Joyous, playful, lazy, and irresponsible, with brutality lurking just below the surface and ready to break out into violence. . . . (He was) childish and excitable, imprudent and improvident, sexually aggressive, and dangerous, but possessed of superb and sustained power to satisfy sexual demands.[7]

The teenager was not consequence oriented nor future oriented. This also increased the large society's pressures of discrimination towards this group.

As the teenager became more and more aware that he shared a distinct status as a member of a group set apart from adult society, he began to adopt and adapt artifacts of popular culture as his own. The early adoptions were drawn, in the main, from black culture and took the forms of (among other things) rhythm and blues music and "jive" talk.

The teenager was not the only one aware of his status and emerging culture. The merchandizers of the larger society soon detected a market and produced artifacts beamed directly at that market. For a great while in the 1950's, a dilemma existed within adult society whether to exploit and allow exploitation of the teenager by supplying him with the materials with which to build his culture, to censor these artifacts (hot rods,[8] rock and roll music, teen movies, *Mad* magazine, and so on) in hopes of "exorcising the evil" inherent in the adult stereotype of the teenager—destroying the culture and "straightening out all these kids."[9]

The resolution of this dilemma seemed, in most cases, to take the form of censoring artifacts that derived from minority cultures (such

---

6. Edgar Z. Friedenberg, "The Image of the Adolescent Minority," in *The Other Minorities,* ed. Edward Sagarin (Waltham, Mass.: Ginn and Co., 1971), p. 96.
7. Ibid., p. 97.
8. Interestingly, the hot rod and drag racer of the 1950's have been assimilated into the mainstream of American mass culture to such an extent that their major use as subcultural symbols in the 1960's is by ethnics in urban street racing and the translation of the values they represent to the emerging cycle culture. Hence, the car has lost its potency in the 1960's as a symbol of youth culture. The alliance of youth to the ecology movement has also helped to detract from the potency of the car as symbol (excepting the VW microbus—symbol of economy— and ecology-minded mobile living).
9. Edgar Friedenberg has noted that "the process by which youth is brought into line in American society is almost wholly destructive of the dignity and creative potential of the young." Edgar Z. Friedenberg, "The Generation Gap," *The Annals of the American Academy of Political and Social Science* (March 1969), p. 41.

as black rhythm and blues music) as well as those that were created by and for teenage culture *(Mad* magazine being one example), yet allowing the exploitation of the youth market to continue *as long as the artifacts were being produced by members of the larger adult society.* This implies control of the dissemination of artifacts—a control actually exercised in the 1950's, one example being the frantic censorship of crime and horror comics instigated and carried out by concerned adults such as Dr. Frederic Wertham.[10]

These aspects of severe control led to a bifurcation of teenage culture. Some (perhaps the majority) of the teenagers had all along accepted many of the goals of the larger adult society. The youths, although accepting these goals of wealth, material success, and high social status, were rebelling against the *means* of attaining the goals (to a great extent because the accepted means were disallowed teenagers by the adult society). Labeled as *vertical deviance* by sociologist John Howard, this form of rebellion refers to a situation where

> power ultimately remains with the privileged. The rulebreaker wants what they have. They can control him by gradually extending prerogatives to him in return for conforming behavior.[11]

Thus, for many teenagers, deviations took the form of clandestine aberrations with respect to alternate *means* of attaining socially approved goals. When detected by adults, these aberrations could be easily controlled: "You can't have the car until I see you destroy those engineer boots myself." Or "You cut the lawn *and* get your hair cut, or you do not get paid this week."

On the other hand, the teenagers who did *not* accept the goals of the larger society (labeled by Howard as *lateral* deviants[12]) were driven "underground," and, while being constantly harassed, served to flesh out the adult stereotype of the youth culture. As these youths grew older, they were neither accepted nor absorbed in adult society— rather they became increasingly the outlaws of America, allying themselves more with the bohemian culture of the beats. As Norman Mailer suggests, when the bohemian and the juvenile came face-to-face with the Negro, the youth "counter culture" was born.

> If marijuana was the wedding ring, the child was the language of Hip for its argot gave expression to abstract states of feeling which all could share. In this wedding of the white and the black it was the Negro who brought the cultural dowry.[13]

---

10. Frederic Wertham, *Seduction of the Innocent* (New York: Rinehart, 1954).
11. John Robert Howard, "The Flowering of the Hippie Movement," *The Annals of the American Academy of Political and Social Science,* (March 1969), p. 52.
12. Lateral deviants *cannot* be controlled by extending rewards for conforming behavior. In this case, the rewards are not valued as such by the deviants. Ibid.
13. Norman Mailer, "The White Negro," *Dissent* (Autumn 1957).

From a combination of this rich cultural dowry and the affluence and leisure of their society, the youth culture of the 1960's has shaped an increasingly important life style, as reflected in the creation of their own artifacts of popular culture—artifacts that reflect their rejection of the goals and values of adult society.

> Although the ethos depends on personal contact, it is carried by underground media, rock music and collective activities, artistic and political, which deliver and duplicate the message; and it is processed through a generation flow. It is no longer simply a constructive expression of dissent and thus attractive because it is a vital answer to a system that destroys vitality; it is culture and the young are growing up under the wisdom of its older generation.[14]

In the following piece, Arthur Berger explores the world of comics in America, tracing their changing influence and forms from the late 1940's to the early 1970's. Although his discussion encompasses much more of America than its youth culture, (and much more of the youth culture than its antithetical elements) Berger is primarily interested in the appeal of the comics to these youth and the changing values of the youthful segment of America that are reflected within the comics. Following Berger's piece, Harvy Pekar discusses the emergence in the 1960's of *comix*. Their prototype forced underground in the 1950's[15] comix have now emerged as an important artifact of the popular culture of youth.

---

14. Michael E. Brown, "The Condemnation and Persecution of Hippies," TRANS-*action* 6, no. 10 (September 1969): 39.
15. In 1954, *Mad* magazine showed an artist (Bill Elder) being dragged away by the men in white coats, while a writer (Harvey Kurtzman) evaded the blue-coats on a street corner, still surreptitiously peddling magazines to a group of grinning kids. The screaming headline read "COMICS GO UNDERGROUND." Leo Daniels, "Comics Under Fire: Dr. Wertham's Revenge," *Fusion,* January 1971, p. 13.

COMICS AND CULTURE

Arthur Asa Berger

I

To be an American is a complex fate, we have been told. It is also to have a certain sensibility. For any American growing up in the forties, the comics and radio programs (now it would be comics and television) were a part of life. On the radio, Monday, Wednesday and Friday it was "The Lone Ranger"; Sunday it was "Counterspy," "The Shadow," "I Love A Mystery," and so on. In the newspaper, there were the daily comic strips; *Dick Tracy, Li'l Abner, Flash Gordon.* All during the week one could luxuriate in stupendous piles of comic books: *Superman, Batman,*

The Flash, Plasticman, etc., etc. These were desperate times: crime was everywhere, mad fiends threatened to take over the world. Things seemed to be coming apart—and would have, no doubt, were it not for the heroics of the various comic strip and comic book characters.

The 'funnies" (which they seldom are nowadays) must have contributed somehow towards fashioning the American imagination. They were an important part of our socialization by virtue of the simple fact that millions of children—and adults—cannot continually be exposed to a form of communication without something happening.

And yet, because of a certain elitist bias in our educational system, scholars have paid relatively little attention to comics. They have been ignored because millions of people read them.

To be sure, there were a few books on the comics, such as David Manning White's *The Funnies* and Steven Becker's *Comic Art in America,* but White's book is an anthology and Becker's is a general history, with little sustained analysis of the social significance of his subject.[1] There were also occasional articles in literary magazines and news magazines, but for the most part comics have been neglected.

Until the past few years, that is. We have now discovered (taking our cue from European scholars who have studied the comics for a long time) that the comic strip is an important form of communication.[2] Comics are not a perfect mirror of society. They do not reflect American society as it is—they have a much higher proportion of heroes and villains, the girls tend to be much better looking, the situations tend to be more dramatic and improbable—but this same criticism could be applied, in fact, to all art forms. Although comics (strips and books) are produced for mass consumption and often cater to simple tastes, it is possible to discover important American values showing through. Perhaps the writers and artists unconsciously let their guards down and, drawing from (literally and figuratively) the American *ethos,* produce material that is culturally significant, though it may be at the same time "junk," as Jules Feiffer puts it.[3]

We now recognize, thanks in part to the Oxford-Cambridge philosophical school, that ordinary language is capable of dealing with profound and complex matters. If the comics are simple, it does not mean that the problems they deal with are necessarily so. Though the comics generally have not in the past been used to create great art, the comic strip form has real possibilities. The existence of strips such as *Krazy Kat, Peanuts* or

---

[1]Stephen Becker, *Comic Art In America* (New York: Simon and Schuster, 1959), and David Manning White and R. Abel, *The Funnies: An American Idiom* (Glencoe, Ill.: The Free Press, 1963).

[2]I will use the term "funnies" to distinguish between newspaper comics and comic books. "Funnies" is dated and not quite correct, but it will serve to distinguish between the two manifestations of the comic strip. I will use "comics" to cover both, for the sake of simplicity.

[3]Jules Feiffer, *The Great Comic Book Heroes* (New York: Dial Press, 1965).

Li'l Abner (at its best) suggests that there have already been significant works in this form. The comics give opportunity for a fusion of art and language which allows ideas to be presented in images that are often emotionally gripping. Verbal wit can be reinforced by pictorial wit, puns by caricatures (which are themselves graphic puns).

There is also great opportunity for social comment under the protection of humor (as in Capp's *Li'l Abner* and Schulz's *Peanuts),* sadism (in Gould's Dick Tracy), fantasy, and whatever you will. If the "intellectual" has de Sade, the middle classes have Mr. Bribery—a modern instance, but no less monstrous.

All of the above lead me to suggest, then, that the comics are worth studying as a sort of window into certain aspects of American society. Though they seem simple and trivial, their combination of graphic art, language, and narration makes them rather difficult to deal with, except on the most superficial and general level. In my *Li'l Abner: A Study in American Satire,* I have tried to show what an in-depth study of a comic strip involves, and what a complicated matter it is.[4] I need not go into detailed discussions of these complications in this essay, however. What I wish to do here is to deal with certain interesting changes that have taken place in the comics —from "funnies" to "comics" (which are not humorous a good deal of the time): the values these funnies and comics reflect, the attitudes about authority and technology found in them and the new kinds of heroes they present.

II

There is a widespread misconception about who reads the funnies. Many people assume that they are essentially a "lower class" phenomenon, and the essential reading fare of juveniles and quasi-illiterate adults. This is wrong. The funnies are read by all classes, but essentially by middle and upper class families for the simple reason that middle and upper class people read more of everything. Young people do read comic books in great numbers, as the following statistics demonstrate:[5]

Age	Percentage
5–7	82%
8–10	92%
11–14	94%
18	60%

Youth are the primary readers of comics, though certain books such as Marvel Comics are now popular with high school and college students. Readership figures for comic strips in newspapers run into the hundreds

---

[4] Arthur Asa Berger, *Li'l Abner: A Study in American Satire* (New York: Twayne, 1970).

[5] Comics Magazine Association of America, *The Soaring Youth Market and Code Approved Magazines* (New York: undated).

of millions *each day,* making comic strips and comic books one of our most popular forms of mass entertainment.

Although we glance at the comic strips in the paper only momentarily, there is reason to believe that the funnies have a considerable impact upon us. In a study of *The Sunday Comics* made by Science Research Associates in 1956, it was suggested that comics are like icebergs, with "the important and significant part of meaning tending to be below the surface and concealed from public view." According to this study, readers use the comics for a variety of purposes including escapism, gaining information about society and human relationships, vicarious experience, nostalgia for childhood days, and the working through of psychological problems.

It might be useful to make a distinction between education and learning at this point. If we consider *education* to be that which we learn in formal circumstances (schools) and learning to be the "education" we get from our various experiences, then it can be seen that we must *learn* from reading the comics—as well as from many other of our activities. (The validity and usefulness of what we learn from the comics, television and other forms of entertainment is another question, which is the subject of considerable controversy.) There is good reason to suspect that any activity as widespread as reading funnies and comics must have a function that is of some importance, even though this function may not be apparent.

For the person without much of an education, reading the funnies may be his only or one of his few literary (or subliterary) experiences. The funnies also are good for girl watching. Many strips are popular because they satisfy certain voyeuristic needs of readers. *Tiffany Jones,* an English import, is a model who often is shown with little on. At times she is seen nude, and regularly is shown with a considerable amount of breast and cleavage, as she pursues her rather banal love adventures and assignments. The same holds true of many other strips. There is, at times, a considerable amount of eroticism in the funnies. There exists a flourishing genre of erotic comics: *Barbarella* and *Jodelle* (from France), and *Zap* and a host of other American imitators.

In addition, there is an element of curiosity which leads us to read the comics to satisfy a need to know what happened next. For the "iterative" strips, the strips which do not have serial adventures but are complete each day (such as *Peanuts* or *Beetle Bailey*), there is the question of how the creator will manage to reach the inevitable conclusions and create the inevitable humorous situations. The characters in the funnies and comics have a "history," so to speak; their activities become more meaningful the more we are acquainted with this history—the longer we've been following the strip. We come to know the heroes and they become part of us. Since the strips are eternal (often continuing after the originator dies) they are one of the few things that carry with us from childhood to old age.

The comforting thing about the comics is that we are always certain of the resolution of the adventure; we don't know the means by which it will be resolved, but we do know that "Tracy will win," for example. Thus, what the comics do is *raise moderate levels of anxiety which they then satisfy.* We keep coming back for more, getting our daily emotional charge, but it is not intense enough to do much more than make us want to read the strip the following day.

There are many factors which are involved in the matter of how the strips and comic books affect us and why we read them.

Age, class, education and the selection carried by the local papers are all important considerations. There is also the element of geographic location. A selection of strips popular in San Francisco might not go over very well in Fargo, North Dakota, at least as far as middle class morning paper readers are concerned. *The San Francisco Chronicle* carried a rather far-out strip, *Odd Bodkins,* for a number of years, but eventually dropped it (despite a storm of protests) for reasons that are not clear.[6]

One of the reasons comics—and the popular arts in general—are denigrated and attacked by various critics and scholars is that supposedly they must appeal to the "LCD," the lowest common denominator, and therefore be inoffensive and uninteresting. Yet the opposite argument can be made: If you have a strip with many readers you can always afford to "lose" some of them for any given day's adventure. This argument was brought to my attention by Charles Schulz, who said he feels quite free to try different things and is not worried about whether some of his readers won't like what he does on any given day.

III

Dealing with the values reflected in comics is complicated by the fact that we don't have a fixed item to analyze; strips are in continuous production and the values found in, say, the first 30 years of a strip may not be found in the most recent examples of it. This is the case with Al Capp, who was once considered quite liberal and now has become considerably more conservative—if not reactionary.

There is also an element of *interpretation* involved in eliciting values from comics, not to mention the question of whether or not the *reader* understands the significance of what is in a given strip. Nevertheless, I believe it is possible to discern values in strips and comics and make a reasonable case for them.

For example, I did some research on Italian and American funnies (which were similar in terms of time of appearance and kind of hero) and discovered that there is a considerable difference between the strips of the two countries, as far as the matter of *authority* is concerned. In the Italian strips, authority of all sorts was seen as valid and attempts to over-throw authority were shown to be futile. On the other hand, the American

---

[6]The increasingly abstract form in which *Odd Bodkins* presented an increasingly harsh brand of social commentary may have been an important factor in this decision *(editor).*

strips were all (with one exception) antiauthoritarian and ridiculed authority figures. My findings happened to correlate with sociological studies made on the same subject—dealing with child rearing, the "strong father" and other treatments of authority in the two countries.[7] This analysis was based on comics covering some 70 years and suggests that there is a considerable amount of continuity in our attitudes about authority; this is probably a reflection of a basic egalitarianism in the American psyche, perhaps stemming from values which became dominant as a result of the Revolutionary War.

On the other hand, the comics also reflect many changes in our values —or, to be more specific, those of the creators and readers of comic books and funnies. Comics also show that different classes in our society vary in the way they respond to such circumstances as, for instance, technology.

In the newspaper funnies, which have to appeal to the family as a whole, the changes have not been as striking. As a matter of fact, one of the remarkable things about the funnies is their resistance to change: Little Orphan Annie and most other characters never age, for instance. Yet there are certain changes reflected in the general *ambiance* of even the family comics, such as the appearance of Hippies in adventures, jazzed up language in *Blondie,* and lots of flesh in the strips featuring nubile young nymphs.

Probably the most significant innovation in comic books is the development of humanized, occasionally neurotic, multi-dimensioned characters, instead of the bland superheroes who were found in the comics of the "old days." The Marvel Comics Group, which publishes *The Amazing Spider Man, The Fantastic Four,* and the *Silver Surfer* (among many many others) probably saved the comic book when it introduced this kind of "real" character. Ben Grimm, one of the *Fantastic Four,* looks like a jigsaw puzzle and is often shown as angry and upset over his looks. In this series women become pregnant and have babies, and frequently biting political comments are made, usually as asides, during the course of the adventures.

There has been an interesting change in the looks and character of Peter Parker, the Spider Man. In the earliest issues he was shown as a rather "square" type of individual with thick glasses. The whole strip actually was rather crudely drawn. In current adventures he looks something like Elvis Presley, rides a motorcycle and is always in the company of beautiful and sexy young women. There are many Negroes in the strips along with much talk about drugs[8] and other social problems.

---

[7]Arthur A.. Berger, "Authority in the Comics," TRANS-*action,* December 1969.
[8]Because of its coverage of drugs, *Spider Man* has been disallowed the Comics Code Seal Of Approval (even though drugs are condemned, the Code does not allow them to be discussed). *(editor)*

The comic books have gained a new audience—high school and college students—have become "relevant," and now deal increasingly with social and political issues. Marvel Comics has an American Indian hero, *Red Wolf,* and two black heroes: *The Falcon* and *The Black Panther,* while *Superman, Batman and Robin,* and many other characters have become modernized and more realistic. If there has been some kind of revolution in American culture, or in American youth culture, this revolution is reflected graphically in these comic books.

It has been argued by Lindsay and Lawrence Van Gelder, in an article appearing recently in *New York* magazine, that the comics have become "radicalized":

> . . . the recognition of the limits of powers among the superheroes, and beyond that ther accelerating social consciousness, their deepening anxiety, the proliferation of their neuroses, their increasing involvement in issues with no clear solutions, and most of all, their burgeoning radicalization, have restored excitement, interest and merit to a once crippled industry.[9]

The changes that have taken place in these heroes are significant in many ways not directly related to the present social problems and conflicts of American society. The diminution and humanization of the superheroes suggests a new and emerging conception of the role in our culture. We have, in effect, rejected the old version of the superhero as the strong father who rescues the weak and powerless from the forces of evil. When one realizes that there isn't any superhero who can intervene at the last moment and straighten everything out, one is on the road to maturity. The weakening of the powers of the superheroes reflects, correspondingly, a new sense of strength in our own abilities and capacities.

In addition, the comics generally show a new conception of the relationship between the individual and society. The old idea of the self-reliant "individualistic" hero who can do everything on his own, with no help from anyone else—who can save the world because he is a Superman, for example, has been replaced by a view of each one's fate being related to the fate of everyone else. It is a much more complex and sophisticated view of man and society than we found in the "caped crusader" comics of the forties and fifties.

IV

The subject of machines and technology is important, and one about which the comics have much to say. There is a considerable difference in attitude, as far as science and technology are concerned, in the works of our elite artists and popular artists in extremes such as the novel and the comic book. The dominant thrust of "high" literature has been a sense of

---

[9]Lindsay Van Gelder and Lawrence Van Gelder, "The Radicalization of the Superheroes," *New York,* October 19, 1970.

revulsion against science and the machine. For some reason our novelists and poets see science and technology almost invariably as a threat to humanity. They recoil against the machine in panic. Thus many contemporary novels are *dystopias,* which see societies of the future as totalitarian and antihuman.

This is due in part to a bias in our higher arts which have traditionally looked toward nature for a source of inspiration and wisdom. *The Fantastic Four* reflects a much different attitude towards science and the machine. Although the various villains are able to use technology for their evil purposes, they are always defeated by heroes who are superior morally and technologically. Rather than refusing to face the contemporary world and returning to the older and simpler days of the pastoral, many comics use science and technology as their subject matter. The victories of the "good guys" (who now have faults of their own) may be, in part, an expression of a fundamental optimism which is said to infuse American culture. The triumph of the heroes reflect an awareness of the potentialities for good and evil in machines and a faith in man's ability to control them—that is, a realism and an awareness of the moral dilemma posed by science and technology.

We can see this if we look at a *Fantastic Four* adventure entitled *This Man . . . This Monster!* (51 June). Here, a machine is given an entire page. There is a sense of threat from the very size of the device, a "radical cube" which dwarfs the figures who are to use it, and from its function—sending people into "subspace." But the purpose of the experiment with the radical cube is to gain information on the "space-time principle" which is needed to defend the human race and the earth, so the size of the machine becomes of secondary importance. *The Fantastic Four* are, in their own way, larger than life, so the cube becomes even less menacing.

The machine sends Reed Richards, the "leader" of the *Fantastic Four,* into subspace, which is represented by a rather magnificent full-page spread of worlds, galaxies and space. The presentation of landscape in *The Fantastic Four* is particularly interesting, with brilliant panoramas of gothic castles and modern super megalopolae. The settings for the adventures tend to be extreme—either urban or primitive—however, urban adventures tend to dominate, reflecting the readers' acceptance of the city as the environment for modern man.

It has been suggested that these comic books, and perhaps science fiction in general, play around with technological gadgetry but do not really exhibit the kind of thinking found in science or an understanding of what science is really about. I'm not so sure such is always the case. But what is at issue is not whether comic book science fiction writers understand science but how they and their public feel about it. A radical cube may be bad science; however, it reflects an attitude about science and technology that is quite positive—though not worshipful. Science can be manipulated by dedicated scientists *or* mad fiends. Progress is a function of moral character as well as intelligence.

We find a definite expression of optimism in these stories, not only in the events which take place in them but in their very form—the comic book format. In a celebrated essay on "The Meaning of Spatial Form," literary critic Joseph Frank discussed the theories of Wilhelm Worringer, whose ideas are relevant here. According to Worringer, there is a continual alternation of naturalistic and nonnaturalistic art styles that is determined by man's sense of his place in the cosmos. In naturalistic periods, man feels himself part of nature and able to dominate it; his art work reproduces natural forms. When man feels he is not in harmony with nature, he develops nonorganic, linear and geometric forms.[10]

If Worringer is correct, the comics reflect a basic confidence in man's ability to dominate the forces of technology and industrialization. For every fantastic monster or problem we find an ingenious solution and remarkable hero. Despite the violence and terror in the comics, they display an underlying confidence about man's possibilities. We may question, then, whether this really is an age of the antihero? It may be for some elements in society, but it does not seem to be the case for millions of Americans who read comics—even though the heroes of Marvel Comics and their imitators are "flawed."

V

It should be obvious by now that clichés about comics being useless dribble cranked out by commercial hacks and fit only for wrapping garbage are not valid. Nor were they ever valid. The comic strip and comic book are art forms, and as such they have served people of genius as well as of mediocrity. I would argue that though there have been only a handful of first-rate comic strip artists, the same can be said about novelists, poets and artists in every medium.

The fact is, comics are a distinctly American idiom and are one of the few things that we all have in common—one of the few things in our society that cuts across class barriers (for the most part), regional differences, ethnic distinctions—whatever you will—to give us a communality of experience and of reference points. There have been major changes in the funnies and the comics, just as there have been significant changes in American society. We have now become urbanized and industrialized, and our comic book heroes have taken on new personalities in the face of new functions which they serve.

There is more than meets the eye in the comics; the fact that increasingly large numbers of people are beginning to read them and study them

---

[10]Joseph Frank, "The Meaning of Spacial Form," in *The Widening Gyre* (New Jersey: Rutgers University Press, 1963).

is, strange as it may seem, a sign of intellectual sophistication and cultural maturity. The Italians have, for a long time, studied American comics assiduously, and sponsor an international colloquium every year dealing with comics and society. The University of Rome has an extensive collection of comics. Perhaps a dozen books have been published in Italy in the past five or ten years on comics—with particular attention paid to American comics. There is also a good deal of work being done in France, Germany and England concerning American comics. And now, thanks in part to the youthful rebellion and the various counter-culture movements, as well as a sudden curiosity about the significance of many everyday aspects of our daily life, we are beginning to mine our own treasures. It's about time.

RAPPING ABOUT CARTOONISTS, PARTICULARLY ROBERT CRUMB

Harvey Pekar

Each bohemian movement has had its own characteristics. Today's is identified with, among other things, rock music, radical politics and experimentation with drugs and communal living. A less well known but interesting development associated with contemporary bohemians is the growth of the underground comic book. There is a vigorous avant garde cartoonists' movement in America today. Most of the artists involved in it are unknown to the general public but one of them, Robert Crumb, has developed a following that extends beyond the hippie subculture into a variety of social classes. I'll discuss Crumb in more detail later but first let's trace the development that led to his emergence.

In the 40's comic books, which are indigenous to the United States, were a national institution; millions were reading them. By the early 50's their quality had deteriorated badly. A mass of tastelessly done crime, horror and romance comics had hit the market. Reformers were claiming that comics were rotting the moral fiber of American youth, and crippling censorship practices were being employed. Creative, exciting comic book art seemed in danger of extinction.

A few years later comics started to make a comeback. The D. C. comic line revived some of its old super heroes (Flash, Green Lantern) and they caught on. The new Marvel Comics brought back some old heroes (Captain America, The Human Torch) and created others (Spider Man, The Hulk) and these proved popular. So, by the middle 60's Americans were becoming comic book readers again. A potential audience for underground comics was available.

That was what was happening in the straight world. The super hero—top comic book drawing card of the 40's—was making a comeback. But let's go back to the early 50's again and follow another stream of comic book development. Things looked bad then, but there was one encouraging development. *Mad* comics. *Mad,* edited by Harvey Kurtzman, was an exciting innovation—an adult comic book whose authors didn't compromise to reach the kiddie market. Still, plenty of teenagers and even some preteens dug it. It featured satire—a comic book and comic strip features, of politicians, of the communications media—it contained some of the freshest American parody ever created.

Mad was eventually published in magazine rather than comic book form and became stale and repetitive. However, its impact on a generation of kids was significant and manifested itself in the work of the avant garde of "underground" cartoonists of the 60's. (A couple of great expressionist comic book artists, Jack Cole, creator of "Plastic Man," and Will Eisner, who did "The Spirit," influenced the creators of *Mad.* Therefore, Cole and Eisner have been, directly or indirectly, very important influences on the avant-garde cartoonists of the 50's and 60's.)

Another hopeful sign during the 50's was the emergence and rise of men like Charles (Peanuts) Schulz and Jules Feiffer who brought psychology and hip social criticism and commentary into cartooning. They were to prove very influential. (Before them, of course, there was Al (Li'l Abner) Capp. Capp is now a self-righteous misanthrope but he was a brilliant commentator on and parodist of American social and political life in the 1940's and early 50's.)

Moving right along into the 60's we find publications like *Help* and *The Insiders Newsletter* using cartoon features. Among the best of these were "Captain Melanin," which dealt with a champion of the civil rights movement, and Gilbert Shelton's story about a pathetic wretch, "Wonder Warthog." Both of these stories parodied the super hero. "Wonder Warthog" (in reality, reporter Philbert Desanex) presents the super hero as a schlemiel. Captain Melanin, "supernaturally gifted pentathlon champion and Amherst Phi-Bet . . . Faster than a presidential penstroke—more puissant than a court order—able to overcome staunch barriers with all deliberate speed" was, in civilian life, Billy Bootblack, shoeshine boy. Billy became Captain Melanin by uttering the name, "Booker T. Washington," much as Billy Batson, boy newscaster, became Captain Marvel by saying, "Shazam.") Out of this background the underground comic book emerged. By now a number of underground comics have been published—*Zap Comix, Bijou Funnies, Radical America Komics, Feds 'n' Heads, Yellow Dog.* Perhaps the best known of them is *Zap,* out of San Francisco, which was created by Crumb in 1967. It was one of the first underground comics to be published, though Crumb himself gives cartoonist Joel Beck, who did "Lennie of Laredo" and "The Prophet," plenty of credit for his pioneering work in the art form.

Owing to the limited financial resources of *Zap's* publishers and attendant distribution problems the book's circulation is not what it might be. Still, its sales have been surprisingly large. When I saw Crumb in May,

1969, he told me that its first four numbers had sold a total of 80,000 copies and that he and his associates had been able to sell as many as they could get printed. If *Zap* enjoyed wider distribution it would probably have plenty of mass appeal because *Zap* has something for everyone—sex, violence, stories about people ranging from hippies to lower middle class characters. It's an All-American publication.

Crumb originally did *Zap* by himself. Later, however, he collaborated on it with a few other cartoonists. The work of all of Zap's contributors is interesting, though it varies quite a bit. S. Clay Wilson's stories are outrageously raunchy; they are reminiscent of those wonderful old pornographic comic books, the "eight pagers," which could be thought of as precursors of today's underground comics. Wilson's characters include folk heroes old ("Captain Pissgums and His Pervert Pirates") and new (Motorcycle gang members), and imaginary beings such as his Checkered Demon.

Victor Moscoso and Rick Griffin are both abstractionists. Their work may not have the popular appeal of Wilson's (sex is a big drawing card in the underground as well as the straight world) but it is fine and should be influential. Both are opening a whole new area for cartoonists. Moscoco's work is sometimes quite lyrical. His handling of space and perspective is very interesting. His use of a kind of motion picture cartoon technique is also notable. He takes shapes and figures and alters them and their relation to each other from panel to panel in such a way as to give the viewer an experience similar to spot checking through a movie by checking every fiftieth frame rather than looking at each frame in succession.

Griffin, too, has used this motion picture cartoon technique. His work, which has a surrealistic quality, is often mystical. He's interested in the Cabala and has employed Hebrew letters and words in his work and he employs cryptic phrases like, "Black is the colour, none is the number" in his things.

In *Zap* #3 the Grand Old Man, Gilbert Shelton, is represented by a fine Wonder Warthog story.

But *Zap* wouldn't have happened if not for Crumb, its originator and one of the finest comic book artists to come to the fore since the 40's.

I met Crumb in Cleveland in 1962. He was still in his teens and had just come to Cleveland from Philadelphia looking for work. He was a jazz record collector like I was and we used to listen to and swap old 78's.

The first time I met him he showed me a project he was working on—a cartoon novel (which is an unusual form in itself) called *R. Crumb's Big Yum Yum Book*. It was about a frog named Ogden, a student at a medieval university, who freaked out and murdered some ladybugs. He buried them, hoping his crime would go undetected, but a huge vine like Jack's beanstalk sprang from their grave. Ogden got scared, climbed the vine, and found himself in an Eden-like land populated by a stupid, naked teeny bopper of Rubensesque proportions. Ogden fell in love with her but, unfortunately, she couldn't stand him; all she wanted to do was eat him. After some weird changes during which he went back down the vine and found that it had engulfed and destroyed the land he came from, Ogden kissed the girl before she could kill him and turned into a man. Naturally she fell for him and they went off to New York together.

I had read a number of comics. I'd had a big collection in the 40's and had started reading them again a couple of years before I met Crumb. But I'd never seen anything like his *Big Yum Yum Book*. Nothing he's done since—and I really dig his more recent work—has impressed me as much.

Crumb got a job in Cleveland at the American Greeting Card Company and eventually worked himself up to designing cards for their Hi-brow line. (Incidentally, his cards are still on the market.)

He was in Cleveland for about two years. During that time his personality didn't change much but he got involved in more things. When I met him he was a quiet, introverted guy who kept pretty much to himself.

His tastes were kind of anachronistic—he was nuts about old things. For example, he liked jazz but not modern jazz or even swing—he was a moldy fig who thought jazz had died around 1932. He was far more interested in comic book art of the 40's than the late 50's and early 60's. (Not that I blame him; the older comics were generally much more interesting, if not as slick.)

When he first got to Cleveland he lived a kind of hermit's life. After awhile, though, he got to hanging with what I laughingly refer to as "Cleveland's underground" and started to get Liberated and to get into the Contemporary Scene.

After leaving Cleveland Crumb went to Europe where he (voluntarily) visited Bulgaria. He did a cartoon feature for Help on Bulgaria, as a matter of fact. It was one of the first things he had published.

He spent some time in New York and came back to Cleveland for awhile in 1966, but in January, 1967, left for San Francisco where he made his name.

Over the years he's contributed to *Cavalier* and various underground newspapers including *Jive Comics,* a paper devoted entirely to cartoons, as well as to *Zap*. He also did some sex things in *Snatch* comics which he describes as a satire on pornography and which were funky enough to cause the publication to be banned in Berkeley. An anthology of his work called *Head Comix* was published by Viking Press, and a collection of his Fritz the Cat stories has been printed by Ballantine. And Crumb did the album cover for the Big Brother and the Holding Company L. P., *Cheap Thrills.*

It's difficult to describe Crumb's style in just a few sentences. He's been influenced by so much; by whole schools of cartooning as well as individual cartoonists. His work is notable partly because of its variety and the way he synthesizes his influences. He digs animal cartoonists like George Harriman, who did Krazy Kat; Walt Disney—especially early Disney and 40's Disney comics, which were done by a variety of cartoonists including the excellent Carl Barks; and Walt (Pogo) Kelly. He did and still does use animal characters like Ogden, Fritz and Dirty Dog.

Crumb also has been impressed by the work of cartoonists who are better appreciated by older teen-agers and adults than by little kids. People like Kelly, a fine political satirist, and Feiffer. The guys who did *Mad* when it was in comic book form (Bill Elder, Jack Davis, Wally Wood) should also be cited as influencing Crumb. Crumb talks about liking to cram a lot of "eyeball kicks" into his work. ("Eyeball kicks" are humorous effects jammed into the panel in some way or another which are ostensibly secondary to the action of the main characters in a comic book or strip story but which still are, hopefully, quite funny in themselves. A good cartoonist can superimpose a series of "eyeball kicks" over his main theme that is as funny as that theme.) Anyway, "eyeball kicks" were a trademark of *Mad's* artists and Crumb probably derived it from them. (Actually "eyeball kicks" were a trademark of the work of Bill Holman, the creator of Smokey Stover, years before Mad existed. He may be called the inventor, or at least one of the most important early users, of this technique.)

"Popeye" also marked the work of Crumb. The lumpy, oddly proportioned characters that Crumb sometimes draws are reminiscent of those in "Popeye." (Crumb is not a virtuoso technician but his art work is very good —it's strong and clean and he's a fine caricaturist. His lettering is neat and bold. Overall, he's a very easy-to-follow cartoonist.) And there's a feature in *Popeye* comics about a crackpot inventor named O. G. Wottasnozzle that is similar to Crumb's "hot-headed old sage," Mr. Natural. Crumb told me he'd never been aware of Wottasnozzle until after he'd created Mr. Natural. Still, the resemblance between the two characters is interesting. Both are old men with beards. Mr. Natural has a disciple named Flakey Fooney whose mind he's always blowing and Wottasnozzle has a landlord he's always involving in crazy projects that backfire.

Crumb's drawing has also been influenced by Basil Wolverton, who worked for *Mad* and before that had a groovy little half-page feature called "The Culture Corner" in *Whiz Comics* during the 40's. (Culture Corner was was presided over by Croucher K. Conk, Q.O.C., i.e., Queer Old Coot.) Some of Crumb's no-neck characters with sausage-like noses, round heads and big, thick hands are very much like Wolverton's.

He also credits colleague S. Clay Wilson with influencing him in that Wilson's wild stuff persuaded him to stop censoring himself.

Of the older comic strip artists Crumb particularly likes Chester (Dick Tracy) Gould and Harold (Little Orphan Annie) Gray. (Of course, he has no use for Gray's reactionary political philosophy.) In fact, Crumb's knowledge of cartoon history extends back into the nineteenth century and he admires Thomas Nast's work quite a bit.

Crumb is a very hip guy with big eyes for what's going on around him. All sorts of things turn him on and it's interesting to consider the number of themes he uses. I imagine there are some people around who are very concerned with interpreting Crumb. (What does he mean by this? What is the hidden significance of that?) But there is no secret key to understanding his work. He's been turned on by a great variety of people and things; consequently his stories have to do with a great variety of people and things.

He lived for some time in San Francisco's Haight-Ashbury section and is involved in the hippie scene so, not surprisingly, he deals with sex and drugs. But partly because he's a little older than most hippies and has had more varied experiences, he's able to see the underground in perspective and deal with it very perspectively.

There's a piece he called "Duck's Yas Yas" about a frantic junkie who cuts out of New York and goes on the road that presents a sensitive portrayal of a very strung-out guy even while parodying itself. Dig some of the dialogue: "Made a decision to go back to my wife . . . Called her but no answer . . . screw the bitch . . . Bopped over to the East Side with a dealer name of 'Teen Age Ric'. . . He invited me to hitch it to the Coast. First ride was a wild young kid in a '51 Hudson. We drank wine all the way to Cincinnati . . . Teen Age Ric moved in with a chick in Iowa City. I hit the road alone and sad . . . Finally wound up on ol' Haight Street. Dropped acid for three weeks. Man, it was intergalactic! Split outa that freak show with a truckload of Zen monks. Doin' the spiritual thing up in the mountains. Whatever's right man! Wow!"

Crumb also does work containing visions that he might have had when he was stoned; e.g., his piece called "Abstract Expressionist Ultra Super Modernistic Comics," which consists of a series of unrelated panels including some that are surrealistic and some that are non-representational.

In addition to stuff about sex and dope there's also some good healthy violence in Crumb's work—Bertrand Russell getting hit with a meatball (nothing is sacred to Crumb), a kid smashing his head against a wall, a sadist biting a girl's toes, a couple of peacefully conversing snails getting squashed by a kid's tennis shoe—all kinds of violence. Perhaps the most savage of all Crumb's published pieces is "Neato Keeno Time," which appeared in the Bantam publication Us #1 and is a parody of comic stories like "Archie." "Neato Keeno Time" deals with the activities of a brutal sadist named Forky O'Donnell, who is shown running over a pedestrian while driving with his girl friend, doing in his girl friend by stabbing her with a fork ,and later, after he and a male friend have had sexual intercourse with her body, telling the counter man at a restaurant not to bother giving him a fork to eat with because he has brought his own, i.e. the one with which he'd stabbed his girl friend. Because the characters in it look like square, clean-cut American young people, such as those that appear in "Archie" and "Freckles and His Friends," the brutality of "Neato Keeno Time" is especially shocking.

There is a mean, cynical side to Crumb's work. This is illustrated in his "How to Get Inside a Teenybopper's Head, Take Over, Develop a Large

Following and Become a Leader of the Scene," which also appears in
Us #1. Dig some of Crumb's comments in it:

> "Teenyboppers aren't very smart. This is your Chief Advantage.
> . . . If you don't get her, somebody else will. . . . They're fun and
> they're beautiful, but they die soon after exposure. They're pathet-
> ically stupid and vulnerable.
>
> "The teenybopper has somehow gotten hold of the notion that
> some big thing is going on that she's missing! She wants to be in
> worse than anything.
>
> All you have to do is prove to the teenybopper that you're right
> where it's at. Be sure you're a member of at least one very in group
> or tribe. . . . Show the teenybopper how utterly nowhere she is. . . .
> Ultimately you must bring her to the realization that you are not
> only the moving force in your in-group, but also the whole universe.
>
> "Before you know it you'll have herds of devoted worshippers.
> You'll be a cult unto yourself!! They'll do anything and everything for
> you. Sound hard to believe? Try it. It's Magic!"

In addition to being funny, this piece contains an accurate description
of teenyboppers and sound advice regarding techniques to use to exploit
them. And Crumb conveys the impression in this piece that he does advocate exploiting them.

Now lets consider the characters that Crumb, a "keen student of
human nature," deals with. He has a sympathy for and is amused by people who are cast as freaks and misfits. This is apparent not only in "Duck's
Yas Yas" but in a sex thing he does about horny Dirty Dog who can't pick
up a girl and gets his kicks by reading skin magazines.

He also does things about up-tight people. His "Whiteman" is the
story of a guy straining against his inhibitions ("I must maintain this
rigid position or all is lost") and his inhibtions straining back. Crumb wants
people to loosen up and have fun.

In "Just Us Kids" Crumb evokes memories of childhood. This story
is a masterpiece because it tells it like it is. Kids are presented not as
adults think they are—gentle and nice—but as they really are—vicious
and destructive. (A kid asks his older brother and a friend where they
got a lifesize cardboard dummy. They answer, "A guy in a shoe store . . .
gave it to us. We're gonna take it over t' my house 'n smash it up.") Also—
Crumb does a great job of portraying an alienated little kid in "Just Us
Kids" through a character that I think is him. Crumb and this character,
who is named Bobby, has an older brother named Chuckie.

One of the better things Crumb's done, "Life among the Constipated,"
in a series of hilariously vulgar vignettes about lower class white America.
Crumb keeps his eye on the proletariat. Actually, Crumb does have a
lower middle class background. His father even worked for awhile as
a chicken plucker. And he's loyal to this class to the point of reverse
snobbery. He told me, only half jokingly, that all great art comes from
the lower middle class. He hates pretentiousness and "arty" art—even fine

"arty" art like great nonrepresentational painting or the better Jefferson Airplane performances. He really digs popular, as opposed to high-brow, culture. He's even interested in lousy popular music and comic books because of what they tell you about the era in which they were produced.

Another thing about Crumb is that he uses the accents and dialects of all sorts of different people in his work, e.g. Lyndon Johnson's accent, black people's accents, 1920's slang, hippies' slang. For fun, get together a collection of Crumb's work and count all the different dialects he uses.

The nature of hipness concerns Crumb. What is it? How does one acquire it? These questions are explored in "Mr. Natural."

I mentioned before that Crumb has a fondness for old things. This is frequently apparent in his work. He really digs old jazz and old jazz slang. "Duck's Yas Yas," the story referred to above, got its title from the name of a record made by Oliver Cobb's Rhythm Kings in 1929. Mr. Natural responds to the remark, "I wish someone would tell me what Diddie-wah Diddie means" by saying, "If you don't know by now, lady, don't mess with it." Actually, this remark has been attributed to Fats Waller in responding to the question of a society matron. "What is jazz?"

Crumb uses rhyming dialogue spoken by a large, constantly changing cast of characters to set up a rhythmic, euphoric groove in "Don't Gag on It . . . Goof on It," which was published in *Jive Comics* and "Stoned," which is in *Head Comix*.

Crumb digs old cars (the '51 Hudson referred to in "Duck's Yas Yas") and old radios. I remember going junk shopping with him once when he was pricing those big old console radios with all the different bands and push buttons. Eventually he bought one of them and an old table model to boot, which he painted all kinds of different colors.

There's a certain amount of science fiction influence in Crumb's work, too, although he doesn't like most super hero characters, feeling that he can't identify with them. He does like to draw robots and weird machines and vehicles, though, and these can be seen in his "City of the Future" and "Abstract Expressionist Ultra Super Modernistic Comics."

The latter is a strange kind of feature. Crumb did it partly to satirize and put down modern art, which he dislikes, but it's good enough to be looked at and enjoyed not only as a parody but as fine, far-out modern cartoon work.

As I tried to suggest earlier, it's a waste of time trying to find a hidden key to Crumb's work. Sure, it's often profound. But remember, he's trying to make you laugh. So when you read his stuff, don't let it put you up tight. Relax and enjoy it.

"Don't gag on it . . . goof on it."

As with many of the underground forms, once Crumb's work was "discovered," its diffusion throughout mass society was swift. *Fritz the Cat* is now a full length (but X-rated) cartoon film production.

The influence of science fiction in Crumb's work is a reflection of the importance of this form of culture to American youth. An increasing concern on the part of youth with the proliferation of technology has led to a search in the literature of science fiction for probable future consequences of technological actions (such as chronicled in Walter Miller's "*A Canticle For Liebowitz*[16]"). Predictably, the novels of social science fiction are very important in the youth culture, as well as are those dealing with alternative solutions to pressing environmental problems (Frank Herbert's ecologically oriented *Dune* being an example of the latter[17]). Popular social science fiction many times affirms cultural values of youth as it chronicles a "new breed" of man—more highly evolved socially—who is continually persecuted by the technological society surrounding him, yet eventually triumphs over it.[18] These themes of science fiction are transmitted not only through the medium of print, but also are reflected in rock music (most noticeably in the works of Frank Zappa and the Jefferson Airplane) and in film *(2001: A Space Odyssey)*.

The concept of man's alternative futures has been represented by the science fiction writer Ray Bradbury in his book *The Illustrated Man*.[19] Utilized in 1958 by Bradbury as a vehicle with which to present a collection of short stories, this tale of the tattooed man, whose tattoos would, when stared at, each come alive and present a vignette of man's future, became popular in the youth culture of the 1960's as symbolic of the alternative futures man holds within himself.[20]

In the following piece, journalist Amie Hill takes a look at the place of tattooing in America today. Do you feel the underlying motives and values as expressed in the piece by both the creator and

---

16. Walter M. Miller, Jr., *A Canticle For Leibowitz* (Philadelphia: J. B. Lippincott, 1959).
17. Frank Herbert, *Dune* (Philadelphia: Chilton, 1965).
18. Two widely read examples are: Arthur C. Clark, *Childhood's End* (New York: Harcourt Brace Jovanovich, 1963); and Robert Heinlein, *Stranger In A Strange Land* (New York: Putnam, 1961).
19. Ray Bradbury, *The Illustrated Man* (New York: Doubleday, 1958).
20. The rejection of the goals, means *and* values of the larger society has led the youth culture in pursuit of alternatives. This search can be seen reflected not only in the popularity of the social science fiction novel, but also in youths' continuing search through the world's religions for alternative values and their forms of expression as evidenced in the many (and short-lived) religious fads of the youth of the late 1960's and the early 1970's, including occultism and witchcraft. This concept of the *viability* of alternatives (there is *not* only one way to do it) is an integral part of the emerging value structure of the culture. The potentiality of man as a creature who can create his own alternatives is becoming an overriding ethic of youth.

wearers of this cultural artifact are *antithetical* to those of the larger society? Does your conclusion lead you to any hypotheses about the place of youth culture within the larger social structure?

TATTOO RENAISSANCE

Amie Hill

Tattooing is how you look at it. The popular concept falls somewhere between Ray Bradbury weird and a sleazy carnival kickback to Uncle Bernie's first glorious navy drunk in Hong Kong. But it wasn't always that way.

Since the invention of the tattooing process, probably more or less coinciding with the discovery of fire, skin design has been used for the most sanctified of religious ceremonies, induction into adulthood, evidence of high social status and/or wealth, not to mention personal adornment, and evidences of it have turned up in the most advanced of early cultures—in China and Japan, among the Incas, Cretans, Aztecs, Mayans and Egyptians. The factor that relegated a perfectly respectable art into its present less-than-exalted state is that common cold of behavioral systems, the Judaeo-Christian-Puritan-goodguy Ethic. Like many another cultural refinement, tattooing represented (and does to this day) a threat to the solidarity of nearly every major Western religious movement. Seeing it as evidence of competition from pagan religions, skittery prelates through the ages have seen fit to ban it on pain of hellfire.

The effect of this, in the earlier days of the great Christian purges, was to force tattooing underground, where, like certain other art forms and cultures, it flourished among its fellow outcasts. Tattooists established themselves on waterfronts and battlefields, in traveling circuses and carnivals, and in the most disreputable quarters of cities, where only brawny seamen, stevedores, adventurous students, and underworld characters (and certainly no self- and life-respecting churchman) dare to roam.

Every once in a while, however, fashion chooses to dispense with dogma, as in late 18th-century Britain on the occasion of Captain Cook's celebrated return from the Polynesian Islands with descriptions and examples of the natives' fascinating art of "Tatu." There followed what has been known as the "Golden Age of Tattooing," with society belles, fashionable gentlemen, and even royalty—Czar Nicholas II, the Prince of Wales, later Edward VII, and his son, later George V—going under the needle.

Now, almost exactly a hundred years later, the evidence is that tattooing is once again undergoing a renaissance. And according to Lyle Tuttle, master-tattooist of San Francisco, this city is in the forefront of the movement as far as sophistication in choice of design and appreciation of the tattoo as an art form are concerned.

Walking through the door under the TATTOO (While-U-Wait) sign into Tuttle's 7th Street emporium, you run into a broad double flight of wooden stairs, with one of the boards halfway-up politely painted "Please Do Not Run" (as if formerly countless galloping numbers had bruised themselves against the stairs in eagerness for the needle). Far from being the sinister, greasy hole that popular fiction associates with tattooing, Tuttle's establishment is almost disappointingly clean and well-lighted. The working area, unstained of the blood of innocent victims, is hospital-spotless behind a gleaming bar of chrome. The place, if you discount the cheerful atmosphere and the walls covered with semilurid "flash" (the trade name for an artist's display sheets of available designs), could pass for a dentist's office.

Up and down the steps trickles a steady streamlet of the curious, the tentative, and the determined; sailors, lured in from looking for action on Market Street; transients, killing time until their Greyhound leaves from the terminal next door; long-haired kids, earnest young couples with babies, motorcyclers, the occasional tourist. Tuttle (a far cry from your greasy little man in the unmentionable undershirt) has a face that could probably sell Marlboros, although the backs of his hands are one of the few places he isn't tattooed, and neat greying mutton-chop sideburns. He greets all comers with the same unfailing politeness, and answers all questions with scholarly thoroughness.

His sleeves are rolled up, ready to work, and incidently displaying an intricate network of tattooed undershirt, neatly cuffed above the wrist. Occasionally one of the onlookers takes a deep breath and dives under the chrome bar to take his or her place under Tuttle's needle, while others look on eagerly, marvel, and wince sympathetically, even when informed, bravely, that "it doesn't hurt—much." (The sensation is something like a tiny, controlled electric shock.) Occasionally a lady wants a design in a more personal place; if she requests it, the door is closed, other visitors ushered out, and only her old man or girlfriend allowed to view the process.

Tuttle's most celebrated tattooee to date has been [the late] Miss Janis Joplin, singer, who proudly wore a tattooed Florentine bracelet on one wrist, and a small valentine-shaped design near to her heart. "It was just a trip," said Janis, who has happily discussed and displayed her tattoos for the *San Francisco Chronicle* and viewers of the Dick Cavett show, among others. "I wanted some decoration. See, the one on my wrist is for everybody; the one on my tit is for me and my friends." A pause and a chuckle. "Just a little treat for the boys, like icing on the cake."

Shortly after her own decoration, Janis threw a party in her Mill Valley house, with Lyle as chief attraction, which resulted in a number of her friends following suit. The party is remembered by at least one person with a certain trepidation: "I thought for sure they were going to pants me," says Lyle, who is tastefully tattooed from stem to stern. "Janis had a lot of big good-looking girl friends, and they all sort of run in a pack. They got really curious about what I had tattooed on the lower half of my body, and they wouldn't let me alone."

Apparently Lyle escaped, with pants and modesty reasonably intact, to tattoo again another day. Since the party, other friends, acquaintances and devotees of the entertainment world have acquired Tuttle tattoos. Sam Cutler, ex-Rolling Stones manager, now with the Grateful Dead, boasts a skull on one arm, and Kent Robertson, editor of New Gravity comics, a dolphin. Some others who have recently come by tattoos are members of the *Rolling Stone* staff and the Grateful Dead family, cartoonist Simon Deitch, Judith Weston, wife of Pacific High recording studio manager Peter, Gayle Hayden of the *Hair* cast (a blushing rose on her blushing bottom), Michael J. Pollard of *Bonnie and Clyde* fame, who had his wife Annie's name permanently engraved inside a heart, and, recently, Lyle found himself obliging an unidentified amazon who wanted "Property of Janis Joplin" tattooed prominently across one breast.

To Lyle Tuttle, all this is just part of the definite change in his clientele and its tattoo tastes which he's noticed in the past few years. Alhough he still gets his quota of servicemen and greasers who want what he calls "the armorplate effect"—massive designs depicting service insignia, eagles, or dripping daggers entwined with stylized snakes—as well as the more traditional naked broads, slavering wolves, cartoon characters, crucifixes, or such delightfully whimsical innovations as a drunken monkey swinging on a parking meter, a growing number of his prospective tattooees have their own ideas. Instead of just wandering in and picking a design from his "flash," many of the new breed of customer are bringing in or designing their own. The new trend, says Tuttle, is for softer, more fanciful, more purely decorative and less violent designs. Signs of the Zodiac, occult and religious markings, and personal totems form a great part of his new business, along with peace symbols, doves, marijuana leaves, the yin-yang, and the Zig-Zag man.

Since tattooing is only slightly more restrictive than say, heavy-pen drawing, almost any design, except those requiring infinite detail, can be reproduced, and Tuttle is willing to go along with almost any whim of creativity. Blacks, he says, occasionally want themselves tattooed with panthers, but often opt for African designs and tribal symbols they've researched out. Chicanos and Mexicans occasionally come in with Aztec or Mayan figures, and American Indians and Samoans have their own "culture marks." Tuttle recalls one or two unique requests along these lines, one from a Marshall-Islander for a portrait of "one of our local gods," and another from a police officer in support of his own local deity—a club-wielding piggie.

Women, who not so long ago would no more have entered a tattoo parlor than stood up to a urinal, now make up an increasing proportion of Lyle's living canvases. For the ladies, he devises butterflies and roses, filigreed hearts, rings, and dainty flower bracelets. Female customers range from Hells Angels' old ladies to middle-aged lady schoolteachers and dewy-eyed debutantes, with the odd college student or chorus girl thrown in.

"The women never faint," says Tuttle, "I've had 200-pound bruisers come in here and keel over when I touch 'em with the needle, but never a woman."

Every once in a while, he says, he receives a request for one of those "obscene" tattoos, the "Fuck You," or "Fuck the Army" on the saluting hand which popular fiction says will get you out of the draft. Lyle invariably refuses, not from any excess of hawkish sentiment, but because authorities would just love to bust him and his fellow artists for aiding and abetting a draft-dodger, or just about anything else, since, as every decent citizen knows, tattooing and immorality go hand in hand. In spite of the fact that tattoo parlors are subjected to the most stringent of health regulations and inspections, the practice of tattooing has been banned in a number of areas, including entire states and the City of New York, where church authorities hold that only "lewd and dissolute persons" would subject themselves to such hideous mutilation. Lyle also refuses to tattoo those under 18 (in accordance with state law), or people under the influence of liquor or drugs, and often offers a little fatherly advice and/or discouragement to those he thinks may be making a major and permanent mistake in choice of design, location, or simply in getting tattooed at all.

Just why does a woman get the urge for a tattoo? Ask the lady who owns one. "I'd wanted to get tattooed since I was a little girl," says a receptionist with a delicate OM engraved on one hand. "I guess it's the age-old urge to decorate your body. I used to play with those little decals you got when you were a kid, the kind that come off with water, and I just made up my mind I was going to have a real one someday."

"It makes people think twice about me," explained Candi, a young model, flashing the sign of Scorpio on one wrist. "They try, especially men, to figure out why I did it. It's not a really chick thing to do, you know, and otherwise I'm very female. It kind of adds another facet to my personality. Also," she added, "it saves on that draggy old 'What's your sign?' bit." According to Candi, once you have a tattoo, it's like being in a club. "You feel an instant rapport with everybody you meet who's tattooed. It's like people who ride the same kind of bike."

"I saw the movie *The Rose Tattoo*," admits the wife of a San Francisco publisher, her own rose tattoo gracing the inside of her left forearm. "It made a big impression on me. Also I read *The Scarlet Letter,* and I really liked the idea of a permanent thing like that." She came into possession of her tattoo several years ago. "I was scared to death to go into the studio. Nobody I knew was doing it then. I expected this awful place, and some greasy old man." Happy to find Lyle just the opposite, she regards her tattoo as a "permanent piece of jewelry," and "a real commitment, one of the most lasting things in my life."

For a writer with a flower-and-filigree ring on the middle finger of her right hand, her tattoo serves a kind of personal-relations barometer: "It seems as though I can actually tell how I'm going to get along with people, and vice-versa, by the way they react to my tattoo. It's more or less expressive of the unconventional side of my character right up front. Most of the people who seem to like me really dig the tattoo, too." Her decision, she says, was sudden and unpremeditated. "I was talking to a chick who'd just gotten one, and decided just like that. It wasn't really a copy-cat thing; it just suddenly seemed like something I'd been thinking about for a long time. I went right down to Lyle's and had it done the same day, and I haven't regretted it once."

The "surprise-your-lovers" syndrome is celebrated by Pam, a secretary whose bottom is decorated with a small yellow and green flower, and her friend Cheryl, a photographer's assistant with a multi-colored butterfly perched on her shoulder. "It really turns guys on the first time they see it," says Pam. "Yeah," agrees Cheryl, "they really think it's a gas. The first thing they want to do is kiss it. And you can bet they'll remember you."

Tattooing like collecting paintings or porcelains, can be slightly addictive, those with one skin design often hankering for more. Psychologists are beginning to be of the opinion that, for some, the slight pain of the needle is sexually pleasing and stimulating. Although Lyle is of the opinion that it's probably disappointing to anyone heavily into sadomasochism, he has his own version, as told to an obnoxiously patronizing social researcher.

"Of course tattooing is sexual. Every night, before I go home, I lock my door. Then I go over and stand by the cash register and look at the little numbers, and then look at the receipts and see how they've turned to great big numbers, and every time I see those great big numbers, I just get right off!"

Since the highly publicized death of Janis Joplin in 1970, the tattooing business in America has taken a remarkable upswing. Tattooing was legitimized by the acceptance (and exploitation) of Janis Joplin in the mass media of America, just as the cartoon work of Robert Crumb was. The cover of Janis' first "major league" recording (cut while she was a member of Big Brother and the Holding Company) was designed by Robert Crumb. The title of the album was to be *Sex, Dope and Cheap Thrills;* however, the recording company vetoed this, labeling the album simply *Cheap Thrills.*

Dope, in the form of marijuana, has long been an important artifact of the youth culture. Ned Polsky has traced the spread of marijuana in American society from its early use by ethnic jazz musicians in the 1950's beats.

The beats' most enduring imprint on American culture appears, in retrospect, to have been precisely this diffusion of marijuana use to many circles of middle- and upper-class whites outside the jazz world.[21]

As Jerry Rubin has noted,[22] the illegality of marijuana, the absurdly harsh penalties for its use, and the media misrepresentation of its effects have aided in strengthening the group identity of the youth culture and its impression that the logic, rules and order of the larger society explain nothing about the reality of the world. The structure and restriction of the state is seen as not only unnecessary and artificial but dehumanizing and dangerous: absurd—but dangerously absurd.[23]

As marijuana diffuses further within the larger society, the penalties involved in its use become less harsh and its effects more widely understood and more realistically presented by the mass media. Consequently, marijuana has been losing much of its status as a totem of youth culture. Just as the youth culture adopted marijuana as a symbolic artifact of group identity from the ethnic jazz musicians (via the beats),[24] so many middle and upper class segments of the larger American society seem now to be on their way to adopting marijuana as an artifact of their mass popular culture.[25] As James Hitchcock has remarked, some radicals are gratified to hear of lawyers and junior executives being secret marijuana users because they feel these persons are preparing to defect from the system. Jerry Rubin feels that if one should legalize marijuana, society would fall apart.[26] This would, however, probably not be the case.

> It is probably more likely that for such people smoking pot is like drinking liquor—precisely that which makes the System bearable, hence that which strengthens it. . . . Should pot-smoking . . . ever become respectable, there is absolutely no reason why businessmen would not be able to adopt (this style) and still remain within the system.[27]

---

21. Ned Polsky, *Hustlers, Beats and Others* (Chicago: Aldine, 1967), p. 162.

22. Jerry Rubin, *Do It!* (New York: Simon and Schuster, 1970).

23. Mark Gerzon, *The Whole World Is Watching* (New York: Viking Press, 1969), pp. 39–48.

24. Who in turn adopted it in the 1920's in New Orleans from the Mexican-American subculture.

25. This diffusion can be traced by noting the spread of the sale of accoutrements of marijuana use (such as pipes, cigarette papers, and incense) in the larger society. George H. Lewis, "Capitalism and the Head Shop," paper presented at the 1971 Annual Meeting of the American Sociological Association, Denver, Colorado.

26. Jerry Rubin, *Do It!*

27. James Hitchcock, "Comes the Cultural Revolution," *New York Times Magazine*, July 27, 1969.

Hand-in-hand with the emerging youth culture came those out to exploit the youth as consumer. One of the more blatant media of exploitation has been film. Richard Staehling, himself a member of the American film community, describes in an article "The Truth About Teen Movies,"[28] the artifacts created by the film companies and beamed at the youth audience. His presentation reveals how the stereotyped images of the 1950's teenager (such as have been discussed earlier in the commentary of this section) were intensified by and for the screen—the juvenile delinquent and outcast in *Blackboard Jungle, Rebel Without A Cause* (James Dean), and *The Wild Ones* (Marlon Brando) as well as the clean all-American teenagers of *Beach Party* (Frankie Avalon and Annette Funicello) and *Where the Boys Are* (Connie Francis). The article also points out how the teen films of the 1950's and early 1960's not only reflected this bifurcation of teenage culture, into "wild" and "mild" stereotypes, but also how they reflected the introduction of many of the values, themes and artifacts that were to come together as the youth culture of the middle to late 1960's—marijuana in *Mary Jane,* LSD in *The Trip,* hard drugs in *High School Confidential,* rock music in *Rock Around the Clock,* surfing in *Ride the Wild Surf,* and motorcycle gangs in *The Wild Angels* are but a few examples.

In the following piece, journalist Nora Sayre discusses Hollywood's 1969–1970 counterpart to the youth exploitation film of the 1950's— the "youth-in-rebellion" film. More specifically, she attempts to capture the whole "aura" of the creation of one of these films: a case study of Stanley Kramer's *RPM*.*

RPM* raises the question of how a commercial firm can market a product that calls for the destruction of the system of which it is a part. Conversely, how can those of the youth culture accept products from the system they oppose—especially when they are helping support the system by paying for these artifacts? As Theodore Roszak has put it in *The Making of a Counter Culture:*

> As has been mentioned, it is the cultural experimentation of the young that often runs the worst risk of commercial verminization—and so of having the force of its dissent dissipated. It is the cultural experiments that draw the giddy interest of just those middle-class swingers who are the bastion of the technocratic order. . . . There is no diminishing the tendency of counter-cultural dissent to fall prey to the neutralization that can come of such false attention. Those who dissent have to be supremely resourceful to avoid getting exhibited in somebody's commercial showcase—rather like bizarre fauna brought back alive from the

---

28. Richard Staehling, "The Truth About Teen Movies," *Rolling Stone,* December 27, 1969.

jungle wilds. . . . On such treacherous terrain, the chances of mis-
calculation are immense. Bob Dylan, who laments the nightmar-
ish corruptions of the age, nevertheless wears his material thin
grinding out a million-dollar album a year for Columbia. . . .

From such obfuscation of genuine dissenting talent, it isn't
far to go before the counter culture finds itself swamped with
cynical or self-deceived opportunists who become, or conveniently let themselves be turned into, spokesmen for youthful dis-
affiliation. Accordingly, we now have clothing designers, hair-
dressers, fashion magazine editors, and a veritable phalanx of pop
stars who, without a thought in their heads their PR man did not
put there, are suddenly expounding "the philosophy of today's
rebellious youth" for the benefit of the Sunday supplements.
. . ."[29]

Those in the youth culture who are serious about cultural revolution must work through the problem of distinguishing *genuine* sub-
versiveness in today's *avant garde* world, in which everything radical
and new—clothes, art, films, books, comics, and drugs, as well as music
—has proved to be a great money maker, in and through the capitalist
system.[30]

---

29. Theodore Roszak, *The Making of a Counter Culture* (New York: Doubleday, 1969), pp. 70–72.
30. James Hitchcock, "Comes the Cultural Revolution." Apparently in the case
of *RPM**, the distinction was made. The film did not have a successful run
at all.

REVOLT FOR FUN AND PROFIT

Nora Sayre

Like some hapless Victorian waif, ripe for rape, the Left has rarely been
lucky in its allies. Besieged from right and center, punctually lacerated
from within, the movement faces yet another swarthy problem: how are you
going to achieve a revolution when your enemies keep joining it? Industry
has long been into revolution, which has already lost some of its language
to ads for lipsticks and vaginal deodorant sprays. And Hollywood—equally
inspired and unnerved by the success of *Easy Rider*— is dilating its efforts
to produce "Now-movies" by making films about "campus disorders." In
The Activist (from the *Ride the Wild Surf* team, Art and Jo Napoleon),
student radicals are smeared with sympathy, as they probably will be in
most revolution-pictures—since Now-movies have to be aimed at the
youth-culture audience. (Hence one film corporation called a special
meeting of all the heads on its staff, to test the taste-vibrations.) MGM has
filmed James S. Kunen's *The Strawberry Statement* and has also bought
Abbie Hoffman's *Revolution for the Hell of It,* Stanley Kramer has produced

and directed *RPM**, footage has been shot for a movie on the Chicago 7, and others are being packaged with a haste that's almost outpacing the politics of genuine protest. Richard Kleindienst has announced that "while Nixon is President, random civil disorder will not be seen in America." But it will be seen in many movies. Perhaps some company may be tempted to belt out a scenario for the life and times of Fred Hampton, or to shoot (the experiences of) the Panther 21.

However, as an independent film maker admits, "The trouble with Now-movies is that they're often Then-movies." What may happen on campus or in the streets before a picture's released may worry the publicists as much as it worries Mrs. John Mitchell. How can your product maintain its nowness and its appeal for those who provide the material? Only fest-films, like *Woodstock*, seem safe in this sphere, since culture isn't changing quite as rapidly as politics.

Moreover, some of the current styles of moviemaking still seem influenced by the techniques of promotion. As many have noticed, slices of both *Easy Rider* and *The Activist* resembled TV commercials: filming attractive bodies within nature at its nicest suggests the hint of menthol, or seems to advertise the life-style that's depicted. (And, although *Easy Rider* was the ultimate Now-movie of 1969, quite a few have remarked that it seems at least ten years old—a nostalgic belch from the Beats and *On The Road*.) But the moral stance for filming revolution will be slippery: are you trying to sell it outright, or must the conclusion deliver an awful warning? Meanwhile, Hollywood's cradle of co-optation will continue to be rocked with desperate sincerity. (Yet good intentions can't validate any movie: as an English critic said of *Blow-Up*, "He got it all so *sensitively* wrong.") In the U.S., those who have been isolated by their profession will keep trying to produce worthy films about the values of a generation which deplores the system which longs to profit from Now-movies. . . . Of course, young radical film makers are also being hired to help the industry to reach the audience which it's trying to portray. As Graham Greene wrote in 1935, "There's always money to be picked up in a revolution."

One movie that's been braving these problems is Stanley Kramer's *RPM**, starring Anthony Quinn and Ann-Margret. The confrontation scenes were filmed at the University of the Pacific in Stockton, California— it's one of the few universities which will permit the miming of revolution on campus.

Like a professional army, the crew and 1200 extras—including many real students from Stockton—stand about on location, where the bushes around the college buildings have been sprayed with yellow paint to make December look like fall. A chorus of response punctuates the shooting.

"Quinn's finished. They knocked him down and they've been kicking him in the head."

"Were there some nice kicks?"

"Yeah, fine."

Policemen scrape dirt and leaves from their uniforms, rub their sore ribs and knees, compare shattered visors and broken clubs; students press ice bags against bruised faces, share bloodied bits of Kleenex for cut lips. Some pat one another's backs or shoulders, others scowl. All wade in succulent mud, which clutches their boots and streaks their thighs. One says, "The vibes are getting ungood." Two crewmen recall the styles of riot control which they once saw in Italy: "We should have the kind of equipment they have. They squirt guns full of red stuff all over the leaders, the inciters—it dyes their skin. Then it's easy to arrest them later."

"That's good. Not messy, you know what I mean?"

The *RPM** script is by Erich Segal, an associate professor of classics and comparative literature at Yale.[1] Anthony Quinn plays the acting college president: one of the world's most distinguished sociologists, author of *Studies in Alienation.* A radical in his fifties, he has been chosen by the students to replace the president they've forced out. (The faculty agreed to his appointment, since the other choices were Che and Eldridge Cleaver. And at least some of them are flexible: one professor admits, "We've been absentee slumlords in the Ghetto of the Mind.") Stanley Kramer, who cheerfully refers to himself as "a discarded liberal," focuses the movie on the long-term rebel who's racked by his conflicts of responsibility when the younger militants outpace him. At one point, the Quinn-president protests, "I marched for the Textile Workers' Union! I fought against Franco. . . . I spoke out *against* McCarthy. . . ." (Throughout, he gets limited comfort from Ann-Margret, cast as a student body, whom he urges to "read Talcott Parsons . . . *and put on a bra!")* He does satisfy most of the radicals' demands, but balks when they insist on hiring and firing faculty and abolishing formal courses. But they acknowledge that they will continue to invent unreasonable demands—as soon as each batch has been answered. They threaten to wreck a 2-million-dollar computer in the building that they've occupied. The president accuses the white student leader of having "a pathological need to destroy." But the latter's unmoved by this analysis, as well as by the president's earlier defense of private property: the student replies, "Private property is the jockstrap of the American conscience." The anguished president orders a friendly police chief to clear the building, stressing that there must be no violence. But as the students are gassed out, a psychotic bad-mouth female activist attacks a cop and inspires a bloodbath. After a giant bust, the president is hissed, booed, and pronounced pig by even the moderate students, who continue to jeer as he walks away. . . .

Sweating beside a swimming pool before Christmas, drenched in steam and cooked by lights: they're shooting an earlier scene in which Quinn mingles with the students just after his appointment. "You gotta

---

[1]Segal followed *RPM** in 1970 with a script aimed at middle America. He was on target with *Love Story*—(editor).

look radical," a makeup man says, pasting sideburns and a moustache on a sulky extra. "Yeh, like one of those goddamn hippies." The one-line actors explain that they were cast as Left or Right according to their looks.

"Oh, but I was Left yesterday and Right today."

"Well, I was Left in my last picture."

Then they talk about the word faggot, its multiple meanings, and what it stems from.

Blue lights are arranged to shine to Quinn's scene with the Right; later, a red glow bathes his consultation with the Left. The two groups assemble at opposite ends of the pool. The conservative students tell Quinn that they deplore the Left's tactics, that the university should stay the way it is: "Love it or leave it." One actor keeps fluffing "Maoist" for "Marxist"—a slip of the Sixties.

Just before I came to Stockton, a couple of young New York revolutionaries were disturbed to hear that such a movie was being made at all. One said, "That really hurts. What will they make of us? Brutes or clowns?" . . .

As a tenth-grade dropout, Quinn describes preparing for this film. "I didn't know what Ph.D. meant, or the function of sociology. I really crammed—I've read 40 books for this part. I even read Abbie Hoffman and those dirty newspapers at Berkeley." He and Stanley Kramer visited universities, questioned many students, attended classes. He says that the theme of RPM* is "where does permissiveness end and authority begin? There comes a point when you have to say, Here's the line. Right, dad, it stops here." (He no longer thinks highly of Dr. Spock. "I think he was well-meaning, like Emily Post—but so many sins have been perpetrated in his name. I just bought his book in Italian and threw it down the toilet.") He praises students for their instincts, their ideals, and their approach to love, but he considers the rebellion to be psychological rather than political. And yet he hopes that a third political party will come out of the student movement. "If the students could ever unite, they could put this country on its ass economically. . . . I don't think a lot of them are morally against the Vietnam war; instead, they know they're being exploited as slave labor. But nowadays you don't needs kids to fight a war—you can have old men pushing buttons. If my generation wants this war, let *them* fight it. With their buttons."

He says that he refuses "to do anything outside the system." Still, he was recently touched when the Brown Berets asked him to be a spokesman for them (he's a Mexican Indian). "If I thought I could be a leader, I'd give up acting. . . ." He visited the Indians who were occupying Alcatraz, has been speaking on their behalf, and was chided by George Murphy for his participation.

Quinn says that he and his family came to Stockton from Mexico when he was a boy, and that they were migrant fruit pickers, traveling in cattle cars with wooden slats. At first they didn't know that the California workers were on strike, that they themselves were being used as scabs. "I do know about hardship. Still, I can't relate to militancy." Now, he says, he's left of center, although "my son thinks I'm one step behind Nixon. . . . But don't make me sound like one of those far-out leftists." And yet: "The public doesn't do anything. . . . If tomorrow a shooting war started, we'd all run and hide." Suddenly, he's furious: "We've reached the same point that Nazi Germany reached when they were killing the Jews!" He's fiercer than I've ever seen him on the screen. Then he shakes his big head; there's a pause; the outrage subsides. He talks quietly about the potential power of economic boycotts: "A 25-million-Negro boycott would really hurt. . . . But I still wonder how far the balloon can stretch—like a balloon, you've got to say, This is all the air I can take. You've got to stay within the balloon, within the system." . . .

Stanley Kramer, whose productions include *Home of the Brave, The Men, High Noon,* and *The Wild One,* and who has directed *Judgment at Nuremberg, It's a Mad, Mad, Mad, Mad World, Ship of Fools, Guess Who's Coming To Dinner,* and *The Secret of Santa Vittoria,* among others, says that he'd like to be "a leader of the counterrevolution"—which means "hope against frustration. Life against death. Many films of the moment have a death-in-life motif at the end." He emphasizes that *RPM**'s student revolutionaries must appear "pure and idealistic. I take very seriously the responsibility of having people understand them. I dig the activists. If I were black I'd be a militant now. And I also think that tyranny is worse than anarchy." However, he feels that some students have carried their tactics too far, and that many are in the grip of fashion. He's already been attacked by some: "I told them, 'I've been fighting the establismment for 30 years, and I can't find out what it is.' And *they* said, 'Because you're it.' " To refute them, he cites some of his earlier films, which were considered radical. The Navy objected to *The Caine Mutiny* as antiAmerican; they protested that the character of Captain Queeg gave them a bad image, and that they'd never had a mutiny. The government refused to lend him a nuclear sub for *On The Beach,* and he had to defend himself before a congressional committee concerning "world guilt" about nuclear weapons. A spokesman from an adjunct of the State Department told him that it was ridiculous to suggest that nuclear war "would wipe out all humanity. Only about 200 million people would be killed, so it wouldn't be the end of the world."

Now, stressing that he dislikes the documentary approach, that no single movie "can tell the whole truth,"and that any film changes constantly while it's being shot, he underlines his identification with the president played by Quinn. "My own concept has always been to give voice to all the things that are bothering me. Yet I'm part of the system that's financing me." He looks momentarily wistful. "Isn't it possible to be someone who has a little compassion and awareness—and work in your own area? Isn't it possible to wait a little while, until things become clear? Before you choose sides?"

I'm up against the wall, standing with my back to a college building: the police are about to charge. That sickening suspense—of waiting to see if and how the cops will move—uncoils from the experience of Chicago, Paris, even Washington—so many confrontations of the past two years. . . . In Chicago, I waited like this against the Hilton, just where the police had told the press to stand. Suddenly, they rammed us against the hotel, smashing random heads ("for no reason that could be immediately determined"—*The New York Times*). Now, as the sun winks on visors and helmets and the revolving red lights of real police cars, I shrink as the uniforms and boots hurtle toward me and past me. But it's only a rehearsal; those who practice tussling with each other have to be reminded not to laugh. *"Please! No* more laughing!" Smoke billows from the windows: it does look exactly like tear gas, and dispels a mildly unpleasant stink of inner tube. I remember how gas can make you hate your own lungs, detest your throat.

Two young cops twirl their rubber guns, fence lightly with their plastic clubs.

One, mishearing directions, says, "Hey, the riot starts now!"

"No, we don't get to be violent until after Christmas."

Most of the cops are from the University of the Pacific's student football team. A black football instructor and the president of the Black Students' Union tell me that U.O.P. is very conservative, very expensive, and that many undergraduates are still apolitical. Atmospherically, the Stockton campus seems a solar distance from most impassioned universities—few of the student-extras seem to have any feelings about the war, the draft, or institutions. However, when the B.S.U. demanded a number of scholarships for minority students, the administration granted more than they asked for. Still, verbal agreements have outstripped tangible action. Meanwhile, the football instructor details the most practical and concrete plans I've ever heard for involving the schools in the community. As for white activists, he says that "their main project is to get rid of football; they forget that it gives scholarships to blacks." He adds that whites at so many universities are particularly isolated from current issues due to their recent discovery of drugs, which absorb so much of their time. "Drugs have done a flip-flop. They were a black thing for years. Now they're white." He and I share a queasy sensation that this movie's being filmed far from the questions of death or suffering, from the ghetto or Vietnam. . . . Yet my own actuality bump is dissolving: at moments, the movie jolts into what one knows so well—at others, it jars because it's so remote. Sometimes the *RPM** company seems to distill most of the opinions and quandries of the whole country, with all of the contradictions that are thickening up around us. Only one ingredient is missing: militants. . . .

Rap-groups tend to form around Gary Lockwood, of *2001: A Space Odyssey* and the TV series, *The Lieutenant:* he now plays *RPM**'s leading white revolutionary. Young actors and extras close around him, arguing, asking questions. He talks about redneck California, the world he grew up in, which is now hostile to the abundance of his (not very long) hair. Shaggy Californians are used to being called dirty faggot hippies, but mere insults in the East can be threats fulfilled in the West. Although *Easy Rider* is not his favorite movie, he and others agree on the validity of the theme: you really can get killed for the way you look. He's regretfully giving up his place on the Colorado River "because of the polarization": those who yell at him when they drive past his house could one day start shooting. . . .

Two crewmen disagree about Vietnam: both fought heavily in World War II. One says we should withdraw. The other insists that we've got to stay. Someone asks him why. "Because of the minerals."

Meanwhile, the local police of Stockton, who patrol the location, are very friendly to the company; they admire the professionalism of Stanley Kramer's staff. They snort with disgust in referring to MGM's *The Strawberry Statement,* which was filmed very freely in Stockton a month ago— the police called it Fruit's Delight. "Those hippies were so disorganized, and they used four-letter words that were 18 inches high." The city hall was used as an administration building, and the city manager was staggered to find his office being occupied by extras. He said that he had to get into his desk, but they said, "We're making a movie, daddy!" (The bona fide policeman loves imitating them; he switches his hips and snaps his fingers.) "And *he* said, 'Let me in or I'll call the *real* cops!' Ha!" . . .

On the set of *RPM**, an echo steadily recurs: so many kinds of Americans can no longer stomach living with one another. Later, several crewmen reminisce about "how the boys who came home from the war cleaned out the zoot-suiters in two weeks—they strung them up and had them hanging from the lampposts in L.A."

"Oh, I don't think they actually *hung* them."

"Well, anyway, they got rid of them."

Bob Yaeger says, "Well, time's scythe has reaped another day."

Gentle and cordial, Ann-Margret is reflective when asked for her views on revolution: "I've never been in a riot," she says, and pauses; "I'm not an intellectual." But she's sympathetic to student protest—"I think it's very healthy"—and says that she can identify with the issues. Still, "I find so many of the kids so mixed up, they don't know what, because the world is going so fast. I wish there were more leaders than followers. The leaders know exactly what they're doing, and sometimes they're doing wrong.

"You get a 16- or 17-year-old kid, seeing their parents into the Martinis and sleeping around, they tell them not to smoke pot, you know, blah, blah, blah, they're so confused, they'll grasp at anything. Some of them find it.

"Lord knows it's ten thousand times harder to go to college now than it was for me." (She went to Northwestern's School of Speech.) "I don't know how the kids remain sane. And some don't, and we know that some freak out and some are insanitary. They've got to have something, or else they'll go completely out of your mind."

Some other conversations within this company imply that the young are corroded—or half-crazed—from being torn apart by politics, or from thinking about politics all the time. Also, some share the conviction that the youngest generation is clamoring for a Disneyish Utopia. Someone says, "They want to make it perfect so that they can just drop out."

Mounting toward the confrontation, a female militant, played by Linda Meiklejohn, yells at the police chief who has ordered the students to leave the building: "Thanks to you, and to our *noble* president, maybe our citizens who are so unmoved by our use of force overseas and in our own cities will wake up when they see hobnailed boots in the Garden of Eden. . . ."

Between takes, Graham Jarvis, of Elaine May's *Adaptation* and *The Fig Leaf,* tells me that he initially hesitated about playing the police chief. He accepted the role when Stanley Kramer assured him that the students "would not appear in a bad light." Now, it does seem likely that the audience may leave the theatre thinking that the rebels are sick adventurists. I know that Stanley Kramer doesn't intend this. But Jarvis and I talk about how easy it is to play into the hands of the Right. After all, this subject is in the public domain—it merely belongs to everyone in the country. But some students will feel that they've been both exploited and put down. . . .

ABC-TV is filming the filming; Gary Lockwood makes some shots with his hand-held camera; a still photographer snaps pictures of Lockwood and ABC filming the filming. Bob Yaeger says, "So this is not just for the B'nai B'rith Bugle."

Teda Bracci is setting her hair for tomorrow's confrontation. She plays the ferocious activist who mauls a cop, shouting, "Pig bastard!" and thereby touches off "the riot." She loves her part. Now, her eyes glow and her excitement kindles as she anticipates the shooting—she throbs like a Tolstoyan heroine looking forward to her first ball, or National Velvet before the great steeplechase. Her bony face ripples with a flurry of rapturous smiles; she has the kind of ripe, husky voice that can slide from a whoop to a croon. Meanwhile, Audrey Hepburn is having nun's trouble on TV. Teda says, "I mustn't have any breakfast, or there'll be something *else* all over the ground." Audrey Hepburn says, "How can I be a good nun if I cannot get the Congo out of my blood?"

Agitation rustles through the location, despite the fiber-glass vests and shin guards, and the plastic skullcaps which some stunt men wear beneath hairy wigs. Waiting for planned chaos pinches some nerves and mouths, tautens the skin stretched over cheeks and around nostrils.

Teda Bracci kicks her cop's feet out from under him, flinging him prone. She's a magnificent fighter; somebody says, "She knows where a man's castanets are." Hundreds race and leap to beat each other's heads against the ground, to wrestle in a mud-rich flesh-pack that grows angrier every hour. Arms, legs, fists, knees, clubs reassemble again and again to punish one another. When the action's cut off by the bark of a gun, they stand panting and gasping and glaring. After all the rehearsals, the preparation, the choreography with stunt men, much of the crowd starts punching from the heart. Later, it was discovered that some who swung hardest weren't even student extras, but were unpaid visitors simply fighting for free.

Many grudges build up through the re-shooting: "Next time, I'll get *him.*" A cop slams a student hard against a car; a student knees a cop repeatedly; many skulls are cracked together; one policeman socks a student six times after a take is finished. The casualty list swells. Blurts of blood glisten through the glycerine and the red paint and lots complain of having been bitten.

Older professionals talk indulgently about "body contact": they think that's what makes the crowd grow wilder. But it's also this period: by the end of 1969, the real students who play students can't help reacting against the symbol embodied by their classmates who play police. And the latter do hate being called pigs. One says he'd *never* join the force: "Like it changes you." Another adds, "I used to wonder why they called cops pigs, and now I know why." A shortish boy in uniform has been jumped five times by the same group. Now, Lockwood's astonished by receiving his first mouse: he was doing elaborate flips and rolls with a stunt man, when a student ran up and belted him in the eye. "Man, I've been in at least five hundred fights and never had a mouse!"

A black student playing a cop says happily, "Pig hit a pig." He explains that a few of the students are actually police trainees, and two have just accidentally clobbered one another. Later, two of the fledgling cops recall the flaming ping-pong balls which they encountered on a stretch of duty in Washington after Martin Luther King was killed. "They're worse than Molotov cocktails. You take a hypodermic needle and inject the ball with fire-lighting fluid. After it's lit, you can bat it through a window with a tennis racket."

"It's not just an amateur thing."

Meanwhile, a cop and a student—who have been pounding each other into the mud—spring up beaming, and slap each other's palms. At least a few remember that this is a movie. But, as the days of shooting have accumulated, many have started weighing the issues that *RPM** has thrust at them. Some seem to have acquired more respect for student revolt: "They're trying to tell us something, but nobody listens, so the next time they try harder. What else can they do?"

Gary Lockwood says, "If enough people are okay financially, there won't be a revolution. And if enough *aren't,* there will be." He talks about ghettos; "Like I'm glad I'm not sort of black, man." Since he was poor for years, he's personally irritated by those who call him a cop-out because he now earns well: "They attack my 80-dollar desk. But why shouldn't I groove on my own?" I press him again about student revolution. "Man, I *gotta* be for it! I just *have* to think it's good. But there's a lot of . . . elements I don't go along with. If you go ripping down the street with your bayonet, chanting from Mao, that's cool, but don't come yelling to me if you get shot. . . . But if this white conservative middle class doesn't come around, then it looks like we're moving toward civil war, man. Sometimes it seems inevitable. But I don't want all those people killed, or the rest of us. I like my old lady, I like my dog, I like me. And I'd like to be seventy, man."

Someone else says, "But what do we *do?*"

Small arguments continue about violence and the perils of inviting repression, plus the likelihood that both will ripen soon. But there are others—including some high-school students—who gleam with sheer exhilaration of the fighting. "We're going to miss this when it's over."

"Man, we've never had such fun."

One murmurs, "Right on," softly, as though he's never said it before.

Later, I learn that it cost over half a million to film the confrontation—including the price of keeping the company at a motel for 26 days. Abbie Hoffman wrote that the Yippies spent under $5000 on the Chicago demonstrations, and that the Yip-In in Grand Central cost $15.

The flesh-pile is heaving and hurting again. Paul Winfield—who plays the key black militant—and I compare our confrontations. He was in the antiwar crowd that was savaged by blue power at the Century Plaza Hotel when L.B.J. visited Los Angeles in 1967. While we agree that most of *RPM*'s* combat scenes are painfully accurate, we're startled when so many students jump on cops' backs, and send them rolling over and over on the ground. We've never seen anyone attack the police so blithely, nor cops who are so easy to knock down. However, today's action is being shot in blur and slow motion, so perhaps the fuzz won't look like such a pushover.

Winfield, who grew up in Watts, describes being shot to death in his last picture, *The Lost Man.* Pellets of pseudo-blood and gunpowder were taped to his body beneath his clothes; when an electric switch was pressed, blood and smoke stains burst through his shirt. He says that it wasn't unpleasant, although the electrical aspect did make him uneasy beforehand.

The last gun is fired to end the shooting. Teda Bracci lies on the ground with a cop in her arms, patting the back of the man she's just been kicking.

The real Stockton police produce a huge cake with blue icing, inscribed, "To the *RPM** Crew,/From the Boys in Blue."

Bob Yaeger gazes benignly around the location. "Well, as they say in the hardware business, god bless 'em and screw 'em."

ROCK CULTURE

At this point, the important question to be asked about the artifacts of youth culture is: Are they antithesis or thesis? Do they serve a counter culture or merely, as one writer in this section puts it, define a "cultural playpen" for the establishment youth of America?

This section can be thought of as a case study, focusing specifically upon one artifact of youth culture—rock music—in an attempt to throw light on this question.[1] The section contains no running commentary. The reader is at this point (and within the background afforded by the broader section on youth culture) urged to make and consider his own "links." Some very brief editorial comments upon the section, however, do appear below.

Joe Ferrandino, from the radical stance, traces the emergence of rock from the teenage musical culture of the 1950's. It is his impression that rock music *is* radical in content, and that it does help establish political awareness in youth (as well as being a cultural link between middle class youth and the working class). Sociologist Robert Rosenstone, from a more establishmentarian perspective, analyzes the lyrical content of protest songs and reaches quite similar conclusions as to the music's effectiveness in establishing social consciousness. The editor then presents his own analysis of the songs of Bob Dylan— pointing to the fact that in a structural sense, a good deal of Dylan's work has been released with a commercial public in mind. Rock critic Michael Lydon then presents the case that rock music has in fact been co-opted and emasculated by the lure of capitalistic rewards. Finally, journalist Sol Stern uses the December 1969 Altamont rock concert to illustrate the lack of commitment and values the youth culture revealed in that instance—a group of amazed middle class kids with no concept of revolutionary or political consciousness at all.

---

1. See D. Duane Braun, *Toward A Theory Of Popular Culture: The Sociology And History Of American Music And Dance, 1920–1968* (Ann Arbor, Mich.: Ann Arbor Publishers, 1969) for an account of the American origins of music and its subsequent institutionalization in the American social structure. See also Charles Keil, *Urban Blues* (Chicago: University of Chicago Press, 1966) as well as Charlie Gillett, *The Sound of the City: The Rise of Rock and Roll* (New York: Outerbridge and Dienstfrey, 1970).

ROCK CULTURE AND THE DEVELOPMENT
OF SOCIAL CONSCIOUSNESS

Joe Ferrandino

THE ROOTS

Rock culture begins in exploitation and appropriation. In the late 1940s
the big band era, which had carried a generation through a war and was
readying them for another, was on the decline. Much of the black big band
sound had been effectively coopted by the Paul Whitemans of the day in
order to make it palatable to the white consumer consciousness. A sound
that began around the turn of the century in New Orleans ghettos, which
evolved into rag time and ultimately into the black big bands, had been,
in effect, turned into its opposite—music by whites for whites—and drained
of any critical social content. (A contemporary example of a similar phenomenon is the Boston Pops treatment of the Rolling Stones.)

At the same time that this sound was collapsing, the more vibrant
elements of black music were coalescing with what was left of the big
band into a new form. These elements included the *blues* (perhaps *the*
foremost contributor to the history of rock), both rural and urban. The
best known of the rural blues singers at the time was Leadbelly, whose
song *Good-night Irene* was number one in 1950—but not by Leadbelly (he
was too black, but Gordon Jenkins and The Weavers were just fine). The
urban blues were simply the rural blues ghettoized as the blacks went
north in search of the promised land and found Chicago instead. Out of
these roots came the great black rock and roll artists of the 1950's—
Chuck Berry, Little Richard, Clyde McPhatter, Ray Charles, Jimmy Reed,
Bo Diddley, Ivory Joe Hunter, etc. (I make references only to those people
who did achieve some degree of recognition in the 50's. It was only in the
middle 60's that people began to "discover" the blues artists who carried
the tradition of urban blues through the 30's, 40's, 50's, and 60's—e.g.,
Howlin' Wolf, Homesick James, Little Walter, Muddy Waters, etc.) The
other elements were *gospel*—always a part of the black history and very
close to the blues; *jazz*—again close to blues and also the black version
of the big band sound—including people like Charlie Parker, Billie Holiday,
Dinah Washington; and lastly, the *boogie piano* (Jimmy Yancy, Meade Lux
Lewis). This piano style was copied almost directly by Little Richard, Fats
Domino and other pianists of the 50's. These elements coalesced in the
late 40's and very early 50's and were given the name rock and roll—two
of the most commonly used terms in late 40's rhythm and blues songs. Alan
Freed, whose function in the 50's was very similar to today's Bill Graham,
manager of the Fillmores—East and West—i.e., rock entrepreneur, coined
the phrase.

At the same time there was developing a large social group whose
consciousness was the receptive element for this music—youth. Their

backgrounds were predominantly new working class. With the exception of the blacks this group was perhaps the most disenfranchised at the time.

These were the formative years of the knowledge factory and defense industry as institutional safety-valves for surplus manpower—primarily youth. The need to absorb surplus manpower into either one of these two industries was not as acute at that time as it was to become in the late 50's and after. As the Rowntrees state in *The Political Economy of Youth:*

> While civilian government employment during 1950-65 increased only 2% as a proportion of adult population, students and military personnel during the same period increased by 6.4% as a proportion of adult population. (Together the change was 8.4%.) These defense and education industries are particularly suited to absorb workers almost indefinitely, and the workers they absorb are primarily young. in 1965, almost three-quarters of the armed forces were under 30 and 56% were under 25. Almost all students are under 35, and about 95% are between the ages of 14 and 24. The task of absorbing the surplus of the U.S. economy has therefore increasingly fallen on the shoulders of young people.[1]

In 1950 the *need* to go to college was not as great among working class youth (especially sons and daughters of factory workers) as it was to be ten years later. This meant for many of them dropping out of high school. In fact it was almost a status symbol to drop out and take a job in a service station. The defense industry was, of course, hard at work in Korea, but the level of social consciousness was so low that again it was almost a status symbol to join up and fight the Communists. (These attitudes are not uncommon in many 'traditional' working class areas today; however, among the working class youth working in the factories or in the armed forces involved in today's youth culture, strong positions against the draft, racism and imperialism are developing.)

The bourgeoisie had effectively taken hold of the cultural apparatus—to such an extent that those being sucked into the capitalist machine had very little if anything in the way of cultural salvation. The barrenness of the cultural scene at the time can perhaps best be seen by the fact that among the most popular TV shows were The Life of Riley and (a little later) Jackie Gleason's The Honeymooners, both of which portrayed "blue collar" workers as a bunch of buffoons totally subservient to their masters. The movies were packed with McCarthyite anticommunism, and shows like South Pacific which defined happiness as "Some Enchanted Evening," were on Broadway. The music scene wasn't much better, with Vic Damone, Vaughn Monroe, Theresa Brewer and Patti Page, and songs like "Forever and Ever" by Perry Como, "Buttons and Bows" by Dinah Shore and other greats like "A Bushel and a Peck," "Our Lady of Fatima," and "Enjoy Yourself, It's Later than You Think" on the charts.

---

[1]John and Margaret Rowntree, "The Political Economy of Youth," REP, p. 9.

Needless to say, under the heel of McCarthyism and (Nixonism) organized labor, and the Old Left had either retreated or moved right to liberalism. There wasn't very much that was happening that spoke in any way to the actual lives of these young people, which is the way the bourgeoisie preferred it. Rock and roll came into being in opposition to this bourgeois culture and although able to relate to youth, the relationships that did obtain were for the most part determined by the bourgeoisie. That is, the analysis that Ewen makes in "Advertising As Social Production" of capitalist productive relations vis-a-vis the *workers* in the 1920's can also be applied to the emerging youth culture of the 50's. The bourgeoisie recognized the necessity to control something potentially dangerous to them (witness the violence at rock and roll show fights, in street gangs, etc.— imagine that coupled with a social consciousness). They also saw the potential for new markets. The latter meant the attempted *destruction* of the liberating aspects of the culture and the *construction* of repressive social relations in order to meet productive needs.

In the formative years of rock and roll this practice on the part of the bourgeoisie took the form of exploitation and appropriation. As indicated, particularly in the case of Leadbelly, the music was appropriated from blacks and done by whites primarily for whites. This became standard operating procedure through the early 50's under the appropriate heading of "cover" records. This meant that the record company would consciously seek out black artists in order to pick up what sounded like saleable tunes which would then be recut and marketed with established white personnel (losing the black content). Some of the most blatant examples were the McGuire Sisters' "Sincerely," originally done by the Moonglows, Kay Starr's "Wheel of Fortune," originally done by the Cardinals, Bill Haley's "Shake Rattle and Roll" originally done by Joe Turner, and Elvis Presley's "Money Honey," originally done by Clyde McPhatter and the Drifters. The exploitative feature added another dimension. It is by now well known how record companies would buy rights to a song mostly from black people and then make millions off it. Billie Holiday's whole life is a testimony to this type of racist exploitation.[2] A more obvious example (and actually one of *the* most famous "cover" records) is Big Mama Thornton's song, "Hound Dog" (written around 1952–53 by Leiber and Stoller). She sold her rights to the song for $500.00. Elvis Presley sold over two million copies and Big Mama Thornton never received another penny.[3]

This type of exploitation/commoditization served a number of purposes from the point of view of the bourgeoisie. First, it took what was

---

[2]Billie Holiday's autobiography, *(Lady Sings the Blues,* N.Y.: Lancer, 1956) is a moving chronicle of this type of exploitation.
[3]This practice still continues. Jesse Fuller's "San Francisco Bay Blues" is a more up-to-date example. As popular as the song was, as of two years ago he had received no money for it.

potentially some of the most critical and subversive music (namely black blues), drained it of its critical content and turned it into its opposite to buttress the status quo. Secondly, by controlling the artists, the media, etc., this "cultural imperialism" was an excellent method for channelling the tension and rage generated by an oppressive system (again gang fights, rock and roll shows, and bourgeois controlled dances and record hops served this purpose). And thirdly, it provided for new domestic markets.

> While agreeing that "human nature is more difficult to control than material nature," ad men nonetheless discovered in such general notions of human self-conception useful tools for advertising, given their desire to predictably control men in order to create new habits and desires for consumer products.[4]

What could be better?—one could control people through their culture and even make money off it. But for the capitalist there were a number of contradictions involved which outline the beginnings of the struggle by youth to find themselves in and through their cultural practice in the face of bourgeois manipulation.

NEW FORMS, OLD CONTENT

Around 1953–54 the contradiction between what the songs were originally and what the songs were as presented by the media was becoming apparent (primarily through the people who really got into the music and began collecting "originals"). The static styles of those who passed for real rock and rollers were no longer tolerable to growing numbers of young people (both white and black and primarily urban oriented) whose whole life style was the antithesis of the Vic Damone death style. As Jonathan Eisen put it: "Rock music was born of a revolt against the sham of Western culture; it was direct and gutsy and spoke to the senses. As such, it was profoundly subversive. It still is."[5]

In 1955 La Verne Baker's (a black woman) original version of "Tweedle Dee Dee" gained a greater popular reception that the white Georgia Gibbs version. La Verne Baker even went so far as to take "the issue of 'covers' to her congressman who decried the practice on the floor of the House but was unable to do anything about it since 'covers' were legal."[6]

This move signalled the recognition of black in rock and roll but it was not at this time the recognition of *black as black*, but *black as white*. That is to say, with the exception of a few artists, almost all the black rock and roll artists who achieved any notoriety whatsoever did not sing about anything that was ever remotely related to the black experience. This was particularly true of most of the "great" groups—The Platters, the Harptones,

---

[4]Stuart B. Ewen, "Advertising As Social Production," *Radical America,* May–June 169, p. 48.
[5]Jonathan Eisen, *The Age of Rock* (N.Y.: Vintage Books, 1969), Introduction, p. XV.
[6]*Eye,* Oct. 1968, p. 51.

Moonglows, Valentines, Four Tunes, Billy Ward and The Dominos, etc. Many of the songs projected an idealism that was almost religious. What had developed was a new *form*, but this form was infused with the old sham content. First of all, most of the problems dealt with in the songs were false problems in the sense that they almost invariably centered around "boy-girl" relations in a false way. They were heavily male chauvinistic—juxtapose Gloria Mann's "Teenage Prayer" to The Videos' "Trickle Trickle" for example. The male is hot and heavy and usually roams a lot. The female is passive and just wishes he would pick her from the others (competing all the time) so that she could become his property as a steady girl and later as a housewife. The situations were super-romantic and tended toward the view that all the problems in the world would be solved "When We Get Married." It would be "Heaven and Paradise," etc. Frankie Lyman and the Teenagers are an excellent example of this phenomenon. A black group—New York City ghetto oriented—they made the grade on such great tunes as "Why Do Fools Fall In Love" and "I Want You to Be My Girl." The cover photo on the album they did for GEE has all five dressed like Yale students—dark trousers, white shirts, white "letter sweaters" with a big T in front, and, of course, processed hair. In fact, since the Establishment had started on the juvenile delinquency kick in an attempt to thwart dissident elements among the youth culture, the Teenagers even felt it necessary to *apologize* in a song titled "I'm Not a Juvenile Delinquent." This is a blatant but certainly not uncommon illustration of the seizure and destruction of a culture by taking the potentially negative elements, denuding them of their negative characteristics, and assimilating them into normal capitalistic social relations. It is therefore not very surprising to learn that Frankie Lyman died from an overdose of heroin two years ago in his late 20's, and that Little Willie John, a victim of the same kind of exploitation, died in jail about the same time as Frankie Lyman.

The focus on interpersonal/boy-girl relations worked well in the interest of the bourgeoisie who could control the youth while at the same time creating mass consumer man (in this case, youth). All of one's energies were channelled into these pseudo-problem areas (in the sense that what is really a social problem was defined in terms of an individual aberration) —the biggest problem was not the *kind of society* that forces the fetishization of one's penis; but simply, can one make it with Marsha on Saturday night? Further, the social relations were of course not healthy ones—i.e., there was almost no real sexuality and everything was defined as neat and clean, malt-shop romances, etc. Given this, the control factor was not very problematic. In "The Affirmative Character of Culture" Marcuse puts it rather well:

> Release of sensuality would be release of enjoyment, which presupposes the absence of guilty conscience and the real possibility of gratification. In bourgeois society, such a trend is increasingly opposed by the necessity of disciplining discontented masses. The inter-

nationalization of enjoyment through spiritualization (i.e., the abstract character of boy-girl relations in this music) therefore becomes one of the decisive tasks of cultural education. By being incorporated into spiritual life, sensuality is to be harnessed and transfigured. From the coupling of sensuality and the soul proceeds the bourgeois idea of love.[7]

At the same time the consumerization (proletarianization) of youth was progressing well. Besides the usual cultural items such as radios, records, etc., one had to have the "right" commodities in order to make it socially (mouthwash, acne cream, hair tonic, etc.). Mass consumer youth was being created. Ewen has an excellent discussion of the rise of social psychology as an ideology for control and consumerization. He quotes social psychologist F. H. Allport: "Our consciousness of ourselves is largely a reflection of the consciousness which others have of us . . . . My idea of myself is rather my own idea of my neighbor's view of me."[8]

PROGRESSIVE DIRECTIONS

Nevertheless, there was struggle and in the face of malt-shop romanticism there emerged with and through this music two semiprogressive elements: sensuality (though channelled) and rebellion (though primitive)—and concomitantly a growing sense of community. That is, in the struggle of the youth culture to become itself in opposition to the attempted mass bourgeoisification can be found the beginning of social consciousness.

The sensual element came primarily through the musical form—especially in the work of black rock and roll artists (although Elvis Presley was also a help). The heavy up-beat rhythms, shouts and screams, and bodily movement in the face of a white musical culture that was totally antisensual was a progressive step. Dancing (as in the jitterbug) was serving to bring to consciousness the recognition of one's body; i.e., it was an unsophisticated attempt to overcome the mind-body alienation. Eldridge Cleaver in Soul On Ice says: "Bing Crosbyism, Perry Comoism and Dinah Shoreism had led to cancer, and the vanguard of white youth knew it."[9]

Though Cleaver's descriptions are primarily directed toward the music of the late 50's and early 60's (as opposed to the earlier 50's), the similarity is evident, particularly in the following passage:

> They "the young" couldn't care less about the old, stiffassed honkies who don't like their new dances: Frug, Monkey, Jerk, Swim, Watusi. All they know is that it feels good to swing to way-out body rhythms instead of dragassing across the dance floor like zombies to the dead beat of mind-smothered Mickey Mouse music.[10]

---

[7]Herbert Marcuse, "The Affirmative Character of Culture," Negations (Beacon Press, 1968), p. 110.
[8]Ewen, "Advertising as Social Production," p. 49.
[9]Eldridge Cleaver, Soul On Ice (Ramparts, 1968), p. 195.
[10]Ibid., p. 81.

Yet it must be kept in mind that the dances were always confined to certain "acceptable" forms and in this respect served as an excellent means of channelling this emerging sensuality.

The Pleasure Principle absorbs the Reality Principle, sexuality is liberated (or rather liberalized) in socially constructive forms. This notion implies that there are repressive modes of desublimation, compared with which the sublimated drives and objectives contain more deviation, more freedom, and more refusal to heed the social taboos.[11]

The history of rock and roll dances is the history of the emergence of a more liberating sensuality until in the late 1960's the dance almost totally rejects all traditional western forms and refuses to be structured even within the standardized confines of dances such as the Jerk, Watusi, etc. As late as 1967 the American Broadcasting Company was still trying to market the "Bugaloo"—dance, dress, TV show, etc. But it was evident at this time that youth were demanding more of their culture than another plastic commodity. The Bugaloo didn't make it.

Most white and black up-tempo rock and roll music evidenced this emerging sensuality in terms of form. Probably the best example artistically was Little Richard. His performances in person were an attempt to introduce the subject into what was purely an object-to-object relation. The song *was* Little Richard—he moved, sweated, screamed and, in general, tried to break through the pseudo-individuality of previous "stars" and assert himself as a real individual. Listen to "Jenny, Jenny." But even here it was still the Little Richard of the diamond rings, the expensive cut-rite suits, and processed hair. The rock-sale system had forced Little Richard to sell himself. In some cases the sensuality also came across in content—usually in a somewhat vulgarized form as in Hank Ballard and The Midnighters' "Work With Me Annie," "Annie Had a Baby," and "Annie's Aunt Fannie." These songs were overt in their sexual references and were consequently banned from radio air play. Nevertheless a type of sexual consciousness was developing and the songs sold well. As usual the conservative bourgeoisie got very nervous. The following are examples of some of the more reactionary measures taken at the time:

Houston—The Juvenile Delinquency and Crime Commission banned over fifty songs in one of its weekly purges.

Chicago—A radio station broke R & R records over the air as a daily ritual.

Iowa—A radio station got so carried away banning "unsuitable" rock records that even songs from the Broadway musical *Damn Yankees* were kept off the air.

---

[11]Marcuse, *One Dimensional Man* (Boston: Beacon Press, 1964), p. 772.

Washington—A Senate Subcommittee began looking into the correlation between R & R and juvenile delinquency.

New York—*Variety*, in an editorial entitled 'A Warning to the Music Business' said, 'The most casual look at the current crop of lyrics must tell even the most naive that dirty postcards have been translated into songs.' Another article in *Variety* stated that R & R would make a 'negative global impression for the U.S.'[12]

The other element that I have termed progressive in this music was the primitive rebellion (as expressed in gut-level social commentary) that helped build a sense of youth solidarity. Most of this social comment was very low-level with an almost total lack of historical analysis—but it spoke to the masses of youth who were experiencing a tremendous sense of alienation. The comments were primarily directed at the authority figures—parents, teachers, and the social system in general. The alternative to this oppressive system was always the youth rock culture (which was for the most part under the control of bourgeois productive relations). Some criticisms however were also directed to the work place—e.g., The Silhouettes' "Get A Job," Fats Domino's "Blue Monday," and the Coasters' "Quarter to Eight"[13] which contained the lines, "I'm tied to my job, my boss is a big fat slob." The bulk of the musical criticism, however, was directed toward the authority figures. Even the police/arrest system came in for some criticism as a Kafkaesque procedure in the Coasters' "Framed."[14] Most of the other Coaster songs dealt with parents ("Yakity Yak") and the school system ("Charlie Brown"). They were speaking to youth who were feeling the same kinds of frustrations the Coasters were describing. But again, the dissent was contained within the traditional structures. Charlie Brown, in opposition to the school authority, instead of becoming a leader of organized resistance, was "the clown." The bourgeoisie wanted to keep it that way.

Chuck Berry transcended this. While never getting quite to the level of the protest songs of the 60's, Berry told it like it was. "No Particular Place to Go" sang of youthful alienation. "Almost Grown" told of having to give up the youth scene to make it in the Establishment. "Sweet Little Sixteen" and "Rock and Roll Music" were fine descriptions of the youth culture. "Too Much Monkey Business" is one of the best pieces of social comment (from the rock culture perspective) at the time. The latter song in both form and content is almost a *direct* parallel to Dylan's "Subterranean Homesick Blues."[15] As the Rowntrees put it: ". . . the young have taken the mark of their oppression—their youth—and turned it into a signal

---

[12]Eye, "Advertising as Social Production," p. 52.
[13]I'm not sure of the exact title of this latter song.
[14]Almost all the Coasters' songs were written by Leiber and Stoller.
[15]Most of these songs can be heard on the album "Chuck Berry's Golden Decade" on Chess.

by which to recognize the fellows with whom they wish to express solidarity."[16]

Chuck Berry was a self-conscious rock and roll artist. One of the few who had a sense of history and who understood and sang about the historical importance of the youth culture. That is, Berry grasped the tension between the culture which contained the elements of liberation and the society which repressed the possibilities of liberation. This tension is captured well in Berry's "School Days." The song documents an extremely repressive and typical school day and then states:

"Soon as three o'clock rolls around
You finally *lay your burden down*
Close up your books
Get out of the seat
Down the hall and into the street
Up to the corner and round the bend
Right to the juke joint you go in." (my emphasis)

This song was one of the most profound criticisms (in the context of the youth culture) of the knowledge factory versus youth culture to come out of the 50's. There is no doubt that Berry was the spokesman for a growing consciousness. In reference to Mann's *Doctor Faustus* Marcuse comments on black music:

> In the subversive, dissonant, crying and shouting rhythm, born in the 'dark continent' and in the 'deep South' of slavery and deprivation, the oppressed *revoke the Ninth Symphony* and give art a desublimated, sensuous form of frightening immediacy, moving, electrifying the body, and the soul materialized in the body.[17] (emphasis mine)

Or, as Chuck Berry put it, "Roll Over Beethoven!"

With this kind of music it was very easy to see how a sense of community was beginning to develop. People began to recognize that the problems that they were experiencing were not just their own individual problems (although the bourgeoisie was working hard at attempting to maintain that image). This musical social comment evolved dialectically. The form of the music came into being in opposition to the traditional forms. Yet this new form contained the same old alienated content. The new form thus required an alteration of the content and as the musical history proceeded and the content became more meaningful, new forms were required, as we shall see.

THE CULTURAL SCENE IN GENERAL

A word about the general cultural scene at the time . . . .How was the music a reflection of the practical cultural activity of youth and vice versa? This time was the most acute in the development of the youth culture. With

---

[16]The Rowntrees, "The Political Economy," p. 20.
[17]Herbert Marcuse, *Essay on Liberation* (Boston: Beacon Press, 1969), p. 47.

few exceptions (noted above), the level of consciousness was at the level of individual consciousness (which is why the kinds of inroads that Chuck Berry was making were very important). The social problems were internalized which led to a false analysis which suggested false solutions. If one couldn't "make it" (sexually, socially, etc.), it was his own fault and not the system's. In other words the connections between seemingly "individual" problems of "adjustment" and an exploitative and oppressive social system had not been made. The bourgeoisie reenforced these attitudes in order to market the mass personality. This type of internalization usually resulted in tremendous feelings of guilt and impotence and frequently manifested itself in self-destructive tendencies (hard drugs, motorcycle and auto races and stunts, gang fights, etc.). Compensation usually took the form of a facade of toughness (e.g., the Cheers' "Black Denim Trousers and Motorcycle Boots") and rebellion against authority.

Although the youth culture did involve youth from the whole new working class (and even in rare cases bourgeois youth), it was primarily among working class youth working in factories, the armed forces or preparing in high school for the same, and among black youth (often unemployed and unemployable) that these characteristics manifested themselves most acutely. This is perhaps due to the fact that they were born into violence and tension—the factory, the family (where the social relations were already strained by the working conditions of the parents, usually resulting in extreme authoritarianism), and the school (where it wasn't the dunce cap but the fist), etc. The violence which characterized the rebellion took many forms (some mentioned above). On the one hand much of it was channelled in the right direction—namely, toward the institutions that were immediately oppressing them, e.g., property (theft and vandalism were extremely common), the family (constant parental disagreements), the educational system (as objectified in the principal or teacher—who would be called names, fought with, spat upon, etc.) and even the police and officers in the armed forces. But, on the other hand, there was no overall social analysis, which meant that much of the violence was misdirected (against each other) and, in this sense, it is understandable that many of the hardiest participants in this "rebellion" are now policemen.

A sense of community was developing which was important but it was a community that was, in many cases, organized around false issues, and therefore, one that was very easily controllable. One's immediate neighborhood and the degree of toughness determined who was a friend. The enemy was usually everyone else. (Dances and rock and roll shows sometimes served to break this down; however, these events also served as good places for the release of intergang antagonisms.) Despite the lack of ownership of private property, the internalization of the master's mentality had taken such hold that *turf* fights became commonplace (many of these along racial lines). Compare this level of social consciousness to those people consciously struggling in defense of People's park.

"HEROES"

The individualism, inarticulateness, guilt, etc. were objectified in some of the 50's "heroes." Marlon Brando in the "Wild Ones" was such a hero. James Dean was another. He was the existential hero/antihero who saw sham and phoniness for what it was. He experienced in his own life, as well as on the screen, the social problems that youth was confronting—but again, it was on an individualistic internalizing basis. "James Dean expresses in his life and films the needs of adolescent individuality which, asserting itself, refused to accept the norms of the soul-killing and specialized life that lie ahead."[18]

As the title of one of his films indicates, James Dean expressed *A Rage to Live* against a society that was dehumanizing people every day.[19] James Dean presents an interesting counter to the bourgeois art critics who consistently demean youth and working class people because they have "inferior tastes." In James Dean youth was able to identify authenticity and relate to it, albeit on an individualistic level, in terms of their own lives.

Another 50's hero was Elvis. His major contribution to the developing culture was the emphasis on sexuality (though well controlled). His negative contributions, however, surpassed his positive one. That is, Elvis Presley served first of all as excellent testimony to the individualistic ethic —that in this society, any poor boy can make it. The bourgeoisie made sure this message was well presented and saw to it that most of Elvis' movies used this as a theme. This move by the bourgeoisie was an attempt at giving further credence to a system that was becoming suspect to many youth. Needless to say, Elvis' being drafted was still another buttress to the system in the form of the rapidly developing 'defense' industries. Secondly, since the myth was that anyone could make it, many of the youth attempted to do so. This again, served the purposes of control (since their primary energies were directed toward singing on the corner in the hope that some producer would find them) and consumerization of the culture (musical instruments, sheet music, copyrights, etc. became important cultural necessities). This type of consumerization grew tremendously in the late 60's. One almost *had* to belong to some sort of singing group, own an electric guitar, amplifier, etc. in order to maintain social acceptance. New needs were created and met within the dominant structure of advanced industrial capitalism. Moby Grape put it well in song when they said:

"Can I buy an amplifier
On time
I ain't got no money now
But I will pay before I die.[20]

---

[18]Edgar Marin, "The Case of James Dean," *Modern Culture and the Arts* (N.Y.: McGraw-Hill, 1967), p. 450.
[19]Ibid., p. 459.
[20]From the song "Naked If I Want To" on Moby Grape's first album.

OTHER THRUSTS

Although rock and roll was the dominant popular musical trend in the 50's, there were a number of other cultural/musical thrusts that should be mentioned. First, there was the Ginsberg/Kerouac phenomenon, which was essentially the working class *angst* at an intellectual level. Their rebellion took more creative forms. Instead of beating up a school teacher, they dropped out, took head drugs, read and wrote poetry and hit the road. They emphasized spontaneity and naturalness in the face of artificial mass culture. But, there was no in-depth criticism and no analysis. Second, there was the urban blues, which did not gain any real audience until the 60's. Third was the other "popular" musical form—namely, country and western. C & W, like rock, contained many contradictions. On the one hand, its roots were honest, straight-forward and human (as in the original Jimmie Rodgers and Hank Williams); but, on the other hand, much of it had been perverted by C & W entrepreneurs and turned into a commodity—all form and no content. The two other musical thrusts at the time were to end up as the continuation of the youth culture of the 50's and the roots for the youth culture of the 60's—folk music and the protest music of the Old Left.

The musical Old Left in the 50's had been unable to relate to the youth of the 50's. Those who did retain some of their original analysis after the McCarthy repression (which moved most of the Old Left right to liberalism[21] were unable to relate that analysis to the new working class—and to youth in general. Their songs and slogans were primarily factory oriented. I think it can be said that Chuck Berry did more to begin to raise social consciousness than any Left artist in the 50's. In fact, as Carl Oglesby points out, much of the thrust of the Beat Movement was due to a lack of any real critique of the quality of life on the part of the Old Left.[22]

As the content of rock and roll began to take on quasi-progressive overtones, new forms began to develop. Youth was beginning to search for newer and more meaningful types of cultural and social relations. In the late 50's "ordinary" rock and roll had reached perhaps its all-time low, both in form and content (Chuck Berry was in jail, and Little Richard had found religion). The best rock and roll music at this time had its roots in C & W and took on the forms called "rock-a-billy" and "Tex-mex" (for which some credit can be given to Elvis).[23] The Everly Brothers and Buddy

---

[21]See James Gilbert's *Writers and Partisans* (Wiley & Sons, 1969).

[22]Carl Oglesby in *Evergreen,* Feb. 1969.

[23]It should be mentioned in fairness however that two strains of "standard" rock of this period did retain *some* of the integrity of the earlier 50's—the music of Phil Spector (though he served the bourgeoisie well as "America's First Teenage Millionaire"—see Tom Wolfe's *Kandy Kolored Tangerine Flake Streamline Baby)* and the music of Motown. The only reason I mention these is that it was this music plus the best of the earlier fifties that the Beatles, Stones, and Dylan were into and much of their earlier music (not Dylan) was almost direct copying of this music.

Holly are the two best examples. Both were able to convey an honesty and straightforwardness in form and content which was opposed to the "rock" that was getting all the hype. Their music also revealed an appreciation for language and message. Parallel with this was the emerging of Hollywood folk music—the Brothers Four, the Highwaymen, Christy Minstrels, Chad Mitchell Trio, Kingston Trio, etc. A new form was evolving—but again, in the way in which it could easily be used to channel and control. The music of these "folksingers" was semi-hip, sometimes funny, but rarely subversive and the artists themselves were neat, clean and certainly American. The bourgeoisie were also busy locating and grooming clean-cut "rock stars" in an attempt to keep the heat off. This was originally done by the smaller record companies, but soon became a big-business practice. Fabian and Frankie Avalon were what they came up with. This type of plastic rock and roll star did take with some of the more unsophisticated elements of the youth culture. But ever-increasing numbers of youth were demanding more from the artists than Fabian's "I'm a Tiger." Those who rejected this plastic package deal sought meaning in the newly emerging forms.

The contradiction in the development of the education industry— namely, that some real understanding of the nature of the beast was beginning to grow—coupled with some of the above cultural developments helped develop the base for the liberal bourgeoisie to start making moves in the late 50's which culminated in the election of Kennedy in 1960. While a majority of the youth culture stayed with rock and roll, many, especially working-class students who attended the more liberal northern universities, as well as what Martin Sklar calls the nonacademic intelligentsia—free lancers, detached artists, etc.[24] took to this new form—folk music. These youth were the vanguard of the struggle against the bourgeoisification of rock and roll. In conjunction with their distaste for "mass culture," they were rapidly becoming aware that the abstract ideals of the U.S.—freedom, justice, equality, etc. were not being realized. This problem was located very conveniently in the South. It was at this point that some liaison between the folk culture and the remnants of the Old Left began to develop —i.e., the youth culture was taking on some overt political content. The new musical forms beginning to emerge in the late 50's/early 60's, reached out to a rediscovery of new cultural roots. Lawrence Goldman put it this way:

> . . . the folk music world was composed to a large extent of the rebel-
> lious children of ex-radical middle-class families. These families had
> once been active, often in support of causes associated with the Com-
> munist Party. They were still sympathetic to radicalism and regarded
> themselves, whether they were active or not, as 'progressives.' It

---

[24]Martin Sklar, "On the Proletarian Revolution and the End of Political-Economic Society," *Radical America,* May-June 1969, p. 19.

should be remembered that in the 1950's the Left consisted of a small band of harried and desperate people, divided by ancient quarrels, persecuted by the McCarthyites, abused by the cold war liberals and betrayed by the Khrushchev Report and the Hungarian Revolution. They were tired, impotent and unsure of where they were going or why they were going there.

To protect and preserve itself, the Left created a series of myths which, though originally based on a careful analysis of the political situation, had become, after a time, a means of avoiding reality. The Left came to talk of the Negro rather than Negroes, of the Worker rather than Workers, of the Thirties rather than the fifties, and of the People rather than people. The folk music world was one of the few places left in American cultural life . . . where those myths still retained their emotional force.[25]

This abstract analysis, while reflecting a more advanced level of social awareness than that of the 50's (in the sense that parts of the system itself were singled out for criticism), was still a liberal view. "Help Others" was the motto. The system in general was fine; all that was necessary was the integration of the disenfranchised (the Southern black) into it. Alliances were made between these youth and the liberal politicians against the "enemy"—Bull Connor and the Southern racists. Again, control of the disenchanted through the culture was assured by always keeping it within the context of reformist politics.

The new music, nevertheless, was clearly an advancement over the old. It re-introduced genuine emotion. Human relations began to take on a different perspective. In fact, much of the thrust of the folk scene can be viewed as a part of this cultural struggle to overcome the enforced capitalist consumer social relations. The immediate appreciation of the Kingston Trio folk types and gradual rejection of them for more "authentic" folk people accomplished two things. First, it indicated that the people involved in this culture were evolving new and higher artistic standards and secondly, it led to a recognition/appreciation of a totally different culture, one almost untouched by the advanced technology and one which involved different, more human ways of being. The folk music was much more articulate than most of the 50's rock and therefore required a much different collective response. Instead of the immediacy of jumping around to loud music, folk music demanded quiet listening, reflection, etc. In this sense, folk music can be viewed as the mediation between the fundamentally inarticulate rock of the 50's and the heavily articulate rock of the 60's.

DYLAN

The folk songs themselves were usually either original folk songs (e.g., "Barbara Allen") or some type of social comment (e.g., Phil Ochs' "Talking Birmingham Jam"). The form was the traditional folk form and the

---

[25]Lawrence Goldman, "Bobby Dylan—Folk-Rock Hero," in *The Age of Rock*, ed. Jonathan Eisen, p. 210.

consciousness was the traditional liberal one. One of the new young folk artists who was able to break through both of these restictions was Bob Dylan. Dylan's development from the early 60's to the present parallels the development of the consciousness of the youth culture and the concomitant development of the New Left. In this sense, Bob Dylan was making history and history was making Bob Dylan.

Dylan's move to the East was primarily a result of his disenchantment with the bourgeois mass culture of the Hibbing (Minn.) working class and petit-bourgeoisie. His own history was one of a constant search for new cultural (musical) forms. He therefore came East as an eclectic—well-steeped in almost all of the musical strains of the 50's. He had a strong feeling for the blues, country and western music (particularly Hank Williams) and the best of the 50's rock and roll. His folk hero was Woody Guthrie, who represented perhaps the best of the Old Left folk tradition ("This guitar kills fascists," was a Guthrie motto) but Dylan himself, along with the other young people, was developing a new genre—a genre struggling not only against the bourgeoisification of popular music and culture, but also against the old folk forms themselves. This new form was the urban folk culture.

During the early stages in the development of this cultural movement, Dylan and other urban folk artists seized upon both the traditional forms and content. Dylan, for example, affected a style and performed the recorded songs much in line with the originals, leaving some room for subjectivity in interpretation (as in Dylan's version of Blind Lemmon Jefferson's "See That My Grave Is Kept Clean"). Dylan, however, along with some of the other folk artists had a tremendous sense of history. He was aware of the contradictions of the society and the limitations of confining oneself to a musical style that was historically obsolete in both form and content. About his subsequent move to more topical music, Dylan said in a letter to Dave Glover:

> I'm singin' and writin' what's on my own mind now—
> What's in my own head and what's in my own heart—
> I'm singin' for me an a million other me's that've
>   been forced t'gether by the same feeling—
> Not by no kind a side
> Not by no kind a category—
> People hung up an' strung out—
> People frustrated an' corked in an' bottled up—
> People in no special form or field—
>   age limit or class—
> I can't sing 'Red Apple Juice' no more
> I gotta sing 'Masters a War'—
> I can't sing 'Little Maggie' with a clear head—
> I gotta sing 'Seven Curses' instead—

I can't sing 'John Henry'
I gotta sing 'Hollis Brown'—
I can't sing 'John Johannah' cause it's
    his story and his peoples' story—
I gotta sing 'With God On My Side' cause it's my
    story and my peoples' story—
I can't sing 'The Girl I Left Behind' cause I know
    what it's like to do it—
I gotta sing 'Boots a Spanish Leather' cause I know
    what it's like to live it
But don' get me wrong now—
Don' think I go way out a my way not t' sing no folk songs—
That aint it at all—
The folk songs showed me the way
They showed me that songs can say somethin' human—[26]

As Dylan's consciousness grew in and through his songs, so did the folk culture. He was, as he put it, singing "his peoples' story"; the story of a cold war, nuclear mentality and John Birch paranoia ("Talkin WWIII Blues," "Talkin John Birch Society Blues"); the story of the coming of age in such a society ("Bob Dylan's Dream"); and, the story of human relations in such a society ("Don't Think Twice"). It was through this infusion of contemporary content into traditional forms that Dylan was able to begin to build a mass base of young people who felt essentially the same way. Gramsci describes this phenomenon: "It is still the culture of a narrow intellectual aristocracy which is able to attract the youth only when it becomes immediately and topically political."[27]

The people who were attracted to the folk culture were those who had been able to retain some sensitivity in the face of massification and who were constantly struggling against massification. Much of this struggle, however, was waged on the basis of the "symptom-disease" confusion. That is, they were aware of many of the symptoms of a diseased society— meaningless unproductive labor, racism, distorted social relations, etc.— but, very infrequently did they get to the real *causes* of these problems.

Many of the folk people were also "socially involved"; that is their *praxis* reflected their distaste for these problems and the attempt to correct them—usually within the system. A great many of these people refused to work—i.e., to perform alienated labor—though many did engage in what they considered to be meaningful labor—organizing, social projects, voter registration in the South, and writing for topical folk magazines (*Broadside, Sing Out* etc. which were the forerunners of underground newspapers).

---

[26]Bob Dylan, *Broadside No. 35,* Nov. 1963.
[27]Antonio Gramsci, "Marxism and Modern Culture," in *The Modern Prince and Other Writings,* p. 85.

They identified with the "folk" (usually in the abstract), and wore folk clothing—work shirts and dungarees—and behaved as "folk" were seen or thought to behave—more humanly/communally, etc. In terms of these social and musical confines, Dylan's struggle as a self-conscious artist with a deep feeling for history can be viewed as an attempt to break through these restrictions, explode the old forms, and create new ones always within the context of a growing social awareness. In "Only A Pawn In Their Game," it was the system that produces racism that was brought to task. In "The Lonesome Death of Hattie Carroll," it was the class nature of justice that was exposed and in "With God On Our Side" and "Masters of War," it was (respectively) the religious buttress of militarism and war profiteers that were indicted. But, as Dylan's development indicates, there was much more to be said and a larger audience to reach.

It must be kept in mind that although the folk culture was growing and the restrictions of both liberalism and the folk music form were being brought into question, the youth actually involved in the folk scene represented only a small minority of the nation's youth. It should also be kept in mind that the civil rights struggle had peaked and was on its way down. The blacks, through people like Malcolm X and Stokely Carmichael, were becoming aware that change in this society is not made by accepting handouts from white liberals, but by organized struggle. At the same time, the war in Vietnam was escalating despite the election of the "peace" candidate Johnson. The Berkeley FSM was also going full blast and beginning to articulate a critique of the university. The Rowntrees capture much of the feelings of these times:

> The off-campus New Left also reached a turning point in 1965. Following Selma, SNCC moved from non-violence to self-defense and black power. . . . It became clear to many young radicals that their emphasis on spontaneity and grass-roots activity had led them into a reformist dead end. Many saw that isolated projects, no matter how radical in themselves could not become spontaneously revolutionary. In the reassessments and reorientations of the last three years, youth have turned their attention back to the schools and to the promotion of the more militant class forms of action that have emerged in recent times.[28]

Musically the Beatles and Stones had hit the nation with "good old rock and roll"—though more amplified and more up to date. Their early music was based on some of the best of the 50's, but was almost totally devoid of content (as in the Beatles' "I Want to Hold Your Hand"). This was the music of the majority of youth and since it and the Beatles (sweatshirts, wigs, etc.) were very easily marketable, this was where the bourgeoisie concentrated their attention. The music was criticized by the folk people as being impure and inarticulate, but this critical perspective was

---

[28]The Rowntrees, *"The Political Economy,"* p. 27.

primarily elitist and essentially bourgeois. The folk purists were interpreting the music, not struggling to change it. Dylan, however, although originally a critic, had moved to a new position. He did see the necessity for
change and struggle right here on the home front, not simply down South.
which was essentially the same kind of ideological development taking
place within the New Left. This precipitated Dylan's move to a new form—
rock and roll, which was again, another instance of the old forms not being
able to contain the new content. Dylan was also very critical at the political
level. His earlier views were primarily within the liberal framework. As
his social consciousness grew, so did his antipathy for liberalism (along
with many others in the Movement). In his first major interview (in the
October 24, 1964 issue of the *New Yorker*) Dylan expressed this antipathy:

> I fell into a trap once—last December—when I agreed to accept
> the Tom Paine award from the Emergency Civil Liberties Committee.
> At the Americana Hotel! In the Grand Ballroom! As soon as I got there
> I felt up tight. First of all, the people with me couldn't get in. They
> looked even funkier than I did, I guess. They weren't dressed right,
> or something. Inside the ballroom, I really got up tight. I began to
> drink. I looked down from the platform and saw a bunch of people
> who had nothing to do with my kind of politics. I looked down and I
> got scared. They were supposed to be on my side, but I didn't feel
> any connection with them. Here were these people who'd been all
> involved with the Left in the thirties, and now they were supporting
> civil-rights drives. That's groovy, but they also had minks and jewels,
> and it was like they were giving the money out of guilt. . . . And then
> I started talking about friends of mine in Harlem—some of them
> junkies, all of them poor. And I said they need freedom as much as
> anybody else, and what's anybody doing for *them?*[29]

Here was not only a critique of liberalism (for Dylan this incident and
his critique of liberalism are expressed in song in 'As I Went Out One
Morning" on *John Wesley Harding*), but an indictment also of the Old Left
forms. Dylan was struggling not only to break through the old *musical*
forms, but also through the old *political* forms, since most of these forms
were predicated on bourgeois social relations. Dylan was practising and
speaking for what Marcuse was to later call the "new sensibility."

Dylan's new form—rock and roll—was criticized by those members
of the folk culture who considered themselves "purists." The "purists"
viewed Dylan and the new culture as their property. At Newport and Forest
Hills in the summer of 1965, he was booed by these people. He responded
in song—"It's All Over Now, Baby Blue." Thus, Dylan's struggle, at this
point, was at many levels. On the musical and cultural level he was attempting to break through the forms that had already become static and in fact
useful to the bourgeoisie. Dylan, the other folk artists, and the whole folk
culture held little threat for the system as long as they were apart from the

---

[29]*The New Yorker,* Oct. 1964, pp. 86–88.

masses. Dylan's response, however, was essentially the same response as the emerging New Left, i.e., to move away from elitism and toward youth or as the title of Dylan's first folk-rock album stated, "Bringing It All Back Home."

The significance of this break should not be underestimated. Even so dynamic a left movement as that centering around the Wobblies in the early 20th century was unable to effect a break with the traditional folk forms—they simply used the traditional forms and inserted new content. Take, for example, two of Joe Hill's most famous songs "Casey Jones and Union Scab" and "We Will Sing One Song" whose tunes were respectively the original railroad ballad "Casey Jones" and Steven Foster's "My Old Kentucky Home." (Cf. Folkways Records FP-2039)

What was Dylan able to accomplish by this move? The topic is worth much more than time and space allows; however, it will be worthwhile to mention at least a few things. First of all, Dylan was able to reach more people. Some of his songs, e.g., "Subterranean Homesick Blues," did get on the radio and more and more people became aware that Dylan was articulating the frustrations, problems, and views on society that these young people were experiencing daily. This, in itself, served a number of purposes. It carried through what had begun to develop in the later 50's: a sense of community. The restrictions imposed by the internalization of problems were being shattered. A genuine critical consciousness was developing. In this way, this music also transcended the mediocrity and plasticity that the rock of the late 50's and early 60's had become, which meant in practice that new forms and new artists—artists who spoke to these people and their experiences—would be required. It also meant that cooptation would have to move to a new level.

It was not only what Dylan said, but also how he said it that character-izes another of his contributions to the development of social awareness. Marcuse has argued that our universe of discourse is closed and that one way of attempting to keep it closed is by a repressive language—a lan-guage that is positively based, static, abstract, and at almost every instance turns the abstract "concepts" of liberation into their opposites in practice. It is, therefore, clear that any culture which attempts to do away with the old will have as one of its major tasks the liberation of language. Here Dylan's work was very important. He was able to take the abstract language that had almost no relation to anything and concretize it within the prac-tical critical experience of an evolving youth culture. In almost every phrase in every song on "Highway 61" and "Bringing It All Back Home," was jam-packed some sort of critical perspective. This type of critique was usually expressed in semi-surreal imagery, but to most of Dylan's following, the world was surreal—bowling balls *were* coming down the road and knocking people off their feet; heart attack machines *were* being strapped across the shoulders of the people in this society; people who sang with their tongues of fire *did* gargle in the rat-race choir, etc. ("Maggie's Farm," "Desolation Row," and "It's All Right Ma, I'm Only Bleeding" are three excellent instances of the almost total indictment of a dehumanized society). In this context, it is interesting to note that Bobby Seale and Huey Newton were also able to relate the black experience to Dylan's "Ballad of A Thin Man" (as Seale recounted in a recent issue of *Ramparts).* George Metefsky points out:

> [Dylan's] surreal rock reached the mass of U.S. youth with a revolutionary message: escape from 'rational, liberal discourse' into real, superintense experience. Instead of slogans, he created poetry that people listened to again and again, straining after the seductive lyric until they freaked right out of middle-class consciousness into sudden understanding.[30]

Marcuse makes a similar point:

> The new sensibility and the new consciousness which are to project and guide . . . [social] reconstruction demand a new *language* to define and communicate the new 'values' (language in the wider sense which includes words, images, gestures, tones). It has been said that the degree to which a revolution is developing *qualitatively* different social conditions and relationships may perhaps be indicated by the development of a language: the rupture with the continuum of domination must also be a rupture with the vocabulary of domination.[31]

It is part of my thesis that Dylan played a major role in the development of this new awareness through a new *way* of language. This is not to say that Dylan is or should be aloof from criticism. Alan Berger in an article "Acid and Revolution" *(Connections,* Jan. 1967, Madison, Wisc.) contends that some of the critique that Dylan offers at this stage does not go far enough in terms of a totally radical perspective, and I agree. (e.g., "Though the rules of the road have been lodged/It's *only* peoples' games that you got to dodge" from "It's All Right, Ma (I'm Only Bleeding).") However, it does seem clear that one cannot overlook Dylan's negation of the old "biology" and his attempt at establishing a new one.

With these breakthroughs evolved new and higher standards amongst the youth for the artists and performers. The music had to be relevant to the developing new man. Topical rock artists were more and more in demand. The Beatles and the Stones had to relate to the times. The Beatles focused on alienation ("Elenor Rigby"), mysticism ("Within You Without You") and fun ("Yellow Submarine"). The Stones were more pointed in their attacks—"Satisfaction" was an almost total social indictment; "Mother's Little Helper" focused on the necessity for drugs as a buffer to an oppressive social system; and "Paint It Black" ended in a kind

---

[30]George Metefsky, "Right On Culture Freeks!" *Kaleidoscope,* Madison, Wisc., Sept. 1969.
[31]Marcuse, *Essay on Liberation,* p. 33.

of nihilism. In terms of capturing the sense of alienation, Simon and Gar-
funkle were perhaps the best (as far as that level of consciousness goes)—
"Sounds of Silence," "Most Peculiar Man," etc. and their "Silent Night 7:00
News" portrayed some of the more apparent social contradictions. Even
plastics such as Sonny and Cher and the Turtles had to tailor their work
to these new forms.

Here again, however, the tension between a culture attempting to
assert itself and a system attempting to destroy it by cooptation once more
emerged. Just as good old rock and roll was subverted as much as possible
in the 50's in order to further inculcate the consumer's mentality, it was
now folk rock that became the vehicle for cooptation. The record companies were doing a grand old business, hip entrepreneurs were popping up
all over, and many of the artists (either due to a lack of integrity or money)
were now spokesmen for Coca-Cola, white levis, and rock and roll equipment. But since this was one side of a contradiction and since capitalistic
greed knows no bounds, it was not infrequent that subversive ideas got
sold. As Metefsky says in regard to Dylan:

> Dylan's use of profit-oriented media to spread this revolutionary
> message established both the dominant pattern of hip activism, and
> the foremost contradiction within the hip movement. Indeed, the con-
> tradiction between liberation and the use of capitalist media is the
> basic problem for any cultural revolution under capitalism.[32]

The Rowntrees argue similarly about the youth culture in general:

"Viewed one way, 'youth culture' is a merchandisers' invention and a
vehicle of false consciousness. However, it also offers support for many
alienated youth that may make it possible for them to translate their disaffection into open revolt."[33]

OTHER DEVELOPMENTS—LOVE AND HAIGHT

Bourgeois culture was producing its own potential grave diggers. As
cooptation and consumerization escalated, so did the social realities—Vietnam, black revolt, etc. and consequently so did the political activism of
the young. Underground newspapers which had begun on an almost total
drug trip (EVO, Oracle, etc.) were not only springing up all over the place
but were also involved in a much more serious kind of politics. Along with
them, antiwar organizing, demonstrating and draft resistance grew. The
blacks were getting their shit together and were being supported by white
youth. More frequent and more critical attacks, both theoretical and practical, were being directed toward educational institutions—college and
high school. And, more generally, a *new life style* was coming into being
—one that was antithetical to the bourgeois massified life style. This life
style manifested itself in many ways: in dress—a looser clothing style

---

[32]Metefsky, "Right On Culture Freeks!"
[33]The Rowntrees, *"The Political Economy,"* p. 23.

nowhere as restrictive as the old; in appearance—long hair, beards, no make-up, etc.; and more importantly in behavior—new, more human, social relations really became the basis for *praxis.* Much of this "feeling for the other," however, lacked a good social analysis and consequently emerged in abstractions—"Love" and "Flower Power."

This ideology reached its apex in San Francisco during the 1967 "Summer of Love" in the Haight-Ashbury community. The lack of good analysis made for a community filled with contradictions. On the one hand, there was the liberating life style. People were trying to live a kind of utopian socialism—communal sharing, lack of private property—based on the new, more human social relations. There was also a refusal to perform alienated labor (keep in mind that these young people were rejecting the positions offered them in "the middle class"). People were dropping out of "straight" society. In this sense, the "new sensibility" was emerging: The social expression of the liberated work instinct is *cooperation,* which, grounded in solidarity, directs the organization of the realm of necessity and the development of the realm of freedom."[34]

But, on the other hand, there were a lot of problems with the scene. One was the view that all one had to do was get his head together and all the problems would be solved. To an extent introspection, self-analysis, etc. were all necessary as a means to a more pervasive social end. But, for many the means were the end. This resulted in the heavy use of drugs (again, not the right drugs used intelligently as a means to greater social awareness, but only drugs used as an end in themselves) in the attempt to have instant freedom. Nicolaus makes the point that drugs also served (and still do serve) as a means for the promotion of internal group solidarity.[35] I would agree in the cases of pot and perhaps acid, but many of the Haight people graduated very readily to harder drugs such as heroin and speed. *Dealers* introjected the capitalist mentality and bought low and sold high, making plenty of money off their "brothers." In practice drugs and the drug ideology also served as an excellent means of controlling potential dissidents (as they have done in the ghetto). In a certain sense the *users* also introjected the bourgeois mentality by attempting to solve their social problems through drugs. Their parents fought alienation, oppression, and frustration with alcohol, tranquilizers and sleeping pills. They did it with LSD, speed and heroin.[36]

These contradictions within the "love movement" were indicative of at least a bad if not false analysis of society. Although most of those involved held that the society in one way or another was badly in need

---

[34]Marcuse, *Essay on Liberation,* p. 91.
[35]Martin Nicolaus, "The Contradiction of Advanced Capitalist Society And Its Resolution," REP, p. 7.
[36]Theodore Roszak in his article "Capsules of Salvation" *(Nation,* Vol. 206, 1968) has a good discussion of this particular phenomenon.

of change, the connections to capitalism were usually not made, thereby resulting in a false positive—love. It was assumed that exemplary gentle love-like behavior could change material conditions. As if throwing flowers at Rockefeller would automatically cause him to give up his oil interests to the people of Latin America. This was brotherhood in the abstract since it failed to take into account the historical conditions which could have served as the practical guide for the direction of these newly developing social relations. The decline of the Haight and the growth of the New Left has, in practice, educated masses of young people to this fact. Frank Zappa and the Mothers of Invention, while themselves more cynical and nihilistic than consciously radical, did provide in song a critique of this notion of love in the abstract and the whole Haight ideology on *We're Only In It For the Money* ". . . psychedelic dungeons cropping up on every street . . . I will love everyone. I will love the police as they kick the shit out of me on the street."

In addition, there was no doubt that the bourgeoisie loved love and flower power since they were very easily turned into a product. Flowers and love became styles—in dress, art, etc. Auto makers put out a car with flowers on it right from the factory. The plastic hippie was created—from $38.00 sandals to the $15.00 leather handbag. Having done their job for the Indian upper classes, Maharishis and Swamis were brought in to sell inner peace for $5 per meditation. The Haight and East Village were turned inside out and instead of becoming real peoples' communities, they became hip tourist attractions where the "hip boutiques" could fleece hippies and tourists alike. Some communal activities did meet with some success— primarily the underground newspapers, communications collectives, Digger Free Stores for food and clothing, etc., but on the whole, most were short-lived. This is not to say that everyone was immediately coopted. On the contrary, many of those who were among the original community organizers were able to see through this and fought against it. The cooptation was aimed at the new people who hadn't at that time achieved the level of consciousness that the others had. In total opposition to this bourgeois destruction of the scene, the most socially conscious of the hippies did a beautiful thing: they declared "The Death of the Hip" and marched through the Haight with a coffin into which were thrown bells, flowers, etc. A new level of social consciousness was beginning to emerge. For many this meant the beginning of radical politics—i.e., the understanding that *social change does not come out of the stem of a flower.* For others, it meant a renewed cynicism and a desire to start anew. These people felt that the big city environment had caused the failure so they split to start communes in the country. (As an aside, it might be worthwhile to mention that some of these commune experiments, e.g., in New Mexico are now being funded by the big foundations, primarily for two reasons: (1) to get rid of the potential dissidents; and (2) to create conflict between the poor Indians and Mexican-Americans on the one hand and hippies on the other, since the former have *no* land and are forced to live a more uptight existence which causes them to view hippies and their "liberating life style" as elite bourgeois.)

The San Francisco music scene pretty much reflected these kinds of contradictions. On the one hand the hip entrepreneur developed (the theater managers, the record company managers and the liaison people), and advertising took on the hip style and bought off many of the more creative film makers, writers, artists, and musicians. But on the other hand, something new to the rock and roll scene developed—peoples' music. This culture was struggling to maintain itself. Therefore, while the bourgeoisie catered to the plastic hippie at $5 a seat in some downtown theater, the peoples' groups played free in the park. They played the music that was totally relevant to these peoples' lives. They played *blues;* they played *head music;* and, they played *political music* because these were all parts of the day-to-day community experience. Of course, the police busts came time and time again (and Columbia records has the audacity to put out a record ad which says "The man can't bust our music," when in fact Columbia is *the man)* which served to educate people more to the reality and not the ideal. The musical groups—Country Joe and the Fish, The Jefferson Airplane, The Grateful Dead, etc. also lived communally, shared their incomes, etc. They were also very involved with the student movement wing of the New Left culture and frequently performed at university rallies and antiwar demonstrations.

The music and culture evolving out of this scene served to break down the alienation between audience and artist (since the artists were the people and the people were artists in the sense that they lived art. Groups like the SF Mime Troupe even went further to involve in their street theater people who were in no way involved with the culture). Along with these developments and the rise of black nationalism, came the appreciation of black music, as black. Blues singers such as Howlin' Wolf, Muddy Waters, BB King, *et al.* who had been around for many years were now being listened to and imitated, primarily, I think, for two reasons: (1) because of the honesty in the music, and (2) to extend a hand to a culture that had struggled and survived despite the many years of cultural, racial and economic exploitation. In this sense the white youth saw in the black blues singer a brother waging the same kind of struggle he was waging. "No matter how many people exploit it, black culture, is a revolutionary peoples' culture, because it developed in opposition to and bitter knowledge of capitalism, and because it enabled blacks (unlike the American Indian) to survive cultural imperailism and grow as a cultural entity."[37]

When in 1968 Dick Clark (American Bandstand) observed the new dance, musical and life styles he remarked, "This music is subversive; these hippies want to change society. It's not like the nice clean music of

[37]Metefsky, "Right On Culture Freeks!"

the fifties." Although the Haight failed and the love balloon burst, that cultural movement served a tremendous educational purpose for the New Left. As Nicolaus puts it:

> [the] style and appeal of hippie subculture may well fade away, but the vision of a practical culture in which man is free from labor, free to begin at last the historic task of constructing truly human relationships, probably has been permanently launched and will continue to haunt capitalist society as the spectre of its own repressed potentialities.[38]

THE PRESENT SCENE

There is no doubt that the present level of social awareness among youth is far above that of the 50's. The Rowntrees make a comparison between the communal aspect of the present culture and the Beat Scene of the 50's: "The communities also offer laboratories for the development of communal, life-affirming forms of living, eating, sharing in, and participating in public activities. Contrast the buoyancy of contemporary youth culture with the nihilism, individualism and withdrawal of the 1950's."[39]

Of course this culture is still engaged in a struggle—a struggle against consumerization, cooptation and neo-romantic ideology. It has been through this struggle that this greater social consciousness has emerged. This emerging consciousness is presently manifesting itself in many ways. There is first of all the ever-growing radical community, i.e., a community composed of people who are transforming themselves through their social practice and at the same time attempting to transform the society at large. The students/hippies have been able to ally themselves with other members of the New Left—workers, blacks, army organizers, etc—through *both* their respective cultural *and* political practices. This growing consciousness is also reflected more precisely in the music, much of which relates directly to the social practice of both the artist and the audience. To cite a few examples—Gordon Lightfoot's "Black Day In July," Bob Seeger's "2 plus 2 Is On My Mind," the Earth Opera's "American Eagle Tragedy," Credence Clearwater's "Bad Moon Rising," and Bobby Darin's (!) "Simple Song of Freedom" sung by Tim Hardin. Listening to almost any black radio station will indicate that black music has also taken on a new relevance. Most of the above music has been heard on Top 40 radio. The "underground music" only heard on LP's and some FM stations goes beyond this to overt political and social critiques.

This distinction between Top 40 and underground or "schlock rock" vs. "good rock" is understood by most members of the youth culture. As emphasized earlier, they are demanding more from the artists (this will perhaps explain part of the reason for the tremendous changes undergone by people like Bobby Darin—from "Splish Splash" to "Simple Song of

---

[38]Nicolaus. "The Contradiction . . .", p. 8.
[39]The Rowntrees, "The Political Economy" p. 24.

Freedom"—and Dion—from "Run-Around Sue" to "Abraham, Martin, and John"). As Tony Taylor of the rock group Grafitti states: "A few years ago people would request bubble gum music that the groups wouldn't dig playing. Now they're asking for the Cream's stuff—good music."[40] The artists therefore have had to undergo changes in order to keep up with the developing culture. The Dave Clark Five faded but Dylan, the Beatles, and the Stones have changed and stayed with these cultural developments.

The Beatles and the Stones are interesting cases in point. They have both evolved dialectically against and with the cultural and political movements. From a heavy dependence on 50's rock, they moved to greater social content, to drugs and finally to the statement of a quasi-political ideology (the forms of the music also requiring drastic changes along the way). For the Beatles this ideology is "Give Peace a Chance" through non-violence and love. For the Stones it's "Street Fighting Man." The album "Beggar's Banquet" is a fine musical statement of contemporary politics. A song like "Factory Girl" indicates not only a tremendous development in both form and content as compared to the lack of political content in the 50's, but also a tremendous development in the Stones' own artistic history (e.g., "Stupid Girl," etc.)

This type of development, as I have maintained, is due in great part to the dialectical relationship between the artist and the cultural/political milieu. The sensitive artist is being led by the cultural/political movements and he, in turn, is in the creative vanguard of these movements. To paraphrase Hegel, the artist comprehends his times in thought. Thus, it is no surprise that much of today's music is directly relevant to the most intense period of political activism in the last three decades.

If it is the case, thus, that the cultural movement is giving direction to the artist and vice versa, what kinds of directions for the movement seem to be emerging? First and most obvious is the thrust of the culture itself. If mass culture does serve both to control man and to direct his needs (i.e., man on and off the job), then it must be this bourgeois culture, as Metefsky claims, that must be smashed in order to awaken people to the repressive reality of the social system. This has been successful (to the extent that it has overcome bourgeois cooptation, consumerization, etc.) as far as many working class young people are concerned—*primarily* those in suburban high schools, the universities, those working in the service industries, street people more and more from blue collar backgrounds, and . . . increasingly, draftees and enlisted men in the armed forces. Through their cultural and social practice they have been able to develop a social critique and attempt to implement change on the basis of it. Witness the rapid growth of coffee houses near army bases, the extensive use of marijuana by the troops, as well as much more developed forms of struggle. Also, it is encouraging that many young factory workers were in attendance at

---

[40]*Jazz and Pop Magazine,* Dec. 1968.

Woodstock. The second point is more specific: exactly where should this cultural thrust be concentrated? Although many of the new working class youth are developing revolutionary potential, it remains the case that these people do not yet comprise the masses of American people whose lives are still controlled and manipulated by the cultural apparatus. If the cultural apparatus controlled by the bourgeoisie can be smashed at this level, then the real possibilities for a social transformation will emerge. ". . . the disorderly, uncivil, farcical, artistic desublimation of culture constitutes an essential element of radical politics: of the subverting forces in transition."[41]

I believe that some of the contemporary artists most sensitive to the cultural/political climate have been attempting to practice cultural subversion—The Rolling Stones by putting "mass man" back into perspective (in the whole of *Beggar's Banquet* especially "Salt of the Earth"); the Band by breaking down the abstract categories associated with "mass man" such as Southerner, Northerner, Worker, Soldier, etc. by singing very sensitively about human beings as real people with real histories (e.g., "The Night They Drove Old Dixie Down"); and, finally, Dylan, who has extended his hand as a representative of a particular new working class background—the college educated urban youth—to other working class people young and old, and to American roots—country people, Johnny Cash, etc. (as in *John Wesley Harding* and *Nashville Skyline*). These thrusts are taking place at a time of intensified social crisis when bourgeois remedies are increasingly failing.

Thus, a two-pronged attack both on and off the job can be made. One of the ways that connections can be made between the same kind of repression on and off the job is through the new culture. For example, a New Left organizer recently told of his experiences organizing in a predominantly white, 'blue-collar' working class neighborhood. He found himself stymied and thwarted until he discovered that both he and the people in the community really dug Dylan's *Nashville Skyline*. The excitement of this common experience provided the catalyst that helped get his organizing project off the ground. The insurgent culture serves as a good way of bringing together disparate social forces—youth, different sectors within the new working class, lumpen people, blacks, etc. Many of those involved in the culture are already transforming themselves in and through their practice.

> The new sensibility has become, by this very token *praxis*: it emerges in the struggle against violence and exploitation where this struggle is waged for essentially new ways and forms of life: negation of the entire Establishment, its morality, culture; affirmation of the right to build a society in which the abolition of poverty and toil terminates in a universe where the sensuous, the playful, the calm,

---

[41]Marcuse, *Essay on Liberation*, p. 48.

and the beautiful become forms of existence and thereby the *Form* of the society itself.[42]

Marcuse is talking about the emergence of the New Historical Subject who is transforming himself right down to his socially conditioned infrastructure. The new culture thus serves a negative function by smashing the old cultural forms which only serve to dominate man. This culture thereby emerges as a new positive force in practice by offering new and liberating cultural forms and ways of being. One of the tasks of the New Left should be to practice and spread in our own day-to-day activities this "new sensibility" with the aim of subverting the repressive culture and building a movement to transform the repressive society at large. I have tried to indicate the very important role that rock culture has played in the historical development of this social consciousness and new sensibility. Woody Guthrie put it this way: "Our songs are singing history."

---

[42]Ibid., p. 24.

THE TIMES THEY ARE A-CHANGIN':
THE MUSIC OF PROTEST

Robert A. Rosenstone

At the beginning of the 1960's, nobody took popular music very seriously. Adults only knew that rock n' roll, which had flooded the airways in the 1950's, had a strong beat and was terribly loud; it was generally believed that teen-agers alone had thick enough eardrums, or insensitive enough souls, to enjoy it. Certainly, no critics thought of a popular star like the writhing Elvis Presley as being in any way a serious artist. Such a teen-age idol was simply considered a manifestation of a subculture that the young happily and inevitably outgrew—and, any parent would have added, the sooner the better.

In recent years this view of popular music has drastically changed. Some parents may still wonder about the "noise" that their children listen to, but important segments of American society have come to recognize popular musicians as artists saying serious things.[1] An indication of this

---

[1]The definition of "popular music" being used in this article is a broad one. It encompasses a multitude of styles, including folk, folk-rock, acid-rock, hard-rock, and blues, to give just a few names being used in the musical world today. It does so because the old musical classifications have been totally smashed and the forms now overlap in a way that makes meaningful distinction between them impossible. Though not every group or song referred to will have been popular in the sense of selling a million records, all of them are part of a broad, variegated scene termed "pop." Some of the groups, like Buffalo Springfield, Strawberry Alarm Clock, or the Byrds, have sold millions of records. Others, like the Fugs or Mothers of Invention, have never had a real hit, though they are played on radio stations allied to the "underground." Still, such groups do sell respectable numbers of records and do perform regularly at teen-age concerts.

change can be seen in magazine attitudes. In 1964, the *Saturday Evening Post* derided the Beatles—recognized giants of modern popular music—as "corny," and *Reporter* claimed: "They have debased Rock 'n Roll to its ultimate absurdity." Three years later the *Saturday Review* solemnly discussed a new Beatles record as a "highly ironic declaration of disaffection" with modern society, while in 1968 *Life* devoted a whole, laudatory section to "The New Rock," calling it music "that challenges the joys and ills of the . . . world."[2] Even in the intellectual community, popular music has found warm friends. Such sober journals as *The Listener, Columbia University Forum, New American Review,* and *Commentary* have sympathetically surveyed aspects of the "pop" scene, while the *New York Review of Books*—a kind of house organ for American academia—composer Ned Rorem has declared that, at their best, the Beatles "compare with those composers from great eras of song: Monteverdi, Schumann, Poulenc."[3]

The reasons for such changes in attitude are not difficult to find: there is no doubt that popular music has become more complex, and at the same time more serious, than it ever was before. Musically, it has broken down some of the old forms in which it was for a long time straight-jacketed. With a wide-ranging eclecticism, popular music has adapted to itself a bewildering variety of musical traditions and instruments, from the classic Indian sitar to the most recent electronic synthesizers favored by composers of "serious" concert music.

As the music has been revolutionized, so has the subject matter of the songs. In preceding decades, popular music was almost exclusively about love, and, in the words of poet Thomas Gunn, "a very limited kind [of love], constituting a sort of fag-end of the Petrarchan tradition."[4] The stories told in song were largely about lovers yearning for one another in some vaguely unreal world where nobody ever seemed to work or get married. All this changed in the 1960's. Suddenly, popular music began to deal with civil rights demonstrations and drug experiences, with interracial dating and war and explicit sexual encounters, with, in short, the real world in which people live. For perhaps the first time, popular songs became relevant to the lives of the teenage audience that largely constitutes the record-buying public. The success of some of these works prompted others to be written, and from the second half of the decade on there was a full efflorescence of such topical songs written by young people for their

---

[2]*Saturday Evening Post* 237 (March 21, 1964): 30; *Reporter* 30 (Feb. 27, 1964): 18; *Saturday Review* 50 (August 19, 1967): 18; *Life* 64 (June 28, 1968) 51.

[3]"The Music of the Beatles," *New York Review of Books*, Jan. 15, 1968, pp. 23–27. See also "The New Music," *The Listener* 78 (August 3, 1967): 129–30; *Columbia University Forum* (Fall 1967), pp. 16–22; *New American Review* 1 (April 1968): 118–39; Ellen Willis, "The Sound of Bob Dylan," *Commentary* 44 (November 1967): 71–80. Many of these articles deal with English as well as American popular groups, and, in fact, the music of the two countries cannot, in any meaningful sense, be separated. This article will only survey American musical groups, though a look at English music would reveal the prevalence of the themes explored here.

[4]"The New Music," p. 129.

peers. These works may be grouped under the label of "protest" songs, for taken together, they provide a wide-ranging critique of American life. Listening to them, one can get a full-blown picture of the antipathy that the young song writers have toward many American institutions.

Serious concerns entered popular music early in the 1960's, when a great revival of folk singing spread out from college campuses, engulfed the mass media, and created a wave of new "pop" stars, the best known of whom was Joan Baez. Yet, though the concerns of these folk songs were often serious, they were hardly contemporary. Popular were numbers about organizing unions, which might date from the 1930's or the late nineteenth century, or about the trials of escaping Negro slaves, or celebrating the cause of the defeated Republicans in the Spanish Civil War. Occasionally there was something like "Talking A-Bomb Blues," but this was the rare exception rather than the rule.[5]

A change of focus came when performers began to write their own songs, rather than relying on the traditional folk repertoire. Chief among them, and destined to become the best known, was Bob Dylan. Consciously modeling himself on that wandering minstrel of the 1930's, Woody Guthrie, Dylan began by writing songs that often had little to do with the contemporary environment. Rather, his early ballads like "Masters of War" echoed the leftist concerns and rhetoric of an earlier era. Yet, simultaneously, Dylan was writing songs like "Blowin' In the Wind," "A Hard Rain's A-Gonna Fall," and "The Times They Are A-Changin'," which dealt with civil rights, nuclear war, and the changing world of youth that parents and educators were not prepared to understand. Acclaimed as the best of protest song writers, Dylan in mid-decade shifted gears, and in the song "My Back Pages," he denounced his former moral fervor. In an ironic chorus claiming that he was much younger than he had been, Dylan specifically made social problems the worry of sober, serious, older men; presumably, youths had more important things than injustice to think about. After that, any social comment by Dylan came encapsulated in a series of surrealistic images; for the most part, he escaped into worlds of aestheticism, psychedelic drugs, and personal love relationships. Apparently attempting to come to grips in art with his own personality, Dylan was content to forget about the problems of other men.[6]

The development of Dylan is important not only because he is the leading song writer, but also because it parallels the concerns of popular music in recent years. Starting out with traditional liberal positions on war, discrimination, segregation, and exploitation, song writers have turned increasingly to descriptions of the private worlds of drugs, sexual experience, and personal freedom. Though social concerns have never entirely faded, the private realm has been increasingly seen as the only one in

---

[5]*Time* 80 (Nov. 23, 1962): 54–60, gives a brief survey of the folk revival.
[6]Willis, "The Sound of Dylan," gives a good analysis of his work.

which people can lead meaningful lives. Today the realms of social protest and private indulgence exist side by side in the popular music, with the latter perceived as the only viable alternative to the world described in the former songs.[7]

In turning to recent protest songs, one finds many of the traditional characters and concerns of such music missing.[8] Gone are exploited, impoverished people, labor leaders, "finks," and company spies. This seems natural in affluent times, with youths from middle class backgrounds writing songs. Of course, there has been one increasingly visible victim of exploitation, the Negro; and the songsters have not been blind to his plight. But egalitarian as they are, the white musicians have not been able to describe the reality of the black man's situation. Rather, they have chronicled Northern liberal attitudes towards the problem. Thus, composer-performer Phil Ochs penned works criticizing Southern attitudes towards Negroes, and containing stock portraits of corrupt politicians, law officials, and churchmen trembling before the Ku Klux Klan, while Paul Simon wrote a lament for a freedom rider killed by an angry Southern mob.[9] Similarly white oriented was Janis Ian's very popular "Society's Child," concerned with the problem of interracial dating. Here a white girl capitulates to society's bigotry and breaks off a relationship with a Negro boy with the vague hope that someday "things may change."[10]

Increasingly central to white-Negro relationships have been the ghetto and urban riots, and a taste of this entered the popular music. Phil Ochs, always on top of current events, produced "In the Heat of the Summer" shortly after the first major riot in Harlem in 1964. Partially sympathetic to the ghetto-dwellers' actions, he still misjudged their attitudes by ascribing to them feelings of shame—rather than satisfaction—in the aftermath of the destruction.[11] A later attempt, by Country Joe and the Fish, to describe Harlem ironically as a colorful vacation spot, verged on patronizing blacks, even while it poked fun at white stereotypes. Still, it was followed by sounds of explosion that thrust home what indifference to the ghetto is doing to America.[12] The most successful song depicting the situation of the Negro

---

[7]It must be pointed out that, in spite of the large amount of social criticism, most songs today are still about love.

[8]This article is concerned almost exclusively with music written and performed by white musicians. While popular music by Negroes does contain social criticism, the current forms—loosely termed "soul music"—make comments about oppression similar to those which Negroes have always made. The real change in content has come largely in white music.

[9]Phil Ochs, "Talking Birmingham Jam" and "Here's to the State of Mississippi," *I Ain't Marching Any More* (Elcktra, 7273); Simon and Garfunkel, "He Was My Brother," *Wednesday Morning 3 A.M.* (Columbia, CS 9049). (Songs from records will be noted by performer, song title in quotation marks, and album title in italics, followed by record company and number in parentheses.)

[10]Dialogue Music, Inc.

[11]Ochs, *I Ain't Marching Any More.*

[12]"The Harlem Song," *Together* (Vanguard, VSD 79277).

was "Trouble Coming Everyday," written by Frank Zappa during the Watts uprising in 1965. Though the song does not go so far as to approve of rioting, it paints a brutal picture of exploitation by merchants, bad schooling, miserable housing, and police brutality—all of which affect ghetto dwellers. Its most significant lines are Zappa's cry, that though he is not black, "there's a whole lists of times I wish I could say I'm not white." No song writer showed more empathy with the black struggle for liberation than that.[13]

While the downtrodden are heroes of many traditional protest songs, the villains are often politicians. Yet, politics rarely enters recent songs. Ochs, an unreconstructed voice from the 1930's, depicts vacillating politicians in some works, and Dylan mentioned corrupt ones early in the sixties. But the typical attitude is to ignore politics, or, perhaps, to describe it in passing as "A yardstick for lunatics."[14] Even those who call for political commitment, caution against trying "to get yourself elected," because to do so you will have to compromise principles—what's worse, you'll have to cut your hair.

It is true that the death of President Kennedy inspired more than one song, but these were tributes to a martyr, not a politician.[15] If Kennedy in death could inspire music, Lyndon Johnson in life was incapable of inspiring anything, except perhaps contempt. In a portrait of him, Country Joe and the Fish pictured the, then, President as flying through the sky like an "insane" Superman. Then they fantasized a Western setting with "Lyndon" outgunned and sent back to his Texas ranch.[16]

One traditional area, antiwar protest, does figure significantly in the music. With America's involvement in Vietnam and mounting draft-calls, this seems natural enough. Unlike many songs of this genre, however, the current ones rarely assess the causes of war, but dwell almost exclusively with the effect which war has on the individual. Thus, both Love and the Byrds sing about what nuclear war does to children, while the Peanut Butter Conspiracy pictures the effect of nuclear testing on everyone—a "firecracker sky" poisoned with radioactivity.[17] Most popular of the antiwar songs was P. F. Sloan's "Eve of Destruction," which, for a time in 1965, was the best-selling record in the country (and which was banned by some patriotic radio-station directors). The title obviously gives the author's view of the world situation; the content deals mostly with its relationship to

[13]Mothers of Invention, *Freak Out* (Verve, 65005).

[14]Strawberry Alarm Clock, "Incense and Peppermints," *Strawberry Alarm Clock* (Uni., 73014); "Long Time Gone," *Crosby, Stills and Nash* (Atlantic, SD 8229).

[15]Phil Ochs, "That Was the President," *"I Ain't Marching Any More"*; the Byrds, "He Was A Friend of Mine," *Turn! Turn!* (Columbia, CS 9254).

[16]"Superbird," *Electric Music for the Mind and Body* (Vanguard, 79244).

[17]Love, "Mushroom Clouds," *Love* (Elektra, EKL 4001); the Byrds, "I Come and Stand at Every Door," *Fifth Dimension* (Columbia CS 9349; Peanut Butter Conspiracy, "Wonderment," *Great Conspiracy* (Columbia, CS 9590).

young men like himself, as it asks why they tote guns if they don't believe in war.[18] There are alternatives to carrying a gun, and defiance of the draft enters some songs, subtly in Buffy St. Marie's "Universal Soldier" and stridently in Ochs' "I Ain't Marching Any More" and Steppenwolf's "Draft Resister."[19] Perhaps more realistic in its reflection of youthful moods is the Byrds' "Draft Morning," a haunting portrait of a young man reluctantly leaving a warm bed to take up arms and kill "unknown faces." It ends with the poignant and unanswerable question, "Why should it happen?"[20]

If many songs criticize war in general, some have referred to Vietnam in particular. The Fugs give gory details of death and destruction being wreaked on the North by American bombers, which unleash napalm "rotisseries" upon the world.[21] In a similar song, Country Joe and the Fish describe children crying helplessly beneath bombs. No doubt, it is difficult to make music out of the horrors of war, and a kind of black humor is a common response. In a rollicking number, the Fugs, with irony, worry that people may come to "love the Russians" and scream out a method often advocated for avoiding this: "Kill, kill, kill for peace."[23] And one of Country Joe's most popular numbers contains an attack on generals who think that peace will be won "when we blow 'em all to kingdom come."[24]

The injustice and absurdity of America's Asian ventures, perceived by the song writers, does not surprise them, for they feel that life at home is much the same. The songs of the 1960's show the United States as a repressive society where people who deviate from the norm are forced into conformity—sometimes at gunpoint; where those who do fit in lead empty, frustrated lives; and where meaningful human experience is ignored in a search for artificial pleasures. Such a picture is hardly attractive, and one might argue that it is not fair. But it is so pervasive in popular music that it must be examined at some length. Indeed, it is the most important part of recent protest music. Here are criticisms, not of exploitation, but of the quality of life in an affluent society: not only of physical oppression but also of the far more subtle mental oppression that a mass society can produce.

YOUTH AS VICTIM

Throughout the decade, young people have often been at odds with established authority, and, repeatedly, songs picture youth in the role of victim. Sometimes the victimization is mental, as when the Mothers of Invention complain of outworn thought patterns and say that children are

---

[18]Trousdale Music Publishers, Inc.
[19]Buffy St. Marie, 'Universal Soldier," Southern Publishing, ASCAP; Ochs, *I Ain't Marching Any More;* Steppenwolf, *Monster* (Dunhill DS 50066).
[20]*The Notorious Byrd Brothers* (Columbia, CS 9575).
[21]"War Song," *Tenderness Junction* (Reprise, S 6280).
[22]"An Untitled Protest," *Together.*
[23]"Kill for Peace, *The Fugs* (Esp. 1028).
[24]"I Feel Like I'm Fixin' to Die," *I Feel Like I'm Fixin' to Die* (Vanguard, 9266).

"victims of lies" which their parents believe.[25] On a much simpler level, Sonny Bono voices his annoyance that older people laugh at the clothes he wears, and he wonders why they enjoy "makin' fun" of him.[26] Now, Bono could musically shrug off the laughs as the price of freedom; but other songs document occasions when Establishment disapproval turned into physical oppression. Thus, Canned Heat tells of being arrested in Denver because the police did not want any "long hairs around."[27] The Buffalo Springfield, in a hit record, describe gun-bearing police rounding up teenagers on Sunset Strip.[28] On the same theme, Dylan ironically shows that adults arbitrarily oppose just about all activities of youths, saying that they should "look out" no matter what they are doing.[29] More bitter is the Mothers' description of police killing large numbers of hippies, which is then justified on the grounds that because they looked "weird" it "served them right."[30] A fictional incident when the song was written, the Mothers were clearly prescient in believing Americans capable of shooting down those who engage in deviant behavior.

Though the songs echo the oppression that youngsters have felt, they do not ignore the problems that all humans face in a mass society. Writer Tom Paxton knows that it is not easy to keep one's life from being forced into a predetermined mold. In "Mr. Blue" he has a Big-Brother-like narrator telling the title character, a kind of Everyman, that he is always under surveillance, and that he will never be able to indulge himself in his precious dreams of freedom from society. This is because society needs him to fill a slot, no matter what his personal desires. And Mr. Blue had better learn to love that slot, or "we'll break you."[31] Though no other writer made the message so explicit, a similar fear of being forced into an unwelcome slot underlies many songs of the period.

The society of slotted people is an empty one, partly described as "TV dinner by the pool."[32] It is one in which people have been robbed of their humanity, receiving in return the "transient treasures" of wealth and the useless gadgets of a technological age. One of these is television, referred to simply as "that rotten box," or, in a more sinister image, as an "electronic shrine." This image of men worshipping gadgets recurs. In the nightmare vision of a McLuhanesque world—where the medium is the message—Simon and Garfunkel sing of men so busy bowing and praying

---

[25]*We're Only in It for the Money* (Verve, 65045).
[26]"Laugh at Me," *Five West Cotillion*, BMI.
[27]"My Crime," *Boogie* (Liberty, 7541).
[28]"For What It's Worth."
[29]"Subterranean Homesick Blues," *Bob Dylan's Greatest Hits* (Columbia, KCS 9463).
[30]*We're Only in It for the Money.*
[31]"Mr. Blue," *Clear Light* (Elektra, 74011).
[32]Mothers of Invention, "Brown Shoes Don't Make It," *Absolutely Free* (Verve, 65013).

to a "neon god" that they cannot understand or touch one another. Indeed, here electronics seem to hinder the process of communication rather than facilitate it. People talk and hear but never understand, as the "sounds of silence" fill the world.[33] Such lack of communication contributes to the indifference with which men can view the life and death of a neighbor, as in Simon's "A Most Peculiar Man."[34] It also creates the climate of fear which causes people to kill a stranger for no reason other than his unknown origins in Strawberry Alarm Clock's "They Saw the Fat One Coming."[35]

Alienated from his fellows, fearful and alone, modern man has also despoiled the natural world in which he lives, has in Joni Mitchell's words, paved paradise to "put up a parking lot."[36] With anguish in his voice, Jim Morrison of the Doors asks "What have they done to the earth?" and then angrily answers that his "fair sister" has been ravished and plundered.[37] In a lighter tone but with no less serious intent, the Lewis and Clark Expedition describe the way man has cut himself off from nature in the great outdoors, where chains and fences keep him from the flowers and trees. With a final ironic thrust, they add that there's no reason to touch the flowers because they are "plastic anyway."[38]

This brings up a fear that haunts a number of recent songs, the worry that the technological age has created so many artificial things that nothing natural remains. Concerned with authenticity, the songsters are afraid that man himself is becoming an artifact, or in their favorite word, "plastic." Thus, the Jefferson Airplane sing about a "Plastic Fantastic Lover," while the Iron Butterfly warn a girl to stay away from people "made of plastic."[39] The image recurs most frequently in the works of the Mothers of Invention. In one song, they depict the country as being run by a plastic Congress and President.[40] Then, in "Plastic People" they start with complaints about a girl who uses "plastic goo" on her face, go on to a picture of teen-agers on the Sunset Strip—who are probably their fans—as being "plastic," too, and finally turn on their listeners and advise them to check themselves, for "you think we're talking about someone else."[41] Such a vision is frightening, for if the audience is plastic, perhaps the Mothers, themselves, are made of the same phony material. And if the whole world is plastic, who can be sure of his own authenticity?

---

[33]"Sounds of Silence," *Sounds of Silence* (Columbia, CS 9269).
[34]*Sounds of Silence.*
[35]*Wake Up . . . It's Tomorrow* (Uni., 73025).
[36]"Big Yellow Taxi," *Ladies of the Canyon* (Reprise, RS 6376).
[37]"When the Music's Over," *Strange Days* (Elektra, 74014).
[38]"Chain Around the Flowers," *The Lewis and Clark Expedition* (Colgems, COS 105).
[39]*Surrealistic Pillow* (Victor, LSP 3766); Stamped Ideas," *Heavy* (Atco, S 330227).
[40]"Uncle Bernie's Farm," *Absolutely Free.*
[41]"Plastic People," *Absolutely Free.*

LOVE RELATIONSHIPS

Toward the end of "Plastic People," the Mothers say that "true love" cannot be "a product of plasticity." This brings up the greatest horror, that in a "plastic" society like the United States, love relationships are impossible. For the young song writers, American love is viewed as warped and twisted. Nothing about Establishment society frightens them more than its attitudes towards sex. Tim Buckley is typical in singing that older Americans are "Afraid to trust in their bodies."[42] Others give graphic portraits of deviant behavior. The Fugs tell of a "Dirty Old Man" hanging around high school playgrounds; the Velvet Underground portray a masochist; and the Mothers depict a middle-aged man lusting after his own 13-year-old daughter.[43] The fullest indictment of modern love is made by the United States of America, who devote almost an entire album to the subject. Here, in a twisted portrait of "pleasure and pain," is a world of loveless marriages, homosexual relationships in men's rooms, venomous attractions, and overt sadism—all masked by a middle-class, suburban world in which people consider "morality" important. To show that natural relationships are possible elsewhere, the group sings one tender love lyric; interestingly, it is the lament of a Cuban girl for the dead Ché Guevara.[44]

The fact that bourgeois America has warped attitudes toward sex and love is bad enough; the songsters are more worried that such attitudes will infect their own generation. Thus, the Collectors decry the fact that man-woman relationships are too often seen as some kind of contest, with a victor and vanquished and in which violence is more acceptable than tenderness.[45] Perhaps because most of the singers are men, criticisms of female sexual attitudes abound. The Mothers are disgusted with the American woman, who lies in bed gritting her teeth, while the Sopwith Camel object to the traditional kind of purity by singing that they don't want their women "wrapped up in cellophane."[46] This is because such a woman will bring you down with her "talking about sin."[47] All the musicians would prefer the girl about whom Moby Grape sings who is "super-powered, deflowered," and over 18.[48]

Living in a "plastic" world where honest human relationships are impossible, the song writers might be expected to wrap themselves in a mood of musical despair. But they are young—and often making plenty of money

---

[42]"Goodbye and Hello," *Goodbye and Hello* (Electra, 7318).
[43]*The Fugs*, "Venus in Furs," *The Velvet Underground and Nico* (Verve, V6-5008); "Brown Shoes Don't Make It," *Absolutely Free.*
[44]*The United States of America* (Columbia, CS 9614).
[45]"What Love," *The Collectors* (Warner Bros.-Seven Arts, WS 1746).
[46]*We're Only in It for the Money*, "Cellophane Woman," *The Sopwith Camel* (Kama Sutra, KLPS 8060).
[47]"Cellophane Woman."
[48]"Motorcycle Irene," *Wow* (Columbia, CS 9613).

—and such an attitude is foreign to them. Musically, they are hopeful because, as the title of the Dylan song indicates, "The Times They Are A-Changin'." Without describing the changes, Dylan clearly threatens the older generation, as he tells critics, parents, and presumably anyone over 30, to start swimming or they will drown in the rising flood-waters of social change.[49]

In another work, Dylan exploits the same theme. Here is a portrait of a presumably normal, educated man, faced with a series of bizarre situations, who is made to feel like a freak because he does not understand what is going on. The chorus is the young generation's comment to all adults, as it mocks "Mr. Jones" for not understanding what is happening all around him.[50]

The changes going on are, not surprisingly, associated with the care-free, joyful experiences of youth. As Jefferson Airplane sings, "It's a wild time" one in which people are busy "changing faces."[51] The most full-blown description of the changing world is Tim Buckley's "Goodbye and Hello," a lengthy and explicit portrait of what the youth hope is happening. Throughout the song the author contrasts two kinds of people and their environments. On the one hand are the "antique people"—godless and sexless—of an industrial civilization, living in dark dungeons, working hard, worshipping technology and money, sacrificing their sons to placate "vaudeville" generals, and blinding themselves to the fact that their "masquerade towers" are riddled by widening cracks." Opposed to them are the "new children," interested in flowers, streams, and the beauty of the sky, who wish to take off their clothes to dance and sing and love one another. What's more, the "antique people are fading away"; in fact, they are already wearing "death masks."[52]

Buckley's vision of the new world that is coming is obviously that of a kind of idyllic Eden before the fall, a world in which men will be free to romp and play and indulge their natural desires for love. It is a pagan world, the antithesis of the Christian ideal that would postpone fulfillment to some afterlife. Elsewhere, Buckley explicitly condemns that part of Christianity which saves pleasure for an afterlife. Similarly, the Doors' Jim Morrison wants to cancel his "subscription to the resurrection," and then shrieks for a whole generation: "We want the world and we want it now."[53]

Though the times may be changing, the songsters are well aware that —despite their brave words and demands—there is plenty of strength left

---

[49]*Bob Dylan's Greatest Hits.*

[50]"Ballad of a Thin Man/Mr. Jones," *Highway 61 Revisited* (Columbia, CS 9189). Though this song has obvious homosexual overtones, it also stands as youth's criticism of the older generation.

[51]"Wild Tyme (H)," *After Bathing at Baxter's* (Victor, LSO-1511).

[52]"Goodbye and Hello," written by Tim Buckley, *"Goodbye and Hello.*

[53]"Pleasant Street," written by Tim Buckley, "When the Music's Over," *Strange Days.*

in the old social order. Obviously, they can see the war continuing, Negro demands not being met, and the continuing hostility of society toward their long hair, music, sexual behavior, and experimentation with drugs. Faced with these facts, the musicians have occasionally toyed with the idea of violent revolution. Some, like the Bank, see it as an inevitable great storm "coming through" the country. Others wish to force the issue. The Doors, claiming "we've got the numbers," call on people to get their guns, for "the time has come," while Jefferson Airplane echoes the same plea in asking for volunteers to change the world.[54]

Yet most musicians have not believed revolution feasible, and more typically they have dealt with the problem of how to live decently within the framework of the old society. Here they tend toward the world of private experience mentioned earlier in connection with Dylan. Many of their songs are almost programs for youth's behavior in a world perceived as being unlivable.

The first element is to forget about the repressive society out there. As Sopwith Camel says, "Stamp out reality . . ." before it stamps you out.[55] Then it is imperative to forget about trying to understand the outside world rationally. In a typical anti-intellectual stance, the Byrds describe such attempts as "scientific delirium madness."[56] Others combine a similar attitude with a strong measure of *carpe diem*. Spirit derides people who are "always asking" for "the reason" when they should be enjoying life, while H. P. Lovecraft admits that the bird is on the wing and states, "You need not know why."[57] What is important is that the moment be seized and life lived to the fullest. As Simon and Garfunkel say, one has to make the "moment last," and this is done best by those who open themselves fully to the pleasures of the world.[58]

The most frequent theme of the song writers is the call to freedom, the total freedom of the individual to "do his own thing." Peanut Butter Conspiracy carry this so far as to hope for a life that can be lived "free of time."[59] Circus Maximus and the Byrds—despite the fact that they are young men—long to recapture some lost freedom that they knew as children.[60] Such freedom can be almost solipsistic; the late Jimi Hendrix claimed that even if the sun did not rise and the mountains fell into the

---

[54]"Look Out, Cleveland," *The Band* (Capitol, STAO-132); "Five to One," *Waiting for the Sun* (Elektra, EKS 74024); "Tell all the People" *The Soft Parade* (Elektra, EKS 75005).

[55]"Saga of the Low Down Let Down," *The Sopwith Camel.*

[56]"Fifth Dimension," *Fifth Dimension.*

[57]"Topanga Window," *Spirit* (Ode, 212 44004); "Let's Get Together," *H. P. Lovecraft* (Phillips, 600-252).

[58]"Feeling Groovy," *Sounds of Silence.*

[59]"Time Is After You," *West Coast Love-In* (Vault, LP 113).

[60]"Lost Sea Shanty," Circus Maximus (Vanguard, 79260); "Going Back," *The Notorious Byrd Brothers.*

sea, he would not care because he had his "own world to live through."[61] But for others, it can lead to brotherhood. H. P. Lovecraft asks all to "Try and love one another right now."[62]

A desire for freedom is certainly nothing new. Neither is the attempt to find freedom far from smoggy cities in the rural world of nature that Dylan has recently celebrated in his 1970 album *New Morning* and that Joni Mitchell depicts in "Woodstock." What is different in the songs is the conviction that freedom should be used by the individual in an extensive exploration of his own internal world. Central to the vision of the song writers is the idea that the mind must be opened and expanded if the truths of life are to be perceived. Thus, the importance of external reality is subordinated to that of a psychological, even a metaphysical, realm. The most extensive treatment of this subject is by the Amboy Dukes, who devote half of a long-playing record to it. Their theme is stated quite simply: mankind would be happy if only people took the time "to journey to the center of the mind."[63] Like any mystical trip, what happens when one reaches the center of the mind is not easy to describe. Perhaps the best attempt is by the Iron Butterfly, who claim that an unconscious power will be released, flooding the individual with sensations and fusing him with a freedom of thought that will allow him to "see everything." At this point, man will be blessed with the almost supernatural power of knowing "all."[64]

Such a journey is, of course, difficult to make. But youth has discovered a short cut to the mind's center, through the use of hallucinogenic drugs. Indeed, such journeys are almost inconceivable without hallucinogens, and the so-called "head songs" about drug experiences are the most prevalent of works that can be classified as "protest."[65] In this area, the songs carefully distinguish between "mind-expanding," nonaddictive marijuana and LSD, and hard, addictive drugs which destroy the body. Thus, the Velvet Underground and Love both tell of the dangers of heroin, while Canned Heat warn of methedrine use and the Fugs describe the problems of cocaine.[66] But none of the groups hesitate to recommend "grass" and "acid" trips as a prime way of opening oneself to the pleasures and beauties of the universe. As the Byrds claim in a typical "head song," drugs can

---

[61]"If 6 Was 9," *Axis* (Reprise, S 6281).

[62]"Let's Get Together," *H. P. Lovecraft.*

[63]"Journey to the Center of the Mind," *Journey to the Center of the Mind* (Mainstream, S 6112).

[64]"Unconscious Power," *Heavy.*

[65]There are so many "head songs" that listing them would be an impossibly long task. Some of the most popular protest songs of the decade have been such works. They include Jefferson Airplane, "White Rabbit," *Surrealistic Pillow;* the Doors, "Light My Fire," *The Doors* (Elektra EKS 74007); Strawberry Alarm Clock, "Incense and Peppermints," *Incense and Peppermits;* and the Byrds, "Eight Miles High," *Fifth Dimension.*

[66]"Heroin," *Velvet Underground;* "Signed D.C.," *Love* (Elektra, 74001); "Amphetamine Annie," *Boggie* "Coming Down," *The Fugs.*

free the individual from the narrow boundaries of the mundane world, allowing him to open his heart to the quiet joy and eternal love which pervade the whole universe.[67] Others find the reality of the drug experience more real than the day-to-day world, and some even hope for the possibility of staying "high" permanently. More frequent is the claim that "trips" are of lasting benefit because they improve the quality of life of an individual even after he "comes down."[68] The Peanut Butter Conspiracy, claiming that "everyone has a bomb" in his mind, even dream of some day turning the whole world on with drugs, thus solving mankind's plaguing problems by making the earth a loving place.[69] An extreme desire, perhaps, but one that would find much support among other youths.

This, then is the portrait of America that emerges in recent popular songs which can be labelled as "protest." It is, in the extreme eyes of those like Steppenwolf, a kind of "Monster" gone berserk, a cruel society which makes war on peoples abroad and acts repressively toward helpless minorities like Negroes, youth, and hippies at home. It is a land of people whose lives are devoid of feeling, love, and sexual pleasure. It is a country whose institutions are crumbling away, one which can presumably be saved by a sort of cultural and spiritual revolution which the young themselves will lead.

Whether one agrees wholly, partly or not at all with such a picture of the United States, the major elements of such a critical portrait are familiar enough. It is only in realizing that all this is being said in popular music, on records that sometimes sell a million copies to teenagers, in songs that youngsters often dance to, that one comes to feel that something strange is happening today. Indeed, if parents fully understand what the youth are saying musically to one another, they must long for the simpler days of Elvis Presley and his blue suede shoes.

If the lyrics of the songs would disturb older people, the musical sound would do so even more. In fact, a good case could be made that the music itself expresses as much protest against the status quo as do the words. Performed in concert with electronic amplification on all instruments—or listened to at home at top volume—the music drowns the individual in waves of sound; sometimes it seems to be pulsating inside the listener. When coupled with a typical light show, where colors flash and swirl on huge screens, the music helps to provide an assault on the senses, creating an overwhelming personal experience of the kind that the songs advise people to seek. This sort of total experience is certainly a protest against the tepid, partial pleasures which other songs describe as the lot of bourgeois America.

---

[67]"Fifth Dimension," *Fifth Dimension.*
[68]See Country Joe and the Fish, "Bass Strings," *Electric Music for the Mind and Body;* or United States of America, "Coming Down," *United States of America.*
[69]"Living, Loving Life," *Great Conspiracy.*

Another aspect of the music which might be considered a kind of protest is the attempt of many groups to capture in sound the quality of a drug "trip," to try through melody, rhythm, and volume to—in the vernacular—"blow the mind" of the audience. Of course, youngsters often listen to such music while under the influence of hallucinogens. In such a state, the perceptive experience supposedly can have the quality of putting one in touch with regions of the mind and manifestations of the universe that can be felt in no other way. Such mysticism, such transcendental attitudes, are certainly a protest against a society in which reality is always pragmatic and truth instrumental.

To try to explain why the jingles and vapid love lyrics of popular music in the 1950's evolved into the social criticism and mystical vision of more recent days is certainly not easy. Part of it is the fact that performers, who have always been young, started writing their own songs, out of their own life experiences, rather than accepting the commercial output of the older members of tin pan alley. But this does not explain the popularity of the new songs. Here one must look to the youthful audience, which decided it preferred buying works of the newer kind. For it was the commercial success of some of the new groups which opened the doors of the record companies to the many that flourish today.

Though one cannot make definitive judgments about this record-buying audience, some things seem clear. Certainly, it is true that with increasingly rapid social change, parents—and adults in general—have less and less that they can tell their children about the ways of the world, for adult life experiences are not very relevant to current social conditions. Similarly, institutions like the school and the press suffer from a kind of cultural lag that makes their viewpoints valueless for youth. Into the place of these traditional sources of information have stepped the youth themselves, and through such things as the "underground" press and popular music they are telling each other exactly what is happening. In this way, the music has achieved popularity—at least in part—because it telegraphs important messages to young people and helps to define and codify the mores and standards of their own subculture. A youngster may personally feel that there is no difference between his parents' drinking and his use of marijuana. Certainly, it is comforting to him when his friends feel the same way, and when popular songs selling mililons of copies deliver the same message, there are even stronger sanctions for his "turning on." Thus, the lyrics of the music serve a functional role in the world of youth.

It is interesting to note that the popular music also puts youth in touch with serious, intellectual critiques of American life. Perhaps it starts only as a gut reaction in the song writers, but they have put into music the ideas of many American social critics. Without reading Paul Goodman, David Riesman, C. Wright Mills, or Mary McCarthy, youngsters will know that life is a "rat race," that Americans are a "lonely crowd," that "white-collar" lives contain much frustration, and that the war in Vietnam is far from just. And they will have learned this from popular music, as well as from their own observation.

The other side of the coin from criticism of contemporary life is the search for personal experience, primarily of the "mind-expanding" sort. As is obvious by now, such expansion has nothing to do with the intellect, but is a spiritual phenomenon. Here a final critique is definitely implicit. Throughout the music—as in youth culture—there is the search for a kind of mystical unity, an ability to feel a oneness with the universe. This is what drugs are used for; this is what the total environment of the light and music shows is about; and this is what is sought in the sexual experience— often explicitly evident in the orgasmic grunts and moans of performers. Through the search for this unity, the music is implicitly condemning the fragmentation of the indivdual's life which is endemic in the modern world. The songsters are saying that it is wrong to compartmentalize work and play, wrong to cut men off from the natural rhythms of nature, wrong to stifle sex and love and play in favor of greater productivity, wrong to say man's spiritual needs can be filled by providing him with more material possessions.

This is obviously a criticism that can only be made by an affluent people, but these youth do represent the most affluent of all countries. And rather than wallow in their affluence, they have sensed and expressed much of the malaise that plagues our technological society. The charge may be made against them that they are really utopians, but the feeling increases today that we are in need of more utopian thinking and feeling. And while one might not wish to follow their prescriptions for the good life, they have caught something of the desire for freedom that all men feel. What could be more utopian and yet more inviting than the future painted by the Mothers, a time when all the lonely people—poor or fat or gray-haired—will feel free to take off their clothes "to sing and dance and love."[70] Of course it is difficult to say how close such a time is. But as Plato wrote and the Fugs have echoed, "When the mode of the music changes, the walls of the city shake."[71] Now the mode has changed and the walls are shaking. Perhaps that future is closer than we think.

[70]"Take Your Clothes Off When You Dance," *We're Only In It for the Money.*
[71]"When the Mode of the Music Changes," *It Crawled* (Reprise, IS 6305).

THE POP ARTIST AND HIS PRODUCT:
MIXED UP CONFUSION[1]

George H. Lewis

Over the past decade there has been an increasing concern with the pop artist as a force in American culture. Articles and books, ranging from the environmental art of Tom Wolfe to the drivel of the "teen mags," from the academics of Robert Rosenstone and Richard Peterson to the cultism of Jann Wenner's *Rolling Stone* magazine, have appeared with increasing regularity. Through most of this diverse material there runs one common theme—that a selected few of the pop artists are, in fact, cultural leaders who set styles and tastes, not only for their mass audiences, but also for lesser lights within their expressive medium. Although some of the students of pop culture (notably the social scientists) recognize the concept of "feedback" and its place in the creation of pop culture artifacts, too often the urge to attribute the creation of mass taste solely to the manipulating media gains the upper hand.

The empirical question becomes: How much influence is exerted by the media in shaping its own future content, with relation to how much of this influence is exerted by the mass audience or its more prestigious representatives. Clearly the answer to this question will involve the concept of feedback and may well be couched within a theoretical structure which posits some sort of "causal loop."[2]

The question of artistic influence becomes even more complex when one examines the role of the pop artist. Can he be thought of as an independent variable contributing input to the "causal loop" as presented above, or is he, in fact, a dependent variable existing entirely within this system? Folk wisdom is likely to define the artist as an independent variable, while scholarly tradition usually sees the artist as synthesizer, existing within the system, yet independently piecing together existing units in new combinations, yielding unique total forms. Within the context of the McLuhan age, are either of these conceptions of any use in understanding the role of the pop artist? It is my contention that the latter conception begins to touch on explanation, yet in its present form is seriously flawed—mainly because the pop artist, in order to remain "pop," has to be constantly aware of the tone of the marketplace in which he is to sell his product. The myth of independent creation seems just that—a myth perpetuated by the mass media in order to legitimate the product as that of a "true" artist.

As the late C. Wright Mills put it, within the present-day American

[1]This is the revised version of a piece that originally appeared in *The Journal of Popular Culture,* Vol 4, Fall 1970, pp. 327–38.
[2]Arthur Stinchcombe discusses the concept of the casual loop cogently in his book *Constructing Social Theories* (New York: Harcourt, Brace and World, 1968), pp. 93–101.

arena the "cultural workman" tends to become either a commercial hack or a commercial star.

> By The Star, I refer to a person whose productions are so much in demand that, to some extent at least, he is able to use distributors as his adjuncts. This role has its own condition and its own perils: The Star tends to be culturally trapped by his own success. . . . As a leader of fashions he is himself subject to fashion. Moreover, his success as a star depends upon his "playing the market"; he is not in any educative interplay with publics that support his development. By virtue of his success, The Star too becomes a marketeer.[3]

In the field of popular music today, there exist three examples of persons generally treated as pop artists (or "Stars"): Bob Dylan, The Beatles (even though they have officially parted ways), and The Rolling Stones. The music of each is acclaimed as highly creative and each have their own series of myths of independence and innovation, fostered by the mass media and nurtured by their mass audience.

Recently, "underground capitalists" have begun illegally to press and release a number of recordings produced by major pop artists which have, up to now, been unavailable for public consumption. Of the three artists mentioned above, the previously unreleased work of Bob Dylan is by far the most voluminous and spans his recording career from 1961 to his 1969 Isle of Wight concert.[4] Taken in conjunction with the material he has officially released, this "underground" material affords a unique opportunity to examine the wares of a major pop artist that are presented to the public by himself and his recording company, in relation to his total artistic output. As Leo Lowenthal has remarked, the starting point for the analysis of popular culture should not be market data—one should ask specific questions concerning formal and informal dictas of media censorship.[5] Although the data necessary for answers to Lowenthal's questions are not at hand (for example, is censorship that of the recording company or the artist himself?), hopefully the comparisons these underground recordings afford will cast new light upon this area—the role of the pop artist within present-day popular culture.

The Bob Dylan myth is an important aspect of this artist—and one that he and his manager, Albert Grossman, have carefully perpetuated. According to the myth, Dylan arrived in New York City in 1961, a vagabond who, with his battered guitar and harmonica, had been roaming America and collecting its essence in his songs. Like Woody Guthrie, his pro-

---

[3]C. Wright Mills, "The Cultural Apparatus," in *Power, Politics and People,* ed. Irving Louis Horowitz. (New York: Oxford University Press, 1963), p. 419.

[4]These underground records, in plain white jackets, include: *Great White Wonder* (double record set), *Great White Wonder, Volume Two* (double record set), *Best of Great White Wonder, Stealin', Troubled Troubadour, A Thousand Miles Behind, At Home* (double record set), *Motorcycle,* and *Isle of Wight.*

[5]Leo Lowenthal, "Historical Perspectives of Popular Culture," *American Journal of Sociology* 55 (1950): 331.

fessed hero and influence, Dylan exhibited a wry sense of humor and outrage at social ills—and expressed these ideas in the traditional folk-and-talkin' blues idioms of the 1930's protest singers. By 1962 Dylan's musical style had begun to change slightly as songs from his public repertoire began to be taken up by other artists, such as Peter Paul and Mary and Joan Baez. Through Peter Paul and Mary's popularizing of "Blowin' In the Wind," Dylan became the folk hero and musical spokes-man of the civil rights movement of the early 1960's youth. Then, in late 1964 and early 1965, came the big change. According to the myth, Dylan "went rock" and "sold out the movement." Indeed, he was jeered from the stage at the 1965 Newport Folk Festival when he attempted to do a set with electric accompaniment. From then on, Dylan performed part acoustic and part electric concerts—the electric portion gaining increasingly more and more of the billing. As Dylan had changed, so went popular music. The myth explains that Dylan, seeing that the true "music of the people" was rock, risked his career by switching from the folk idiom in which he was safe, to the more "truthful" rock idiom.[6] Recently, the same type of explanation has been proposed to explain the Nashville sound of Dylan's latest commercial albums, Nashville Skyline, Self Portrait, and New Morning.[7]

How much truth lies in the Dylan myth?, which casts the artist in the role of an independent variable influencing the system. Although, in speaking of a feedback system, causality is difficult to prove, speculation concerning the degree of this independence is certainly permissible.

The most important aspect of the Dylan myth is the alleged transfor-mation from folk to rock and the resulting explanation of this shift. Much has been written concerning this shift—the majority of which has utilized the myth as its factual base. Indeed, only the release of Dylan's unre-corded material lends empirical substance to the speculations that all is not what it seems.

Music may be examined and classified in a number of ways. Un-fortunately for the researcher, isolating aspects of the material for classi-fication does injustice to the whole—as many should realize who perform content analysis on rock lyrics and attempt to explain the influence of the music in terms of their data.[8] However, some means of breaking the data down must be attempted if any empirical analysis is to be done at

---

[6]A Marxian-tinged explication of this aspect of the myth can be found in Joe Fer-randino's "Rock Culture and the Development of Social Consciousness," Radical America, November 1965, official publication of Students for a Democratic Society, Madison, Wisconsin. This article is reproduced in this volume, pp. 263–290.

[7]The Bob Dylan myth can be seen reflected in (among many others) the following treatments of the artist's career: Carl Belz, The Story of Rock (New York: Oxford University Press, 1969); "Bobby Dylan—Folk-Rock Hero," by Lawrence Goldman in The Age of Rock, ed. Jonathan Eisen (New York: Random House, 1969), pp. 208–13; Daniel Kramer, Bob Dylan (New York: Citadel Press, 1967); and Sy and Barbara Ribakove, Folk-Rock: The Bob Dylan Story (New York: Dell Books).

[8]This problem is well illustrated in the 1969 study by John Robinson and Paul Hirsch, "Teenage response to rock and roll protest songs," unpublished manuscript.

all. The researcher must be aware of this dilemma in his work. Furthermore, he must acknowledge the probable shortcomings of his research, whatever empirical resolution of the dilemma he chooses.

Pop researchers and rock critics have tended to distinguish between "folk" and "rock" (Labeled "folk-rock" by many) in their analyses of Dylan's artistic output. A review of their material brings to mind three possible means of song classification (although this statement does not mean these researchers have necessarily employed or even recognized the following classificatory schemes). They are: (1) the type of musical structure of the piece, (2) the type of lyrical content of the piece, and (3) the means by which the piece is presented. Most pop researchers seem confused about what base their classificatory scheme will rest upon.

At times these researchers point out that the content of Dylan's lyrics changed when he "sold out" the folkies in 1965. This does not seem to be as much the case as some wish to make it. If one wishes to examine Dylan's lyrics, one finds two major categories of songs:[9] (1) love songs and (2) protest songs. Dylan's protest songs did not cease in 1965; they merely shifted focus from the specific concerns of the civil rights movement ("Oxford Town") to more general concerns with total society ("Desolation Row").[10] Of the 103 songs Dylan had recorded for Columbia Records by December 1969, 80 are concerned with one or the other of these two themes: 37 (46 percent) concerning relationships with women and 43 (54 percent) concerning social protest. Prior to Newport 1965, Dylan had recorded 15 songs (39 percent) concerning relationships with women and 23 (61 percent) concerning social protest. From Newport 1965 to December 1969, he had recorded 22 (52 percent) songs concerning relationships with women and 20 (48 percent) concerning social protest— hardly a significant shift in context, if one considers the small number of cases.

The second type of classification that pop researchers tend to utilize is that of acoustic-electric. They equate the type of song with its mode of presentation, labeling acoustic songs as folk and electric songs as rock. One has only to note Dylan's recent performances of some of his more popular acoustic songs backed by the electric instruments of the Band and his original acoustic performances of "Mr. Tambourine Man" (considered a "rock" song) to point up the absurdity of this classificatory approach. Dylan's first officially released song in early 1962 (deliberately ignored by the myth and for years unavailable on the market) was recorded with electric instruments.[11]

---

[9]Lyrics for content analysis were taken, whenever possible, from M. Witmark and Sons publications of Dylan material.

[10]Although, as Stephan Goldberg has pointed out, Dylan's visions of societal ills were usually couched within the context of personal salvation. See Stephan Goldberg, "Bob Dylan and the Poetry of Salvation," *Saturday Review,* May 30, 1970.

[11]The song was "Mixed Up Confusion"—released early in 1962 with Bob Dylan on piano; Bruce Langhorne, guitar; Gene Ramey, bass; and Herb Lovelle, drums. Columbia took it off the market by 1963.

In analyzing the songs of Bob Dylan, I will use the musical structure of the piece as a basis for classification. In so doing, I realize the injustice this does to the song as a totality; however I feel the method is a more viable one than either presented above. From his first performances, Dylan has exhibited as strong a preference for rhythm and blues as he has for the folk styles. Although it is a nearly impossible task to place many Dylan songs into one or the other of these categories (because of stylistic overlap and fusion), I have attempted to do so. I have used certain criteria as broad guidelines,[12] but have also had to use subjective judgment in some cases. (How would one categorize "My Back Pages"?)

In examining Fig. 1, it is immediately apparent that there have been far more rhythm and blues songs commercially unreleased than there have been folk songs commercially unreleased. If the totals are compared with the figures for commercial releases, one immediately notices that Dylan has recorded more rhythm and blues than folk, not the other way around, as the commercial releases would show. Figures 2 and 3 show how these songs are distributed along the time line of Dylan's recording career.[13, 14]

	folk	rhythm & blues	total
commercially recorded	56	47	103
commercially unrecorded	37	65	102
total	93	112	205

Fig. 1. Recorded Bob Dylan Songs by Type
—January, 1961 to December, 1969

Figure 2 shows how Dylan's commercial releases have accentuated the yearly trends of his total output (especially in terms of his folk output).

---

[12]The major criterion for rhythm and blues is whether the song is of the traditional 12-bar progression or some variation of this progression. Dylan's "rock" material (or as he calls it, "tone poems") derives mainly from this form (see "Like a Rolling Stone"). Folk criteria include the traditional ballad form ("Girl From the North Country," the music of which is the traditional "Scarborough Fair"), as well as the decision to classify talkin' blues as folk.

[13]The switchover in 1968 from rhythm and blues to folk, in terms of the commercial releases, takes place because of the great number of songs of folk structure that appear on Dylan's *John Wesley Harding* album. The reason this shift is not seen in the total recordings for that year is because of the infamous "Basement Tape," (mainly rhythm and blues) recorded by Dylan and The Band and never commercially released.

[14]This analysis does not include material found on the *Self-Portrait* and *New Morning* albums for two reasons: (1) This material chronicles Dylan's shift into country-pop (mainly with "covers" of other artists' materials) and his subsequent flounderings in search of the commercial mainstream he seems to have lost sight of. As such, it is irrelevant to the analysis at hand. (2) Because of the mass of underground recordings already released, recording security has been stepped up and there have been no underground albums released containing material more recent than the Isle of Wight concert (1969) with which to compare Dylan's commercial output.

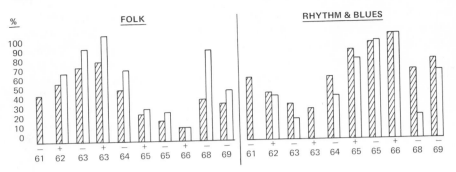

Legend:

⬜ commercial releases

▨ total recordings

— first six months of year

+ last six months of year

Note that some six month periods are missing. This is because Dylan recorded no material during these periods.

Fig. 2 Percentage of Songs Per Year, January, 1961 to December, 1969, Classed as Folk or Rhythm & Blues

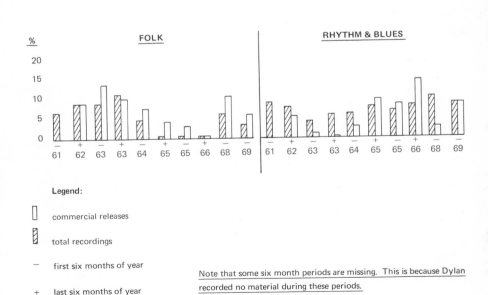

Legend:

⬜ commercial releases

▨ total recordings

— first six months of year

+ last six months of year

Note that some six month periods are missing. This is because Dylan recorded no material during these periods.

Fig. 3. Percentage of All Songs, January, 1961 to December, 1969, Classed as Folk or Rhythm & Blues

Notice that in late 1964 and early 1965, when Dylan's shift to electric instruments is posited, his shift in percentage of songs of each type per year has already taken place—rhythm and blues is fast climbing and the percentage of folk material has dropped off sharply. In comparing Dylan's output per year to national trends, it is interesting to note, as many writers have, that the commercial success and artistic content of rock and roll music fell off sharply around 1961, to be replaced with a "rebirth of popularity" of the folk song.[15] This trend continued until the end of 1963, when the Beatles and the Rolling Stones burst upon the American scene, showing that their own brand of electric rhythm and blues was not only artistically satisfying but also hugely successful commercially.

In examining Fig. 3, which graphs the total number of Dylan songs per type to appear each year, things become perhaps more clear. Again, Dylan's commercial output reflects his "dramatic shift" from folk to rock. However, when one examines the totality of Dylan's output, it is apparent that Dylan has *always* been writing and recording rhythm and blues songs. What is more, his production of them has been relatively constant from the beginning of his career. Dylan's production of folk material can now be seen as that which has shifted drastically over the years—indeed, he began recording about equal numbers of each type of song in 1961, then began to increase his folk output without substantially altering the absolute number of rhythm and blues songs he was recording per year. However, during the period when folk music enjoyed its immense popularity, Dylan released few rhythm and blues songs. When rock (in the form of the rhythm and blues revival of the Beatles, Animals, and Rolling Stones) became commercially successful, Dylan stopped recording folk material. His production of rhythm and blues numbers, although on a slight upswing, remained relatively the same as it had always been. Dylan just began releasing this type of song commercially.

What does this mean in terms of the pop artist and his product? Although there is no way of determining how much responsibility was that of Dylan and how much his recording company, it is clear that Dylan's commercial releases have been the type of pop song that is most commercially successful at the time of their release. Again, how much Dylan's releases further increased the popularity of whatever type of song he was recording is a question that cannot be answered here. As I have stated, causality within a feedback loop is hard to prove. There is evidence, however, that Dylan was not a pioneer in the placing of new song structures on the market.[16] As he himself said, when asked about how he wrote his songs, "It

---

[15]See Carl Belz, *The Story of Rock* and Greil Marcus, *Rock and Roll Will Stand* (Boston: Beacon Press, 1969).

[16]Here I am not speaking of the lyrical content of Dylan's songs. Dylan's main contribution to rock music, like John Lennon's, was that of the free-form symbolic lyric that he had developed over his years of playing with words in his poetry and earlier musical material.

was also what the audience wanted to hear, too . . . don't forget that. When you play in front of an audience, you know what they want to hear. It's easier to write songs then."[17]

As has been previously mentioned, Dylan's first recording was a rhythm and blues song with an electric accompaniment. When folk music began gaining in popularity, and Dylan's first album (all acoustic) was praised as a folk album, the electric rhythm and blues song was taken off the market. Indeed, Dylan's first producer, John Hammond, Sr., recalls that at that time (early 1962) Bob Dylan wasn't sure whether he wanted to be a "rock and roll star," but that late in 1962 Dylan was in touch with Robbie Robertson and the electric rock group that is today known as The Band. By 1963, Dylan was playing regularly with The Band.[18] Further, Griel Marcus recalls early talk of Dylan touring with Bobby Vee and Buddy Holly (early rock stars) prior to his 1961 arrival in New York City.[19] Taken with the empirical charting of Dylan's material over the years, it does not seem unreasonable to conclude that Dylan was always very interested in rhythm and blues (or rock and roll), and that his folk period was the anomaly, rather than the bedrock from which he sprang (as the myth claims).

Dylan did not suddenly switch to rock in 1965. There were many hints of this switch, even in his commercially recorded material, before he publicly appeared with electric instruments at Newport. A number of songs on Dylan's 1964 album, *Another Side of Bob Dylan,* were of the rhythm and blues variety, even though acoustically recorded. And on that album, in a talkin' blues song entitled "I Shall Be Free," Dylan explains a Beatles-type rhythm and blues riff he is doing as "somethin' I learned over in England." It seems possible that Dylan was trying, in 1964, to determine if he could keep his folk market while he shifted his commercial output to the rhythm and blues type of song that was commercially burning up the charts with the release of albums by the Beatles and the Rolling Stones. Further evidence of this might be the fact that Columbia signed a rock group called the Byrds in late 1964 and had them put out a rock version of Dylan's "Mr. Tambourine Man."[20] However, the Byrds were not allowed to play the instrumental accompaniment on this recording—it was done by the Columbia studio musicians. This immensely popular recording was released while Dylan was performing the song acoustically and prior to his commercial release of it with an electric backup. Taken in this light, Dylan's public switch to electric instrumentation at Newport in 1965 may be thought of as the logical culmination of a well-planned campaign to shift Dylan's product to the commercial pop mainstream, rather than as the bold step forward the Bob Dylan myth claims it to be.

---

[17]From Jann Wenner's interview with Bob Dylan, *Rolling Stone,* November 29, 1969.
[18]Interview with John Hammond, Sr., in *Fusion,* October 31, 1969.
[19]*Rolling Stone,* November 29, 1969.
[20]John Hammond, Sr., *Fusion* interview.

In the light of Dylan's 1969 shift to country music and his 1969–1970 public affiliation with Johnny Cash, it is interesting to note that the major commercial shift to the pop Nashville sound took place in 1968, a year before the release of Dylan's *Nashville Skyline* album.[21] Further, Bob Dylan and Johnny Cash were good friends as far back as 1962.[22] Again, it seemed Dylan's musical position was the result of another well-planned campaign to shift his music back into the commercial pop mainstream. It is interesting to note that, after the critical failure of the country-pop–oriented *Self Portrait* album. Dylan immediately released *New Morning*—containing among other things attempts to "get back" to his previously successful *avant garde* rock (in itself, a contradiction). Unfortunately, Dylan's efforts were so simplistic in concept and so blatant in execution as to sound like a parody of himself—he had come full circle and as Ben Gerson remarked; "In this new morning, Dylan emerges as just another musician."[23]

In conclusion, I would note the seeming importance of "the myth" in perpetuating the notion of the pop artist as independent contributor and creative genius. When dealing with the mass audience, the mass media must satisfy the audience's expectations or create artificial expectations which they can satisfy. Those pop artists who realize this may succeed—though their success will last only so long as they can juggle their myths and productive output to conform with what is expected of them, both by the media and its audience.

---

[21]Some claim Dylan's earlier *John Wesley Harding* (1968) contained the roots of the Nashville shift—however he himself has declared he was attempting on that album to get a "Gordon Lightfoot sound." (Gordon Lightfoot is a Canadian artist who has only recently [1970] recorded in Nashville). With respect to Nashville-based musicians, Dylan had been utilizing them in his recordings since his first electric album ventures of 1965. No one has labeled their playing on these recordings as "Nashville-country," nor should they do so. It is pure rock.
[22]John Hammond, Sr., *Fusion* interview.
[23]Ben Gerson, "Bob Dylan," *Fusion,* December 11, 1970, p. 17.

ROCK FOR SALE

Michael Lyndon

In 1956, when rock and roll was just about a year old, Frankie Lymon, lead singer of Frankie Lymon and the Teenagers, wrote and recorded a song called "Why Do Fools Fall in Love?" It was an immediate million-selling hit and has since become a rock classic, a true golden oldie of the sweet-voiced harmonizing genre. The group followed it up with other hits, starred in a movie, appeared on the Ed Sullivan Show, toured the country with Bill Haley and the Comets, and did a tour of Europe. Frankie, a black kid from Harlem, was then 13 years old. Last year, at 26, he died of an overdose of heroin.

Despite the massive publicity accorded to rock in the past several years, Frankie's death received little attention. It got a bit more publicity than the death in a federal prison of Little Willie John, the author of "Fever," another classic, but nothing compared to that lavished on the breakup of the Cream or on Janis Joplin's split with Big Brother and the Holding Company. Nor did many connect it with the complete musical stagnation of the Doors, a group which in 1967 seemed brilliantly promising, or to the dissolution of dozens of other groups who a year or two ago were not only making beautiful music but seemed to be the vanguard of a promising "youth cultural revolution."

In fact these events are all connected, and their common denominator is hard cash. Since that wildly exciting spring of 1967, the spring of *Sgt. Pepper's Lonely Hearts Club Band,* of be-ins and love-ins and flower-power, of the discovery of psychedelia, hippies and "doing your thing"—to all of which "New Rock," as it then began to be called, was inextricably bound—one basic fact has been consistently ignored: rock is a product created, distributed and controlled for the profit of America (and international) business. "The record companies sell rock and roll records like they sell refrigerators," says Paul Kantner of the Jefferson Airplane. "They don't care about the people who make rock or what they're all about as human beings any more than they care about the people who make refrigerators."

Recently, the promoters of a sleazy Southern California enterprise known as "Teen Fair" changed its name to "Teen Expo." The purpose of the operation remains the same: to sell trash to adolescents while impressing them with the joys of consumerism. But nine years into the '60s, the backers decided that their '50s image of nice-kid teenagerism had to go. In its place, they have installed "New Rock" (with its constant companion, schlock psychedelia) as the working image of the "all new!" Teen Expo.

By the time the word gets down to the avaricious cretins who run teen fairs, everybody has the message: rock and roll sells. It doesn't make money just for the entertainment industry—the record companies, radio stations, TV networks, stereo and musical instrument manufacturers, etc.— but for law firms, clothing manufacturers, the mass media, soft drink companies and car dealers (the new Opel will "light your fire!"). Rock is the surest way to the hearts and wallets of millions of Americans between 8 and 35—the richest, most extravagant children in the history of the world.

From the start, rock has been commercial in its very essence. An American creation on the level of the hamburger or the billboard, it was never an art form that just happened to make money, nor a commercial undertaking that sometimes became art. Its art was synonymous with its business. The movies are perhaps closest to rock in their aesthetic involvement with the demands of profitability, but even they once had an arty tradition which scorned the pleasing of the masses.

Yet paradoxically it was the unabashed commerciality of rock which gave rise to the hope that it would be a "revolutionary" cultural form of expression. For one thing, the companies that produce it and reap its profits have never understood it. Ford executives drive their company's cars but Sir Joseph Lockwood, chairman of EMI, the recording company which, until Apple, released the Beatles' records, has always admitted that he doesn't like their music. The small companies like Sun and Chess Records which first discovered the early stars like Elvis Presley and Chuck Berry were run by middle-class whites who knew that kids and blacks liked this weird music, but they didn't know or really care why. As long as the music didn't offend the businessmen's sensibilities too much—they never allowed outright obscenity—and as long as it sold, they didn't care what it said. So within the commercial framework, rock has always had a certain freedom.

Moreover, rock's slavish devotion to commerciality gave it powerful aesthetic advantages. People had to like it for it to sell, so rock had to get to the things that the audience really cared about. Not only did it create a ritualized world of dances, slang, "the charts," fan magazines and "your favorite DJ coming your way" on the car radio, but it defined, reflected and glorified the listener's ordinary world. Rock fans can date their entire lives by rock; hearing a "golden oldie" can instantaneously evoke the whole flavor and detail of a summer or a romance.

When in 1963-64 the Pop Art movement said there was beauty in what had been thought to be a crass excreta of the Eisenhower Age, when the Beatles proved that shameless reveling in money could be a stone groove, and when the wistful puritanism of the protest-folk music movement came to a dead end, rock and roll, with all its unabashed carnality and worldliness, seemed a beautiful trip. Rock, the background music of growing up, was discovered as the common language of a generation. New Rock musicians could not only make the music, they could even make an aesthetic and social point by the very choice of rock as their medium.

That rock was commercial seemed only a benefit. It ensured wide distribution, the hope of a good and possibly grandiose living style, and the honesty of admitting that, yes, we are the children of affluence: don't deny it, man, dig it. As music, rock had an undeniably liberating effect; driving and sensual, it implicitly and explicitly presented an alternative to bourgeois insipidity. The freedom granted to rock by society seemed sufficient to allow its adherents to express their energies without inhibition. Rock pleasure had no pain attached; the outrageousness of Elvis' gold lamé suits and John Lennon's wildly painted Rolls Royce was a gas, a big joke on adult society. Rock was a way to beat the system, to gull grown-ups into paying you while you made faces behind their backs.

Sad but true, however, the grown-ups are having the last laugh. Rock and roll is a lovely playground, and within it kids have more power than they have anywhere else in society, but the playground's walls are carefully maintained and guarded by the corporate elite that set it up in the first place. While the White Panthers talk of "total assault upon the culture by any means necessary, including rock and roll, dope and fucking in the streets," *Billboard,* the music trade paper, announces with pride that in 1968 the record industry became a billion-dollar business.

Bob Dylan has described with a fiendish accuracy the pain of growing up in America, and millions have responded passionately to his vision. His song, "Maggie's Farm," contains the lines, "He gives me a nickel, he gives me a dime, he asks me with a grin if I'm having a good time, and he fines me every time I slam the door, oh, I ain't gonna work on Maggie's farm no more." But along with Walter Cronkite and the New York Yankees, Dylan works for one of Maggie's biggest farms, the Columbia Broadcasting System.

Mick Jagger, another adept and vitriolic social critic, used rock to sneer at "the under assistant west coast promotion man" in his seersucker suit; but London Records used this "necessary talent for every rock and roll band" to sell that particular Rolling Stones record and all their other products. For all its liberating potential, rock is doomed to a bitter impotence by its ultimate subservience to those whom it attacks.

In fact, rock, rather than being an example of how freedom can be achieved within the capitalist structure, is an example of how capitalism can, almost without a conscious effort, deceive those whom it oppresses. Rather than being liberated heroes, rock and roll stars are captives on a leash, and their plight is but a metaphor for that of all young people and black people in America. All the talk of "rock revolution," talk that is assiduously cultivated by the rock industry, is an attempt to disguise that plight.

Despite the aura of wealth that has always surrounded the rock and roll star, and which for fans justified the high prices of records and concerts, very few stars really make much money—and for all but the stars and their backup musicians, rock is just another low-paying insecure and very hard job. Legend says that wild spending sprees, drugs, and women account for the missing loot; what legend does not say is that most of the artists are paid very little for their work. The artist may receive a record royalty of 2½ percent, but the company often levies charges for studio time, promotion and advertising. It is not uncommon for the maker of a hit record to end up in debt to the company.

Not surprisingly, it is the black artists who suffer most. In his brilliant book, *Urban Blues,* Charles Keil describes in detail how the blues artist is at the mercy of the recording company. It is virtually impossible, he states, for an unknown artist to get an honest contract, but even an "honest" contract is only an inexpensive way for a company to own an artist body and soul.

A star's wealth may be not only nonexistent, but actually a fraud carefully perpetuated by the record company. Blues singer Bobby Bland's "clothes, limousine, valet, and plentiful pocket money," says Keil, "are image bolsterers from Duke Records (or perhaps a continual 'advance on royalties' that keeps him tied to the company) rather than real earnings." And even cash exploitation is not enough; Chess Records last year forced Muddy Waters to play his classic blues with a "psychedelic" band and called the humiliating record *Electric Mud.*

Until recently, only a very few stars made any real money from rock; their secret was managers shrewd to the point of unscrupulousness, who kept them under tight control. Colonel Parker molded the sexual country boy Elvis into a smooth ballad singer; Brian Epstein took four scruffy Liverpool rockers and transformed them into neatly tousled boys-next-door. "We were worried that friends might think we had sold out," John Lennon said recently, "which in a way we had."

The musicians of New Rock—most of them white, educated, and middle-class—are spared much of what their black and lower-class counterparts have suffered. One of the much touted "revolutions" New Rock has brought, in fact, has been a drastic increase in the power of the artist vis-à-vis the record company. Contracts for New Rock bands regularly include almost complete artistic control, royalties as high as 10 percent, huge cash advances, free studio time, guaranteed amounts of company-bought promotion, and in some instances control over advertising design and placement in the media.

But such bargaining is at best a futile reformism which never challenges the essential power relationship that has contaminated rock since its inception. Sales expansion still gives the companies ample profits, and they maintain all the control they really need (even the "revolutionary" group, the MC5, agreed to remove the word "motherfucker" from an album and to record "brothers and sisters" in its place). New Rock musicians lost the battle for real freedom at the very moment they signed their contracts (whatever the clauses) and entered the big-time commercial sphere.

The Doors are a prime example. Like hundreds of New Rock musicians, the four Doors are intelligent people who in the early and mid-'60s dropped out into the emerging drug and hip underground. In endless rehearsals and on stage in Sunset Strip rock clubs, they developed a distinctly eerie and stringent sound. The band laid down a dynamo drive behind dramatically handsome lead singer Jim Morrison, who, dressed in black leather and writhing in anguish, screamed demonic invitations to sensual madness. "Break on through," was the message, "yeah, break on, break on through to the other side!"

It was great rock and roll, and by June 1967, when their "Light My Fire" was a number-one hit, it had become very successful rock. More hits followed and the Doors became the first New Rock group to garner a huge following among the young teens and pre-teens who were traditionally the mass rock audience. Jim Morrison became rock's number-one sex idol and the teeny-boppers' delight. The group played bigger and bigger halls—the

Hollywood Bowl, the garish Forum in Los Angeles, and finally Madison Square Garden last winter in a concert that netted the group $52,000 for one night's work.

But the hit "Light My Fire" was a chopped-up version of the original album track, and after that castration of their art for immediate mass appeal (a castration encouraged by their "hip" company, Elektra Records), the Doors died musically. Later albums were pale imitations of the first; trying desperately to recapture the impact of their early days, they played louder and Morrison lost all subtlety: at a recent Miami concert he had to display his penis to make his point.

Exhausted by touring and recording demands, the Doors now seldom play or even spend much casual time together. Their latest single hit the depths; *Cashbox* magazine, in its profit-trained wisdom said, "The team's impact is newly channeled for even more than average young teen impact." "Maybe pretty soon we'll split, just go away to an island somewhere," Morrison said recently, fatigue and frustration in his voice, "get away by ourselves and start creating again."

But the Doors have made money, enough to be up-tight about it. "When I told them about this interview," said their manager, Bill Siddons, sitting in the office of the full-time accountant who manages the group's investments (mostly land and oil), "they said, 'Don't tell him how much we make.'" But Siddons, a personable young man, did his best to defend them. The Doors, he said, could make a lot more money if they toured more often and took less care in preparing each hall they play in for the best possible lighting and sound; none of the Doors lives lavishly, and the group has plans for a foundation to give money to artists and students ("It'll help our tax picture, too"). But, he said, "You get started in rock and you get locked into the cycle of success. It's funny, the group out there on stage preaching a revolutionary message, but to get the message to people, you gotta do it the establishment way. And you know everybody acquires a taste for comfortable living."

Variations on the Doors' story are everywhere. The Cream started out in 1966 as a brilliant and influential blues-rock trio and ended, after two solid years of touring, with lead guitarist Eric Clapton on the edge of a nervous breakdown. After months of bitter fighting, Big Brother and the Holding Company split up, as did Country Joe and the Fish (who have since reorganized, with several replacements from Big Brother). The Steve Miller Band and the Quicksilver Messenger Service were given a total of $100,000 by Capitol Records; within a year neither one existed in its original form and the money had somehow disappeared.

Groups that manage to stay together are caught in endless conflicts about how to make enough money to support their art and have it heard without getting entangled in the "success cycle." The Grateful Dead, who were house and bus minstrels for Ken Kesey's acid-magical crew and who have always been deeply involved in trying to create a real hip community, have been so uncommercial as to frustrate their attempts to spread the word of their joyful vision.

"The trouble is that the Grateful Dead is a more 'heard of' band than a 'heard' band," says manager Rock Scully, "and we want people to hear us. But we won't do what the system says—make single hits, take big gigs, do the success number. The summer of '67, when all the other groups were making it, we were playing free in the park, man, trying to cool the Haight-Ashbury. So we've never had enough bread to get beyond week-to-week survival, and now we're about $50,000 in debt. We won't play bad music for the bread because we decided a long time ago that money wasn't a high enough value to sacrifice anything for. But that means that not nearly enough people have heard our music."

The Jefferson Airplane have managed to take a middle route. A few early hits, a year of heavy touring (150 dates in 1967), a series of commercials for White Levis, and the hard-nosed management of entrepreneur Bill Graham gave them a solid money-making popular base. A year ago they left Graham's management, stopped touring almost entirely, bought a huge mansion in San Francisco and devoted their time to making records (all of them excellent), giving parties, and buying expensive toys like cars and color TVs. They've gone through enormous amounts of money and are now $30,000 in debt. But they're perfectly willing to go out and play a few jobs if the creditors start to press them. They resolve the commercial question by attempting not to care about it. "What I care about," says Paul Kantner, "is what I'm doing at the time—rolling a joint, balling a chick, writing a song. Start worrying about the ultimate effect of all your action, and in the end you just have to say fuck it. Everybody in the world is getting fucked one way or another. All you can do is see that you aren't fucking them directly.

But the Airplane also profess political radicalism, and, says Kantner, "The revolution is already happening, man. All those kids dropping out, turning on—they add up." Singer Grace Slick appeared in blackface on the Smothers Brothers show and gave the Black Panther salute; in a front window of their mansion is a sign that reads, "Eldridge Cleaver Welcome Here." But Kantner said he hadn't really thought about what that meant: would he really take Cleaver in and protect him against police attack, a very likely necessity should Cleaver accept the welcome? "I don't know, man. I'd have to wait until that happened."

Cleaver would be well-advised not to choose the Airplane's mansion for his refuge. For Kantner's mushy politics—sort of a turned-on liberalism that thinks the Panthers are "groovy" but doesn't like to come to terms with the nasty American reality—are the politics of the much touted "rock revolution." They add up to a hazy belief in the power of art to change the world, presuming that the place for the revolution to begin and end is inside individual heads. The Beatles said it nicely in "Revolution": "You say that it's the institution, we-ll, you know, you better free your mind instead."

Jac Holzman, president of Elektra Records, said it in businessman's prose: "I want to make it clear," he said, "that Elektra is not the tool of anyone's revolution. We feel that the 'revolution' will be won by poetics and not by politics—that poetics will change the structure of the world. It's reached the kids and is getting to them at the best possible level."

There is no secret boardroom conspiracy to divert antisocial youthful energy into rock and thus render it harmless while making a profit for the society it is rebelling against, but the corporate system has acted in that direction with a uniformity which a conspiracy probably could not have provided. And the aware capitalists are worried about their ability to control where kids are going: "There is something a bit spooky, from a business point of view," a *Fortune* issue on youth said recently, ". . . in youth's widespread rejection of middle-class styles ('Cheap is in') . . . If it . . . becomes a dominant orientation, will these children of affluence grow up to be consumers on quite the economy-moving scale as their parents?"

So the kids are talking revolution and smoking dope? Well, so are the companies, in massive advertising campaigns that co-opt the language of revolution so thoroughly that you'd think they were on the streets themselves. "The Man can't bust *our* music," read one Columbia ad; another urged (with a picture of a diverse group of kids apparently turning on): "Know who your friends are. And look and see and touch and be together. Then listen. *We* do." (Italics mine.)

More insidious than the ads themselves is the fact that ad money from the record companies is one of the main supports of the underground press. And the companies don't mind supporting these "revolutionary" sheets; the failure of Hearst's *Eye* magazine after a year showed that the establishment itself could not create new media to reach the kids, so squeamish is it about advocating revolution, drugs and sexual liberation. But it is glad to support the media the kids create themselves, and thereby, just as it did with rock, ultimately defang it.

The ramifications of control finally came full circle when *Rolling Stone,* the leading national rock newspaper, which began eighteen months ago on a shoestring, had enough money in the bank to afford a $7000 ad on the back page of *The New York Times.* Not only was this "hip rock" publication self consciously taking its place among the communication giants ("NBC was the day before us and *Look* the day after," said the 22-year-old editor), but the ad's copy made clear the paper's exploitive aim: "If you are a corporate executive trying to understand what is happening to youth today, you cannot afford to be without *Rolling Stone.* If you are a student, a professor, a parent, this is your life because you already know that rock and roll is more than just music; it is the energy center of the new culture and youth revolution." Such a neat reversal of the corporate-to-kids lie into a kids-to-corporate lie is only possible when the kids so believe the lie they have been fed that they want to pass it on.

But rock and roll musicians are in the end artists and entertainers, and were it not for all the talk of the "rock revolution," one would be led to expect a clear political vision from them. The bitterest irony is that the "rock revolution" hype has come close to fatally limiting the revolutionary potential that rock does contain. So effective has the rock industry been in encouraging the spirit of optimistic youth take-over that rock's truly hard political edge, its constant exploration of the varieties of youthful frustration, has been ignored and softened. Rock musicians, like their followers, have always been torn between the obvious pleasures that America held out and the price paid for them. Rock and roll is not revolutionary music because it has never gotten beyond articulation of this paradox. At best it has offered the defiance of withdrawal; its violence never amounted to more than a cry of "Don't bother me."

"Leave me alone; anyway, I'm almost grown"; "Don't step on my blue suede shoes"; "There ain't no cure for the summertime blues"; "I can't get no satisfaction": the rock refrains that express despair could be strung out forever. But at least rock has offered an honest appraisal of where its makers and listeners are at, and that radical, if bitterly defeatist, honesty is a touchstone, a starting point. If the companies, as representatives of the corporate structure, can convince the rock world that their revolution is won or almost won, that the walls of the playground are crumbling, not only will the constituents of rock seal their fate by that fatal self-deception, but their music, one of the few things they actually do have going for them, will have been successfully corrupted and truly emasculated.

ALTAMONT: PEARL HARBOR TO THE WOODSTOCK NATION

Sol Stern

"The Festival turned out to be history's largest happening. As the moment when the special culture of U.S. youth of the '60s openly displayed its strength, appeal and power, it may well rank as one of the significant political and sociological events of the age."
—*Time* Magazine on Woodstock,
August, 1969

Berkeley and San Francisco have been the epicenters, both symbolic and real, for a decade of change. The Free Speech Movement, the Haight-Ashbury, rock bands, the be-ins, trips festivals, Peoples' Park—in a sense, the sixties were partly defined by events which began there. And during the last months of the old decade, it seemed to come full circle. Instead of the promised counter-community getting stronger and more together, it was rapidly fragmenting, atomized, helpless to stop the violence it was doing to itself and unable to do anything about the commercial rape of its own cultural revolution.

The lionized "counter-culture" of the sixties which was born and weaned in the Bay Area, received its belated coming out at Woodstock in the summer of 1969. A pre-McLuhan Greek chorus led by *Life, Time, Newsweek* and the *New York Times* suddenly discovered the existence of a free, dope-smoking, cooperative, nonviolent, antipolitical—though potentially culturally revolutionary—counter-community of youth which was cemented together by rock music, but retained enough good middle-class manners to clean up after itself. This rather happy view of the "Woodstock Nation" was something the other, over-30 nation could live with. But those millions of readers of the popular press who knew all about Woodstock were never told about Altamont.

Pearl Harbor eve, Saturday, December 6, 1969—on the barren land outside a semi-abandoned dragstrip 30 miles east of Berkeley, the popular myth of Woodstock died an untimely and unreported death. Upwards of half a million of the supposed citizens of Woodstock Nation were present in those last hours, but the national media which gave its birth a rave review have yet to run even a funeral notice.

The occasion was the groovy, free, all-day concert at Altamont racetrack given by the Rolling Stones and billed by its promoters as Woodstock West. When it was all over these incomplete casualty lists were assembled:

> —Four people were dead. One, an 18-year-old black youth, was killed in a ritual stabbing by several aging Hell's Angels 25 feet from the stage as Mick Jagger sang "Sympathy for the Devil." Two others were run over by cars driven by unknown people. The fourth drowned in a puddle.
> —Some 100 people had their heads bloodied or ribs cracked or were otherwise pummelled and violated by the Hells Angels, semi-official border guards of the concert.
> —A reported 700—there were more likely thousands—people were treated at the site for nightmarish bad acid trips.
> —One musician, Marty Balin of the Jefferson Airplane, was knocked unconscious and bloodied while on stage performing. Another musician Denise Jewkes of the Ace of Cups, six months pregnant and on stage observing, was hit in the head by an empty beer bottle thrown from the crowd and wound up in the hospital with a fractured skull.

In the immediate shocked aftermath of Altamont, many of the big name bands, like the Jefferson Airplane and Crosby, Stills, Nash and Young, said they wouldn't play any more at big Woodstock-type festivals. The Grateful Dead, who had helped plan the concert, were so shaken they wouldn't talk to any outsiders for weeks. Thousands of believers in the Woodstock ethic were emotionally, almost physically, shaken as by no other event of the decade. The entire hip underground radical community in the Bay Area was on a monumental bummer and couldn't talk about anything else for weeks. Several people I know have serious anxiety attacks whenever they think of that day. One girl, a graduate student at Berkeley who witnessed the stabbing from the stage, is now afraid to go near any large crowd.

"Stones Concert Ends it—America Now Up For Grabs," the *Berkeley Tribe,* the most widely read of the Bay Area's underground newspapers, headlined. And that's what Altamont symbolized to the hip Bay Area. It meant the end of the love-community ethic at base of the rock counter-culture.

Neither *Time* nor *Life,* both orgiastic over Woodstock, carried a word about Altamont. *Newsweek,* which went ape over Woodstock in two consecutive issues, finally ran a story three weeks late; it was full of misinformation about the Hell's Angels and said almost nothing about the concert. The *New York Times,* which had covered Woodstock as if the Mafia had held an upstate convention, ran a short dispatch on the inside pages of its late Sunday edition. The editors of these publications at least must be presumed to have heard of those weird stories of killings, stompings and total disaster and disorientation at Altamont. But the deflation of the Woodstock myth—so soon after they had helped inflate it—was apparently something the masters of the mass media were not up to.

"Believe in the magic. It will set you free. . . ."

—The Lovin' Spoonful

Eighteen of us made the 30-mile trek from Berkeley to Altamont, a varied collection of Berkeley radicals and rock freaks, more or less friends and comrades, who had shared real battles such as Peoples' Park as well as a mythical belief in a counter-community which had never really materialized.

We went together partly for logical convenience, but also because of a herding instinct, a sense that we were going into something unpredictable where it would be good to be close to friends. The rock radio stations called the free concert "Woodstock West," but it already felt different. Chaos was written into the event from its vague inception when rumors started that the Stones wanted to give a free concert in San Francisco when their national tour was over.

But soon there were conflicting and confusing stories about the concert. One of the rock stations announced, on reliable information from the Stones, that the concert was "definitely set" for December 6 in San Francisco. The next day however, a city official stated that as far as the city was concerned there would be no concert since no one had officially applied for a permit.

Three days before the scheduled date, the Stones announced that they had obtained a site outside of San Francisco, at the Sears Point Raceway in Sonoma County, about 40 miles north of the Golden Gate Bridge. The radio stations began to give directions to the raceway, a stage started to go up and workers began to pour onto the site.

Then, chaos again. The owners of the raceway, Filmways Corporation of Los Angeles, charged that the Stones' management hadn't lived up to the terms of their agreement and said the concert was off. The Stones insisted that it was all being worked out and the concert would be held. Different radio stations were carrying conflicting reports (the radio was the only effective source of communication about the concert, since the newspapers were too slow to keep up with all the changes).

At noon on December 5, just 24 hours before it was supposed to start, it was officially announced that the concert would instead be held at Altamont, an obscure semi-abandoned racing strip far east of Berkeley in the Alameda County hills. Meanwhile, at Sears Point, the hundreds of people who had labored for three days and nights to construct a stage and install chemical toilets and other rudimentary facilities began to tear everything down and engage the logistical horror of moving everything 60 miles south and setting it up again overnight.

It was madness. And as we gathered in Berkeley on Friday night, making sandwiches and rolling sleeping bags for the next day, we knew that all of us, radicals or just plain rock freaks, were victims of that madness. Some of the radicals called the Stones "capitalist pigs" for charging $7 per ticket for their concerts; "those fuckers are making $2 million on the tour and Mick Jagger practically spit in Abbie Hoffman's face when Abbie asked him for some bread for the Chicago 8," a girl said over coffee in a Telegraph Avenue restaurant. But all of us got stoned listening to Jagger singing "Street Fighting Man," and for all the teasing ambiguity of the song, we dreamed a dream of revolution in the streets.

We were easy victims because things hadn't been going too well in our "counter-community" lately. After the initial high of Peoples' Park, there was a sense of defeat and frustration in Berkeley. On the University of California campus, the political radicals could hardly outdraw the Hare Krishna religious devotees who sang and danced at Sproul Plaza.

On the cultural front, it was much the same. The Wild West Festival— a proposed combination hip world's fair and rock festival—had been shot down in the intense factional infighting that was pervading the rock world. Old friends were calling each other dirty names, and a sense of disintegration was in the air. Berkeley, the cradle of the New American Revolution, was one of the quietest places in the country in the fall and early winter of 1969, waiting for the next turn-on.

The Stones promised magical rejuvenation, an energy center that would bring it all together again—hundreds of thousands of people merging into an instant community, even if only for one day. As we gathered in a big house in Berkeley on Friday night, each of us invested our peculiar hopes and fantasies in this existential event called by some millionaire British Pied Pipers.

Someone in our group discovered, to his delight, that Altamont was just a few miles from Santa Rita, the prison farm where several hundred people had been taken and brutalized by the Alameda County Sheriff's deputies during the Peoples' Park fighting in Berkeley. "Far out," said one of the more imaginative Berkeley activists. "Why don't we turn the whole thing into a march on Santa Rita after the concert and demand that all the prisoners be freed." And for several minutes, some of us were captivated by the image of several hundred thousand marching rock enthusiasts approaching the prison, chanting "free the prisoners."

At 1 a.m., we piled our sandwiches, sleeping bags and fantasies into a huge rented white van and started towards Altamont. No one knew the way, but maps weren't necessary. We just got onto the freeway and followed the traffic.

At 3 a.m., with the help of a Rolling Stones Concert Tour button belonging to rock journalist Mike Lydon, we breached the none-too-tight security leading to the backstage area, rolled up our sleeping bags and piled out, rubbing our eyes from drowsiness and the sudden shock of the beautiful eerie scene we encountered.

The moon overhead was a thin silver scimitar against a black sky, and the only light was coming from two tall towers casting powerful spotlights outward from the racetrack: a pallid yellow light that illuminated a bowl-shaped valley gently sloping back from the stage for almost three-quarters of a mile, at least four city blocks wide on the sides. Towards the rear, hundreds of abandoned, twisted, wrecked cars, once used on the dragstrip, were piled in heaps. The valley floor was a hard, ugly, rutted surface, and trucks were wheeling over it in chaotic fashion. In the yellow light, the place looked like an Army encampment in the desert. At the valley's lowest point, the already completed stage was the center of additional frantic construction work. Five 75- to 100-foot-high skeleton-like scaffolds were going up in a semicircle around the stage. In front of the stage about 2,000 people were stretched out in neat rows of sleeping bags or blankets, like a sleeping battalion.

Those who couldn't or wouldn't sleep stood near the stage in small, quiet groups, passing joints around like hot coffee, marveling at the seemingly spontaneous creation going on around them. Workers scrambled up the scaffolding like monkeys up a jungle gym. A half mile up the hill, hundreds of chemical toilets were being unloaded off trucks.

There didn't seem to be anyone in charge.

We knew that somehow, impossible as it seemed, out of all this chaos everything would get done. We were at the mercy of the unsung, faceless geniuses of the rock scene, the stage managers and electronic technicians who transformed rock from music for the few into huge public rituals, like the one we would witness in the morning.

By 4 a.m., a small group of us, mostly journalists and rock camp followers, were huddling around a fire, unable to sleep. Something strange was beginning to happen, but no one dared to put it into words. What were we gathered at this weird site for? An Antonioni movie? A religious ritual? A sermon?

A pretty blonde girl named Elaine, maybe 18 years old, was warming her hands at the fire. You had seen her at nearly every rock dance in the Bay Area, dancing frantically near the front of the stage, usually topless. Now she was muttering about the astrological signs for the day, which she said foreshadowed heavy vibrations.

At 7 a.m., with the sun peeking over the tops of the hills, a loud roar went up at the back of the valley. The gates were open. Within minutes, thousands of kids were pouring down the hills from the back and side, running and jumping, letting out Indian war whoops, pressing in close to grab a few inches of sacred earth near the stage, tromping on sleeping bags which still contained sleepers. It was a young, hard-looking, scruffy vanguard, the 40,000 to 50,000 who would push closest to the stage for the rest of the day. No plastic weekend hippies these, but lots of working-class kids, in shabby army coats and work shirts, and many already stoned-out freaks. If the kids at Woodstock were distinctive of the part-time drop-outs of the American middle class, Altamont seemed to have more of the sons and daughters of the silent majority. People going to Woodstock thought they would have to spend upwards to $20 in admission fees. Altamont, however, because of its proximity to the Bay Area industrial center and because it was free, attracted more working-class kids, kids in the streets, the kind of kids you see at drive-ins, those kids just making the shift from wine to grass, who had heard of the free and lovely life of Woodstock and were now about to experience it first-hand.

The first disastrous experience of the day came to the Berkeley radicals who tried to relate to the crowd in a political way. Some of them circulated with buckets collecting money for the Black Panthers' legal defense fund (Fred Hampton had been murdered by Chicago police just days before) and met with indifference and even hostility from the solidly anti-political rock audience.

For 14 members of the COPS (Committee on Public Safety), a Berkeley political commune that had been self-consciously trying to bridge the gap between the political and cultural revolutionaries, Altamont became Waterloo. When the commune members first heard about the concert they tried to organize a free food stand, like the Hog Farm commune had done at Woodstock. All they got for their trouble was a big run-around from the concert organizers, and finally they had to give up and come to Altamont as consumers just like everyone else. Around 10 a.m., vendors selling food, peanuts, soda and coffee at outrageously inflated prices started circulating through the crowd. The people from COPS, still hoping to carry out the spirit of Woodstock Nation, decided that commercialism had no place in a free concert. To make that political point clear to the crowd, they began to harass the vendors to make them give the food away. Seven or eight political people surrounded two middle-aged, nondescript-looking men, obviously working-class and hard up for money, who were selling old Rolling Stones programs from a table.

"Hey, man," said one of the communards, "this is a free concert. There shouldn't be anything for sale."

At first the vendors told the kids to mind their business, but the kids persisted and threw some of the programs into the crowd. One of the vendors, frightened that the kids would actually attack him, picked up a table to defend himself. Finally, somewhat terrified, the two men cut out, leaving most of their programs behind with the crowd, which couldn't care less.

It was a foolish and demeaning thing, and later most of the COPS people realized that what was wrong with the day had nothing to do with a few hapless old men trying to make a few bucks. Some members of COPS, among the most sensitive and together people in the Berkeley political scene, were literally physically sickened by Altamont.

By mid-morning everything seemed up for grabs. There was not a uniform in sight. If there was to be any order, or law, it would have to come from the massive community that had gathered so suddenly. As the sun moved toward the official noon starting time and the tension and expectation increased, only a mythical political category such as the State of Nature seemed to apply. The normal restraints and structures were gone—there were only the people, and the drugs and the music to come and the feeling of incredible energy already beginning to radiate from the empty stage.

Until slightly past noon, the only restraint between that fragile, four-foot-high stage and the pressing, surging crowd was the melodious British voice of Sam Cutler, the road manager of the Stones. Cutler looked as improbable as his name: tall and thin, straight black hair falling nearly to his shoulders, a thin mustache, a long beaked nose, high cheekbones, beady dark eyes. He was wearing a tight-fitting brown leather coat and white turtle-neck sweater. The tension was getting almost unbearable as the last piece of equipment was put in place and Cutler moved to the mike and said, "Ladies and gentlemen, we give you Santana. The first band in the best party in 1969."

The crowd, contained for hours, responded with a roar that rumbled half a mile back.

For the reality of what's happening in America, we must go to rock 'n roll, to popular music."

—Ralph J. Gleason

For at least five minutes, it was almost pure ecstasy. Turning around, all I could see were people as far back as the clear blue horizon. In front was the music, evil but beautiful, coming from huge, perfect amplifiers at the sides of the stage, enveloping us in a protective coat of mind-shattering sound. It was like being in the eye of a hurricane, with energy and turmoil all around.

Considering what was to come off that stage the rest of the day, Santana was a poetically perfect way to open the program. Their loud music throbs with the violence of the city. Few vocals, mostly deep down Latin-type voodoo rhythms backed up by two conga drummers. The members of the band look like a bunch of knife fighters just off the streets of Spanish Harlem. As they did their first number, I thought everything was going to be all right, that the power of the music would keep it all in balance.

Then suddenly we went over the edge. Ugliness and meanness erupted all around, all at once. Up front, a huge handfull of pills were being passed down the row. No one knew what they were—"probably bad acid," someone yelled out—but kids were popping them anyway. To the right of the stage, about 20 rows back, a repulsively fat man, a huge circus freak, stood naked, his enormous belly hanging down in ripples which almost obscured his tiny penis. He half stumbled, half danced toward the stage, and groans went up from the people he trampled on as he moved forward.

Behind us fear was rising. A two-year-old baby was sobbing as her stoned-out mother screamed at her to shut up. To our left an acid freakout —mad, frightened, screaming. Someone was desperately trying to get out of the jammed-in crowd—but there was no escape except over the stage. Watching from the front of the stage was Timothy Leary, who had something to do with the way it all began. He was apparently too busy digging the music to help any of the kids who were freaking out on acid.

A fight broke out around the grotesque fat man. Some people, beginning to panic, raised their hands in the "V" sign. The unusual thought occurred that perhaps we needed a few cops.

Then three Hell's Angels, carrying five-foot pool cues, crossed the stage, moving from left to right, divined the location of the scuffle, and dove in, feet first, as if into a swimming pool. A huge circle cleared to accommodate them. Women began screaming and chants of "peace, peace" erupted as the Angels got their man. Two Angels stood over the fallen fat figure pounding down with the pool cues, hard, well-aimed blows with both hands coming down over their heads, as if they were beating the dust from an old mattress. A man rushed to the assistance of the figure on the ground, but he went under quickly in a hail of stomping and kicking Angels. The lesson took with the crowd, and no one tried to be a hero again.

The Angels are the cops! The unspoken thought chilled me. The State of Nature had been short-lived, and we now had law and order of sorts. But the Angel-cops had no jail to take people to or judge or jury to try them. So for the rest of the afternoon, if the Angels decided you broke the law, they did only what they do best—wiped you out, making certain you didn't do it again.

Who had elected them? Not us. No one from the stage had mentioned anything about Angel-cops. (Later, we were to find out that the Angels had been hired as a security force in return for $500-worth of beer. Sam Cutler, good old gentle Sam, had made the arrangements. Later, he was to maintain that the Angels were not supposed to guard the stage but only serve as personal security for Mick Jagger and the Stones. The Angels denied this, saying they had been told explicitly that their job was to protect the stage, and that version was backed up by several others involved in the concert.)

The Angels waded into the crowd at least half a dozen times during Santana's 45-minute set. Each time a circle would open for them while they beat a couple of people bloody with their pool cues or motorcycle boots, sometimes utilizing both. The victims were varied: a freaked kid who tried to get up on the stage, a photographer the Angels didn't like, a bystander who just happened to get in the way. Each time half a dozen Angels would face off the several thousand witnesses who stared on in impotent horror.

Later, Carlos Santana, leader of the band, told a rock reporter:

> "It all happened so fast, it just went right on before us and we didn't even know what was going on. There were lots of people just fucking freaked-out. During our set I could see a guy from the stage who had a knife and just wanted to stab somebody. I mean, he really wanted a fight. Anybody getting himself in the way of anybody had himself a fight whether he wanted it or not. There were kids being stabbed and heads cracking the whole time. We tried to stop it the best we could by not playing, but by the time we got into our fourth song, the more we got into it, the more people got into their fighting thing."

Every time a circle opened up in the tightly packed crowd, people were pushed closer together. When the fight was over, others from the back would inch forward to fill up the circle. Soon people were packed in so tight they couldn't sit down. For hundreds of yards around the stage it was like a New York subway at rush hour—but there were 10,000 people on the train and no doors to let you out.

It took me about 20 minutes to work my way around backstage. I stumbled past a roped-off area that was being used as a medical center, and was reminded of the previous night's feeling of being in an army encampment. Here was a battlefield hospital. Several doctors were sewing people up inside the brown tent, and outside was a long line of stretchers bearing blood-spattered people. From the tent came the periodic screams of bad acid trips.

Fifty yards behind the stage, though, the sun was warming the hills and people were spread out picnic-style with their kids playing in the grass. From the stage came the muted sounds of the Jefferson Airplane. Occasionally they would stop in the middle of a song ,and we would know there was more trouble. Even their "Revolution" song, with its "up against the wall, motherfucker" refrain, was brought to a stop.

It was during the Airplane's set that the Angels completely took over the stage. Lead vocalist Marty Balin made the mistake of trying to reassert the power and prerogatives of the music. A black man at the back of the stage was being stomped, and Balin stopped playing and waded into the melee, trying to pull the Angels off. Down he went, bloodied and laid out by one of the Angels. When Paul Kantner complained about the treatment Balin was getting, he nearly got himself smashed too. Only the soothing feminine presence of Grace Slick kept the Angels from decking the whole band.

Crosby, Stills, Nash and Young, the hottest new band in the country, came on at about 4 p.m. The sun was down behind the hills at the back of the valley, and it was getting cold again. A hundred yards from the stage, you could see the Angels smashing away with their pool cues. The harmonious, lyrical, soft sound of Crosby, Stills and Nash seemed to be affected more than any other by the violence. They played very badly, and it was obvious that they wanted to get off the stage as soon as possible.

Watching Crosby's discomfort on the stage, I remembered that the same group had played in Golden Gate Park at the November Vietnam Moratorium before a quarter of a million peace marchers. Crosby had taken an obvious slap at some of the political speakers who had preceded him—Black Panther David Hilliard, Dolores Huerta of the Delano grape strikers and Rennie Davis of the Chicago 8. The musician told the crowd, "We don't need any politicians, politics is bullshit." He implied that all we needed to get everything right was the music. But at Altamont his music failed him; it was unable to affect the violence that was engulfing his band, and he watched dumbfounded as the Angels kicked his fans in front of his stage.

At least Crosby could get out. He and his band finished up and immediately climbed aboard a waiting helicopter, leaving behind their fans—300,000 by the most conservative estimates, and much closer to a half million. It was 5 o'clock in the afternoon, and getting dark and cold very fast.

We were all waiting for the Rolling Stones, a wait that seemed interminable. Rumors spread through the crowd that they had refused to play because of the violence. You didn't know whether it was more likely that there would be a riot if they played or if they didn't.

The Angels sauntered around all over the littered stage. Every few minutes Sam Cutler took the mike to repeat: "The Rolling Stones are here to play but they won't play until this stage is cleared and that means Hell's Angels, too." The crowd screamed its hostility at every mention of the Angels, who weren't moving for anyone. Actually, the attempt to clear the Angels off the stage was all bullshit. Cutler was merely stalling for time so that the Stones would come out when it was completely dark—getting the full dramatic impact of the elaborate lighting setup. So the crowd waited—restless, frightened, depressed, alienated—but unable to leave without hearing the Stones.

It was now pretty much the Angels' show; if they had elected to close the concert and order everyone to go home, I believe most people would have gone. The Angels teased the crowd, and showered us with contempt. While we were waiting, one of them, wearing a wolf's head, took the microphone and played the flute for us—a screeching, terrible performance; no one dared protest or shut off the microphone.

We hated them, hated them and envied them all at the same time. For all of their brutality and ugliness they had a definition of themselves and their purpose that showed us up. We had all talked about a counter-community for years—and now, with that community massed in one place, we couldn't relate to anything. In their primitive way, and without talking much about it, the Angels were so together that less than 100 of them were able to take over and intimidate a crowd of close to a half-million people. We had talked about solidarity but they, not us, were willing to go down for each other in a showdown. We had the music but they had a purpose, and everyone in that atomized, alienated mass in front of the stage knew it, and that was their incredible power over us.

> *"They call me Lucifer and I'm in need of some restraint"*
> —Mick Jagger, "Sympathy for the Devil."

By 7 p.m. we were sitting in darkness with the only lights coming from garbage fires people were setting all over the hills to keep warm, danger-ous fires that were befouling the air and threatening the dry grass at the back of the valley. Suddenly the bank of colored stage lights and the huge spotlights on the surrounding scaffolding went on in one flash of hot, red brilliance. The Stones, led by Jagger wearing an Uncle Sam hat, a black and orange cape draped over both shoulders, silver pants and thigh-high black boots with three-inch heels, walked into their places through a pro-tective gauntlet of Hell's Angels. On Jagger's shirt was the Greek letter Omega—the end.

The whole thing had been staged for this precise moment. The Stones, backstage in a tent, let the violence mount as they waited for their beloved darkness. We had pushed and shoved each other, been humiliated by the Angels, destroyed the landscape, fouled the air, all just to see this moment, and even now no one could get up, say it wasn't worth it and go home. Most of the crowd had never seen the Stones in a live performance, but the mystique of Mick Jagger, perhaps the most exciting stage performer of our time, and his tantalizing evil-beauty songs cast a terrible magic over that blood-spattered stage.

Mick Jagger began dancing dervishly about the stage, his cape flapping behind him like an orange and black butterfly. Many kids were muttering, desperately wondering if they would be able to hear the music for just one hour without any interference from the Angels. They got their music and it *was* beautiful. The amplification was incredibly clear; illumi-nated by the brightly colored lights against the dark sky, the Stones looked and sounded out of this world.

But the devil, if that's what Jagger represented, had his price. Violence came with the music. It was more savage and more sustained than anything we had yet witnessed, and acts of hostility built in crescendo with the erotic pulsation of the songs.

The horror built slowly. During the first three songs there were a few scuffles, but not enough to stop the music. Then Jagger leeringly started singing "Sympathy for the Devil"—"Permit me to introduce myself, I'm a man of wealth and taste. . . ." A few more bars and, suddenly the music stopped. To the right of the stage a huge, fearful circle had begun to ripple through the crowd.

In the spotlights you could plainly see the Angels chasing someone through the screaming, stampeding crowd. Mick Jagger, trying to pick up on what was happening, said pleadingly, "Hey, brothers and sisters, come on now. Cool out. Everyone cool down." More soothing words came from Jagger: "We always have something very funny happen when we start this number," he said, again beginning "Sympathy."

There was another commotion next to the stage, and again Jagger stopped singing. The audience could tell someone was badly hurt; people were trying to pass a body up to the stage. Mick Jagger, panic now in his voice, pleaded, "Hey, we need a doctor here." After 10 more minutes of turmoil near the stage, the Stones finally finished the song.

While Jagger kept singing "Sympathy for the Devil," directly in front of him the Angels were stabbing to death 18-year-old Meredith Hunter, a black youth from Ashby Avenue in Berkeley.

The violence seemed just another stage setting for the Stones' routine. They continued to play, mostly uninterrupted, while the fights flared again and again across the front of the stage. Some people in the crowd were sufficiently angered to tempt the Angels by kicking at their bikes, and one was actually set on fire. The Angels dove into the crowd in front of their bikes, flailing away with their pool cues to protect their wheels.

The Stones played on through all this, spurred on by a fear that seemed to make their music more urgent, more beautiful. Jagger danced around the stage, weaving through the snarling Angels, propelled by some inner, powerful motor which caused him to lash out at the violence around him with his most popular songs. After a long hour of hard singing he ended with "Street Fighting Man":

> But what can a poor boy do/Cept sing in a rock'n roll band?/In sleepy London town./There's just no place for/A street fighting man.

It was over by 8 p.m. The Stones headed back to "sleepy London town," and 300,000 confused Americans cleared out of desolate Altamont like the British evacuating Dunkirk.

The fear and hysteria had become so pervasive that the Grateful Dead, scheduled to go on after the Stones, did not even play. The Dead, more than any other major rock group, really believed in the spontaneous power and beauty of the large crowds who came to the concerts. For them the dream has crashed down perhaps the hardest.

Back at the van, our Berkeley group reassembled, each of us with a horror story to tell. But all we did was to look at each other and pile into the van for a quick getaway. Instead of following the mass of traffic back to the Bay Area, we made a wide, swinging circle, adding 50 miles onto our route. It didn't matter—all we wanted to do was get away from that damned dragstrip.

> It was like a time warp snapping shut—zap! There we were back in the 1950's, rock and roll disk jockey Rick Beban said later, trying to make sense out of what had happened. The dragstrip is the symbol of the fifties' youth culture. And so are rock and roll riots like the ones that used to happen at Bill Haley's concerts. San Francisco was the birth of a new culture, but it took us only five years to get back into that old star trip.

Rolling Stone newspaper ran a long solid reportorial story on the concert, but the closest they came to making a judgment was to call it "perhaps rock and roll's all-time worst day." But the rock culture's leading paper could never quite get it together to say why it happened. Instead, it quoted at length some of its favorite music people like rock promoter Bill Graham, David Crosby and rock columnist Ralph Gleason—all of whom put the blame almost exclusively on the paper's British namesakes.

After initially devoting two of his columns in the San Francisco Chronicle to blaming the Stones, Gleason two weeks later published a more thoughtful piece, which allowed that there might be larger dimensions to the disaster: "What started as a dream on Haight Street in 1965 may very well have ended in Meredith Hunter's blood in front of the bandstand at Altamont on December 6 when Mick Jagger sang 'Sympathy for the Devil' as Hunter died."

The political people saw it another way. Frank Bardacke, one of the Oakland Seven and a leader of the Peoples' Park Struggle, who had gone to Altamont in our white van said, "I think the killing of Meredith Hunter was to our community what the Kitty Genovese murder was to the straight community.

"It showed that if you're going to have a new nation in which you make up new rules, then you have to have more than shared needs. You have to have shared values. Out there we didn't have those shared moral values and so we didn't have the courage to stop the violence that led to the murder of a black man."

For me the utter disaster of Altamont was summed up by one macabre bit of irony. We had started out on our trip dreaming a fantasy of marching on Santa Rita with our community of 300,000, ripping off the Alameda County Sheriffs and freeing the prisoners. The reality was that when we beat a hasty retreat from Altamont, we left behind the body of Meredith Hunter, one of our people, a kid many of us had probably nodded to on Telegraph Avenue. And the only ones who cared for that battered body, made sure it got from the coroner's office to a funeral parlor, informed the parents, and now the only ones trying to bring the killers to justice, are the Alameda County Sheriffs.

"The za-za world of rock is almost entirely an uptown plastic dome. Up at Woodstock it meant living at the Concord Hotel or the Holiday Inn in

*Liberty and buzzing in stoned out of your head in a helicopter. It meant
being hustled under guard to a secluded pavilion to join the other aristo-
crats who run the rock empire. Here one could dig the whole spaced-out
scene and dine on California grapes and champagne, just 40 yards below
the Field Hospital where a thousand screaming freakouts were happening
and cats with barbed wire through their feet were moaning on the cots."*
                                          —Abbie Hoffman, Woodstock Nation.

Altamont was more than the crack-up of a dream; it was the culmination of the erosion of a vision. The process of decay had begun long before the big media discovered that there were an enormous number of
young kids who smoked dope, took acid, sometimes took off their clothes
and fucked in public, and who found a community of sorts around an intensely powerful music. By the time that *Time* got around to reporting
this, certain changes had already occurred in the Woodstock life style
which made it much less of a community, though more populous.

Part of the change was simply due to the size of the crowds. Only
three years before Woodstock, 20,000 people showing up in Golden Gate
Park in 1967 for the first be-in was considered a monumental happening.
Four months after Woodstock, the Rolling Stones almost literally snapped
their fingers and brought close to half a million people to a desolate, out of
the way place with only a few hours' notice.

At the first be-ins and large rock concerts particularly in the Bay
Area, the audience was as important as the bands, and observers spent
at least as much time discussing the people who danced, wore beautiful
costumes, and made a kind of music of their own as they did discussing
the performers. There was no sense of distance between the stage and
the people; the bands were just part of a larger show which included political speeches, poetry, dancers and poster makers.

The dream that developed from these early experiences was not the
later and much abused pop sociological concept of "counter-culture,"
but the vision of an organic community that through its music, drugs, co-
operatives and open sexuality could subvert the existing societal structure. To a kid growing up in Kansas City or New York, what was coming
out of San Francisco in those early days was a real possible alternative,
not only to the mainstream cultural and political structure, but even to an
exclusively political way of opposing the society. There was politics there
of a sort, definable perhaps as a "politics of joy." Kids could now consider
themselves rebels or revolutionaries while they smoked dope, lived communally, gave out free food with the Diggers, watched the Mime Troupe and
listened to bands like the Grateful Dead and the Jefferson Airplane, all for
free, every Sunday in the parks.

The hardened political radicals from across the Bay in Berkeley might
dismiss it all as irrelevant to the real tasks at hand, but the smartest and
most sensitive of them know that a legitimate, if utopian and disorganized,
vision was emerging from the Haight-Ashbury's head shops, the Diggers'

free stores and the Grateful Dead's house on Pine Street. They realized that in some way they would have to come to terms with that vision. When Jerry Rubin, then an uptight politico, spoke at the great 1967 Human Be-in in Golden Gate Park he had the cool not to say a word about straight politics, but sounded more like Columbus than a leader of the VDC, muttering something along the lines of, "I have come from the old world to the new world."

The early bands, too, were different from the world that had developed by the time of Woodstock and Altamont. Rock journalist Michael Lydon defined the essence of that nonviolent, loving, turned-on vision: "In that community, everyone looked like a rock star and rock stars began to look like people, not gods on the make."

Then rock burst out all over, like June in the song of a far-away decade. Rock was a commercial success, rock was big time show business, and finally rock was an industry. Rock stars got their pictures on the covers of magazines stacked in suburban dentists' offices, made the Ed Sullivan Show, hired chauffeurs and publicity agents. The changes came quickly and thunderously; the bands and individual performers became more important than the community and the cultural explosion which gave birth to them. The distance between the stage and the spectators kept expanding, and soon all the music came from the stage and very little energy came to the stage from the crowds.

Country Joe and the Fish, for example, self-consciously billed itself in its early Berkeley days as a "political band." Barry Melton, the lead guitarist, was in the radical guerrilla puppet theater of the San Francisco Mime Troupe, and on the Robert Scheer for Congress campaign. The band was an unofficial part of the Vietnam Day Committee, and composed, "Feel Like I'm Fixing to Die Rag," which for two years was the national anthem of the antiwar movement. But then the Fish made it big—big tours, big records, big money—and became unavailable for "political" performances.

Some rock groups, such as the Grateful Dead, fought the trend, and tried to continue living communally and keep that special relationship with their audiences. (It was the Dead, to their credit, who originally thought that the Stones' concert ought to be a fair in Golden Gate Park with full community participation. The Dead wanted the Monterey Pop Festival to be free, or have the profits turned over to the Diggers.) They organized their own tours, cutting out the commercial middlemen. The Dead and the Jefferson Airplane tried to organize a cooperatively run, community-controlled dance hall at the Carousel Ballroom in San Francisco, in competition with Bill Graham's Fillmore. The Dead were good visionaries but not very good entrepreneurs, and the Carousel floundered on mismanagement and inefficiency. When it collapsed, Bill Graham moved in to pick up the pieces, renamed the Carousel Bill Graham's Fillmore West, and put it on a sound basis. Talk of "the community" was drowned out by the noisy machines of tight profit-and-loss bookkeeping.

The success of Graham as a rock entrepreneur is symptomatic of the fundamental change in the scene that could make an Altamont out of Woodstock. Graham organized the first big San Francisco rock dance as a benefit for the Mime Troupe. Graham saw the gold in the rock hills, quit Mime Troupe and began to run the concerts on a regular commercial basis. A sharp, tough businessman with a keen sense of organization, he demonstrated that the business ethic was a more efficient way of organizing music for the people than the communal ethic.

A similar development took place in rock publishing. *Crawdaddy,* the first good rock magazine (named after the club in Richmond, just outside of London, where the Rolling Stones first played) was started in 1966 by Paul Williams, a young, sensitive Swarthmore College dropout. *Crawdaddy* was a sometimes brilliant, often erratic monthly that achieved a circulation of 25,000 but was badly organized, often missed issues and didn't bother to pursue record company ads. Williams, more interested in the whole experience of rock and the people who listened to it than in gossip about the stars, eventually went off to the country to live in a commune and do his own writing.

Crawdaddy was quickly superseded by *Rolling Stone.* Where *Crawdaddy* had messed up, *Rolling Stone* was right on top of things. Like Graham's enterprises, it was at once a natural outgrowth of the growing commercialization of the rock world and at the same time accelerated the trend. It soon became the "industry" newspaper, and the principal source of information and gossip for the growing rock audience around the country. The paper pushes the star system and a kind of rock imperialism that sees the music industry as the center of the revolution. Yet as far as relating to the original idea of a self-conscious counter-community, the *Rolling Stone* is a disaster.

When Jerry Rubin organized the Yippies' demonstration in Chicago two summers ago and was trying to encourage rock groups to participate, Jann Wenner, *Rolling Stone's* clever young editor, who had been nurtured in the Berkeley scene around the days of the FSM, wrote a front page editorial putting Rubin down for having the effrontery to think that rock groups might want to play at anything like a political event. Wenner's editorial about the relation of rock music to the larger revolution stands as a fairly complete statement of those who seriously believed—at least until Altamont—that the rock music scene's antipolitics represented some sort of a political alternative in itself:

> Rock and roll is the *only* [Wenner's italics] way in which the vast but formless power of youth is structured, the only way in which it can be defined or inspected. The style and meaning of it has caught the imagination, the financial power and the spiritual interest of millions of young people.
> It is indeed so powerful and full of potential as all that, and more. It has its own unique morality. And as difficult as it is for even

the most knowledgeable, literate observers to define and explain it (and if you have to keep asking why, you'll never understand) it is nonetheless there and it is slowly taking an actionable form.

This is the kind of obscurantist rhetoric that *Rolling Stone* still uses to push the idea that rock, only rock, is the revolution, and to put down the many attempts to unite it with a wider political perspective. As rock bloomed as an industry, the new people who tuned in did so entirely as consumers, not participants. And the only "actionable form" that rock and roll was taking by itself was higher ticket prices for more and bigger concerts.

Those early visionaries of the rock counter-culture could control the contours of their world when its population was largely contained in the Haight-Ashbury, Golden Gate Park and the old Fillmore. But they couldn't cope when the American tradition of marketing, consumerizing and, eventually, assimilating all original and radical life styles rocketed the rock world into the big time thing. While retaining the goal and rhetoric of cultural salvation, rock culture had become just another business, and practical cats such as Wenner and Graham have surfaced to lead the new wave. They still give voice, at times eloquent, to that vision of rock as the center of a new counter culture, but in actual practice their tight, consumer-oriented way of establishing what is feasible and "right" in the scene has helped move it progressively further away from the communal experience that was essential to the possibility of providing a mass social, and perhaps political, alternative to the dreariness of society-as-usual.

Eventually, people stopped dancing in front of the bands, not just at big events like the Woodstock and Altamont but at the Fillmore, where it all started. Dances became concerts, and at one recent New York event, Janis Joplin had to cajole the kids to come up front and dance.

Similarly, but on a titanic scale, there was no music emanating from the crowd at Altamont. All the energy flowed from the stage; in that alienation and passivity, we were asking for whatever came down from that stage to us.

> *Wenner:* Many people—writers, college students, college writers—all felt tremendously affected by your music and what you're saying in the lyrics.
> *Dylan:* Did they?
> *Wenner:* Sure. They felt it had a particular relevance to their lives . . . I mean, you must be aware of the way that people come on to you.
> *Dylan:* Not entirely. Why don't you explain it to me.
> *Wenner:* I guess if you reduce it to its simplest terms, the expectation of your audience—the portion of your audience that I'm familiar with—feels that you have the answer.
> *Dylan:* What answer?
> *Interview in Rolling Stone, November, 1969.*

The rhetoric of the counter-community was both persuasive and indiscriminate; it even made some people believe that a group of outlaw motorcyclists who had a long history of running over people could become part of a cooperative counter-community because they dug rock music and turned on to acid. Ralph Gleason, for instance, once wrote that the vibrations coming from the rock scene were so groovy that it ". . . results in the Hell's Angels being the guardians of the lost children at the Be-in and the guarantors of peace at dances."

That, of course, was two years ago. After Altamont, self-righteous accusations abounded. Gleason laid out the blame in this syllogism: the Angels killed a man. The Stones plus Rock Scully of the Grateful Dead and ex-Digger Emmett Grogan had arranged for the Angels to be hired as a security force. Therefore, asked Gleason rhetorically, "Are Mick Jagger, Sam Cutler, Emmett Grogan and Rock Scully any less guilty of that black man's death than Sheriff Madigan is of the death of James Rector?"

The *Rolling Stone,* of which Gleason is also an editor, agreed: "Gleason raised the real questions about Altamont more forcefully than anyone else had dared." But one must make a distinction between the myth of Woodstock and the dream. The myth was never more than promoters' hype, and absurd claims for the power of the music. The dream, if only one of hope and possibilities, was real. There was something there to be killed.

It is there in Tom Wolfe's *Electric Kool Aid Acid Test:* the Merry Pranksters and Ken Kesey and the Hell's Angels, using acid and music and psychedelic buses, traveling around the country, turning people on with their energy and, for a brief moment, realizing the potential of a subversive, magical, ecstatic community in the belly of fat America. Wolfe, the journalist not the mythmaker, cautiously understood the dream as a possibility, real but tentative.

> So it was wonderful and marvelous, an unholy alliance, the Merry Pranksters and the Hell's Angels . . . [but] . . . The Angels were like a time bomb. So far, so good—one day the Angels even swept and cleaned up the place—but they were capable of busting loose into carnage at any moment. It brought the adrenaline into your throat. The potential was there, too, because if the truth were known, there were just a few of the Pranksters who could really talk to the Angels. . . .

Wolfe's description of perhaps the most vital and exciting part of the San Francisco rock psychedelic scene ironically suffered at the hands of the very McLuhanesque theory of which Wolfe himself was a popularizer. By the time his manuscript had gotten through the creaky Gutenberg publishing system, the scene he reported was already dated. Most of the younger kids at Altamont didn't know who Tom Wolfe was, let alone Merry Pranksters.

That original counter-culture is a hopeless shipwreck. The Haight-

Ashbury is now a boarded-up slum where violent death is commonplace. The Diggers are gone, too, and Emmett Grogan has gone off riding with the Angels. Ken Kesey is back to Oregon, and most of the Pranksters have vanished. The rest of the people have gone to the country, leaving basically the music people and the political radicals and street people, who had their bloody high noon over the proposed Wild West Festival last summer. On one side of the street were the festival's organizers (some of the band managers and, of course, Bill Graham, Ralph Gleason, and Jann Wenner); and on the other were the street people, the political radicals and the San Francisco Mime Troup—one of the few groups left from the old scene that believes there is nothing wrong with artists sharing a revolutionary social and political perspective.

Ronnie Davis of the Mime Troupe led the questioning of the promoters with embarrassing questions about priorities: Why was money being spent on fancy equipment? Why was admission to be charged for the star performers at a supposedly free festival? Why weren't peoples' groups from the ghettos involved? The questions were loud, boisterous and occasionally disruptive. Columnist Ralph Gleason denounced Davis and friends as a pack of political crazies who wanted to destroy beautiful things and who had no program. Anyway, said Gleason, they didn't represent the multitudes. That is no doubt true, as, I suppose, is the fact that Wenner, Graham and Gleason represent the sensibilities of the power of the elite of the rock and roll industry. But there was no one to represent the hundreds of thousands of people at Altamont, who clearly failed to exhibit the very "nonpolitical" revolutionary force that Wenner and Gleason and other theoreticians of a rock-based counter-culture have argued is somehow inherent and inevitable in the togetherness and the music.

At Altamont, the crowd totally failed to define itself in any other way than the hype of "groovin' to the music," and ended up as target practice for the Hell's Angels and fodder for the promoters (including the high-powered camera crew, filming the Stones' free concert for profit, which used even the murder of that Berkeley kid as an unexpected extra in a best-selling movie). Despite Altamont, the heavies in the rock culture and operators like Wenner and Graham, and musicians like David Crosby, still maintain that the kids don't need any politics—only the music. The "politics is bullshit" line is neat and easy. It keeps the rock world something very special and removed. You don't ask embarrassing questions of those who are doing you the favor of bringing you magic. And if no one asks embarrassing questions, you can get away with nonsense like the following written by Ralph Gleason:

"The Beatles aren't just more popular than Jesus, they are also more potent than the SDS.

"What do you think Dylan is doing up there in Woodstock? Counting his money? You don't resign from being an artist. Not until you're dead.

No. He and the Beatles started something which is beyond politics, past the programs of the planners and out there in McLuhanland changing the heads of the world.

"Out of it will come the programs. Out of it will come the plans. When the time is right."

Well, maybe the time isn't right yet, but we haven't got much time. Things have been coming down heavy lately. So far the only programs to come from the Beatles is John Lennon and Yoko spending 24 hours in bed and John spending thousands of dollars on an ad in the *New York Times* which said, "The war is over if you want it."

Unfortunately, the poor, depoliticized, atomized kids of Altamont were still waiting for the "programs and the plans." And while they waited, they got stomped by their old friends the Hell's Angels.

STREET THEATER AS POPULAR CULTURE

If rock music has been co-opted (has it?) and along with it, its sizable following in the youth culture, are those who act out culture and politics in the streets any more successful in producing antithetical artifacts of popular culture? James Hitchcock has claimed that historically, although cultural and political revolution have occurred together, in every instance culture has "followed upon the heels of politics." The revolution itself has been rooted in objective political and economic conditions.[1] Today in America, however, this traditional order seems to be giving away to the conviction in the minds of the New Left that a cultural revolution must be effected before the political and economic institutions can be undermined.

The nature of the cultural revolution is left deliberately vague, but at a minimum it includes unrepressed sensuality, a contempt for the established categories of rational thought, speech, drugs, dress and design, rejection of organized work and support for the extreme *avant garde* in art.

> Our life style is our politics. Our activity is aimed at liberating the human soul. . . . We are cultural revolutionaries. LSD is our textbook, Day-Glo our weapon and orgasm our victory. Older people find it hard to imitate our dance, impossible to understand our music and afraid to experience our drugs. . . . Attempts at reaching the middle-aged middle-class community are fruitless. We should rather direct our efforts toward our potential brothers, the young, the blacks, the bikers, hippies and junkies.[2]

The strategy of revolution can be found in the writings of persons such as Susan Sontag, Abbie Hoffman and Jerry Rubin with their emphasis on the revolutionary uses of unconventional clothes, speech, music, and sexual behavior in the context of what is known as *street theater.*

---

1. James Hitchcock, "Comes the Cultural Revolution," *New York Times Magazine,* July 27, 1969.
2. Ronald McGuire, "Cry of the Wild," *Observation Post,* January 30, 1969.

I began thinking about HUAC (House UnAmerican Activities Committee) as theater: I knew that I could not play on their stage, because they hold power in their gavel. I had to create my own theater to mindfuck HUAC and capture the nation's attention. But how?

I tossed out to Ronnie Davis of the San Francisco Mime Troupe the idea of coming to the hearings wearing the hat of an American Revolutionary War soldier.

"Why just the hat?" Ronnie asked. "Why not the whole uniform?"

Lightning bolt!

HUAC as a Costume Ball.[3]

Since the early days of Jerry Rubin's confrontations with HUAC, the concept of the revolutionary use of clothing in street theater has become widely diffused in the youth underground. Hunter Thompson, who campaigned in 1970 for sheriff of Pitkin County, Colorado, has remarked on the uses of the costume within the political context.

The costume signals a deliberate refusal to play the conventional compromise game of straight candidates. In my campaign, for example, I wore shorts, greaser glasses, and weird medals—a regular Dr. No. . . . The costume in politics jolts the opposition. . . . After that jolt, the costume becomes a joke, a bridge, even a weapon with which to cope with heavy hostility and spook judgments. The easiest level on which to beat the straights is to set up a straw man with the costume, then destroy it on their terms. Mocking your own demented image seems like a concession to them. . . . Politics is a mean and cynical trade with definite rules. The costume breaks those rules and all the preconceptions and misconceptions they represent.[4]

Perhaps the best known cultural revolutionaries are the Yippies. Garry Wills discusses the formation and content of Yippie culture— viewing the Yippie use of street theater as the advance guard of American popular culture.

---

3. Jerry Rubin, *Do It!* (New York: Simon and Schuster, 1970), pp. 59–60.
4. Blair Sabol and Lucian Truscott IV, "The Politics of the Costume," *Esquire*, May 1971, p. 124.

THE MAKING OF THE YIPPIE CULTURE

Garry Wills

In Chicago, with the nomination of "Pigasus" for President, Americans were exposed to the playful fringe around the edges of our radical youth movement. It has always been there, though it rarely gets as much attention as it did in Chicago. The freaks and crazies have a para-political role to play. The difference between them and staid radicals like Rennie Davis and Tom Hayden was symbolized when the University of Chicago's administration building was occupied early in 1969. Inside were the real guerrillas; outside was a group that called itself Chickenshits, who were afraid to go in. They wore yellow armbands, and carried a yellow flag, and played kazoos (popular instrument with the freaks). When they crashed administration hearings, it was to read parts of *Catch-22*. Instead of seizing the Dean's files, they went and *asked* him for them. When he turned them down, they dropped to the floor and crawled out mumbling, "Grovel, grovel, grovel, who are we to ask for power?"

Most such guerrilla theatre is not merely propaganda for the revolution, enacting little moral lessons (though there are some dead-serious propaganda teams like the San Francisco Mime Troupe). The spirit of play, of put-on, is important for its own sake, and related to the nonpolitical "Merry Pranksterism" in groups like Ken Kesey's and the Hog Farm, groups that did not even bother to go to Chicago. The Yippies' heroes are Antonin Artaud (for his "poetry of festivals") and Marshall McLuhan ("Myth means putting on the audience"). Even the pig as candidate was not meant solely as a symbol of the cops, of Daley, of Humphrey, of Nixon ("There would be a pig in the White House in '69, no matter what"). It was also a symbol of the Yippie movement ("We love the pig, our candidate and hero"). The original plan was to roast and eat him as a kind of communion rite. Death of the Pig meant the death of Yippie—and to kill Yippie was the stated purpose of the Yippies' trip to Chicago. A funeral was actually held on Thursday, Paul Krassner presiding.

There had been earlier funerals for Hippie and the Flower Children. The first thing the freak movement must do, once it establishes itself, is kill itself off. Abbie Hoffman wrote, after Chicago: "There never were any Yippies and there never will be. It was a slogan YIPPIE! and that exclamation point was what it was all about. It was the biggest put-on of all time." Krassner writes: "The Crazies have a rule that in order to become a member one must first destroy his official membership card." There should be nothing surprising in all this, if we remember Dada and the Surrealists. The Yippies—wearing American Revolution uniforms to H.U.A.C. hearings, exorcising the Pentagon, burning money at Wall Street, nominating Pigasus, trying to turn Chicago on with LSD in the water supply (it was counteracted by chlorine), holding an "In Hoguration" in Washington, calling for Indecency Rallies, taking the arms off the clock in Grand Central Station (perhaps their best symbolic blow at the System)—are modern Dadaists. And Dada was always devoted to the destruction of Dada. Its principles were often enunciated: The real Dadaists are against Dada. Everyone is a leader of Dada. No one is a leader of Dada. The Dadaists and Surrealists wanted to kill Art, which degenerates inevitably into Culture. But Dada's own gestures were continually being framed off as artifacts and hailed as "the new art," so the movement had to keep killing itself ("Dada is not new, not modern, not art"). This was the time when Duchamp made a practice of "incompleting" works; and at a Dada "manifestation," André Breton went along behind Francis Picabia, erasing the drawings he had just made. The Dada manifestation was like modern street theatre, even in details— death's heads, toy guns, mocking use of uniforms, elaborate put-ons, gestures obscene or obscure, incantations, nudity. At the International Dada Fair in 1920, the principal attraction was a dummy in German officer's uniform, topped with a stuffed pig's head—the first incarnation of Pigasus.

Like Dadaists, Yippies represent the aesthetic side of a revolutionary movement. It was the custom to distinguish between "radicals" at the Chicago convention, and Yippies, and liberal McCarthy kids. The distinction is real, but partial—more a question of mood, of style, than of doctrinal divisions. In fact, the code of the Yippies is simply Castroism applied to art. Fidel's view of revolution is that one acts and, through action, discovers the aims of the revolution. Only by forswearing ideology—even the revolutionary ideology of Marx—does one discover radically new roles for society. Dada took the same approach to art; only by forswearing art does one open up new creative worlds: "Thought is made in the mouth" (Tristan Tzara). The Yippies' form of antipolitics is not simple negation (curse the pig). It is also support for all antipolitical symbols (we *love* the pig). Antipolitics becomes a positive thing. In just this way, Dadaists lionized the piggish Père Ubu, creation of their favorite ancestor, Alfred Jarry.

The Yippie events take place within an aesthetic context established over the last decade or so, beginning with the motion from Action Painting to Pop Art and Happenings. A trickle-down effect spread Happening philosophy out from the Reuben Gallery onto the street. The critical rationale of the movement was popularized by Susan Sontag in her essay *Against Interpretation,* which criticizes "the hypertrophy of the intellect at the expense of energy." She is merely picking up the standards of Dada and Surrealism, which tried to free energy from the trammels of Art. But more to the point today ,she is giving us a Castro aesthetic, the artistic equivalent of Debray's maxims: he wrote, "The intellectual will try to grasp the present through preconceived ideological constructs and live it through books. He will be less able than others to invent, improvise. . . ." Since interpretation sets up categories of the possible before all the possibilities have been broached, Miss Sontag claims that "a great deal of today's art may be understood as motivated by a flight from interpretation." Just as a great deal of radical action is motivated by a flight from ideology. "Abstract painting is the attempt to have, in the ordinary sense, no content; since there is no content, there can be no interpretation. Pop Art works by the opposite means to the same result; using a content so blatant, so 'what it is,' it, too, ends by being uninterpretable." Rubin and Hoffman and Krassner, when they are not making fun of ideology, portray themselves by put-on as "Commie freaks." In Chicago Hoffman passed out dime-store bits of paper with Chinese figures on them, to show his "tails" that he was one of Mao's men. This is making a message so blatant that it is uninterpretable.

The Surrealists, too, wanted to bo "beyond art" by a destruction of Culture, which is an elaborate set of expectations—expectations that limit, structure, contain experience much as ideology hedges revolutionary action. But where Dadaists depended, like the street kids, on direct unstructured action, Surrealists relied on the newly discovered subconscious. If the aim is to "cut back content" by living entirely in one's first virgin grasp of things, the subconscious becomes a kind of preprimary grasp of reality, existing before actual sensation. Thus the Surrealists concentrated on dream-reporting, on automatism, on cultivated delirium and hysteria (Dali's "paranoia-criticism"). They even threw a birthday party for hysteria, on the fiftieth anniversary of its discovery. Action Painting was, on one side of it, a return to such automatism.

The Surrealists even *sound* like today's kids. Breton pointed to "the conviction that here we all share—i.e., that modern society survives by a compromise so serious as to justify any excess on our part." The second-generation Surrealist magazine, *Le Grand Jeu,* declared: "Our discoveries are those of the explosion and dissolution of all that is organized." The artists had a joint interest in astrology, in Eastern mysticism. They demanded an end to military service and release of all "political prisoners." They indulged in what came later to be known as Camp; Maurice Nadeau recounts how they sought out vapid popular performances: "The most ridiculous shows were the most prized, for they put on stage the popular sentiments and emotions that had not yet been spoiled by culture." And they were resolutely Against Interpretation: *La Révolution surréaliste* proclaimed that "Surrealism does not present itself as the exposition of a new doctrine. Certain ideas which serve it today as a point of departure must not be allowed to prejudice its later development."

If the Yippies are the advance guard of the youth culture, the youth culture is the advance guard of our popular culture. And the whole thing is anticipated and embodied in an official culture of the museums. We are living through an aesthetic revolution that is entirely Castroite. That was borne in on me during a 1969 stroll through the museums clustered in one block on West Fifty-third Street. The Museum of American Folk Art had a show of Pennsylvania artifacts from the eighteenth and nineteenth centuries—intricate toys, large wedding chests, rich mazy samplers like postage-stamp Renaissance tapestries. The most interesting thing was the mechanical bent of the artists—sprocketed, wheeled, drilled, dowel-in-hole smooth rub of wood on wood; axle turn, mesh, catch; windmills, whirligigs, model grinding wheels; seesaw worked up and down (and dwarfed) by a huge wheel-and-pulley apparatus; a wrought-iron squirrel cage, big ribbed drum swinging easily. The artists obviously liked to invent little worlds of programmed action for real or imagined small denizens, worlds outside their maker, controlled by him.

A few doors east on Fifty-third, the Museum of Contemporary Crafts had a show called "Feel It," where one moved in a suspended April rainstorm, sunlit, of translucent clinging plastic strips (two hundred fifty miles of the stuff cut up into lengths that just brushed the floor, decending everywhere in dazzling sheets). There were murky revelations made by mirrors, blipping electric lights and sounds, lucite cones and coils. Here was a new squirrel cage which the artist builds to *enter,* along with his audience (who all become artists). It is the perfect way to escape interpretation. What is the artifact to be interpreted—the strips of plastic? the lights or mirrors? But these do not function until people stir and intercept them, are tangled or reflected in them. If there is an artifact, it is put together, disassembled, redone constantly in each person as he gropes, snow-blind in the lucite, toward or away from others. Not only is the audience the artist. The artist is also audience: Allan Kaprow says of his Happenings, "I need to be part of it to find out what it is like myself." And both audience and artist are, as well, the artifact—hundreds of discrete "products" of the process, successfully defying interpretation. Miss Sontag wrote: "Interpretation takes the sensory experience of the work for granted, and proceeds from there. This cannot be taken for granted, now." The Feel-In neatly solves that problem: it offers *nothing but* the sensory experience. "Our task is to cut back content." A task accomplished, here. Art is now an experiment one performs upon oneself—not standing outside or above it, like the makers of toy wooden worlds in Pennsylvania. The promise of the new art, like that of the new politics, is that you need not make a revolution; the revolution, if you simply act, will make you. The artist need not make an artifact. Art, if you simply act, will shape the true, the authentic artifact within you. This was the new element Action Painting added to Surrealist concepts of automatism. The painting is not so much a product as an act—paint*ing.* This means the audience must be present at the act, either actually or in imagination, or with the help of TV or movie cameras. The Japanese Gutai painters became a kind of repertory theatre of painting, and developed many of the props used in Happenings (transparent walls to be painted on, balloons, smoke). When the French action-painter Mathieu painted the Battle of Bouvines, he did it in period costume on the battle's anniversary, with an audience and with the cameras grinding.

The big gallery on Fifty-third was still waiting for me—the Museum of Modern Art, then holding its popular exhibit on The Machine. That term was stretched to include many things. There, for instance, was Duchamp's piston-slide blurred nude of mechanical outline, clicking her way downstairs, perfectly audible across the room despite trip-hammer sounds of metamatics and other chugging devices. There were walls of Futurist paintings trying to be movies. Photographs (not themselves machines, but the result of mechanical play with sunlight). Léger's mechanics made extensions of the machines they work on. Dada machines for doing nothing. Their ideal was finally achieved in Claude Shannon's Little Black Box, which involves the audience (one must throw the box's switch to an On position) and erases the artist-audience effort (all the On switch does is activate a hand that pops out of the box and turns the switch back Off). Drawings and photographs of Jean Tinguely's Homage to New York, a vast happening-contraption, a "self-destroying machine," part of which was meant to drag itself over to the museum pool and drown itself; appropriately, it did not make it all the way to the water (Tinguely said he was constantly thinking of New York as he put together his guilty and suicidal Frankenstein of a "city").

But there were real machines, too: one of the six surviving "Golden Bugs," the finest car ever made—chassis by Bugatti, coach by Weinberger, tires by Royal. TV sets (tubes by RCA). Lights by G.E. There was even a perfect working model of an elevator button cleverly placed beside the elevator. The famous car by Kienholz still has its rickety lovers in the backseat, their papier-mâché passion wired in taut frustration. But they were not nearly as good as the crumpled papery figures in the museum restaurant, masterpieces of a jaundiced realism (sneakers by Keds). There were Coke bottles on the restaurant tables, too, much better in that setting than the one on the second floor of the museum, where a section is devoted to design: Trimline phones, stainless-steel knives, racing helmet. The racing helmet goes with Andy Granatelli's STP car, downstairs in the Machine exhibit. And the omnipresent Coke bottle reappeared down there in Claes Oldenburg's green plastic profile of a Chrysler Airflow, which looks like a Coke bottle sawed in half.

But Oldenburg's most spectacular contribution to the show was his Giant Soft Fan, the old propeller sort inside its cage, with flabby blades drooping in the droopy cage, ready to stir in any breeze, reversing the order of things ("I am a technological liar," says Oldenburg). It was perfect in detail, but bloated and gone soft like a dream fan, dwarfing passersby. It is not so much an artifact, enclosed, as a dream prop creating an aura, around it, of life thrown off-scale, grown weirdly malleable, marshmallowy. Walk into the magic zone, and you are back in Feel It, doing experiments on yourself.

And the true masterpiece of the show was not the puffy Oldenburg fan; it was a Soft Girl made, it seemed, of mattresses—thermal underwear, shepherd boots, sheeps'-wool cape. She too seemed to inhabit, hypnotically, a dream: I followed her; it was a working model that dragged itself *all the way* to the pool—I mean the door. And on out where, in the New streets, she looked perfectly at home, endangered—another self-destroying machine.

Our whole culture is a kind of street theatre. That was the real point of the machine exhibit, mixing everyday artifacts with the new art's anti-artifacts. If one cannot say *what* art is (cannot "interpret"), then one cannot even say *that* it is; cannot define it, find its boundaries, seal it off as something separate, to be judged. The Dadaists were right: the only way to get free of art is to destroy it. Back to Breton-Picabia: now an "Erased de Kooning by Robert Rauschenberg" is exhibited. Yet one cannot destroy Art—all the attempt does is turn *everything* into art, into a giant squirrel cage man runs in, having experiences, a huge laboratory for doing experiments on himself. The world of the Feel It show is also that of a nightclub like Cerebrum, where one is to float, seen and seeing, in diaphanous stuff; of the Joffrey Ballet and its dance-rub through plastic bubbles and tunnels; of Barbarella's adventures in the same stuff; of an increasing number of shows where one froths through a suds of various synthetics—for that matter, the world of a rock concert, where one is immersed in dense undulant sound; or the world of disorienting light thrown off by strobes, mixed media, Expo '67 camera work all around one. Yoko Ono, a veteran of Happenings before she moved on to bed-ins with John Lennon, put it simply: "I think they should turn everywhere into a museum. It is a museum. They just need to put a label on it all, don't you think?"

Our aesthetics is Castroite because our culture, like radical politics, drifts toward total empiricism, where all norms are provisional, to be tested; where no authority exists except majority will at the moment (and our majority seems, for the moment, to have no will). There is no *a priori* set of standards; one must pick up or produce a set for oneself, *ambulando.* Seen in this light, the youth rebellion is not a monstrous incursion from nowhere; it is just the next step, a little more thorough, a little more honest, on the way our society is moving. Life is being absorbed into street theatre, devoted to what Tzara called "the poetry of the street." As Richard Goldstein says, the Living Theatre turns every building where it performs into a street (even when it does not, as in New Haven, actually take to the street). Yayoi Kusama has given up museum work (phalloi pinned to couches) for the painting of polka-dot nudes—real nudes—in the street. When the brothers Berrigan, priest war-protesters, lugged draft records into the street to pour napalm and blood on them, it was treated as a kind of Action Painting—Pollock doing his famous drip act—and given "reviews": Paul Velde wrote, "The details, it is clear, are those of a guerrilla action, the smallness of the numbers, suggestive of professional cadre, an underground; the very apparent concern of the participants with the media possibilities of their action, with the outrageous; surprise, shock, blatant symbol manipulation." Even church services are now happenings with a touch of Yippie gesture: at St. Clement's Episcopal Church, according to the New York *Times,* "Communicants were blindfolded, ordered to take off their shoes and led through a 40-minute maze that included a period of crawling on their hands and knees over bread crumbs as a sign of 'humble access' to the Holy Communion." *(Grovel, grovel grovel, who are we to ask. . . .)* At one of the more famous Happenings of modern recent years, the march on the Pentagon, Norman Mailer one-upped the Yippies' exorcism rite by turning the whole thing into a movie of him-as-hero writing about him-as-hero getting arrested. It was action-art carried to its logical goal—as if Mathieu had a camera watching him paint the Battle of Bouvines *at the actual Battle of Bouvines.*

As the rest of society is drawn into the ongoing street drama, the impresarios react in various ways. Some see such participation as a threat —as when Abbie Hoffman complained that Bobby Kennedy's ghetto appearances were turning into better shows than his own troupe could supply. Others welcome the "conversion" of society to their norms—Jerry Rubin, for example, wrote: "The cops are a necessary part of any demonstration theatre. When you are planning a demonstration, always include a role for the cops. Cops legitimize demonstrations." The cops, of course, played the main role (though not the hero's) in the well-managed morality play on Chicago streets. When Robert Brustein protested to Judith Malina, "That's not theatre, it's politics," she answered, "You can't separate the two, can you?" Rubin criticizes the university by reviewing the classroom as theatrical set: "You can always tell what the rulers have up their sleeves when you check out the physical environment they create. The buildings tell you how to behave. . . . They designed classrooms so that students sit in rows, one after the other, hierarchically, facing the professor who stands up front talking to all of them. . . . Classrooms should be organized in circles, with the professor one part of the circle."

The experimental character of our culture has a number of facets. the most obvious of which can be listed:

1. Perhaps the first sign of a constant need for fresh experience in our people is the power of youth fashion to set all fashions. In the past, teen-agers left behind a world of nursery rhymes and children's books in order, progressively, to listen in on adult talk and entertainment. The big bands, the pop singers of the Thirties, belonged to adults and were merely shared by teen-agers. In Elvis and The Beatles, the kids possessed, briefly, a culture of their own. But only briefly; for the situation is now reversed, and adults listen in on the kids' world. Clothes, decorations, music, literature—all take standards and new directions from the young. And the leaders of the youth culture are under terrific pressure to keep changing, starting over, reconstructing themselves in radical ways—following the example of Bob Dylan and The Beatles. There is more to this than America's tendency to look on itself as a young nation; more to it than liberal openness to one's children or modern permissiveness. A society that has lost its own certitudes and sense of self is coming to rely on the defiance, the bluff

and arrogance, of a newly found or asserted self; on adolescents. Even things that were part of a criminal subculture, like drugs and violent protest, are moved up to respectability through the filter of the youth subculture. Extremes become part of a spectrum that grades imperceptibly toward the official center of fashion. The activism of radicals and the theatrical "act" of Yippies are two different readings of the same experimental approach to life. This is underlined by the way Jerry Rubin "updated" Tom Hayden's famous opening to the Port Huron Statement. The original went this way: "We are people of this generation, bred in at least modest comfort, housed now in universities, looking uncomfortably to the world we inherit." Rubin's version: "We are a new generation, species, race. We are bred on affluence, turned on by drugs, at home in our bodies, and excited by the future and its possibilities." One could construct a series of such creeds moving out from the Yippies to the whole Beatlemaniac youth culture and from there to the universities, movie houses, museums, theatres, and suburbs of America—each giving the doctrine a different inflection, but working from the same text.

2. Another sign of our empiricism is the need for participation. If experience is the only authentic test of reality, then one cannot simply be told something. One must undergo it. The classroom must become a circle, eliminating the gap between teacher (who only tells things) and students (who get told). The gap must be eliminated everywhere—between artist and onlooker in the museum, actors and audience in the theatre, leaders and followers in the street, "newsmakers" and crowd in the televised event. When Robert Brustein told members of the Living Theatre they were destroying drama as the arena of supremely gifted individuals, he got a shouted reply, "We are all supremely gifted individuals." This, too, was the code of Dada and Surrealism; both movements adopted Lautréamont's slogan, "Poetry must be made by all, not one."

The techniques of participation are being developed and expanded on all sides. Group therapy, "sensitivity training," social dynamics are extended from clinical to everyday use. Scenarios are written for domestic fights; the "games people play" are thought of as street theatre or bedroom theatre—at any rate, as role-playing, enactment, drama. Even that key word "scenario," used by the war-gamers, suggests the way society is conceived as a laboratory in which we all do experiments on ourselves. The Rand Corporation, advertising its simulated wars "to guard the nation and the free world"—wars that are waged constantly "in our labyrinthine basement, somewhere under the Snack Bar"—invites members of the general public to sign up as hypothetical missile commanders: "To understand the game one should participate, for understanding is 'in the experience.' "

The ruling metaphor behind social thought like McLuhan's is of society as a mechanical arrangement of meshing parts that must give way to an electronic field of forces. Men must become attuned to each other (rather than mesh), become remote-control extensions of their own TV sets, adjust the circuitry of their nerves to history's shift from mechanics to electronics. To "tune in," to join the global village, to become part of our whole culture's message (which *is* its electronic structure), we must, above all else, participate.

3. A third sign of this empiricism is the spread, out of a subculture and into the main culture, of shocking life-styles (exotic clothes, drugs, unkempt and hirsute experiments with the human shape and its sexual differentiations). And one extreme of this—as such, a good test of it—is the shocking use of nudity in street theatre, then in legitimate theatre, and then in the fashion world at large. Nudity has always been a weapon in the arsenal of shock. Both Dadaists and Surrealists used it—the former, for instance, in the Picabia-Satie event, Relâche, the latter when they opened a Paris show with a banquet eaten off a naked girl. There is a combination of risk and challenge, of vulnerability and effrontery, in the act of public nudity that makes it a natural experiment for a culture that is, precisely, devoted to performing experiments on itself, testing its own reactions, trying everything out. Nudes often appeared in Happenings. Then nudity (as opposed to *Playboy's* pastry bare breasts) spread through the underground press, where it was often used as a political weapon. Finally, it went onto the street in "guerrilla theatre" performances and demonstrations—first on the West Coast, then at the Chicago convention and in New York, as well as at the Washington Inauguration. Significantly, nudity first made a timid appearance on Broadway as part of a simulated "Be-In" by the young cast of *Hair.* Then, as happens with most youth fads, it spread to the rest of our culture. One of the style-setting plays of 1968 was especially good at presenting nudity as a human *experiment.* In Terrence McNally's *Sweet Eros,* a deranged fellow captures a girl, ties her in a chair, undresses her, and for a long time studies her as a laboratory specimen, going over her with a magnifying glass, watching her reactions, referring to her as an insect. For the audience, too, she was an object, an alien "prop" on the stage, so unusual was complete nudity at the time. Author and director did not allow her to move or react for a long period. Only after the novelty wore off, both for her dramatic captor and for the audience, was she by stages "humanized," becoming a character in the play rather than a shocking part of the decor. It was an experiment performed on the audience, making it overcome a whole series of distractions and obstacles to accept her as simply another person in the story.

Then several groups invited audience participation to the point of shared nudity—accepting a new dare, performing a new experiment. And, always, there is the note of menace or insult: the boy whipping his penis out at the Guardsman in Chicago, kids coming forward nude and with a pig's head to insult Professor Galbraith—mocking others who will not be so exposed, so free, so "committed." Richard Goldstein heard one breathless woman, who had stripped during a Living Theater performance, murmur as she put her bra back on: "I feel like I've done something. You know,

I can't stand the war. They're killing babies over there." *She'll* get even with the napalmers. *She'll* show them. *She'll*—take off her panties!

The logic seems elusive, but is not. Though the stripping takes place under a rationale of openness and love, it gets its real edge of excitement as an antisocial defiance of "Establishment" norms. It is a political act, and it keeps its vitality only in groups (like the Beck's Living Theater) that are openly revolutionary. This is not, despite the vapid apologia offered for it, a nudity of the health clubs, offered as something natural and normal. It is a defiance of norms—a push off into normlessness which the true empiricist hopes will open up new worlds. That is why the stripping grows out of a litany of frustrations and resentment in the Becks' show *("I am not allowed* to travel without a passport. *I am not allowed* to smoke marijuana. I don't know how to stop the war. *I am not allowed* to take my clothes off"). The nudity comes in a froth of blood and slaughter in *Dionysus in '69.*

4. A fourth sign of the empirical society is a reversion to superstition, magic, astrology, fortune-telling, tarot cards, I Ching, omens, spells ("Om"), Vedanta, witchcraft, mysticism. Not only do these supply a street theatre of liturgy, symbol and vestments; they are also, like all magic, basically experimental. Magic is a way of getting certain things done. Say the right spell, and an automatic response is assured. Be born under the right star, and things will demonstrably happen. When authority has been drained from conventional religion, when the social symbols no longer signify anything, no longer promote communication, men are forced to invent private myths; they are thrown back on their own resources, no longer saying a social creed based on pure faith, on undemonstrable mysteries. Belief in astrology is mere acceptance of a working hypothesis, which allows endless experiment, verification, personal adaptation, analogical extension. Magic is also "against interpretation." Who knows what machinery makes the doors swing wide at "Open Sesame"? And who cares? The real question is not how astrology works, but whether it works; and that is a question each person must answer in his own case, by experiment, by the daily lab work of checking one's life against one's horoscope.

5. Another sign of the spontaneous culture—acute interest in community as such—might seem to be at odds with the egocentric ethic of "authenticity." But the conflict is only apparent. Since the total empiricist is not bound to others by social-contract doctrines, the ties with others must be existential, based on experiences shared; a oneness that stands (in theory) apart from ideological agreement, principles negotiated, demands met or compromised. Thus arranging for the experience of community becomes a great concern of the empirical culture. Mechanisms must be set up for acquiring shared experience: group gropes, be-ins, feel-ins, festivals of life, Esalen Institute, Om circles, group therapy, living theatre, hippie communes, all leading up to the overarching experience of participatory democracy. New rituals must be invented, hieratic dress, symbols of shared experience. As James Kunen says, defending his long

hair and hippie dress, "I like to have peace people wave me victory signs and I like to return them, and for that we've got to be able to recognize each other."

6. The most ominous sign of the empiricist society is a taste for violence. The need always to test oneself by new experience leads almost inevitably to shocks greater than nudity, nonconformity, or verbal violence. It leads to actual violence. Breton, the "Pope" of Surrealism, said, "The simplest surrealist act would be to go out into the street, revolver in hand, and fire at random into the crowd." Lafcadio's murder as a gratuitous act, Raskolnikov's murder as an experiment performed on himself, haunt the Surrealists, and must always fascinate any explorer of the nerves' boundaries, of one's own system's tolerance (not to mention the tolerance of *the* System). For Lafcadio and Raskolnikov, violence is a form of asceticism, of self-testing. Stavrogin cruelly marries the crippled girl, as Auden's Tom Rakewell marries Baba the Turk, to *defy* desire, to exist "beyond desire." The gratuitous act is the only way to achieve this superman status. An act not "corrupted" by considerations of desire or morality, selfishness or altruism—the random pistol shot in the crowd—is the only act that is demonstrably "disinterested"; and to avoid covert moralism or cowardice one must seek out the revolting, the dangerous, the violent.

A culture bent on authenticity and self-experiment is bound to move toward violence. Seen in this light, the young assassins of our time—not only Oswald and Sirhan, but Charles Whitman and Richard Speck—are explained less by TV violence than by the whole stimulus-culture of which TV is only a part. Both Oswald and Sirhan were egocentric, compulsive diarists, students of themselves, performers before the mirror. They resemble the generation of European terrorists in the Eighties and Nineties of the last century—a group of introspective young people Camus analyzed as "fastidious assassins." These assassins were students, disoriented, idealistic, "trying to escape from contradiction and to create the values they lacked." Obsessed with themselves, they hardly recognized the existence of their victims as people; the *delendi* were merely symbols—which is why they turned out to be heads of state or other "charismatic" figures. The assassins did not act from hatred—as Perry Smith did not hate Nancy Clutter, Charles Whitman could not have hated individually all those he shot—but to test a wavering reality by testing themselves. They had to pursue the Feel It experience to the point where they not only witnessed the violence of our times but participated in it. Perhaps wielding that power would give them some power over it, make them less the audience and more the author-artists of this unstructured world of cruel experience. "Necessary and inexcusable—that is how murder appeared to them (the fastidious assassins)."

The Surrealists took as one of their heroines—and applied to her Baudelaire's saying, "Woman is the being who projects the greatest shadow of the greatest light in our dreams"—Germaine Berton, who murdured the royalist Marius Plateau. The original terrorists made a Joan of

Arc out of Vera Zassulich, who shot General Trepov in 1878. American students have not, of course, made a hero of Oswald—perhaps because of his target. But what if he had succeeded in his first assassination attempt, on General Walker? It was more than a joke, with some people, to ask during Johnson's last months in power, "Where are you, Oswald, now that we need you?" The underground press was full of targets superimposed on Johnson's face, and Humphrey's; of "Wanted" signs describing various members of the military-industrial bogey. A sense of vicarious assassination was being created in the Movement; and it was probably a normal enough college student who cried with ecstatic hope, when he saw a fire down the street in Chicago, "Is it a *pig* car?"

Violence is now openly defended on the Left, and rather lovingly analyzed. Jack Newfield found that more than half the S.D.S. members he canvassed on their reading habits had read some Frantz Fanon, the apologist for terrorism in Algeria. Fanon, a psychiatrist, constructed a simple hydraulics of violence, which he imagines as seeking its own level. All the violence of colonialism's history must be quantitatively balanced off by anticolonial violence. This is the equivalent, in psychological terms, of "purging" and the balance of humors in a primitive medicine; for Fanon thinks violence is a psychic necessity for those who have been colonized. Only a therapeutic rage and catharsis of destruction can give back to "the wretched of the earth" their pride and manhood, make them throw off the alien culture imposed on them, that white mask on their black faces which does violence to their natures. Che said that revolution educates a man; first act, and out of action will come enlightenment. Fanon makes the same promise for violence; first be violent, and wisdom will blossom from that explosion: "Violence alone, violence committed by the people, violence organized and educated by its leaders, makes it possible for the masses to understand social truths and gives the key to them."

It is not surprising that anger and frustration should bring forward such a spokesman in the time of the Algerian tortures and official acts of terror. It would be useless to criticize Fanon "outside the situation"—his purge-theory of the mind's health, his belief that history's violence can be cut into quantitatively exact segments and balanced off, his hope that violence is healing rather than addictive. All these matters were explored centuries ago, when Aeschylus wrote his trilogy of "justified counter-violence" leading to an endless "chain of crimes." But the truly fascinating thing about Fanon is the willingness of our young people to transfer his analysis from Algeria to America. The obvious analogue, partially justified, is the position of the black man still suffering the historical violence of slavery and discrimination, the institutional racism still evident in American life. But the students take the matter much farther: middle-class rebels at the best universities, resorting to tactics of force, claim *they* are the oppressed, the wretched of the earth, who are merely returning a violence first inflicted on them. This violence, of course, has to be described as covert and diffuse—the institutionalized militarism and imperialism of our system; the manipulative, exploitative, brainwashing influence of the political parties and mass media; the inbuilt essential violence of capitalism; even the "violence" of liberal compromise and negotiation. In the students' view, American imperialism is not ony exercised against the Vietnamese, who, like Fanon's Algerians, are justified in a counter-terrorism of guerrilla war and torture. It is exercised also, even especially, against the American students, who are not merely spokesmen of the exploited Vietcong, but are themselves exploited. The System, not those who resist it, is responsible for all violence. In Marcuse's words: "The students have said that they are opposing the violence of society, legal violence, institutional violence. Their violence is that of defense. They have said this, and I believe it is true."

The terrorists Camus described were—like our current apologists of violence—Leftists; not so much because of political doctrine, but because the terrorists must strike out at the Establishment. That means, in America as it did in nineteenth-century Russia, revolution from the Left: it was the Bay of Pigs that made Oswald lump Kennedy with General Walker. Russia and Cuba were the logical outlets for his flight from America. Sirhan wrote in his diary: "I advocate the overthrow of the current president of the f—ing United States of America . . . I firmly support the Communist cause and its people—wether [sic] Russian, Chinese, Albanian, Hungarian or whoever."

But murder as self-experiment is not inherently political. It can come from the Right, too—as it did when Germany's Dada and Surrealist period came to an end with the collapse of the Weimar Republic. Students then were taking the lead in society, forming the backbone of new parties, making demands on the university, asking for changes in the curriculum (especially the introduction of courses on race). Many people, in 1968 and 1969, read with a shudder of recognition Peter Gay's description of these young people in his book, *Weimar Culture:* "But all *Wandervogel* except the most casual attached an enormous importance to their movement, an importance dimly felt but fervently articulated; as solemn, rebellious bourgeois—and they were nearly all bourgeois—they saw their rambling, their singing, their huddling around the campfire, their visits to venerable ruins, as a haven from a Germany they could not respect or even understand, as an experiment in restoring primitive bonds that overwhelming events and insidious forces had loosened or destroyed—in a word, as a critique of the adult world. . . . Hans Breuer, who compiled the songbook of the youth movement . . . insisted . . . that he had gathered his folk songs for 'disinherited' youth, a youth 'sensing in its incompleteness—*Halbheit*—the good, and longing for a whole, harmonious humanity.' What, he asks, 'What is the old, classical folk song? It is the song of the whole man, complete unto himself.' . . . The *Wandervogel* sought warmth and comradeliness, an escape from the lies spawned by petty bourgeois culture, a clean way of life unmarked by the use of alcohol or tobacco. . . . The result was a peculiarly undoctrinaire, unanalytical, in fact unpolitical socialism—it was a 'self-evident proposition,' one observer noted, for all people in the youth movement to be Socialists. Young men and women, seeking purity and renewal, were Socialists by instinct; the *völkisch,* right-wing groups demanded the 'reawakening of a genuine Germanness—*deutsches Volkstum*—in German lands,' while the left-wing groups called for 'the restoration of a *societas,* a communally constructed society.' Everywhere, amid endless splintering of groups and futile efforts at reunion, there was a certain fixation on the experience of youth itself; novels about schools and youth groups exemplified and strengthened this fixation. . . . Flight into the future through flight into the past, reformation through nostalgia—in the end, such thinking amounted to nothing more than the decision to make adolescence itself into an ideology. . . . The hunger for wholeness was awash with hate; the political, and sometimes the private, world of its chief spokesmen was a paranoid world, filled with enemies; the dehumanizing machine, capitalist materialism, godless rationalism, rootless society, cosmopolitan Jews, and that all-devouring monster, the city."

All the needs of that society were soon met. The cult of youth became a celebration of the "new man" who would rule a thousand years. The need to participate was satisfied in therapeutic group rallies. The thirst for shock and primitiveness came about through state terrorism. Superstition was fed with the myth of a magic race. Community became the invincible *Volk.* And violence was *Blitzkrieg.* It was, as the kids say, "Beautiful."

The last thing left, to a society that rejects imposed standards as unauthentic, is the aesthetic sense. Even those far gone in nihilism have a feel for the striking, the dramatic, the gesture made with flair. Fascism was, in this way, a substitution of aesthetics for ethics: Aryanism was a code of the beautiful, enacted with uniforms, gestures, music, lights and rallies. Mussolini's neo-Renaissance of *Italianitá* went along with Hitler's chiaroscuroed world of Leni Riefenstahl visions, Wagnerian "moments." In retrospect, it is difficult to understand what made men like Mussolini and Hitler respected and loved. They were not great political thinkers or admirable beings; not even very talented schemers. What were they, then? They were both, unquestionably, masters of street theatre.

The violence that Garry Wills points out as inherent in the empiricist society has been revealed in the Chicago street confrontations of 1968, as well as in the more recent underground bombing tactics of the Weathermen and the various attempts on the part of radical youth groups to destroy, by fire, establishment institutions (such as ROTC buildings and branches of the Bank of America).

The Yippie emphasis on the *confrontational* aspect of street theater is less in evidence in the street theater performed by traveling teams, such as the San Francisco Mime Troupe. These teams are concerned with the dissemination of their radical products and messages in ways that will *not* involve establishment distribution systems. In contrast, the Yippie ethic of confrontation is *designed* to attract the attention of the commercial media. Jerry Rubin has remarked as to how indebted he is to establishment institutions (including the United States Government) for taking it upon themselves to disseminate his street theater throughout America.

> The media does not *report* "news," it *creates* it. An event *happens* when it goes on TV and becomes myth. . . . Television keeps us escalating our tactics; a tactic becomes ineffective when it stops generating gossip or interest. . . . You can't be a revolutionary today without a television set . . . every guerrilla must know how to use the terrain of the culture that he is trying to destroy.[5]

Groups such as the Mime Troupe also draw distinctions between themselves as performers and the audience to whom they are attempting to communicate (even as the audience is one of participation).[6] The Yippies, on the other hand, "write everyone in," feeling that all are "actors in the same play."

> Theater has no rules, forms, structures, standards, traditions —it is pure, natural energy, impulse, anarchy. . . . The only role of theater is to take people out of the auditorium and into the streets. The role of the revolutionary theater group is to make the revolution.[7]

The task of the Yippie, then, is to insure that the play is revolutionary, while the task of the Mime Troupe member is to retain his own sense of revolution and not succumb to commercial cooption (as

---

5. Rubin, *Do It!* pp. 107–8.
6. Richard Schechner has compiled the following chart that focuses on the differences between street theater such as that of the Mime Troupe and the traditional theater. Richard Schechner, *The Public Domain* (New York: Avon, 1970), p. 156.

Traditional Theater	*Street Theater*
Plot	Images/events
Action	Activity
Resolution	Open-ended
Roles	Tasks
Theme/thesis	No pre-set meaning
Stage distinct from house	One area for all
Script	Scenario or free form
Flow	Compartments
Single focus	Multi-focus
Audience watches	Audience participates
Product	Process

7. Rubin, *Do It!* pp. 132–33.

have many of the "revolutionary" rock bands). Which tactic do you feel to be potentially more successful? Why?

REVOLUTION OR TOMATOES?

Barbara Falconer

"Ladeeeeeez and Gentlemen. We're going to go on a short parade. Then we're going to sneak up behind you. So don't look."

The San Francisco Mime Troupe, in ponchos and flat World War I helmets camouflaged with the brightest scraps in the rag bag, take a few last-minute licks from a shared strawberry ice cream cone and march off to the other side of Washington Square Park. The Gorilla Band plays *Pomp and Circumstance* and follows it with *La Cucaracha.*

It's Saturday not long after the shootings at Kent and Augusta. A brisk wind carries off the last traces of yesterday's orangish smog. Old-time North Beach dwellers sit on benches at the park's perimeter getting some sun and eyeing the younger North Beach set, apparent hippies, sprawled on the grass with blankets and picnic lunches.

A baby in yellow creepers crawls across the Mime Troupe's grassy stage toward a German shepherd-boxer dog who sleeps in the shade of the Troupe's puppet theater, a string of eucalyptus pods around its neck.

Suddenly the Mime Troupe sneaks up on us. The Gorilla Band, led by a drum majorette in a safari hat bellows, "First, I'd like to invite you all to move up. Get uptight together."

The crowd obeys.

Then, rising on tiptoe, she announces: "The San Francisco Mime Troupe, Gutter Puppets and Gorilla Marching Band offer you one half hour of filthy and subversive puppet shows for your ed-i-fi-ca-shunnnnn and amusement."

Two live faces pop into the puppet theater.

"You are a fine specimen of cattle and this board has seen fit to classify you A-1 prime!" says a muscle-lipped military man to a draftee. "Or, by our new lottery system, better known as Bingo!"

The draftee, following Mime Troupe tradition, twists mouth and eyebrows into an exaggerated grimace visible all the way across the park.

"You have a stake in the future!" sputters the military man.

"Ha, ha, ha, ha, ha," from the audience.

On Sunday, the same show. A girl in a 1930's mink coat suns on the grass, her boyfriend, bare-chested, lays with his head on her lap.

Across the street, the cathedral bells chime.

"You have a stake in the future," says the military man. And again the North Beach crowd laughs affectionately.

The church bells chime some more and a bride in white and her groom, in a white dinner jacket, emerge followed by bridesmaids in long yellow dresses.

"Ladies and gentlemen, we would like to thank the church across the street for providing the introductory music for our next number, based on a medieval play, *Everyman*. We call it *Eco-Man*."

The bridesmaids line up to have their pictures taken.

"Alas and Goddamit," says an actress with a beautiful face. She's Earth and she's not feeling well.

Enter Eco-Man, hand in the peace sign. The Gorilla Band strikes up with his theme song. "All we are saaaaaaaying is blaaaaaa, bla, bla bla."

The crowd grows. There are perhaps 500 in the park, listening raptly.

To save Earth, Eco-Man calls upon The Government. The Government, it turns out, is an alkie and not interested in saving Earth.

"Better sick than Bolshevik," he says.

With that, Eco-Man calls upon Business, a bright-faced P.R. man who explains that "problems are our most important product."

At this point, a little girl in a jeweled red velvet vest and a tiny black kitten in her arms walks onto the stage and stands in front of Eco-Man.

"But we're going have a big ecology fair," continues Business. "Everybody will be picking up candy wrappers for a month."

More laughter. As usual, the Mime Troupe is funny enough to get away with making its audience—and today many are ecology-minded— the brunt of its jokes.

Modern Science next, but Earth is fed up. The only solution is revolution, she says.

Eco-Man winces. "Does it have to be violent?"

Earth's response is coy. "Thomas Jefferson said 'Heaven forbid we should be 20 years without a revolution.'"

After the show, the actors go around collecting money in their helmets, "We don't get money from liberal foundations, and the radical money goes to places like the Panthers."

A group on tour from Harlem, The Third World Revelationists, perform next. The Mime Troupe is a hard act to follow. The crowd thins.

A man with a black V-neck and a starched blue shirt puts a five dollar bill in a passing helmet, takes three dollars change. Says he's originally from New York, is "in the employment business. I get people jobs."

Of the Mime Troupe: "I really like them. They're really professional."

"Do you agree with the Mime Troupe's political line?"

"I really can't answer that question. Homo sapiens are animals. We are always going to have war."

"It was pretty good," say a man with a Spanish accent, who'd come up from the San Joaquin Valley three months ago. He works days and goes to school nights. "They've got my way of talking. Their trip is my trip."

Monday. The Mime Troupe has its studios in a warehouse on Alabama Street in the bakery district.

Upstairs, there are six sunlit rooms, the walls freshly painted white. There's an inviting clutter of worn, overstuffed, upholstered chairs, desks, posters and potted plants. In one corner, a clean-up chart—a list of names and assigned chores. A Vietnamese flag hangs from the ceiling of the center room, and nearby an American flag.

Ronnie Davis is no longer the head of the company, so Sandy Archer (Earth), who has been with the Mime Troup longest, gives a ten-minute history of the group.

It started in 1959 as an adjunct to the Actors Workshop, she says. Ronnie was an assistant director and had a company of five or six trained mimes, which became the R. G. Davis Mime Troupe. That group survived, Sandy feels, because it stopped doing indoor theater and went out-of-doors, into the parks. The Parks Commission gave the Mime Troupe permission to perform in the parks twice during its first year.

"The second year they requested five to ten performances, but the Parks Commission wouldn't give a permit and warned the Mime Troupe that there would be arrests if they performed in the parks again."

The Mime Troupe considered "prior censorship" and challenged it in Lafayette Park when Ronnie Davis got up and said, "The San Francisco Mime Troupe presents for you An Arrest." Sure enough, he was arrested.

There was a benefit show to raise bail money—The Committee, The Warlocks (who changed their name that night to The Grateful Dead), Jefferson Airplane and The Quicksilver Messenger Service. It lasted nine hours and was so successful that Bill Graham, then associated with the Company, organized a second benefit at the Fillmore.

"We could get the Fillmore for 60 dollars a night and charge next to nothing. More groups performed and they were paid this time. Graham said, 'This is what can support us from now on. We'll have a rock benefit festival every week and we can put ourselves on salary.' The Company said no, and continued to do the shows in the parks. . . . Since 1966 we haven't been friendly with Bill Graham. . . . We won the court case against the Parks Commission for prior censorship. From then on we've performed in the parks and opened them up for other groups."

The Mime Troupe is also no longer "friendly" with Jefferson Airplane, Quicksilver Messenger Service, and in some ways, Ronnie Davis.

Sandy Archer continues. "The Company found it could make money touring colleges, which allowed it to perform in the parks for free. In 1967, it took *L'Amant Militaire* to New York. In 1968, it did *Patelin* and *Ruzzante* and in 1969, *Congress of Whitewashers*.

"Every gesture of the Mime Troupe is to direct consciousness—to move people toward change. We use comedia as a means." With the Troupe, the medium is *not* the message: "The comedia form sucks you in but the content antagonizes," says Sandy. "Each year we present a vanguard position on issues. Right now, we have a women's liberation play in the form of a melodrama. . . ."

Each member of the Troupe has a creative function, a paper-work assignment and a housekeeping job. By the looks of the studio, clean-up is taken as seriously as art.

"We work six days and earn $30 a week," says Linda, the promotional and publicity person. "There are political education classes, physical work-outs, acting classes . . . We serve lunch for 25 cents. Once a week, on Mondays, when there's an evening meeting, dinner is served for 50 cents."

Linda shows me the library (a red star on the door), which was set up to make required political reading available to the Company. "We decided last week to chuck all the science fiction."

Joannie (Gloria), still in lipstick, rouge and eyeshadow, has ex-changed her Victorian lady getup for a pair of dungarees and a leather vest. She wields a fat string mop in the foyer.

The sight reminds Linda of Mao. She points at a quotation on the wall. "Everything reactionary is the same; if you don't hit it, it won't fall. Where the broom does not reach, the dust will not vanish of itself."

A little later I have an opportunity to copy down some of the graffiti in the lavatory:

"We are the people our parents warned us against."

"Viva Women's Lib! No passivism!"

Much of the graffiti is illegible, blurred in the course of recent scrub-down.

Dinner's set for 6:00 and a creative workshop for 7:00. At 7:15, the dinner bell rings. Danny (The Draftee) has made Meatballs Buttermilk and spinach cooked from fresh leaves. The dinner routine is carefully egali-tarian.

Soon all 18 members of the Company, plus Gypsy, are seated around the library, tapping boot heels and wooden-soled clogs, each in a dif-ferent variation on the same rhythm. Danny comes around with the dinner money bowl. The backsliders pay up.

Two filmmakers are here from the Workshop. They want to know whether the Mime Troupe would like to go to the country to make a movie with the Jefferson Airplane and Quicksilver Messenger Service.

"What are you going to say?" asks one of the Company.

"Well, no message," is the reply. "It will be its own message."

"Ha, ha, ha. The medium is the message," jibes one. "Ha, ha."

"Is this going to be another *Woodstock?*" says someone else.

"No," says one of the filmmakers carefully. He does not seem to know what he's said wrong.

Joannie says, "I wonder whether you have seen us lately?"

Well, no. Neither filmmaker had seen the Mime Troupe perform in a couple years.

"Why did you choose us?"

"Because of your political leanings. Your reputation," says one of the filmmakers. He's uncomfortable.

"Why is it going to be in the country?" someone else asks. The struggles are in the city.

The filmmakers are beginning to catch on to what the Mime Troupe wants the film to be.

"It's going to be propaganda," one says. "But we want to show people like us when we are having a good time."

"I haven't been to the country in years," says Danny.

"Us can't go see *Woodstock,*" says Joannie. "We only earn $30 a week."

"You say the world can see this movie, but can the world see it on three dollars?" Danny persists. "Can you show it on the side of a building?"

"We are going to have problems in distribution," one of the filmmakers concedes.

"All the rock festivals were reviewed in the hip media as 'This is it. The revolution is here,' " says Joan Holden, who wrote '*L'Amant Militaire.* She wears cowboy boots and a bandana around her head. 'Maybe what you'd get would be a confrontation between the music freaks and the politicos."

"That would be an event," is the reply.

"Yeh," says Joannie, "You could call it *A Bummer in the Country.*"

"How are you going to distribute this?" Sandy asks.

Warner Brothers."

"Can we get the TV rights?" another asks.

The filmmakers smile. "Sounds like a capitalist organization."

The Mime Troupe does not smile.

"We need to learn how to use the media."

The TV rights would be arranged. But the filmmakers are right to smile. Could the Mime Troupe push Mao on television? Come out against Ecology, *Woodstock* and rock music?

"Where we come from," says on the the Company, getting back to the question of content. "The politics come before the art."

He's corrected by Sandy. "I thing it's synonymous."

"We are interested in creating an arm of communication for the culture of today," the filmmakers say. "It's not going to be a staged thing. We are setting the environment, that's all."

"But you must have a reason for doing what you're doing," says Joannie.

The filmmakers play their last card:

"Who's the bigger rip-off?" one says. "The pigs? Or Jefferson Airplane and Quicksilver Messenger Service?"

"Jefferson Airplane and Quicksilver Messenger Service, of course," says Danny. The rock groups are the bigger rip-off "because everybody respects them."

The conversation is over. The Company wil decide later whether to make the movie. But first, Sandy gets a promise that the deal would include transportation to the country for the Company.

Sure, sure, food too, says the filmmakers. Everything will be taken care of.

The two men are invited to stick around while the Company works on a new skit called *Strike*. Those sitting at one end of the room move somewhere else and that space becomes the stage. The Company has to decide whether to show the skit this weekend at Fort Collins.

Steve plays a pacifist student shot in a march on the ROTC building. Joannie has pulled her denim shirttails out of her jeans for the role of rock-throwing militant.

"The San Francisco Mime Troupe presents *Pacifism Kills* or *Woodstock West*."

Steve is shot. He clutches his hands to his breast and calls upon the name of Ghandi.

"Oh, it's nothing but a shoulder wound," says Joannie.

Steve's forgotten his lines. He adlibs "A shoulder wound? Not in the middle of my chest," he giggles. It's late; everyone else giggles too until Joannie says "If you're not against the pigs, you're for them" and goes into a lengthy political rap.

"All right, do we take this to Fort Collins?" says Sandy.

Joan Holden thinks the pacifist should get killed.

"But then you make a martyr out of him."

It's finally decided to call Fort Collins, find out what the issues are there and write them into the script tomorrow.

Sandy announces that the State Department is going to send a South Korean official to talk to the Mime Troupe and see them perform. Everybody wonders why.

"We got Seoul," says Steve.

"Ha, ha, ha, ha, ha."

It's agreed that the Government is using the Company to prove its liberality and that the group will not co-operate with it in the future.

A member of the Third World Revelationists arrives. He's Puerto Rican and wears a white shirt, a worn black ski parka and a narrow-brimmed hat. Everyone had been getting punchy but the group settles down and grows respectful when he arrives. The best times in his collective, he says, are when there is trust within the group, trust built on mutual sacrifice.

"Did eleven of you come out here in that van?" one of the Mime Troupe asks.

"Eleven," replies the Puerto Rican.

"Yeh, I don't think we could do that yet . . ." the actor replies, enviously.

Later the Puerto Rican says. "I don't think your performances did anything yesterday."

The Company seems to agree that it "performed" without actually changing anything.

"It's true that we go into a place and leave it," says Steve. "That we don't carry out the things we counsel."

"Maybe the parks idea is stale," says a woman who's wardrobe mistress. "Maybe we should be going to the universities where things are happening."

The conversation shifts and shifts, from money to whether to keep playing in the parks, to communality. But the Mime Troupe's greatest worry is whether to be professional theater or agit-prop.

"We have to get off being theatrical, 'We played Las Vegas,' " one man says. "Like when I speak I feel like Lenny Bruce. I tell a few jokes, then leave."

"Like Abbie and Jerry," another says.

The workshop's over. It's nearly midnight. The conversation on the way out of the studio is about repression and how it will be necessary to know how to deliver babies and grow tomatoes on the roof.

Ronnie Davis talks about why he left the Mime Troupe ("temporarily"). It was to set up Praxis, which will distribute movies, records, video tapes, theater and speakers.

"The key to what goes on in this country is the means of distribution, not the means of production," he says. "Praxis is trying to find ways to distribute radical products in order to avoid the commercial distributors." There are a lot of radical records and movies not being made because there's no central distribution network for them.

As for the Mime Troupe itself: "I am not sure whether I want to work on that level any more." Ronnie says he doesn't disagree with street theater, but the Mime Troupe can only produce so many products. And Ronnie Davis is ready for larger scale operations.

There's a further difference between Ronnie and members of his Troupe—over some other mass media showmen, the Chicago Seven. "I left the Mime Troupe because there was a need to do a show in Chicago," he says. "A big road show with the Conspiracy, all seven guys in a four-hour condensation of the trial." He worked on that roadshow for two months.

Is is true that Ronnie and the Mime Troupe split because of male chauvinism on his part? "That's a lie. There is no Women Liberation in the Mime Troupe. . . . Joan Holden hasn't had a problem with Women's Liberation until this year when she got into it." Of course, neither had Ronnie.

Nor does Ronnie share the Mime Troupe's feeling for the Third World Revelationists. Such groups are comunal rather than professional; they don't perform for an audience, they conduct public group therapy. If you are a family and the family comes first, then you can't demand professional performances of your members.

A few days after the *Independent Female* opened, Sandy Archer followed Ronnie Davis and left the Mime Troupe. She's currently working on a film with Saul Landau in Chile. The *Chicago Seven Road Show* has not come off, nor apparently has Praxis.

Walter and some others have left the Troupe, but on the whole its membership remains unchanged. The group feels that Ronnie had tended to be dictatorial and that decisions ought not be made by "leaders."

The split has led to legal battles. The Mime Troupe is a nonprofit organization and Ronnie Davis, Sandy Archer and Saul Landau constitute its board of directors. Both sides have hired lawyers.

As of now, the Company plans only one tour, a month-long tour of the Midwest in November, playing *Independent Female, Telephone, Eco-man* and possibly some pieces still in workshop on Los Siete and BART, the Panthers and the Soledad Brothers.

Also in the making is a Revolutionary Rock Band, featuring a female drummer.

With the exception of the sexist issues, Ronnie agrees that the Mime Troupe is asking itself the same question as every other radical group, big or small, in the country. Do you play to North Beach hippies or Berkeley activists or to the telephone operators at Bell? Are you communal or professional? Do you tell a few jokes and leave, or do you stick around and get you head busted? Do you like Bill Graham (and Ronnie Davis?) and make money selling groovy products to the young? Or do you preach revolution and grow tomatoes on the roof?

Just as the issues of cooptation and exploitation loom large in the thinking of groups such as the Mime Troupe, so do they also in the minds of many attempting reevaluations of the "star trips'" of spokesmen for the cultural revolution. As drama critic Robert Brustein has remarked in his *Revolution As Theatre:*

> Developments of this kind are inevitable in a culture where fame is replacing money as the animating drive of ambitious men and the cardinal sign of achievement. "In five years," as Andy Warhol has cogently observed, "everybody in the world will be famous for fifteen minutes ... one of the current formulas for finding fame is theatricalized revolution—revolution for the hell of it—designed to capture attention for an individual through some extraordinary antic. This impulse may help account for the mindlessness of the movement, and may explain why radical thinkers like Christopher Lasch, Paul Goodman, Eugene Genovese, Bayard Rustin, and Irving Howe are such isolated figures these days, and so unpopular with the revolutionary young. When performance is considered more important than the script, hard economic solutions and practical programs are abandoned for mass media confrontations which lead no-

where except to further publicity. In place of thought, we are given expletives and imprecations, used so indiscriminately that they have lost their meaning even for those who employ them. And what may have been originally stimulated by a desire to dramatize a cause for the sake of curing an injustice now often seems like theatre for its own sake, destructive in its aim, negative in its effect, performed with no particular end in mind. . . . It is the age of seething grievance, when everyone is joining an undifferentiated chorus of complaint on so many subjects that one is hard put to separate out the real from the phony issues.[8]

As Nikki Giovanni pointed out within the context of the black revolution, this sort of an ego hustle for the ear of the enemy may lead to individual income and prestige—but it also leads to a fragmentation of the movement and perhaps to the ride "on a pink damn cloud to the concentration camps" as well. Do you agree?

Street theater has taken another, less political and more social, form—radical community.[9] Groups such as the Third World Revelationists do not perform for an audience as do the Mime Troupe. Rather, they conduct "public group therapy" (as Ronnie Davis put it)—an attempt to create a communal sense of cultural identity.

We need to build radical communities in order to provide alternate life styles. We need radical communities to provide staging grounds for our struggle and bases of operation for that struggle. We need radical communities to further enjoy those experiences denied to us by the society. . . . (At the same time) we must guard against our communities becoming havens for dropouts. Communities must be movement centers in the real sense of the word. If a community attempts to remove itself from confrontations in the society then it becomes irrelevant as a force for change. . . . We are not an underground, but we must prepare to be an underground. . . .[10]

The Hog Farm is just such a radical community; its members practicing the "Merry Pranksterism" of Ken Kesey[11] as they take their brand of street theater to America. Our final piece is an account by

---

8. Robert Brustein, *Revolution As Theatre* (New York: Liveright, 1971), pp. 21, 22, 25.
9. Radical community is not to be confused with the retreatist ideal of the "hippie" segment of the youth culture—that which has found expression in the creation of costumes and which is essentially separatist and nonpolitical in nature.
10. Ronald McGuire.
11. An account of Kesey's Merry Pranksters as a mobile community can be found in Tom Wolfe, *The Electric Kool-Aid Acid Test* (New York: Farrar, Strauss, and Giroux, 1968).

Hugh Romney of the Hog Farm's trek from Los Angeles to New York. How *does* the radical community operate? And how does it relate to the larger society within the contexts of street theater and popular culture?

THE HOG FARM

Hugh Romney

The Hog Farm is an expanded family, a mobile hallucination, a sociological experiment, an army of clowns . . . we are 50 people on a perpetual trip, citizens of earth. We have six converted school buses, some vans and pickups, one for our pet pig, Pigasus, who now weighs 400 pounds and has learned to roll over.

The farm was once located on a mountaintop in the San Fernando Valley of California. It is now relocated 110 miles from New York City on the banks of the Delaware River—a journey of 3,000 miles, 7 months in the making—and *this* (taaa daah!) is the story of *that.*

It seems like it was almost yesterday . . . we had been living on this Pig Farm about two years . . . feeding 40 real primordial pigs breakfast and dinner in exchange for free rent. Just a few people in the beginning, in the mud, hanging windows on the wind, fixin up the joint after years of vandalism and neglect . . . also our bodies and brains . . . trying to get it together . . . some kind of Hog Consciousness.

And others started comin in. All kinds of people. At first we had separate jobs on the hill. Like I was working at Cal State University with brain-damaged children and teaching movie stars at Columbia Pictures how to improvise; my wife Bonnie Jean was in television; Paul Foster was a computer engineer; David Le Braun was finishing his last year in cinematography at UCLA.

Several local heads began to migrate. Evan Engber split from his commune in Topanga to join *what?* Nobody knew. Just sandpainting in the wind. People remodeled old farm shanties, pitched tents, or set up in the main house. Just groovin' out their hole. That place you lay down yer haid an' rest. And when that was done we went to work on the land and each other . . . trying to make *it* work . . . seeing what the hell we were here for.
. . .

To equalize the division of work and save wear and tear on the available vehicles, we instituted the dance master program. Our dance master ran the farm and the dance mistress ran the kitchen, and each day it was some different person working off this wheel with everybody's name. We could feed 30 people on $3 a day combined with a garbage run at local super markets. In California they throw away a lot of stuff; tons of near fresh fruits and vegetables plus scooter pies and other goodies.

We also instituted the FANTASY BOX into which people would place ideas of stuff the group could do . . . and it could be anything that you would agree to do under hypnosis. Whenever a given fantasy had been completed (build a meditation dome on the point, start a hog farm band of home-made instruments for sunsets, clean the ceiling, etc) we would, lightnin' fast, draw out another.

First we start with an Open Sunday for Los Angeles. Each Sunday with a theme. Always a celebration. Lots of food and music. One Sunday it's kites and we have people and kites from everywhere . . . but no wind till sunset . . . so kite day is kite night and we sent up flashlights and mirrors and bells on their tails and it was do dark you couldn't tell if someone was holding a kite or putting you on.

And Tiny Tim Sunday where the audience built a theatre for Tim to perform in. And Mud Sunday (use what you got). And Dress Like Kids Day with silly shorts and water pistols and no girls allowed in the boys club house, and a formal croquette party held in a pig pen, the hog farm state fair with the bake-off and freak show and who can stay under the water longest. Learning how to play hard.

Bus. Some part of the hog had completed a secret mission earning the farm a bus. On Christmas morning with only one star it drove up the mountain and announced itself. Both Paul Foster and I had been and still are, I guess, Merry Pranksters and lived on Furthur with Ken Kesey. I felt this bus was Furthur's baby. Machines don't make me horny but Furthur made me come. Maybe this bus . . . 1947 White Superpower *Bus* Bus.

Driver, the United States of America, and step on it!

Everybody is really turned on by this fantasy. The whole Hog has lit up for the first time. When any fantasy can light up the whole Hog, that seems to be what's happening. It's the bus ride to the *show* show. Reports are pouring in. Lots of action on the other end. The Everybody Paint the Bus Sunday. Followed by the mechanical show under the bus. Sure it's all a show. Even a flat tire can be a show if we use *joy*. . . .

Get a couple buses. Lumber for the bunks. Projectors, Fix everything. Get new stuff. Hit the road.

First drive up to Oregon to pick up Babbs. Ken Babbs and Gretchen Fetchen his slim queen and old lady plus their babies Mouse and Squeek. Babbs was a strong force within the Merry Prankster trip and if we could get him to some along . . . we talked on the phone lots and he agreed to come. The bus is moved to Keseys farm to finish off the interior carpentry work. Lockers that are benches open to double bunks . . . trying to get the most out of the least.

This bus, called The Road Hog, can now comfortably sleep and board a crew of 14 and is starting to acquire a personality. Everybody paints on her and the ceiling begins to acquire a collage.

In New Mexico we did a hauna prayer which we learned from a wise man in the Sierra Madre. It works like this. Lots of people in a circle. Some-body says, Put your whole consciousness at the base of your spine. Feel it in your blood. Feel it in your stomach.

Whole consciousness guided through the body . . . heart throat head and out to merge with other consciousness in the circle . . . getting stronger . . . becoming whole *whole* consciousness *consciousness.* Then send it out all together at the same time as light love sound, "aaaaaaaaaaahhhhhhhhh-ooooooooooooom." Coinciding with the first sprinkle of the season.

"Rain without snakes," somebody murmurs and runs off to tell the Indians.

Sunday is the big day of the festival and I have my first official wed-ding to perform. Paul Foster is getting married. To Laura. I have just become an ordained minister to one of Southern California's many mini-religions. Traveling in community it is handy to have someone on the trip who can do that stuff.

This is what happened. I come out with Paul, Laura, and Babbs who is best man and can hold up Paul Foster who is actually wearing ice skates. We begin by lighting incense as a simple sacrifice to the elements . . . planting of ancient beans . . . the sharing of water and food . . . the couple chose to exchange pork chops . . . then the vows.

We discovered months later the marriage was consummated with a cantaloupe fight.

The next morning we lite out for El Rito and the 4th of July. Hog Farm buses are pulling in all the time. Not to mention Peter Whiterabbit's bus called The Queen Midtown Tunnel of Love. He had been waiting some time in Santa Fe. Back when we didn't even know we were coming. It's like meeting yourself in the street . . . and El Rito began with a street parade with all the buses and vans and a lot of Volkswagen campers.

Everybody but the drivers get out and walk or dance, play music and wave. El Rito is a very tiny town. Mostly Spanish American with a few Anglo artists. We—the pig in the lead wearing an Uncle Sam hat and a skirt of stars on an endless leash held by me and the children. Finally the hog is exhausted and we load her into a place of honor and speed out to camp. Followed by the town of El Rito.

We have a forestry permit and have already set up the big dome. Everybody grabbed a musical instrument and started to cook. Except for the natives who ringed the scene wide-eyed and cling to their cool, belting beers. Only their children were super free . . . join in music and dance and here comes the rain.

The evening light show was scarey and beautiful. Our light show screening is a series of triangles which grommet to the dome frame form-ing a covering similar to the Hollywood Bowl . . . that night the wind tore up the screens and they're flapping all over but those light show guys they just keep projecting and the whole thing is another first.

Beautiful accident . . . while the natives chugged beer in pickup trucks facing the light show screens full of butterflies and buddhas all flapping in the wind like a drive-in on the moon . . . the rock music made em crazy those drunk guys in the pickups and they started running around yellin and beatin on things, so we slipped on a Tiny Tim tape and a couple of ragas and everybody went home.

The camp moved in and around that general area for some time and the population swelled to about 150 stomachs. The kitchen in the woods show had really gotten nifty. With a sink and pump from this stream with elaborate log shelves for pots and spice and staples and counters made by a lot of guys . . . and keeping it clean and together was a giant's dance.

The food ran out fast . . . the Hog Farm had brought staples to last 30 people a couple of months but with all these people eatin it really upped the drama. I remember we had this dramatic nighttime meeting on the road hog and everybody was worried about the food except Babbs who gives this impassioned speech about giving everything away and everybody gets real excited except the pig who had just eaten my sleeping bag.

The camp show is more than a food flap and psychedelic sauna, it is crafts and workshop and music and the fire at night and music and singing and talking into the fire. We decide to hold our next celebration at Los Alamos . . . the Atomic City . . . Love-in at Los Alamos . . . a lurid title to a funny fantasy. Of course they'd never allow it . . . but maybe it just might happen.

Tom Law and I shuttled up in his bus to look around. It is situated on the top of an enormous plateau amid breathtaking country. Picked purposely by Oppenheimer for these reasons and a few others. You can feel old death in the air. We go straight to the Chamber of Commerce.

There is a white-collar teenybopper working in the office and the director has gone home. When he hears words like *light show domes* and *electric music* he gets very excited. Nothing like that ever happened in Los Alamos. He takes it as a personal challenge . . . shows us land, talks of a community sponsor. Nothing can happen in Los Alamos without a sponsor. We exchange lots of phone numbers and return to camp.

The mechanics have been working all day on our old army generator. It is an enormous machine with its own trailer that Evan Engber brought from Topanga. An erratic beast at best, the generator was capable of enough wattage to run our entire scene . . . light show, band, etc. However, world war two was a while ago and the machine was looking for a discharge. After the mechanics fixed it there was an afternoon shower and somebody tossed on a tarp while it was still running. The generator ate the tarp and destroyed itself. This put the mechanics and everybody else on a fantastic bummer.

Which brings us around to The Great Generator Exorcism. It was a spontaneous event to heal the crimp of people and machine . . . starting out with Paul Foster sticking sparklers all over the motor and the mechanics beating on it with rocks. The thing began to snowball. Every body adorning the generator with personal mojo like buddhas and godseyes and great strands of beads and painting on it and praying to it and somebody lit a couple of flares and next thing you know there's maybe 50 or 60 people dancing around the drums and guitars and even a saxophone.

Most folks were beating on the machine with sticks, feeding it incense and oranges, and singing and chanting their ass off. After the first hour or two the vibes were tremendous with no sign of let-up. *Heal,* you son of a bitch machine *heal.* Nobody really noticed the Lincoln Continental slip up the rutted road and park.

In between whacks and shouts I chance to look up and over and under the flares and the moon I see this big beautiful old gentleman with long white hair, twinkley eyes, semi-straight clothes, with a 10-pound lump of green jade hanging round his neck on a chain, and he's hunched over beating on this generator just like I am. I dig him to be Bill Tate, the Justice of the Peace from Truchas, a little town high in these mountains. I also heard he was a fine painter, ran a gallery, and was the only Anglo in America to be a practicing Penatente, an obscure sect that each year physically enacts the passion of Christ. Far out!

I disappear in waves of holy generator joy. A long time later his secretary or something tries to pull him away but it takes a couple tries cause he's totally spun out . . . dissolved into the rest of us. When he finally drives away he leaves an ancient tin rattle of the Penatentes, a promise of return, and a powerful presence of something eternal. We discovered that the next day he called up some general with the New Mexico National Guard and told him how nifty we are, and about our Celebrations, and how we really need this generator to turn on the people of New Mexico, and after a couple science fiction phone calls the Army agrees to fix our generator.

The next night a baby is born in camp. Born in the back of a 1952 International Harvester truck. Her name is Cueva and she weighed about 6 pounds. Ken Babbs played the doctor. Somebody else played the guitar.

The rules are simple. A lead vehicle, preferably the slowest, sets the pace, with each driver minding the vehicle behind it. If there is a hang-up flash your lights and the message will relay through the convoy and everybody will pull onto the shoulder. Sounds easy if your lights work, if everybody is paying attention, and if there is a shoulder to pull off on.

Before we leave on a mission there is usually a drivers' meeting where the route is discussed and everybody gets high. If possible a contact phone number is passed out to use if you are hopelessly lost and haven't lost the phone number. All good clean drama. Thrills and spills and 30 miles an hour. Into the sunset.

Around the bend we run into Evan Engber and his old lady Bonnie sitting in a Bread Van full of avocados watching the sun set. They were a month late having broke down in Needles, California. And now we're all together. The Road Hog, Chances Van—the big Pig, Arts truck towing Pigasus and the generator, the band bus (a gift from Synanon) with Wilson Smith who was our band, his lady Sue (now Chipmont Sue, having adopted an orphan in El Valle), and here comes Peter Whiterabbit's Queens Mid-Town Tunnel of Love Bus, followed by the Light Show Bus, Tom Law's Juke Savage Machine built from parts gathered at the Atomic junk yard in Los Alamos, the Bread Van full of Evan and avocados, Eloi's and Nancy's pick-up with newborn baby Cueva and their 4 other kids, plus countless campers and sedans . . . into the night with a trail of lights through the woods looking like rush hour on the Ventura Freeway.

You can just imagine the gas station show! Pulling into Espanola around 8 o'clock on Saturday night a little loaded and looking to pee. One hundred freaks spill from thirsty machines in quest of an Almond Joy or a Juke Savage cantaloupe and still no sign of the chuckwagon or the white-rabbit bus or the volkswagen riding drag. When the news hits in the person of Calvin—an organic farmer in bib overalls, shirtless and tanned to the top of his balding brain . . . face framed in gray mutton chop whiskers all a'quake and jumping up and down for all his maybe 50 years spewing blubber mumble goon about how the chuckwagon went *over a cliff* but everything was cool with the white bus standing by . . . he secretly called the police and fire departments and was never seen again.

The result was mass confusion with everybody flapping around . . . the what went over the what? Sirens in the distance. The word slowly gets around. Calvin says its cool, nobody hurt. Babbs is there. Babbs is together. Babbs will take care of it.

We later discovered most of the information was Calvin's hallucination. Babbs could have stood a little help . . . with all our worldly dinners drib-bling down this mountain side and Terry Scout going mad at the switch and throwing washing machines and stove parts further down the mountain cursing our karma in the person of Peter Blackrabbit nee Chuckwagon for refusing brake fluid back in camp and being a shitty driver . . . Babbs is laughing his ass off which is his habit when the world falls off and nobody gets hurt.

So when the natives arrive with their perpetual beer show he and the Whiterabbits and even Terry Scout get good and stinking drunk. The cops say the late Chuckwagon needs a tow which is $70 that they pull from Judge Tate who answered his door in a nightshirt with pistola. So they all go to live at Judge Tate's house as voluntary hostages.

Meanwhile back at the gas station everybody's gassed and pissed and candied up and waiting for at least some kind of news, and the gas station guys get nervous cause there's no room for anybody else. So we move into this Safeway parking lot and start waiting. But it's Saturday night and the whole town is out driving around like they always do except they re-route Main Street to the Safeway parking lot of their own accord just to check us out and it's really a scene.

David Butcovitch has assumed his police identy and is outside blowing his whistle and directing traffic . . . when who should he whistle up but the police chief who also has a whistle and has just about swallowed it. My wife Bonnie Jean is the police commissioner because she is very pretty and has talked to a lot of police. She went to cool the captain while we stashed Butcovitch in the belly of the bus. We had 10 minutes to get out of town. Oh well, Babbs had a map and Calvin must be with him using the Volks for shuttle. We all hook up at the Hot Springs tomorrow.

The rainy season was upon us as we played the swamp show. Second night in camp the Band Bus ran amuck . . . sheered its moorings and ran over some strange cat . . . having never been run over by a bus before he was somewhat shaken but quite whole the only casualty being his guitar which resembled a Picasso in cubes.

The Band Bus came to rest with only its nose in the river as if testing the temperature like some chickenshit Florence Chadwick. Somewhere around that time the peyote arrived. From the Texas Plains with bulging gunny sacks came Federal Fred our Psychedelic Santa Claus to kick off the *Great Peyote Geeze.*

Now personally I smoke grass to get giddy and psychedelics are a sacramental serious scene and some of my brothers and sisters are on a similar trip . . . and others can go either way . . . and still others will consume whatever's around whenever they can. Announcing the great peyote eating contest with our boy Butch pulling in top honors with 40 buttons under his brain . . . followed by a peyote fight in the yellow dome. It was a pretty noisy show and me and my old lady slipt up to the bus and fell out.

That's the Hog Farm for you. The full spectrum. Do anything you want as long as nobody gets hurt.

Kesey used to say, "The trouble with the super hero is—what to do between phone booths." No time for that now. It's telephone time in Los Alamos. Let's bottle up and go. It's a long ascent for the convoy, stretching splendid ribbons of rubber and day-glo into the mesa side.

Los Alamos was a closed city till about ten years ago. The guard towers are ominous and deserted. The town looks a lot like Scarsdale with residential cottages—east coast style. On each house there is a plaque like TA 714-648B, etc. White picket fence and chicken every Sunday. Freckled kids ride Schwinn bikes down Avenues of elm trees on a mesa in New Mexico. Not an adobe in sight. Only death merchant Americana.

The cops are there already and they got an attitude. Teenage kids informed us the police had boasted we'd never be allowed to set up the show but the persistent Unitarians saved the day. So here we are . . . and there they are . . . to protect and serve.

I plod over to the peace officers to see if I can cool them on. They are wearing mirrored sunglasses and I am wearing a jester's hat. I adjust my bells in their eyes. "Hi ya, you guys, what can we do to make things groovy? I mean if there's any hassle we can fix just let us know up front, okay? And after a gruff and a grumble they're goin for it . . . saying something about the parking show. So I appoint myself parking commissioner and official greeter with a lot of hand signals and a how do you do . . . de do de dootie!

It's a pretty good gig and I get to meet everybody personally. They share a similar affection for beer as the rest of the inhabitants of the land of enchantment . . . and they're pushy with it. Each carful getting a can for the greeter, and putting a gentle lurch in the side of my peyote buzz. I give the cops a wink and a giggle and they are semi-amused. The first breakthrough. After a while I get some relief and go check out the show-show.

The band is all set up and everybody is helping set up the big dome. Not just us but farmers and physicists and freaks all working together, and that's what the show is about. The Ladies Auxiliary has set up shop around the side of the white bus and they're doing a hell of a business. Psychedelica is a rare bird is Atomicsville.

Night fell. The light show was beautiful, the music was grand, and everybody felt responsible. Cuz they had helped. They explored the buses . . . exchanged hugs and hellos and we were all just one big happy family . . . of man. Earth people at a party. Even the police were kissing cousins. After the show they escorted us to a nearby parking lot, saving the striking of equipment for Monday morning. They also copped food for our pig.

The clean-up show the next morning was really a wonder with every hog in action. Not a gum wrapper left standing. This is always a mindblower for local officials who have never seen a freak at work . . . let alone for free. The response is always generous with food and gee-gaws . . . smiles and even tears. And so we bid a fond farewell to Los Alamos USA and it's a satisfied man that lumbers back to Pilar and the river for after-the-show layup and general recuperation.

Our next show is set for the Santa Fe Rodeo Grounds and is to be a real wheeler-dealer event with lots of advance radio and newspaper publicity. It will be a benefit for the Santa Fe Repertory Theatre and an opportunity to do our thing on a whole other level . . . rent fancy equipment and give the freaks a good name.

We have never charged money before and it's against our basic principles but it's not for us and what the hell . . . let's see what happens. We move the camp into the mountains just above Santa Fe and make ready. The show-show is a horror with belligerent cowboys . . . a sparse attendance . . . and a bunch of rock hounds on an ego trip . . . it is a stiff lesson.

The next day a couple of us picked up the generator from the national guard. It had been entirely rebuilt and as a special surprise painted dayglo and stenciled with love. They were honestly embarrassed about Chicago[1] and it was a touching scene as we towed that brightly colored

---

[1]This was at the time of the 1968 Democratic convention in Chicago (ed.).

machine out of all that olive drab. Two different armies passing in review. A couple of weeks went by and some psychedelic dope appeared in camp. A kool-aid was prepared and those of us that were hearty enough took a little busride heh heh heh!

Ken Babbs has taken off with his big army bus to rescue the light show bus in Albuquerque. Where he was taken off to jail for calling this prick cop a prick cop. Babbs is digging the jail show and refuses bail for a while. "Just another experiment."

Communications broken down with the slippery LeBraun bus, the Hog Farm rushes to Albuquerque to reason with Babbs. We are in town ten minutes when we hook into LeBraun who has scheduled our celebration at the University of New Mexico. A lady playground designer offers up her vacant lot with a promise of hot showers. Hot showers are a hot item in any bus community.

Everything starts coming together. The jail has had enough of Babbs just being Babbs . . . and we have the pig installed in this lady's back yard doll house. Our host (an architect) & hostess were holding up rather well under the onslaught. Something happens when the hog farmers walk into your house. I mean there's just so many of us . . . babies, kids, dogs and big folks . . . that you kind of disappear. I mean you become part of this hot squirming organism looking for this and that.

You see they thought we had come to live in Albuquerque—5 buses full of squeaky freaks, with only Babbs to go on. Fifty Babbses? Call the cops! Then they heard we're only passing through. After the show at the college. Heading for wherever that is. Those cops were really happy and stopped the stopping of our buses. "Just turn your head and wave, Sergeant, they're leaving town in a week."

Our first college celebration was a super success with thousands of people getting into stuff. We had all kinds of equipment supplied by the college which made for a very rich palate. Many mikes, speakers, projectors and amps. The ladies Auxiliary sold a ton of "native crafts" which we converted into gasoline and groceries.

Vigilantes, drunken cowboys, and hostile heat drive us out of Evergreen, Colorado. Temporary sanctuary is found in a local hippie bushes. Meanwhile diapers are changed, oatmeal is burned, socks are darned . . . just like everybody else . . . except it's compressed and expanded. Like a billion balloons in a shoebox.

The Hog Farm floats into Boulder Colorado looking for a parking place . . . and ends up on the outskirts, in a campground, out of sight. That night we all make an appearance at the University of Colorado. It's a meeting of SDS and we just walk in. The whole family. It is good timing because all the students were politically exhausted. Everybody is flashing on our celebration and we get lots of sponsors. Not just the SDS but the sophomore and senior class and the interfraternity council and a lot of student groups I can't remember. This means a bigger budget which means more toys. A richer palate.

The Boulder Police chased us out of the outskirts and we are given sanctuary on a university parking lot. The life show and show-show are coming closer together. Students popping in and out at all hours and always holding. Our free store overfloweth. Incredible garbage runs net mountains of chicken and doughnuts. Girls' dormitories offer up showers and the engineers are interested in our domes.

Too much is yet too much and more! After a series of administrative hassles we are awarded an enormous field for our frolic. A professional nonstudent named Scott Holazar starts hanging out and helps us in our dealings within the university power structure. Thousands of leaflets are distributed with the wrong date. Another debacle. Everybody runs around makin changes, meeting people, and it's even better because of our bungle.

Ten thousand people attend our celebration throughout the course of the day and night. Helping with the equipment. Sprouting domes. Swapping sandwiches. Painting paintings. Just like we dreamed it. Only better. The art department has donated a 50-foot long inflatable plastic hot dog that people can crawl inside of and turn red. It has been previously used at a college happening where a red smoke bomb had left a rub off residue. Turning cowboys into Indians. There are lots of children around to help the big folks get it off. . . .

Night time found everybody gathered in and around the big dome waiting for the lightshow and electric music. We had several local bands who had volunteered to play and were busy hooking up equipment with the usual delays. The hype was tremendous. Thousands of people clapping and whistling and . . . this one incredible whistle . . . I grab a working mike and trace it down.

This student does bird calls. He is brought forward with deafening applause. This kid is so hot to do his thing he chips his tooth on the mircophone. After each bird call everybody claps like hell . . . behind it is all so bizarre. Meanwhile the last minute electrical hassles have all been solved, the band is poised, and the whole place is set to explode.

At that moment I am grabbed from behind and tossed to the ground. A hose is stuck into my mouth and I am filled with nitrous oxide. As I change dimensions I catch a glimpse of Kesey. This is Prankster business. I am handed a microphone and tossed on stage. The same for Babbs and Bucavitch and other hogs. We are pumped full of gas and wired for sound. Our synchronized scream is a cosmic cartoon.

The light show erupts, the band takes off, and 10,000 people are dancing and prancing like New Years Eve, V.J. Day, and the legalization of marijuana. We slip out unnoticed in quest of Kesey. He's got a white Cadillac full of nitrous oxide and a tennis racket. Just passing through! We tour and explore and everything is running itself . . . a snowball in the summer. That's when it's really best. When the momentum of what went down can carry the show and we weary hogs can sit back and enjoy the enjoyment of everybody else.

The next day is the big clean-up show with lots of students helping out. A telephone call has been made to the Department of Agriculture by Red Dog. He says there's apple picking for everyone in Missouri. We really want a bunch of money to continue our trip. The road hog needed a ring job and New York was a long way off . . . so we bid a fond farewell to colorful Colorado and a hearty hello to the *Great Apple Show.*

Missouri living is slidy and slow and just like ther rollin river here come the hog farm. Our first job is picking apples off the ground after the tree guys had passed through. Big golden balls of apple destined for cider and sauce. We crawl under trees and fill bushel baskets then empty them into big boxes. A couple bucks each box. Then we move up in the world. Our next gig takes us into the trees and the apples are red and our stomachs are bulging with bites.

It was a sweet gig with the whole family pitching apples . . . apple baseball, apple tennis, and a squishy apple fight. We had a stark scene with the orchard owner who didn't want us to leave. However the rains were upon us and we persevered, picked up our bread and a couple of apples and hit the road. The cop shows of Kansas were amiable, the highways flat and easy on the buses. It was also difficult to get lost. We camped evenings at State Lakes which were left over WPA projects and we always drew a crowd. One time we showed our movies on the back of a gas station wall.

The last lap to Ann Arbor was really shaky and about dawn after getting directions from some mean police we find the warehouse which is big and new and ready to house a lazer factory. The board of directors run us out of there the next day and we seek sanctuary in a tiny farmhouse in Ypsilanti. . . .

The road going out of the farm has a full blockade and they are busting anything that moves. A reporter from the *Detroit Free Press* joins our convoy . . . and we decide to run the blockade, with all our legal vehicles . . . leaving our other equipment in the bushes till later on.

We crank it all up and start the music and it's really exciting. There are police cars in front and behind every vehicle and they are following along waiting for us to make a mistake but we are hip to their trip and are very legal. At the county line they stop us anyhow with a police car almost totaled by a semi on that final curve.

So the ritual begins with drivers licenses and registrations, tail lights and horns . . . and we pile out with our movie cameras and groovy cameras our babies and kazoos. Bonnie Jean is standing on the kitchen stove playing *Home on the Range.* We get ticketed for our tires, snap pictures of policemen and they snap pictures of our pictures.

It is snowing softly and the kazoos sing *Silent Night* in the afternoon.

It is a tender sight, all us scruffy day-glo hog farmers bunched with our babies and buses and holy kazoos. A couple choruses and we are cut loose with two tickets. The kazoo is the Hog Farm secret weapon.

The Michigan show was a bit of a dance . . . everything on campus is unionized and turning on anything except students cost a fortune. It was a 2-day fete featuring the MC5 on the first night. They are a revolutionary rock experience dedicated to kicking out the jams while turning my ears to electric jelly. It seems they were having equipment hassles causing feed-back of feedback. Great sheets of audio pain. My brain began to drain like a science fiction sinus. When it was over it was still going on. The audience deserved to be decorated. When their wires are connected the band is grand. Trans-love energies, the commune of which they are an integral part, is as active and dedicated as any in the country. . . .

We spend Thanksgiving living at the tricooperative student commune in Ann Arbor. After meetings and greetings and turkey and ping pong we mend our machines and move on to Detroit . . . for new recurits. Barry and Moe have been to our show at Canterbury. They got a school bus with a rubber floor ripped off from an abandoned sponge factory. Like White-rabbit in Santa Fe they have always been family . . . before formal marriage . . . a clog in the hog. There are lots of people in this world we haven't met yet but their shades and their shadows trail off of our convoy like magnets that lead to their blood. We're coming, you guys. Keep a candle in the garage.

We pulled the whole show in back of Barry's house and it was a squeeze. Like slipping 60 circus midgets in a phone booth . . . in the snow. Barry and Moe sold their clothes and worldly mush and we hooked up with the Grateful Dead for a western reunion. Babbs is back after driving in triangles for a month. Also Paul Foster and Laura who were playing a one-week stand in Athens, Ohio.

There is a fantasy afoot to mobilize the Dead and everybody else into a fantastic convoy of maybe 500 souls. A circus tent that holds 10,000. We have a pow-wow with Jerry Garcia and it sounds too good to be true. That night the Dead are booked into the Grande Ballroom, Detroit's psychedelic cavern of funk with the Hog Farm pushing soft piles of people sailing paper saucers, blazing birthday candles for buddha. Anything to get it off.

A gentle glow pervadeth the cash register. Owsley is smiling. "I love you, but Jesus loves you the best. And I bid you good night . . . good night." Sleep tight little piggies. Tomorrow Babbs and the Dead go west . . . and we saddle up the Hog and head for New York City.

Saul suggests we stop for a day at this little farmhouse in Montrose, Pennsylvania. The Living Theater laid up there while playing Harper College. Sounds nifty and false dawn finds us flapping for directions. We get some to this one place that sends us somewhere else.

Sanctuary at last. A snug little spot with down home dayglo. A haven for a couple of hospitable heads. We figure on dinner, some shut-eye and maybe the road . . . when we're ready. The rice sets to boil, our guitars start to thaw, and just when we're full up and purrin *in come the policemen* through windows and doors and the cracks in the floors with their wives and their brothers and dogs.

We figure everybody's clean and join in the excitement. Start bangin and twanging and thumping up music. A sound track for the Cop Show. Now we're not scared of cops, bein stopped every 30 miles for the last 3,000. And they are scared of us not being scared and we try to reassure them. They got a search warrant that looks like *War and Peace*. So we help em search with searching music and everybody crawling around looking under stuff. It was really bizarre.

The warrant says this little house has been watched for six months and our "Psychedelic" buses are what's used to move tons of dope from Mexico to Montrose. This was the big drop. Thousands of kilos to be converted to Popsicles. Slipped to the kiddies who tie up the mammas and pappas. Take over the town. Glue marshmallows to the fire house. Hang bananas on the flag. This is the first dope raid in the county and these people are really jacked up. They finally discover a skinny assed joint under this guy's bed. I produce a dusty mircroscope and (square business) they give it a peek.

I have lost all link with reality and have been eaten by this small town movie. The next frame shows our host being busted. Reel two. It's after midnight and snowing like an exploding popcornfactory. The cops are outside searching the buses . . . cutting open sacks of soybeans and grain below zero. On the white bus they find a dusty leather bag. Inside is an Indian chillum. This is a form of ethnic paraphernalia used by Afghanistanians to get stoned. By scraping the sides they obtain a residue.

Paul Fleming is sleeping on the bus. They wake him up. "What's this stuff?" they query. "Achoo!" sneezes Paul, reducing the residue and he is busted for destroying evidence. Once again they scrape on the chillum. With one quarter gram of burned marijuana memory they march into the house and pop sleeping Peter Whiterabbit who is registered owner of a bus that sleeps 12. "Bust us all, bust us all," cry we piggies and they are tossing us out of their police cars as fast as we can get in. They got what they came for and start to drive away. We crank up the convoy to follow the cop cars and it's another debacle. The buses just won't start. One ragged ass Cadillac full of mammas and babies make it to jail and are tossed out again.

After a series of scenes too surreal to surmise we slither into Binghamton, New York just across the state line. Actual sanctuary is achieved at the Unitarian Church. The minister there is a Magic Christian whose eyes dig deeper than dayglo . . . down to the heart of the hog. It's warm in that church with a real kitchen and food flows full in our bellies. Thank god. A church full of Christians is a rare find in the free world. Like finding an egret in an eclair.

Round about now which was then we start to work on our formal presentation for love and money at N.Y.U. We send invitations to rich relations, foundations, and wallets we don't even know. The fantasy is to stash the checkbooks in the balcony leaving the main floor wide open for folks.

Backstage I discover three spades and 20 purses. "Well, you know man, we're just sittin around talkin about the revolution while we watch these chicks' bags from New Jersey." I slip out for help but nobody's handy and when I return with some heavies the dudes have departed leaving a lot of empty pocketbooks.

Paul Krassner is held up in the men's room. "Give us all your money, man" and he did so. While walking down the hall he is accosted by other cats who whisper, "Don't tell anybody." These guys are the looters of love-ins . . . the vultures of free. Five microphones are also ripped off, literally cut at the cords . . . for the revolution, baby. Can you dig it? Not me. No siree. Boosting's bad karma in front . . . but on a free night, forget it.

We all shuffle on to Buffalo and the Lemar Convention. The Legalization of Marijuana sounds like a pipe dream but the college has mailed us the gas and we're moving again where we never have been and where there's dope there's hope. All the name heads are coming together like Ginsberg and Leary and Metzner and Kesey (who never shows up when he's supposed to) not to mention Jerry Rubin, Abbie Hoffman, Bob Fass, Paul Krassner, and the MC5. Man alive, even the Motherfuckers and the Hog Farm. I secretly suspect the FBI of invisible nets to cast us all over the falls.

The first day is lectures and terribly dull interspersed by occasional weirdness. Abbie Hoffman tosses 500 carefully rolled joints of catnip in the middle of a seminar. Stuart Brand's semi-spontaneous slide show called "War-God" is ultra nifty. So is Stuart Brand. A part-time Prankster, it was he who organized the San Francisco Trips Festival which kicked off the psychedelic revolution. He is now editing *The Whole Earth Catalog* and running a truck store.

The night-time show at Buffalo was dedicated to Psychedelics and the Arts. The gym is jammed and full of dopey chairs. They got a speakers platform on stage along with an impressive array of amplifiers belonging to the MC5. Allan Ginsberg on crutches hobbles humbly to the mike followed by Peter Orlovsky. They start chanting to Krishna and it is a bit of a drag but in my eyes he is a semi-saint and can sing *Mairze Doates* if he wants to . . . but the Motherfuckers aren't going for it. They're beating on bongos and looking to boogie. After a lot of yelling one of the Motherfuckers grabs a microphone and states his case which is this isn't India and we got our own chants which keep changing and why doesn't he get up to date.

This is kind of crude and tasteless but terribly to the point. Krassner tries to intervene and they tell him to fuck off. It's kind of scary and intense with everybody shouting at everybody else. I slip up on stage in my jump suit and jester's hat and attempt to make the peace. "War is a complicated way of getting acquainted." After a bit of a tongue dance we all hook up for a gong bong. It's really together now and we empty out all the chairs with a human chain stretching clear to the basement. The MC5 plugs in and Buffalo is boogie city. The band is grand with everything working and people are dancing up the walls.

Try to get out of New York City. That is our advice to all New Yorkers. The south-west furthers. Start gradually. Rent a farm upstate with a couple other families. Not too close to Pookipsee. Share the refrigerator. The first lesson begins with the belly. Get your gang together and decide what you want to do. You can do anything if its together. Split it up and they start picking you off. The Hog Farm has changed to Invisible Inc. We live in Total Commitment, wherever that is.

SYNTHESIS?

It is a commonplace among critics of the modern capitalist economy, young and old, that it is dependent upon the artificial acceleration of the demand for goods. Advertisers have found that they can best stimulate this demand by constantly overheating the atmosphere—by convincing people that they can attain happiness by reaching out for continually new and improved products and by warning them that not to reach out is to fall out of step with the times to allow themselves to become obsolete. The great enemy of capitalist growth is consumer contentment. . . . Radicals are very sensitive to some of the specific debasements and vulgarizations of advertising, but they do not reflect that their own mood fits closely with the general atmosphere which Madison Avenue hopes to sustain. Admen, too, regard contentment and attachment to tradition as unthinkable. They, too, exhort us to change our ways; they, too, seek a state of bewildering and unending flux, in which men are vulnerable to the preachments for various kinds of panaceas.

James Hitchcock, "Comes the Cultural Revolution,"
New York Times Magazine, July 27, 1969

What is not illusionary is the reality of a new culture of opposition. It grows out of the disintegration of the old forms, the vinyl and aerosol institutions that carry all the inane and destructive values of privatism, competition, commercialism, profitability and elitism. The new culture has yet to produce its own institutions on a mass scale; it controls none of the resources to do so. For the moment it must be content—or discontent— to feed the swinging sectors of the old system with new ideas, with rock and dope and love and openness. Then it all comes back, from Columbia Records or Hollywood or Bloomingdale's in perverted and degraded forms. But something will survive, because there's no drug on earth to dispel the nausea. . . . Mass politics, it's clear, can't yet be organized around the nausea; political radicals have to see the cultural revolution as a sea in which they can swim, like black militants in "black culture." But the urges are roaming, and when the dope freaks and nude swimmers and loveniks and ecological cultists and music groovers find out that they have to fight for love, all fucking hell will break loose.

Andrew Kopkind, "Woodstock Nation,"
Hard Times, October 1969

FURTHER READINGS

The following are recommended for those who wish to pursue further the topics raised in the present volume.

CONCEPTS AND ISSUES

Gans, Herbert J. "Popular Culture In America." In *Social Problems: A Modern Approach*, edited by Howard S. Becker, pp. 549–620. New York: John Wiley & Sons, 1967.

Huizinga, Johan. *Homo Ludens: A Study of the Play Element in Culture*. Boston: Beacon, 1955.

Jacobs, Norman. *Culture For the Millions?* New York: D. Van Nostrand Co., Inc., 1961.

Lowenthal, Leo. "Historical Perspectives of Popular Culture." *American Journal of Sociology* 55 (1950): 323–32.

McLuhan, Marshall. *Understanding Media: The Extensions of Man.* New York: McGraw-Hill, 1964.

———, *Culture is Our Business*. New York: McGraw-Hill, 1970.

Nye, Russel. *The Unembarrassed Muse: The Popular Arts In America.* New York: The Dial Press, 1970.

José Ortega Y Gasset, *The Revolt of the Masses.* New York: W. W. Norton & Co., 1932.

Rosenberg, Bernard and David Manning White. *Mass Culture: The Popular Arts in America.* 1st Edition. New York: The Free Press, 1957.

Rosenberg, Bernard and David Manning White. *Mass Culture Revisited.* New York: Van Nostrand Reinhold Company, 1971.

Sontag, Susan. *Against Interpretation.* New York: Farrar, Straus and Giroux, 1966.

Toffler, Alvin. *Future Shock.* New York: Random House, 1970.

THESIS

Browne, Ray B., Larry N. Landrum, and William K. Bottorff. *Chal-*

lenges In American Culture. Bowling Green, Ohio: Bowling Green Popular Press, 1970.

Bryle, R. H. *Sport—Mirror of American Life.* Boston: Little, Brown & Co., 1963.

Cavan, Sherri. *Liquor License: An Ethnography of Bar Behavior.* Chicago: Aldine, 1969.

Cawelti, John G. *The Six-Gun Mystique.* Bowling Green, Ohio: Bowling Green Popular Press, 1971.

Daniels, Les. *Comix: A History of Comic Books In America.* New York: Outerbridge & Dienstfrey, 1971.

Denney, Reul. *The Astonished Muse.* Chicago: University of Chicago Press, 1957.

Faulkner, Robert R. *Hollywood Studio Musicians.* Chicago: Aldine-Atherton, 1971.

Green, Arnold W. *Recreation, Leisure and Politics.* New York: McGraw-Hill, 1964.

Greene, Theodore P. *American Heroes: The Changing Models of Success in American Magazines.* New York: Oxford University Press, 1970.

Grissim, John. *Country Music: White Man's Blues.* New York: Paperback Library, 1970.

Klapp, Orrin E. *Heroes, Villains and Fools.* Englewood Cliffs, N.J.: Prentice-Hall, 1962.

Larrabee, Eric. and Rolf Meyersohn. *Mass Leisure.* New York: The Free Press, 1958.

Larson, Otto N. *Violence and the Mass Media.* New York: Harper & Row, 1968.

Lynes, Russell. *The Tastemakers.* New York: Harper's, 1954.

Sagarin, Edward. *Sex and the Contemporary American Scene.* New York: Dell, 1970.

Truzzi, Marcello. *Sociology and Everyday Life.* Englewood Cliffs, N.J.: Prentice-Hall, 1968.

White, David Manning. *The Funnies: An American Idiom.* New York: The Free Press, 1963.

Wolfe, Tom. *The Kandy-Kolored Tangerine-Flake Streamline Baby.* New York: Farrar, Straus and Giroux, 1965.

———, *The Pump House Gang.* New York: Farrar, Straus and Giroux, 1968.

———, "Radical Chic." *New York* magazine, 1970.

ANTITHESIS

Belz, Carl. *The Story of Rock*. New York: Oxford University Press, 1969.

Braden, William. *The Age of Aquarius*. Chicago: Quadrangle, 1970.

Braun, D. Duane. *Toward A Theory of Popular Culture: The Sociology and History of American Music and Dance, 1920–1968*. Ann Arbor, Mich.: Ann Arbor Publishers, 1969.

Brustein, Robert. *Revolution As Theatre*. New York: Liveright, 1971.

Cleaver, Eldridge. *Soul On Ice*. New York: Dell, 1968.

Fishwick, Marshall. *Remus, Rastus, Revolution*. Bowling Green, Ohio: Bowling Green Popular Press, 1971.

Friedenberg, Edgar Z. *The Dignity of Youth and Other Atavisms*. Boston: Beacon, 1965.

Gerzon, Mark. *The Whole World Is Watching*. New York: Viking Press, 1969.

Gillett, Charlie. *The Sound of the City: The Rise of Rock and Roll*. New York: Outerbridge and Dienstfrey, 1970.

Glessing, Robert. *The Underground Press In America*. Bloomington, Indiana: Indiana University Press, 1970.

Halisi, Clyde. and James Mtume, *The Quotable Karenga*. Los Angeles: US Organization, 1967.

Herskovits, Melville J. *The Myth of the Negro Past*. Boston: Beacon, 1958.

Jones, LeRoi. *Blues People*. New York: Morrow, Williams and Co., 1963.

Keil, Charles. *Urban Blues*. Chicago: University of Chicago Press, 1966.

Meltzer, Richard. *The Aesthetics of Rock*. New York: Something Else Press, 1970.

Nuttall, Jeff. *Bomb Culture*. New York: Dell, 1968.

Powers, Thomas. *Diana: The Making of a Terrorist*. Houghton-Mifflin, 1971.

Reynolds, *Freewheelin' Frank*. New York: Grove Press. 1967.

Roszak, Theodore. *The Making of a Counter Culture*. New York: Doubleday, 1969.

Rubin, Jerry. *Do It!* New York: Simon and Schuster, 1970.

Somma, Robert. *No One Waved Good-bye*. New York: Outerbridge and Dienstfrey, 1971.

Thompson, Toby. *Positively Main Street: An Unorthodox View of Bob Dylan*. New York: Coward-McCann, 1971.

Williams, John A. and Charles F. Harris. *Amistad 2*. New York: Vintage Books, 1971.

Wolfe, Tom. *The Electric Kool-Aid Acid Test*. New York: Farrar, Straus and Giroux, 1968.